business ethics

business
ethics

**Managing Corporate
Citizenship and Sustainability
in the Age of Globalization**

Fourth edition

ANDREW CRANE
DIRK MATTEN

OXFORD
UNIVERSITY PRESS

OXFORD
UNIVERSITY PRESS

Great Clarendon Street, Oxford, OX2 6DP,
United Kingdom

Oxford University Press is a department of the University of Oxford.
It furthers the University's objective of excellence in research, scholarship,
and education by publishing worldwide. Oxford is a registered trade mark of
Oxford University Press in the UK and in certain other countries

First edition 2004
Second edition 2007
Third edition 2010
Impression: 3

Published in the United States of America by Oxford University Press
198 Madison Avenue, New York, NY 10016, United States of America

British Library Cataloguing in Publication Data
Data available

Library of Congress Control Number: 2015944382

ISBN 978–0–19–969731–1

Printed in Great Britain by
Bell & Bain Ltd., Glasgow

OUTLINE CONTENTS

PART A

Understanding Business Ethics   1

PART B

Contextualizing Business Ethics   227

The Corporate Citizen and its Stakeholders

DETAILED CONTENTS

PART A

Understanding Business Ethics

PART B

Contextualizing Business Ethics
The Corporate Citizen and its Stakeholders

LIST OF FIGURES

LIST OF BOXES

Ethics on Screen

Ethics Online

HOW TO USE THIS BOOK

■ Who is it for?

This book is suitable for MBA students, advanced undergraduates, masters students, as well as participants on executive courses. It has been specifically written from an international perspective, so it can be enjoyed by students from any country, and can be used effectively for courses in Europe, North America, Australasia, Asia, Latin America, or Africa.

One of the main differences between this and many other business ethics textbooks is that it adopts a broad perspective on business ethics and integrates issues of globalization, corporate citizenship, and sustainability throughout. As such, it has been designed to be used as a core recommended text for courses in business ethics, corporate responsibility, business and society, or stakeholder management. It can also be successfully used for modules focusing specifically on sustainable business, marketing ethics, supply-chain ethics, and other specialist subjects.

■ Structure of the book

The book consists of two parts, as shown in **Figure A**:

- **Part A** presents the key conceptual foundations of business ethics. This enables you to gain a thorough understanding of the subject's main theories and tools.

- **Part B** explores business ethics in the context of key stakeholder groups. Each chapter explains the specific stakeholder relationship involved, the main ethical issues that arise, and then how each stakeholder can be examined through the lenses of globalization, corporate citizenship, and sustainability.

Most courses will tend to use Part A as a foundation and then selectively use chapters or sections from Part B to suit the aims and structure of the particular course. The book has been specifically designed to accommodate this modular approach, and each of the sections in Part B can be used as a standalone component to support individual courses.

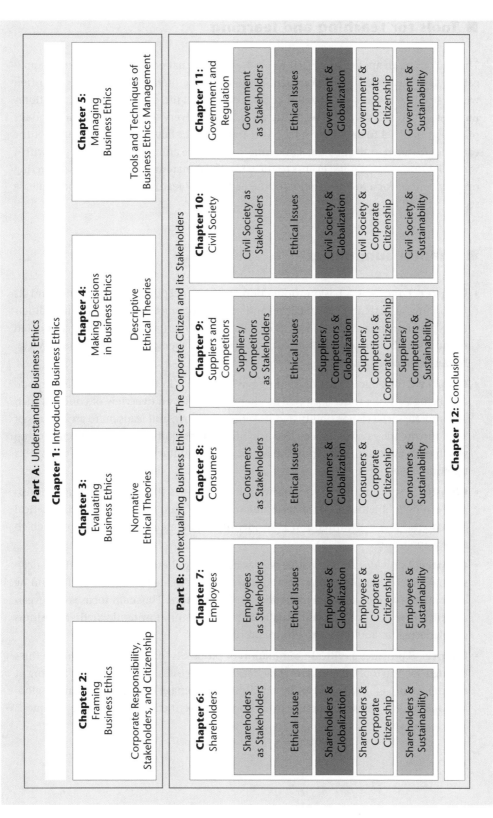

Figure A Structure of the book

■ Tools for teaching and learning

The book takes an applied approach to business ethics that emphasizes real-world application. This means that it is grounded in the academic literature but has been written with a strong emphasis on practical problems and real-life examples and illustrations. Business ethics issues seem to be in the media almost every day, so there is no shortage of current material to draw on. In fact, you are certain to have come across many of the examples featured in the book at some time—and Crane and Matten provide you with a way of linking those real-life events to the conceptual material that you will be covering on your course. For a full description of the pedagogical features used in the book please see pp. xx–xxii.

■ Chapter summaries

- **Chapter 1** provides a basic introduction to the concept of business ethics and its importance at both an academic level and in terms of practical management in different types of organizations. As well as explaining the international perspective adopted in the book, this chapter introduces two of the main themes of the book, namely globalization and sustainability.

- **Chapter 2** introduces ways of framing business ethics in the context of the corporation being part of a wider society. The chapter provides an overview of concepts such as corporate social responsibility and stakeholder theory, and leads on to an analysis of key contemporary concepts such as corporate accountability and corporate citizenship which offer important conceptual space for understanding business ethics beyond its traditional boundaries.

- **Chapter 3** sets out the key normative ethical theories that can be applied to business ethics problems, both in terms of traditional and contemporary theoretical approaches. The main intention is to identify a pragmatic, pluralistic approach to theory application.

- **Chapter 4** provides an alternative way of addressing these questions of ethical decision-making by looking at how decisions are actually made in business ethics, and by assessing the various descriptive theories in the literature. The main focus is on revealing the different individual and situational influences on how (and whether) business people recognize and deal with ethical problems.

- **Chapter 5** provides a critical examination of proposals for managing business ethics through specific tools, techniques, practices, and processes. This is done by looking at the importance of, and problems in, attempting to manage business ethics in the global economy, and the development over time of different ethics tools and techniques.

- **Chapter 6** sets out the rights and responsibilities of *shareholders*, emphasizing the ethical issues that arise in the area of corporate governance including insider trading, executive remuneration, and ethics of private equity. It also highlights the different corporate governance models across the globe, and the specific role played by shareholders in socially responsible investment. It concludes with a discussion of alternative forms of corporate ownership as a basis for enhanced sustainability.

- **Chapter 7** examines ethical issues in relation to *employees*. It discusses the various rights and duties of this stakeholder group, and presents the global context of workers' rights. Moves towards corporate citizenship and sustainability in relation to employees are discussed in the context of issues such as workplace democracy, work–life balance, and sustainable employment.

- **Chapter 8** considers the ethical issues arising in the context of *consumers*. It examines the question of consumer rights, the ideal of consumer sovereignty, and the role of ethical consumption in shaping corporate responsibility. The chapter concludes by examining problems and solutions around moving towards more sustainable models of consumption.

- **Chapter 9** explores the ethical issues arising in relation to firms' *suppliers* and *competitors*. The chapter examines problems such as conflict of interest, bribery, and unfair competition and moves on to discuss the global supply chain and ethical sourcing. Finally, the challenge of sustainable supply-chain management and industrial ecosystems are explored.

- **Chapter 10** considers the relationships between businesses and *civil society organizations* (CSOs), addressing the changing patterns of relationships between these traditionally adversarial institutions. Key issues examined here include the ethics of pressure group tactics, business–CSO collaboration, and social enterprise.

- **Chapter 11** covers *government* and *regulation*. Government as a stakeholder is a very multi-faceted group, which we unpack at various levels, functions, and areas. The chapter explores problems such as corruption and corporate lobbying and also examines the shifting relationships between regulation, government, and business, stressing the increasingly important role played by corporations in the governance of the global economy.

- **Chapter 12** provides a review and integration of the previous chapters in terms of key topics such as corporate citizenship, sustainability, and globalization. It also discusses the potential conflicts between different stakeholder groups discussed in Part B and draws conclusions about the future relevance of business ethics issues.

GUIDE TO THE BOOK

Each chapter includes the following pedagogical features:

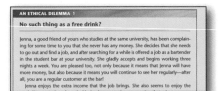

Learning Objectives

Each chapter starts with a set of bulleted learning outcomes, which indicate what you can expect to learn from the chapter, including specific key concepts and skills.

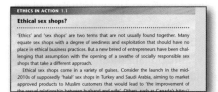

Key Concepts

A new feature in the fourth edition, in each chapter there are definitions of key concepts that you need to remember, all highlighted in the margin for easy reference.

☑ **Skill check**

Skill Check

Another new feature, these are call-outs throughout the text to indicate where there are key skills that you will need to develop to become a business ethics expert. These include academic skills and practical business skills.

Ethics in Action

These are short articles, primarily drawn from *Ethical Corporation* magazine, which showcase current ethical problems faced by business, leading-edge initiatives, or high-profile scandals that have hit the headlines.

An Ethical Dilemma

These describe a hypothetical ethical scenario, mainly derived from real-life incidents, and provide you with the opportunity to think about what you would do in a typical business ethics situation in a structured way.

Ethics on Screen

These provide reviews of topical films or TV series selected because they help to bring to life some of the key issues discussed in the respective chapters.

Ethics Online

These provide explanations of how business ethics issues discussed in the chapter have been dealt with on the internet and through social media.

Case Studies

At the end of each chapter is an extended case study that describes the ethical issues faced by well-known companies. They provide an excellent opportunity to use the material covered in the chapter to conduct a critical analysis of a real-life situation.

Think Theory

Throughout the text are call-out boxes that encourage you to stop and think about how the theories discussed in the book apply to real-world examples.

Chapter Summary

The chapter summary provides a brief overview of the issues covered in a particular chapter, helping you to review what you have learned.

Study Questions and Research Exercise

At the end of each chapter we provide readers with the opportunity to test their knowledge and understanding of the material covered so far, in a format commonly used in course assignments and exams.

Key Readings

At the end of each chapter we select two articles that we believe provide the best insight into some of the issues we have discussed. Annotated with helpful comments about their content, these will help prioritize additional reading and research.

HOW TO USE THE ONLINE RESOURCE CENTRE

www.oxfordtextbooks.co.uk/orc/cranebe4e/

To support this text, there is a wide range of web-based content for both teachers and students.

All of these resources can be incorporated into your institution's existing Virtual Learning Environment.

■ For students

Film trailers

Trailers of movies featured in Ethics on Screen boxes.

Film list

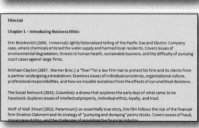

A chapter-by-chapter list of relevant movies to guide you in learning more about the issues covered in the book.

Think Theory solutions

Attempt to answer them yourself and then check your knowledge with suggested solutions for all of the Think Theory questions posed in each chapter.

Annotated weblinks

Links to websites relevant to all of the Cases, Ethics in Action, Ethics on Screen, and Ethics Online features included in the chapters, providing you with the opportunity for exploring issues in more depth and getting updates of latest developments.

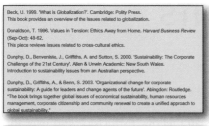

Recommended reading

Annotated links for additional readings providing you with orientation through the literature in order to enhance your understanding of key conceptual issues and selected applications.

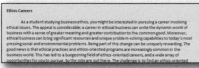

Ethics careers

Information about the careers that are available to you in the field of business ethics.

Crane and Matten blog

Follow the authors' commentary on all the latest business ethics issues and trends, and take the opportunity to contribute your own perspective through online comments.

■ For registered adopters

Powerpoint slides

A full set of chapter-by-chapter lecture slides including all of the main points and figures in the text, fully customizable to suit your own presentation style.

Teaching notes

Suggested answers, teaching suggestions, and further resources for all Ethics in Action features, Ethical Dilemmas, Ethics on Screen, and end-of-chapter Cases.

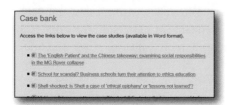

Case bank

Repository of all the cases (with teaching notes) from the previous editions of Crane and Matten, so that you can still get access to all the tried and tested cases you have used in the past.

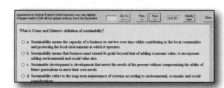

Test bank

A ready-made electronic testing resource to help assess your students' learning of the key points in the text. The test bank can be customized to meet your teaching needs.

Sample course outline

A sample course outline for instructors specifying course aims, student skills, weekly subjects, and key readings.

ACKNOWLEDGEMENTS

First off, we would like to thank all the students and fellow instructors who over the years have provided such great feedback in developing the successive editions of *Business Ethics*. We are also grateful to the legions of anonymous OUP reviewers who have taken the time to provide detailed comments and suggestions on the book throughout its four editions. We would also like to thank Angela Brugger, Akhil Kohli, and Sheryl Shibu for research assistance on the new edition.

Our sincere thanks go to the Schulich School of Business for providing us with the time, resources, and support without which the book would not have been possible. We would also like to thank Cameron Sabadoz for all his hard work in updating the Online Resource Centre materials, and David Mba, Stephanie Peca, and Redzep Ferati for assisting with permissions and other administrative details. Others who have provided help are acknowledged at the relevant places in the book. Finally, we would like to thank the team at OUP, especially our dedicated editor Lucy Hyde, as well as Siân Jenkins and Tristan Jones, who were responsible for production and marketing respectively. We are always surprised by how much work each new edition entails for us as authors, but our team at OUP always provides wonderful support and service along the way.

Andrew Crane and Dirk Matten
May 2015

Front cover: A labourer wears rudimentary, homemade goggles to protect his eyes when working on ships at a shipbuilding yard in Dhaka. Workers get around Tk300 (about GBP2.45) per day for working at the yard, where ships are built for domestic and export markets. The Bangladesh shipbuilding industry has been growing in recent years, due in part to its low labour costs. However, as this photo shows, worker safety standards remain a serious concern. For more on different standards of protection for workers in developing countries, see Chapter 7, especially the section on *Employing people worldwide: the ethical challenges of globalization* (pp. 317–324).

Credit: G.M.B. Akash/Panos

Paper: This book is printed on paper that has been accredited by the Forest Stewardship Council. FSC members comprise a diverse group of representatives from environmental and social groups, the timber trade, paper industry, forestry profession, indigenous people's organizations, community forestry groups, and forest product certification organizations from around the world. It is their job to ensure that the forests are managed to protect wildlife habitat and respect the rights of local communities.

All products carrying the FSC Logo have been independently certified as coming from forests that meet the internationally recognized FSC Principles and Criteria of Forest Stewardship. Certification involves inspection and auditing of the land from which the timber and pulpwood originate and tracking it through all of the steps of the production process until it reaches the end user. The Forest Stewardship Council (FSC) is an international non-profit organization founded in 1993 to support the world's forests. It is an example of a business–CSO collaboration, as discussed in Chapter 10. See pages 467–473 for more information.

Unless otherwise stated, all websites mentioned in the text were last accessed on July 27 2015.

PART A

Understanding Business Ethics

Introducing Business Ethics

Having completed this chapter you should be able to:

■ Provide a basic definition of business ethics.

■ Describe the relationship between business ethics and the law.

■ Distinguish between ethics, morality, and ethical theory.

■ Evaluate the importance of business ethics as an academic subject and as a practical management issue in organizations.

■ Specify ethical challenges in different types of organizations.

■ Describe how globalization represents a critical context for business ethics.

■ Elaborate on different international perspectives on business ethics, including European, Asian, and North American perspectives.

■ Explain how the 'triple bottom line' of sustainability is a key goal for business ethics.

Key concepts and skills:

Concepts	Skills
• Business ethics	• Defining business ethics
• Globalization	• Comparative analysis of business ethics
• Race to the bottom	• Triple bottom line analysis
• Sustainability	

■ What is business ethics?

'A book on business ethics? Well that won't take long to read!'

'You're taking a course on business ethics? So what do you do in the afternoon?'

'Business ethics? I didn't think there were any!'

These are not very good jokes. Still, that has not stopped a lot of people from responding with such comments (and others like them) whenever students of business ethics start talking about what they are doing. And even if these are not particularly funny jokes, nor even very original, they do immediately raise an important problem with the subject of business ethics: some people cannot even believe that it exists!

Business ethics, it is often claimed, is an oxymoron (Duska 2000). By an oxymoron, we mean the bringing together of two apparently contradictory concepts, such as in 'a cheerful pessimist' or 'a deafening silence'. To say that business ethics is an oxymoron suggests that there are not, or cannot be, ethics in business: that business is in some way unethical (i.e. that business is inherently bad), or that it is, at best, amoral (i.e. outside of our normal moral considerations). For example, it has been said that the 'game' of business is not subject to the same moral standards as the rest of society, but should be regarded as analogous to a game of poker, where deception and lying are perfectly permissible (Carr 1968).

To some extent, it is not surprising that some people think this way. A long list of scandals have highlighted the unethical way in which some firms have gone about their business. However, just because such malpractices take place does not mean that there are not some kinds of values or principles driving such decisions. After all, even what we might think of as 'bad' ethics are still ethics of a sort. And clearly it makes sense to try and understand why those decisions get made in the first place, and indeed to try and discover whether more acceptable business decisions and approaches can be developed.

Revelations of corporate malpractice should not therefore be interpreted to mean that thinking about ethics in business situations is entirely redundant. After all, as various writers have shown, many everyday business activities require the maintenance of basic ethical standards, such as honesty, trustworthiness, and co-operation (Collins 1994; Watson 1994; Duska 2000). Business activity would be impossible if corporate directors always lied; if buyers and sellers never trusted each other; or if employees refused to ever help each other. Similarly basic principles of fairness help ensure that people in business feel adequately rewarded for working hard rather than being evaluated on irrelevant criteria such as how good they are at golf or how nice their hair is.

It would also be wrong to infer that scandals involving corporate wrongdoing mean that the *subject* of business ethics was in some way naïve or idealistic. Indeed, on the contrary, it can be argued that the subject of business ethics primarily exists in order to provide us with some answers as to *why* certain decisions should be evaluated as ethical or unethical, or right or wrong. Without systematic study, how are we able to offer anything more than vague opinions or hunches about whether particular business activities are acceptable?

Whichever way one looks at it, there appears to be good reason to suggest that business ethics as a phenomenon, and as a subject, is not an oxymoron. While there will inevitably be disagreements about what exactly constitutes 'ethical' business activity, it is possible at least to offer a fairly uncontroversial definition of the subject itself. So, in a nutshell, we regard the subject of **business ethics** as the study of business situations, activities, and decisions where issues of right and wrong are addressed.

It is worth stressing that by 'right' and 'wrong' we mean morally right and wrong, as opposed to, for example, commercially, strategically, or financially right or wrong. Moreover, by 'business' ethics, we do not mean only commercial businesses, but also government organizations, pressure groups, not-for-profit businesses, charities, and other organizations. For example, questions of how to manage employees fairly, or what constitutes deception in advertising, are equally as important for organizations such as Wikimedia, Seoul National University, or the German Christian Democrat Party as they are for Facebook, Samsung, or Deutsche Bank (for detailed discussion of ethics in different types of organizations see Business ethics in different organizational contexts, p. 15).

Business ethics
The study of business situations, activities, and decisions where issues of right and wrong are addressed.

? THINK THEORY

A good definition is an important starting point for any theory. The one we have given for business ethics is mainly a definition of business ethics as an *academic subject*. If you were trying to define an *organization*'s business ethics, what definition would you use? Try writing it in the form, 'An organization's business ethics are . . .'.

VISIT THE ONLINE RESOURCE CENTRE for a short response to this feature

☑ **Skill check**

Defining business ethics. Establishing what you mean by business ethics is an important skill for managing the issues in practice. Definitions help to provide shared understandings and clarify the scope of what you are trying to achieve.

Business ethics and the law

Having defined business ethics in terms of issues of right and wrong, one might quite naturally question whether this is in any way distinct from the law. *Surely the law is also about issues of right and wrong?*

This is true, and there is considerable overlap between ethics and the law. In fact, the law is essentially an institutionalization or codification of ethics into specific social rules, regulations, and proscriptions. Nevertheless, the two are not equivalent. Perhaps the best way of thinking about ethics and the law is in terms of two intersecting domains (see **Figure 1.1**). The law might be said to be a definition of the minimum acceptable standards of behaviour. However, the law does not explicitly cover every possible ethical issue in business—or for that matter outside of business. For example, just as there is no law preventing you from being unfaithful to your significant other (although this is perceived by many to be unethical), so there is no law in many countries preventing businesses from testing their products on animals, selling landmines to oppressive regimes, or preventing their employees from joining a union—again, issues that many feel very strongly about.

Similarly, it is possible to think of issues that are covered by the law but which are not really about ethics. For example, the law prescribes whether we should drive on the right or the left side of the road. Although this prevents chaos on the roads, the decision about which side we should drive on is not an ethical decision as such.

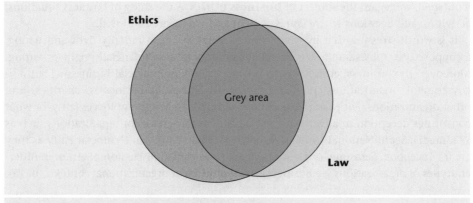

Figure 1.1 The relationship between ethics and the law

In one sense then, business ethics can be said to begin where the law ends. Business ethics is primarily concerned with those issues not covered by the law, or where there is no definite consensus on whether something is right or wrong. Discussion about the ethics of particular business practices may eventually *lead* to legislation once some kind of consensus is reached, but for most of the issues of interest to business ethics, the law typically does not currently provide us with guidance. For this reason, it is often said that business ethics is about the 'grey areas' of business, or where, as Treviño and Nelson (2014: 39) put it, 'values are in conflict'. **An Ethical Dilemma 1** presents one such situation that you might face where values are in conflict. Read through this and have a go at answering the questions at the end.

AN ETHICAL DILEMMA 1

No such thing as a free drink?

Jenna, a good friend of yours who studies at the same university, has been complaining for some time to you that she never has any money. She decides that she needs to go out and find a job, and after searching for a while is offered a job as a bartender in the student bar at your university. She gladly accepts and begins working three nights a week. You are pleased too, not only because it means that Jenna will have more money, but also because it means you will continue to see her regularly—after all, you are a regular customer at the bar!

Jenna enjoys the extra income that the job brings. She also seems to enjoy the work. You are rather pleased with developments since you notice that whenever you go up to the bar, Jenna always serves you first regardless of how many people are waiting.

After a short while though, it becomes apparent that Jenna is not enjoying the job quite as much as she did. Whenever you see her, she always seems to have a new story of how the bar manager has mistreated her. She tells you how she has been getting the worst shifts, always getting chosen to do the least-popular jobs (like cleaning the washrooms), and being constantly reprimanded for minor blunders that seem to go uncensored for the rest of the staff.

This goes on for a short while and then one day, when you are in the bar having a drink with some of your other friends, Jenna does something that you are not quite sure how to react to. When you go up to pay for a round of four drinks for you and your other friends, she discretely only charges you for one drink. Whilst you are slightly uncomfortable with this, you certainly do not want to lose the opportunity to save some money, or even worse, to get your friend into any kind of trouble by refusing. And when you tell your friends about it, they think it is very funny and congratulate you for the cheap round of drinks! In fact, when the next one of your friends goes up to pay for some drinks, he turns around and asks you to take his money, so that you can do the same trick for him. Although you tell him to get his own drinks, Jenna continues to undercharge you whenever it is your turn to go to the bar.

This goes on for a number of visits. You are happy to get the cheap rounds at the bar but you are not 100% comfortable with what is going on. You decide to at least say something to your friend when no one else is around. However, when you do end up raising the subject she just laughs it off and says, 'Yeah, it is great isn't it? They will never notice, and you get a cheap night out. Besides, it is only what this place deserves after the way I have been treated.'

Questions

1. Who is wrong in this situation—Jenna for undercharging you, you for accepting it, both of you, or neither of you?

2. Confronted by this situation, how would you handle it? Do nothing, or ask Jenna to stop undercharging you? If you take the latter option, what would you do if she refused?

3. To what extent do you think that being deliberately undercharged is different from other forms of preferential treatment, such as Jenna serving you in front of other waiting customers?

4. Does the fact that Jenna feels aggrieved at the treatment she receives from her boss condone her behaviour? Does it help to explain either her actions or your actions?

As we shall see many times over in this book, the problem of trying to make decisions in the grey areas of business ethics, or where values may be in conflict, means that many of the questions we face are equivocal. What this suggests is that there simply may not be a definitive 'right' answer to many business ethics problems. It is often not just a matter of deciding between right and wrong, but between courses of action that different actors, for different reasons, both believe are right—or both believe are wrong. Consider the case of bottled water. Critics, such as *The Story of Stuff Project*'s Annie Leonard (2010), argue that it promotes needless consumption, creates waste, and has been deceptively advertised as superior to tap water. Proponents, such as Nestlé, contend that it meets customers' need for convenience, it encourages more healthy lifestyles (by substituting for sugary drinks), and has a low carbon footprint compared to other bottled drinks (Kitts 2013).

With issues such as bottled water, as well as countless others including sweatshop working conditions, executive compensation, or corporate tax avoidance, we can see that business ethics problems tend to be very controversial and open to widely different points of view. In this sense, business ethics is not like subjects such as accounting, finance, engineering, or business law where you are supposed to learn specific procedures and facts in order to make objectively correct decisions. Rather, it is about gathering relevant evidence, and systematically analyzing it through particular lenses and tools (as discussed in more detail in Chapter 3) in order to come to an informed decision that has taken account of the most important considerations. So studying business ethics should help you to make *better* decisions, but this is not the same as making unequivocally *right* decisions. Business ethics is principally about developing good *judgement*.

Defining morality, ethics, and ethical theory

Some of the controversy regarding business ethics is no doubt due to different understandings of what constitutes morality or ethics in the first place. Before we continue, it is important for us to sort out some of the terminology we are using.

In common usage, the terms 'ethics' and 'morality' are often used interchangeably. This probably does not pose many real problems for most of us in terms of communicating and understanding things about business ethics. However, in order to clarify certain arguments, many academic writers have proposed clear differences between the two terms (e.g. Crane 2000; Parker 1998b). Unfortunately though, different writers have sometimes offered somewhat different distinctions, thereby serving more to confuse us than clarify our understanding.[1] Nonetheless, we do agree that there are certain advantages in making a distinction between 'ethics' and 'morality'. Following the most common way of distinguishing between them:

> Morality is concerned with the norms, values, and beliefs embedded in social processes which define right and wrong for an individual or a community.

> Ethics is concerned with the study of morality and the application of reason to elucidate specific rules and principles that determine morally acceptable courses of action. Ethical theories are the codifications of these rules and principles.

According to this way of thinking, morality precedes ethics, which in turn precedes ethical theory (see **Figure 1.2**). All individuals and communities have morality, a basic sense of right or wrong in relation to particular activities. Ethics represents an attempt to systematize and rationalize morality, typically into generalized normative rules that

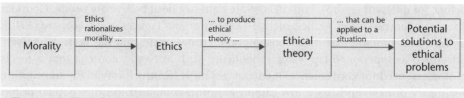

Figure 1.2 The relationship between morality, ethics, and ethical theory

supposedly offer a solution to situations of moral uncertainty. The outcomes of the codification of these rules are ethical theories, such as rights theory or justice theory.

A word of caution is necessary here. The emergence of the formal study of ethics has been aligned by a number of authors (e.g. Bauman 1993; Parker 1998b; Johnson and Smith 1999) with the modernist Enlightenment project, and the idea that moral uncertainty can be 'solved' with recourse to human rationality and abstract reasoning. As we shall show in Chapters 3 and 4, this has come under increasing attack from a number of quarters, including feminists and postmodernists. However, it is important at this stage to recognize that *ethics* is about some form of rationalization of *morality*. The importance of this distinction will hopefully therefore become clearer, and will certainly become more pertinent, as we start to examine these and other theories (in Chapter 3), as well as assessing how they feed into ethical decision-making in business (in Chapter 4). Indeed, contributing to the enhancement of ethical decision-making is one of the primary aims of this book, and of the subject of business ethics more generally. In the next section, we shall briefly review this and some of the other reasons why studying business ethics is becoming increasingly important today across the globe.

■ Why is business ethics important?

Business ethics is currently a very prominent business topic, and debates surrounding the subject have attracted a lot of attention from various quarters, including consumers, the media, non-governmental organizations (NGOs) and, of course, companies themselves. This attention to ethics confronts organizations whatever line of business they might be in.

Ethics in Action 1.1, for example, provides an illustration of how the sex industry has responded to ethical concerns with the emergence of 'ethical sex shops', which have positioned themselves as responsible alternatives to the more seedy operators that the industry is primarily known for.

There are many reasons why business ethics might be regarded as an increasingly important area of study, whether as students interested in evaluating business activities or as managers seeking to improve their decision-making skills. Consider the following:

1. **Business has huge power within society**. Business affects almost every aspect of our lives, and can even have a major impact on the democratic process of government. Evidence suggests that many members of the public are uneasy with such developments. For instance, one recent poll revealed that a large majority of the US population believe that lobbyists (71%), major companies (67%), and banks and financial institutions (67%) have too much power.[2] This raises a host of ethical questions and suggests we need to find new answers to the question of how we can either restrain this power or ensure that it is used for social good rather than exploitation of the less powerful.

2. **Business has the potential to provide a major contribution to our societies**. Whether in terms of producing the products and services that we want, providing employment, paying taxes, acting as an engine for economic development, or solving complex social problems, business can be a tremendous force for good. How, or indeed whether, this contribution is actually realized in practice goes to the heart of

VISIT THE
ONLINE
RESOURCE
CENTRE
for links to
useful sources
of further
information

ETHICS IN ACTION 1.1

Ethical sex shops?

'Ethics' and 'sex shops' are two terms that are not usually found together. Many equate sex shops with a degree of seediness and exploitation that should have no place in ethical business practices. But a new breed of entrepreneurs have been challenging that assumption with the opening of a swathe of socially responsible sex shops that take a different approach.

Ethical sex shops come in a variety of guises. Consider the launch in the mid-2010s of supposedly 'halal' sex shops in Turkey and Saudi Arabia, aiming to market approved products to Muslim customers that would lead to 'the improvement of the sexual relationship between husband and wife'. Others, such as Canada's http://sensual-intelligence.ca, focus more on eco-friendly, non-toxic sex toys, while some look to cover a range of ethical issues, including policies on everything from fair trade to diversity, and animal welfare to charitable giving. For example, the Berlin-based sex shop Other Nature only stocks products that do not contain animal products and that have not been tested on animals, including leather-free whips, and certified vegan sex aids. It markets itself as 'a feminist, queer-oriented, eco-friendly, vegan sex shop', which in case you were in any doubt means 'we are not your average sex shop'. Some, like the French 'eco-erotic' store Divinextases, are online only while others such as the US-based Babeland chain operate bricks-and-mortar stores alongside an online catalogue.

It is not just ethical products that distinguish the new breed of ethical sex shops. Many also specifically focus on providing a welcoming environment to women and other customers who are marginalized by the mainstream sex industry. It is perhaps no coincidence that a lot of ethical sex shop entrepreneurs are women, or that their product selection, courses, and in-store information are often targeted to women. Consider Halal Sex Shop, which claims that 'our store puts women at the center, offers information, and provides answers to frequently asked questions on sex'. Or Toronto's Good For Her, which markets itself as a 'cozy, comfortable place where women and their admirers can find a variety of high quality sex toys, books, DVDs, workshops, great advice and much more.' Although open to all, the store also 'offers women and trans only hours for those who feel more comfortable in an environment that is created especially with them in mind.'

Ethical sex shops also tend to offer their clientele a range of advice and information to encourage safe sex and to help customers achieve a satisfying sex life. The Babeland chain, for example, offers in-store advice and workshops, as well as an entire section of their website dedicated to 'sex info' with everything from 'how to find the G-spot' to 'green your sex life' and a 'women's guide to porn'. It even operates a philanthropic programme, 'Come for a Cause', that supports a range of organizations involved in sexual health, sex education, and civil liberties.

For some, the whole idea of trying to marry business ethics with the business of sex might be too much of a contradiction in terms to make any real sense. There is a significant portion of society that would simply brand the whole endeavour as objectionable and obscene. So in much the same way that the anti-smoking lobby will not countenance the possibility of there being an ethical cigarette firm, so too there are problems in establishing the idea that there can be any such thing as an ethical sex shop.

However, it is clear that ethical sex shops have found a unique niche within the less-than-salubrious sex industry, and some are showing that good ethics can pay off in terms of business profitability. Babeland has been operating now for more than 20 years and has four US stores and a thriving web business. Good For Her has been open for more than 15 years, about the same length of time as its Toronto neighbour, the world's only worker-co-operative sex store, Come as You Are, which operates with a 'democratic, egalitarian, and feminist mandate'. And as the halal sex shops have shown, it is not just in the permissive West where such shops are thriving. China also has its own 'inclusive female-owned' sex shop chain, Amy's Bedroom, which operates in Shanghai and online.

On the other hand, ethical sex shops have not been immune to social and economic pressures, which has led to several casualties in recent years. The Pennsylvania women's sex store Feminique, run by the 'sexologist' Dr. Jill, closed its doors in 2013, partly as a result of what the proprietor called 'repeated harassment' from local residents offended by its sex-positive message on the high street. And Coco de Mer, the upmarket 'erotic emporium' started up by Sam Roddick, the daughter of the Body Shop founder Anita Roddick, was sold in 2011 because of poor financial performance. This resulted in the closure of two of its three physical stores and a notable reversal in its ethical positioning. No longer does the firm's website include the claim that 'We have very strong and clear ethics at Coco de Mer' or that 'all our products are made with the consideration of environmental and human rights'. This means that products such as sustainable wood spanking paddles and fairly traded condoms are no longer part of the range on offer. Also gone is the firm's 'activist arm', Bondage for Freedom, which Roddick set up to provide a free creative service for organizations fighting for human or environmental rights. The message seems to be that just as sex does not *always* sell, nor does ethical sex.

Sources

Gerrard, J. 2013. Feminique Owner Closing Store in West Chester. *Daily Local News*, 4 November 2013: http://www.dailylocal.com/general-news/20131104/feminique-owner-closing-store-in-west-chester.

Morrison, A. 2015. Halal Sex Shop Opening for Muslims in Mecca, Saudi Arabia: Report. *International Business Times*, 20 April 2015: http://www.ibtimes.com/halal-sex-shop-opening-muslims-mecca-saudi-arabia-report-1888564.

Wallop, H. 2011. Sam Roddick Sells Coco de Mer to Lovehoney. *Telegraph*, 21 November 2011: http://www.telegraph.co.uk/finance/newsbysector/retailandconsumer/8904239/Sam-Roddick-sells-Coco-de-Mer-to-Lovehoney.html.

http://www.babeland.com.

http://www.coco-de-mer.com.

http://www.divinextases.fr.

http://other-nature.de.

http://sensual-intelligence.ca.

VISIT THE
ONLINE
RESOURCE
CENTRE
for a short
response to this
feature

> **? THINK THEORY**
>
> If, as we have argued, business ethics is not an oxymoron, then is it necessarily true of *any* business, regardless of the industry it is in? Think about the reasons for and against regarding an ethical sex shop as an ethical organization. Would the same arguments hold for an 'ethical' landmine manufacturer, or an 'ethical' animal-testing laboratory?

the business ethics debate. As a global survey conducted by McKinsey showed, only about 50% of business executives actually think that corporations make a mostly or somewhat positive contribution to society, while some 25% believe that their contribution is mostly or somewhat negative (*McKinsey Quarterly* 2006).

3. **Business malpractice has the potential to inflict enormous harm on individuals, communities, and the environment**. When the Rana Plaza building collapsed in Bangladesh in 2013, more than 1,000 garment workers stitching clothes for suppliers of Western retailers died having been forced to return to work after the building was evacuated and declared unsafe (Yardley 2013). Through helping us to understand more about the causes and consequences of these malpractices, business ethics seeks, as the founding editor of the *Journal of Business Ethics* has suggested, 'to improve the human condition' (Michalos 1988).

4. **The demands being placed on business to be ethical by its various stakeholders are becoming more complex and challenging**. It is critical to understand these challenges and to develop responses to them that address the demands of stakeholders but also enable firms to perform their economic role effectively. Getting this balance right remains a critical challenge for managers.

5. **Employees face significant pressure to compromise ethical standards**. For example, a survey of 500 financial services professionals in the UK and the US found that more than one in four had observed wrongdoing in the workplace, while a quarter of respondents agreed that financial services professionals might need to engage in unethical or illegal conduct in order to be successful.[3] Studying business ethics provides us with a way of looking at the reasons behind such infractions, and the ways in which such problems might be dealt with by managers, regulators, and others interested in improving ethical practice.

6. **Business faces a trust deficit**. Globally, only 18% of the general population trusts business leaders to tell the truth and just 19% trust them to make ethical decisions.[4] Enhancing business ethics will be a critical component in restoring that trust in the future.

Having identified some of the reasons why business ethics is important, we should also make it clear that this does not mean that there are not also a number of problems with the subject of business ethics. The limits of the business ethics discipline have been a subject of discussion for decades (e.g. Stark 1994; Sorrell 1998), even prompting one team of business ethics textbook authors to admit that 'we are not particularly fond of "business ethics"' (Jones et al. 2005: 1). After all, despite many years of business ethics being researched and taught in colleges and universities, ethics problems persist and the public remains sceptical of the ethics of business. However, in the main, these concerns are directed at how theories of business ethics have been developed and applied, rather than questioning the importance of business ethics as a subject *per se*.

There appears to be a growing consensus regarding the importance of addressing questions of business ethics, whether on the part of students, academics, governments, consumers, or, of course, businesses. Modules in business ethics are now being run in universities across much of the world. As *Businessweek* magazine put it, ethics and profits is the 'B-Schools' new mantra' (Stonington 2011). There has also been an outpouring of books, magazine, journal, and newspaper articles on the subject, as well as web pages, blogs, and other electronic publications—amazon.com currently lists more than 26,000 books related to business ethics, while a Google search on 'business ethics' returned more than 2 million hits at the time of writing. Even through television and cinema, business ethics issues are reaching a wide audience. Movies such as *The Wolf of Wall Street*, the subject of **Ethics on Screen 1**, raise a number of critical business ethics issues and have played them out to millions of viewers across the globe.

Similarly, the last few years have witnessed significant growth in what might be regarded as the business ethics 'industry', i.e. corporate ethics officers, ethics consultants, ethical investment trusts, ethical products and services, and activities associated with ethics auditing, monitoring, and reporting. One annual UK survey, for instance, estimates the country's 'ethical market' (i.e. consumer spending on ethical products and services) to be worth something like £78 billion annually.[5] The ethical market ranges from organic and fair trade foods to responsible holidays, energy efficient products, ethical banking, and ethical clothes. As **Ethics Online 1** shows, organizations such as Ethics Girls have sprung up to help consumers navigate these new market niches—and to promote the idea that ethics is also for those who 'love to shop'!

▲ **ETHICS ONLINE** 1

Ethical fashion for ethics girls

Want to buy a new pair of skinny jeans, but also care about how much the workers were paid to make them? Think there may be space in your life for an iPhone case made from upcycled fire hose and reclaimed parachute silk? Well, being ethical does not have to mean being unfashionable any more, at least not according to the Ethics Girls, a UK-based organization launched online in 2007. The Ethics Girls website seeks, as they put it, to 'set the example' in 'ethical fashion, shopping and ideas'. Featuring a shop, magazine, and even the opportunity to become a member of the Ethics Girls co-operative the site promises to 'take the guilt out of ethical consumption, to make life and our choices simpler'.

Unlike some ethical shopping sites, such as the Ethical Consumer organization's online buyers' guides (which provide detailed scorecards for a wide range of products in numerous categories), Ethics Girls do not claim to have a particularly robust research methodology. Their approach is style led rather than research led, with an emphasis on lifestyle journalism and the promotion of positive choices among young women. And perhaps more than anything, it shows the continuing transformation and maturation of the internet as a place for ethical shoppers of all kinds—and not just diehard activists—to go for advice, information, and inspiration.

Sources
Ethics Girls website: http://www.ethicsgirls.co.uk.
Ethical Consumer website: http://www.ethicalconsumer.org.

▼

VISIT THE ONLINE RESOURCE CENTRE for links to useful sources of further information

ETHICS ON SCREEN 1

The Wolf of Wall Street

[An] exhilarating orgy of excess.

Keith Uhlich, *Time Out New York*

The amorality of modern business, and of the finance industry in particular, has been a common theme in Hollywood over the years (see also Ethics on Screen 2 and 6). *The Wolf of Wall Street* ramps up the intensity with a romp through the coke-snorting, pill-popping, sex-fuelled debauchery of convicted stock swindler Jordan Belfort, played by Leonardo DiCaprio. The movie is based on Belfort's memoir, describing how he built a multi-million dollar trading firm, Stratton Oakmont, in the 1990s and defrauded millions of dollars from unsuspecting investors in the process.

The movie presents a first-person narrative from Belfort, taking us from his beginnings as a trainee at a big Wall Street firm in the late 1980s right through to his ultimate conviction for money laundering and securities fraud in the early 2000s. Along the way he loses his job as a newly minted trader as a result of the Black Monday stock crash of 1987, and ends up selling penny stocks in a ramshackle trading operation in a strip mall in Long Island.

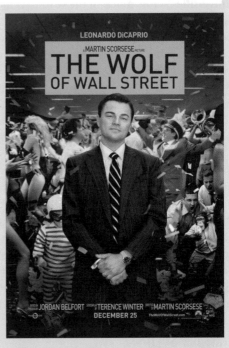

Edward R. Pressman film/The Kobal Collection

Despite the down-at-heel surroundings, Belfort's talent for selling largely worthless stocks to unwary investors soon has him pulling in thousands of dollars in commission every week, to the amazement of his co-workers. Before long, Belfort starts up his own trading firm along with his partner Donnie Azoff (played by Jonah Hill), who he befriends after Azoff marvels at how much money Belfort seems to be making, and quits his job on the spot.

Their first hires are a bunch of Belfort's old friends, whose most relevant business experience to date involves selling drugs—talents that Belfort soon shapes into a potent, if decidedly unscrupulous, sales force. The firm prospers, growing to become a booming trading floor employing more than a 1,000 brokers, with ever more wealthy clients, and a remarkable ability to generate enormous

profits out of seemingly thin air. They perfect a form of fraud known as 'pump and dump' which involves buying up cheap stock, talking it up to gullible investors, and then selling it high and reaping in the commissions.

DiCaprio's Belfort is a charismatic, larger-than-life personality; his talent for selling worthless stock is matched only by his appetite for money, drugs, and sex. The Bacchanalian lifestyle of Belfort and his traders makes for entertaining, if at times somewhat uneasy, viewing, but it also serves to illustrate the supposed moral bankruptcy of the finance industry. The mantra is money—'enough of this shit'll make you invincible' claims Belfort. 'See money doesn't just buy you a better life, better food, better cars, better pussy, it also makes you a better person'.

The movie shows Stratton Oakmont as a wild, testosterone-driven environment, where there is no place for the faint of heart or those with a conscience. The crazed culture of the trading room crowds out any potential concern for the unfortunate investors who they pressurize into ill-advised deals. As the real-life Belfort says in his book on which the movie is based: 'It was the essence of the mighty roar, and it cut through everything. It intoxicated you. It seduced you! It fucking liberated you! It helped you achieve goals you never dreamed yourself capable of! And it swept everyone away, especially me.'

Nowhere is this 'mighty roar' more evident that in the traders' language—the movie allegedly holds a record for the most utterances of the word 'fuck' in a non-documentary feature film—and the poor treatment meted out to women—the main female roles in the film being either those of the long-suffering wives of Belfort and his friends or the many prostitutes that service the traders in their wild parties.

Director, Martin Scorsese, who is perhaps best known for his gangster epics such as *Goodfellas*, in fact presents Wall Street in much the same way that he does the mafia—a system of organized crime made up of wisecracking tough guys who enjoy a life of excess whilst maintaining a casual disregard for the law and anyone outside the close-knit 'family' of the organization.

Therefore, despite its ethically charged subject material, some critics have accused *The Wolf of Wall Street* of being morally ambivalent and glamorizing rather than condemning Belfort's antics. Certainly the film avoids any earnest moralizing, choosing instead to adopt a more darkly comic approach. Notably, DiCaprio won a Golden Globe for his portrayal of Belfort in the category of Best Actor in a Musical or Comedy rather than the more usual Best Actor in a Drama award.

Perhaps then it is no surprise that the film met with an enthusiastic mainstream audience. It brought the legendary director his best-ever box office return. And even the supposed villains of the piece, the traders in the world's financial capitals, reportedly loved the movie. Rather than being dismayed by their representation as incorrigible cheats, bankers set up special screenings of the movie, whooping and cheering Belfort's worst excesses. As one reporter concluded: 'it would be a real shame if Martin Scorsese just accidentally inspired the future Jordan Belforts of the world.'

Sources

Kolhatkar, S. 2013. Jordan Belfort, the Real Wolf of Wall Street. *Bloomberg Businessweek*,
    7 November 2013: http://www.businessweek.com/articles/2013-11-07/jordan-belfort-the-real-
    wolf-of-wall-street.
Perlber, S. 2013. We Saw 'Wolf of Wall Street' with a Bunch of Wall Street Dudes and It Was
    Disturbing. *Business Insider*, 19 December 2013: http://www.businessinsider.com/banker-pros-
    cheer-wolf-of-wall-street-2013-1#ixzz2zugDvytc.
http://www.thewolfofwallstreet.com.

What is clear then is that business ethics has not only been recognized as increasingly important, but has also undergone rapid changes and developments during the past decade or so. This has been the case not only in large corporations, but also in small and medium-sized enterprises (SMEs), and in public and non-profit organizations too. Let us now take a closer look at how business ethics issues might be manifested in these rather different organizational contexts.

■ Business ethics in different organizational contexts

It should be clear by now that whatever else we may think it of it, business ethics clearly matters. It matters not just for huge multinational corporations like McDonald's, Nestlé, Shell, or HSBC, but also for a range of other types of organizations. Some of the issues will inevitably be rather similar across organizational types. **Figure 1.3**, for example, shows that employees from business, government, and civil society organizations (by this we mean non-profit, charity, or non-governmental organizations) observe similar types of ethical misconduct in the workplace—and at similar intensities. Indeed, despite some historical differences, the level of ethical violations observed by employees in different sectors appears to be converging (Ethics Resource Center 2008). Nonetheless, there are also a number of critical differences, which are worth elaborating on a little further (and which are summarized in **Figure 1.4**).

Business ethics in large versus small companies

Small businesses (often referred to as SMEs or small and medium-sized enterprises) typically differ in their attention and approach to business ethics compared to large firms. As Laura Spence (1999) suggests, these differences include the lack of time and resources that small business managers have available to focus on ethics, their autonomy and independence with respect to responsibilities to other stakeholders, and their informal trust-based approach to managing ethics. They have also been found to assess their employees as their single most important stakeholder (Spence and Lozano 2000).

Large corporations, on the other hand, tend to have much more formalized approaches to managing business ethics. They have considerably more resources available to develop sophisticated ethics and compliance management programmes. That said,

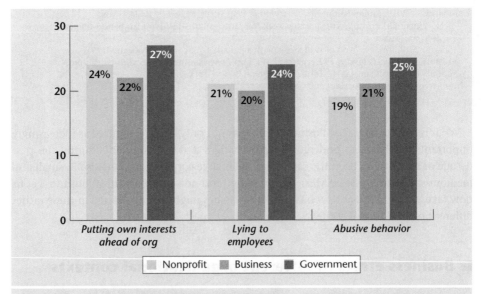

Figure 1.3 Types of misconduct across sectors

Source: 2007 National Nonprofit Ethics Survey: An Inside View of Nonprofit Sector Ethics, Arlington, VA: Ethics Resource Center: p. 16. Reprinted with permission.

	Large corporations	Small businesses	Civil society organizations	Public sector organizations
Main priorities in addressing ethical issues	Financial integrity, employee/ customer issues	Employee issues	Delivery of mission to clients; integrity of tactics; legitimacy and accountability	Rule of law, corruption, conflicts of interest; procedural issues, accountability
Approach to managing ethics	Formal, public relations and/ or systems-based	Informal, trust-based	Informal, values-based	Formal, bureaucratic
Responsible and/or accountable to	Shareholders and other stakeholders	Owners	Donors and clients	General public, higher level government organizations
Main constraints	Shareholder orientation; size and complexity	Lack of resources and attention	Lack of resources and formal training	Inertia, lack of transparency

Figure 1.4 Differences in business ethics across organizational types

they are constrained by the need to focus on profitability and shareholder value, as well as the very size and complexity of their operations.

Business ethics in private, public, and civil society organizations

While private sector companies will tend to be responsible primarily to their shareholders or owners, the main responsibilities of civil society organizations (CSOs) are to the constituencies they serve (and to a lesser extent their donors). In the public sector, more attention is paid to higher-level government and the general public. Typical ethical issues prioritized by government agencies will be those of rule of law, corruption, conflicts of interest, public accountability, and various procedural issues involved in ensuring that resources are deployed fairly and impartially (Moilanen and Salminen 2007). This is usually reflected in a formalized and bureaucratic approach to ethics management.

CSOs, on the other hand, will often be more informal in their approach, emphasizing their mission and values. CSOs may be limited in terms of the resources and training they may typically be able to deploy in relation to managing ethics, whereas government organizations are often restricted by a heavy bureaucracy that breeds inertia and a lack of transparency to external constituencies.

A summary of some of the differences in business ethics across organizational contexts is provided in **Figure 1.4**. Although brief, this sketch should give you some of the flavour of the challenges that managers may face in each type of organization. In this book, we will generally focus more on large corporations than the other types—principally because most of our readers will probably end up working in such organizations. However, as we go through, we will also highlight issues pertinent to small firms, and in the latter part of the book in particular we will discuss in much fuller detail business ethics issues in CSOs (Chapter 10) and government (Chapter 11). Before we move on though, we need to consider another important context—namely the global nature of business ethics today.

■ Globalization: a key context for business ethics?

Globalization has become one of the most prominent buzzwords of recent times. Whether in newspaper articles, politicians' speeches, or business leaders' press conferences, the 'G-word' is frequently identified as one of the most important issues in contemporary society. In the business community, in particular, there has been considerable enthusiasm about globalization. Businesses search for new employees worldwide, supply chains span multiple continents, and global brands such as Coca-Cola, Adidas and Toyota are now an everyday feature even in the remotest African village. But as much as many businesses (as well as many consumers and employees) have enjoyed the fruits of globalization, they have also experienced a downside. As William Parrett, the former Chief Executive Officer of Deloitte Touche Tohmatsu (one of the 'Big Four' accounting firms), commented at the World Economic Forum (WEF) in Davos:

> One effect of globalization has been that risk of all kinds—not just fiscal, but also physical—have increased for businesses, no matter where they operate. Information travels far and fast, confidentiality is difficult to maintain, markets are interdependent and events in far-flung places can have immense impact virtually anywhere in the world.

So, globalization clearly has some negative effects, even for the business community. But beyond this, it is significant that over the past two decades a significant 'anti-globalization' protest movement has also emerged. Some meetings of global organizations such as the WEF, the World Trade Organization (WTO), or the G8, for example, have been accompanied by criticism and occasionally even violent protest. Hackers have targeted global companies such as Amazon and Sony, while successive battles over fair trade, poverty, food prices, water access, and financial stability have kept the ethical spotlight on the process of globalization. The 'Occupy' movement, which itself morphed into a global phenomenon within just a few weeks in 2011, also revitalized a strident critique of 'corporate globalization'.[6]

Race to the bottom
A process whereby multinationals pitch developing countries against each other by allocating foreign direct investment to countries that can offer them the most favourable conditions in terms of low tax rates, low levels of environmental regulation, and restricted workers' rights.

In the context of business ethics, this controversy over globalization plays a crucial role. After all, corporations—most notably multinational corporations (MNCs)—are at the centre of the public's criticism on globalization. They are accused of exploiting workers in developing countries, destroying the environment, and, by abusing their economic power, engaging developing countries in a so-called '**race to the bottom**'. However true these accusations are in practice, there is no doubt that globalization is the most current and demanding arena in which corporations have to define and legitimatize the 'rights and wrongs' of their behaviour.

What is globalization?

Globalization is not only a very controversial topic in the public debate; it is also a very contested term in academic discourse.[7] This is partly due to controversy about its merits and downsides, as we have just alluded to. Moreover, it often gets mixed up with similar ideas such as 'internationalization', 'Westernization', or 'homogenisation' (Scholte 2005). While we can say that globalization has many facets, it is useful to understand why it is new and—in the context of this book—what its influence is on the role of business. Let us first consider some recent examples that get to heart of what globalization is.

- The countries of the European Union have been in various states of financial crisis since 2008. In particular, the fiscal problems of Greece, Ireland, Spain, and Italy have at different times had a substantial effect not only on the wider system of state finances in the countries of the eurozone, but far beyond in global financial markets. Globalization entails that *events, which have local roots, have knock-on effects far beyond* in seemingly disconnected places.

- Global climate change has gradually been acknowledged as a critical problem to address across the world. While some companies have taken steps to reduce their emissions and a number of countries have issued regulations limiting greenhouse gas emissions, it is clear that solutions to this global problem can only be achieved if we develop global agreements. The Kyoto Protocol was a first step, but the spate of intergovernmental conferences in Cancun, Copenhagen, Durban, Doha, and Warsaw over recent years make it very clear that *global problems need global solutions*—and finding these solutions has become one of the big unresolved challenges in managing global issues.

- Luckily, most of us have not been personally affected by acts of terror. But we all are affected by terrorism as we have to go through enhanced security checks in airports, public buildings or mass events, or have encountered difficulties in getting a foreign visa—just to name some examples. Globalization has led to a situation where *events, people or ideas from faraway places can have a very palpable effect on people in otherwise unconnected locations and situations.*

The new and game-changing feature 'globalization' is that it makes real-time social, political, economic, and cultural exchanges possible between people or organizations without any need for direct physical contact. **Globalization** makes these interactions possible regardless of how close or how far away the different partners are actually located from each other.

To get a good grasp on what globalization means, two main developments in the last few decades are particularly important.

The first development is *technological* in nature. Modern communications technology, from the telephone through to the internet, open up the possibility of connecting and interacting with people despite the fact that there are large geographical distances between them. Furthermore, the rapid development of global transportation technologies allows people to easily meet with other people all over the globe. While Marco Polo had to travel for many months before he finally arrived in China, people today can step on a plane and, after a passable meal and a short sleep, arrive some time later on the other side of the globe. Territorial distances play a less and less important role today. The people we do business with, or that we make friends with, no longer necessarily have to be in the same place as us.

The second development is *political* in nature. Territorial borders have been the main obstacles to worldwide connections between people. Only 25 years ago it was still largely impossible to enter the countries in the Eastern bloc without lengthy visa procedures, and even then, interactions between people from the two sides were very limited. With the fall of the iron curtain and substantial liberalization efforts elsewhere (for instance within the EU),

Globalization
The ongoing integration of political, social, and economic interactions at the transnational level, regardless of physical proximity or distance.

national borders have been eroded and, in many cases, have even been abolished. In Europe, you can drive from Lapland to Sicily without stopping at a single national border.

These two developments mainly account for the massive proliferation and spread in supra-territorial connections. These connections may not always necessarily have a global spread in the literal sense of worldwide coverage. The new thing about these connections is that they no longer need a geographical territory to take place, and territorial distances and borders no longer restrict them (Scholte 2005).

We all enjoy various elements of globalization already. For instance, due to the modern communication infrastructure, many of us could closely follow the 2014 FIFA World Cup or the 2016 Olympics in Brazil live on TV—regardless of our actual location at the time. Such events are global not in the sense that they actually happen all over the world, but in the sense that billions of people follow them, and to some extent take part in them, regardless of the fact that they are in Milan, Manchester, or Manila. Or think of many of our consumption decisions: we can potentially drink the same Heineken beer, drive the same model of Toyota car, or buy the same expensive Rolex watch almost wherever we are in the world—we do not have to be in Amsterdam, Tokyo, or Geneva. Certain global products are available all over the world and if we go out to eat 'Chinese', 'Mexican', or 'French' we normally do not have to travel to a certain geographical territory. Or think of the way we do our personal banking: our banks no longer store or provide access to our money in a single, geographic location. Most people have a credit card that allows them to withdraw money all over the world, or we can pay our bills via internet banking at home in Istanbul or while sitting in a cafe in India.

Global communications, global products, and global financial systems and capital markets are only the most striking examples of globalization in the world economy. There are many other areas where globalization in this sense is a significant social, economic, and political process. As we shall now see, globalization also has significant implications for business ethics.

Globalization and business ethics: a new global space to manage

Globalization as defined in terms of the closer integration of economic activities is particularly relevant for business ethics, and this is evident in three main areas—culture, law, and accountability.

Cultural issues

As business becomes less fixed territorially, so corporations increasingly engage in overseas markets, suddenly finding themselves confronted with new and diverse, sometimes even contradictory ethical demands. Moral values that were taken for granted in the home market may get questioned as soon as corporations enter foreign markets (Donaldson 1996). For example, attitudes to racial and gender diversity in North America may differ significantly to those in Middle Eastern countries. Similarly, Chinese people might regard it as more unethical to sack employees in times of economic downturn than would be typical in Europe. Again, while Scandinavians tend to regard child labour as strictly unethical, some South Asian countries might have a different approach. Or consider the case of IKEA, which in 2012 was found to have edited out pictures of women in the Saudi Arabian edition of their otherwise globally homogeneous catalogue.[8] Was IKEA right to adapt to local standards or was it wrong to compromise its own standards of anti-discrimination and human rights?

The reason why there is a potential for such problems is that while globalization results in the 'deterritorialization' (Scholte 2005) of some processes and activities, in many cases there is still a close connection between the local culture, including moral values, and a certain geographical region. For example, Europeans largely disapprove of capital punishment, while many Americans appear to regard it as morally acceptable. Women can freely sunbathe topless on most European beaches, yet in some states of America they can be fined for doing so—and in Pakistan they would be expected to cover up much more. This is one of the contradictions of globalization. On the one hand, globalization makes regional difference less important since it brings regions together and encourages a more uniform 'global culture'. On the other hand, in eroding the divisions of geographical distances, globalization reveals economic, political, and cultural differences and confronts people with them. This dialectical effect has been a growing subject for research over the past decade (see, for instance, Boli and Lechner 2000).

? THINK THEORY

Capital punishment and topless sunbathing are interesting issues to think about when considering globalization theory and cultural dimensions of ethics, but they have little to do with business responsibility as such. Can you think of some similar examples that a business might have to deal with?

VISIT THE ONLINE RESOURCE CENTRE for a short response to this feature

---

Legal issues

A second aspect is closely linked to what we said previously about the relationship between ethics and law. The more economic transactions lose their connection to a certain territorial entity, the more they escape the control of the respective national governments. The power of a government has traditionally been confined to a certain territory; for example, French laws are only binding on French territory, UK laws on UK territory, and so on. As soon as a company leaves its home territory and moves part of its production chain to, for example, an emerging economy, the legal framework becomes very different. Consequently, managers can no longer simply rely on the legal framework when deciding on the right or wrong of certain business practices. If, as we said earlier (see Business ethics and the law, pp. 5–8), business ethics largely begins where the law ends, then globalization increases the demand for business ethics because globalized economic activities are beyond the control of national (territorial) governments. One striking example of how companies might skilfully benefit from these confines of the law are the tax avoidance strategies of Apple, Google, Starbucks, and Amazon, who were all criticised in the 2010s for paying only marginal amounts of tax. Through a complex system of transfer pricing between subsidiaries and by exploiting differences in tax legislation in various countries of operation these companies were able to minimize their tax payment without breaking the letter of the law in any particular jurisdiction.[9]

Accountability issues

Taking a closer look at global activities, it is easy to identify corporations as a dominant actor on the global stage: multinationals own the mass media that influence much of the information and entertainment we are exposed to, they supply global products, they pay our salaries, and they pay (directly or indirectly) much of the taxes that keep governments running. Furthermore, one could argue that MNCs are economically as powerful as many governments. For example, in 2012 the gross domestic product (GDP) of Poland, South Africa, and Finland was about the same as the revenue of Shell, BP, and Chevron (respectively) (Steger 2013). However, whereas the Polish government has to be accountable to the Polish people and must face elections on a regular basis, the managers of Shell are formally accountable only to the relatively small group of people who own shares in the company. The communities in the Netherlands, the UK or Nigeria that depend directly on those companies' investment decisions, however, have next to no influence on them and, unlike a regional or national government, Shell, BP and Chevron are, at least in principle, not legally accountable to these constituencies.

What this means is that the more economic activities become global, the less governments can control them, and the less they are open to democratic control by the people affected by them. Consequently, the call for direct (democratic) accountability of MNCs has become louder in recent years, as evidenced, for example, by the Occupy movement that we mentioned above. Put simply, globalization leads to a growing demand for *corporate accountability*. We shall examine this argument fully in Chapter 2, but this is a clear example of why business ethics is in demand since it offers the potential for corporations to examine and respond to the claims made on them by various stakeholders. Indeed, globalization can be seen to affect *all* stakeholders of the corporation, as we shall discuss in Part B of this book. Some examples of these impacts are presented in **Figure 1.5**.

Globalization and business ethics: new local challenges to address

So far in this section we have accentuated the homogenizing effects of globalization: it creates a new space where business faces similar ethical questions worldwide. Paradoxically though, globalization also has an opposite effect on business: the more business becomes global, the more it gets exposed to regions and countries where ethical values and practices are still vastly different. From this perspective it is important to note that the formal academic subject of business ethics is largely a North American invention and has most of its roots and a large part of its traditions in the US, while, for instance in Europe, it only became visible from the beginning of the 1980s (van Luijk 2001). In presenting a text from an international perspective, we believe that although many of the original ideas in business ethics have been, and still are, very useful in, say, the African, Latin American, or Asian context, there are definite limits to the transfer of North American approaches into the rest of the world. For instance, the European context poses some distinctly different questions, which are not necessarily on the agenda from an American perspective (Spence 2002). Likewise, Asia has quite a distinct historical, philosophical, and religious legacy, giving rise to a different approach to the study, as well as the practice, of business ethics in Asia (Romar 2004; Elankumaran, Seal, and Hashmi 2005; Ip 2009). At another level, it is also critical to think beyond developed countries in shaping our knowledge and understanding of business ethics. After all, it is in emerging economies and the developing world where many ethical issues in business are most pressing (Visser 2008), and insights from Asian, African, and Latin American ethical perspectives are therefore essential for situating business ethics in a truly global context.

Stakeholders	Ethical impacts of globalization
Shareholders	Globalization provides potential for greater profitability, but also greater risks. Lack of regulation of global financial markets, leading to additional financial risks and instability.
Employees	Corporations outsource production to developing countries in order to reduce costs in global marketplace—this provides jobs but also raises the potential for exploitation of employees through poor working conditions.
Consumers	Global products provide social benefits to consumers across the globe but may also meet protests about cultural imperialism and Westernization. Globalization can bring cheaper prices to customers, but vulnerable consumers in developing countries may also face the possibility of exploitation by MNCs.
Suppliers and competitors	Suppliers in developing countries face regulation from MNCs through supply chain management. Small scale indigenous competitors are exposed to powerful global players.
Civil society (pressure groups, NGOs, local communities)	Global business activity brings the company in direct interaction with local communities thereby raising the possibility for erosion of traditional community life. Globally active pressure groups emerge with aim to 'police' the corporation in countries where governments are weak and corrupt.
Government and regulation	Globalization weakens governments and increases the corporate responsibility for jobs, welfare, maintenance of ethical standards, etc. Globalization also confronts governments with corporations from regions with different cultural expectations about issues such as bribery, corruption, taxation, and philanthropy.

Figure 1.5 Examples of the ethical impacts of globalization on different stakeholder groups

International variety in approaches to business ethics

Various authors have claimed that there are certain fundamental differences in the way in which business ethics is practised and studied in different parts of the world. Much of this work initially focused on Europe and North America (e.g. van Luijk 1990; Vogel 1992, 1998; Koehn 1999), but there have also been studies emerging since then on Africa (Rossouw 2005; Visser et al. 2006), Australasia (Moon 1995; Kimber and Lipton 2005), Latin America (Haslam 2007; Puppim de Oliveira and Vargas 2006), and Asia (Kimber and Lipton 2005; Donleavy et al. 2008; Ip 2009). In this section, we shall look at these differences in relation to six key questions and discuss some of the specifics of business ethics in various regions or countries globally. An example of this discussion with regard to three key regions is summarized in **Figure 1.6**. In so doing, we recognize that, given their cultural diversity and geographical spread, some regions such as Africa or Asia are perhaps harder to generalize about than Europe or North America. **Ethics in Action 1.2** provides a flavour of the differences and commonalities of business ethics in East Asia. However, the point is not to make an absolutely definitive statement about business ethics in different regions of the world, but to show that any approach to business ethics is likely to be driven by the cultural and historical context of the region or country.

	Europe	North America	Asia
Who is responsible for ethical conduct in business?	Social control by the collective	The individual	Top management
Who is the key actor in business ethics?	Government, trade unions, corporate associations	The corporation	Government, corporations
What are the key guidelines for ethical behaviour?	Negotiated legal framework of business	Corporate codes of ethics	Managerial discretion
What are the key issues in business ethics?	Social issues in organizing the framework of business	Misconduct and immorality in single decisions situations	Corporate governance and accountability
What is the dominant stakeholder management approach?	Formalized multiple stakeholder approach	Focus on shareholder value	Implicit multiple stakeholder approach, benign managerialism

Figure 1.6 Regional differences from a business ethics perspective: the example of Europe, North America, and Asia

VISIT THE
ONLINE
RESOURCE
CENTRE
for links to
useful sources
of further
information

ETHICS IN ACTION 1.2   http://www.ethicalcorp.com

Local rules in east Asia
Paul French, 2 May 2013

While China seems to be the centre of attention of many debates on business ethics, it is instructive to look beyond to east Asia in general, as these countries are facing many of the same corporate responsibility problems as China.

In most places, however, local issues take precedence. Malaysia's Astro, the country's largest Pay TV service, has been behind a major deep-sea cleaning process in Sabah on the Borneo coast involving 139 divers cleaning the seabed and relocating precious coral. Astro has of course televised much of the underwater action, raising awareness of seabed conservation. Corporate responsibility has been promoted in Malaysia in recent years through the actions of the Kuala Lumpur stock exchange, pushing companies to include corporate responsibility statements in their filings. Consequently, many Malaysian main board-listed companies have a prominent corporate responsibility policy. However, James Pereira, a local reputation and marketing consultant, believes many companies have a way to go yet, saying that a lot use corporate responsibility activities as a tax write-off and have a 'been there, done that' attitude.

Singapore has an advanced corporate responsibility sector, as might be expected of a modern service-oriented economy. Certainly the rush of new global companies, especially in the finance sector, that have expanded their operations there in recent years has boosted this responsibility trend.

Many have been seeking to be good community citizens. For instance, the local DBS Bank has undertaken a programme to open up the Marina Bay harbour to the public. The company has sponsored the DBS Marina Regatta and a DBS Social Enterprise event, working with the government and community organisations, including the Urban Redevelopment Authority, the Singapore Dragon Boat Association and the Singapore Sailing Federation.

Across in Indonesia corporate responsibility is at a slightly earlier stage than in Malaysia or Singapore, and still more focused on philanthropy. One interesting initiative is from the country's largest pawnshop operator, Pegadaian, a state-run company. Aware of the fact that pawnshops don't always have the best reputation among many consumers, being seen by some as part of the problem of poverty rather than a solution, Pegadaian (which is highly profitable) recently donated an ambulance to a charity for the poor and announced the provision of free health services in central Jakarta. The company also sponsors three orphanages.

Other firms operating in Indonesia also suffer from poor PR and have been ramping up their efforts to counter the negative publicity their operations attract. The oil and gas industry is one such sector, with land acquisitions a particularly contentious issue. Pertamina EP, part of the state energy firm, is one company that has run into local community objections over land acquisitions. After some demonstrations and problems between guards and local communities in Palembang, Pertamina has significantly increased its stakeholder engagement activities, liaising with local groups. Critics say it is just trying to buy off local objectors, but others see this as the start of a possibly more progressive outreach programme by the energy giant.

Cambodia, Laos, and Vietnam are attracting attention as alternative sourcing points for China. However, issues as diverse as workers' rights and preservation of heritage are all appearing. For instance, the Angkor Gold Corporation, an American publicly traded gold explorer operating in Cambodia, has launched a corporate responsibility programme after locals voiced concerns about its activities.

Angkor Gold is sponsoring elected village development committees as well as planting fruit trees, digging wells and running family planning and health educations sessions.

In communist Vietnam, corporate responsibility faces many of the challenges seen in China. But that doesn't mean that nothing is happening. The Hanoi-based Vietnam Chamber of Commerce and Industry has started monitoring the local corporate responsibility situation and instituted an annual awards scheme. It seems foreign companies will lead the way—for instance, HSBC recently partnered with the Dariu Foundation and Maison Chance to work with disadvantaged Vietnamese children through projects worth $500,000.

This is a pattern becoming more common across southeast Asia—initiatives are popping up in response to local issues, both in developed economies and, perhaps more importantly, in those emerging markets where corporate responsibility has previously been a very secondary consideration.

Sources

Ethical Corporation, Paul French, 2 May 2013, http://www.ethicalcorp.com. Reproduced with the kind permission of Ethical Corporation.

VISIT THE
ONLINE
RESOURCE
CENTRE
for a short
response to this
feature

> **? THINK THEORY**
>
> Looking at different east Asian countries, what are common themes in responsible business practices? Also, reflect on the differences between these countries. Discuss potential reasons for both the commonalities and differences.

Who is responsible for ethical conduct in business?

North America is typically said to exhibit a strong culture of individualism, suggesting that individuals are responsible for their own success. Hence, if there are demands for solving ethical questions, it would be the individual who is usually expected to be responsible for making the right choices. There is some impressive literature dealing with individual ethical decision-making emanating from the US (as we shall discuss in Chapter 4), and many US textbooks focus on decision-making at this level (Ferrell et al. 2012; Treviño and Nelson 2014). In Asia, however, hierarchy is much more important, and so top management is typically seen as responsible for ethical conduct. Similar perspectives can be found in Africa or India, where long-standing tribal and close-knit family-based communities tend to embed the individual in a broader social context in which responsibility for decisions is more a collective than an individual matter. Somewhat similarly, in Europe it has traditionally been thought that it is not the individual business person, nor even the single company, that is primarily expected to be responsible for solving ethical dilemmas in business. Rather, it is a collective and overarching institution, usually the state. European business ethics has therefore tended to focus more on the choice *of* constraints compared with the North American approach of focusing on choice *within* constraints (Enderle 1996). A specific flavour of this approach can then be found in Central Europe and post-communist countries where individuals tend to assign responsibility for ethical behaviour primarily to the larger collective or bureaucratic entities that govern economic or social life (Lewicka-Strzalecka 2006).

> ☑ **Skill check**
>
> **Comparative analysis of business ethics.** Understanding the differences in cultural norms and moral values between different countries and regions is an important skill in business ethics. Comparative analysis helps you to understand that key issues, actors and guidelines for ethical conduct always need to be understood in the specific geographic context where a business operates.

Who is the key actor in business ethics?

In North America, in most (but not all) areas, the institutional framework of business ethics has traditionally been fairly loose so that the key actor has tended to be the corporation. This, at least partly, explains the rather practical approach to business ethics evident in the North American approach (Enderle 1996). Similarly, given that business ethics is particularly important when the law has not yet codified the 'right' or 'wrong' of a certain action, this would also seem to partially explain the longer legacy of business ethics as an academic subject in North America. However, the identification of the corporation as the key actor in North America also means that corporate misconduct tends to face greater enforcement and harsher penalties (Vogel 1992).

Conversely, in most European countries there is quite a dense network of regulation on most of the ethically important issues for business. Workers' rights, social and medical care, and environmental issues are only a few examples where it could be said that European companies have not traditionally had to give much consideration to the moral values that should guide their decisions. These questions have, at least in principle, been tackled by the government in setting up a tight institutional framework for businesses. Examples range from the Scandinavian welfare state to the German codetermination system and the strong position of trade unions and workers' rights in France (Matten and Moon 2008).

In Europe, governments, trade unions, and corporate associations have therefore been key actors in business ethics. A similar focus on government tends to be evident in the Asian perspective, although it is corporations rather than trade unions that have typically been involved with governments in this activity. For example, in Japan, firms are interconnected with one another and with the government through *keiretsu* arrangements, while South Korea exhibits a similar *chaebol* structure. In China, many large corporations are still state owned. Hence, engagements with business ethics in Asia often look to both governments and corporations as key actors.

Moving to developing countries in Africa or Latin America, however, the so-called 'third sector', i.e. non-governmental organizations (NGOs), is often a key player within the arena of business ethics. One of the reasons for this lies in the fact that governments in these regions often are underfunded or even corrupt, and therefore provide limited guidance or legal frameworks for ethical decision-making. In Latin America, for instance, NGOs are the key players in organizing, incentivizing, or co-ordinating ethical initiatives by business (Haslam 2007). NGOs also partner with business (and governments) in public-private partnerships to address urgent ethical issues, such as poverty, disease, or lack of education—as we will discuss in more detail in Chapter 10.

What are the key ethical guidelines for ethical behaviour?

The differing character and extent of the legal frameworks globally to some degree necessitates different approaches to business ethics. Similarly, it also suggests that whereas the key practical guidelines for ethical behaviour in some regions, such as in Europe, tend to be codified in the negotiated legal framework of business, in Asia there is greater managerial discretion, giving rise to a more organic and flexible approach to ethical decision-making that places considerable emphasis on personal virtues and collective responsibility and relationships (Koehn 1999). Notably, personal and professional life are not seen to be distinct, as is typically the case in North America and Europe (Parker 1998a: 128). Indeed, in North America, there is a strong reliance on rules and guidelines for business conduct, but rather than coming from government (as in Europe), these tend to come from businesses themselves in the form of corporate codes of ethics and internal compliance programmes (Enderle 1996). Nonetheless, these are often put in place to avoid the potentially hefty fines that accompany breaches of the US federal sentencing guidelines (Vogel 1992).

As the Asian context suggests, these differences become even more pronounced once we leave the context of Western and industrialized countries. Deon Rossouw (2005: 98), for instance, argues that business ethics in the African context is predicated on the philosophy of *Ubuntu*, a value system in which the 'commitment to co-existence, consensus, and consultation' is prized as the highest value in human interaction. While Rossouw infers that *Ubuntu* explains the absence of shareholder supremacy in African corporate governance, the somewhat similar Chinese notion of *guanxi* exposes a general tension with these traditional values: they sometimes fly in the face of certain fundamental Western ethical beliefs. The *guanxi* idea puts close, reciprocal, trusting interpersonal ties at the core of human interaction, which has led some commentators to mistakenly question whether in Chinese business relations, the *guanxi*-informed practice of gift-giving in fact amounts to little less than an indifference to bribery (Ho and Redfern 2010).

What are the key issues in business ethics?

This contrast is often manifested in the types of issues deemed important within business ethics in different contexts. This becomes evident when looking at contemporary US business ethics textbooks, since they tend to accord a considerable amount of space to issues such as privacy, workers' rights, salary issues, and whistleblowing, to name just a few. These are deemed to be the responsibility of the individual company, since the state, in principle, does not take full responsibility for regulating these issues.

The European approach, in contrast, has tended to focus more on social issues in organizing the framework of business. Hence, European business ethics textbooks have tended to include greater consideration of subjects such as the ethics of capitalism and economic rationality (Enderle 1996). In Asia, concerns about the responsible organization of business have given rise to a focus on ethical issues in relation to corporate governance and the accountability of management for practices such as mismanagement and corruption. Specifically in China, the latter issue is high on the agenda of the government, exemplified by the fact that some of the biggest business ethics scandals to hit the country have led to arrests and even the execution of corrupt officials (Ip 2009).

In the developing world in general, there seems to be a predominant focus on the ethical obligations of business to provide jobs that pay a living wage, and to provide fairly priced goods and services (Visser 2008). Next to these basic economic functions of business, ethical considerations in the developing world place a particular expectation on multinationals—particularly foreign ones—to contribute to local development, health care, and education.

What is the most dominant stakeholder management approach?

Another important aspect that follows from the above is the variety in institutional arrangements shaping the form and purpose of corporations in different countries (Morgan et al. 2010). European corporations in general are smaller than their North American counterparts, and may be more likely to see multiple stakeholders (as opposed to simply shareholders) as the focus of corporate activity. European, African, and Asian models of capitalism are not so dominated by the drive for shareholder value maximization compared with North American companies. European companies are often managed by large executive and supervisory boards, with a considerable amount of interlocking ownership structures between companies and close bank relations (van Luijk 1990). Asian companies also feature a great deal of structural integration, but the interests of employees and other stakeholders are often promoted through cultural norms of trust and implicit duties, rather than formal governance mechanisms (Johnson, Whittington, and Scholes 2011). This sort of arrangement might be thought of as a form of 'benign managerialism' (Parkinson 2003: 493), an approach that has a long-standing tradition in countries such as India, where companies like Tata have attempted to honour ethical obligations to multiple stakeholders for decades (Elankumaran et al. 2005). This approach is also visible in Latin America, where much of the economy is dominated by smaller, often family-owned firms and where the key stakeholder from a business ethics perspective is the employee (Vives 2007).

Sources of difference between different regions globally

From where have such differences emerged? Comparing the US and Europe—two otherwise very similar contexts seen from a global perspective—can serve as an instructive backdrop in answering this question. Many of these differences in business ethics are rooted in the differing cultural, economic, and religious histories of the Europe and the US (Palazzo 2002). One argument here is that the influence of the Catholic and Lutheran Protestant religions in Europe led to a collective approach to organizing economic life, whereas the individual focus of the Calvinist-Protestant religion in the US led to the rise of a distinctly different capitalist economic system (Weber 1905). Even though today we tend to talk about much of Europe and North America as secularized, there are significant differences in the religious legacies of the two regions—which in turn have a significant impact on the different approaches to business ethics in different regions.

This becomes even more pronounced in other parts of the world where the active practice of religion is sometimes still more embedded than in the West. In Asia, the influence of Hinduism, Buddhism, and Confucianism, for example, could be said to have led to a more pragmatic, relational, and flexible approach to ethical decision-making (Koehn 1999). The Muslim world, although diverse in its spread over three continents, is characterized by a number of ethical principles, of which justice/fairness, trusteeship and integrity ('unity') can be considered core (Rice 1999). Such religiously informed ethical values sometimes can have far-reaching implications for business, as the example of Islamic financial systems shows (Nomani 2008) (see Chapter 6).

Next to religious influence, differences in business ethics can also have other historic roots. Georges Enderle (1996) suggests that the interest in broader macro issues of business ethics in Europe can also be partly traced to the need to rebuild institutions after the Second World War and in the aftermath of economic and political restructuring in Eastern Europe. Moreover, Vogel (1992) argues further that the focus on individual action and codes of conduct in the US has been substantially driven by the impact of widely publicized corporate scandals that have focused attention on the need to avoid ethical violation at the firm level (see also Verstegen Ryan 2005). In a similar vein, many of the specific challenges for business ethics in the developing world, be it poor governance, extreme poverty, or violence, can be understood as a heritage from colonial times (Banerjee 2009), as is particularly visible in countries such as South Africa, Brazil, or Myanmar (Burma). In some countries such as Canada or Australia, it is mining companies—rather than just governments—that are exposed to ethical claims, based, for instance, on past and current discrimination against indigenous groups (Lertzman and Vredenburg 2005).

Globalization and the assimilation of different global regions

As we can see then, there are a number of reasons that can be advanced to explain differences in business ethics across countries and regions of the globe. But does this mean the differences are likely to be sustained given the ongoing processes of globalization? Certainly, globalization has mitigated some of the peculiarities of business systems globally. Therefore, however important it is to see the differences between different regions, there is a clear tendency towards some degree of assimilation in the different business systems. In Europe, this has been manifested in a decrease in the importance of (especially national) governmental regulation for business. Globalization has resulted in a rapid and comprehensive move towards deregulation of business activities, which increasingly puts businesses in contexts similar to the American version of capitalism (Matten and Moon 2008). This is even more noticeable if we focus on Central Europe and former communist countries: economies in transition are typically characterized by a weak state and a deficit in law enforcement, which together leave a growing number of ethical issues to be tackled by businesses (Lang 2001). This trend towards a greater convergence of business systems and firm characteristics is visible in most parts of the world (Whitley 1999); however, we also see that certain fundamental characteristics and differences remain and will continue to have relevance (Sorge 2005; Yoshikawa and Rasheed 2009).

In this book, we therefore provide the following balance between the different positions on the main variations in business ethics evident in different parts of the globe:

- Rather than selecting either one or the other, we will consider both the individual decision-maker and the corporation itself as responsible for ethical conduct—and consider top managers as well as rank-and-file organization members. Although it is clearly individuals in organizations who ultimately make business ethics decisions, many non-US perspectives suggest that we also have to look at the context that shapes those decisions. Moreover, most of us quite naturally regard corporations as significant actors in business ethics. If there is an incident of industrial pollution or it is revealed that children are being used in an overseas factory, it is usually the company as a whole that we criticize rather than any specific manager(s).

- We will focus on the corporation in its relations with other key actors such as government, NGOs, and trade unions.

- We will provide a critical perspective on both managerial discretion and ethical guidelines (such as codes of conduct), and broader forces shaping ethical decision-making, such as product and financial markets, supply chains, civil society, and systems of governance.

- The morality of single business situations will be considered in the context of corporate governance and the broader organizing framework of business.

- A multiple stakeholder approach that includes shareholders as a particularly important constituency will be taken. As we will outline in Chapter 2, this assumes some intrinsic rights for stakeholders rather than focusing only on their role in affecting shareholder value.

■ Sustainability: a key goal for business ethics?

At the same time that these new challenges of globalization have emerged, considerable interest has also been directed towards the development of new ways of addressing the diverse impacts of business in society. Many of these impacts are far-reaching and profound. To mention just a few, one only needs to think of impacts such as:

- The environmental pollution, in particular the effects on climate change, caused by the production, transportation, and use of products such as cars, refrigerators, or newspapers.

- The ever-increasing problems of waste disposal and management as a result of excessive product packaging and the dominance of our 'throwaway culture'.

- The devastating consequences for individuals and communities as a result of plant closures, 'downsizing', or 'outsourcing' as experienced throughout Europe and North America.

- The erosion of local cultures and environments due to the influx of mass tourism in places as diverse as Thai fishing villages, Swiss alpine communities, or ancient Roman monuments.

Faced with such problems (and many more besides), it has been widely suggested that the goals and consequences of business require radical rethinking. Ever since the Rio Earth Summit of 1992, one concept in particular appears to have been widely promoted (though not unilaterally accepted) as the essential new conceptual frame for assessing not only business activities specifically, but industrial and social development more generally. That concept is *sustainability*.

Sustainability has become an increasingly common term in the rhetoric surrounding business ethics, and has been widely used by corporations, governments, consultants, pressure groups, and academics alike. **Figure 1.7** provides some examples of sustainability being used in the corporate reports and websites of some major multinational firms. Despite this widespread use, sustainability is a term that has been utilized and interpreted in substantially different ways (Dobson 1996). Probably the most common usage of sustainability, however, is in relation to sustainable development, which is typically defined as a 'strategy of social development that meets the needs of the present without compromising the ability of future generations to meet their own needs' (World Commission on Environment and Development 1987).

This, however, is only the core idea of an elusive and widely contested concept—and one that has also been subject to a vast array of different conceptualizations and definitions (Gladwin, Kennelly, and Krause 1995; Starik and Rands 1995). So while we would caution against any unreserved acceptance of any particular interpretation, at a very basic level, sustainability appears to be primarily about system maintenance, as in ensuring that our actions do not impact upon the system—for example, the Earth or the biosphere—in such a way that its long-term viability is threatened. By focusing sustainable development on the potential for future generations to satisfy their needs, sustainability also raises considerations of *intergenerational equity*, i.e. equality between one generation and another.

With its roots in environmental management and analysis, sustainability for some is largely synonymous with environmental sustainability. Crucially, though, the concept

Company	Sustainability Statement	Source
DeBeers	'Everything in our business is long term. Therefore, sustainability is in our best interests. It makes perfect business sense, and it means we must continue to push the boundaries of best practice in sustainability, being open, acting on our commitments and encouraging positive behaviour across the diamond value chain – from mine to finger.'	http://www.debeersgroup.com 2015
H&M	'Our planet is facing scarcity issues on many fronts and too many people still live in poverty. Clean water, climate change, textile waste, wages and overtime in supplier factories are some of the key challenges in our industry. Making more sustainable fashion choices available, affordable and attractive to as many people as possible is our starting point. We want to use our scale to bring about systemic change to our industry and across the lifecycle of our products.'	H&M Sustainability Report, 2014
Samsung	'Integrating corporate management and sustainable development is an issue of increasing importance in the business world, amid increasing rising expectations for social and environmental responsibility. In response, we have been improving the process of collecting stakeholders' ideas and setting up a corporate-wide vision and strategies for sustainable development.'	http://www.samsung.com 2015
Shell	'Our role in sustainability is to help meet current energy needs in a responsible way. We do this by operating in line with international standards, our own stringent frameworks and best practice. We also participate in shaping a path towards a lower-carbon energy future.'	Shell Sustainability Report, 2014
Volkswagen	'Our aim is to create lasting value: for the Company, its employees and its shareholders, but also for the countries and regions in which we operate. This all-embracing view of sustainability is shared by all twelve brands, our companies and all our employees across the Group. Together we work to find solutions for the challenges of the future – and make no mistake, those challenges are substantial: markets are shifting, resources are becoming scarcer, emissions regulations are tightening up all over the world, and booming cities call for new and intelligent traffic and mobility concepts. We consider it part of our responsibility to find the right answers to these trends.'	http://www.volkswagenag.com 2015

Figure 1.7 Corporate commitments to sustainability

of sustainability is now more commonly thought of in broader terms to include not only environmental considerations, but also economic and social considerations (Elkington 1999). This is shown in **Figure 1.8**.

This extension of the sustainability concept arose primarily because it is not only impractical, but even sometimes impossible, to address the sustainability of the natural environment without also considering the social and economic aspects of relevant communities and their activities. For example, while environmentalists have opposed road-building programmes on account of the detrimental impact of such schemes on the

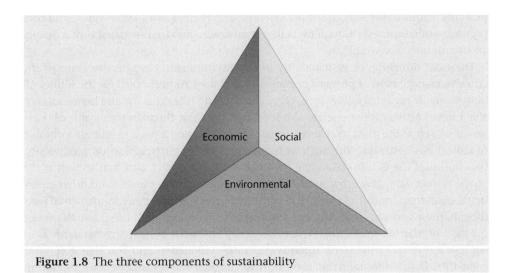

Figure 1.8 The three components of sustainability

environment, others have pointed to the benefits for local communities of lower conges-tion in their towns and extra jobs for their citizens. Another argument for this extension is the consideration that if equity is to be extended to future generations, then logically it should also be extended to all those in the current generation. Hence, one of the pri-mary espoused aims of the World Commission on Environment and Development was the eradication of world poverty and inequity. As we see it then, **sustainability** can be regarded as comprising three components—environmental, economic, and social.

While we regard this idea of sustainability as the long-term maintenance of systems according to social, economic, and environmental considerations as sufficient for de-termining the essential content of the concept, it is evident that sustainability as a phe-nomenon also represents a specific goal to be achieved. The framing of sustainability as a goal for business is encapsulated most completely in the notion of a 'triple bottom line'.

Sustainability
The long-term maintenance of systems according to environmental, economic, and social considerations.

The triple bottom line

The triple bottom line (TBL) is a term coined by the sustainability thought leader John Elkington. His view of the TBL is that it represents the idea that business does not have just one single goal—namely adding economic value—but that it has an extended goal which necessitates adding environmental and social value too (Elkington 1999). From this perspective, it should be clear why we have highlighted sustainability as a poten-tially important new goal for business ethics. However, in order to develop a clearer picture of just what the three components of sustainability actually represent in terms of a goal for business ethics, we shall have to examine each of them in turn.

Environmental perspectives

As we mentioned briefly above, the concept of sustainability is generally regarded as hav-ing emerged from the environmental perspective, most notably in forestry management and then later in other areas of resource management (Hediger 1999). Indeed, it would probably be true to say that, at the present moment, there is still a fairly widespread conception within business (though we believe a mistaken one) that sustainability is mainly an environmental concept.

The basic principles of sustainability in the environmental perspective concern the effective management of physical resources so that they are conserved for the future. All biosystems are regarded as having finite resources and finite capacity, and hence sustainable human activity must operate at a level that does not threaten the health of those systems. Even at the most basic level, these concerns suggest a need to address a number of critical business problems, such as the impacts of industrialization on biodiversity, the continued use of non-renewable resources such as oil, steel, and coal, as well as the production of damaging environmental pollutants like carbon dioxide and other greenhouse gases from industrial plants and consumer products. At a more fundamental level though, these concerns also raise the problem of economic growth itself, and the vexed question of whether future generations can really enjoy the same living standards as us without a reversal of the trend towards ever more production and consumption. Most companies have understandably been slow to consider the reversal of consumption in their sustainability strategies, but one company that has adopted an interesting position on this is the US outdoor clothing business Patagonia, which in the 2010s campaigned to persuade its customers to buy less, including adverts imploring customers 'Don't Buy This Jacket!'

Economic perspectives

The economic perspective on sustainability initially emerged from economic growth models that assessed the limits imposed by the carrying capacity of the earth.[10] The recognition that continued growth in population, industrial activity, resource use, and pollution could mean that standards of living would eventually decline led to the emergence of sustainability as a way of thinking about ensuring that future generations would not be adversely disadvantaged by the activities and choices of the present generation. Economists such as Kenneth Arrow (Arrow and Hurwicz 1977), Herman Daly (Daly and Cobb 1989; Daly 1991), and David Pearce (1999) have since been highly influential in advancing the agenda for a macroeconomic understanding of sustainability.

The implications for business ethics of such thinking occur on different levels. A narrow concept of economic sustainability focuses on the economic performance of the corporation itself: the responsibility of management is to develop, produce, and market those products that secure the long-term economic performance of the corporation. This includes a focus on those strategies that, for example, lead to a long-term rise in share price, revenues, and market share rather than short-term 'explosions' of profits at the expense of long-term viability. An example of an unsustainable approach in this perspective would be the financial crisis of 2008 which revealed that many financial services providers had engaged in highly risky transactions for short-term gains in profits and executive bonuses.

A broader concept of economic sustainability would include the company's attitude towards and impacts upon the economic framework in which it is embedded. Paying bribes or building cartels, for instance, could be regarded as economically unsustainable because these activities undermine the long-term functioning of markets. Corporations that attempt to avoid paying corporate taxes through subtle accounting tricks might be said to behave in an unsustainable way: if they are not willing to fund the political institutional environment (such as schools, hospitals, the police, and the justice system), they erode one of the key institutional bases of their corporate success. This issue was brought to wider attention in 2012 when it surfaced that Starbucks had paid no corporation tax on its £398 million revenues of the previous year in the UK. Similar accounting practices were reported in respect of Amazon, Facebook, and Google in the UK. While these incidents of tax avoidance were perfectly legal, they nevertheless met a public that perceived such corporate behaviour immoral, causing Starbucks to offer a 'voluntary tax payment' of £20 million.[11]

Social perspectives

The development of the social perspective on sustainability has tended to trail behind that of the environmental and economic perspectives (Scott, Park, and Cocklin 2000) and remains a challenging area of development. The explicit integration of social concerns into the business discourse around sustainability can be seen to have emerged during the 1990s, primarily in response to concerns regarding the impacts of business activities on indigenous communities in less-developed countries and regions. It would be wrong to assume though that this means that, until this time, local community claims on business (and other social issues) went entirely unheard by business or unexamined by business ethics scholars. Indeed, in Chapter 2 we shall be tracing the rather impressive literature dealing with such issues. However, the inclusion of social considerations such as these within the specific domain of sustainability marked a significant shift in the way that notions of community relations and sustainability were conceptualized.

The key issue in the social perspective on sustainability is that of *social justice*. This applies, first, to the global level, where currently around 80% of the world's GDP is enjoyed by 1 billion people living in the developed world while the remaining 20% is shared by the 6 billion people living in developing countries. More recently though, social sustainability has also been put on the agenda in many developed countries. Most notably in the US there was a rise of the 'Occupy Wall Street' movement in 2011, which quickly spread to hundreds more cities across the globe. The central issue highlighted by the protest was the widening gap in wealth between the top 1% and the rest of society. Globally, the top 10% of people own 86% of the global wealth (Credit Suisse 2013), with countries such as the US, Mexico, and Turkey leading the inequality statistics according to the OECD.[12] This problem has grown over time and has particularly challenged the notion of a middle class in the US: while in 1983 the poorest 47% in the US owned on average $15,000, by 2009 their wealth had gone down to zero. As Robert Reich (2012) has argued in his book and subsequent movie[13] such inequality is unsustainable, threating not only the balance of the economy but also the long-term stability of social and political institutions in the country.

Such issues of social sustainability are of utmost importance to business. Reich's suggestions to address this problem, be it reform of the financial system, the strengthening of worker's rights or a reining-in of corporate influence in politics, all point to private business as one key target of reform. Throughout this book we will discuss a number of these issues and analyse business's responsibility for its impacts on society in a variety of contexts.

VISIT THE
ONLINE
RESOURCE
CENTRE
for a short
response to this
feature

? THINK THEORY

Think about inequality in terms of the definition for sustainability provided above. To what extent do you think inequality is relevant for the maintenance of social, economic, or environmental systems?

☑ **Skill check**

Triple bottom line analysis. To understand the simultaneous economic, social, and environmental impacts of business decisions is crucial. A triple bottom line analysis helps to evaluate this performance and to manage not only these different business goals but also to manage the trade-offs between the three areas.

Implications of sustainability for business ethics

Given this extended set of expectations placed on business according to the triple bottom line of sustainability, there are clearly significant implications for how we should look at business ethics. Issues of an ethical nature, be they plant closures, product safety issues, or industrial pollution, demand that we think about a diverse and complex range of considerations and concerns. However, to achieve genuine sustainability in any of the three areas, let alone in *all* of them, is perhaps expecting too much. After all, there are few, if any, products, businesses, or industries that can confidently claim to be sustainable in the full sense of the word. However, with the notion of sustainability widely promoted by governments, businesses, NGOs, and academia, it is clearly vital that we understand its full implications and evaluate business ethics practices according to their performance along, and trade-offs between, the different dimensions of sustainability. As Elkington (1999) suggests, the TBL is less about establishing accounting techniques and performance metrics for achievements in the three dimensions (which we shall look at in Chapter 5), and more about revolutionizing the way that companies think about and act in their business. It is these challenges, as they are framed according to each of the corporation's stakeholders, that we shall be examining in the second part of the book.

■ Summary

In this chapter we have defined business ethics and set it within a number of significant contemporary debates. First, we have shown the importance of business ethics to current business theory and practice, suggesting that knowledge of business ethics is vital in the contemporary business environment. Next, we have argued that business ethics has been fundamentally recontextualized by the forces of globalization, necessitating a distinctly global view of ethical problems and practices in business. Finally, we have identified sustainability as a crucial concept that helps to determine and frame the goals of business activities from an ethical perspective. In the rest of the book we shall revisit these themes of globalization, international diversity, and sustainability many more times in order to expand, refine, and contextualize the initial arguments put forward here. In Chapter 2 though, we shall move on to consider specifically the social role and responsibilities of the corporation, and examine the emerging concept of corporate citizenship.

Study questions

1. Critically evaluate the proposition that business ethics is an oxymoron.

2. 'Business ethics is of no practical importance to managers. Debates about right and wrong should be left in the classroom.' Critically evaluate this statement using examples where appropriate.

3. What is the relationship between business ethics and the law?

4. 'Business ethics do not really matter to small firm owners. They will get away with whatever they can in order to succeed.' Critically examine why such a view of small firms might be pervasive and whether it is likely to be accurate.

5. What is globalization and why is it important for understanding business ethics? Select one multinational corporation based in your home country and set out the different ways in which globalization might have implications for business ethics in that corporation.

6. What is sustainability? To what extent do you think it is possible for corporations in the following industries to be sustainable? Explain your answers.

   (a) Tobacco industry.

   (b) Oil industry.

   (c) Car industry.

Research exercise

Business ethics issues are reported on regularly in the media. Conduct a thorough investigation of all the incidents that have been reported on the web during the past two weeks in your home country.

1. List the incidents that you have unearthed, and identify the main issues and criticisms in each case.

2. To what extent is it possible to classify these as ethical as opposed to legal violations?

3. Which companies have been implicated in each case? Are these large or small companies, local or international in scope? Explain your findings.

4. In which country has each incident taken place? Can you identify any national or regional influences on the types of cases that have come to light?

VISIT THE
ONLINE
RESOURCE
CENTRE
for links to
further key
readings

Key readings

1. Collins, J.W. 1994. Is business ethics an oxymoron? *Business Horizons*, September-October: 1–8.

   This paper is very readable and provides a good overview of the challenge facing business ethics. It goes on to identify a route forward that emphasizes the importance of managers in building trust and creating value.

2. Cullum, L. , Darbyshire, C.C. , Delgado, R. , and Vey, P.C. 2005. Executives behaving badly. *Harvard Business Review*, September: 106–7.

   Humour is a great way to start thinking about business ethics. This article presents cartoons focusing on the theme of executives behaving badly in the work environment, and provides a good platform for thinking about why the idea that business ethics is an oxymoron is so embedded in organizational life. Read the cartoons, have a laugh, and then consider what needs to change in organizations in order to get people to take ethics more seriously.

VISIT THE
ONLINE
RESOURCE
CENTRE
for links to
useful sources
of further
information on
this case

Case 1

Global McEthics: should McDonald's ethics be standardized across the globe?

This case examines ethical criticisms of the US fast-food giant McDonald's, and explores demands for the company to extend its efforts to maintain legitimacy across the globe. The case focuses on the problems of obesity and unhealthy eating that have confronted the company, which are presented in the context of the broader critique of the chain. These issues cover many of the key concepts around ethics, globalization, and sustainability that are discussed in Chapter 1.

McDonald's is truly a multinational corporation. By 2014, the firm was operating some 33,000 restaurants in 119 countries, serving over 64 million customers a day. The market leader in its industry, and one of the most vigorous exponents of a global business approach, McDonald's has pioneered an innovative business model that has since been widely imitated in the fast-food industry and beyond. McDonald's is also hugely popular with its core customer base for providing cheap, fun, convenient food, earning it a range of affectionate nicknames around the world including Maccy D's in the UK, Donken in Sweden, McDo in France, Macca's in Australia, and Makku in Japan. With 57 million likes, McDonald's is one of the most liked companies on Facebook.

However, McDonald's has also faced enormous criticism of its business practices across the world since the 1980s. In the US and Europe, McDonald's has been one of the main corporate targets of environmentalists, animal welfare activists, nutritionists, and social justice campaigners. Not only does the company have the distinction of being the subject of England's longest ever trial—the legendary 1990s McLibel case—but it was also the unwitting subject of the Oscar-nominated *Super Size Me* movie, one of the top 20 highest grossing documentaries of all time. McDonald's has probably faced more store occupations, protests, and online campaigns against it than almost any other company.

Nutritionists and healthy-eating campaigners continue to roundly criticize the company for its standard fare of high-calorie burgers and fries that many see as a major cause of spiralling obesity rates, especially among young people. Even its more recent attempts to introduce healthier menu options have often been greeted with scepticism or hostility, either because they are seen as too little too late, or simply not as healthy as they are purported to be. Meanwhile, with increasing affluence in Asia and Latin America leading to a wave of diet-related problems similar to those in North America and Europe—such as escalating rates of obesity and diabetes in children and young adults—many have suggested that the new directions that McDonald's has taken in some countries should be replicated everywhere it does business.

Big Mac under attack

When the epic McLibel trial came to an end after more than three years in 1997, the McDonald's corporation must have thought that things could not get any worse. Although the company was partly vindicated by the judge's verdict concerning the veracity of some of the claims made by an obscure London activist group in the late 1980s, the two unemployed campaigners that the huge company had spent millions of dollars taking to court were ruled to have proven several of their claims. These included accusations that the company 'exploits children' with its advertising; was 'culpably responsible' for cruelty to animals; was 'strongly antipathetic' to unions; paid its workers low wages; falsely advertised its food as nutritious; and risked the health of its most regular, long-term customers—hardly a positive message to be sending to its millions of customers and critics across the world. The trial attracted massive international publicity, and even sparked the publication of an acclaimed book, TV programme, and a movie. Most damaging of all, the McSpotlight website was launched, which immediately made a wealth of information critical of McDonald's, much of it used in the trial, freely available to an international audience, even to this day.

More trouble soon came from across the channel when anti-globalization campaigners made international headlines for attacking McDonald's stores in France and other parts of Europe—a theme which then extended to other parts of the world between 2000 and 2010 due to an upsurge in anti-American feeling following the Iraq invasion. At the same time, a major thorn in the company's side in its North American heartland was People for the Ethical Treatment of Animals (PETA) which launched its McCruelty campaign in 1999 to try and force the company to alleviate animal suffering in its supply chain. Having placed a moratorium on its campaign in 2000 after McDonald's agreed to make improvements, it was reactivated in 2009 due to the firm's refusal to adopt less-cruel slaughter methods.

However, probably the biggest ethical challenge faced by McDonald's across the globe has been around issues of health and nutrition. With critics claiming that a diet of fast food had been a major contributor to escalating rates of obesity, McDonald's, as the world's leading fast-food company, has inevitably found itself first in the firing line. Among the arguments made by its critics over the years are that the company has failed to provide a balanced menu, that it provides insufficient nutritional information and guidance, and that it actively encourages consumers (especially children) to make unhealthy choices, for example by promoting 'supersize' portions.

Meanwhile, governments also started to tackle the fast-food industry in an effort to address health and nutrition issues. In 2007, France introduced a legal requirement for all advertising of unhealthy food and drink to bear a health message. In 2009, New York City enacted a law requiring restaurant chains to display calorie information on their menus—which in turn became federal law in the US in 2010. The UK government introduced a voluntary pledge on calorie labelling, signed by McDonald's amongst others, in 2011. Ireland, meanwhile, banned all advertising for food high in fat, sugar, and salt during children's programming in 2013.

Big Mac slims down

In the face of such events, McDonald's has not stood idly by, especially once profits looked to be at risk. Not only were activists and governments focusing more attention on healthier food choices, customer preferences were also clearly changing. The chain launched a substantial turnaround strategy in 2003 where, to many people's surprise, the firm dropped its supersizing options, and put a range of new healthy options on the menu, including salads and grilled chicken flatbreads, oatmeal for breakfast, and even the opportunity for concerned parents to replace fries with carrot sticks and fruit in the ubiquitous children's 'happy meals'. Advertising campaigns emphasizing the firm's fresh and healthy new approach accompanied the menu changes and extended in-store and online nutritional labelling also followed—moves once vigorously resisted by the company.

Beyond its own stores, McDonald's has also launched a swathe of exercise and sports initiatives especially targeted at young people. Promoted under the theme of 'balanced lifestyles', the company has sought to show young people the two sides to a healthy lifestyle—a balanced diet and exercise. McDonald's websites in countries across Europe began including sports sections in addition to the usual information about stores and menus, and these have now become a standard feature on national websites. For instance, since 2007 McDonald's Germany has partnered with DFB, the German football association, in a programme to provide soccer badge clubs for children and young people, which has reached more than a million participants.

Such developments have met with considerable scepticism from some of the company's critics. This has especially been the case when it has been revealed that some of the firm's new menu items, such as particular salads or oatmeal flavours, have more fat and calories than the much-maligned hamburger. However, to this and many other criticisms the company has typically been quick to respond with rebuttals or further refinements in the menu. For example, the firm further refined its Happy Meals formula in US stores in 2012 by reducing the quantity of fries and automatically adding apples.

Over time it has become clear that the shifts under way at McDonald's are part of a long-term strategic realignment towards the changing societal values and expectations it is facing. This was further emphasized by a commitment to serve Rainforest Alliance-certified sustainably grown coffee in its restaurants, which is now in place in much of Europe and in Australia and New Zealand, as well as some coffee options in the US. In 2013, the company also announced that it would be the first US chain to label all of its fish products with the widely accepted Marine Stewardship Council sustainable fish logo, and subsequently announced that it would next start purchasing verified sustainable beef in 2016.

Surprising to many has also been the firm's gradual embracing of greater transparency, such as through its 'Open for Discussion' blog about sustainability and the 'Our Food. Your Questions' initiative that was launched in Canada in 2012. The 'Our Food. Your Questions' campaign allows people to submit any kind of questions about McDonald's food to a dedicated website, which it then commits to post online and answer in an open and honest manner. The campaign is an explicit attempt by the company to dispel what it regards as myths about its food, and inform the public better about its products, because as its website acknowledges, 'we haven't always done a great job of answering questions'. The campaign was hugely successful in Canada, generating thousands of questions, millions of views, and billions of social impressions, as well as garnering multiple industry awards. In 2013, McDonald's Australia went one step further with a 'Track my Macca's' app that enables consumers to scan their burger's container to discover the source of the food and where it was processed.

In most respects, McDonald's strategy appears to have been a success. Trust in the brand has improved in the face of campaigns such as 'Our Food. Your Questions', and because the menu is healthier, families have a greater opportunity to provide their children with a more balanced meal under the golden arches. Even the firm's fiercest critics seem to have lost some of their momentum in the firm's heartlands in North America and Europe.

Big Mac goes east

Despite the apparent success of the McDonald's ethical turnaround in North America and Europe, many of the same threats to its reputation have returned to haunt the company in Asia. With increasing prosperity in emerging economies such as India and China, the demand for eating out and for a whole range of convenience foods has expanded substantially since the turn of the century. This has come at a time when Western markets for traditional fast food have become saturated with little opportunity for significant growth. Capitalizing on growth in Asia, McDonald's has targeted major store expansion in the region, with the firm's China business expanding faster than any other market in the early 2010s.

But as eating habits have changed, so too have health considerations. Rates of obesity in China and India have rocketed since the turn of the century. Although only a few decades ago famine was a more common threat, the region is said now to be facing an oncoming obesity epidemic. Other diet and exercise-related problems such as diabetes and heart disease are also on the rise.

To date, activists and regulators have not challenged fast-food companies such as McDonald's to the same extent that they were attacked in Europe and North America, but growing pressure is clearly evident. In China, researchers have shown that the discourse around McDonald's has increasingly shifted from one focused on it being a cheap, modern place for the young, to also incorporating concerns about 'junk food', health and environmental considerations, food safety, and associations with Western imperialism. *Ethical Corporation* magazine revealed that, although widespread in Europe, nutritional information was absent on McDonald's websites for the Philippines, Hong Kong, and China. Moreover, practices now halted in North America and Europe appeared to be much in use in Asia—such as dedicated online kids' zones where the company has been accused of targeting young children with unhealthy food.

The company this time has been less slow to respond to its critics—a healthy option corn soup has emerged on the menu in China, vegetarian burgers feature in India, and the games, competitions, and special offers featured on the company's Asian kids' zones have largely been scaled back. But calories are not yet typically posted on menu boards in Asia as they are in the UK or the US, and transparency clearly lags behind developments in Canada and Australia. In general, the overall emphasis on healthy eating, exercise, and a balanced lifestyle has yet to be actively promoted in Asia to anything like the same extent as in North America and Europe, even if countries such as Malaysia and Singapore now feature such programmes. However, signs that the company is moving towards a more globally integrated approach to health and nutrition emerged in 2013 when the company announced that it would start offering healthy options as part of its 'value meals' in all of its 20 major global markets by 2020. The company simultaneously announced plans to promote and market only water, milk and juice as the beverages in its children's Happy Meals.

Questions

1. Set out the main criticisms that have been levelled at McDonald's in the West. To what extent are these criticisms likely to be replicated in Asia? What differences can be predicted?

2. Describe and evaluate the tactics used by McDonald's in responding to its critics in the past. Will these work to the same degree in Asia?

3. Should McDonald's offer healthy alternatives to the same extent in all of the countries in which it operates, or just those where it has been criticized in the past, or is it expecting further regulation? What if customers overseas do not want healthy options?

4. How could McDonald's seek to avoid further criticism in the future? Can the company realistically present itself as an ethical corporation?

5. How sustainable is the fast-food industry from the point of view of the triple bottom line?

Sources

Baertlein, L. 2013. Want fruit with your burger? McDonald's expands anti-obesity push. *Reuters*, 26 September: http://www.reuters.com/article/2013/09/26/us-mcdonalds-menu-obesity-idUSBRE98P1DI20130926.

Chhabara, R. 2008. Brand marketing—catering for local tastes. *Ethical Corporation*, 13 November: 20–21.

Gao, Z. 2013. Revisiting the golden arches in China: the Chinese discourse on McDonald's between 1978 and 2012. *Journal of Macromarketing*, 33: 288–305.

The Economist 2004. Big Mac's makeover—McDonald's turned around. *The Economist*, 16 October: www.mcdonalds.com, www.mcdonalds.ca, www.mcdonalds.de, www.mcdonalds.com.my, mcdonaldsindia.com, www.mcdonalds.com.sg.

Notes

1. For example, Kelemen and Peltonen (2001) analyse the different usage of the concepts of 'ethics' and 'morality' in the writings of Michel Foucault and Zygmunt Bauman, two leading authors in the area of postmodern business ethics. They reveal strikingly different distinctions that in fact virtually provide a direct contradiction to one another.

2. 'Americans Decry Power of Lobbyists, Corporations, Banks, Feds', Gallup Politics, 11 April 2011: http://www.gallup.com/poll/147026/Americans-Decry-Power-Lobbyists-Corporations-Banks-Feds.aspx (accessed 25 November 2013).

3. 'Financial Services Professionals Feel Unethical Behavior May Be a Necessary Evil and Have Knowledge of Workplace Misconduct, According to Labaton Sucharow Survey', Labaton Sucharow, 10 July 2012: http://www.labaton.com/en/about/press/Labaton-Sucharow-announces-results-of-financial-services-professional-survey.cfm (accessed 25 November 2013).

4. 2013 Edelman Trust Barometer: http://www.edelman.com/insights/intellectual-property/trust-2013/ (accessed 12 April 2013).
5. *The ethical consumerism report 2014*. http://www.ethicalconsumer.org/portals/0/downloads/ethical_consumer_markets_report_2014.pdf.
6. http://www.occupy.com/article/occupy-language-its-time-debunk-few-words (accessed 10 April 2013).
7. There is a wide range of literature addressing globalization and its meaning. A good introduction is provided by Scherer and Palazzo (2008a).
8. http://online.wsj.com/article/SB10000872396390444592404578030274200387136.html (accessed 10 April 2013).
9. http://www.theguardian.com/business/2012/dec/03/amazon-google-starbucks-tax-avoidance (accessed 17 December 2013).
10. For an early articulation of this relationship, see Meadows et al. (1974). While many of their initial predictions of growth limits proved to be overly pessimistic, the basic principle of carrying capacity has become largely accepted.
11. http://www.bbc.co.uk/news/business-19967397 (accessed 10 April 2013).
12. http://www.oecd.org/els/soc/OECD2013-Inequality-and-Poverty-8p.pdf (accessed 18 December 2013).
13. http://www.inequalityforall.com (accessed 17 December 2013).

2

Framing Business Ethics

CORPORATE RESPONSIBILITY, STAKEHOLDERS, AND CITIZENSHIP

Having completed this chapter you should be able to:

- Explain why corporations have social responsibilities.
- Explain corporate social responsibility in terms of its levels, strategies, and outcomes.
- Explain the stakeholder theory of the firm.
- Apply accurately the concepts of corporate citizenship, accountability, and transparency to the political role of corporation.
- Critically evaluate the implications of applying these theories and concepts to different international contexts.

Key concepts and skills:

Concepts

- Corporate social responsibility (CSR)
- Stakeholder theory
- Corporate citizenship
- Corporate accountability
- Corporate transparency

Skills

- Applying the CSR pyramid
- Designing a CSR strategy
- Stakeholder analysis
- Corporate citizenship analysis

■ Towards a framework for business ethics

In Chapter 1 we defined the subject of business ethics as 'the study of business situations, activities, and decisions where issues of right and wrong are addressed'. In order to address issues of right and wrong, the crucial starting point for businesses is the question of whether companies are actors that have to make decisions beyond simply producing goods and services on a profitable basis. After all, if companies provide us with great products that we want to buy, employ workers to produce them, and pay taxes to government, are they not already providing a sufficient contribution to society? It is the definition and justification of these potentially wider responsibilities that is the subject of this chapter.

We begin by addressing the fundamental nature of the modern corporation in order to answer the question of whether corporations can have a moral responsibility in the same way as individual people do. We then proceed to discuss key themes in the literature on the social role of business, namely corporate social responsibility, stakeholder theory, and corporate accountability. We finish the chapter by exploring the notion of corporate citizenship. We argue that although this is a new concept to have emerged from the literature, and it can be interpreted in a number of different ways, in its fullest sense it can be extremely useful for framing some of the problems of business ethics in the global economy that were raised in Chapter 1.

■ What is a corporation?

It may seem like an obvious question, but the practical and legal identification of the corporation within any given society has significant implications for how, and indeed whether, certain types of responsibility can be assigned to such an entity. Corporations are clearly not the same as individual people, and before we can decide what responsibilities they might have, we need to define exactly what they are and why they exist in the first place.

The corporation is by far the dominant form of business entity in the modern global economy. Although not all businesses (such as sole traders) are corporations, and many corporations (such as charities and universities) are not-for-profit businesses, we shall be concentrating primarily on business in the corporate form.

Key features of a corporation

So what is it that defines a corporation? A corporation is essentially defined in terms of legal status and the ownership of assets. Legally, corporations are regarded as independent from those who work in them, manage them, invest in them, or receive products or services from them. Corporations are separate entities in their own right. For this reason, corporations are regarded as having *perpetual succession*, i.e. as an entity, they can survive the death of any individual investors, employees, or customers—they simply need to find new ones.

This legal status leads to the second key defining feature of corporations. Rather than shareholders or managers owning the assets associated with a corporation, *the corporation owns its own assets*. The factories, offices, computers, machines, and other assets operated by, say, Samsung, are the property of Samsung, not of its shareholders. Shareholders simply own a share in the company that entitles them to a dividend and some say in certain decisions affecting the company. They could not, for instance, arrive at Samsung's HQ and try to remove a computer or a desk and take it home, because it is Samsung that owns that computer or desk, not the shareholder. Similarly, employees, customers, suppliers, etc., deal with and agree contracts with the corporation, not with shareholders.

The implications of this situation are significant for our understanding of the responsibilities of corporations:

- **Corporations are typically regarded as 'artificial persons' in the eyes of the law**. That is, they have certain rights and responsibilities in society, just as an individual citizen might.

- **Corporations are notionally 'owned' by shareholders, but exist independently of them**. The corporation holds its own assets, and shareholders are not responsible for the debts or damages caused by the corporation (they have limited liability).

- **Managers and directors have a 'fiduciary' responsibility to protect the investment of shareholders**. This means that senior management is expected to hold shareholders' investment in trust and to act in their best interests. As we shall see in Chapter 6, the exact nature of the duty this imposes on managers and how it is legally structured actually varies across different parts of the world.

This establishes a legal framework for corporations to be open to questions of responsibility in that a company is legally responsible for its actions in the eyes of the law. However, this is not quite the same as assigning a *moral* responsibility to corporations. After all, it is one thing to say that a person feels a sense of moral responsibility for their actions, and can feel pride or shame in doing the right or wrong thing, but clearly we cannot claim the same for inanimate entities such as corporations. Hence, we need to look a little more closely at the specific nature and responsibilities of corporations.

Can a corporation have social responsibilities?

In 1970, just after the first major wave of the business ethics movement in the US, the Nobel-Prize-winning economist Milton Friedman published an article that has since become a classic text, questioning the alleged social role of corporations. Under the provocative title 'The social responsibility of business is to increase its profits', he vigorously protested against the notion of social responsibilities for corporations. His arguments, which have been rehearsed by many corporate responsibility sceptics over the years (see for example Karnani 2010), boil down to three concerns:

- **Only human beings have a moral responsibility for their actions**. The first substantial point is that corporations are not human beings and therefore cannot assume true moral responsibility for their actions. Since corporations are set up by individual human beings, it is those human beings who have moral responsibility for the actions of the corporation.

- **It is managers' responsibility to act solely in the interests of shareholders**. The second concern is that as long as a corporation abides by the legal framework society has set up for business, the only responsibility of the managers of the corporation is to make profit, because it is for this task that the firm has been set up and the managers have been employed. Acting for any other purpose constitutes a betrayal of their special responsibility to shareholders and thus essentially represents a 'theft' from shareholders' pockets.

- **Social issues and problems are the proper province of the state rather than corporate managers**. The critics' third main point is that managers should not, and cannot, decide what is in society's best interests. This is the job of government. Corporate managers are neither trained to set and achieve social goals, nor (unlike politicians) are they democratically elected to do so.

We will deal with the second and third points shortly. First, however, we will examine the proposition that a company cannot be morally responsible for what it does, since its decisions are essentially those of individual people.

Can a corporation be morally responsible for its actions?

Is a corporation just a loose collection of individuals who work together under the same roof, or is it a distinct entity of its own which can actually assume moral responsibility for the rights and wrongs of its actions? We suggest four considerations that have contributed to a situation where most scholars, and indeed the wider public, would nowadays answer this question in the affirmative.

- **Legal identity**. Perhaps the strongest case for assigning responsibility to a corporation comes from the legal perspective because corporations have a distinct legal identity. Corporations enter into contracts, they are subject to a host of legal requirements, including paying taxes, ensuring the safety of their products and meeting environmental obligations. Corporations can sue other entities, and vice versa, and they can be subject to all sorts of legal prosecutions. Corporations can also claim a number of rights. Indeed, the scope of corporate rights in the US has been significantly enlarged in recent years through rulings that grant corporate rights to free speech under the First Amendment, including the ability to limitlessly fund political campaigns.[1]

- **Agency**. Corporations can also be said to decide and act independent of their members (Moore 1999). This argument is based on the idea that every organization has a *corporate internal decision structure* that directs corporate decisions in line with predetermined goals (French 1979). Such an internal decision structure is manifested in various elements—such as corporate policies and procedures—that, acting together, result in the majority of corporate actions being regarded as the result of corporate, not individual, decisions. This does not completely deny individual agency and there are still quite a number of decisions that can be directly traced back to individual actors. The crucial point is that corporations have an organized framework of decision-making that establishes an explicit or implicit *purpose* for these decisions.

- **Organizational culture**. A further argument supporting the moral dimension of corporate responsibility is the fact that all companies not only have an organized corporate internal decision structure, but also a set of beliefs and values that set out what is generally regarded as right or wrong in the corporation—namely, the *organizational culture* (Moore 1999). As we shall see in Chapter 4, these values and beliefs are widely believed to be a strong influence on the individual's ethical decision-making and behaviour. Hence, many of the issues discussed in this book for which corporations receive either praise or blame can be traced back to the company's culture. For example, the executive director of Ethisphere, which produces an annual list of the 'world's most ethical companies' argues that 'a culture of ethics is crucial to sustainable excellence' (Smith 2013).

- **Functional identity**. Finally, on a more general level we observe that corporations present themselves and interact with customers and other stakeholders as if they were distinct persons. Often associated with their brand, companies interact with customers as objects of affection (e.g. McDonalds' 'I'm lovin' it' slogan), or companionship (e.g. Jack Daniels' 'Become a friend of Jack' feature)—or just put up a human face as the brand to begin with, such as Colonel Sanders (Kentucky Fried Chicken) or Mr Clean (Procter & Gamble). As we will see later in this chapter, many corporations refer to themselves as corporate 'citizens' and espouse the aspiration to act as a good neighbour and partner with other members of society.

We can therefore conclude that corporations do indeed have some level of moral responsibility that is more than the responsibility of the individuals constituting the corporation. In the following sections, we will take a closer look at the second argument brought forward by Friedman (and many of his followers). This questions any social responsibilities a corporation might have beyond those that are based on the duty to produce profits for shareholders. In order to do so, we shall primarily discuss the two most influential concepts to have arisen from the business ethics literature to date: corporate social responsibility and stakeholder theory.

■ Corporate social responsibility

The systematic reasoning about a conceptual framework for corporate social responsibility (CSR) started in the US more than half a century ago (Carroll 2008). During this time many different concepts and principles have been aired and debated in relation to CSR. Such debates have focused on two key questions:

1. Why might it be argued that corporations have social as well as financial responsibilities?

2. What is the nature of these social responsibilities?

Let us look at each of these two questions in turn.

Why do corporations have social responsibilities?

This first question has raised enormous amounts of controversy in the past, but it is by now fairly widely accepted that businesses do indeed have responsibilities beyond simply making a profit. This is based on a number of distinct, but related, arguments, many of which tend to be couched in terms of *enlightened self-interest*, i.e. the corporation takes on social responsibilities insofar as doing so promotes its own self-interest. Such a 'business case for CSR', is commonly advanced using four main arguments (Davis 1973; Mintzberg 1983; Smith 2003; Kurucz et al. 2008):

- **Enhance (long-term) revenues**. Corporations perceived as being socially responsible might be rewarded with extra and/or more satisfied customers, while perceived irresponsibility may result in boycotts or other undesirable consumer actions. Just consider the commercial success that automotive companies Toyota and Tesla have had with hybrid and electric cars, respectively. Similarly, employees might be more attracted to, and committed to, corporations perceived as being socially responsible, giving such companies more effective workforces (Greening and Turban 2000).

- **Reduce costs**. CSR can reduce costs as it helps in saving energy, reducing waste and cutting out inefficiencies. Wal-Mart, for instance, is expected to have achieved savings of $1 billion by 2020 due to such CSR-related measures in particular with regard to enhancing its environmental performance.[2]

- **Manage risk and uncertainty**. Voluntarily committing to social actions and programmes may forestall legislation and ensure greater corporate independence from government (Moon and Vogel 2008). A more responsible approach to the safety of their offshore drilling might have saved BP the $20 billion it had to spend in the aftermath of the Deepwater Horizon Accident in the Gulf of Mexico in 2010. Furthermore, in the aftermath of the Rana Plaza factory collapse in 2013 in Bangladesh, many Western retailers with links to suppliers there feared damage to their brands and reputation.

- **Maintaining the social licence to operate**. A considerable driver for CSR in resource-based industries is the necessity for gaining and maintaining the consent of local communities, employees, and governments. Such actors can effectively provide or revoke a social licence to operate to business. More broadly, making a positive contribution to society might be regarded as a long-term investment in a safer, better-educated and more equitable community, which subsequently benefits the corporation by creating an improved and stable competitive context in which to do business (Porter and Kramer 2006).

These are primarily good *business* reasons why it might be advantageous for the corporation to act in a socially responsible manner. **Case 2** provides an example of American Apparel, a company that positions itself clearly as a responsible company in the fashion industry and that has reaped some success in doing so. In arguing against CSR, Friedman (1970) in fact does not dispute the validity of such actions, but rather says that when they are carried out for reasons of self-interest, they are not CSR at all, but merely profit-maximization 'under the cloak of social responsibility'. This may well be true, and to a large extent depends on the *primary motivations* of the decision-maker (Bowie 1991). It is not so much a matter of whether profit subsequently arises from social actions, but whether profit or altruism was the main reason for the action in the first place. However, corporate motives are difficult, sometimes impossible, to determine. Also, despite numerous academic studies, a direct relationship between social responsibility and profitability has been almost impossible to unambiguously 'prove'.[3] Even though the overall weight of evidence seems to suggest some kind of positive relationship, there is still the issue of causality (Orlitzky 2008). When successful companies are seen to be operating CSR programmes, it is just as reasonable to suggest that CSR does not contribute to the success, but rather the financial success frees the company to indulge in the 'luxury' of CSR.

Hence, in addition to these business arguments for CSR, it is also important to consider further *moral* arguments for CSR:

- **The externalities argument**: Externalities are the positive and social impacts of an economic transaction that are borne by those other than the parties engaging in the transaction. Corporations create a variety of externalities of one sort or the other. Whether through the provision of products and services, the employment of workers, or through their ubiquitous advertising—corporations cannot escape responsibility for these impacts, whether they are positive, negative, or neutral. Many regard corporations to have a moral responsibility to deal with, in particular, the negative externalities they cause, such as pollution, resource depletion, or community problems, insofar as these are not dealt with by governments.

- **The power argument**: Another important argument is that as powerful social actors, with recourse to substantial resources, corporations should use the power and resources responsibly in society. Some refer to this as the Spiderman maxim: 'with great power comes great responsibility'.

- **The dependency argument**: Corporations rely on the contribution of a much wider set of constituencies, or stakeholders in society (such as consumers, suppliers, local communities), rather than just shareholders, and hence have a duty to take into account the interests and goals of these stakeholders as well as those of shareholders.

Given this range of moral and business arguments for CSR, the case for CSR is on a reasonably secure footing, although as we shall discuss later in the chapter, there are also problems with this, particularly in terms of the accountability of corporations (see Implications of CC: corporate accountability and transparency, p. 76). Our next question though is: if corporations have some type of social responsibility, what form does that responsibility take?

VISIT THE ONLINE RESOURCE CENTRE for a short response to this feature

> **? THINK THEORY**
>
> Theories of CSR suggest there are both business and moral reasons for engaging in social initiatives. Go to the website of one or two companies of your choice and find the section dealing with social issues (the page may be headed CSR or sustainability, or perhaps corporate citizenship) and see what kinds of reasons the corporations give for their involvement in CSR. Is there a balance of business and moral reasons, or does one type of reason predominate? How do you explain this?

Corporate social responsibility
The attempt by companies to meet the economic, legal, ethical, and philanthropic demands of a given society at a particular point in time.

What is the nature of corporate social responsibilities?

Probably the most established and accepted model of CSR that addresses our second question is the 'Four-part model of corporate social responsibility', as initially proposed by Archie Carroll (1979), and subsequently refined in later publications (e.g. Carroll 1991; Carroll and Buchholtz 2015). This model is depicted in **Figure 2.1**.

Carroll regards **corporate social responsibility** as a multilayered concept, which can be differentiated into four interrelated aspects—economic, legal, ethical, and philanthropic responsibilities. He presents these different responsibilities as consecutive layers

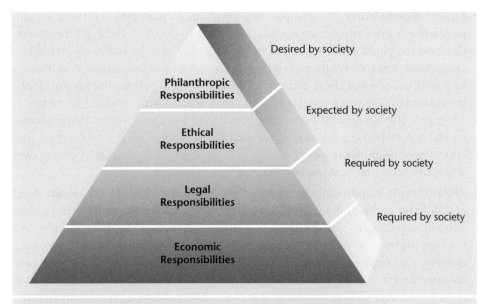

Figure 2.1 Carroll's four-part model of corporate social responsibility

Source: Adapted from Carroll, A.B. 1991. The pyramid of corporate social responsibility: toward the moral management of organizational stakeholders. *Business Horizons*: 42, Fig. 3.

within a pyramid, such that 'true' social responsibility requires the meeting of all four levels consecutively, depending on the expectations present in society at the time.

- **Economic responsibility**. Companies have shareholders who demand a reasonable return on their investments, they have employees who want good jobs, and they have customers who want their products to satisfy their needs. So the first responsibility of business is to be a well-functioning economic unit and to stay in business. This first layer of CSR is the basis for all the subsequent responsibilities, which rest on this (ideally) solid basis. According to Carroll (1991), the satisfaction of economic responsibilities is thus *required* of all corporations. In the extreme this leads to the idea that some large banks are 'too big to fail' because their basic economic functions are so vital to society that they should be 'bailed out' by governments and taxpayers when in trouble.

- **Legal responsibility**. The legal responsibility of corporations demands that businesses abide by the law and 'play by the rules of the game'. Laws, as we have seen in Chapter 1, are the codification of society's moral views, and therefore abiding by these standards is a necessary prerequisite for any further reasoning about social responsibilities. In some ways this may sound trivial if we talk about CSR, but the frequent news about court cases against corporations show that compliance with the law is by no means self-evident. Consider the scandals around mislabelled meat in Europe in 2013, faking of safety certificates in the Korean nuclear industry, or the massive $13 billion fine JP Morgan accepted in the US for misleading investors in mortgage-backed securities[4]—legal responsibilities appear to be an ongoing challenge in discharging CSR. As with economic responsibilities, Carroll (1991) suggests that the satisfaction of legal responsibilities is *required* of all corporations seeking to be socially responsible.

- **Ethical responsibility**. These responsibilities oblige corporations to do what is right, just, and fair even when they are not compelled to do so by the legal framework. Consider the public's scrutiny of the tax policies of companies like Apple, Starbucks, Google and Amazon. While exploitation of loopholes and international differences in legislation allowed these companies to legally avoid substantial tax payments, governments, customers and the general public reacted with outrage.[5] As we saw in Chapter 1, globalization, if anything, has extended this space where companies face ethical expectations in the absence of legal frameworks. Carroll (1991) argues that ethical responsibilities therefore consist of what is generally *expected* by society over and above economic and legal expectations.

- **Philanthropic responsibility**. Lastly, at the tip of the pyramid, the fourth level of CSR looks at the philanthropic responsibilities of corporations. The Greek word 'philanthropy' means literally 'the love of the fellow human'. By using this idea in a business context, the model incorporates activities that are within the corporation's discretion to improve the quality of life of employees, local communities, and ultimately society in general. This aspect of CSR addresses a great variety of issues, including things such as charitable donations, the building of recreation facilities for employees and their families, support for local schools, or sponsoring of art and sports events. According to Carroll (1991: 42), philanthropic responsibilities are therefore merely *desired* of corporations without being expected or required, making them 'less important than the other three categories'.

The benefit of the four-part model of CSR is that it structures the various social responsibilities into different levels, yet does not seek to explain social responsibility without acknowledging the very real demands placed on the firm to be profitable and legal. In this sense, it is fairly pragmatic.

However, its main limitation is that it does not adequately address the problem of what should happen when two or more responsibilities are in conflict. For example, the threat of plant closures and/or job losses often raises the problem of balancing economic responsibilities (of remaining efficient and profitable) with ethical responsibilities to provide secure jobs to employees. A typical example is a company that relocates its operations from the global North to a developing country. While this satisfies the economic level in terms of boosting profits for shareholders and providing employment for hitherto unemployed workers in the developing world, it can clash with ethical responsibilities in terms of abandoning long-standing ties to workers and communities in the North and exploiting lower environmental or social standards overseas.

☑ **Skill check**

Applying the CSR Pyramid. The pyramid of CSR is a useful tool for analysing the specific societal expectations that a corporation faces. Effective application of the pyramid enables a more refined and comprehensive analysis of relevant social responsibilities.

CSR in an international context

CSR as a view of business responsibility in society has been particularly prominent in the US, from where much of the literature, authors, and conceptualizations have emerged. In other parts of the globe, however, the concept of CSR has only recently become so influential. The main reason for this is that the US tends to leave more discretion to companies over their social responsibilities. This has led to a model of *explicit* CSR, which means CSR as a distinct, named activity of private companies. Other countries have operated more of an *implicit* CSR model that sees social responsibilities of business tightly embedded in the legal and institutional framework of society (Matten and Moon 2008). In Europe this has been achieved mainly through regulation, whereas in Africa or Asia other, softer institutions such as religious, customary, or tribal traditions have shaped expectations on business. Generally, then, while one could argue that all levels of CSR play a role outside the US, they clearly have different significance and, furthermore, are interlinked in a somewhat different manner.

- The aspect of *economic* responsibility in the US is strongly focused on the profitability of companies and thus chiefly looks at the responsibility to shareholders. As we shall explain in more detail in Chapter 6, the dominant model of capitalism in much of Europe and Asia has traditionally been somewhat different. This model tends to define economic responsibility far more broadly and focuses, to varying degrees, on the economic responsibility of corporations to employees and local communities as well. Examples include the fairly extensive health care and other social provisions by German or French companies, encompassing a very elaborate system of mandatory workers' rights and collective bargaining.

- The element of *legal* responsibility is often regarded as the basis of every other social responsibility in Europe, particularly given the prominent role of the state in regulating corporate practice. Continental European thinking tends to see the state in the role of enforcing the accepted rules of the game, whereas in the Anglo-American world view, governmental rules are more likely to be regarded as an interference with private liberty. In many developing countries with weak or corrupt governments, compliance at the legal level is often not a very reliable standard of responsible behaviour.

- As we discussed in Chapter 1, different regions of the world vary significantly as to local *ethical* values and preferences. For instance, it has been found that Europeans tend to exhibit greater mistrust in modern corporations than North Americans do, while people in developing countries have far greater levels of trust in business (Edelman 2014). As a result, certain issues such as nuclear power, genetic engineering, and animal testing have always been far higher up the public agenda in Europe than in other parts of the world (Dawson 2005). In the developing world in general, as Visser (2008) has argued, ethical expectations are less prevalent compared to the expectation that corporations assume their economic and philanthropic responsibilities.

- With regard to *philanthropic* responsibility, the US has a long-standing tradition of successful companies or rich capitalists such as Bill Gates donating large sums to the funding of the arts, higher education, or local community services—just to name a few examples (Brammer and Pavelin 2005). In Europe, by contrast, income and corporate taxes are generally higher than in the US and funding of these activities is more an expectation directed towards governments. In developing countries we see that against the backdrop of widespread poverty, companies are increasingly expected to 'share' their wealth with local communities. A good example is the World Instant Noodles Association, whose members are dominantly from developing/emerging economies in Asia, who on a regular basis provide substantial aid to victims of natural disasters, most recently in the aftermath of the earthquake in the Philippines in 2013.[6]

As we can see, while the four levels of responsibility are still largely valid in most international contexts, they take on different nuances, and may be accorded different significance. Thus, CSR, even if neatly defined along the lines of Carroll's model, still lacks some precision. It does however become more concrete if we break it down into different corporate social strategies.

VISIT THE
ONLINE
RESOURCE
CENTRE
for a short
response to this
feature

> **? THINK THEORY**
>
> Think about the concept of CSR in the context of a multinational. To what extent can a multinational corporation operate a global CSR programme, or is it necessary for such companies to operate CSR on a more national or regional basis?

Strategies of CSR

The way companies prioritize different levels of CSR depends on their overall strategy. While there is a rich literature discussing CSR strategies under the label of 'corporate social responsiveness' (Carroll 1979; Wood 1991), and 'strategic CSR' (Burke and Logsdon 1996; Porter and Kramer 2006) we will focus on two basic options, as illustrated in **Figure 2.2**.[7]

'Traditional CSR' is a rather long-standing approach to social responsibility, which in some ways has been practised since the industrial revolution, but is still widespread around the globe. It considers CSR as part of a strategy where a company generates its profits without too much consideration for wider societal expectations. However, once the profit is generated, the company then distributes some of the value created to projects, activities and causes that are important to stakeholders and will ultimately enhance

	Traditional CSR	**Contemporary CSR**
Focus	Risk	Reward
Driver	Image, Brand, Public Acceptance	Performance, Markets, Products
Relation to the bottom line	No direct contribution: CSR is value distribution	Integral goal: CSR is value creation
Responsiveness	Reaction, Defence	Accommodation, Pro-action
Motto	'CSR is bolt-on'	'CSR is built-in'

Figure 2.2 Basic types of CSR strategies

the wider image of the company and bolster its brand identity. Thus, CSR is 'bolted on' to the firm but without any real integration with its core business. In Carroll's model, CSR for these companies is mostly about philanthropy and has very little to do with the other, lower levels of the pyramid. Typically, companies will adopt a defensive or reactive approach to new societal demands, seeking to protect the company and denying responsibility for the social issues at stake (Carroll 1979).

In the 'Contemporary CSR' approach companies see responsible behaviour as an opportunity to generate profits while at the same time living up to expectations of society. Rather than unilaterally 'dishing out' money, they work with stakeholders to understand their interests and expectations, and attempt to cater to their needs by offering business solutions that drive additional value for the firm and their constituencies. CSR for these companies is integral, or 'built in' to core business. Companies that are active in green technologies, develop new or cheaper health-care products, invest in more humane workplaces—just to name some examples—would attempt to proactively integrate social expectations directly into their core operations and ultimately see CSR as a way to drive new business at a profit. **Ethics in Action 2.1** provides an example from the banking sector where BNY Mellon is integrating CSR directly in its business operations.

Both strategic approaches ultimately then ask for ways of conceptualizing observable outcomes of business commitment to CSR, namely *corporate social performance*. After all, companies are eager to assess whether philanthropic donations have indeed led to tangible results or whether new products or new technologies adopted have had the desired societal impact.

☑ Skill check

Designing a CSR strategy. This is a key skill to develop because it sets the entire CSR direction of the company and determines the policies, programmes, and impacts that will be included.

Outcomes of CSR: corporate social performance

If we are able to measure, rate, and classify companies on their economic performance, why should it not be possible to do the same with its social performance as well? The concept of *corporate social performance* (CSP) has, again, generated a long and varied debate about adequate constructs and measures (Gond and Crane 2010). Donna Wood (1991) has presented a model that is widely regarded as the state-of-the-art and has been extensively cited in the CSR literature. Following her model, corporate social performance can be observed as the *principles* of CSR, the *processes* of social responsiveness (or 'CSR strategy' as we have called it), and the *outcomes* of corporate behaviour. These outcomes are delineated in three concrete areas:

• **Social policies**—explicit and pronounced corporate social policies stating the company's values, beliefs, and goals with regard to its social environment. For example, most major firms now explicitly include social objectives in their mission statements and other corporate policies. Some corporations also have more explicit goals and targets in relation to social and environmental issues, such as Unilever and its 'Sustainable Living

VISIT THE
ONLINE
RESOURCE
CENTRE
for links to
useful sources
of further
information

ETHICS IN ACTION 2.1   http://www.ethicalcorp.com

Interview: Jim McEleney, BNY Mellon
Ethical Corporation (EC) Newsdesk, 7 February 2014

McEleney is chief operating officer (COO) for Europe, the Middle East, and Africa (EMEA), based in London at BNY Mellon, a global financial services company. It operates in 35 countries and serves more than 100 markets. It has $27.6 trillion in assets under custody and administration as of 31 December 2013.

EC: It's interesting to be speaking to a chief operating officer (COO) on corporate social responsibility issues (CSR). It's not an issue that falls into the brief of most of your COO colleagues. How does your role relate to corporate responsibility?

McEleney: CSR is certainly important to us in terms of our role as a major global institution. Part of my role as COO is to coordinate our efforts across all of Europe, the Middle East and Africa (EMEA). CSR is about the wellbeing and strength of our workforce, our role in local communities, as well as the day-to-day service that we provide to our clients. These are all a key focus of my role and in my work with our CSR team.

One of our corporate priorities has been around driving excellence. This really comes down to what we do as a provider of investment management and investment services. We're working across the region to improve risk management, productivity, the quality of our operations—so these are all things that I spend my time on.

And more and more we're linking things up to our own CSR agenda. For example, we're simplifying our delivery platforms, investing in technology and so forth, but all in the most resource efficient way possible.

EC: What are the big CSR issues for BNY Mellon specifically?

McEleney: In the past year, we've introduced an approach to CSR which concentrates on materiality and three main areas: first, market integrity; second, our people; and then third, the world.

We've found these are the areas that are most important and relevant to our stakeholders. And more and more we've been linking them into the future of our business.

Within the category of market integrity, for example, our view is that the industry really needs to continue to address issues around governance, ethics and transparency. This could involve addressing regulation, helping to inform and educate others, particularly our clients, on these evolving global regulations, and also how to respond to regulation across the investment lifecycle.

We also really need to focus on operational resiliency for our clients. In our company, we've had several examples of having to focus on resiliency and why the benefits are paying off for us.

We have a pretty major presence, for example, across the Northeast and Mid-Atlantic seaboard in the United States. Hurricane Sandy proved the importance of resilience and BNY Mellon showed very well in that. We definitely link that into our CSR agenda.

EC: Do you feel financial institutions are contributing enough in their immediate communities?

McEleney: In our case, yes, I believe so. Our employees overall are passionate about supporting charities in the cities and neighbourhoods where they live and work.

In fact, we had over 80,000 hours volunteered by employees last year. We see this as a way we can really make a real difference for youth and the people who need it most. It also gives us an opportunity to be role models and enable young people in our communities to consider new possibilities—potential roles or careers—that they hadn't thought they could aspire to, for instance.

EC: Looking at the bigger picture for your industry, do you think structural reforms are required to ensure standards and ethics are met or has enough been done already?

McEleney: I think when we look back, we will see that the industry is undergoing a major transformation. We focused a lot on setting industry standards to reform critical elements of the capital markets infrastructure. We're really working to create an environment that encourages healthy dissent and helps employees to raise concerns. I think BNY Mellon has a unique role in our industry. Given our size, we're sometimes a natural leader in helping to set the standards.

We work with investors along every stage of the investment lifecycle. So there's a role for us given that our clients have different challenges and with our services and expertise we can help them see this through a different lens.

EC: Can you provide a concrete example of how this kind of engagement works?

McEleney: Sure. In the past year, for example, we've actually reconstituted and created a global collateral services business. Part of why we created this business comes from the recognition that our clients really need help to recognize and address risk. We saw an opportunity to provide a solution to this need that would really aid them around the levels of transparency and resiliency that regulators and others are now asking for.

EC: Going forward, what changes do you think are required to create a better culture among the most senior levels of the financial services?

McEleney: Among other things, greater diversity at the top ranks would certainly help. We named our first female president, Karen Peetz, and we've been around for more than 220 years. It's those kinds of changes that are not only set the tone, but bring new ideas and fresh approaches to problems. This is ultimately going to affect the culture around what's accepted, what's acceptable and how decisions are made within the organisation.

EC: Is it really possible to balance your duty to society with your financial duties to your shareholders?

McEleney: Definitely. Financial services really do serve a purpose in society. With the right behaviours and controls in place, I think this industry absolutely has a role to play in not only providing global stability, but also in helping to create prosperity.

Bringing it back to BNY Mellon, we touch nearly a quarter of the world's assets on any given day. So we're absolutely a player in this. We welcome the opportunity that comes with that role, but it is a big responsibility. We believe this whole question extends beyond pure economics, and we treat it as such.

Sources

Ethical Corporation, Ethical Corporation (EC) Newsdesk, 7 February 2014, http://www.ethicalcorp. com. Reproduced with the kind permission of Ethical Corporation.

VISIT THE
ONLINE
RESOURCE
CENTRE
for a short
response to this
feature

> **? THINK THEORY**
>
> Explain how BNY Mellon is implementing a 'contemporary CSR' approach across its various initiatives.

Plan'. Here, the company commits to specific goals for the year 2020, for instance to reduce greenhouse gases by 50%, provide 500 million people with drinking water, or to source 100% of raw material from sustainable sources.[8] In regular updates Unilever then reports on its performance toward these targets indicating whether the company is on track for achieving them in the given time frame.

- **Social programmes**—specific social programmes of activities, measures, and instruments implemented to achieve social policies. For example, many firms have implemented programmes to manage their environmental impacts, based around environmental management systems such as ISO 14000 and EMAS (Environmental Management and Auditing Scheme) that include measures and instruments that facilitate the auditing of environmental performance, or ISO 2600 the international CSR standard.

- **Social impacts**—social impacts can be traced by looking at concrete changes that the corporation has achieved through the programmes implemented in any period. Obviously this is frequently the most difficult to achieve, since much data on social impacts is 'soft' (i.e. difficult to collect and quantify objectively), and the specific impact of the corporation cannot be easily isolated from other factors. Nevertheless, some impacts can be reasonably well estimated. For example: policies aimed at benefiting local schools can examine literacy rates and exam grades; environmental policies can be evaluated with pollution data; employee welfare policies can be assessed with employee satisfaction questionnaires; and equal opportunity programmes can be evaluated by monitoring the composition of the workforce and benchmarking against comparable organizations.

Clearly then, while the outcomes of CSR in the form of CSP is an important consideration, the actual measurement of social performance remains a complex task. We shall be discussing some of the potential tools and techniques for achieving this in more detail in Chapter 5. **Ethics Online 2** provides an example of one important implication of the discussion on corporate social performance: we have been witnessing a rise in the number and prominence of rankings and awards that measure and benchmark responsible corporate behaviour and have led to a highly competitive environment for companies who see value in positioning themselves as good CSR performers. A key element in this is to define not only what the corporation is responsible for, but who it is responsible to. This is the task of stakeholder theory.

■ Stakeholder theory of the firm

The stakeholder theory of the firm is probably the most popular and influential theory to emerge from business ethics (Stark 1994). While the use of the term 'stakeholder' in relation to business was first noted in the 1960s, the theoretical approach was popularized by Edward Freeman (1984) in the 1980s. Unlike the CSR approach, which strongly focuses on the corporation and its responsibilities, the stakeholder approach starts by looking at various groups to which the corporation has a responsibility. The main starting point is the claim that corporations are not simply managed in the interests of their shareholders alone, but that there is a whole range of groups, or stakeholders, that have a legitimate interest in the corporation as well.

Although its basic premise is simple and readily understood, there are numerous different definitions as to who or what constitutes a stakeholder, some of which are shown in **Figure 2.3**. This range of definitions makes it difficult to get a generally agreed upon idea of what a **stakeholder** actually is. To determine who in a specific situation can be considered as a stakeholder, Evan and Freeman (1993) suggest we can apply two simple principles. The first is the *principle of corporate rights*, which demands that the corporation has the obligation not to violate the rights of others. The second, the *principle of corporate effect*, says that companies are responsible for the effects of their actions on others.

> **Stakeholder**
> An individual or a group that, in the context of a specific situation, is either harmed by, or benefits from, the corporation, or whose rights the corporation should respect.

This clarification makes clear that the range of stakeholders differs from company to company, and even for the same company in different situations, tasks, or projects. Using this definition, then, it is not possible to identify a definitive group of relevant stakeholders for any given corporation in any given situation. However, a typical representation is given in **Figure 2.4**.

Figure 2.4(a) shows the traditional model of managerial capitalism, where the company is seen as only related to four groups. Suppliers, employees, and shareholders provide the basic resources for the corporation, which then uses these to provide products for consumers. The shareholders are the 'owners' of the firm and consequently they are the dominant group whose interests should take precedence.

In Figure 2.4(b), we find the stakeholder view of the firm, where the shareholders are one group among several others. The company has obligations not only to one group,

Author	Definition of stakeholders
Stanford memo 1963 (cited in Freeman 1984)	'those groups without whose support the organization would cease to exist'
Rhenman (1964, English trans 1968)	'are depending on the firm in order to achieve their personal goals and on whom the firm is depending for its existence'
Freeman 1984	'can affect or is affected by the achievement of the organization's objectives'
Evan and Freeman 1988	'benefit from or are harmed by, and whose rights are violated or respected by, corporate actions'
Hill and Jones 1992	'constituents who have a legitimate claim on the firm … established through the existence of an exchange relationship' who supply 'the firm with critical resources (contributions) and in exchange each expects its interests to be satisfied'
Clarkson 1995	'have, or claim, ownership, rights, or interests in a corporation and its activities'

Figure 2.3 Some early definitions of stakeholders

VISIT THE ONLINE RESOURCE CENTRE
for links to useful sources of further information

▲ **ETHICS ONLINE 2**

Exploiting the competitive gene: the world of CSR Awards

Ever since the rise of CSR practices in business we have seen the parallel phenomenon of a burgeoning number of CSR-related awards and rankings. In such rankings, the 'most responsible', 'most sustainable' company, or the 'best corporate citizen' gets recognized for their performance and progress in the area of CSR. Most appear online on an annual basis, and provide an overview of the most active companies in the field of responsible business. Unsurprisingly, firms take them seriously, not least because they are widely promoted and discussed online, giving firms a great opportunity to boast about their CSR credentials.

There is considerable diversity in what actually gets assessed as responsible behaviour across the different awards and rankings. Most look at a host of issues, including environmental performance, treatment of employees, community relations, or how well the company avoids irresponsible behaviour (e.g. corruption). But it is also interesting to see the differences between rankings. While the European CSR Award Scheme mostly focuses on partnerships between business and other actors in society, the Asian CSR Awards focus on how well a company contributes to local 'education improvement', 'poverty alleviation', or 'health enhancement'. The awards thus reflect regional differences in what stakeholders expect from a company. In a similar vein, two of the North America-based rankings, the Global 100 and the 100 Best Corporate Citizens lists explicitly include responsible financial management, good corporate governance and the pay gap between CEO and average worker—which clearly reflects some of the key concerns of the North American public in the wake of the financial crisis.

The initiative to conduct these rankings is equally telling. Some of them are conducted by media organizations, such as Corporate Knights, Ethical Corporation, or Corporate Responsibility Magazine. The awards help to boost readership as well as providing a way

of encouraging companies to enhance their CSR performance. Indeed, many rankings are published by business-led organizations that were set up with the goal to further the implementation of CSR in a particular country or region. *CR Magazine* is the voice of the US-based Corporate Responsibility Officers Association, which like Business in the Community (BITC) in the UK or CSR Europe at the EU level, aims to promote responsible business practices among its members. Increasingly, we also see consulting firms and think tanks occupying this space, such as Corporate Register or Sustainia, which both use the internet to solicit entries and publicize winners. Finally, the European CSR Award Scheme is heavily backed by the EU Commission, a pan-European representation of government.

Next to these differences in criteria and the sponsoring organization, we can also observe an increasing diversity in the data used to rank companies. Corporate Register, for instance, focuses exclusively on ranking CSR/non-financial reports of companies and selects winners based on voting by its members. Another influential ranking, the CSR RepTrak 100 Study by the Reputation Institute in New York, instead focuses on the reputation of companies as responsible organizations among a broad panel of stakeholder groups. Others, such as Ethical Corporation's Responsible Business Awards rely on entrants to enter reports of specific initiatives that are then judged by a panel of experts.

The meaning and relevance of these rankings is not uncontested though. There is no shortage of social media criticism each time a ranking or award gets announced. This is because nearly all of the rankings include companies that in some of their operations raise serious concerns. For example, the Global 100 ranking of the world's most sustainable companies features two oil companies among its top six companies, despite their focus on non-renewable fossil fuels. Most rankings also

▼

focus almost exclusively on large, publicly listed companies whose footprint is inevitably larger than that of their smaller counterparts. This, at least, is starting to change with the emergence of two new rankings for small and medium companies—the B Corporation 'Best for the World' ranking of the top 10% of its certified member companies, and Corporate Knights' 'Future 40' ranking of Canadian companies with revenues under $2 billion.

Probably the most important effect of the rankings is that corporations are benchmarked against their competitors and thus feel the need to maintain their standing and, if at all possible, outcompete other companies on the list. Since they are so easily accessible on the internet, most rankings are also increasingly important tools for decision-making by consumers, potential employees, governments and even investors. The demands of the latter stakeholder group has taken the idea of rankings to another level in that many new stock market indices, such as the Dow Jones Sustainability Index or the FTSE4Good, effectively rank companies according to their performance as responsible businesses.

Sources

100 Best Corporate Citizens List, Corporate Responsibility Magazine (USA): http://www.thecro.com/content/2013-100-best-corporate-citizens-list.

Asian CSR Awards (Philippines): http://www.asianforumcsr.com/awards/background.

Best for the World, B Corporation (US): http://bestfortheworld.bcorporation.net.

Corporate Reporting Awards (UK): https://www.corporateregister.com/crra/.

CSR RepTrak 100 Study, Reputation Institute (US): http://www.reputationinstitute.com/thought-leadership/csr-reptrak-100.

Ethical Corporation Responsible Business Awards (UK): http://events.ethicalcorp.com/awards/.

European CSR Award Scheme (EU): http://www.europeancsrawards.eu.

Future 40, Corporate Knights Magazine (Canada): http://www.corporateknights.com/report-types/future-40-responsible-corporate-leaders-canada.

Global 100 Most Sustainable Companies, Corporate Knights Magazine (Canada): http://global100.org.

Sustainia Awards (Denmark): http://www.sustainia.me/sustainia-action-forum/sustainia-award-2013/.

The Responsible Business Awards (UK): http://www.bitc.org.uk/services/awards-recognition/responsible-business-awards.

WorldBAES Award Management (Australia): http://www.worldbaes.com/main/.

but also to a whole variety of other constituencies that are affected by its activities. The corporation is thus situated at the centre of a series of interdependent two-way relationships.

It is important to remember though that stakeholder groups also might have duties and obligations to their *own* set of stakeholders, and to the other stakeholders of the corporation. This gives rise to a *network model* of stakeholder theory (Rowley 1997), which is shown in Figure 2.4(c).

? THINK THEORY

The network model of stakeholder theory suggests that firms have indirect relationships with a whole range of constituencies via their immediate stakeholders. To what extent should corporations also have to respect the rights of these indirect stakeholders? Think, for example, about the case of a company's supply chain and all the different tiers of supplier stakeholders that are involved. Does a company have responsibilities to suppliers at all tiers?

VISIT THE ONLINE RESOURCE CENTRE for a short response to this feature

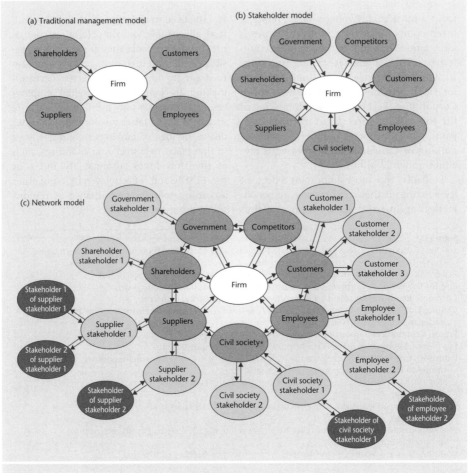

Figure 2.4 Stakeholder theory of the firm

Why stakeholders matter

If we go back to our discussion earlier in the chapter regarding Milton Friedman's arguments against social responsibility, his second main objection was that businesses should only be run in the interests of their owners. This correlates with the traditional stockholder model of the corporation, where managers' only obligation is to shareholders. Indeed, in legal terms, we have already seen that in most developed nations, managers have a special *fiduciary relationship* with shareholders to act in their interests. Stakeholder theory therefore has to provide a compelling reason why other groups also have a legitimate claim on the corporation.

Freeman (1984) himself gives two main arguments. First, on a merely descriptive level, if one examines the relationship between the firm and the various groups to which it is related by all sorts of contracts, it is simply not true to say that the only group with a legitimate interest in the corporation are shareholders. From a *legal perspective*, there are far more groups apart from shareholders that appear to hold a legitimate 'stake' in the corporation since their interests are already protected in some way. There are not only legally binding contracts to suppliers, employees, or customers, but also an increasingly dense network of laws and regulations enforced by society, which make it simply a matter of fact that a large spectrum of different stakeholders have certain rights and claims on the corporation. For example, EU social contract legislation protects certain employee rights in relation to working conditions and pay, suggesting that, from an ethical point of view, it has already been agreed that corporations have certain obligations toward employees. Of course, among this broader set of obligations and rights, there are also obligations toward investors, but from a legal perspective this does not remove the obligation that the corporation has to other stakeholders.

A second group of arguments comes from an *economic perspective*. An important aspect here is the *agency problem*: one of the key arguments for the traditional model is that shareholders are seen as the owners of the corporation, and consequently managers have their dominant obligation to them. This view, however, only reflects the reality of shareholders' interests in a very limited number of cases (Stout 2012). The majority of shareholders do not invest in shares predominantly to 'own' a company (or parts of it), nor do they necessarily seek for the firm to maximize its long-term profitability. In the first place, shareholders often buy shares for speculative reasons, and it is the development of the share price that is their predominant interest—and not 'ownership' in a physical corporation. In his trenchant critique of shareholder dominance, the late management guru Sumantra Ghoshal (2005: 80) therefore argued that 'most shareholders can sell their stocks far more easily than most employees can find another job'. Hence, it is not evident why the highly speculative and mostly short-term interests of shareowners should preside over the often long-term interests of other groups such as customers, employees, or suppliers. The controversy around stakeholder versus shareholder dominance is ongoing and flared up publicly again in the financial crisis of the late 2000s. Among the most noted voices was the one of former General Electric CEO Jack Welch—a long-standing poster child of shareholder value advocates—telling the *Financial Times* that shareholder value maximization as a strategy 'is a dumb idea' and that 'your main constituencies are your employees, your customers and your products' (Guerrera 2009).

☑ Skill check

Stakeholder analysis. Being skilled at stakeholder analysis enables you to answer the question of who exactly the company has a social responsibility to in a specific situation.

A new role for management

According to Freeman, this broader view of responsibility towards multiple stakeholders assigns a new role to management. Rather than being simply agents of shareholders, management has to take into account the rights and interests of all legitimate stakeholders. While they still have a fiduciary responsibility to look after shareholders' interests, managers must integrate this with the interests of other stakeholders for the long-term survival of the corporation, rather than maximizing the interest for just one group at a time. We shall look at some of the ways in which managers can achieve this in Chapter 5, but clearly the task of balancing different stakeholder expectations is a major challenge. **Ethics on Screen 2** provides a contemporary example of how—for better or for worse—corporations attempt to engage with stakeholders in the specific context of hydraulic fracturing or 'fracking'.

VISIT THE ONLINE RESOURCE CENTRE for links to useful sources of further information

ETHICS ON SCREEN 2

Promised Land

An entertaining anti-corporate thriller, … a tract on Machiavellian corporate behaviour and their employees' self-deception.

Andrew Pulver, *Guardian*

Fracking has become a major concern in many parts of Europe and North America. Hydraulic fracturing—as it is properly called—is a novel technique by which gas hitherto unavailable for extraction can be extracted from beneath rocky earth formations. The process of releasing natural gas from shale deposits involves blasting underground drilling beds with water and sand. Not only does this technique have an impact on groundwater levels and the ground ecology of an area, it also deposits a host of chemicals and toxic substances into the ground that represent a potential threat to humans, animals, and vegetation.

This topic has been picked up in a number of critical documentaries, most notably the controversial 'Gasland' and 'Gasland 2' directed by Josh Fox. *Promised Land*, however, represents a fictional exploration of the fracking experience, directed by Gus Van Sant and based on a story by the author and journalist Dave Eggers. The movie stars Matt Damon and Frances McDormand as corporate executives who come to a small town in the American Midwest with the brief to make the local farmers sign over mineral rights so that their company can start fracking. The town is rather typical for many in the 'Rust Belt' with a declining population, few economic opportunities, and farming as the only, but diminishing, base of survival.

The movie then immerses the viewer immediately into the approaches of stakeholder engagement of modern corporations. Damon and McDormand's characters are initially quite successful at pitching their com-

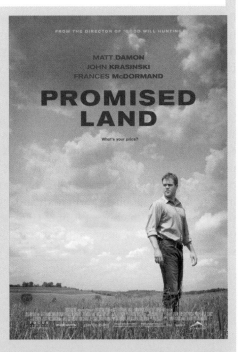

Focus Features/The Kobal Collection

pany's project to local farmers since they can provide the poor farmers with a much-needed, sudden boost of income. However, after a short period of success, resistance grows within the local community, led by a local teacher who raises concerns over the safety of fracking for the local community. Further problems arise for the frackers when an NGO activist, played by former *The Office* star John Krasinski, enters the picture providing evidence of environmental pollution at other sites, including his own family's dairy farm.

The movie provides a dramatic illustration not just of the complexities of firm–stakeholder relations, but also of the dynamics between different stakeholder groups and their respective networks. It also exposes the challenges of corporate engagement and 'management' of those stakeholder relationships and the often disconcerting experiences this may entail for individual corporate managers far away from the security of the office environment at headquarters.

The twists and turns of the story are entertaining and the film helps to bring the different perspectives of firms and their stakeholders to life. However, Promised Land met with rather mixed reviews, partly because it caricatures somewhat these differences for dramatic effect. It certainly does little to rescue the 'bad guy' reputation of fracking companies, but then NGOs also end up receiving a blow to their credibility. Perhaps the most significant aspect is that fracking and the different stakeholder positions around the issue have evidently become accepted Hollywood fare. This all points to the fact that the impact and responsibility of business for local communities, the environment, its employees, and other stakeholders is now firmly embedded in the public eye.

Sources

French, P. 2013. Promised Land—*review. Guardian*, 21 April 2013.
Pulver, A. 2013. Promised Land—first look review. *Guardian*, 8 February 2013.
http://www.focusfeatures.com/promised_land.
http://www.gaslandthemovie.com.

Furthermore, since the company is obliged to respect the rights of all stakeholders, this could suggest a further obligation to allow stakeholders to take part in managerial decisions that substantially affect their welfare and their rights. In this sense, there is a case for suggesting some model of *stakeholder democracy* that gives stakeholders an opportunity to influence and control corporate decisions—although, as we shall see later in the book, different stakeholders will have different expectations in this respect and different forms of participation in the corporate decisions will be possible (see Matten and Crane 2005). This also includes the idea of a model or a legally binding code of *corporate governance*, which codifies and regulates the various rights of the stakeholder groups. This, as we shall now see, appears to be more developed in other parts of the world than it is in the US, where stakeholder theory was popularized.

Stakeholder thinking in an international context

Stakeholder theory is a relatively simple and pragmatic approach to management. Therefore, in the second part of the book we will have a detailed look at major stakeholders of the company and provide an in-depth analysis of the company's obligations and managerial approaches towards these different stakeholders. Nevertheless, it is important at this stage to consider the international variations in stakeholder thinking as these have a significant impact on the way that stakeholder theory is engaged with in different contexts.

As we indicated above, the shareholder-dominated model of managerial capitalism has never been as strongly developed in continental Europe or Asia as it has in the Anglo-American tradition. Therefore, a general 'shift' towards other stakeholders has not been seen as so much of a necessity in these other parts of the world. Furthermore, with state influence on corporations—or even direct ownership—still playing a considerable role in countries such as France, Germany, or China, one of the major 'shareholders', government, automatically represents a large variety of 'stakeholders'—at least in principle.

The implications of this are that the rights of groups other than the direct contractual partners of the firm have traditionally been fairly well respected anyway in these countries. This typically applies to European countries such as France, Germany, or Sweden, but also to many Asian economies, in particular Japan. It also applies to many economies in transition from communism, where the large state-owned industrial entities typically had a strong commitment to all sorts of groups other than their owners—a pattern that still survives to some extent despite the recent phase of privatization (Edwards and Lawrence 2000; Crotty 2014).

In a certain sense then, one could argue that although the *terminology* of stakeholder theory may often be relatively new outside the US, the general principles have actually been *practised* in many countries for some time. Let us consider three examples:

- The vision of stakeholder democracy reads as something of a blueprint for the German model of industrial relations: at least one-third of the members on the supervisory board of large public shareholder-owned corporations have to be representatives of the employees—and in some industries they even have up to 50% of the votes. Furthermore, there is a very dense 'corporate law' of governance that codifies far-reaching rights of co-determination within the company. Although one might argue that this is only focusing on one stakeholder group, namely employees, this example is representative of a broader orientation of corporations towards stakeholders in many European countries.

- In many parts of Asia, particularly in Japan but also to a lesser degree in China, India, Korea, and Taiwan, we see a specific form of conglomerate business organization (Carney 2008). These are networks of banks, manufacturing companies, suppliers, and service providers (e.g. *keiretsu* in Japan, *chaebol* in Korea), which reflects a view of the firm where suppliers, creditors, and customers represent the most important stakeholders. In Japan and Korea, this wider focus on who could be important stakeholders has also included employees, since many companies traditionally offered lifetime employment so that 'salary men' worked for just one company throughout their entire life.

- Scandinavia has been recognized as having an important influence on the emergence of stakeholder thinking, and in contrast to other regions, the language of stakeholder management has long been incorporated into management teaching and practice. This is reflected in the stronger attention to co-operation in Scandinavian business, such as through participative management, employee involvement, and consensus building. This has been labelled a 'Scandinavian cooperative advantage', whereby contemporary Scandinavian companies such as H&M, IKEA, and Novo Nordisk tend to adopt stakeholder engagement that emphasizes 'jointness of interests, cooperative strategic posture, and rejection of a narrowly economic view of the firm' (Strand and Freeman 2014).

Although some of these entrenched patterns of stakeholder orientation have waned in the process of globalization, this absence of shareholder dominance is still notable. We will look at further aspects of stakeholder management, inclusion, and participation in the second part of the book, when we move on to focusing on each stakeholder group individually. However, at this stage, it is important to recognize that there are not only different ways in which a stakeholder approach can be implemented, but there are actually quite different *forms* of the theory itself.

Different forms of stakeholder theory

The popularity of stakeholder theory in the business ethics literature has meant that quite different forms of the theory have emerged, and it is important to be able to distinguish between them.[9] Thomas Donaldson and Lee Preston (1995) provide a convincing argument that there are in fact three forms of stakeholder theory:

- **Normative stakeholder theory**—this is theory that attempts to provide a reason why corporations *should* take into account stakeholder interests.

- **Descriptive stakeholder theory**—this is theory that attempts to ascertain whether (and how) corporations *actually do* take into account stakeholder interests.

- **Instrumental stakeholder theory**—this is theory that attempts to answer the question of whether it is *beneficial for the corporation* to take into account stakeholder interests.

In the preceding discussion, we have mainly used the first two types of argument to present the case for a stakeholder approach—that managers should and indeed do (at least to some extent) take into consideration interests beyond narrow shareholder concerns. However, we will develop a deeper normative basis for our arguments regarding specific stakeholder groups in Part B of the book. The instrumental argument—that considering the interests of stakeholders is in the best interests of the corporation—is largely akin to the argument for enlightened self-interest that we presented earlier in this chapter (see Why do corporations have social responsibilities? on pp. 48–50), and will be explored in more detail in Chapter 5.

By now it should be fairly evident that Friedman's (1970) first and second arguments against the social role and responsibilities of the corporation face considerable dissent from those advocating a CSR and/or stakeholder position. However, there is still one final aspect of his argument that we have not yet addressed, namely whether corporate managers should be involved in decisions about public welfare.

■ Corporate citizenship—the firm as a political actor

In Friedman's view, corporations should not undertake social policies and programmes because this is the task of government. Governments are elected by the public to pursue social goals whereas corporate managers are acting on behalf of shareholders, so their accountability is primarily to shareholders not to the public. Friedman therefore proposes a strict political division of labour in society—corporations to pursue economic goals, governments to pursue social goals. Although it could potentially be argued that Friedman's argument was defensible when his article was published, more recently the question of the wider responsibilities of business has become far more vexed. The main challenge to Friedman's view comes from the fact that corporations today have taken on a role in society that overlaps and interferes quite substantially with that of governments. Let us consider three main areas where this has happened:

- **Governments retreating from catering to social needs**. Throughout the twentieth century, many societies saw the provision of water, electricity, education, health care, basic transportation, public safety or telecommunication as part of what governments provided to their citizens. In many countries, however, these services have been privatized and are now in the hands of private companies. It is very clear then that companies that take responsibility for people's health, for heating their homes or keeping them safe have a somewhat more complex social responsibility. In fact, companies in these new areas face many of the social expectations hitherto directed at governments and the political sphere in general.

- **Governments unable or unwilling to address social needs**. In some contexts, especially in less-developed countries, business often faces governments that lack the resources to cater effectively for basic social needs. Mining companies that build roads, housing, schools and hospitals for the communities where they operate often do this for the 'business case' reasons for CSR discussed earlier. As a result though corporations often 'play government' in these contexts and face social expectations that in Western democracies would be placed on the government.

- **Governments can only address social problems within their reach**. When we discussed globalization in Chapter 1 we already encountered some of the limits of governments. Global financial markets, the climate of the planet, or the internet are new social spaces that no single government can reach. On the contrary, these spaces are often influenced and governed by businesses. Hence the expectation towards business in addressing climate change, internet privacy or uncontrollable financial markets are a natural consequence of their global reach.

All three basic developments have led to a situation where it is business that today often finds itself facing many social expectations that are similar to those usually reserved for political authorities. This raises a host of ethical problems for businesses and for those who work in or with them. **An Ethical Dilemma 2**, for example, describes a situation where business has become involved in the funding of universities (previously a purely governmental function in most countries), and the ethical challenges this can raise for university employees such as professors. It is from this perspective that the business ethics literature has increasingly started to reconsider again the political division of labour between business and government (Mäkinen and Kourula 2012). A key concept addressing this shift is corporate citizenship (CC).

VISIT THE
ONLINE
RESOURCE
CENTRE
for a short
response to this
feature

? THINK THEORY

Think about the concept of globalization that was discussed in Chapter 1, and our characterization of globalization as 'the ongoing integration of political, social and economic interactions at the transnational level'. How might this influence the failing of government and increasing power of corporations?

The concept of corporate citizenship

Towards the middle of the 1990s, the term 'corporate citizenship' emerged as a new way of addressing the social role of the corporation. Initially favoured primarily by practitioners (Altman and Vidaver-Cohen 2000), CC has also increasingly been introduced into the academic literature. Although again, the shift in terminology largely started in the US, numerous companies in Europe, Asia, and elsewhere have since committed themselves to CC (see **Figure 2.5**), and various consultancies and research centres based around the concept of CC have been founded across the globe.

However, as the literature on CC is relatively new, there seems to be quite a variety of usages of the terminology (Matten and Crane 2005; Crane, Matten, and Moon 2008). In a 'limited view' of CC many refer to philanthropy as the main activity of a virtuous corporate citizen that shares its wealth with its 'fellow citizens'. Others refer to CC in a way that mainly is synonymous to CSR, equating good neighbourly behaviour to a responsible role of business in society. In the context of the political nature of the corporations as outlined so far in this section, however, we prefer to use the 'extended view' of CC proposed by Matten and Crane (2005) which deliberately embraces the political elements of business ethics (also sometimes referred to as 'political CSR', see Scherer and Palazzo 2011). The extended view of CC takes as its starting point the notion of 'citizenship', and the dominant idea in most industrialized societies that citizenship is defined as a set of individual rights (Faulks 2000: 55–82). Following the still widely accepted categorization by T.H. Marshall (1965), liberal citizenship comprises three different rights:

- **Social rights**—these provide the individual with the *freedom to* participate in society, such as the right to education, health care, or various aspects of welfare. These are sometimes called 'positive' rights since they are entitlements towards third parties.

- **Civil rights**—these provide *freedom from* abuses and interference by third parties (most notably the government); among the most important are the rights to own property, to engage in 'free' markets, or exercise freedom of speech. These are sometimes called 'negative' rights since they protect the individual against the interference of stronger powers.

- **Political rights**—these include the right to vote or the right to hold office and, generally speaking, enable the individual to participate in the process of governance beyond the sphere of his or her own privacy.

The key actor for governing these rights for citizens is the government. Thus, at first glance, it is somewhat hard to make any sense of something like 'corporate citizenship' since citizenship is about relations between individuals and governments. Although, as we saw earlier, corporations are regarded as 'artificial persons' and so do enjoy some of the rights and obligations of other citizens (rights to own property, for example), it is hard to imagine corporations claiming most of the social and political rights that individual citizens enjoy. However, corporations enter the picture not because they have an entitlement to certain rights as a 'real' citizen would, but as powerful public actors that—for better or for worse—can have a significant impact on those 'real' citizens' rights. That is, the failure of governments to fulfil some of their traditional functions, coupled with the rise in corporate power, has meant that corporations have increasingly taken on a role in society that is similar to that of traditional political actors. Hence, corporations enter the arena of citizenship at the point where traditional governmental actors fail to

AN ETHICAL DILEMMA 2

When good results are bad results

Professor Ballistico is scratching his head. Looking at the results of last month's series of experiments has brought on a distinct feeling of unease. He has been sitting in his office for hours now trying to analyse the spreadsheets from every possible angle— but without success. He even had an argument with his research assistant, accusing her of having prepared the results incorrectly—but she had been right all along.

Not that Ballistico is unhappy about the project itself. It is actually quite a success- ful piece of research looking at the various side effects of food additives in frozen food. The two-year project has already produced some very good publications; he has even been invited several times to give interviews on television about the results. However, the latest round of results has got him wondering.

The reason for Ballistico's unease is that according to the results of the latest tests, two substances involved in the study, called 'Longlife' and 'Rotnever', appear to significantly increase the risk of human allergies for long-time consumers of the addi- tives. And however he interprets the results, his assistant really seems to have deliv- ered solid work on the data analysis.

Normally such surprising results would be good news. Solid results of this kind would make for sensational presentations at the next conference of the World Food Scientist Federation. On top of that, 'Longlife' and 'Rotnever' are very common addi- tives in the products of the large food multinational Foodcorp, which is the market leader in frozen food in his country. His results could really make big headlines.

There is one problem though: Professor Ballistico is director of the Foodcorp Cen- tre for Food Science at BigCity University. Three years ago, Foodcorp donated €2.3 million to BigCity University in order to set up the research centre and to fund its activities. The company felt that as 'a good corporate citizen we should give some- thing back to society by funding academic research for the benefit of future genera- tions'. It also signalled that it saw this as a continuous engagement over time … and Ballistico is only too aware that the decision about the next €2 million funding will be imminent three months from now.

Professor Ballistico has a major dilemma: if he publishes his results, Foodcorp might get into serious trouble. He also knows that this will be quite embarrassing at the next meeting with his sponsor, and it will most certainly influence the company's decision to further fund the centre. And he hardly dares to think of his next meeting with the president of the university, who is always so proud of BigCity having such excellent ties to companies and scoring highest in the country in terms of its ability to secure external funding. Should he therefore just tell Foodcorp privately about his results so that it can take appropriate action to deal with Rotnever and Longlife, or should he go public with his findings?

Questions

1. What are the main ethical issues for Professor Ballistico here?
2. What options are open to him? How would you assess these options?

> 3. How should Ballistico proceed, and what can he realistically do to prevent similar problems arising in the future?
>
> 4. What are the wider ethical concerns regarding corporate involvement in funding universities and other public institutions?
>
> 5. In light of this example, give a critical assessment of the benefits and drawbacks of corporations stepping into roles often played by governments, such as the funding of higher education.

be the only 'counterpart' of citizenship. Quite simply, corporations can be said to partly take over those functions with regard to the protection, facilitation, and enabling of citizens' rights. Let us consider some examples:

- **Social rights.** Many companies have pursued initiatives formerly within the province of the welfare state: feeding homeless people, helping head teachers in managing school budgets, enhancing the employability of the unemployed, or improving deprived neighbourhoods. For example, the British retailer Marks and Spencer has for more than a decade operated its 'Marks and Start' programme to help people facing barriers to employability (such as single parents, people with disabilities, and the homeless) to gain work experience and skills that improve their employment prospects.[10] Similarly, in developing countries where governments simply cannot (or do not want to) afford a welfare state, the task of improving working conditions in sweatshops, ensuring employees earn a living wage, providing schools, medical centres, and roads, or even providing financial support for the schooling of child labourers are all activities in which corporations such as Shell, Nike, Levi Strauss, and others have engaged under the label of CC.

- **Civil rights.** Governmental failure again becomes particularly visible in developing or transforming countries in the arena of civil rights. Corporations can sometimes play a crucial role in either discouraging or encouraging governments to live up to their responsibility in this arena of citizenship or directly protecting or infringing people's civil rights. Consider Facebook, which faced several court cases in the 2010s because of alleged infringements of the rights to privacy of its users.[11] On the other hand, companies such as Google have sometimes held themselves up as guardians of people's rights to free speech in the face of government restrictions. As a global space not governed by any single government, the internet is therefore a good example of one of those areas where corporations are exposed to dealing with core civil rights of individuals.

- **Political rights.** Voter apathy in national elections has been widely identified in many industrialized countries, yet there appears to be a growing willingness on the part of individuals to participate in political action *aimed at corporations rather than at governments* (Hertz 2001a). Whether through single-issue campaigns, anti-corporate protests, consumer boycotts, or other forms of sub-political action, individual citizens have increasingly sought to effect political change by leveraging the power, and to some extent vulnerability, of corporations. Returning to the McEthics case in Chapter 1, when anti-obesity campaigners have sought to draw attention to the social problems of poor health and nutrition among young people, they have achieved international coverage for their efforts not by tackling national governments, but by attacking the McDonald's corporation.

Company	Industry and Country of Origin	Corporate citizenship statement (*emphasis added*)	Source
BMW	Automobiles, Germany	*Corporate citizenship* is an integral part of the BMW Group's identity as a company. Our activities concentrate on areas where we can best apply our core expertise to achieve concrete and measureable improvements. The focus of our strategy is on intercultural innovation and social inclusion, as well as responsible use of resources.	http://www.bmwgroup.com 2015
Citibank	Financial Services, US	*Citizenship* at Citi means recognizing the impact we have on the world and ensuring our business is enabling progress in the communities we serve. We focus our efforts on the promotion of financial inclusion and economic progress and the advancement of environmental sustainability.	http://www.citigroup.com, 2015
Microsoft	Software, US	Microsoft has an enduring commitment to working to fulfill our public responsibilities and to serving the needs of people in communities worldwide. Fundamental to this commitment is the role we serve as a responsible global *corporate citizen*. As our company has grown, this commitment has extended far beyond our own products and services and has been amplified many times over through our network of partners, including governments, nonprofits and other organizations.	http://www.microsoft.com, 2015
Panasonic	Electronics, Japan	Panasonic is promoting *corporate citizenship* activities (social contribution activities) and working to solve social issues around the world, based on the philosophy of education and coexistence while focusing on two key areas: the environment and energy and the next generation. We carry out our *corporate citizenship* activities not as distribution of profit but as investment in society, and to ensure the sustainable continuation of activities in the two key areas.	http://www.panasonic.com, 2015

Figure 2.5 Commitments to corporate citizenship

Hence, given this emerging role for corporations in the administration of civil, social, and political rights, the extended view suggests that **corporate citizenship** is essentially about how corporations govern the rights of individual citizens.

These rights are governed by the corporation in different ways. With regard to social rights, the corporation basically either supplies or does not supply individuals with social services and hence largely takes on either a *providing* or an *ignoring role*. In the case of civil rights, corporations either capacitate or constrain citizens' civil rights, and thus can be viewed as assuming more of an *enabling* or a *disabling role*. Finally, in the realm of political rights, the corporation is essentially an additional conduit for the exercise of individuals' political rights—hence, the corporation primarily assumes a *channelling* or a *blocking role*. This extended conceptualization of CC is shown in **Figure 2.6**.

It is evident that corporate citizenship may be the result either of a voluntary, self-interest-driven corporate initiative, or of a compulsory, public pressure-driven corporate reaction—either way it places corporations squarely in a political role rather than just an economic one. Most firms actually claim to not want to take on such a political role in society, yet it seems that increasingly they do, either because of pressure from activists or sometimes simply out of necessity. If an apparel company needs to make sure the children of its staff working in a poor African community get an education, it may need to build its own schools centre because the local authorities may not have the resources to do so. The point is that we do not need to know the motivation to label something an act of 'extended' CC. This is because this view of CC is essentially a *descriptive* conceptualization of what does happen, rather than a *normative* conceptualization of what should happen. **Ethics in Action 2.2** provides the opportunity to examine this perspective in the context of corporate initiatives in developing countries.

Corporate citizenship
The corporate role in governing citizenship rights for individuals.

☑ Skill check

Corporate citizenship analysis. A CC analysis is a useful tool in a situation where corporations face expectations from society that are similar to those normally directed towards governments. Analysing the three types of citizenship rights will help you to identify the extra expectations society places on corporate activities in this context.

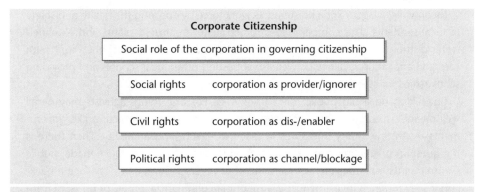

Figure 2.6 An extended view of corporate citizenship

VISIT THE
ONLINE
RESOURCE
CENTRE
for links to
useful sources
of further
information

ETHICS IN ACTION 2.2

Private, but public

Mike Valente and Andrew Crane, 23 March 2009

When companies set up shop in developing countries, they often find that they have to do a lot more than just run a business. In many of these countries, local institutions cannot meet basic needs, from health care and education to roads and reliable electricity. But companies cannot operate without a healthy, productive work force and solid infrastructure—so, more and more of them are taking matters into their own hands. Companies are laying down roads and water pipes, setting up schools and hospitals and bankrolling a range of social programmes. In other words, increasingly companies are taking on functions typically handled by the public sector.

This new role, however, is not easy. Companies are struggling to figure out how to help locals without making them too dependent, while finding ways to placate shareholders back home who may not see the value of all these pricey investments.

Into the breach

In many cases, companies directly take on public-service roles, even when these have little relationship to their core business. For instance, a mining company might build schools, health-care facilities or general infrastructure—things that have nothing to do with the job of mining but are essential to creating an environment for doing business.

Consider Magadi Soda Co. When the mining company—a part of India's TATA Chemicals Ltd.—set up operations in Kenya, it discovered that almost all government-funded public programmes in the region were centred on the city of Nairobi. But the company was outside city limits—and lacked the infrastructure it needed for its operations. So, Magadi Soda started building. It extended the 75-mile (120-kilometre) road from the southern edges of Nairobi to the company's facilities in Lake Magadi, and built and operated an extension of the Kenyan railway line to transport soda ash to the port of Mombasa. It also introduced a passenger coach to offer transport services to the public along the route. The road and railway are now used by Kenyans with little relationship to the company, and the company helps the community maintain rural access roads.

Meanwhile, Magadi Soda bolstered its work force by ensuring the health and safety of local residents. The company constructed water-treatment plants and extended water distribution to surrounding communities. It also built up local housing, health care and education facilities, as well as supporting other local schools and providing scholarships for students.

But taking on a big public role carries risks. For one thing, activists may derail well-meaning programmes by questioning why companies are acting like governments—with few, if any, measures in place to ensure accountability. Then there is the question of creating dependency among local communities. Once made, public commitments may escalate and be difficult to reverse. Companies can face a backlash if they retrench investments because of difficult financial times, or pressure from shareholders or a parent firm.

One way to avoid these concerns is to take on a sweeping role only when the lack of public services represents an immediate threat to the surrounding community or the company, such as a famine or drought. In fact, that is the strategy some big companies favour in developing countries. Still, even if companies are not planning long-term social efforts, just emergency relief, they should keep community concerns in mind and involve locals in decision making as early as possible.

Working through others

Another solution to the problems encountered above is to rely on other organizations to provide necessary services. With this approach, companies help establish local groups, or bolster existing ones, that make decisions about public welfare and implement social programmes. These groups take on the responsibility and accountability for providing necessities, leaving the company in a purely support role, such as providing funds. This might not be an answer to immediate problems—such as helping a community deal with drought—but it can build up long-term capabilities, so communities can eventually handle crises themselves.

That is what Magadi Soda ended up doing. The company eventually became uncomfortable with the government-like role it was playing. So, senior executives helped set up a county council and brought the local community on board to prioritize the company's public programmes. This reduced the company's costs and minimized its obligation to operate activities in which it had little expertise.

Or consider a Russian aluminum producer that found itself facing a host of problems in the communities where it operated. Pressure was on to hire and source supplies locally. But public health and education were deteriorating—hurting the potential work force—and there were few small businesses to draw on. The company decided to help the communities help themselves. It organized nongovernmental organizations, or NGOs, and community foundations in and around the regions it operated, and then provided funding for critical programmes. The result? The groups partnered with local communities to launch educational and health-care facilities, and nurture small businesses that ended up in the company's supply chain.

Again, though, companies that adopt this approach face a number of challenges. Unlike the strategy Magadi Soda used at first, which brings immediate results, this approach requires a longer-term investment of resources. And that can lead to grumbling from shareholders back home or local communities in need. What is more, companies must be careful to build good relationships in the community. If they do not take the time to learn local concerns, they may end up fostering groups and programmes that do not really address what communities need, potentially leading to friction. In our research in Africa, for instance, CEOs commented on the importance of regularly visiting communities and senior chiefs to gain sensitivity to their ways of life.

Sources

Valente, M. and Crane, A. 2009. *Wall Street Journal*, 23 March. Reproduced with kind permission.

VISIT THE
ONLINE
RESOURCE
CENTRE
for a short
response to
this feature

> **? THINK THEORY**
>
> In which way are the companies in Kenya and Russia mentioned in this case implementing the 'extended view of corporate citizenship'? What are the new responsibilities arising from this role and what are the limits of this approach?

Implications of CC: corporate accountability and transparency

The debate on such a proposed political role of the firm has been quite rich and controversial (Scherer and Palazzo 2007, 2008b, 2011; Crane et al. 2008; Willke and Willke 2008; Néron 2010). The central problem behind such a role is clearly visible though: does political involvement by companies represent a risk to democracy? Since many important decisions appear to be no longer taken by governments (and hence also no longer indirectly by individual voters) but by corporations (who are not subject to a democratic vote), there is considerable unease with the implications this has for democratic accountability.

Corporate accountability
A concept that refers to whether a corporation is answerable in some way for the consequences of its actions.

The question of **corporate accountability** is therefore integral to assessing the pros and cons of any shift to extended CC. The central points here are the questions of *who controls corporations* and *to whom are corporations accountable*. There are those like Friedman, as discussed above, who see it as a given that corporate managers are only accountable to their shareholders, provided they comply with the laws of the countries in which they do business. Governments are accountable to the public and therefore it is they who are the 'proper guardians of the public interest … accountable to all citizens' (*The Economist* 2005). However, there are also good arguments for the view that since corporations now shape and influence so much of public and private life in modern societies, in effect they are already *de facto* political actors, so they *have* to become more accountable to society.

One avenue for greater corporate accountability is the market itself. Hertz (2001a) and others suggest that given the power of large corporations, there is more democratic power in an individual's choice as a consumer (for or against certain products) than in their choice at the ballot box. As Craig Smith (2014) contends, consumption choices are to some extent 'purchase votes' in the social control of corporations. However, as we shall discuss in more detail in Chapter 8 when we cover business relations with consumers, one should also recognize the limitations of the individual's power to affect corporate policy through purchase choices. There is little guarantee that consumers' social choices will be reflected in their consumer choices, or that such social choices will be even recognized, never mind acted on, by corporations. After all, not only do corporations benefit from a massive power imbalance compared with individual consumers, but consumers are also constrained in executing their voting rights by the choices offered by the market. Perhaps most importantly, consumers are just one of the multiple stakeholders that corporations might be expected to be accountable to.

This has led to further questions regarding how corporations can be made more accountable to the broad range of relevant stakeholders for their actions. One important stream of literature has examined the possibility for corporations to audit and report on their social, ethical, and environmental performance through new accounting procedures, such as environmental accounting and social reporting (Owen and O'Dwyer 2008). Another important stream of literature has looked at broader issues of communication with stakeholders, and development of stakeholder dialogue and stakeholder partnerships (e.g. Bendell 2000; Crane and Livesey 2003). We shall look at these developments in more detail later in the book, most notably in Chapters 5 and 10. However, the key issue here is that in order to enhance corporate accountability, corporate social performance should be made more visible to those with a stake in the corporation. The term usually applied to this is **corporate transparency**.

Although transparency can relate to any aspect of the corporation, demands for corporate transparency usually relate primarily to social as opposed to commercial concerns, since traditionally corporations have claimed that much of their data are commercially confidential. However, it is evident that many social issues cannot be easily separated from commercial decisions. For example, Nike long claimed that the identity and location of its suppliers could not be revealed because it was commercially sensitive information that Nike's competitors could exploit. However, concerns over working conditions in these factories led to demands for Nike to make the information public, which in 2005 it eventually agreed to do.

According to Schnackenberg and Tomlinson (2014) the quality of corporate transparency depends on three elements:

- **Disclosure**—whether relevant information is made available in a timely and accessible manner.

- **Clarity**—the degree to which information is understandable to relevant stakeholders.

- **Accuracy**—whether the disclosed information is correct and reliable.

Calls for increased transparency—i.e. enhanced disclosure, clarity and accuracy in how companies communicate their social impacts—are all about being able to hold corporations accountable for their actions. Only if stakeholders know what companies are doing can they seek to influence them to change their behaviour or make decisions about whether to continue to support them.

For example, most consumers believe that 'ingredient transparency' is an important factor in their purchase decisions across a range of product categories including food, household products, and beauty products.[12] Frequently, however, providing credible information is difficult for companies in the realm of social and political impacts, because they do not always know the facts themselves. Consider the case of mica, a mineral commonly used in cosmetics. The largest deposit is in the Indian state of Jharkhand, where the remote jungle landscape means that monitoring programmes are unable to determine whether child labour is used in its production. As a result, the UK cosmetics firm Lush announced in 2014 that it was committed to removing mica from its products because it could no longer guarantee transparency in its supply chain (Fearn and Nesbitt 2014).

While increased transparency is certainly no panacea for restoring public trust (see, for example, O'Neill 2002), the tenor of current demands for greater openness from corporations suggests that increased attention to issues of transparency might no longer be just an option for many corporations. Increasingly, corporate accountability and transparency are being presented as necessities, not only from a normative point of view, but

Corporate transparency
The degree to which corporate decisions, policies, activities, and impacts are acknowledged and made visible to relevant stakeholders.

also with regard to the practical aspects of effectively doing business and maintaining the trust of stakeholders (Schnackenberg and Tomlinson 2014).

Assessing CC as a framework for business ethics

Having set out the concept of CC and explored some of its implications in terms of accountability and transparency, we need to consider whether the concept of corporate citizenship really represents a useful new way of framing business ethics—or at least whether it offers us anything different or better compared with CSR, stakeholder theory, and the other concepts we have discussed in this chapter. CC does seem to add something significant that helps us frame business ethics in new ways:

- The extended view of CC helps us to see better the *political role* of the corporation and clarifies the demand for *corporate accountability* that is such a prominent feature of contemporary business ethics thinking.

- By providing us with a way of understanding business in relation to common rights of citizenship across cultures, CC in this sense also helps us to better understand some of the challenges presented by the context of *globalization*.

- These rights of citizenship, which include rights to equality, participation, and a safe and clean environment, also have strong links to the goal for business ethics of *sustainability*.

- Finally, although the notion of CSR has been widely adopted all over the world, the extended view of CC provides us with a more critical perspective on the social role of business.

Of course, one downside to the extended view of CC is that it is both new and not yet widely accepted within the mainstream discourse of business ethics. However, that is changing as it becomes increasingly apparent that the traditional concepts of CSR and stakeholder theory may not be adequate to deal with broader changes in the roles of business, government, and civil society.

■ Summary

In this chapter we have discussed business ethics in relation to the social role of the corporation. We have outlined the nature of corporations and argued that confining corporations to their initial purpose of producing goods and services in a way that yields a maximal profit for the shareholders of the corporation is too limited. We subsequently analysed different perspectives on CSR, stakeholder theory, and CC, and assessed their relevance in an international context.

Our argument is that the shifts and changes in the global economy in recent years have brought to the surface the necessity for a new framing of business ethics. The extended perspective on CC—which ultimately sees the corporation as a political actor governing the citizenship of individual stakeholders—helps to bring some much-needed definitional clarity to the CC debate. Perhaps more importantly though, it helps us to conceptualize the emerging role of corporations in the global economy, as well as to clarify the ethical expectations increasingly placed upon them.

Study questions

1. What are the main implications of the *legal status* of corporations for notions of corporate social responsibility?

2. 'Only human beings have a moral responsibility for their actions.' Critically assess this proposition in the context of attempts to ascribe a moral responsibility to corporations.

3. What is enlightened self-interest? Compare and evaluate arguments for corporate social responsibility based on enlightened self-interest with more explicitly moral arguments.

4. According to Archie Carroll, what are the four levels of corporate social responsibility? How relevant is this model in a European, Asian, or African context?

5. Explain the difference between normative, descriptive, and instrumental versions of stakeholder theory. To what extent do stakeholders have intrinsic moral rights in relation to the management of the corporation?

6. Define the extended view of corporate citizenship. Give examples to illustrate the concept.

Research exercise

Select one of the following companies:

    (a) Microsoft (www.microsoft.com).

    (b) BMW (www.bmwgroup.com).

    (c) Panasonic (www.panasonic.com).

Investigate the company's website and set out the main aspects of its corporate citizenship programmes. Which aspects of its programmes might be said to be formerly governmental responsibilities? What are the benefits and drawbacks of the corporation taking over these responsibilities?

Key readings

VISIT THE ONLINE RESOURCE CENTRE for links to further key readings

1. **Carroll, A.B. 2008. A history of corporate social responsibility: concepts and practices. In A. Crane, A. McWilliams, D. Matten, J. Moon, and D. Siegel (eds.), *The Oxford handbook of corporate social responsibility*: 19–46. Oxford: Oxford University Press.**

   This provides a broad overview of the development of CSR theory and practice (albeit from a predominantly US perspective) from one of the field's most well-known scholars.

2. **Matten, D. and Crane, A. 2005. Corporate citizenship: towards an extended theoretical conceptualization. *Academy of Management Review*, 30(1): 166–79.**

   This article sets out the main arguments presented in the last part of this chapter in more detail and is useful if you want to follow up the citizenship perspective more fully.

VISIT THE
ONLINE
RESOURCE
CENTRE
for links to
useful sources
of further
information on
this case

Case 2

American Apparel: a new fashion for CSR?

This case examines American Apparel's unique approach to social responsibility in the apparel industry. The case discusses the firm's 'sweatshop-free' made-in-the-USA philosophy as applied to clothing design and manufacturing, and also explores the company's unusual commitment to political campaigning on immigration and sexual orientation causes. You have the opportunity to evaluate the potential risks and rewards of its social responsibility strategy and to consider how such practices might help or hinder the company's financial performance.

Although it is a fixture along with Zara, Gap, and H&M on high streets across much of the world, in terms of corporate social responsibility American Apparel is unlike virtually all of its counterparts in the apparel industry. While almost all global clothing companies outsource the production of their products to suppliers in emerging economies, American Apparel has steadfastly stuck to a made-in-America philosophy, promising that its clothes are resolutely 'sweatshop free'. Many have wondered about the business logic of such an approach when American Apparel's competitors can enjoy such drastically lower labour costs. Is this a case of 'ethics pays', or is American Apparel ultimately doomed to failure?

Vertically integrated and sweatshop free

Since the 1990s, apparel companies in Europe, North America and much of the rest of the developed world have reorganized the way that clothes get produced. No longer do mass market branded apparel companies like Gap, Levi's, H&M, or Zara manufacture their own clothes. Instead such companies subcontract their entire manufacturing process—from dying to cutting and stitching—to third-party contractors. Almost always these contractors are located in emerging economies such as Bangladesh, China, India, Turkey and Vietnam. Because factories in these countries rely on local labour and employ working conditions that are very different from factories in Europe and North America, they typically enable big brands to produce at considerably lower unit cost than if they manufactured closer to home.

For example, in 2013 while the minimum wage in the US guaranteed workers at least $1,250 per month, Chinese workers were only guaranteed about $200 monthly. Meanwhile, according to the International Labour Organization, workers in rival Asian exporters Vietnam and Cambodia earned around $80 monthly while the minimum monthly wage for garment workers in Bangladesh was a rock bottom $39. As a result, labour costs have been reduced to a fraction of the cost of a piece of clothing sold in a high street store. One estimate suggested that a $14 T-shirt sold in the store would cost a retailer about $5.70 to produce. Of this, labour costs would comprise no more than $0.12, or 2% of the total production cost and under 1% of the price paid at the checkout (see Table C2.1).

Salaries are not the only way that overseas factories can save money for apparel companies. Contractors in developing countries also operate with very different rules and norms on working conditions, which further reduces costs compared to producing closer to home. Overseas manufacturing typically means lower levels of environmental, health, and safety protection than that enjoyed in North America and Europe, and a greater likelihood of forced overtime, arbitrary pay deductions, child labour, sexual harassment, and other abuses. Although many overseas factories meet internationally agreed minimum labour standards, reports of violations are common.

	Cost ($)	Percentage of total cost of production ($5.67)	Proportion (%) of final price paid by consumer ($14)
Factory overhead	0.07	1.2	0.5
Labour	0.12	2.1	0.9
Agent	0.18	3.2	1.3
Factory margin	0.58	10.2	4.1
Freight, insurance, and duties	1.03	18.2	7.4
Finishing and materials	3.69	65.1	26.4
Total	**5.67**	**100.0**	**40.6**

Table C2.1 Cost breakdown of a $14 T-shirt

Source: Original data from O'Rourke Group Partners LLC (2011), reported in Westwood, R. 2013. What does that $14 shirt really cost? *Macleans*, 1 May 2013: http://www2.macleans. ca/2013/05/01/what-does-that-14-shirt-really-cost/.

American Apparel operates a substantially different model. Rather than sourcing its clothes from third-party suppliers in emerging economies, the company utilizes a vertically integrated model. This means that all of its manufacturing (including dying, cutting, knitting, and stitching) is completed in-house, as are design, marketing, accounting, retail, and distribution. All of these activities take place at American Apparel facilities in Southern California, and most of it right in its downtown Los Angeles factory, the largest garment manufacturing facility in North America.

Perhaps the most remarkable aspect of American Apparel's unique business model though is that it enables the firm to be, or so it claims, 'sweatshop free'. Workers are paid well above the average compared to typical US rates of pay in the apparel industry. The average American Apparel stitcher earns more than $2,000 monthly, almost double the US federal minimum wage. Workers are also guaranteed full-time employment and promotion opportunities rather than the precarious, part-time and casual work typical of the industry. Also available are a range of employee benefits including subsidized health insurance, an on-site medical clinic, subsidized public transport, and even free on-site massages! Because so many of its workers are immigrants to the country (typically from Mexico and other parts of Latin America), the company also provides English classes.

Such an unusual approach to doing business in the apparel industry does not come cheap. Producing with decent working conditions in the US incurs significant costs in terms of overhead, labour, capital, and training costs. According to the company, however, its vertically integrated business model in fact offers certain efficiencies because everything is completed in-house. The company claims that it enables better quality control and provides for a faster response to the rapid changes in the fashion industry. It also reduces some shipping and transport costs of products from their place of manufacture and keeps the firm's carbon footprint relatively low. Its claims to be 'sweatshop free' and 'made in the USA' might also appeal to its young consumer base and drive greater sales— but to date, these have not been major elements of its marketing strategy.

All in all, American Apparel acknowledges that its sweatshop-free approach is 'not the easy road to travel'. Regardless of the benefits it claims it brings, the company remains a conspicuous outlier in an industry that has wholeheartedly embraced the cost savings of global outsourcing. Nonetheless, the firm claims on its website that its model will stand the test of time: 'Manufacturing in America requires risk taking and long-term investment. We think it's well worth it. The apparel industry's reliance on low wages cannot be sustained over time, ethically or fiscally. As labor and transportation costs increase worldwide, exploitation will not only be morally offensive, it will not even be financially viable.'

Political activism

A socially responsible approach to manufacturing is not the only area where American Apparel stands out from the pack in terms of corporate responsibility. The company also takes a distinctly unusual approach to political activism. Where most apparel companies either avoid any real political engagement or look to carry out political lobbying behind the scenes, American Apparel takes a much more public stance. For many years, the firm has actively pursued two hot-button political causes in the US—immigration reform and gay rights—both of which have proved to be popular with some and highly controversial with others.

The company's 'Legalize gay' campaign emerged in response to efforts to outlaw same-sex marriage in California, and has spread to the protection of gay rights more generally. The firm has given away more than 50,000 of its 'Legalize Gay' T-shirts to lesbian, gay, bisexual, and transgender (LGBT) groups and organizations across the world and has featured the T-shirts in its stores during LGBT demonstrations and celebrations. The firm has also partnered in organized protests and run gay rights advertisements in the US. It even stocks the often-explicit gay publication, Butt Magazine, in its stores, despite occasional bouts of media controversy.

The 'Legalize LA' initiative, on the other hand, advocates for immigration reform in the US. Like much of the world, immigration issues in the US have been very politically sensitive, but as the company's former CEO Dov Charney argued in support of his company's involvement:

> Despite the fact that so many experts agree that the productivity and hard work of immigrants improves our economy, the issue has been grossly misrepresented by the media and certain politicians. Businesses are generally afraid to speak out because they're frightened of reprisals by government agencies, but at American Apparel we have not been able to sit in the shadows while the facts get distorted.

The campaign focuses on the company's hometown of Los Angeles, which has one of the largest concentrations of immigrants in the US. American Apparel itself hires a large proportion of its staff from the city's immigrant community, and features a number of them in video clips hosted on its Legalize LA webpages. The firm produces a hard-hitting pamphlet, distributes T-shirts printed with the Legalize LA motto, and raises funds for immigrant organizations, among other things. But many questioned the business logic of such a stance when the company was investigated by US immigration officials in 2009 and forced to fire some 1,800 immigrant workers, almost a quarter of its workforce, for 'irregularities' in their immigration documents.

Controversies and catastrophes

American Apparel is clearly a leader in some areas of corporate responsibility, but its unusual approach coupled with its outspoken boss also caused it a whole host of problems along the way. To begin with, the company has often been criticized for its overtly sexual advertising, featuring scantily dressed young girls (and occasionally men) in provocative, borderline pornographic poses. The use of nudity in adverts (and more recently, visible pubic hair on its mannequins) has clearly been successful in courting publicity, but it has also threatened the firm's appeal, especially amongst many parents of its sizeable teenage market. However, the firm also purports to be promoting a more open approach to sexuality, using advertising that eschews airbrushing and comes straight from the firm's headquarters rather than via an advertising agency. It may have risks, but American Apparel's edgy aesthetic clearly has its legions of fans.

One of the more visible risks of its 'sex sells' approach has been a series of sexual harassment claims made against former CEO Charney beginning in 2005. Although so far these have all been dismissed or settled, Charney became a divisive figure who not only encouraged romantic relationships in the workplace (unlike much of corporate America, which prohibits them), but actively promoted a highly charged sexual atmosphere. In one now legendary encounter, he even masturbated in front of a journalist while being interviewed in his office. According to one account: 'He's short, hairy and absolutely unapologetic about loving sex—any time, anywhere, with anybody he comes across, up to and including his own company employees.' Even to his supporters, he is something of a 'a tarnished hero'. Ongoing investigations into sexual harassment at the firm eventually led to Charney being fired in 2014.

But it is not just ethical controversies that have plagued American Apparel. Even more of a threat to the ongoing health of the company has been its multitude of financial problems. After years of strong growth and one of the fastest international retail expansions in history, American Apparel started to run into problems around 2009. Its run-in with the immigration authorities led to staff shortages and supply hold-ups, whilst its supercharged expansion left the company short of cash during the financial downturn. A hike in global cotton prices then drastically cut into the firm's profitability.

As a result, the firm twice faced bankruptcy (in 2009 and 2012), only to be saved by last-minute loans from investors. It was even at one point threatened with delisting from the New York Stock Exchange due to financial mismanagement and delays in its filings. Lawsuits from investors followed. From a high of $15 in December 2007, its stock tumbled to below $0.50 in 2014.

A turnaround strategy, including a new management team (and eventually the ousting of CEO Charney), a retrenchment of its retail operations, and debt refinancing helped American Apparel to arrest its precipitous decline. However, by 2015 the company still had not managed to turn an annual profit since 2009. With the company still operating at a loss and burdened by heavy debts, many analysts questioned whether the turnaround would ultimately be successful while the company still clung to its high-cost 'Made in the USA' approach. However, although some suggested the company should rethink its strategy and offshore jobs to Asia, others regarded it as a non-starter. 'They've essentially painted themselves into a red-white-and-blue corner,' one analyst was quoted in 2014. 'They can't get out of it. It would be viewed as hypocritical.'

Questions

1. What are the main CSR issues faced by an apparel company such as American Apparel and what has it done to address them?

2. How would you characterise the overall CSR strategy adopted by American Apparel?

3. Who are the main stakeholders of American Apparel and how has the firm prioritised them? Is it right to prioritise them in this way?

4. What are the potential risks and rewards of American Apparel's political activism on immigration reform and gay rights? Are there ways that it could improve its approach?

5. To what extent do you think that American Apparel has been successful in managing its various social responsibilities? What would you advise it to do now?

Sources

Gumbel, A. 2006. Dov Charney: The hustler and his American dream. *Independent*, 23 December 2006: http://www.independent.co.uk/news/people/profiles/dov-charney-the-hustler-and-his-american-dream-429627.html.

Li, S., Hsu, T. , and Chang, A. 2014. American Apparel, others try to profit from domestic production. *LA Times*, 10 August 2014: http://www.latimes.com/business/la-fi-american-apparel-made-in-usa-20140810-story.html#page=1.

Millman, E., Ghebremedhin, S., and Effron, L. 2012. American Apparel CEO Dov Charney: A tarnished hero? *ABC News*, 27 April 2012: http://abcnews.go.com/Business/american-apparel-ceo-dov-charney-tarnished-hero/story?id=16229958.

Minato, C. and Edwards, J. 2013. American Apparel's first profit in years put the CEO's sex scandals in the rearview mirror. *Business Insider*, 9 March 2013: http://www.businessinsider.com/american-apparels-first-profits-in-years-put-the-ceos-sex-scandals-in-the-rearview-mirrow-2013–3?op=1.

http://www.americanapparel.net.

Notes

1. Specifically, the *Citizens United v. Federal Election Commission* (No. 08-205) (2010) case on political funding.

2. *Citizens United v. Federal Election Commission* (No. 08-205) (2010) http://tech.fortune.cnn.com/2013/04/30/wal-mart-sustainability/.

3. This relationship has been examined at least since the early 1970s, with interest apparently unabated despite (or perhaps because of) the somewhat equivocal findings so far. Overviews of some of its problems are provided by Margolis and Walsh (2003) and Gond and Crane (2010), with a meta-analysis of previous studies provided by Orlitzky et al. (2003).

4. See the 'Top Ten Corporate Responsibility Stories of 2013' in the Crane and Matten Blog: http://craneandmatten.blogspot.ca/2014/01/top-10-corporate-responsibility-stories.html.

5. See for example the 'Tax Gap' series run by the *Guardian* newspaper:http://www.theguardian.com/business/series/tax-gap.

6. https://instantnoodles.org/noodles/disaster-relief.html.

7. There is an abundance of literature arguing along the lines of this suggested dichotomy. See for instance Porter and Kramer (2002) for a very clear cut critique of the 'traditional' view. Good reference points are also Porter and Kramer (2011) and Visser (2010). See also Grayson and Hodges (2004) from where we acknowledge taking the 'built in versus bolt on' metaphor.

8. http://www.unilever.com/sustainable-living/.

9. There are a number of excellent papers that offer reviews of stakeholder theory, in particular Donaldson and Preston (1995) and Stoney and Winstanley (2001). A 25-year review of the concept is provided by Phillips (2011).

10. For more information see http://marksandspencer.com.

11. For example, in 2014 Facebook lost an appeal regarding a privacy case in Germany relating to its 'Friend Finder' service (see Knibbs 2014). An earlier 2011 case forced the company to settle with US regulators, committing the company to 20 years of independent audits of its privacy procedures (Bartz and Oreskovic 2009).

12. http://bbmg.com/news/consumers-rank-ingredient-transparency-among-important-issues-brands/.

3

Evaluating Business Ethics

NORMATIVE ETHICAL THEORIES

Having completed this chapter you should be able to:

- Explain the role of normative ethical theory for ethical decision-making in business.
- Identify the international differences in perspectives on normative ethical theory.
- Understand and apply Western modernist ethical theories, i.e. utilitarianism, ethics of duty, and rights and justice.
- Understand and apply alternative ethical theories, i.e. virtue ethics, feminist ethics, discourse ethics, and postmodernism.
- Conduct a pluralist business ethics evaluation.

Key concepts and skills:

Concepts	Skills
• Normative ethical theory	• Utilitarian analysis
• Egoism	• Applying the categorical imperative test
• Ethics of duty	
• Utilitarianism	• Applying the UN Guiding Principles on Business and Human Rights
• Human rights	

Concepts	Skills
• Justice	• Applying Rawls' justice test
• Virtue ethics	• Conducting ethical discourse
• Feminist ethics	• Pluralist ethical analysis
• Discourse ethics	
• Postmodern ethics	

■ Introduction

In our everyday lives, we constantly come up against situations where values are in conflict and where we have to make a choice about what is right or wrong. Maybe it is a question of whether to lie about something in order to protect a friend's feelings, or driving over the speed limit when rushing to avoid being late for a date, or perhaps deciding whether to report a classmate you have seen cheating on their assignment. The point is that we all have some prior knowledge of what is right or wrong that helps us to decide what to do. Most of the situations that we are faced with in our personal lives are pretty much within the scope of what a typical person would be able to decide. In a business context, however, situations might become considerably more complex.

Consider the case of a multinational company intending to establish a subsidiary in a developing country. There are a number of ethical problems that may arise—maybe the local public authorities expect to receive bribes for granting planning permission, perhaps labour standards in the country are particularly low, or possibly workplace discrimination is much more common than back home. There is also the additional problem that a variety of people will be involved, all of whom might have different views and attitudes towards these issues. Consequently, coming to an ethical conclusion in business situations is far more complex than in most of the situations where we as private individuals have to make ethical decisions.

Perhaps more importantly, in a business context there is often a need for these decisions to be based on a systematic, rational, and widely understandable argument so that they can be adequately defended, justified, and explained to relevant stakeholders. Similarly, if we believe that an organization has acted unethically in responding to these issues, we need some concrete basis from which to argue our case. After all, at what point can we say that a particular behaviour is more than just *different* from what we would have done, but is in some way actually *wrong*? This is the point where **normative ethical theories** come into play. By normative, we mean ethical theories that propose to prescribe the morally correct way of acting.

Normative ethical theories
The rules and principles that determine right and wrong for a given situation.

In this chapter we will take a look at the major ethical theories and analyse their value and potential for business ethics. To begin with, though, we first need to be clear about how exactly we shall be using ethical theory in the context of this chapter and in the rest of the book that follows.

■ The role of ethical theory

In locating a place for ethical theory in business, Richard De George (1999) suggests that two extreme positions can be imagined:

- **Ethical absolutism**. On one side of the spectrum would be a position of ethical absolutism, which claims that there are eternal, universally applicable moral principles. According to this view, right and wrong are *objective* qualities that can be rationally determined.

- **Ethical relativism**. The other extreme would be a position of relativism, which claims that morality is context-dependent and *subjective*. Relativists tend to believe that there are no universal right and wrongs that can be rationally determined—it simply depends on the person making the decision and the culture in which they are located. In its most well-known form, the notion of relativism occurs in international business issues, where it is argued that a moral judgement about behaviour in another culture cannot be made from outside because morality is culturally determined. Ethical relativism is different from *descriptive relativism*: while the latter merely suggests that different cultures *have* different ethics, the former proposes that both sets of beliefs can be equally *right*. Ethical relativism then is still a normative theory (De George 1999).

? THINK THEORY

Think about the concepts of absolutism and relativism in the context of bribery. How would each theory conceptualize the problem of bribery and what course of action might they suggest for someone faced with a corrupt official?

VISIT THE ONLINE RESOURCE CENTRE for a short response to this feature

Most traditional *Western modernist* ethical theories tend to be absolutist in nature. They seek to set out universal rules or principles that can be applied to any situation to provide the answer as to what is right or wrong. Contemporary ethical theories provide us with some *alternative perspectives* on ethical theory. They often tend towards a more relativistic position. However, in the course of this chapter we want to show that for the practical purposes of making effective decisions in business, both of these positions are not particularly useful.

Our position therefore is one of *ethical pluralism*. This occupies something of a middle ground between absolutism and relativism. Pluralism accepts different moral convictions and backgrounds, while at the same time suggesting that a consensus on basic principles and rules in a certain social context can, and should, be reached. Ethical theories, as we shall show, can help to clarify different moral presuppositions of the various parties involved in a decision—one person may tend to think in terms of one theory, while another might think in terms of a different theory. In making good business decisions, we need to understand this range of perspectives in order to establish a consensus on the solution to ethical problems (Kaler 1999b). Rather than establishing a single universal theory, in this chapter we will present the different theoretical frameworks as complementary resources or conceptual tools that help us make a practical, structured, and systematic assessment of the right and wrong in particular business decisions. Theory can help to clarify these situations and each theory highlights different aspects that need to be considered.

This view rests on two basic things that John Kaler (1999b) suggests we already know about morality before we even try to introduce ethical theory into it. First, morality is foremost a *social phenomenon*. We apply morality because we constantly have to establish the rules and arrangements of our living together as social beings. It seems reasonable to accept the argument of *descriptive relativism*—that there is a diversity of moral convictions, be they religiously, philosophically, or otherwise ideologically grounded, is a given. Hence, even if there were one and only one 'objectively' right moral conviction, it is simply a matter of fact that this is not widely agreed upon.

It only takes a quick visit to the pub or café to listen in to the conversations around us to discover that people from the same street or place of work differ considerably in their moral views and convictions. From a business angle, this gets even more important due to globalization, since this multiplies the relevant 'supply' of moralities by the sheer number of different cultural contexts playing a role in business decisions.

As morality seeks to solve questions of right and wrong in organizing social life, we cannot therefore realistically rely on an absolutist position, since empirically we can see a variety of moral perspectives. If we are to make good decisions that are acceptable to others, we obviously need to develop some knowledge of the different moralities that we are likely to face.

The second of Kaler's (1999b) assumptions is that morality is primarily about *harm and benefit*. Right and wrong are largely about avoiding harm and providing benefits. After all, if we did not dislike harm or value benefits, there would simply be no need for morality. As we will see further on, 'benefit' and 'harm' are matters that are conceptualized differently by various ethical theories. Nevertheless, there is a certain consensus about the fact that morality should ultimately help a society to avoid harm and provide benefits for its members. Given this focus, it is possible to partly refute the position of the relativists and assert that morality is more than a subjective feeling or opinion since it is about actual harms and benefits that we need to address. Ultimately, the logic of relativism is that everything is just different and nothing is wrong (Donaldson 1996). This 'anything goes' approach to morality is not very helpful when we see genuine harm being inflicted on people.

The value of ethical theories lies in the fact that they help to rationalize and understand the hunches or gut feelings we all have about what is right or wrong. Furthermore, they make it possible to engage in a rational discourse between individuals whose moral values are different from each other. Nowhere is this diversity more evident than on the web where every conceivable moral position on business ethics is articulated. **Ethics Online 3** provides an overview of numerous blogs on business ethics where one can see how different ethics experts apply their knowledge of theory and principles to address real-life events in the business ethics world.

■ Normative ethical theories: International origins and differences

In Chapter 1 we argued that business ethics thinking varies across the world. This is particularly the case in the use of ethical theories. However, it is probably fair to say that the academic debate on business ethics has so far been largely dominated by thinking originating in Europe and North America. In fact, more narrowly, most of

VISIT THE ONLINE RESOURCE CENTRE for links to useful sources of further information

ETHICS ONLINE 3

Business ethics blogs

The growth of the blogosphere has not gone unnoticed by the business ethics community. There are now a considerable number of blogs concerned with applying ethical theories and principles to the latest business issues and scandals, both in English as well as increasingly in other languages too, such as French, German, Spanish, or Portuguese.

The value of following these blogs for business ethics students is manifold. Many business ethics blogs comment on current events using the types of theories and concepts discussed in this chapter. They also feature interesting links, provide opinion, and offer food for thought—all of which helps to highlight the contemporary relevance of the topic. Blogs can be very helpful for applying what you read in your business ethics textbook, or what you learn in your ethics class, to what is happening right now in the business world.

Not all business ethics blogs showcase the theoretical thinking discussed in this chapter, but those written by academics tend to offer the most thorough ethical analysis—

and are often the most relevant for applying the lessons learnt in the classroom. The specific value of those blogs is that they refer to daily events. Be it the Bangladesh factory collapse in 2013, the controversies around the rights of gay and lesbian athletes at the Winter Olympic Games in Russia in 2014, or the use of slave labour in the build up to the 2022 Qatar World Cup—many of the blogs provide a great opportunity to get an insightful analysis from an ethical perspective that typically does not get too much airtime in the mainstream media.

Most bloggers, however, are not academics—and yet in their assessment of business ethics issues, many of the ideas discussed in the classroom tend to get aired. Popular bloggers outside academia are mostly professional commentators or journalists. Such blogs may be light on ethical theory, but they have plenty of practical insight and advice, and help to give a more rounded picture of the business ethics issues currently hitting the headlines.

Featured blogs
http://blog.iese.edu/ethics/ (IESE Business School, Barcelona)
http://businessethicsblog.com/ (Chris MacDonald)
http://craneandmatten.blogspot.com (Andrew Crane and Dirk Matten)
http://knowledge.wharton.upenn.edu/category/business-ethics/# (Wharton Business School, University of Pennsylvania)
http://tobiaswebb.blogspot.ca ('The Smarter Business Blog', Toby Webb)
http://www.mallenbaker.net/csr/blog.php (Mallen Baker)

the literature available in English is more or less dominated by an Anglo-American view, whereas many of the continental European or Asian approaches are less widely received since most of the literature is published in languages other than English. And although we find several continental European approaches also in American and UK textbooks, the general use and the necessity for theory in business ethics is fairly different on both sides of the Atlantic. Though our core focus in this chapter is on European and North American approaches, we acknowledge that there is a growing debate and literature on African, Asian, and Latin-American perspectives on business ethics.

We believe it is helpful, then, to highlight some relevant differences in the mainstream debate in Europe and North America as they most commonly appear in the published literature (see Palazzo 2002)—albeit with a note of caution about the dangers of general-izing such a rich and diverse body of work.

- **Individual versus institutional morality**. As we saw in Chapter 1, some approaches to studying business ethics tend to have a more individualistic perspective on moral-ity while others tend to focus more on the economic system and the wider governing institutions. Therefore, normative ethical theories in the US tend to be more applica-ble to *individual behaviour*, whereas in Europe the *design of institutions* in the economic system seems to be the main influence in developing and applying theory.

- **Questioning versus accepting capitalism**. Most of the mainstream business ethics literature in the US does not particularly question the existing framework of manage-ment, but rather sees ethical problems occurring *within the capitalist system*, which it treats as a given. In Europe, relevant parts of business ethics focus on *questioning the ethical justification of capitalism*. Hence, considerable effort in business ethics theory has been dedicated to defending or refining the ethical legitimacy of capitalist eco-nomic thought. Although one has to say that not all of this work has been immediate-ly helpful in solving day-to-day issues in business life, it nevertheless helps to develop a more critical and distanced approach to the institutions that govern and determine business decisions, and therefore provides help in understanding certain ethical dilem-mas in business, including corporate governance, employee rights, and stakeholder involvement.

- **Justifying versus applying moral norms**. Europe is characterized by a strong plural-ism of moral convictions and values. Therefore, the challenge for business ethics on the theoretical level often involves the *justification and ethical legitimation of norms* for addressing ethical dilemmas in business situations. In the US, however, judging by most American business ethics textbooks, these issues do not seem to take such a dominant position: apart from a section on normative theories in business, most text-books treat the question of which moral values are appropriate as a given and chiefly focus on the *application of morality* to business situations.

Notwithstanding these differences, it is important to recognize that no single normative theory can be 'claimed' or attributed to any individual country or region. As we shall now see, most of the traditional theories routinely embraced by American authors are in fact European in origin. And, as indicated in Chapter 1, there is of course a wealth of ethical thinking in business beyond the North American and European context. However, in terms of theoretical approaches to the field, the debate beyond this context is rather limited, albeit with some important additions concerned with Asian and other approaches to business ethics.

A key difference to the approaches discussed later in this chapter is that much of the thinking in Asian business ethics, for example, is either informed by religion, such as Islam (Wienen 1999) or Buddhism (Gould 1995), or traditional community values, such as the Chinese *Guanxi* approach (Chenting 2003). European and North American approaches, in contrast, are mainly based on philosophical arguments, as we will discover in the following sections. So before we explain these philosophical arguments, let us briefly look at the difference between our normative ethical theories and religious ethics.

■ Normative ethical theories and religion

Religious teaching about ethics and normative ethical theory from philosophy both tend to have the same aim when applied to business, namely how to decide what is the right thing to do when faced with moral problems in commerce. Both are therefore focused on ensuring that business is responsible, avoids doing harm and contributes to societal benefits. However, there are two main differences between the approaches:

- **Source of rules and principles**. Religions typically invoke a deity or an organized system of belief (e.g. the teachings in the Qu'ran or the Talmud) as the source of determining right and wrong. Therefore, faith is the critical requisite for acting ethically. Philosophical theories, on the other hand, are based on the belief that human reason should drive ethics. Thus, rationality is the critical requisite for acting ethically.

- **Consequences of morality and immorality**. Acting ethically according to normative philosophical theory is primarily considered a matter of creating tangible social benefits and harms for others. While these are still important in religious teaching, there is also an important element of spiritual consequence for the decision-maker. These consequences might include salvation, enlightenment, reincarnation, or damnation.

Of course, different religions often have very different things to say about how to go about achieving the goals of ethical business. Followers of Judaism, for example, tend to exhibit some distinctive business practices that can be directly traced back to basic tenets of their faith (Tamari 1997). One such form of Jewish observance is specific periods of abstinence from economic activity. In Jerusalem, this has given rise to a long-running 'Sabbath war' between secular and orthodox residents over whether shops, cinemas, and bars should remain open on the Jewish day of rest (Linthicum 2014). Islam also provides certain rules about appropriate business practices, which has even given rise to a distinct system of banking consistent with the principles of Sharia Law that forbids the charging the interest, often referred to as 'Islamic banking' (Ariff and Iqbal 2011).

In many parts of the world, the influence of religious principles is less direct, but they continue to shape business conduct, even if most economic actors are not devout followers. This is nowhere more visible than with the Protestant work ethic that has shaped large parts of the global economy, especially Northern Europe and North America, where it has been found to give rise to self-discipline, hard work and honesty (Jones 1997).

It is important, however, not to overemphasize differences in religious principles when it comes to business. Interfaith groups have long promoted their common cause of improving ethical practices in business. The Interfaith Centre for Corporate Responsibility, for example, seeks to use the collective influence of values-based investors to improve corporate attention to social and environmental issues, regardless of denomination.[1] Similarly, the Interfaith Declaration, an accord between Christian, Jewish and Muslim leaders, established an influential set of business principles based on commonalities across their religions. It emphasizes the shared commitment to justice, mutual respect, stewardship, and honesty across the three religions.[2] Ultimately, although religious principles continue to be influential on the institutional fabric of economic life, their direct effect on business culture and practice is significant in only certain regions of the world. This is because substantial processes of secularization—i.e. movement towards a *non-religious* form of organizing—have taken place in many workplaces across the globe. As such, normative ethical theories, based on philosophical principles, remain at the cornerstone of business ethics for much contemporary business.

■ Western modernist ethical theories

In Western societies, the ethical theories traditionally regarded as appropriate for application to business contexts are based on philosophical thinking generated in Europe and North America beginning with the enlightenment in the eighteenth century. This age is often referred to also as 'modernity' as it modernized a lot of traditional thinking dominated by religious approaches throughout the Middle Ages. We refer to these theories therefore as 'Western modernist'. They generally offer a certain rule or principle that one can apply to any given situation—hence, they are *absolutist* in intention. These theories are normative because they start with an assumption about the nature of the world, and more specific assumptions about the nature of human beings. Consequently, the degree to which we can accept the theory and the outcome of its application to particular business situations depends chiefly on the degree to which we share their underlying assumptions. As they have a rather well-defined rule of decision, the main advantage of these theories is the fact that they normally provide us with a fairly *unequivocal solution* to ethical problems.

These theories generally can be differentiated into two groups (see **Figure 3.1**). On the right-hand side of Figure 3.1 we have theories that base moral judgement on the outcomes of a certain action. If these outcomes are desirable, then the action in question is morally right; if the outcomes of the action are not desirable, the action is morally wrong. The moral judgement in these *consequentialist theories* is thus based on the intended outcomes, the aims, or the goals of a certain action. Therefore, consequentialist ethics is often also referred to by the term *teleological*, based on the Greek word for 'goal'.

On the other hand, we have those theories that base moral judgements on the underlying principles of a decision-maker's motivation. An action is right or wrong, these theories suggest, not because we like the consequences it produces, but because the underlying principles are morally right. These *non-consequentialist* approaches are quite closely linked to Judeo-Christian thinking and start from reasoning about the individual's rights and duties. These philosophic theories, also called *deontological* (based on the Greek word for 'duty'), look at the desirability of principles, and based on these principles, deduce a 'duty' to act accordingly in a given situation, regardless of the desirability of the consequences.

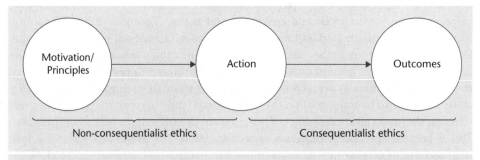

Figure 3.1 Consequentialist and non-consequentialist theories in business ethics

	Egoism	Utilitarianism	Ethics of duties	Rights and justice
Contributors	Adam Smith Milton Friedman	Jeremy Bentham John Stuart Mill	Immanuel Kant	John Locke John Rawls
Focus	Individual desires or interests	Collective welfare	Duties	Rights
Rules	Maximization of desires/ self-interest	Act/rule utilitarianism	Categorical imperative	Respect for human beings
Concept of human beings	Humans are actors with limited knowledge and objectives	Humans are motivated by avoidance of pain and gain of pleasure ('hedonist')	Humans are rational moral actors	Humans are beings that are distinguished by dignity
Type	Consequentialist	Consequentialist	Non-consequentialist	Non-consequentialist

Figure 3.2 Major normative theories in business ethics

In the following, we will have a closer look at both families of philosophical theories and analyse their potential for solving various business decisions. **Figure 3.2** gives a short overview of the relevant philosophical schools and the basic elements of their thinking. In explaining these theories, we shall use them to reflect on a particular business problem, as presented in **Ethical Dilemma 3**. We suggest you read this before continuing with the chapter.

Consequentialist theories

Here we shall look at two main consequentialist theories:

- Egoism.

- Utilitarianism.

Both of these theories address right and wrong according to the outcomes of a decision. However, we shall see that they address those outcomes in different ways—egoism by focusing on the outcomes for the *decision-maker*, utilitarianism by focusing on the wider *social outcomes within a community*.

Egoism

Egoism is one of the oldest philosophical ideas, and it was already well known and discussed by ancient Greek philosophers such as Plato. In the last three centuries, it has been quite influential in modern economics, particularly in relation to Adam Smith's (1723–90) ideas about the design of liberalist economics, and Milton Friedman's advocacy of free markets with limited government.

The justification for **egoism** lies in the underlying concept of humans: as we have only limited insight into the consequences of our actions, the only suitable strategy to achieve a good life is to pursue our own desires or interests. A common interpretation of Adam Smith's (1793) economic thought is that the pursuit of individual self-interest is

Egoism
A theory that suggests that an action is morally right if in a given situation all decision-makers freely decide to pursue either their (short-term) desires or their (long-term) interests.

AN ETHICAL DILEMMA 3

Producing toys—child's play?

You are the product manager of a confectionery company that includes small plastic toys with its chocolate sweets. Having met a potential Thai manufacturer of these toys at a trade fair in Europe, you now visit the company in the north-eastern part of Thailand to finalize a two-year supply contract. Arriving there and talking to the sales manager, you are able to arrange a deal that supplies you with the toys at a third of the cost currently charged by your Portuguese supplier, but with equivalent quality and supply arrangements.

In order to check the reliability of the manufacturing process you ask the manager to show you around the place. You are surprised to find out that there is no real workshop on the premises. Rather, the production process is organized such that at 6am, about 30 men line up at the company's gate, load large boxes with toy components on their little carts or motor-scooters and take the material to their homes.

Your prospective supplier then takes you to one of these places where you see a large family, sitting in a garage-like barn assembling the toys. Not only are the mother and father doing the job, but also the couple's six children, aged five to 14, who are working busily—and from what you see, very cheerfully—together with the parents, while the grandmother is looking after the food in an adjacent room. In the evening, at around 8pm, the day's work is done, the assembled toys are stored back in the boxes and taken to the workshop of the company, where the men receive their payment for the finished goods. At the end of the week, the toys are shipped to the customers in Europe.

As you have never come across such a pattern of manufacturing, your Thai partner explains to you that this is a very common and well-established practice in this part of the country, and one that guarantees a good level of quality. Satisfied, you tell the Thai manager that you will conclude the paperwork once you get back home, and you leave the company offices happy in the knowledge of the cost savings you are going to make, and quietly confident that it will result in a healthy bonus for you at the end of the year.

On your way back, while buying some souvenirs for your five- and seven-year-old nieces at the airport, you suddenly start wondering if you would like to see them growing up the same way as the child workers that you have just employed to make your company's toys.

Questions

1. Reading the case and putting yourself in the role of the product manager, what would your immediate gut reaction be?

2. Based on your spontaneous immediate decision, can you set out the reasons for your choice? Also, can you relate those reasons back to some underlying values or principles that are obviously important to you?

acceptable in the economic system because it produces a morally desirable outcome for society through the 'invisible hand' of the marketplace.[3] This argument may thus be summarized as saying that one is likely to find a moral outcome as the end-product of a system based on free competition and good information. That is, everyone must be free to pursue their own self-interests, unencumbered by market imperfections such as monopolies or limited knowledge of the products and prices available in the market. In this way, everyone gets to participate equally in the market, and any bad behaviour will quickly be punished.

For example, if a producer makes and sells shoddy or faulty products, then consumers may suffer in the short term as a result of the inadequacy of the products that they have bought. However, in the longer run, providing consumers know about alternative choices, the producer's trade will suffer as consumers turn to other producers. Hence, the producer will avoid producing shoddy goods for their own self-interest, thus producing a situation that is beneficial to all. Because of his aim to produce wider social benefits, some have likened Smith's theory to 'egoist practices for utilitarian results' (Beauchamp and Bowie 1997: 18).

It is important to distinguish egoism based on desire from *selfishness*. Whereas the egoist can be moved by pity for others in seeking to remove his own distress caused by their plight, the selfish person is insensitive to the other. So, for example, a firm donating to charity to improve the reputation of the company can be perfectly in line with an egoistic philosophy, whereas ignoring the charity and spending the funds on a self-promotional advertising campaign that has the same effect on reputation would be more about selfishness.

Within moral philosophy, an important criticism of egoism *based on desire* is that it renders patently different approaches to life as being equivalent; therefore, the life of the student who just gets drunk every night in the bar is as admirable as the student who works hard for a first class degree, providing both followed their desire. Therefore, within this school of philosophy, an egoism *based on the pursuit of interests* is the ultimate rendering of this concept (Graham 1990). The idea of interests based on the pursuit of one's long-term well-being enables one to distinguish between the life of the hard-drinking student and that of the hard-working student. In this formulation, a gap opens up between desire (or longing) and what is in one's ultimate interests, such that one can say that it is not in the interest of the drinking student to give in to immediate desires. An egoism based on interests therefore approaches the idea of objective value—as in, that one way of acting is objectively better or 'more ethical' than another.

This leads to the notion of '*enlightened egoism*', which is quite often discussed in the context of business ethics. We have come across it already in Chapter 2 when discussing 'enlightened self-interest'. For example, corporations might invest in the social environment, for instance by supporting schools or sponsoring a new ambulance for the local health service, because an improved level of social services is in the interest of workforce retention and satisfaction.

If we apply the theory of egoism to the case in Ethical Dilemma 3, we would have to look at the actors involved and analyse whether they freely pursue their own desires or interests in engaging in the deal. This certainly applies to the manager and his Thai partner, and by the looks of the case, it could also apply to the parents of the family business. As for the children, it could be that they are quite happy to help the parents and just take it for granted that things work like this in their world. From this perspective, an egoistic look at the situation might consider the deal as morally acceptable. One might, however, wonder if it is in the children's long-term interest to engage in this type of work: although one could argue that it prevents them from being forced into far less desirable forms of work, moral concerns arise when considering that this type of work prevents them from gaining a decent education, enjoying time for play, and exposes them to fairly long working hours, all of which casts some doubt on whether they really are able to freely pursue their own interests. The latter considerations then would tend to suggest that from an egoistic point of view this action might be immoral.

It does not take much thought to discover certain weaknesses in egoist ethics. To begin with, this theory works fine if there is a mechanism in society that makes sure that no individual egoist pursues their own interests at other egoists' expense. In Adam Smith's thinking, this mechanism would be the market. Although we can see that the market usually works quite well, there are numerous situations where this does not seem to be the case, and where the egoism of single actors leads to unfavourable results. Current concerns about growing income inequality, for example, are fuelled by the idea that markets are not functioning perfectly and we thus witness a heavily skewed distribution of wealth to the top 1% of earners in society. Another example would be the sustainability debate: the victims of today's resource depletion or global climate change are future generations, which are not yet present to take part in any kind of market. This clearly shows some initial limitations of egoist theory. **Ethics on Screen 3** discusses some of

VISIT THE ONLINE RESOURCE CENTRE
for links to useful sources of further information

ETHICS ON SCREEN 3

Margin Call

Margin Call is one of the strongest American films of the year and easily the best Wall Street movie ever made.

David Denby, *New Yorker*

In the aftermath of the financial meltdown of the late 2000s a spate of movies were released that dealt with the world of finance and the inner workings of Wall Street. Documentary-style films such as '*Too Big to Fail* or *Inside Job* as well as dramatic features such as *The Wolf of Wall Street* or *Wall Street: Money Never Sleeps* (see Ethics on Screen 1 and 6) have all attempted to explain the crisis or at least expose the world of finance as ruthless, instrumental, and the last place on earth to look for ethics.

Margin Call is something of an exception. For starters, with a prime cast (starring among others Kevin Spacey, Jeremy Irons, Paul Bettany, Demi Moore, and Stanley Tucci) and a sharp script that was nominated for best original screenplay at the 2012 Oscars, it is highly engaging to watch—whether you are looking to gain some insights into the mechanics of the financial crisis or not. But it also stays largely clear of stereotyping or even judging the individual actors in the story—even though the moral mazes in modern finance are expertly brought to screen.

Before the Door Pictures/
The Kobal Collection

The film plays out in the final days preceding the 2008 financial collapse. It starts with a scene where whole swathes of the workforce of a Wall Street investment bank are ruthlessly fired. The main plot, however, revolves around the late-night discovery by a junior analyst that the bank's 'toxic assets' (i.e. those mortgage-based securities whose demise caused the crisis to unfold) are putting the entire existence of the company at risk—unless the firm finds a way to get rid of them as soon as possible.

A central scene unfolds in a 2am meeting convened by the CEO John Tuld (Jeremy Irons)—Tuld being a thinly disguised reference to the infamous Lehman Brothers CEO, Dick Fuld. He summons his senior staff and demands to know what they should do with this 'greatest pile of odiferous excrement in the history of capitalism' (like *The Wolf of Wall Street*, the film captures well the brutal jargon of the industry). The chief trader Sam Rogers (Kevin Spacey) makes an eloquent argument that selling worthless assets to their as yet unsuspecting clients would fundamentally threaten the market, and could ultimately put the company out of business. After all, those clients would soon enough discover that they had been sold 'junk bonds'—an argument which could not better demonstrate an ethics of 'enlightened egoism' that dominates much of the workings of business.

Tuld, however, sticks to a much narrower, less 'enlightened' ethical viewpoint. All that matters is the immediate survival of the firm, regardless of who gets hurt along the way. Raw corporate self-interest thus drives the firm to rapidly offload its toxic assets before the market can even fully realize what is happening. Still, Tuld presents this not as dishonest ('I don't cheat' he clearly states to his team), but as simply 'being first' among their competitors in anticipating the market and 'selling to willing buyers at the current fair, market price'. Of course, unlike their own traders, the firm's clients do not know how worthless the securities are when they buy them from the firm, meaning that the 'market price' is anything but fair. It is a reflection of incomplete information rather than the price that a truly informed buyer would pay.

Sam ultimately goes ahead with the rapid disposal of the toxic assets despite his misgivings and is even convinced by Tuld not to quit afterwards because, as he admits, he 'needs the money'. Tuld, however, continues to see things differently. 'It's just money,' he says over dinner on the top floor of the building overlooking Manhattan. 'It's made up. It's not wrong, and it's certainly no different today than it's ever been.' His point is that in financial markets, self-interest is the only game in town, and in fact it is this self-interest that has driven the success of Wall Street, and made New York one of the richest places on earth. Stock market crashes are just one of the costs along the way. It is a common variant of the 'egoist means for utilitarian ends' argument, even if it does require him to conveniently ignore the evidence that he has just destroyed more value than he has created.

Watching the movie as a business ethics student suggests a number of important lessons. Chief among them is that egoist thinking is powerful in business, but not always in its genuine 'ethical' form (where everyone gets to freely and fairly participate in the market), or still less in its more enlightened form (where concern for others is seen as part of the firm's long-term self-interest). It is a powerful worldview that even those, like Sam, who are given to different ethical viewpoints, find hard to resist.

Sources
Denby, D. 2011. All that glitters. *New Yorker*, 31 October 2011.
French, P. 2012. Margin Call—review. *Guardian*, 8 January 2012.
http://margincallmovie.com.

these issues around egoism in the context of the movie *Margin Call*, which explores the events leading up to the financial meltdown of the late 2000s.

Utilitarianism

The philosophy of utilitarianism has been one of the most commonly accepted ethical theories in the Anglo-Saxon world. It is linked to the British philosophers and economists Jeremy Bentham (1748–1832) and John Stuart Mill (1806–73) and has been influential in modern economics in general.

Utilitarianism
A theory which states that an action is morally right if it results in the greatest amount of good for the greatest amount of people affected by the action.

The basic foundation of **utilitarianism** is the '*greatest happiness principle*'. This is the ultimate consequentialist principle as it focuses solely on the consequences of an action, weighs good outcomes against bad outcomes, and encourages the action that results in the greatest amount of good for everyone involved. Unlike egoism, it does not only look at each individual involved, and ask whether their individual desires and interests are met, but it focuses on the *collective welfare* that is produced by a certain decision.

The underlying concept in utilitarianism is the notion of utility, which Bentham sees as the ultimate goal in life. Humans are viewed as hedonists, whose purpose in life is to maximize pleasure and minimize pain. In this hedonistic rendition of utilitarianism, utility is measured in terms of *pleasure and pain* (the 'hedonistic' view). Other interpretations of utility look at *happiness and unhappiness* (the 'eudemonistic' view), while others take a strongly extended view that includes not only pleasure or happiness, but ultimately all *intrinsically valuable human goods* (the 'ideal' view). These human goods would typically include aspects such as friendship, love, trust, etc. The latter view in particular makes utilitarianism open to a great number of practical decision situations and prevents it from being rather narrowly focused on pleasure and pain only.

Utilitarianism has been very powerful since it puts at the centre of the moral decision a variable that is very commonly used in economics as a parameter that measures the economic value of actions: 'utility'. Regardless of whether one accepts that utility really is quantifiable, it comes as no surprise to find that utilitarian analysis is highly compatible with the quantitative, mathematical methodology of economics. So, in analysing two possible options in a single business decision, we can assign a certain utility to each action and each person involved, and the action with the highest aggregate utility can be determined to be morally correct. Ultimately utilitarianism then comes close to what we know as *cost-benefit analysis*.

Typical situations where utilitarian analysis can be very helpful are analyses of proposed initiatives, such as social and environmental impact assessments of mining or infrastructure projects. These assessments take into consideration all of the likely positive and negative impacts of a given project, including the impact on employment, community development, and environmental quality with a view to determining whether the project will have an overall benefit to society. For example, in most developed countries new mining projects have to undergo extensive social and environmental impact assessments before they can get permission to begin operations. Such permitting long prevented the opening of Europe's largest proposed gold mine around the town of Rosia Montana in Romania since studies had demonstrated the likelihood of significant social, environmental, and cultural damage. In 2013 a mass protest movement arose in the country after the Romanian Government proposed a new law that would enable the Rosia Montana Gold Corporation to finally start operations after years of failing to acquire the necessary environmental permits.

	Action 1: doing the deal		Action 2: not doing the deal	
	Pleasure	**Pain**	**Pleasure**	**Pain**
Product manager	Good deal for the business; potential for personal bonus	Bad conscience; possible risk for company reputation	Good conscience; less risk	Loss of a good deal
Thai dealer	Good deal			Loss of a good deal; search for a new customer in Europe
Parents	Secure the family's income	Limited prospects for children		Search for other sources of income
Children	Feeling of being needed, being 'grown up'; approval of the parents	Hard work; no chance of school education	No hard work; time to play and go to school	Potentially forced to do other, more painful work
Grandmother	Family is able to support her			Loss of economic support

Figure 3.3 Example of a utilitarian analysis

If we apply this theory to the situation described in An Ethical Dilemma 3, we first have a look at all the actors involved and analyse their potential utility in terms of the pleasure and pain involved in different courses of action, say either going ahead with the deal (action one) or not doing the deal (action two). We could set up a simple balance sheet, such as that depicted in **Figure 3.3**.

After analysing all of the good and bad effects for the persons involved, we can now add up 'pleasure' and 'pain' for action 1, and the result will be the *utility* of this action. After having done the same for action 2, the moral decision is relatively easy to identify: the greatest utility of the respective actions is the morally right one. In our hypothetical case, the decision would probably go in favour of action 1 (doing the deal) as it involves the most pleasure for all parties involved, whereas in action 2 (not doing the deal), the pain seems to dominate the analysis.

This example demonstrates some of the complications with utilitarian analysis. Proponents and critics of proposed practices can both summon a host of benefits and harms to support their cases, making any comparative assessment difficult. **Case 3**, for example, elaborates the controversies around the exploration of the oil sands in Canada where a longstanding debate on the pros and cons of development has so far not led to a conclusive outcome. This points to some core *problems with utilitarianism*:

• **Subjectivity**. Clearly when using this theory you have to think rather creatively, and assessing such consequences as pleasure or pain might depend heavily on the subjective perspective of the person who carries out the analysis.

• **Problems of quantification**. Similarly, it is quite difficult to assign costs and benefits to every situation. In the example, this might be quite easy for the persons directly involved with the transaction, but it is certainly difficult to do so for the children involved, since their pleasure and pain is not quantifiable. Especially in these cases, it might be quite difficult to weigh pleasure against pain: is losing a good contract really comparable to forcing children into labour? Similarly, under utilitarianism, health and safety issues in the firm require 'values' of life and death to be quantified and calculated, without the possibility of acknowledging that they might have an intrinsic worth beyond calculation.

- **Distribution of utility**. Finally, it would appear that by assessing the greatest good for the greatest number, the interests of minorities are overlooked. In our example, a minority of children might suffer so that the majority might benefit from greater utility.

Of course, utilitarians were always aware of the limits of their theory. The problem of subjectivity, for example, led to a refinement of the theory, differentiating between what has been defined as 'act utilitarianism' versus 'rule utilitarianism':

Act utilitarianism looks to single actions and bases the moral judgement on the amount of pleasure and the amount of pain this single action causes.

Rule utilitarianism looks at classes of action and asks whether the underlying principles of an action produce more pleasure than pain for society in the long run.

Our utilitarian analysis of Ethical Dilemma 3 used the principle of act utilitarianism by asking whether just in that *single situation* the collective pleasure exceeded the pain inflicted. Given the specific circumstances of the case, this might result in the conclusion that it is morally right, because the children's pain is considerably small, given the fact, for instance, that they might have to work anyway or that school education might not be available to them. From the perspective of *rule utilitarianism*, however, one would have to ask whether child labour *in principle* produces more pleasure than pain. Here, the judgement might look considerably different, since it is not difficult to argue that the pains of child labour easily outweigh the mainly economic benefits of it. Rule utilitarianism then relieves us from examining right or wrong in every single situation, and offers the possibility of establishing certain principles that we then can apply to all such situations.

☑ Skill check

Utilitarian analysis. You should now be able to conduct a basic utilitarian analysis, often referred to as a cost-benefit analysis in business. To be a true utilitarian analysis you have to include all relevant stakeholders and the likely impacts on them.

Non-consequentialist theories

The other main branch of traditional ethical theory is non-consequentialism. Here we shall look at the two main types of non-consequentialist ethical theories that have been traditionally applied to business ethics:

- Ethics of duties.
- Ethics of rights and justice.

These two approaches are very similar, stemming from assumptions about basic universal principles of right and wrong. However, while rights-based theories tend to start by assigning a right to one party and then advocating a corresponding duty on another party to protect that right, ethics of duties *begin* with assigning of the duty to act in a certain way.

Rights and duty have also been central to many religious perspectives on business ethics, and remain important influences on business decision-makers worldwide, especially in regions with high rates of religious adherence, such as Latin America, the US, the Middle East, and Africa. Such approaches start from the basis of divine revelation, as found, for instance, in the religious tracts of the three monotheistic religions of Judaism, Christianity, and Islam, which ascribe enduring duties of humans to God, or conversely, 'God-given rights'. In such a revelation of what is right or wrong, human behaviour has its divine, eternal validity—regardless of whether the outcomes in a given situation are in anybody's self-interest (egoism) or result in more pleasure or pain (utilitarianism), as consequentialist approaches would suggest. In secular societies, the ideas of rights and duties are equally as strong and have been enshrined in various norms and laws, including everything from a doctor's duty of care to a citizen's right to privacy.

Ethics of duties

In business ethics, the most influential theory to come from the perspective of **ethics of duty** derives from the work of the German philosopher Immanuel Kant (1724–1804). Kant argued that morality and decisions about right and wrong were not dependent on a particular situation, let alone on the consequences of one's action. For Kant, morality was a question of certain abstract and unchangeable obligations—defined by a set of *a priori* moral rules—that humans should apply to all relevant ethical problems. As a key Enlightenment thinker, Kant was convinced that human beings do not need God, the church, or some other superior authority to identify these principles for ethical behaviour. He saw humans as *rational* actors who could decide these principles for themselves. Hence, humans could therefore also be regarded as independent *moral actors* who made their own rational decisions regarding right and wrong.

Kant subsequently developed a theoretical framework through which these principles could be derived, called the '*categorical imperative*'. By this he meant that this theoretical framework should be applied to every moral issue regardless of who is involved, who profits, and who is harmed by the principles once they have been applied in specific situations.

The categorical imperative gives rise to three key principles that, taken together, constitute a 'test' of whether a particular action should be deemed ethical:

- **Consistency**. An action can only be regarded as right if the rule guiding that behaviour should be followed consistently by everyone in all cases, without contradiction. So, for example, murder is an immoral action because if we allowed everybody to murder there would be no possibility of human security on earth; lying is immoral, because if everybody were allowed to lie, the entire notion of 'truth' would be impossible, and an organized and stable human civilization would not be imaginable.

- **Human dignity**. Kant states that you should always act so that you treat other humans 'always as an end and never as a means only.' Humans deserve respect as autonomous, rational actors, and this essential human dignity should never be ignored. We all use

Ethics of duty
Ethical theories that consist of abstract, unchangeable obligations, defined by a set of rationally deduced *a priori* moral rules, which should be applied to all relevant ethical problems.

people as means, as soon as we employ them or pay them to provide us with goods or services. However, this does not mean we should *only* treat them as means to achieve what we want and just forget about their own needs and goals in life, and their expectations to make their own choices.

- **Universality**. The rules guiding our actions should also be, according to Kant, 'universally lawgiving.' That is, they have to be acceptable to every rational human being, not because they have been told to accept them but because they are rationally acceptable. 'Because reason is the same for all rational beings, we each give ourselves the same moral law' (De George 1999: 88). This element of the test therefore tries to overcome specifically the risk of *subjectivity* inherent in utilitarian analysis, since it asks us to check if other rational actors would autonomously come to the same judgement. In other contexts, this point has been referred to as the '*New York Times* test' (Langvardt 2012: 383)—namely, if you would be uncomfortable that your actions were reported in the press it means that you believe others disagree with the rules guiding your actions, and so you can be fairly sure that the rules are of doubtful moral status.

As some have argued, Kant's categorical imperative, in particular the principle of consistency, comes close to a core tenet of many religions, otherwise also referred to as the 'golden rule': 'treat others as you wanted to be treated yourself' (Brammer et al. 2007: 231). This core principle is more or less explicitly embedded not just in the three monotheistic religions, but also in Buddhism, Hinduism, and Confucianism amongst others (Romar 2004). **Figure 3.4** in fact shows that the golden rule is a common feature of various belief systems across the world.

The core difference between a religious and a Kantian approach to the golden rule is that while religion 'recognizes God as the ultimate source of value' (Pava 1998: 604), Kant's approach reflects a different assumption: if God is the creator of rational human beings, then these human beings should also be able to rationally understand and decide whatever is the morally right or wrong thing to do in a given situation—rather than just being told what to do by a divine authority.

If we apply Kant's moral 'test' to Ethical Dilemma 3, we get the following insights:

- According to the principle of *consistency*, the first question would be to ask if we would want everybody to act according to the principles of our action in all circumstances. Obviously, as the product manager you are already uncomfortable about applying the principle of exploiting child labour from a third-world context to your own family back home in Europe. You probably would not like this to become a law that is consistently applied, which would then suggest that this activity could be deemed immoral on the basis of inconsistency.

- Regarding the principle of *human dignity*, it is questionable whether the children have freely and autonomously decided to work. By making use of their labour, you could be said to be largely treating them as cheap labour for your own ends rather than as 'ends in themselves', suggesting that their basic human dignity was not being fully recognized and respected.

- Looking at the principle of *universality*, there is also the question of whether you would expect your friends and family to apply the same rule. In other words, it would seem rather doubtful that all other rational human beings would come to the

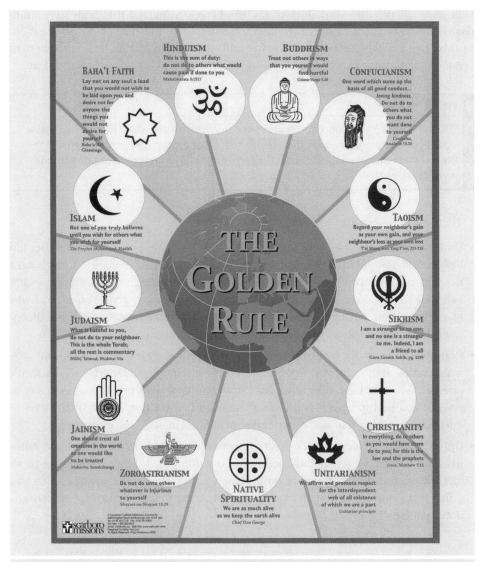

Figure 3.4 The Golden Rule in different belief systems
Source: Reproduced with permission from Scarboro Missions.

same conclusion that child labour is a principle that should be followed on a general basis.

Kant's theory has been extensively examined in relation to business (Bowie 2013), but for the purpose of this book, we do not want to dig any deeper beyond these three basic principles. But already these can be quite helpful in practical situations and have had a considerable influence on business ethics thinking. For example, in Chapter 2 we discussed the *stakeholder concept* of the firm. Evan and Freeman (1993) argue that the ethical basis of this concept has been substantially derived from Kantian thinking. Hence, in order to treat employees, local communities, or suppliers not only as means, but also as constituencies with goals and priorities of their own, Evan and Freeman suggest that firms have a fundamental *duty* to allow these stakeholders some degree of influence on the corporation. By this, they would be enabled to act as free and autonomous human beings, rather than being merely factors of production (employees) or sources of revenue (consumers), etc.

VISIT THE ONLINE RESOURCE CENTRE for a short response to this feature

> **? THINK THEORY**
>
> Stakeholder theory has also been considered from other theoretical perspectives. How would you apply utilitarianism for instance to the concept of stakeholder theory? Do you think that the two different perspectives would suggest different obligations towards stakeholders?

There are, however, also *problems with ethics of duty*:

- **Undervaluing outcomes.** Obviously one of these problems is that there is rather too little consideration of the outcomes of one's actions in ethics of duty. Although Kant would argue that you can consider consequences providing you would agree that everyone should do so when faced with similar situations, it gives you no real way of assessing these outcomes, and they do not form a fundamental part of the theory itself. They *may* be incorporated, but then again, they may not.

- **Complexity.** Secondly, while the basic idea of ethics of duty is quite simple—basically, is this action right, and is it my duty to do it—specific formulations such as Kant's categorical imperative can be quite complicated to apply. His principles-based way of evaluating a decision requires a certain amount of abstraction and it is this level of intellectual scrutiny that one cannot take for granted in each and every case.

- **Optimism.** Furthermore, Kant's theory is quite optimistic: his view of man as a rational actor who acts consequently according to self-imposed duties seems more of an ideal than a reality with regard to business actors. In contrast, the strength of egoism is that it is a concept of humans that is generally quite well confirmed by the conventional pattern of business behaviour.

☑ Skill check

Categorical imperative test. This is a key skill in conducting ethical analysis based on principles, namely consistency, human dignity, and universality. Any rule that does not meet all three principles would be regarded as unethical according to the ethics of duty.

Ethics of rights and justice

In Chapter 2 we briefly discussed the notion of citizenship in terms of a set of individual rights. Actually, this notion of rights goes back to an entire philosophical school initially linked to another modernist thinker, the British philosopher John Locke (1632–1714). He conceptualized the notion of 'natural rights', or moral claims, that humans were entitled to, and which should be respected and protected (at that time, primarily by the state). Among the most important rights conceived by Locke and subsequent rights theorists were *rights to life, freedom, and property*. These have since been extended to include rights to freedom of speech, conscience, consent, privacy, and the entitlement to a fair legal process, among others. Most people now talk of '**human rights**' rather than natural rights, with the assumption that all humans, irrespective of their gender, race, religion, nationality, or any other factor, should be able to universally enjoy such rights.

Human rights
Basic, inalienable entitlements that are inherent to all human beings, without exception.

The general significance of the notion of rights in terms of an ethical theory lies in the fact that these rights typically result in the duty of other actors to respect them. In this respect, rights are sometimes seen as related to duties, since the rights of one person can result in a corresponding duty on other persons to respect, protect, or facilitate these rights. My right to property imposes a duty on others not to interfere with my property or take it away. My right to privacy imposes a duty on others to refrain from gathering personal information about my private life without my consent. Rights and duties are therefore frequently seen as two sides of the same coin.

This link to corresponding duties makes the theory of rights similar to Kant's approach. The main difference is that it does not rely on a complex process of determining the duties by applying the categorical imperative. Rather, the notion of rights is based on a certain axiomatic claim about human nature that rests mostly on various philosophical approaches of the Enlightenment, often backed up by certain religious views, such as the approach of Catholic social thought. Human rights are based on a certain consensus about the nature of *human dignity*.

Despite its lack of a complicated theoretical deduction—or maybe even just because of its rather simple and plausible viewpoint—the rights approach has been very powerful throughout history and has substantially shaped the constitutions of many modern states. This includes the Declaration of the Rights of Man that was influential during the period of the French Revolution (1789), and the American Constitution, which is largely based on notions of rights. These ideas have also led to the United Nations Declaration of Human Rights, issued in 1948, which has been a powerful standard of worldwide endorsement of various rights, as well as the European Union's Charter of Fundamental Human Rights which was agreed as part of the Nice Treaty in 2000.

It is this background that makes the entire notion of human rights one of the most common and important theoretical approaches to business ethics on a practical level. Corporations, especially multinationals, are increasingly judged with regard to their attitude to human rights and how far they respect and protect them. More than 7,000 companies, for example, have signed up the UN Global Compact, which includes human rights obligations as its first two principles (see Ethics in Action 11.2). These are that 'businesses should support and respect the protection of internationally proclaimed human rights' (Principle 1) and that 'business should make sure that they are not complicit in human rights abuses' (Principle 2). Many companies are also increasingly seeking to develop their own human rights policies. The Business and Human Rights Resource Centre, for example, established that nearly 350 companies had published policies on human rights by 2014,[4] some examples of which are given in **Figure 3.5**.

The most important recent development in the implementation of human rights in business have been the so-called 'Ruggie Principles', which have been adopted by the United Nations and increasingly shape the engagement of global businesses with human rights issues. **Ethics in Action 3.1** provides an overview.

Company	Human rights statement	Source
Body Shop	As a global business, we respect local, cultural, and political differences, but will always insist that our business activities adhere to *basic human rights*, as enshrined in the *Universal Declaration for Human Rights*. We will assess all our business activities to determine where we have direct or indirect impacts, ensure compliance with *human rights legislation* and strive to have a positive impact on our stakeholders and on society at large. We will use objectively measurable standards that reflect *internationally recognized human rights standards and conventions*.	'Human Rights Principles': http://www. thebodyshop.com
Shell	To conduct business as responsible corporate members of society, to comply with applicable laws and regulations, to support *fundamental human rights* in line with the legitimate role of business, and to give proper regard to health, safety, security and the environment.	'General business principles': http://www.shell.com
General Electric	GE, as a business enterprise, promotes respect for *fundamental human rights*. We support the principles contained in the *Universal Declaration of Human Rights*, remaining mindful that the Declaration is addressed primarily to nations. GE has joined with other companies to find practical ways of applying within the business community the broad principles established in the Declaration.	'Human Rights': http://www. gecitizenship.com
Tata Steel	The Tata Steel Group is proud of its longstanding reputation as a fair and caring employer, and respects *all human rights* both within and outside the workplace. The Tata Code of Conduct stipulates that all employees have a personal responsibility to help preserve the *human rights* of everyone at work and in the wider community.	'Ethical behaviour': http://www.tatasteel.com
Toshiba	Toshiba Group Companies shall accept the different values of individuals and respect differences in character and personality based on a fundamental respect for *human rights*.	'Toshiba Group Standards of Conduct': http://www.toshiba.com

Figure 3.5 Human rights statements by multinationals (emphasis added)

VISIT THE ONLINE RESOURCE CENTRE for links to useful sources of further information

ETHICS IN ACTION 3.1   www.ethicalcorp.com

Business and human rights: rolling out the Ruggie principles

Stephen Gardner, 2 June 2012

• •

The 'United Nations Guiding Principles on Business and Human Rights', formulated under the steady hand of Harvard law school professor John Ruggie, were six years in the making, and were finally endorsed by the UN Human Rights Council on June 16, 2011. As the name suggests, the guiding principles are designed to make more concrete an earlier piece of work, also by John Ruggie, which was the definition of a broad framework for **human rights** based on three over-arching principles:

1. The **state** has a duty to protect against human rights abuses by third parties, including business.

2. **Companies** have a responsibility to respect human rights.

3. Victims of abuses should have access to effective **judicial** and **non-judicial** remedies.

One year on from their formal adoption, the Ruggie Guiding Principles on Business and Human Rights are being slowly absorbed by governments, business federations and companies.

This next phase will be 'a process of some years,' says Caroline Rees, formerly Ruggie's lead adviser. The Ruggie framework 'is not a quick plug-in solution'. For a large multinational, Rees says, three to five years will be needed to fully grasp and adopt the principles into management practices.

The gradual nature of the take-up means that, one year on from the formal endorsement of the guiding principles, groundbreaking initiatives and projects might seem to be distinctly lacking. But it would be a mistake to think that the principles have been left on the shelf. Their establishment in practice is like the construction of several spiders' webs, with the end result hopefully being to catch all.

Companies and business associations have started to align their practices with the principles, Ruggie told Ethical Corporation magazine. 'Key elements have also been adopted by the Organisation for Economic Cooperation and Development, the European Union, the International Organisation for Standardisation (in ISO 26000) and the International Finance Corporation. Other regional bodies, including ASEAN [Association of Southeast Asian Nations] and the African Union, are also in the game. Each of these has its own implementation modalities and knock-on effects. The roll-out of the principles will continue to roll on.'

Three pillars

The guiding principles rest on three pillars. The first concerns governments: that they have a duty to protect against human rights abuses by third parties, including businesses. The second concerns companies: that they must respect human rights. The third concerns both: that there should be effective grievance procedures.

The most visible initiatives in the year since the adoption of the guiding principles have been taken by groups of states. The European commission, the EU's executive arm, for example, in an October 2011 policy paper on corporate social responsibility, promised to work with specific sectors on the guiding principles. The commission also asked EU governments to submit by the end of 2012 national action plans showing how they would implement the principles.

Business federations are tailoring the guiding principles to their particular sectoral needs, but again, the trickle down to actual examples of the principles in practice has barely started. The International Council on Mining and Metals, for example, recently published a guide on 'integrating human rights due diligence into corporate risk management processes'. This explains the implications of the guiding principles for mining companies, and deals with some sensitive issues, such as operating in conflict zones or trying to maintain the corporate stance on human rights in countries with repressive regimes.

Miguel Pestana, vice-president for global external affairs at Unilever, which has supported the development of the guiding principles from an early stage, says that Ruggie's work 'has been the main catalyst' for promoting corporate risk assessment of exposure to human rights problems. The principles promote good business practice by making the risk assessment more systematic.

A review of operations in the light of the guiding principles is likely to show that a corporation is already doing many things right. Pestana gives the example of gender equality. 'For Unilever that is seen as a factor in retention of our people, rather than strictly an element of human or labour rights,' he says.

In other cases, difficult issues might arise. For example, a supplier might be found to be using child labour, but simply cutting the contract without consideration of the impact it would have might undermine the broader human rights cause. 'You have to make an assessment on a case by case basis,' Pestana says. The guiding principles are 'very useful in helping us make some of those determinations'.

Companies such as Unilever have done vast amounts of work already on corporate responsibility. In Unilever's case, this has been distilled into the company's Sustainable Living Plan, adopted at the end of 2010, and which already includes elements such as 'sustainable sourcing' and 'better livelihoods' for developing country smallholders and small-scale distributors.

The company does not want to establish parallel procedures to take account of the guiding principles, but would rather integrate them into what exists already. 'This is a work in progress for us,' Pestana says.

Rory Sullivan, a senior research fellow at the University of Leeds, says the principles are a 'management framework' that 'fit into an enlightened management perspective'. Implementation of the guiding principles, either through the development and imposition of standards by governments, or through the reviewing of processes by companies, needs more than the year that has passed so far since their UN-level endorsement.

But even once the management framework has been upgraded, another process will have to start, Sullivan says. A rigorous connection between the guiding principles and the real world will have to be established through performance standards, which will need to be monitored and enforced at different levels. And that will be another long-term process.

Sources

Ethical Corporation, Stephen Gardner, 2 June 2012, http://www.ethicalcorp.com. Reproduced with the kind permission of Ethical Corporation.

VISIT THE ONLINE RESOURCE CENTRE for a short response to this feature

? THINK THEORY

The Ruggie principles assign a central role to business in respecting human rights. Which of the rights set out in Chapter 3 would companies be most likely to have to respect in their business operations?

☑ **Skill check**

Applying the UN Guiding Principles on Business and Human Rights.
Understanding and applying the Ruggie principles helps to determine what a company's human rights obligations and risks should be.

The perspective of human rights certainly provides the most straightforward answer to Ethical Dilemma 3. In using child labour, the product manager could be said to violate the rights of the children to education, and arguably to infringe the right to freedom of consent. Furthermore, a human rights perspective would cast doubt on the issue of an individual's right to a living wage, as it would appear that poor wages could have necessitated the engagement of the entire family in employment over long hours of work rather than paying one parent a suitable wage to provide for his or her family.

Ethical theories based on rights are very powerful because of their widely acknowledged basis in fundamental human entitlements. However, the theoretical basis is one of plausibility rather than a deep theoretical methodology. Moreover, perhaps the most substantial limitation of this approach is that notions of rights are quite strongly located in a Western view of morality. A considerable amount of friction might occur if these ideas were to be directly transferred, if not imposed, on communities with a different cultural and religious legacy.

The problem of justice

Whenever two parties enter an economic transaction there has to be agreement on a fair distribution of costs and benefits between the parties. Such agreements are usually handled by contracts or left to market forces to resolve. Various questions about the equity of such distribution inevitably arise, however:

- How should a company pay its shareholders, executives, office workers, and manual staff so that everybody gets fair compensation for their input into the corporation?

- How should a company take into account the demands of local communities, employees, and shareholders when planning an investment with major impacts on the environment?

- How should a government allocate money for education so that every section of society gets a fair chance of a good education?

We could easily multiply these examples, but what becomes clear is that individual rights have to be realized in such a way that they are addressed equally and fairly. This is where the issue of **justice** arises, since justice is all about how fairly individuals are treated so that they get what they deserve.

Justice
The simultaneous fair treatment of individuals in a given situation with the result that everybody gets what they deserve.

The crucial moral issues here are what exactly 'fairness' should mean in a particular situation and by what standards can we decide what a person might reasonably deserve. According to Beauchamp and Bowie (1997), theories of justice typically see fairness in two main ways:

- **Fair procedures**. Fairness is determined according to whether everyone has been free to acquire rewards for their efforts. This is commonly referred to as *procedural justice*.

- **Fair outcomes**. Fairness is determined according to whether the consequences (positive and negative) are distributed in a just manner, according to some underlying principle such as need or merit. This is commonly referred to as distributive justice.

Most views of justice would ideally seek to achieve both types of fairness, but this is not always possible. Consider the case of access to higher education. Say it was discovered that certain ethnic groups were under-represented in your university's degree programmes. Given that ethnicity is not correlated with innate intelligence, we might seek to solve this problem by reserving a certain number of places for under-represented groups to make sure that educational rewards were *distributed* fairly amongst these different sections of society. However, this would impose a potentially unfair *procedure* on the university's admissions, since 'over-represented' groups would be excluded from applying for the reserved places. This is an ongoing debate in India where a quota system reserving more than 20% of available places for lower caste Hindus in government-funded academic institutions has long been in operation but continues to generate controversy.

Notions of justice have been widely applied in business ethics problems, notably in relation to employment practices and the question of discrimination, as we shall examine in more depth in Chapter 7. Justice has also been a key feature of debates about globalization and sustainability. Here, the main concern is about issues of social and economic justice—themes that have long pervaded reasoning about the ethics of economic systems.

This problem of a just distribution of wealth in and between societies has been addressed in numerous ways, although historically answers have tended to fall somewhere between two extreme positions: *egalitarianism and non-egalitarianism.*

The *egalitarian* approach claims that justice is the same as equality—burdens and rewards should be distributed equally and deviations from equality are unjust (Beauchamp and Bowie 1997). Examples for such apparent injustices abound: at the World Economic Forum 2014 the charity Oxfam released a report that described the distribution of wealth globally with a striking image: the 85 richest individuals in the world—a group one could easily fit in a London double-decker bus—has as much wealth as half of the global population (Oxfam 2014). The most common example of an egalitarian position in designing a just economic system may be seen in the work of Karl Marx (see Wray-Bliss and Parker 1998). Living during the industrial revolution in nineteenth-century Britain and Germany, Marx identified the exploitation of the 'working class' in a labour process that provided excess wealth to the owners of the means of productions ('the capitalists'). As an ultimate solution to this problem, Marxist thinking suggests that a just society would be one where the working classes would collectively own the means of production themselves and thus would be the immediate beneficiaries of the economic outcomes of their work in the production process.

With the collapse of the Eastern bloc and China's opening up to market reforms at the end of the twentieth century, Marxist thinking, at least in its real-world manifestations, has somewhat lost momentum. Recently though, Marx's ideas have been reinvigorated in the context of globalization, where the relations between, for instance, consumers and workers in the global South and large Western MNCs mirror fairly closely his initial analysis of the oppression of the working classes by capitalism (Jones et al. 2005: 96–111).

However, egalitarian approaches have problems with the fact that there are differences between people. For instance, should someone who works hard earn the same as a lazy person? Are all skills really worth the same? Egalitarian approaches also tend to be inefficient, since there are no incentives for innovation and greater efficiency because everyone is rewarded equally anyway.

The *non-egalitarian* approach, at the other end of the spectrum, would claim that justice in economic systems is ultimately a product of the fair process of free markets. Actors with certain needs would meet actors who can answer their needs, and if they agree on a transaction, justice is determined by the market forces of supply and demand. One of the more influential thinkers in business ethics along these lines is Robert Nozick (1974). He argues that a distribution of wealth in society is just as long as it has been brought about by just transfers and just original acquisition. For example, Bill Gates' personal wealth as one of the richest individuals on the planet would be perfectly justifiable if the way he had set up Microsoft initially was without fraud or coercion and all other subsequent business transactions had been compliant with the same standards. Nozick's theory is often dubbed 'entitlement theory', as he considers wealth distribution as morally acceptable as long as 'everyone is entitled to the holdings they possess' (Nozick, cited in Boatright 2009: 75).

The notion of the market presupposes equal participants in the market in order to produce a just system. But insofar as people differ in income, ability, health, social and economic status, etc., markets can lead to results that some people would no longer regard as fair. On a global level, this has become visible when poor, underdeveloped countries have tried to compete with highly industrialized countries. It is as if in Formula One we allowed a bicycle to start next to a Ferrari: even with the fairest rules, the driver on the bicycle is doomed to lose.

Obviously, the two extreme answers to the question of what exactly justice means in an economic context are unsatisfactory. The answer might well lie in between the two. A popular approach to this problem has been proposed by John Rawls (1971). In his book *A theory of justice* Rawls suggests two criteria—two 'tests' as it were—to decide whether an action could be called just. According to Rawls, justice is achieved when:

1. Each person has an equal right to the most extensive total system of basic liberties compatible with a similar system of liberty for all.

2. Social and economic inequalities are arranged so that they are both:

   (a) to the greatest benefit of the least advantaged; and

   (b) attached to offices and positions open to all under conditions of fair equality of opportunity.

The first criterion is the most important one: before allowing for any inequalities, we should ensure that the basic freedoms are realized to the same degree for everyone affected by the decision. The first condition thus looks to general human rights and requires their fulfilment before we can proceed to the next step.

The second criterion is based on the assumption that inequalities are unavoidable in a free and competitive society. However, two conditions should be met. First, an arrangement is just when even the one who profits least from it is still better off than they would be without it. This, for example, would suggest that high salaries for corporate leaders might be acceptable providing that employees at the bottom of the corporate hierarchy were also better off as a result—say, because the high salary for the leader led to better corporate performance, which in turn could be translated into higher wages for the least paid. The second condition, again following this example, would be met if not only a privileged few could ascend the corporate ladder, but everyone had a fair chance of doing so, regardless of gender, ethnicity, etc.

☑ Skill check

Applying the Rawls justice test. This is an important skill because the Rawls justice test is a useful tool to help you determine whether an action can be regarded as just or unjust according to two relatively straightforward criteria.

There are, of course a couple of more considerations, conditions, and elements to Rawls' theory that we will not go into here. Even in this simplified form, though, we can usefully apply these basic principles to various business situations in order to determine 'just' treatment of stakeholders.

If we look to our example in Ethical Dilemma 3, the first test would be to ask if all people involved (including the product manager) were in possession of the same basic liberty. Apart from the cultural differences between Europe and Thailand, this is certainly not the case for the children, since they are obviously not allowed to have even a basic education. The second principle could conceivably allow for a more tolerant approach to child labour: the first criterion for inequality would be to ask if the children are better or worse off with the arrangement. One might reasonably argue here that children are often forced into worse things in developing countries than assembling plastic toys. Prostitution, begging, and theft might be other alternatives, suggesting that the children would be better off if you concluded the deal. However, if concluding your deal meant that the children would miss schooling that they otherwise would have had, the arrangement is definitely not benefiting the least well off. The second criterion, though, poses even more of a problem, since without access to education the children do not have a realistic chance of achieving the position that the better-off parties, such as you, have. Hence, they are definitely not 'under conditions of fair equality of opportunity'.

If we extend our view slightly more broadly, Rawls' view of justice can actually be used to justify multinationals' exploitation of low wages and poor conditions in less-developed countries—at least under certain conditions. For example, some MNCs have taken it upon themselves to provide education or basic health care for their workers in less-developed countries. In this way, MNCs still take advantage of lower wages in these countries, but by providing a 'system of basic liberties compatible with a similar system of liberty for all' and creating 'conditions of fair equality of opportunity' (at least on a local level), one might argue that the resulting inequalities are still 'to the greatest benefit of the least advantaged'. After all, without the manufacturing plant, local people would probably face greater poverty and less opportunity for development than they would with it.

VISIT THE
ONLINE
RESOURCE
CENTRE
for a short
response to this
feature

> **? THINK THEORY**
>
> In Chapter 2, in the context of the extended conceptualization of corporate citizenship, we have discussed the role of companies in the provision of basic entitlements such as water, security, and health. From the perspective of John Rawls' theory of justice, could you imagine a situation in which the involvement of private corporations in the provision of public services (such as the provision of water) could be considered as morally just?

Limits of Western modernist theories

If we look back to these major Western modernist ethical theories, we could argue that they present quite a comprehensive view of humans and society, and based on various assumptions they come up with actionable principles to answer ethical questions. In presenting such a closed 'model' of the world, these theories have the substantial advantage that they claim to provide a solution to every possible situation. However, they have the big disadvantage that their view of the world only presents one aspect of human life, while reality normally tends to be rather more complex.

In the previous discussions we have outlined some of the main benefits and drawbacks of each of these main ethical theories. However, the very approach of *all* Western modernist theories is open to criticism. As largely absolutist theories based on objective reason, a number of drawbacks for approaching business ethics problems through theory of this sort can be identified.

The main criticisms of Western modernist ethical theories are:

- **Too abstract**. Stark (1994) suggests that traditional ethical theories are too theoretical and impractical for the pragmatic day-to-day concerns of managers. In real life, managers are unlikely to apply abstract principles derived from long-dead philosophers when dealing with the concrete problems of business. Normative theories 'lack power, persuasiveness and effectiveness' because they do not deal enough with the question of how businesses might actually operate in practice (Brenkert 2010: 709).

- **Too reductionist**. Kaler (1999b) argues that each theory tends to focus on one aspect of morality at the cost of all the rest of morality. Why choose consequences, duties, *or* rights when *all* are important?

- **Too objective and elitist**. Parker (1998b) suggests that ethical theories attempt to occupy a rarefied high ground, such that those specialist ethicists and philosophers who know and understand the theories can pronounce on the right and wrong of other people without any subjective experience of the situation they are faced with. Just because Crane and Matten know the difference between utilitarianism and justice, why should that mean that we can decide for you whether a product manager in Thailand is doing the right thing?

- **Too impersonal**. By focusing on abstract principles, traditional ethical theories do not take account of the personal bonds and relationships that shape our thoughts and feelings about right and wrong (Gilligan 1982).

- **Too rational and codified**. Ethical theories try and distil right and wrong down to codified rational rules of behaviour. Bauman (1993) contends that this suppresses our moral autonomy and denigrates the importance of our moral feelings and emotions, all of which he claims are crucial for acting morally towards others. Rorty (2006) suggests that what we need is better moral imagination and ethical stories rather than moral reasoning.

- **Too imperialist**. Why assume that ethical theories from the West are suitable for business people everywhere else in the world? What about the ethical teachings of classical Asian or traditional African philosophy, for instance—do these not also have something useful to say about modern-day business ethics?

Clearly, then, there are certain problems associated with these Western modernist theories (see also Jones et al. 2005). Many of these stem from their emphasis on the more absolutist approach to ethical theory. As a result, there have been a number of more recent attempts to develop or resurrect alternative ethical theories that emphasize greater flexibility, as well as including consideration of decision-makers, their context, and their relations with others, as opposed to just abstract universal principles. Although the theories we are going to discuss now are also open to criticism, they help to enrich the choice of perspectives we could take on ethical issues in business.

■ Alternative perspectives on ethical theory

Alternative, more contemporary perspectives on ethical theories are those that have either been developed or brought to prominence in the business ethics field over the past two decades or so. As such, they appear much less commonly in business ethics texts, yet we would suggest that they offer an important alternative perspective that should not be ignored, and which, we would suspect, may become increasingly more influential in the business ethics literature. We shall be looking at four main contemporary ethical theories:

- Ethical approaches based on character and integrity.
- Ethical approaches based on relationships and responsibility.
- Ethical approaches based on procedures of norm generation.
- Ethical approaches based on empathy and moral impulse.

Ethical approaches based on character and integrity

Up to now, we have chiefly looked at right and wrong according to the ethics of particular *actions*. However, much attention in recent years has focused on approaches that start from a different perspective: rather than checking every single action according to its outcomes or its underlying principles, these approaches look to the character or integrity of the *decision-maker* (Nielsen 2006). Focusing on the integrity of individuals clearly has a strong resonance in a business context, especially when considering the ethics of professionals such as doctors, lawyers, and accountants who rely on their moral probity for maintaining legitimacy and gaining clients. Attention to character as a foundation for business ethics has also arisen in non-Western contexts, such as Africa, where it has been argued that a humanistic approach is more easily acceptable in African culture than rules-based approaches (Gichure 2006). Similarly, Woods and Lamond (2011) contend that 'refinement of one's character' is central to Confucianism, with its emphasis on cultivating virtues such as benevolence (ren), righteousness (yi), ritual propriety (li), wisdom (zhi), trustworthiness (xin), and filial piety (xiao).

Virtue ethics
A theory that contends that morally correct actions are those undertaken by actors with virtuous characters, and that the formation of a virtuous character is the first step towards morally correct behaviour.

Character and integrity-based approaches to business ethics have mainly drawn on one of the earliest ethical theories, that of **virtue ethics**. In virtue ethics, the main message is that 'good actions come from good persons', where good persons are defined in terms of certain traits or characteristics, namely 'virtues'.

Virtues are 'traits of character that constitute praiseworthy elements in a person's psychology' (Audi 2012: 273). Virtues can be differentiated into *intellectual virtues*—'wisdom' being the most prominent one—and *moral virtues*, which comprise a long list of possible characteristics such as honesty, courage, friendship, mercy, loyalty, modesty, patience, etc. All these virtues are manifested in actions that are a habitual pattern of behaviour of the virtuous person, rather than just occurring once or in one-off decisions. As these traits are not ours by birth, we acquire them by learning and, most notably in business, by being in relationships with others in a community of practice (MacIntyre 1984).

Central to the ethics of virtue is the notion of a 'good life'. For Aristotle, one of the original proponents of virtue ethics, this consists of happiness—not in a limited hedonistic, pleasure-oriented sense, but in a broader sense. This most notably includes virtuous behaviour as an integral part of the good life: a happy business person would not only be one who makes the most money, but one who does so while at the same time savouring the pleasures of a virtuous manner of achieving their success. In a business context, the 'good life' means far more than being a profitable company. Virtue ethics takes a more holistic view by also looking at the way this profit is achieved, and most notably by claiming that economic success is just one part of the good business life—with satisfaction of employees, good relations among all members of the company, and harmonious relations with all stakeholders being equally important (Collier 1995).

From this point of view, the virtuous product manager in Ethical Dilemma 3 could take in different perspectives depending on the community from which the notion of a virtuous manager was derived. On the one hand, you could be compassionate and considerate with the situation of the suppliers. Taking into account their need for work and money, as well as the children's need for education, perhaps you would try to do business with them while, at the same time, assuming responsibility for the children's education. For instance, you could support a local school, or pay sufficiently high wages to allow the family to send their children to school, rather than making use of them as cheap labour. On the other hand, you might also think that the 'good life' in rural Thailand might in fact consist of an entire family working happily together and that Western concepts of education, professionalization, and efficiency are a different concept of a 'good life' that might not be appropriate to the Thai approach to life. Typically, though, virtue ethics in a business context such as this would suggest that the solution to many of the problems faced by managers are located in the culture and tradition of the relevant community of practice. The product manager should determine what a 'virtuous' product manager would do from their professional code of conduct, from virtuous role models, or from professional training.

It does not take long to see what the main drawback of virtue ethics is (see also Jones et al. 2005: 56–68): how do we determine which community ideal of good practice to consult? And, in the absence of a clear code of conduct from our relevant communities, how do we translate ideas of virtuous traits into ethical action? Still, the relevance of virtue ethics for business ethics is that it reminds us that right and wrong cannot simply be resolved by applying a specific rule or principle, but that we need to cultivate our knowledge and judgement on ethical matters over time through experience and participation (Nielsen 2006).

Ethical approaches based on relationships and responsibility

This eschewal of a principle-based approach to ethical problems has also been taken up by other alternative frameworks, which focus not on character but on relationships. One notable example of this approach is *feminist ethics*, which starts from the assumption that men and women have fairly different attitudes towards organizing social life, with significant impact on the way ethical conflicts are handled (Gilligan 1982). In addressing ethical problems, traditional ethical theory has looked for rules and principles to be applied in a fair, objective, and consistent way. This approach has been almost exclusively established and promulgated by male philosophers and thinkers such as Kant, Locke, Bentham, Smith, and Mill. The 'ethics of rights', as this view sometimes is called (Maier 1997), tries to establish legitimate grounds for claims and interests of individuals in situations of social conflicts.

Feminist ethics
An approach that prioritizes empathy, harmonious and healthy social relationships, care for one another, and avoidance of harm above abstract moral principles.

Feminist ethics, on the other hand, has a different approach that sees the individual deeply embedded in a network of interpersonal relations. Consequently, responsibility for the members of this network and maintenance of connectedness, rather than allegiance to abstract moral principles, is the predominant concern of feminist ethics. This approach, often therefore called an *ethics of care*, consequently results in significant differences in the view of ethical issues (Maier 1997; Rabouin 1997). Moral problems are conflicts of responsibilities in relationships rather than conflicts of rights between individuals and therefore can only be solved by personal, subjective assessment that particularly stresses the importance of emotion, intuition, and feeling. While traditional approaches would focus on 'fair' results, feminist perspectives stress social processes and particularly aim at the achievement of harmony, empathy, and integration with regard to ethical issues. The main goal is to avoid harm and maintain healthy relationships.

While some of the literature on feminist perspectives on business ethics—as outlined above—focuses on gender differences and embeds the ethical approach in a gender-specific context (e.g. Maier 1997), the more recent debate has moved beyond these ways of essentializing a 'female' approach to ethics. Rather, as Janet Borgerson (2007) has argued, feminist perspectives on business ethics highlight some general principles that are relevant beyond a narrow concern with 'gender', 'care', or other simple reductions of a feminist perspective. Key elements of a feminist approach then would include the following (Borgerson 2007):

- **Relationships**. While many of the Western modernist theories focus on the individual person trying to enact ethical behaviour, feminist perspectives put an emphasis on the fact that ethical decisions are taken in a specific context of personal human interrelations. Such a perspective emphasizes the impact of ethical decision-making on the web of interpersonal relations of the decision-maker.

- **Responsibility**. Rather than just 'having' responsibility in a given context, feminist perspectives would suggest that ethical decision-making asks for an active 'taking' of responsibility. Thus, in a given situation, rather than defensively living up to external demands or pressures, feminist perspectives suggest an *active* involvement in and assumption of responsibilities for the ethical implications of business activities.

- **Experience**. Feminist perspectives highlight the fact that in decision-making, including ethical decisions, human beings are intricately determined by past experiences. So rather than applying 'principles' or 'rules' in an abstract way, this approach would encourage one to learn and develop from experiences in the past.

VISIT THE
ONLINE
RESOURCE
CENTRE
for a short
response to this
feature

? THINK THEORY

Think about the ethical arguments used by family members, friends, or colleagues. Can you see any differences between the arguments used by men and women? What does this say about the potential contribution of feminist ethics?

This focus on relationships and responsibilities is also evident in some non-Western ethical frameworks. For example, in *Buddhist approaches to business ethics*, as Gould (1995) points out, there is an emphasis on considering 'everyone as our father, mother, brother, or sister', blaming yourself rather than others, and focusing on personal growth and fulfilment as basic tenets of ethical decision-making. Ultimately, the Buddhist perspective highlights the interconnectedness and web of relationships in which ethical decision-making takes place. Similarly, there is a focus on relationships as the basis for ethical conduct in *Confucian approaches to business ethics* (Romar 2004). As Ip (2009) suggests, 'social relationships and their harmony are of utmost importance' in Confucian business ethics.

Applying a relationships approach to the case in Ethical Dilemma 3 would in a certain sense require far more knowledge about the case than we can acquire from just reading about it. A relationships-oriented perspective would cause the product manager to try to get a closer view of the family involved and see if the children are really happy in this situation. It would also involve a better understanding of the social and economic constraints that cause the family to embark on this particular production pattern. Ironically, a feminist perspective would not necessarily argue categorically against any involvement of children in the process, as long as the inter-familiar relationships are functioning well and the children are not forced, exploited, or compelled to work beyond their physical capacities. As the latter conditions might not be fulfilled, relational approaches would probably tend to object to child labour as well—however, not so very much because it violates certain (Western) principles, but because of the likely distress and suffering of the children. Furthermore, feminist theories would also look at the situation of the other actors involved and scrutinize, for example, the question of how the money earned by the assembling of toys is spent and how the income in the family is distributed, etc.

Ethical approaches based on procedures of norm generation

All of the theoretical approaches we have discussed so far start from a certain perspective on humans, on the values or goals governing their decisions, and a few other assumptions that in essence are all normative in nature. By normative, remember that we mean prescriptions of right and wrong action. However, it is worth taking a step back for a minute and asking if the starting point of prescriptions is, in fact, a very useful way to solve ethical conflicts in business. After all, we cannot take it for granted that everybody shares, for instance, the notion of humans being hedonistic, or of rights or feminist values being the most appropriate ones to address ethical problems in business. This is already problematic in a group of relatively homogeneous people; say the marketing department of a Swedish furniture company. But it gets even more complicated if there is a meeting of all marketing directors of the company worldwide, since this could conceivably include participants as diverse as evangelical fundamentalists from the US, atheists from Russia, Muslims from Egypt, and Buddhists from Japan. In these situations, the most significant problems arise from the diverging normative perspectives that the different people might bring to the table.

It is at this point that theoretical approaches based on norm generation might come into the picture. These approaches seek ethical behaviour not in applying ethical principles, but in generating norms that are appropriate and acceptable to those who need to resolve a particular problem. There are various forms that such practices could take, including for instance the traditional African institution of the palaver, where the relevant parties would be brought together under a 'palaver tree' and allowed to speak freely in order to generate appropriate principles for decision-making (Gichure 2006). However, probably the best-known approach to norm generation in business ethics is that of **discourse ethics**.

Discourse ethics
An approach that aims to solve ethical conflicts by providing a process of norm generation through rational reflection on the real-life experience of all relevant participants.

The philosophical underpinning of discourse ethics is the argument that norms ultimately cannot be justified by rational arguments, but that they have to be generated and applied to solve ethical conflicts on a day-to-day basis (Preuss 1999). Horst Steinmann and Albert Löhr (1994), who are among the main proponents of a discourse approach to business ethics, argue that ethical reflection has to start from real-life experiences (rather than belief systems, which could be too diverse). They contend that the ultimate goal of ethical issues in business should be the *peaceful settlement of conflicts*.

With this goal in mind, different parties in a conflict—say a business and its stakeholders—should meet and engage in a discourse about the settlement of the conflict, and ultimately provide a solution that is acceptable to all. This 'ideal discourse', as it is usually called, is more than an occasional chat or business meeting; it has to answer certain philosophical criteria, such as impartiality, non-persuasiveness, non-coercion, and expertise of the participants (Habermas 1983). This includes the injunction that those who are more powerful should refrain from imposing their values on others and using their power to solve the ethical conflict according to their own views. Such an approach should ideally lead to the emergence of norms for addressing the problem that are an expression of the consensus of all the represented parties. In establishing a rational 'ideal discourse' about specific problems, this approach is thus supposed to be *norm generating*.

Discourse ethics, then, is more a recipe for practical conflict resolution than an ethical theory comparable to those discussed above. In simple terms, it assumes that ethical business should be rooted in stakeholder dialogue based on equal participation and conducted without domination or coercion by any party. An ethically correct decision is one that has been reached in the right way, with the agreement of all, irrespective of what the actual decision itself is.

There are understandably certain practical limits to this approach, especially the considerable amount of time it involves, and its fairly optimistic assumptions about rational human behaviour, and the avoidance of self-interested, strategic engagement in dialogue (Noland and Phillips 2010). **Ethics in Action 3.2**, for instance, explores developments in stakeholder engagement among mining companies and indigenous community groups, demonstrating some of the opportunities as well as the challenges in creating genuine 'ideal discourses'. Nevertheless, discourse ethics has been the underlying concept for the settlement of numerous disputes about corporate environmental impacts, in which various stakeholders with completely divergent value systems have come to common decisions on certain controversial projects (Renn et al. 1995). It has also been proposed as a useful yardstick for assessing corporate accountability (Scherer and Palazzo 2011) as well as potentially providing an ethical basis for web 2.0 approaches that focus on open access and inclusive decision-making (Mingers and Walsham 2010).

If we apply a norm-generating approach such as discourse ethics to Ethical Dilemma 3, it lies in the nature of the concept that we are not able to say if this would influence in any way the resulting decision of the parties involved. It would, however, have much to say about the right procedure to be adopted. That is, it would suggest that all parties involved, starting with the Thai trading company, the confectionery manufacturer, the parents, the children, but potentially also the consumers in Europe, should meet together to enter a 'norm-generating' discourse on the topic. Apart from the fact that this shows some of the practical difficulties of the concept, the idea does open the way to a solution that could be closest to the interests of all parties involved.

☑ **Skill check**

Conducting ethical discourse. Knowing how to engage ethically with stakeholders is a critical skill for corporate responsibility managers. Applying the principles of discourse ethics provides a practical framework for establishing these rules of engagement.

Ethical approaches based on empathy and moral impulse

Finally, there is a school of thought in business ethics that takes the rejection of normative approaches yet further. Often referred to as **postmodern ethics,** this school of thought fundamentally questions the link between rationality and morality that is inherent in all the Western modernist ethical theories discussed earlier in this chapter. These traditional theories have their origins in modernism, which emerged roughly during the eighteenth-century Enlightenment era. 'Modern' thinkers strove for a rational, scientific explanation of the world and aimed at comprehensive, inclusive, theoretically coherent theories to explain nature, man, and society. In the area of the social sciences, one of the results of this was the development of various theories, commonly in the form of certain '-isms', such as liberalism, communism, socialism, rationalism, capitalism, etc. Postmodern thinkers contend that these comprehensive theories, these 'grand narratives' of society (Lyotard 1984), are too ambitious, optimistic, and reductionist, ultimately failing to explain the complex reality of human existence.

While postmodernism tends to embrace a whole range of theoretical propositions and arguments, postmodern thinkers have been particularly influential in ethics, since they identify the specific danger of rational approaches to morality. Zygmunt Bauman (1993), one of the best-known proponents of postmodern ethics, argues that by codifying morality within specific rules and codes of behaviour (as, for example, exemplified in bureaucratic organizations), rational approaches deny the real source of morality, which is rooted in a 'moral impulse' towards others. This is a subjective, emotional conviction that humans have about right and wrong, based on their experiences, sentiments, and instincts. Moral judgement, then, is a gut feeling more than anything else, but this is inevitably nullified when people enter organizations and become distanced from the people who are actually going to experience the consequences of their decisions, such as consumers, investors, suppliers, and others.

Ultimately, postmodernists are rather sceptical about the entire venture of business ethics (ten Bos and Willmott 2001), since ethical theories aim to find 'rules and principles that determine right or wrong' (our definition in Chapter 1). Postmodernists tend to suggest otherwise, such that 'the foolproof—universal and unshakably founded—ethical code will never be found' (Bauman 1993). A postmodern perspective on business ethics does not then provide us with any rule or principle, not even a procedure for ethical decision-making, such as discourse ethics. However, postmodern ethics have quite

Postmodern ethics
An approach that locates morality beyond the sphere of rationality in an emotional 'moral impulse' towards others. It encourages one to question everyday practices and rules, and to listen to one's emotions, inner convictions, and 'gut feelings' about what is right and wrong.

VISIT THE
ONLINE
RESOURCE
CENTRE
for links to
useful sources
of further
information

ETHICS IN ACTION 3.2   www.ethicalcorp.com

Indigenous peoples and the extractive sector: NGOs that know what they want

Oliver Balch, 11 July 2012

More than three-fifths of the world's poorest people live in countries rich in natural resources. Far too few ever get to have a say on how these resources are exploited, Oxfam and others argue. Central to the arguments of indigenous groups and their representatives is not the *fact*, but the *manner*, in which mining projects go ahead.

Pivotal here is the issue of **consent**. Fiona Watson, field and research director at human rights group Survival International, maintains that her organization is not against mining 'per se'. 'It only asks if the community has been heard and whether consent has been given fairly with all the independent information to hand,' she says. Accurate information is clearly a prerequisite to any fair negotiation, as Oxfam's Right to Know demand indicates. Watson adds to that the recognition of the collective land rights of indigenous groups. 'Without that you simply can't achieve FPIC,' she says, in reference to the widely used acronym for free, prior and informed consent, adopted by the International Finance Corporation.

Along these lines, Oxfam America's Right to Know, Right to Decide campaign challenges international extractive companies to respect a community's right to decide if or how they want resource-led development to take place in their community, and their right to know about the impacts and benefits of these projects.

- **A community's right to know**: Companies must provide complete and timely information about how their work affects communities—environmentally, socially, and economically. They must also disclose how much they are paying governments for natural resources so that poor communities get a fair share of the profits.

- **A community's right to decide**: Companies must obtain the free, prior, and informed consent (FPIC) of communities affected by extractive operations. For indigenous people in particular, respect for FPIC is a critical means of protecting sacred lands and cultural identity.

A complicated process

Exactly how to obtain consent is not straightforward. Transparency, honesty, equity and fairness are all cited among the core principles espoused by NGOs. So too is inclusivity. Get as many interest groups around the table as possible, says Emily Greenspan, extractive industries policy and advocacy adviser at Oxfam America.

Clearly, it is imperative for companies to respect traditional decision-making processes. At the same time, Greenspan insists, marginalized groups should not be overlooked. 'A lot of companies are realising [that] one of the ways to address this challenge of "who makes the decision?" is to have an inclusive process,' says Greenspan. She also advocates a consultation process that takes in wider interests than merely those facing immediate material impacts. Regional and national indigenous federations, for example, usually have extensive experience and insights into consultation processes. 'Consultation is a critical element of FPIC,' says Survival International's Watson. 'But in the end, it's important that communities have the right to withhold their consent. If it's just consultation then you lose that power.'

Should an indigenous community agree in principle to an extraction project, then the debate shifts to the terms on which that project might go ahead. Naturally, indigenous groups insist that they derive socio-economic benefits. Alongside typical corporate social investments, such as education and health infrastructure, most mutual benefit agreements now include demands for revenue-sharing as well.

Legal action is not the answer

While civil society groups have played a critical role at the level of individual projects, they have also set their sights on shaping the industry as a whole. That starts with the norms that govern mining companies. In general, NGOs warmly welcomed the introduction of FPIC by the International Finance Corporation in January 2012. Yet the fact that only 20 governments have so far recognized FPIC makes it easy for companies to 'pay lip service', according to Chris Albin-Lackey, senior researcher at Human Rights Watch.

Despite the uphill struggle in achieving legal redress, indigenous groups have become increasingly sophisticated and aggressive in pursuing their claims through the courts. Mining companies across the world are finding themselves bound up in litigation. US oil company Chevron provides an emblematic case. In 1994, a coalition of indigenous groups in the Ecuadorian Amazon filed a lawsuit for alleged environmental pollution. Nearly two decades later, the oil major was eventually ordered to pay $18bn in compensation. There are other successful cases. In May 2012, Colombia's constitutional court upheld a 2009 decision to suspend the Mande Norte mining project in Afro-Colombian and indigenous territories of northern Colombia. The decision rested on the failure of the developer, Muriel Mining, to properly consult the local population.

Such successes are the exception, however. Human rights activists such as Gopalakrishnan are consequently cautious about taking the litigation route. Not only can court cases become unwieldy and protracted, but they invariably favour those with deep pockets and time to play with: namely, companies.

But the downside for corporations here is reputational pressure. The indigenous rights movement is nothing if not media savvy. Groups such as Amazon Watch and Cultural Survival have led the way in using communications technology to grab international press attention. All too often, the defence of indigenous rights comes only in the wake of vocal protest. That need not be the case. Early and honest engagement by companies can mitigate this threat of social conflict. And that is surely in the interest of industry and indigenous people alike.

Sources

Ethical Corporation, Oliver Balch, 11 July 2012, www.ethicalcorp.com. Reproduced with the kind permission of Ethical Corporation.

VISIT THE
ONLINE
RESOURCE
CENTRE
for a short
response to this
feature

> **? THINK THEORY**
>
> To what extent are the consultations discussed here an example of discourse ethics? How do you think they could be redesigned to more clearly reflect the basic principles of discourse ethics?

significant implications for ethical decisions in business.[5] Gustafson (2000: 21), for example, suggests that postmodern business ethics emphasizes the following:

- **Holistic approach**. As morality is an inner conviction of individual actors, there is no separation between the private and professional realm. Postmodernists argue that modernist theories of ethical behaviour lead to an abstract and distant view of ethical issues that ultimately causes actors to follow different standards in their professional and private lives. For business organizations, such a view of ethical decision-making could unleash a quite subversive potential to business ethics, as it might question the beliefs and practices held by the organization (Bauman 1993).

- **Practices rather than principles**. As morality is not based on rational theories, ethical reasoning is not embodied in principles and rules. Rather, it is based on narratives of experience, metaphors to explain inner convictions, and practices that help individuals understand and overcome the unquestioned rules that constrain or dominate them (Crane et al. 2008; Weiskopf and Willmott 2013).

- **'Think local, act local'**. Modernist theories and '-isms' are aimed at general principles that are applicable to each and every situation. Postmodernists think that ethical reasoning has to be far more modest: it would only be realistic to expect ethics to come up with local rules applicable to specific issues and situations. Rather than finding one principle for multiple situations, business ethics focuses on deciding one issue after another. This does not mean that postmodernists do not take their decisions seriously and could decide on an issue in one way today and in another way tomorrow. It rather highlights the fact that no one situation is the same, and that different actors, power relations, cultural antecedents, and emotional contexts might lead to different judgements in situations that could, in the abstract, be regarded as being in the same 'class' and subject to the same 'principles'.

- **Preliminary character**. Postmodern ethicists are often seen as more pessimistic than their modern counterparts. They know that ethical decisions are subject to non-rational processes, and thus less controllable and predictable. Ethical reasoning therefore is a constant learning process, an ongoing struggle for practices that have a better fit, or for reasoning that just makes more sense and works better than the approaches tried out so far.

From the nature of a postmodern view on business ethics, it might already be clear that the notion of discussing the abstract case of Ethical Dilemma 3 is a nearly impossible venture. Indeed, postmodernist thinkers are sceptical of the vignette or hypothetical case method of learning about business ethics, preferring instead to engender moral commitment to others through real-life encounters (McPhail 2001). We would at best only be able to come up with some form of judgement if we travelled to Thailand, visited the site, talked to the people, and emphatically immersed ourselves in the real-life situation.

We would then have a 'moral impulse' about what to feel about the situation and could come up with what we would regard as the moral way to decide in this situation.

However, the example does gives us a few indications, and as good postmodernists, we would be well aware of the limitations of our present view on the issue and would try to suggest a preliminary view of what we would do in the situation of the product manager. We might, for example, at least suggest that we as the product manager have made the right first move in actually going to the site of production and facing those who will be affected by our decisions rather than staying at home and simply dismissing them as faceless 'suppliers'. We might also point to our attempt to make our own autonomous decision based on the situation faced in the specific culture of Thailand, rather than relying on a corporate code of ethics, particularly one that is intended to have universal application. However, postmodernists would also question the extent to which you as the product manager are so steeped in a corporate mentality that you immediately think in terms of costs and bonuses, rather than people and their lives.

Ultimately, it is of the nature of postmodernism that we are not able to finally decide on the situation for the manager, since we lack the contextual nuances of the situation and we are not aware of the extent to which a genuine 'moral impulse' is possible in this context.

■ Summary: towards a pragmatic use of ethical theory

The array of ethical theories discussed in this chapter provides us with a rich source of assistance in making morally informed decisions. However, the discussion of our case, Ethical Dilemma 3, has brought to the surface a variety of different views and normative implications depending on the theoretical approach that has been chosen. Sometimes these views provide widely contradictory results.

As we have indicated earlier in the chapter, we will not suggest one theory or one approach as the best or true view of a moral dilemma. **Figure 3.6** shows this approach, where ethical theory is seen as a kind of 'lens' through which to focus ethical decision-making on a specific consideration, such as rights, duties, discourse, or whatever.

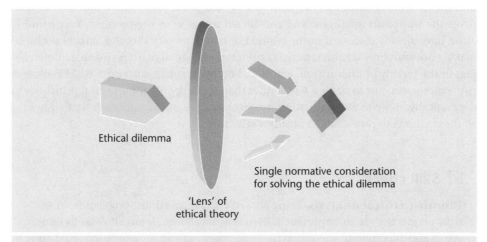

Ethical dilemma

Single normative consideration
for solving the ethical dilemma

'Lens' of
ethical theory

Figure 3.6 A typical perspective on the value of ethical theory for solving ethical dilemmas in business

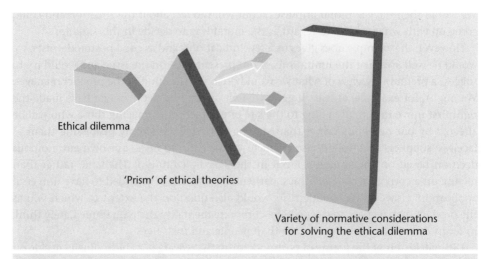

Figure 3.7 A pluralistic perspective on the value of ethical theories for solving ethical dilemmas in business

Alternatively we suggest that all of the theoretical approaches we have discussed throw light on the problem from different angles and thus work in a complementary rather than a mutually excluding fashion. **Figure 3.7** elucidates this role of ethical theories: by viewing an ethical problem through the 'prism' of ethical theories, we are provided with a variety of considerations pertinent to the moral assessment of the matter at hand. Based on this 'spectrum' of views, the business actor is able to fully comprehend the problem, its issues and dilemmas, and its possible solutions and justifications.

By using theory in this non-dogmatic way we take up the notion of pluralism discussed earlier in the chapter to propose that the best way of approaching ethical problems in business is through a *pluralist analysis*. This acknowledges that real business decisions normally involve multiple actors with a variety of ethical views and convictions that feed into the decision. Ethical theories help to articulate these views and a pluralist analysis paves the way to an intelligent and considered response to the problem. Furthermore, as we have already discussed in the context of contemporary theories, ethical decision-making does not only rely on rational considerations. Moral matters embrace human beings in the totality of their reason, emotion, bodily existence, social embeddedness, and past experiences, just to name a few. Rather than looking only for universal principles to dogmatically apply to every situation, we suggest a pragmatic approach that allows for all these aspects to play a role in business ethics.

☑ Skill check

Pluralist ethical analysis. Being able to analyse an ethical problem from multiple perspectives is an important skill in business ethics. It enables you to understand and incorporate the different moral perspectives of people involved in a particular situation in a rigorous and structured way.

Consideration	Typical question you might ask yourself	Theory
One's own interests	Is this really in my, or my organization's, best long-term interests? Would it be acceptable and expected for me to think only of the consequences to myself in this situation?	Egoism
Social consequences	If I consider all of the possible consequences of my actions, for everyone that is affected, will we be better or worse off overall? How likely are these consequences and how significant are they?	Utilitarianism
Duties to others	Who do I have obligations to in this situation? What would happen if everybody acted in the same way as me? Am I treating people only to get what I want for myself (or my organization) or am I thinking also of what they might want too?	Ethics of duty
Entitlements of others	Whose rights do I need to consider here? Am I respecting fundamental human rights and people's need for dignity?	Ethics of rights
Fairness	Am I treating everyone fairly here? Have processes been set up to allow everyone an equal chance? Are there major disparities between the 'winners' and 'losers' that could be avoided?	Theories of justice
Character and integrity	Am I acting with integrity here? What would a decent, honest person do in the same situation?	Virtue ethics
Relationships and responsibility	How do (or would) the other affected parties feel in this situation? Can I avoid doing harm to others? Which solution is most likely to preserve healthy and harmonious relationships among those involved?	Feminist ethics
Procedures of norm generation	What norms can we work out together to provide a mutually acceptable solution to this problem? How can we achieve a peaceful settlement of this conflict that avoids 'railroading' by the most powerful player?	Discourse ethics
Empathy and moral impulse	Am I just simply going along with the usual practice here, or slavishly following the organization's code, without questioning whether it really feels right to me? How can I get closer to those likely to be affected by my decision? What do my emotions or gut feelings tell me once I'm out of the office?	Postmodern ethics

Figure 3.8 Considerations in making ethical decisions: summary of key insights from ethical theories

Figure 3.8 provides a summary of the main consideration raised by each theory discussed in this chapter. Although we would draw back from advocating something akin to a 'ten-point plan' for ethical decision-making, you might want to use this figure as a checklist of potential ways of addressing business ethics problems and dilemmas.

Study questions

1. What are ethical theories and why, if at all, do we need them?

2. Is ethical theory of any practical use to managers? Assess the benefits and drawbacks of ethical theory for managers in a global economy.

3. Define ethical absolutism, ethical relativism, and ethical pluralism. To what extent is each perspective useful for studying and practising business ethics?

4. What are the two main families of Western modernist ethical theories? Explain the difference between these two approaches to ethical theory.

5. Which ethical theory do you think is most commonly used in business? Provide evidence to support your assertion and give reasons explaining why this theoretical approach is more likely than others to dominate business decisions.

6. Read the following case:

You are the manager of FoodFile, a busy city-centre restaurant catering mainly to local office workers at lunchtimes and an eclectic, fashionable crowd of professionals in the evenings. You are proud of your renowned food and excellent service. Most of your staff have been with you since you opened three years ago—unusual in an industry characterized by casual labour and high turnover. You consider this to be one of the key factors in your consistency and success. Now, your head chef has come to you and told you, in confidence, that she is HIV positive. She is very distressed and you want to reassure her. However, you are troubled about her continuing to work in the kitchens and are concerned about the effect this news could have on the other staff, or even on your customers should they find out about her situation.

(a) Using Figure 3.8, set out the main ethical considerations that are suggested by each of the theories covered in this chapter.

(b) Which theories are most persuasive in dealing with this dilemma?

(c) What would you do in this situation and why?

Research exercise

Select a business ethics problem or dilemma that you have faced or which has arisen in an organization of which you have been part, either as an employee, a student, or a manager.

1. Briefly describe the basic details of the case, and identify and discuss the main business ethics issues involved.

2. Set out the main responses, solutions, or courses of action that *could* have been considered in relation to this problem.

3. Evaluate these options using theory discussed in this chapter.

4. What decision was finally made? To what extent do you believe that this was the best option, and why?

Key readings

1. Rorty, R. 2006. Is philosophy relevant to applied ethics? *Business Ethics Quarterly*, 16 (3): 369–80.

This article provides a rather challenging approach to understanding and studying business ethics. Though primarily written for teachers of the subject, its core arguments are powerful for every student of business ethics. Richard Rorty—one of the most influential American philosophers of his time—argues that ultimately philosophical theories are just pragmatic tools to unearth and describe what humanity has learned about right and wrong over the course of history. The paper is based on Rorty's last public talk before he passed away and has led to widespread debate in the business ethics community.

2. Brenkert, G. 2010. The limits and prospects of business ethics. *Business Ethics Quarterly*, 20 (4): 703–9.

This short article from a former editor of one of the field's premier journals provides a useful critique of normative ethics, arguing that its usefulness will be limited unless we can show how business will actually change in line with the prescriptions from theory. For this, he argues, we need to complement normative analysis with a better understanding of the social and political role of firms.

VISIT THE ONLINE RESOURCE CENTRE for links to further key readings

Case 3

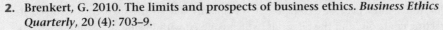

Canada's oil sands: 'most destructive project on Earth' or 'ethical oil'?

This case outlines the ethical controversies surrounding the development of the Canadian oil sands. It sets out the pros and cons of the oil sands, and examines the role that these factors play in broader political decisions in the US and Europe about supporting imports from the Canadian oil industry.

VISIT THE ONLINE RESOURCE CENTRE for links to useful sources of further information on this case

The oil industry is no stranger to controversy, yet Canada's oil sands have become probably the most hotly contested development in decades. Extracting oil from the heavy, extremely viscous mixture of sand, clay, water and bitumen has only recently become economically viable, but critics argue that the social and environmental costs are excessively high. Tar sands extraction requires much greater quantities of water than for conventional oil, it imposes a far higher burden of carbon emissions, and has been associated with a range of other pollutants, including mercury contamination. According to the Sierra Club, the largest environmental NGO in the US, the oil sands produce 'the most toxic fossil fuel on the planet'. However, oil sands development also has its legions of supporters, especially in Canada where most commercial extraction takes place. Rather than being branded a dirty oil, the Canadian Environment Minister has argued that the oil sands should in fact be seen as an 'ethical' source of energy. Since it generates enormous economic benefits for many, and is from a country that upholds democracy, human rights, and environmental protection, so goes the argument, output from the oil sands should really be recognized as 'ethical oil'.

Canada's oil sands industry

Oil sand is a naturally occurring substance that can be found in several locations around the globe, including Kazakhstan, Russia, and Venezuela. However, the deposits in the western Canadian province of Alberta are, so far, the largest and also the most commercially developed source in the world. Alberta's oil sands are located in an area of around 140,000 square kilometres in the north of the province, with Fort McMurray being the main urban hub for the industry and supporting services.

The Albertan oil sands have long been known to the local First Nations in the region who used the bitumen to seal seams on their canoes. European explorers provided the first written accounts of the oil sands in the eighteenth century, and the first patent for commercial separation processes to extract crude oil was awarded as early as the 1920s. However, commercial operations only began seriously in the late 1960s with the establishment of the first oil sands mine. Development initially occurred relatively slowly with the second and third mines only opening in the late 1970s and early 2000s, respectively.

The initial slow pace of development was mainly due to the high cost involved in extracting crude oil from the oil sands, which coupled with low oil prices and relatively abundant supply from other sources, made the oil sands unattractive economically. With the spike in oil prices that began around the turn of the century, and the rush to secure greater energy independence in the face of an unsettled middle east and dwindling supplies elsewhere, investment flowed into the Albertan oil sands. More than $100 billion has been invested in oil sands development since the turn of the century, with current investment levels running into something like $20 billion every year. From just over half a million barrels of bitumen a day in 1997, the oil sands industry in 2014 produced almost 2 million barrels of bitumen every day. By 2022, production is projected to reach 3.8 million barrels per day and the Canadian Association of Petroleum Producers expects the industry will surpass 5 million barrels a day by the end of 2030.

Most major companies now have operations in the oil sands, with over 50 energy companies having some kind of stake in mining and production facilities in the region. This includes Canadian companies such as Suncor Energy, which opened the first mine site some 45 years ago, and Syncrude, the second company to establish operations in the area, both of which now operate some of the largest oil sands mining operations. They have been joined by a swathe of global players such as Shell, Chevron, Total, Statoil, Exxon, and ConocoPhillips. Increasingly, Asian energy companies have also made investments in the oil sands, including the Korean National Oil Company and CNOOC, China's largest producer of offshore crude.

The oil sands development has catapulted Canada up the table of countries with proven reserves of crude oil. Even just counting the 9% of total oil sands volume that is currently recoverable using existing technology, Canada now has the third-largest proven oil reserves after Saudi Arabia and Venezuela. This constitutes some 11% of total global oil reserves, prompting Canadian Prime Minister Stephen Harper to claim that the country is an 'energy superpower'.

The pros and cons of the oil sands

The rapid expansion of the oil sands has brought a host of economic benefits to the local Albertan economy and to Canada as a whole. According to the Canadian Energy Research Institute (CERI), almost every community in Canada has been touched by oil sands development through the stimulating impact it has on job creation and economic growth. Some of the headline impacts promoted by oil sands supporters include:

- Employment in Canada as a result of new oil sands investments is expected to grow from 75,000 jobs in 2010 to 905,000 jobs in 2035.

- The energy sector (oil and gas extraction/mining) accounted for 11% of jobs in Alberta and over 22% of Alberta's GDP in 2012.

- New oil sands development is expected to contribute over $2.1 trillion to the Canadian economy and $521 billion to the US economy over the 25-year period from 2010 to 2035.

- The oil sands industry will pay an estimated $783 billion in provincial and federal taxes and royalties between 2010 and 2035.

- Oil sands development creates thousands of jobs for First Nations communities—there were more than 1,700 Aboriginal employees in permanent operations jobs in the oil sands industry in 2010 (10% of the total workforce).

- Oil sands companies regularly contract more than $1 billion of business with Aboriginal-owned businesses every year. This was as much as $1.8 billion in 2012. Oil sands companies have also provided anywhere from $5 million to $12 million a year to support Aboriginal community programmes between 2010 and 2012.

On the other hand, many critics have highlighted the significant environmental problems caused by oil sands development. Although all oil sands developments must meet Canada's environmental protection regulations, since production began ramping up in earnest after the turn of the century, environmentalists and other critics have pointed to a litany of negative environmental impacts. For example, some of the studies conducted by researchers and environmental groups conclude that:

- Average greenhouse gas emissions for oil sands production (extraction and upgrading) is 3.2 to 4.5 times more per barrel than for conventional crude oil production. Overall, emissions per barrel have been increasing since 2006.

- Oil sands emissions accounted for 7% of Canada's greenhouse gas emissions in 2010 and are forecasted to be 14% in 2020. Canada is now among the top ten greenhouse gas producers on an absolute and per capita basis.

- Water monitoring being conducted by the Regional Aquatic Monitoring Program, a joint industry-government environment body, appears to be inadequate. For example, a 2010 academic study found that levels of pollutants cadmium, copper, lead, mercury, nickel, silver, and zinc in areas around the oil sands exceeded federal and provincial guidelines.

- Another academic study in 2013 found that oil sands development was polluting nearby Alberta lakes with rising levels of toxic carcinogens, refuting long-standing industry claims that waterway pollution in the region was largely naturally occurring. Contaminated water is a particular problem for local First Nations communities who rely on fishing.

- The current water withdrawal management framework prioritizes industry use over aquatic protection. Water allocations from the nearby Athabasca River have nearly doubled between 2000 and 2010. In 2011, the oil sands industry used 170 million cubic metres of water, equivalent to the residential water use of 1.7 million Canadians.

- Tailings, the waste by-product from oil sands extraction processes, are toxic and are stored indefinitely in open lakes that cover an area approximately 50% larger than the city of Vancouver. These tailings lakes seep, but the exact amount of seepage is either not known or has not been made public. One estimate suggests approximately 11 million litres of seepage a day.

- Only 0.15% of the area disturbed by oil sands mining is certified as reclaimed—much of the peatlands and old growth forests that have been destroyed will never return to their natural state.

These and many other environmental criticisms have continued to plague oil sands companies despite some companies investing considerable resources into environmental enhancements of various kinds including better water efficiency at mine sites and new technologies such as carbon capture and storage (whereby waste carbon dioxide is captured and stored to prevent it being released into the atmosphere).

Most environmental groups remain unconvinced that these improvements are making a tangible difference given the speed and scale of development in northern Alberta. Many have taken a strong position against any further development, with groups like the Canadian NGO Environmental Defence labelling the oil sands 'the most destructive project on Earth', while Greenpeace is 'calling on oil companies and the Canadian government to stop the tar sands'. Some more moderate voices, such as the Pembina Institute, have a goal to advance what they call 'responsible oil sands development', which involves a cap on environmental impacts and a reduced environmental footprint per barrel of oil produced. Even the terminology of the oil sands remains contentious with critics typically labelling it the 'tar sands' whilst industry and the Canadian government prefer the more benign sounding 'oil sands'.

The oil sands export problem

The majority of oil sands crude is sold to Canadian and US refineries. But with such vast reserves, Canada has increasingly looked to expand its export markets. Between 2002 and 2012 the oil sands increased their share of US oil imports from about 16% of all US imports in 2002 to an estimated 28% by the end of 2012—albeit at a time when overall US imports reduced in the face of growing domestic energy production. Despite the increase in its share of US imports, the oil sands have become increasingly vulnerable to US efforts to green its energy mix. US environmental groups have long been fighting to restrict US imports of 'dirty' oil sands oil and President Barack Obama made fighting climate change a key plank of his inaugural address in 2013.

The issue of the US's relationship with the oil sands crystallized in the long-running debate about the Keystone XL pipeline extension, which was designed to bring more oil sands crude to refiners in the US. The project became mired in controversy during the 2010s due to its own potential environmental impacts (the risk of spills into ecologically sensitive terrain) as well as the divisive issue of bringing oil sands crude, and its heavier greenhouse gas burden, into the US energy mix at a time when the country was looking to reduce rather than increase its emissions. As President Obama said in 2013:

Allowing the Keystone pipeline to be built requires a finding that doing so would be in our nation's interest. And our national interest will be served only if this project does not significantly exacerbate the problem of carbon pollution. The net effects of the pipeline's impact on our climate will be absolutely critical to determining whether this project is allowed to go forward.

Meanwhile, with exports to the US threatened, Canada's oil sands also found itself fighting to maintain its reputation in Europe. A proposed EU directive aimed at cutting emissions from the transport sector threatened to single out oil sands oil as especially dirty compared with other forms of energy. Not only would this seriously impact exports to Europe by effectively imposing an import tax on Canadian crude, but oil sands advocates were also concerned that it would set a precedent for discriminating against their product that could have global repercussions. 'It could stigmatize the oil from Canada and impact on our access to some markets' the Canadian Natural Resources Minister said in 2013.

The 'ethical oil' makeover

In the face of such challenges to the reputation of the oil sands, one particularly controversial approach to restore its tarnished image has been to focus on the country of origin of competing sources of crude. That is, in addition to all of the supposed economic benefits of oil sands development, some also highlight that buying oil from Canada is more responsible than buying from many other oil-producing countries. The basic point here is that because the oil sands are in Canada, they are properly and democratically regulated, they do not fall foul of corruption and abuses common in oil rich countries—and the proceeds do not go into funding terrorism.

Exponents of this argument need only point to the countries with the largest current reserves of oil to make their point (see **Table C3.1**). Apart from Canada, most other states in the top ten have relatively poor records of democracy and upholding human rights. The Canadian-based NGO Ethicaloil.org, which is the most vociferous promoter of this argument, argues that oil-producing countries should therefore be divided into those producing 'ethical oil' and those producing 'conflict oil': 'Countries that produce Ethical Oil uphold human rights and have high environmental standards. They ensure economic justice and promote peace. By contrast, Conflict Oil countries oppress their citizens and operate in secret with no accountability to voters, the press, or independent judiciaries.'

Rank	Country	Reserves (billions of barrels)
1	Venezuela	298
2	Saudi Arabia	268
3	Canada	173
4	Iran	155
5	Iraq	141
6	Kuwait	104
7	United Arab Emirates	98
8	Russia	80
9	Libya	48
10	Nigeria	37

Table C3.1 Top 10 countries by proven oil reserves

Source: Central Intelligence Agency, *The World Factbook*: https://www.cia.gov/library/publications/resources/the-world-factbook/.

The book *Ethical Oil: The Case for Canada's Oil Sands* written by Ezra Levant, a Canadian lawyer and talk-show host that popularized the idea, became a best-seller in Canada and ended up winning the National Business Book Award. Levant went on to set up Ethicaloil.org, which is widely believed to benefit from oil industry funding and support—or as one Greenpeace spokesperson put it, is 'a front group for Big Oil'. The Canadian government was also quick to throw its support behind the idea in order to support its case to potential importers, especially the US. As the Canadian Prime Minister, Stephen Harper said, 'the reality for the United States, which is the biggest consumer of our petroleum products, is that Canada is a very ethical society and a safe source for the United States in comparison to other sources of energy'.

The 'ethical oil' debate quickly ignited controversy in Canada, not least because it looked to many like an attempt to airbrush out the problematic aspects of the oil sands. John Bennett, executive director of Sierra Club of Canada explained that 'the fact that the Saudis or Nigerians or others are worse in human rights and environment is not relevant. We can't do anything about that; we can deal with our oil sands and we are not.' Others, such as the renowned Canadian environmentalist David Suzuki remarked simply that, 'in today's world, all fossil fuels are unethical. There is no such thing as ethical oil.'

Questions

1. Which actors have a stake in deciding whether the oil sands are an ethical source of oil and why do you think they differ so much in their assessments?

2. How would you go about conducting a utilitarian analysis of the oil sands for the purpose of deciding whether it is an ethical source of oil? Provide a provisional assessment based on the data in the case and outline what other data you would need to make a full assessment.

3. How would this assessment differ if you focused primarily on non-consequentialist ethics (duties, rights and justice)? What issues take precedence now and do they give a reasonable perspective on the problem?

4. How would you compare oil sands oil to other sources of oil from an ethical perspective?

5. Consider the case for saying that all oil is unethical. What theory or principle might support such an assertion? Is it a useful position to take, and if so, for who?

Sources

Alberta Energy website/oil sands: www.energy.alberta.ca/oilsands/791.asp.
Alberta Government website/oil sands: www.oilsands.alberta.ca/region.html.
Austen, I. 2013. In Canada, pipeline remarks stir analysis. *New York Times*, 26 June 2013: http://www.nytimes.com/2013/06/27/business/energy-environment/in-canada-pipeline-remarks-stir-analysis.html?_r = 0.
Canadian Association of Petroleum Producers 2014. Oil sands today/aboriginal peoples: www.oilsandstoday.ca/topics/Aboriginal/Pages/default.aspx.
CBC News 2010. Oilsands mining linked to Athabasca River toxins. *CBC News*, 30 August 2010: http://www.cbc.ca/news/technology/oilsands-mining-linked-to-athabasca-river-toxins-1.877292.
Chase, S. 2011. Harper's embrace of 'ethical' oil sands reignites 'dirty' arguments. *Globe and Mail*, 7 January 2011: www.theglobeandmail.com/news/politics/harpers-embrace-of-ethical-oil-sands-reignites-dirty-arguments/article563356/.

Ethicaloil.org website: www.ethicaloil.org.

Honarvar, A., Rozhon, J., Millington, D., Walden, T., Murillo, C.A., and Walden, Z. 2011. *Economic Impacts of New Oil Sands Projects in Alberta (2010–2035)*. Canadian Energy Research Institute: www.ceri.ca/images/stories/CERI%20Study%20124.pdf.

Kurek, J., Kirk, J.L., Muir, D.C.G., Wang, X., Evans, M.S., and Smol, J.P. 2013. Legacy of a half century of Athabasca oil sands development recorded by lake ecosystems. *Proceedings of the National Academy of Sciences* 110 (5): 1761–66.

Pembina Institute website/oil sands: www.pembina.org/oil-sands.

Sierra Club Canada/oil sands: http://www.sierraclub.ca/en/tar-sands.

Suzuki, D. 2011. Can oil be ethical? David Suzuki Foundation: www.davidsuzuki.org/blogs/science-matters/2011/10/can-oil-be-ethical/.

Notes

1. In fact, although the ICCR began as a coalition of faith-based investors, its 'current membership has grown beyond the universe of religious investors to include like-minded mainstream institutional investors who recognize the moral and ethical repercussions of their financial decisions. Affiliation with a faith tradition is not a requisite for ICCR membership.' See http://www.iccr.org/our-approach/connection-between-faith-investing.

2. For the full text, go to http://institute.jesdialogue.org/fileadmin/bizcourse/interfaithdeclaration.pdf.

3. It is worth noting that Smith's work itself does not only emphasize self-interest and that he also espouses broader moral virtues, including justice and the importance of prudence in exercising one's economic desires. See Werhane (1999).

4. See http://www.business-humanrights.org.

5. In some ways, then, postmodern approaches to ethics resonate quite substantially with some Asian ethical frameworks, particularly those such as Buddhism or Taoism. Rather that the monotheistic 'book religions', which in different degrees have entire dogmas of right and wrong built around them, these Eastern philosophies seek to go beyond rationality and instead emphasize qualities such as compassion or spontaneity.

4

Making Decisions in Business Ethics

DESCRIPTIVE ETHICAL THEORIES

Having completed this chapter you should be able to:

- Explain why ethical and unethical decisions get made in the workplace.
- Specify the characteristics of a decision with ethical content.
- Understand a basic ethical decision-making model and delineate key elements of individual and situational influences on ethical decision-making.
- Critically evaluate the role of individual differences in shaping ethical decision-making.
- Critically evaluate the role of situational influences on ethical decision-making, including both issue-based and context-based factors.
- Identify points of leverage for improving ethical decision-making in business.

Key concepts and skills:

Concepts	Skills
• Descriptive ethical theory	• Modelling the ethical decision-making process
• Cognitive moral development	
• Personal values	• Implementing ethics pledges
• Personal integrity	• Cultivating moral imagination

Concepts

- Whistleblowing
- Moral framing
- Authority
- Bureaucracy
- Organizational culture

Skills

- Analysing individual influences on ethical decision-making
- Analysing situational influences on ethical decision-making

■ Introduction

One of the biggest business ethics scandals of recent years was the downfall of investment banker Bernard Madoff. Over a period of more than two decades, Madoff defrauded his clients of an alleged $65 billion in a 'ponzi scheme' constituting the largest fraud in US history. When Madoff finally turned himself in to the police he was widely depicted as the ultimate business villain, or even a 'monster', that callously abused the trust of his clients. The assumption was that Madoff had acted independently without the knowledge of his business partners, employees, clients, or even his family. His eventual prison sentence of 150 years symbolically reflected a conviction that Madoff's actions were, as the sentencing judge put it, the result of an 'extraordinarily evil' individual (Frank and Efrati 2009).

Since that time, however, the Madoff story has taken on a different spin. In 2014, not only did his key banking partner JP Morgan agree to pay a $1.7 billion penalty for its involvement in the scandal but also five more individuals were sentenced for collaborating in Madoff's fraud (Lappin 2014). Madoff now appears to have had many crucial collaborators and found a business environment—including his credulous clients—that encouraged and enabled his fraud to continue.

Madoff's story raises the question of whether unethical behaviour is simply a matter of individual human ingenuity to do wrong, or whether we can also put such problems down to external factors. Perhaps corruption is as much due to the culture of certain industries as it is to personal characteristics. And the escalating incidence of ethical misconduct uncovered in the aftermath of the financial crisis could be more attributable to institutionalized norms of behaviour on Wall Street or in the City of London than any individual wrongdoing.

This chapter looks at the issue of ethical decision-making in organizations to begin to answer some of these questions about the causes of misbehaviour. In so doing, we will seek to provide the tools to explain why some business people make what appear to be the right ethical choices, while others do things that are unscrupulous or even illegal. We will also address the question of whether people who make these unethical decisions are inherently bad, or whether there are other reasons that can explain the incidence of ethics problems in business. The chapter provides a way of addressing these questions by examining **descriptive ethical theory**.

Descriptive ethical theories provide an important addition to the *normative* theories covered in Chapter 3: rather than telling us what business people *should* do (which is the intention of normative theory), descriptive theories seek to tell us what business people *actually* do—and more importantly, they will help to explain *why* they do those things.

Descriptive ethical theory Theory that describes how ethical decisions are actually made in business, and explains what factors influence the process and outcomes of those decisions.

Understanding the reasons why people make certain decisions is clearly important from a business ethics perspective, not least because it helps us to comprehend the factors that lead to ethical and unethical decisions. From a practical point of view, though, this is also useful for managing business ethics. Obviously, we first need to know what shapes ethical decision-making before we can try and influence it. Therefore, descriptive theories can be said to provide a practical understanding of how the ethical theories covered in the previous chapter can be applied, as well as assisting in identifying points of leverage for managing business ethics, as will be discussed in Chapter 5.

We begin by looking at what exactly an ethical decision is and then go on to examine the various models that have been put forward to explain the process of ethical decision-making in the workplace. This shows us that although ethical decision-making is very complex, extensive research over the years from psychologists, sociologists, management scholars, and others has provided us with a relatively clear picture of the important stages and influences that are central to understanding the ethical decision-making process. We proceed to summarize and evaluate current knowledge about these stages and influences, covering the cognitive and emotional processes that individuals go through in making ethical evaluations, as well as the situational influences that shape the decisions and actions they actually come to make.

■ What is an ethical decision?

On the face of it, this is a very simple question. After all, we have already said in Chapter 1 that ethical decisions are concerned with a judgement about right and wrong. But as Morris (2004) suggests, by using the language of right and wrong, we have already identified that a situation is moral in nature. So, there is an important process of identification that goes *before* this, whereby we examine situations and determine whether they are characterized by such considerations in the first place.

Imagine, for example, a situation where you are downloading a copy of Arcade Fire's latest album from your friend. Are you faced with a moral dilemma? Is this an ethical decision? Perhaps, for you, this is simply a normal practice that has no apparent moral dimensions. But Mercury Records, Arcade Fire's record label, may take a very different view. They may argue that there is an important moral dimension to this decision, since you are not only breaking the law, you are 'stealing' intellectual copyright for free and depriving the company and the artists of their rightful return on their investment. So how do we objectively decide whether a situation should be assigned moral status in the first place?

There are a number of factors that we might identify here, the most important of which are these:

• **The decision is likely to have significant effects on others**. As we saw in Chapter 3, two of the most critical aspects of morality are that it is concerned with harms and benefits, and that it is about considerations of social good, i.e. considerations of others beyond the self. Even egoism is concerned with others in that one is expected to act in one's own self-interest because that is for the *good of society*. Copying an album does have material affects on others, namely the record label, the musicians, and other organizations that have contributed their time and effort to its production.

- **The decision is likely to be characterized by choice, in that alternative courses of action are open**. A moral decision requires that we have a choice. For argument's sake, if you accidently copied the Arcade Fire album without realizing it, then you could not be said to have had much of a choice in the matter. In the normal course of affairs, however, you have the option to copy it or not copy it. When decision-makers actually recognize that they have ethical choices, then they face an *ethical dilemma*.

- **The decision is perceived as ethically relevant by one or more parties**. Regardless of whether the decision-maker sees a decision as having ethical content, if others do, then the decision immediately incurs some degree of ethicality. When a bank provides a loan for a new infrastructure project, this might seem like an ethically neutral act, but campaigners against the project who are concerned about its impacts on local people and the environment might regard it as highly ethically significant. Similarly, just because someone copies albums all the time without ever considering it to be an ethical decision, that does not mean they are engaging in an ethically neutral act.

Now that we have identified the basic characteristics of an ethical decision, let us look at how we can model the decision process that we go through in responding to the decision.

■ Models of ethical decision-making

If we think about times when we have been confronted with an ethical dilemma, we might well now be able to recognize what kind of normative principles we were employing—perhaps we were mainly concerned with possible consequences, or maybe we were thinking mainly about rights or relationships. However, we are probably less likely to know why we thought about it in this way, or why we even saw it as an ethical issue in the first place. This, however, is the purpose of descriptive models of ethical decision-making. Various models have been presented in the literature, and by far the most widely cited ones have been derived from the work of psychologists.

In general, these models primarily seek to represent two things:

- The different stages in decision-making that people go through in responding to an ethics problem in a business context.
- The different influences on that process.

We shall briefly look at each of these two aspects in turn and link them together to form a framework for understanding ethical decision-making in business.

Stages in ethical decision-making

The most frequently used framework for conceptualizing ethical decision-making in business is the four-stage process of ethical decision-making introduced by James Rest (Treviño et al. 2006; Craft 2013). According to this model, individuals move through a process whereby they:

1. Recognize a moral issue.
2. Make some kind of moral judgement about that issue.

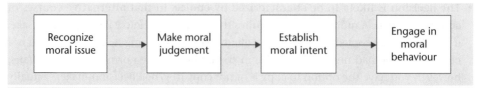

Figure 4.1 Ethical decision-making process

Source: Derived from Rest (1986), as cited in Jones, T.M. 1991. Ethical decision making by individuals in organizations: an issue-contingent model, *Academy of Management Review*, 16: 366–95. Reproduced with permission from the Academy of Management, conveyed through Copyright Clearance Center, Inc.

3. Establish an intention to act upon that judgement.

4. Act according to their intentions.

This is shown in **Figure 4.1**. As Jones (1991) suggests, these stages are intended to be conceptually distinct, such that although one might reach one stage in the model, this does not mean that one will necessarily move onto the next stage. Hence, the model distinguishes between *knowing* what the right thing to do is and actually *doing* something about it; or between *wanting* to do the right thing, and actually *knowing* what the best course of action is. So, for example, even though a salesperson might know that lying to customers is wrong (a moral judgement), for one reason or another—such as needing to meet aggressive sales targets—they might not actually always tell the truth (a moral behaviour). Similarly, although a purchasing manager may realize that receiving personal gifts from suppliers is ethically questionable (a moral recognition), they may defer making a judgement about the problem (a moral judgement) until someone actually questions them about it.

☑ Skill check

Modelling the ethical decision-making process. Being able to understand and apply the ethical decision-making model helps you to identify the relevant stages and influences involved in ethical and unethical decisions.

Relationship with normative theory

The role of normative theory (which is the type of theory we discussed in Chapter 3) in these stages of ethical decision-making is primarily in relation to *moral judgement*. Moral judgements can be made according to considerations of rights, duty, consequences, etc. While there has been very little research actually examining the types of normative theories used by people in business, there is some evidence to suggest that commercial managers tend to rely primarily on consequentialist thinking (Premeaux and Mondy 1993). This is perhaps not surprising given that, as we saw in Chapter 3, much economic and business theory is itself largely predicated upon consequentialism (Desmond and Crane 2004), and that, in general, most people are consequentialists, especially those that are young, university-educated, and have high incomes (Johansson-Stenman 2012).

An interesting example of this type of consequentialist reasoning is given by Joel Bakan (2004: 61–5) in his book *The Corporation*. He describes the decision-making process at General Motors in the face of a design problem with its Chevrolet Malibu model. The company decided to reposition the fuel tank on the car, despite knowing that this would increase the possibility of passengers being harmed in fuel-fed fires if the car was involved in a rear-end collision. A 1970s report produced by a GM engineer had simply multiplied the 500 fatalities that such collisions caused each year by $200,000—an estimate of the cost to GM in legal damages for each potential fatality at the time. Then, by dividing that figure by the number of GM vehicles on the road (41 million) the engineer concluded that each fatality cost GM $2.40 per car. In his report, the calculation appeared like this:

$$\frac{500 \text{ fatalities} \times \$200,000 \text{ / fatality}}{41,000,000 \text{ automobiles}} = \$2.40 \text{ / automobile}$$

Given that the cost to GM of preventing such fires was estimated to be $8.59 per car, the company reckoned it could save $6.19 ($8.59 – $2.40) per car if it allowed people to die rather than changing the design—and so went ahead with the dangerous design anyway.

This type of cost-benefit analysis is extremely prevalent in organizational decision-making. Another well-documented example is the notorious Ford Pinto that happened around the same time as the Malibu case (Gioia 1992), or more recently, General Motors' experience in 2014, when the CEO had to explain to a congressional hearing why it took the company ten years to recall a small switch worth 57 cents which had led to many accidents including at least 13 deaths (CBCnews 2014). Indeed, in the Malibu case a subsequent court case against GM in the 1990s by fire victims received a crucial deposition from the US Chamber of Commerce that held up this type of cost-benefit analysis as a 'hallmark of corporate good behaviour'. Bakan (2004: 64) goes on to quote the philosopher Alasdair MacIntyre who argues that the executive 'has to calculate the most efficient, the most economical way of mobilizing the existing resources to produce the benefits . . . at the lowest costs. The weighing of costs and benefits is not just his business, it is business.'

This could be seen as a rather pessimistic vision of organizational life. However, the issue of *whether* and *how* normative theory is used by an individual decision-maker depends on a range of different factors that influence the decision-making process, as we shall now see.

? THINK THEORY

Think about the prevalence of consequentialist approaches to decision-making, such as cost-benefit analysis, in organizations that you have worked in. Is such reasoning as inevitable as Bakan and MacIntyre suggest or is it possible to invoke ethics of rights, duties, or justice, for example? Does it make any difference what type of organization you are considering—large or small, public or private, for profit or not for profit?

VISIT THE ONLINE RESOURCE CENTRE for a short response to this feature

Influences on ethical decision-making

Models of ethical decision-making generally divide the factors that influence decisions into two broad categories: individual and situational (Ford and Richardson 1994).

- **Individual factors**. These are the unique characteristics of the individual actually making the relevant decision. These include factors that are given by birth (such as age and gender) and those acquired by experience and socialization (such as education, personality, and attitudes).

- **Situational factors**. These are the particular features of the context that influence whether the individual will make an ethical or an unethical decision. These include factors associated with the work context (such as reward systems, job roles, and organizational culture) and those associated with the issue itself (such as the intensity of the moral issue or the ethical framing of the issue).

Taken broadly, these two groups of factors help to explain why certain business decisions get made, and why people behave in ethical and unethical ways in business situations. This gives rise to the framework in **Figure 4.2**, which is the one that we shall use to structure our discussion in this chapter. In the rest of this chapter we shall examine the two sets of factors in much more detail, with the intention of providing the basis for assessing their relative importance to ethical decision-making. Before we do, however, it is worth offering a brief word of warning about using a model such as this to structure our discussions.

Limitations of ethical decision-making models

As we have said, the model depicted in Figure 4.2 is very useful for structuring our discussion and for seeing clearly the different elements that come into play within ethical decision-making. However, such an approach is not without its problems, and as we go

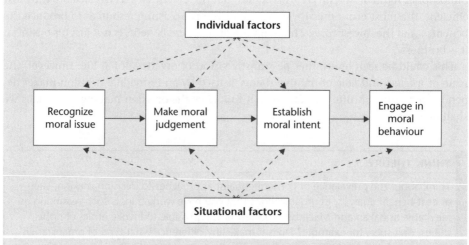

Figure 4.2 Framework for understanding ethical decision-making

through the chapter you might notice that it is not always particularly straightforward (nor some would argue, sensible) to break down these various elements into discrete units. Many of the various stages and influences are, to differing degrees, related, perhaps even interdependent. It can thus seem quite optimistic at times to separate out an individual factor and attempt to identify its unique role in the process of ethical decision-making. Nonetheless, these are criticisms that can be levelled at *all* models of this type, and we feel that as long as one is aware that the model is intended not as a definitive representation of ethical decision-making but as a relatively simple way to represent a complex process, such problems are not too serious. Finally, it is also worth mentioning that ethical decision-making models have largely originated in the US, and this can sometimes give a national or cultural bias to the types of issues and considerations that might be included. Let us just briefly review the different international perspectives before continuing.

International perspectives on ethical decision-making

In Chapter 1 we discussed some of the global differences in business ethics (especially between those in Europe, North America, and Asia), and we will again meet some of these in this chapter about ethical decision-making. As we mentioned in Chapter 1, in the US and Asia the central focus of the business ethics subject tends to be individual actors and their behaviour, whereas in Europe there is more interest in the design of economic institutions and how they function in a morally desirable way and/or encourage moral behaviour of business actors. This difference in perspective becomes quite visible with the topic of ethical decision-making since we could argue that research on *individual factors* influencing ethical decision-making has a strong North American bias, while *situational factors*, on the other hand, have been subject to a lengthy debate principally originated by European authors. The significance of this difference is that a focus on individual factors is consistent with the North American focus on choice *within* constraints, while a focus on situational factors reflects the more European concern with the *constraints* themselves.

To begin with, the very founders of modern organizational theory in Europe have stressed the influence of *social contexts* on ethical decision-making. For example, in the nineteenth century, the French sociologist Emile Durkheim (1993) discussed the emergence of, and necessity for, new work-related moral communities due to the effects of the industrial revolution on the erosion of traditional value systems that held societies together (Thompson and McHugh 2002). Similarly, the German sociologist Max Weber, to name another prominent example from the early twentieth century, shed a critical light on the ethical basis and influence of bureaucratic organizations (du Gay 2000). He distinguished between actions that were guided by an 'ethics of ultimate ends' and an 'ethics of responsibility'.[1] While the first would represent an idealistic view of man, reflecting a person's real moral convictions rooted in social good, the latter is an ethics that sees responsibility for the pursuit of the organization's goals as the ultimate moral imperative (Parkin 1982).

We will discuss the influence of bureaucratic organizations on individual actors in more detail later in the chapter. However, along these lines, the Polish sociologist Zigmunt Bauman (1991) has argued that there is not only an *influence* of bureaucratic organization on the morality of actors, but he regards the two as *mutually exclusive*. We have already come across Bauman in Chapter 3 as one of the key thinkers in postmodern ethics. As such, he contends that organizational dynamics act to neutralize the 'moral impulse' of the individual. Rational organizations require loyalty, discipline, and obedience, all of which, Bauman contends, stifle the personal and emotional aspects that are crucial for a sense of morality to exist (ten Bos and Willmott 2001). In contrast, US-based researchers have tended to focus more on the importance of individual agency in ethical decision-making. Although, as we shall see later in the chapter, important contributions to our understanding of the institutional basis of ethical decision-making have been made by American social psychologists such as Philip Zimbardo, business ethics researchers from the region have tended to focus on individual-level differences. Asian business ethics researchers, meanwhile, have also tended to replicate this approach by concentrating mainly on studies of managers and the cultural values that drive their ethical perception and choices (e.g. Christie et al. 2003; Ho and Redfern 2010). We will explore some of these different influences on ethical decision-making later on in this chapter. We will start, though, with an examination of key individual influences.

■ Individual influences on ethical decision-making

What is it about you or your classmates that causes you to act in different ways when confronted by the same ethical dilemmas? Individual influences on ethical decision-making relate to these facets of the individual who is actually going through the decision-making process. Clearly all employees bring certain traits and characteristics with them into an organization, and these are likely to influence the way in which the employee thinks and behaves in response to ethical dilemmas. For example, evidence suggests that entrepreneurs and small business owners may think and act differently than others in response to ethical issues because they tend to be more achievement-oriented, autonomous, opportunistic, and risk tolerant (Solymossy and Masters 2002). Although this could be taken to suggest that some people, such as small business owners, are simply more ethical than others, this is rather too simplistic a view. Individual factors can more readily account for why some people are perhaps more swayed than others into unethical conduct because of the influence of their colleagues. Similarly, individual factors can help to explain why some people perceive particular actions to be unethical while others do not. Hence, the issue is not so much about determining the reasons why people might be more or less ethical, but about the factors influencing us to think, feel, act, and perceive in certain ways that are relevant to ethical decision-making. Over the years, researchers have surfaced a number of important individual influences, as we shall now see. The factors and their likely influence on ethical decision-making are summarized in **Figure 4.3.**

Age and gender

A good place to start in examining the individual influences on ethical decision-making is to consider some basic demographic factors, such as age and gender. For example, one common question is whether men or women are more ethical. This is no doubt an interesting question, and gender has in fact been one of the individual influences on ethical decision-making in business most often subjected to investigation (O'Fallon and Butterfield 2005; Craft 2013). However, overall the results have been less than

Factor	Influence on ethical decision-making
Age and gender	Very mixed evidence leading to unclear associations with ethical decision-making.
National and cultural characteristics	Appear to have a significant effect on ethical beliefs, as well as views of what is deemed an acceptable approach to certain business issues.
Education and employment	Somewhat unclear, although some clear differences in ethical decision-making between those with different educational and professional experience seem to be present.
Psychological factors: Cognitive moral development	Small but significant effect on ethical decision-making.
Locus of control	At most a limited effect on decision-making, but can be important in predicting the apportioning of blame/approbation.
Personal values	Significant influence—empirical evidence citing positive relationship.
Personal integrity	Significant influence likely, but lack of inclusion in models and empirical tests.
Moral imagination	A relatively new issue with potential, but largely untested, explanatory potential.

Figure 4.3 Individual influences on ethical decision-making

conclusive, with different studies offering contradictory results, and often no differences found at all (Loe et al. 2000; O'Fallon and Butterfield 2005; Craft 2013). For example, ten of the 38 studies reported by Craft (2013) concluded that women are more ethical than men, while other studies demonstrated that men were more consistent in their ethical decision-making or were stricter when making ethical judgements.

Perhaps, though, the problem is more with the studies themselves and the questions they seek to answer (Loe et al. 2000). As we have said, it is rather simplistic to assume that some people are just more ethical than others, and even if this could be claimed, there seems no obvious reason why gender would be an important determinant. However, as we saw when discussing feminist ethics in Chapter 3 (which we shall return to shortly below), there is evidence to suggest that the way in which men and women think and act in response to ethical dilemmas might differ.

Another basic factor we might look at is whether age makes any difference to ethical decision-making. However, a similar problem is present with age as with gender. Empirical tests have tended to report very mixed results, with no clear picture emerging on the influence of age on ethical beliefs and action (Craft 2013). Indeed, again it would seem to be too generalized to categorize certain age groups as 'more ethical' than others, although certain *experiences* might in themselves shape the way in which we recognize and respond to ethical problems.

National and cultural characteristics

Another basic demographic characteristic is nationality. When we meet people from different countries and cultures, either at home or overseas, it does not take long before we start to see certain differences in what they perceive as ethical or unethical, or how they might go about dealing with ethical issues. Issues of nationality, ethnicity, and religion have therefore been of increasing interest to researchers of ethical decision-making, as one might expect, given the trends towards globalization identified in Chapter 1.

As we argued previously, people from different cultural backgrounds are still likely to have different beliefs about right and wrong, different values, etc., and this will inevitably lead to variations in ethical decision-making across nations, religions, and cultures. There is again a problem here with assuming that people from particular nations, religions, or ethnic groups can simply be deemed to be 'more ethical' or 'less ethical' in their decision-making than others. However, research has suggested that nationality can have a significant effect on ethical beliefs as well as views of what is deemed an acceptable approach to certain business issues.[2] These differences have been noted not just in the somewhat obvious cases of managers from developed and from less-developed countries, but also between those from different countries within Europe, those from Europe and the US, or even between those from different ethnic groups in the same country.

Geert Hofstede's research has been extremely influential in shaping our understanding of these differences (Hofstede 2001; Hofstede et al. 2010). Based initially on surveys completed by IBM employees throughout the world, Hofstede suggests that differences in cultural knowledge and beliefs across countries—our 'mental programming'—can be explained in terms of six dimensions:

- **Individualism/collectivism**. This represents the degree to which one is autonomous and driven primarily to act for the benefit of one's self, contrasted with a more social orientation that emphasizes group working and community goals.

- **Power distance**. This represents the extent to which the unequal distribution of hierarchical power and status is accepted and respected.

- **Uncertainty avoidance**. This measures the extent of one's preference for certainty, rules, and absolute truths.

- **Masculinity/femininity**. The extent to which an emphasis is placed on valuing money and things (masculinity) versus valuing people and relationships (femininity).

- **Long-term/short-term orientation**. This addresses differences in attention to future rewards, where long-term-oriented cultures value perseverance and thrift, while short-term ones emphasize more preservation of 'face', short-term results, and fulfilment of social obligations.

- **Indulgence**. This measures the degree to which societies permit or suppress gratification of basic and natural human drives related to enjoying life and having fun.

Hofstede's dimensions can be seen to explain certain differences in ethical decision-making. For example, someone from an individualist culture, such as are found in northern Europe and America, might be more likely to reflect on ethical problems alone in order to make their own independent decision, while someone from a collectivist culture, such as are found in southern Europe and Latin America, might be more likely to consult with the wider group. Similarly, a high power distance culture (i.e. one that respects and accepts stratification in power and status) like Japan or China might be less willing to question the orders given by their superiors, even if they felt they were being asked to do something ethically questionable. Empirical work has generally tended to support these sorts of relationships (e.g. Jackson 2001; Christie et al. 2003), although Hofstede's framework remains open to criticism (Baskerville-Morley 2005).

Clearly though, with the eroding of the territorial basis for business activities—exemplified by rising international trade, frequent international business travel, and growth in expatriate employment—the robustness and consistency of beliefs and values inherited simply from our cultural origin is likely to be increasingly weakened. For example, a Greek IT consultant with an MBA from Manchester University and five years' experience working for an American bank in Frankfurt might be expected to differ significantly from a Greek IT manager who has always lived and worked in Athens. This suggests that education and employment might also play a significant role in shaping our ethical beliefs and values.

? THINK THEORY

Think about Hofstede's 'mental programming' theory of culture in terms of its relevance for ethical decision-making. In the text, we have explained how the dimensions of individualism/collectivism and power distance might influence decision-making. What are the likely influences of masculinity/femininity, uncertainty avoidance, long-term orientation, and indulgence? Is this a helpful way of exploring the cultural influences on ethical decision-making?

VISIT THE ONLINE RESOURCE CENTRE for a short response to this feature

Education and employment

The type and quality of education received by individuals, as well as their professional training and experience, might also be considered to be important individual influences on ethical decision-making. For example, research reveals that business students not only rank lower in moral development than students in other subjects such as law, but are also more likely to engage in academic cheating, such as plagiarism (McCabe et al. 1991; McCabe and Treviño 1993)! Business students have also been found to be driven more by self-centred values than other students (McCabe et al. 1991). Similarly, individual values may shift as a result of exposure to particular working environments. During the financial crisis of the late 2000s, figures as diverse as US President Barack Obama, the Archbishop of Canterbury, Rowan Williams, and Rajan Zed (the president of the Universal Society of Hinduism) criticized the 'culture of greed' that many commentators suggested had allegedly 'poisoned' those working in the banking and finance industry.[3]

Clearly, business training devoid of ethics can reinforce the 'myth of amoral business' (De George 1999)—the idea that business is not expected to be concerned with questions of morality. Hence, although some aspects of individual morality may be developed through upbringing and general education, there is also a place for ethics training in enhancing people's ability to recognize and deal with ethics problems in the workplace (Treviño and Nelson 2014). Overall then, while the relationships between ethical decision-making and employment experience and education still remain somewhat unclear (Loe et al. 2000), some definite differences between those with different educational and professional experience seem to be present. Our hope is certainly that by studying business ethics in the critical and pluralistic fashion we advocate here, you might expand and refine your analytical skills in dealing with ethical issues and problems.

Psychological factors

Psychological factors are concerned with cognitive processes, in other words, how people actually think. From an ethical decision-making point of view, knowing about the differences in the cognitive processes of individuals can clearly help us to improve our understanding of how people decide what is the morally right or wrong course of action. We shall look at two of the most prominent psychological factors: cognitive moral development and locus of control.

Cognitive moral development

Cognitive moral development
A theory explaining the different levels of moral reasoning that an individual can apply to ethical issues and problems, depending on their cognitive capacity.

The most common theory to have been utilized to explain these cognitive processes comes from the psychology discipline, namely Lawrence Kohlberg's (1969) theory of **cognitive moral development** (CMD). Kohlberg developed CMD theory to explain the different reasoning processes that individuals would use to make ethical judgements as they matured through childhood into adulthood. He suggested that three broad levels of moral development could be discerned, namely:

- **Level one**. The individual exhibits a concern with self-interest and external rewards and punishments.

- **Level two**. The individual does what is expected of them by others.

- **Level three**. The individual is developing more autonomous decision-making based on principles of rights and justice rather than external influences.

Kohlberg identified two specific stages within each of the three levels, giving six stages of moral development altogether. **Figure 4.4** sets out these six stages, providing an illustration of how each stage might be manifested in business ethics decisions.

CMD theory proposes that as one advances through the different stages, one is moving to a 'higher' level of moral reasoning. The important thing to remember about CMD theory, however, is that it is not so much *what* is decided that is at issue, but *how* the decision is reached in terms of the individual's reasoning process. Two people at different levels could conceivably make the same decision, but as a result of different ways of thinking. All the same, Kohlberg argued that the higher the stage of moral reasoning, the more 'ethical' the decision.

Empirical research by Kohlberg and others[4] has led to the conclusion that most people tend to think with level II reasoning (hence its 'conventional' tag). Research into the cognitive schema of business managers has also tended to place them at level II (e.g. Weber 1990). This means that most of us decide what is right according to *what we perceive others to believe*, and according to *what is expected of us by others*. As Treviño and Nelson (2014: 82) suggest, '[Most] individuals aren't autonomous decision-makers who strictly follow an internal moral compass. They look up and around to see what their superiors and their peers are doing and saying, and they use these cues as a guide to action.'

As we shall see shortly, this implies that the situational context in which employees might find themselves within their organization is likely to be very influential in shaping their ethical decision-making—although according to Kohlberg, this influence will vary according to whether employees are at sub-stage 3 or 4 in moral development.

Although CMD theory has been very influential in the ethical decision-making literature, there have been numerous criticisms of the theory. It is worth remembering that the theory was initially developed in a non-business context, from interviews with

Level	Stage	Explanation	Illustration
I Preconventional	1 Obedience and punishment	Individuals define right and wrong according to expected rewards and punishments from authority figures.	Whilst this type of moral reasoning is usually associated with small children, we can also see that businesspeople frequently make unethical decisions because they think their company would either reward it or let it go unpunished (Treviño and Brown 2004).
	2 Instrumental purpose and exchange	Individuals are concerned with their own immediate interests and define right according to whether there is fairness in the exchanges or deals they make to achieve those interests.	An employee might cover for the absence of a co-worker so that their own absences might subsequently be covered for in return – a 'you scratch my back, I'll scratch yours' reciprocity (Treviño and Nelson 2014: 78).
II Conventional	3 Interpersonal accord, conformity and mutual expectations	Individuals live up to what is expected of them by their immediate peers and those close to them.	An employee might decide that using company resources such as the telephone, the internet and email for personal use whilst at work is acceptable because everyone else in their office does it.
	4 Social accord and system maintenance	Individuals' consideration of the expectations of others broadens to social accord more generally, rather than just the specific people around them.	A factory manager may decide to provide employee benefits and salaries above the industry minimum in order to ensure that employees receive wages and conditions deemed acceptable by consumers, pressure groups or other social groups.
III Post-conventional	5 Social contract and individual rights	Individuals go beyond identifying with others' expectations, and assess right and wrong according to the upholding of basic rights, values and contracts of society.	The public affairs manager of a food manufacturer may decide to reveal which of the firm's products contain genetically modified ingredients out of respect for consumers' rights to know, even though she is not obliged to by law, and has not been pressurized into doing so by consumers or anyone else.
	6 Universal ethical principles	Individuals will make decisions autonomously based on self-chosen universal ethical principles, such as justice, equality, and rights, which they believe everyone should follow.	A purchasing manager may decide that it would be wrong to continue to buy products or ingredients that were tested on animals because he believes this does not respect animal rights to be free from suffering.

Figure 4.4 Stages of cognitive moral development
Source: Adapted from Ferrell et al. (2014); Kohlberg (1969); Treviño and Nelson (2014).

young American males—hardly representative of the vast range of people in business across the globe! Hence, according to Fraedrich et al. (1994), the most notable criticisms of CMD are the following:

- **Gender bias**. Perhaps the most well known of Kohlberg's critics is one of his former students, Carol Gilligan, who claimed that the theory was gender biased due to its emphasis on the abstract principles esteemed by Kohlberg and his male subjects. As we saw in Chapter 3, Gilligan (1982) argued that women tended to employ an 'ethic of care' in deciding what was morally right, emphasizing empathy, harmony, and the maintenance of interdependent relationships, rather than abstract principles.

- **Implicit value judgements**. Derry (1987) and others have expanded Gilligan's criticism to suggest that CMD privileges rights and justice above numerous other bases of morality, such as those discussed in Chapter 3. Kohlberg has thus interjected his own value judgements regarding the 'most ethical' way of reasoning into what is essentially supposed to be a descriptive theory of how people *actually* think.

- **Invariance of stages**. Kohlberg's contention that we sequentially pass through discrete stages of moral development can be criticized if we observe that people either regress in CMD or, more importantly, if they use different moral reasoning strategies at different times and in different situations. Studies by Fraedrich and Ferrell (1992) and Weber (1990), for example, both revealed cognitive inconsistency amongst managers across work and non-work situations when making ethical decisions. Essentially, we do not always use the same reasoning when we are at work as we do at home or on the sports field. This is the reason why in this chapter we highlight the context dependency of business people's reasoning about ethical problems.

Despite these criticisms, CMD appears to be widely accepted as an important element in the individual influences on ethical decision-making. Various empirical studies have suggested that it at least plays some role in the decision-making process (e.g. Treviño and Youngblood 1990; Goolsby and Hunt 1992), although its influence appears to be rather more limited than that proposed by Kohlberg.

Locus of control

The second psychological factor commonly identified as an influence on ethical thinking is *locus of control*.

> An individual's locus of control determines the extent to which he or she believes that they have control over the events in their life.

So someone with a high *internal* locus of control believes that the events in their life can be shaped by their own efforts, whereas someone with a high *external* locus of control believes that events tend to be the result of the actions of others, or luck, or fate. You might think of this in terms of how you might respond if you received a grade for your business ethics exam that was lower than you expected. If you had an external locus of control, you might automatically blame your professor for setting a difficult test, or you might blame Crane and Matten's book for not preparing you properly. If you had an internal locus of control, however, your first thoughts would probably be more along the lines of questioning whether you had really done enough preparation for the exam.

In terms of ethical decision-making, Treviño and Nelson (2014) suggest that those with a strong internal locus of control might be expected to be more likely to consider the consequences of their actions for others, and may take more responsibility for their actions. Internals may also be more likely to stick to their own beliefs, and thus be more resistant to peer-group pressure to act in a way that violates those beliefs. However, there has not actually been a great deal of empirical research on the effects of locus of control on ethical decision-making in business. What research has been conducted, though, gives a generally mixed picture: while some studies have discerned no significant effect (e.g. Singhapakdi and Vitell 1990), others have identified a noticeable influence (e.g. Chiu 2003).

Overall, even among the individual factors, it would appear that locus of control has, at most, only a relatively limited effect on ethical decision-making. Nonetheless, understanding whether your co-workers have internal or external loci of control can be important for predicting how they will respond to business ethics problems, and particularly how they apportion blame or offer approbation when faced with the consequences of those decisions.

Ultimately, factors such as demographics, experience, psychological factors, and other personality factors can only ever tell us so much about ethical decision-making, perhaps because they only have a relatively indirect effect on how we might actually decide in any given situation. A more immediate relationship to decision-making is perhaps provided by our next three individual factors—values, integrity, and moral imagination.

Personal values

Conventionally speaking, **personal values** might be regarded as 'the moral principles or accepted standards of a person'.[5] This makes sense superficially, but such a view does not capture what is distinctive about values and sets them apart from, say, principles or standards. Sociologists, psychologists, philosophers, and others have therefore invested a great deal of work in defining, identifying, and even measuring the values that we have, giving rise to a diverse and multifaceted literature. Probably the most frequently cited definition from a psychological point of view comes from Milton Rokeach (1973: 5) who stated that a personal value is an 'enduring belief that a specific mode of conduct or end-state of existence is personally or socially preferable to an opposite or converse mode of conduct or end-state'.

This means that values are about the behaviours and things that we deem important in life, but crucially, Rokeach identifies that values (i) persist over time (i.e. they are 'enduring'); (ii) influence behaviour (i.e. they are concerned with 'conduct' and 'end-states'); and (iii) are concerned with individual and/or collective well-being (i.e. 'personally or socially preferable'). Hence, common values include examples such as self-respect, freedom, equality, responsibility, and honesty.

Personal values have long been argued to be influential in the type of decisions we make in organizations (Agle and Caldwell 1999). This is particularly true of ethical decisions since values are key repositories of what we regard to be good/bad and right/wrong. For example, it has been shown that the values of executives influence the extent to which they will encourage CSR initiatives in their companies (Chin et al. 2013; Hemingway 2013). However, knowing that values are important influences is one thing, but finding out exactly what values people have, and which ones influence which decisions, is fraught with difficulty and represents a tricky conceptual and empirical

Personal values
Individual beliefs about desirable behaviours and goals that are stable over time and which influence decision-making.

endeavour (Meglino and Ravlin 1998). After all, researchers such as Rokeach (1973) have suggested that people typically have more than 70 operative values, and even amongst these, some values will be more influential on behaviour than others. Moreover, there is a great deal of disagreement among researchers even over whether values can be relied upon to predict behaviour or whether environmental influences should be given greater emphasis (Meglino and Ravlin 1998). Researchers have also found that although individuals may espouse certain values, they also have a number of unconscious biases that shape their decision-making (Banaji et al. 2003). That is, although most people might consciously abhor racism or sexism, many of us actually make racist or sexist decisions without even knowing it. As Banaji et al. (2003) conclude, it turns out that most of us are not nearly as ethical as we think we are!

Whatever the case, values are clearly an important aspect of ethical decision-making, and corporations are increasingly recognizing that they cannot simply ignore their employees' personal values in tackling ethical problems in their business. PIC, the biotechnology multinational whose business 'is the genetic improvement of pigs', puts it this way: 'personal values describe the way we operate as individuals—we expect them to guide the decisions and behaviour of our employees around the world'. The company has identified three personal values—integrity, respect, and innovation—that its employees should possess, stressing that 'we are honest and ethical in all aspects of our business'.[6]

This kind of attention to values has been particularly evident at the level of corporate or *organizational values*. Many companies have attempted to set out what values their organization has or stands for and, as we will see in Chapter 5, values statements, and codes of conduct based on core organizational values have probably been the most common approaches to managing business ethics over the years. Perhaps unsurprisingly, an alignment of personal and organizational values is typically seen as an ideal basis for developing good working relations and for retaining and motivating staff (Posner 2010). However, it is unclear whether such a situation is necessarily better for encouraging ethical decision-making. For example, employees in professions such as education, medicine, pharmacy, accountancy, and journalism might see dangers in aligning their professional ethics with the increasingly market-oriented values of their organizations. As such, employees are often called upon to exercise personal integrity in the face of such ethical challenges.

Personal integrity

Personal integrity
An individual's adherence to a consistent set of moral principles or values.

Integrity is typically seen as one of the most important characteristics of an ethical person, or, as we saw in Chapter 3, of a 'virtuous' decision-maker. As such, it is no surprise that **personal integrity** has increasingly surfaced in relation to ethical decision-making. Although a variety of meanings are applied to integrity, the most common meaning refers to integrity as *consistency* (Brown 2005: 5).

The original meaning of the word 'integrity' is concerned with unity and wholeness, and we can see that an adherence to moral principles essentially means that one maintains a consistency or unity in one's beliefs and actions, regardless of any inducement or temptation to deviate from them. Another way of looking at this is to consider integrity as being a matter of 'walking the talk', i.e. being consistent in word and action (Brown 2005). An interesting example of how some students and businesses have tackled this issue is in signing some kind of integrity pledge, as discussed in **Ethics Online 4**.

ETHICS ONLINE 4

Ethics pledges

Making career choices can be hard when you want to make a difference. What if a potential employer seems to be offering you a great position but you are not convinced that it shares your values? One way that prospective business graduates have been addressing this problem is by making an ethics pledge, a phenomenon that has increasingly spread across the web.

Emanating originally in 1987 from Humboldt State University in the US, the Graduation Pledge of Social and Environmental Responsibility is probably the oldest and best-known business student pledge. It is based around a simple commitment 'to explore and take into account the social and environmental consequences of any job' that signers might consider, and commits signers 'to try to improve these aspects of any organizations for which [they] work'. Individuals can sign up online, and the initiative's website enables potential organizers to learn about how to organize on-campus campaigns, and to download posters, wallet cards, and other resources (see illustration).

More than a hundred schools and colleges are using the graduation pledge, but other initiatives have also emerged, including the MBA Oath out of Harvard Business School which has garnered a great deal of media attention. The initiative involves a more substantial set of commitments than the graduation pledge, but despite this it has attracted more than 6,000 signatories, all of which are listed on its website. The initiative has also spawned a book and a partner project, The Oath Project, aimed at broader professionalization of management based on integrity and social responsibility.

While these initiatives are mostly for academic institutions and their students, there is an emerging movement of such pledges for business leaders too. A good example is the Business Ethics Pledge, which begins: 'I pledge allegiance, in my heart and soul, to

the concepts of honesty, integrity, and quality in business'. Pledges like this are typically voluntary, and may, like the Business Ethics Pledge, even be used for marketing purposes. However, the Netherlands recently took the unprecedented step of legally requiring all Dutch bankers to swear an oath regarding ethical behaviour, and to do their 'utmost to maintain and promote confidence in the financial-services industry'.

Those who subscribe to such initiatives clearly believe in the importance of personal integrity and of the power of individuals to make a difference. As the Business Ethics Pledge founder, Shel Horowitz, says, 'This is about changing the world! About creating a climate where businesses are expected to behave ethically, and where executives who try to drag their companies into the unethical swamplands find that nobody's willing to carry out their orders.' Rakesh Khurana and Nitin Nohria from Harvard's Oath Project argue that such an oath is nothing short of the equivalent for business what the Hippocratic oath has been to the medical profession for hundreds of years.

The actual effect of pledges, however, is contested. As Dan Ariely (2012: 39–44) has found in his empirical experiments with students, just signing an honour code has no long-term positive effect on ethical behaviour. However, if recalling an oath acts as an 'ethical reminder' immediately prior to facing a moral decision, it does typically have a positive effect on ethical behaviour. This suggests that ethics pledges will not be effective unless they become embedded and visible in an organization on an ongoing basis.

Sources

Ariely, D. 2012. *The (honest) truth about dishonesty*. New York: HarperCollins.
van Gaal, M. 2014. Dutch Bankers Swear to God as Trust in Lenders Slumps. *Bloomberg News*,
    6 February 2014.
Business Ethics Pledge website: http://www.business-ethics-pledge.org.
Graduation Pledge Alliance website: http://www.graduationpledge.org.
The MBA Oath website: http://mbaoath.org,http://theoathproject.org.

> ## ☑ Skill check
>
> **Implementing ethics pledges**. This is a key skill to develop because ethics pledges, when implemented effectively, can be useful tools to raise the awareness of basic ethical rules and moral values in a profession or in an organization.

Whistleblowing
Intentional acts by employees to expose, either internally or externally, perceived ethical or legal violations by their organization.

Integrity frequently plays a central role in incidents of **whistleblowing**, which refers to acts by employees to expose their employers for perceived ethical violations. If, for instance, an engineer identifies a safety problem with one of their firm's products, they may decide to tell their work colleagues or their boss. As a result, the engineer may be encouraged to ignore the problem or desist from taking any further action as their superiors have taken on responsibility for the issue. However, if the problem persists, even after further warnings from the engineer, they may choose to reveal the problem—or 'blow the whistle'—by approaching an industry regulator, a journalist, or some other outside agency.

Although there are clearly various other factors involved, such acts of external whistleblowing often require the employee to maintain their personal integrity or commitment to a set of principles despite being confronted with numerous difficulties, obstacles, and opposition. This is because the organizational context within which individuals elect to blow the whistle can act as a powerful force in suppressing personal integrity in favour of the priorities and goals of the organization. Also, whistleblowers are often faced with a range of negative consequences for their actions. This includes victimization by colleagues or superiors as a result of their 'betrayal'; being passed over for promotion; job loss; even 'blacklisting' to prevent them getting another job in the same field (Rothschild and Miethe 1999).

Figure 4.5 provides some prominent examples of whistleblowers. It is worth noting that some of the more spectacular cases have occurred in governmental organizations, reiterating the relevance for business ethics in other sectors of society beyond public companies.

Acts of ethical decision-making like these, especially where the consequences for the individual are so severe, are clearly driven by a considerable degree of personal integrity on the part of the whistleblower. But even more commonplace ethical violations, which have much less potential downside, require significant adherence to a set of principles in order for people to report on them. Think, for example, of a situation where all of your work colleagues habitually steal small items of company property from the storeroom. A group can easily see this as acceptable simply because everyone does it. If this was something that you thought was wrong, it might require some degree of integrity—that is, adherence to your moral principles—to register your disapproval with your colleagues, and it may need some courage to report it to a superior whose reaction you cannot easily predict.

The exercising of integrity therefore often requires some level of protection from possible recrimination. For example, in some countries, regulators have sought to provide legal protection for whistleblowers. In the US, Sarbanes–Oxley regulations require companies listed on US stock exchanges to adopt methods for anonymous reporting of ethical and legal violations to an audit committee of the board of directors. In Europe, companies listed in the US are also covered by this legislation, but overall the picture is somewhat confused, especially since some US companies found that their global whistle-blower procedures actually contravened EU data protection law! While in some countries there is an institutional structure that facilitates free disclosure by employees (e.g. 'openness laws' in Sweden, and works councils in Germany), others, such as Norway, Romania, and the UK, have specific whistleblower protection laws.

Despite increasing attention to the importance of the issue of integrity, especially in the context of ethical leadership (e.g. Bauman 2013), most descriptive models of ethical decision-making have not tended to include it as a factor influencing how we decide in business ethics matters. While it would appear that this might be likely to change as we start to learn more about its role and effects, for the moment business ethics scholars seem to be somewhat uncertain as to how and why personal integrity affects the process of ethical decision-making.

Moral imagination

Finally, another individual factor that has been accorded increasing attention in business ethics over the past few years is moral imagination. Moral imagination is concerned less with whether one has, or sticks to, a set of moral values, but more with whether one has 'a sense of the variety of possibilities and moral consequences of their decisions, the ability to imagine a wide range of possible issues, consequences, and solutions' (Werhane 1998: 76). This means that moral imagination is the creativity with which an individual is able to reflect about an ethical dilemma.

Interest in moral imagination has been driven by the recognition that people often disregard their personal moralities and moral considerations while at work (Jackall 1988). According to Werhane (1998), higher levels of moral imagination can allow us to see beyond the rules of the game that seem to be operating in the workplace, and beyond the day-to-day supposed 'realities' of organizational life, so as to question prevailing ways of framing and addressing organizational problems. Thus, rather than accepting the usual organizational recipe for looking at, prioritizing, and dealing with things, those with greater moral imagination should be able to envisage a greater set of moral problems, perspectives, and outcomes.

☑ Skill check

Cultivating moral imagination. This is a key skill as it enables you to think 'outside the box' in relation to ethical problems and provides a richer choice of moral perspectives, options, and outcomes.

As with personal integrity, moral imagination has yet to be included in typical models of ethical decision-making, but it is gradually being subjected to empirical testing. For example, Godwin (2012) found that individuals who exercised moral imagination were more likely to generate mutually beneficial outcomes for business and society than those who did not. More broadly though, moral imagination also holds significant potential

Name and year	Context	Consequences	
		Short term	Long term
Daniel Ellsberg 1971	As a military analyst at the **RAND Corporation** he leaked classified documents about the Vietnam War from the US Ministry of Defense to the *New York Times* (the 'Pentagon Papers'); these revealed that the US government did not believe it could win the war despite still publicly defending it.	• Court case with the threat of 115 years in prison (dismissed) • Wiretapping, break-in at his psychiatrist's office to obtain his mental health records	• Life-long civil rights campaigner • Numerous awards • Movies: *The Pentagon Papers, The Most Dangerous Man in America*
Christoph Meili 1997	Working as a night guard at **UBS** in Zurich, he discovered the shredding of records about assets of Jews (and others) who died in Nazi Germany; leaked them to a Jewish organization which handed them to the Swiss police.	• Was investigated for breaking Swiss bank secrecy laws • After death threats left Switzerland • Received political asylum in the US	• Supported by Jewish organization to get a college education • Volatile personal life, incl. divorce from his wife • 2009 return to Switzerland; unconfirmed reports of homelessness
Harry Markopolos 2000–2005	As a portfolio manager with a Boston investment firm, he discovered that competitor **Bernard Madoff's** financial statements were fraudulent and that Madoff was operating a 'ponzi scheme'; filed three reports to the SEC over five years.	• His filings were ignored by the SEC	• Upon breaking of the Madoff scandal became popular on TV (e.g. *60 Minutes*) • Testified before US Congress • Documentary movie *No One Would Listen*
Sherron Watkins 2001	Alerted **Enron** CEO Ken Lay about accounting irregularities; went public with it five months later.	• Initially no reaction	• Testified before US Congress • 'Person of the Year 2001' by *TIME* magazine

Figure 4.5 Famous whistleblower cases

Chelsea Manning (formerly Bradley Manning) 2010	US Army intelligence analyst who leaked thousands of secret diplomatic cables incl. top secret video footage of US soldiers committing potential war crimes in Iraq. WikiLeaks eventually published the material.	• Revealed his identity to a chat partner, who reported him to the FBI • Arrested and spent one year in solitary confinement in a US military prison • Sentenced to 35 years in prison • Announced gender transition on day of sentencing
Michael Woodford 2011	Upon being promoted to CEO of the Japanese electronics manufacturer **Olympus** discovered and subsequently exposed fraudulent transactions of around $1 billion.	• Two weeks after being appointed he was fired as CEO • Due to fear for his life he left Japan for the UK • Was paid $17 million in an out-of-court settlement by Olympus • Numerous awards, incl. Businessman of the Year • Consulting and charity work
Edward Snowden 2013	Working for **Booz Allen Hamilton** as a contractor of the US **National Security Agency** Snowden released thousands of classified documents to the newspapers the *Guardian* and *The Washington Post*. The material exposed mass surveillance and intelligence gathering by the US and other governments.	• Quit his job and travelled to Hong Kong prior to releasing the documents • Fled to Russia • Charged under the US Espionage Act • Remains indefinitely in asylum in Russia at an undisclosed location • Numerous international awards and honours, incl. for the newspapers and journalists that published the material (e.g. Pulitzer Prize)

Figure 4.5 Continued

for helping us to uncover why some people are more likely to just follow the herd in relation to ethical issues while others are able to think about different alternatives and perspectives. This is a vital issue if we are to understand the relative influence of our two sets of factors, individual and situational. Hence, it would seem timely now to consider in more depth the second of our sets of factors, namely those dealing with the situation in which the decision is taking place.

> ☑ **Skill check**
>
> **Analysing individual influences on ethical decision-making**. This is a key skill because it helps you to assess the reasons why some individuals are more or less inclined to decide ethically based on their specific individual characteristics.

■ Situational influences on decision-making

The preceding section sought to examine the influence of various differences between individuals on the decisions they make when faced with ethical problems. However, as we saw, these decisions, and perhaps more importantly, the things people in business actually do, cannot be successfully explained simply in terms of such individual traits. After all, many people appear to have 'multiple ethical selves' (Treviño and Nelson 2014: 252)—that is, they make different decisions in different situations. In fact, most evidence we have points to situational influences being at least equally important, and probably *more* important, in shaping our ethical decision-making. **Ethics in Action 4.1** discusses the case of the 'rogue trader', Kweku Adoboli, who ran up huge losses at the Swiss bank UBS through covert trading activities in the financial market—and shows that even here, individual factors are not always the whole story.

There are a number of important factors to consider regarding situational influences. For a start, the decision process we go through will vary greatly according to what type of issue it is that we are dealing with. Some issues will be perceived as relatively unimportant, and will therefore prompt us into fairly limited ethical decision-making, whereas issues seen as more intense may well necessitate deeper, and perhaps somewhat different, moral reflection. For example, if you worked in a bar, you might think rather more deeply about the morality of taking €20 out of the cash register for yourself than you would pouring your friends a couple of unauthorized drinks 'on the house'. These differences in the importance we attach to ethical issues are what we call *issue-related factors*.

At another level, we must also remember that we are, after all, 'social animals'. Hence our beliefs and actions are largely shaped by what we see around us: the group norms, expectations, and roles we are faced with; the nature of the climate in which we work; and the rewards and punishments that we can expect as a consequence of our actions. After all, we have already seen that Kohlberg's theory of cognitive moral development suggests that the majority of us are at a conventional level of morality, which prompts us to seek guidance from those around us. These types of influences are called *context-related factors*.

Type of factor	Factor	Influence on ethical decision-making
Issue-related	Moral intensity	Evidence suggests significant effect on ethical decision-making.
	Moral framing	Most studies show strong influence on some aspects of the ethical decision-making process, most notably moral awareness.
Context-related	Rewards	Strong evidence of relationship between rewards/punishments and ethical behaviour, although other stages in ethical decision-making have been less investigated.
	Authority	Good general support for a significant influence from immediate superiors and top management on ethical decision-making of subordinates.
	Bureaucracy	Significant influence on ethical decision-making well documented, but actually exposed to only limited empirical research. Hence, specific consequences for ethical decision-making remain contested.
	Work roles	Some influence likely, but lack of empirical evidence to date.
	Organizational culture	Strong overall influence, although implications of relationship between culture and ethical decision-making remain contested.
	National context	Limited empirical investigation, but evidence suggests a clear influence at least for some types of decision.

Figure 4.6 Situational influences on ethical decision-making

Accordingly, we can identify two main types of situational influences:

- Issue-related factors.
- Context-related factors.

The principal factors in these two categories, and their likely influence on ethical decision-making, are presented in **Figure 4.6** and are discussed in more detail in the following sections.

Issue-related factors

Although initially absent from many models of ethical decision-making, issue-related factors have been increasingly recognized as important influences on the decisions business people make when faced with ethical problems. At one level, we need to consider the nature of the ethical issue itself, and in particular its degree of *moral intensity*—that is, how important the issue is to the decision-maker. However, it is also evident that, regardless of the intensity of an issue, we need also to consider how that issue is actually represented within the organization, in that some issues will be presented as important ethical issues while others may not. Hence, we need to also consider the issue's *moral framing*. Such issue-related factors have been shown to influence both whether an

VISIT THE
ONLINE
RESOURCE
CENTRE
for links to
useful sources
of further
information

ETHICS IN ACTION 4.1

Rogue trader, latest edition

Shortly after graduating, Kweku Adoboli landed his dream job as an analyst at UBS, the Swiss-based global financial services company. Money, excitement, and fame were waiting for him—though he could not have imagined just how spectacularly famous he would become just five years later. By 2011, Adoboli was front-page news across the world and had earned himself the now familiar epithet of a 'rogue trader' having accumulated $2.3 billion in losses for his employer due to 'unauthorized trading' in the firm's London investment banking division. This gave Adoboli the dubious honour of a position at number 3 in the all time Rogue Trader Top 10, well behind Jérôme Kerviel at number 1 (with nearly $7 billion in losses), but close to Yasuo Hamanaka at number 2 ($2.6 billion) and well in front of Nick Leeson at number 4 ($1.3 billion).

As soon as the story broke about Adoboli's exploits, intense media speculation started focusing on the derivatives trader at the heart of the scandal. Surely, a person capable of such exceptional crimes must be an exceptionally evil person! This narrative of the 'rogue trader' in the media is a seductive one in making sense of events like those at UBS. A lone trader going off the rails, committing fraud to make himself rich—what could be a simpler explanation? But as with Kerviel, Leeson and others before him, Adoboli does not appear to have been seeking to profit directly from the unauthorized trades (although clearly he would benefit indirectly in terms of a higher bonus if the gamble paid off). In reality it was more a case of taking an illegal route to try and make *the firm* more money.

Adoboli also hardly fitted the stereotype of the evil genius that many will picture when thinking of a rogue trader. By all accounts the young Ghanaian-born trader was pretty unremarkable. He liked art and photography. He was said to be 'very polite', 'very loyal' to his employers, a 'really nice guy' according to the neighbours. Even his former landlord spoke highly of him. He went to private school and graduated from a respectable university (full disclosure: actually he studied at the University of Nottingham and graduated whilst Crane and Matten were teaching there—but he did not, we might add, attend our ethics class).

Still, the damage wrought by Adoboli's deeds was serious. UBS's share price dropped by 10% after the losses were reported, and with almost the entire quarterly earnings of the firm wiped out, the bank reportedly accelerated a major restructuring of its business, involving thousands of job losses. Clearly, a good share of the blame for UBS's losses rests on the person who cooked the books to keep his spiralling losses secret. In 2012, Adoboli was sentenced to seven years in prison, which he is currently serving on Verne Island off the English south coast.

But this is not the entire story. UBS was fined £29.7 million by the British Financial Services Authority for failure to control Adoboli. It was the view of the regulator that UBS itself certainly has to take a large proportion of the responsibility. After all, what kind of financial institution does not realize that one of its employees is taking such wildly speculative positions and then cooking the books to hide it? Adoboli appears to have made unauthorized trades at least since since 2008. In the end it was the trader himself who blew the whistle on his activities, not those who were responsible for exercising financial control. Internal and external auditing, back-office controls, risk management, compliance—organizations like UBS have all kinds of systems in place to stop this sort of thing happening.

The rating agency Moody's also pointed at 'ongoing weaknesses' in the bank's risk management. 'We have continued to express concerns with regards to the ability of management to develop a robust risk culture and effective control framework,' the agency said in the aftermath the initial disclosures. But this was hardly news for a bank like UBS that lost $37 billion in the sub-prime mortgage crisis and had to be bailed out by Swiss taxpayers.

Myret Zaki, the author of a best-selling book on the bank, presented the situation as 'a never-ending story repeating itself'. 'I'm not surprised at all about this,' she told the UK newspaper the *Telegraph*.

[UBS CEO] Oswald Grübel kept advocating an increase in risk-taking. When you have a CEO talking like that, you are not in a climate where you feel restricted as a trader. He was on the side of continuing to make money on the markets, even though wealth management was employing 30% fewer staff for double the profitability.

Others, such as Richard Abbey, the senior managing director of financial investigations at Kroll, pointed to UBS's earlier downsizing as a factor: 'It's no coincidence that after downsizing and lay-offs these type of losses are more common. There may not be enough people to physically control checks and balances. It may be institutions are too reliant on computer controls and they are the easiest to bypass'. In many respects then this was a time bomb waiting to go off—with Adoboli as much the symptom as the cause. Some argued it was more a case of 'rogue bank' rather than 'rogue trader'.

Taking a broader perspective on the scandal, it is also important to look beyond Adoboli and UBS. As with the recent financial crisis, there is also the deeper-rooted problem of the financial services industry as a whole. According to the *Telegraph*, 'unauthorized' trading could be considerably more widespread than the occasional huge rogue trader incident suggests: 'experts and insiders warn the amount of risky unauthorised trading is difficult to quantify and often not brought to the public eye unless losses are huge enough to be announced'. The paper went on to quote a 'senior trader' at a London bank: 'People are fired every year for having stuff on their book that they shouldn't. All the banks tend to know what has happened and why someone has left, but it doesn't get publicised. It's usually only a couple of million bucks.' So while Adoboli may be number 3 in the rogue trader top ten, we never even get to hear about all those entries lower down the charts. Jérôme Kerviel, who is still there at the top of the list, has suggested that companies like Société Générale, his then employer, may even tacitly endorse such trades as long as they are making the bank money. It is only when they start registering huge losses that the controls really kick in. As even the *Wall Street Journal* quipped at the time: 'what do you call a "rogue" trader who makes $2 billion? A Managing Director!'

These may of course be little more than jokes, rumours and groundless accusations. But clearly the financial services industry has a major task ahead of it to clean up its reputation and regain the trust of its stakeholders, which the events at UBS made that much harder. All of this suggests that with Adoboli, we did not just have another rogue trader on our hands but, according to some, maybe even a rogue industry.

Sources

Anon 2011. Rogue trader: Kweku Adoboli was a 'nice guy', says former landlord. *Telegraph*, 15 September 2011.

BBC News 2011. UBS 'rogue trader': Loss estimate raised to $2.3bn. *BBC News*, 18 September 2011.

Hodges, J. 2013. Adoboli Loses Bid to Appeal Unauthorized Trading Sentence. *Bloomberg News*, 30 July 2013.

Mason, R., Armitstead, L., and Wilson, H. 2011. 'Rogue trader' losses engulf UBS. *Telegraph*, 17 September 2011.

Weidner, D. 2011. What Do You Call A 'Rogue' Trader Who Makes $2 Billion? A Managing Director. *Wall Street Journal*, 15 September 2011.

VISIT THE ONLINE RESOURCE CENTRE for a short response to this feature

? THINK THEORY

Think about the Adoboli case in terms of the individual factors set out in models of ethical decision-making. How important do you think these are for explaining his actions, and which other factors might also be at play here?

individual actually recognizes the moral nature of a problem in the first place (i.e. the moral recognition stage) and also the way that people actually think about and act upon the problem (the subsequent stages in the ethical decision-making process).

Moral intensity

The notion of moral intensity was initially proposed by Thomas Jones (1991) as a way of expanding ethical decision-making models to incorporate the idea that the relative importance of the ethical issue would itself have some bearing on the process that decision-makers go through when faced with ethical problems. Jones (1991: 374–8) proposes that the intensity of an issue will vary according to six factors:

• **Magnitude of consequences**. This is the expected sum of the harms (or benefits) for those impacted by the problem or action. Obviously, an issue will be felt more intensely if the consequences are significant, such as health problems or death as a result of a faulty product.

• **Social consensus**. This is the degree to which people are in agreement over the ethics of the problem or action. Moral intensity is likely to increase when it is certain that an act will be deemed unethical by others.

- **Probability of effect**. This refers to the likelihood that the harms (or benefits) are actually going to happen.

- **Temporal immediacy**. This is concerned with the speed with which the consequences are likely to occur. When outcomes are likely to take years to have much effect, decision-makers may perceive the moral intensity to be much lower—for example in the case of the long-term effects of smoking or other 'unhealthy' products.

- **Proximity**. This factor deals with the feeling of nearness (social, cultural, psychological, or physical) the decision-maker has for those impacted by their decision. For example, poor working conditions in one's own country might be experienced as a more intense moral issue than poor conditions in a far away country.

- **Concentration of effect**. Here we are concerned with the extent to which the consequences of the action are concentrated heavily on a few or lightly on many. For example, many people may feel that cheating a person out of €100 is much more morally intense than cheating the same sum out of a large multinational with millions of shareholders.

Jones' (1991) original formulation of moral intensity is theoretical (based largely on social psychology), but we can see its relevance in real cases of business ethics. Consider the collapse of the Rana Plaza garment factory building in Bangladesh in 2013. The social consensus around 'sweatshop' labour conditions already gave the issue a relatively high degree of intensity, but the factory collapse brought unprecedented global attention because of the magnitude of the consequences (more than a thousand deaths), their temporal immediacy, and the concentration of effects (it all happened in one building). And even though the events happened in a country far away from Western consumers, the fact that major brand logos (such as Benetton, Joe Fresh, and Primark) appeared in the news, and online coverage of the accident gave the event a strong 'virtual' proximity. Boosted by those factors, the moral intensity of this event resulted in a comprehensive private industry agreement, the 'Accord on Fire and Building Safety in Bangladesh' which has been signed by more than 150 companies globally.[7]

Moral intensity's role in ethical decision-making has also been exposed to empirical testing, providing good support for Jones' original propositions. O'Fallon and Butterfield (2005), for example, reviewed 32 such studies and concluded that there was strong support for the influence of moral intensity on ethical decision-making, especially with respect to magnitude of consequences and social consensus. However, we would suggest that the intensity of an issue is not necessarily an objective, factual variable, but rather depends on how the issue and its intensity are understood and made meaningful within and around organizations. This is where moral framing comes in.

Moral framing

While it may be possible to determine the degree of intensity that a moral issue should have for decision-makers according to Jones' (1991) six variables, it is clear that people in different contexts are likely to perceive that intensity differently. The same problem or dilemma can be perceived very differently according to the way that the issue is framed. For example, imagine that a student talks about 'cutting and pasting some material from the internet' into their assignment. This may sound quite innocuous. But imagine that if instead the student says, 'I plagiarized something I found on the internet', or even,

'I stole someone's ideas and passed them off as my own'! This would give a very different impression, and would make us sense a deeper moral importance about the student's actions. The **moral framing** of an issue—i.e. the language used to expose or mask the ethical nature of the issue—is therefore a key influence on ethical decision-making.

Moral framing
The use of language to expose or mask the ethical nature of certain behaviours or decisions. It is mostly used to make an unethical action look more acceptable to oneself and/or third parties.

As we can see from the example above, probably the most important aspect of moral framing is the language in which moral issues are couched. This is because using moral language—whether negative terms such as stealing or cheating, or positive terms like fairness or honesty—is likely to prompt us to think about morality because the words are already associated with cognitive categories that consist of moral content. The problem is that many people in business are reluctant to ascribe moral terms to their work, even if acting for moral reasons or if their actions have obvious moral consequences. Bird and Waters (1989) describe this as *moral muteness*. In a widely cited research project based on interviews with managers, they found that groups of managers tend to reframe moral actions and motives, and talk instead of doing things for reasons of practicality, organizational interests, and economic good sense. According to Bird and Waters (1989), managers do this out of concerns regarding perceived threats to:

- **Harmony**. Managers believe that moral talk disturbs organizational harmony by provoking confrontation, recrimination, and finger-pointing.

- **Efficiency**. Managers feel that moral talk clouds issues, making decision-making more difficult, time consuming, and inflexible.

- **Image of power and effectiveness**. Managers believe that their own image will suffer since being associated with ethics is typically seen as idealistic and utopian, and lacking sufficient robustness for effective management.

These are very real concerns for people employed at all levels in companies, and the dangers not only of moral talk but of being seen as overly involved in business ethics can impact negatively on employees working in organizations where such issues are viewed with suspicion. Andrew Crane's (2001) study of managers involved in environmental programmes highlights some of these concerns and problems, suggesting that fears of being marginalized can lead managers to engage in a process of *amoralization*. That is, they seek to distance themselves and their projects from being defined as ethically motivated or ethical in nature, and instead build a picture of corporate rationality suffused with justifications of corporate self-interest. On the positive side, this means that managers may well be able to make what they see as morally good decisions, even ones driven by a strong set of personal values, providing they couch the decision in business terms (Watson 2003). On the flip side, the process of amoralization may mean that even ostensibly 'intense' ethical issues may be seen by co-workers and others as simply a business problem rather than a moral one.

Moral framing can also occur after a decision has been made or an act carried out. It is important therefore to look not just at what people decide, but how they then justify their decisions to themselves and others. Anand et al. (2004: 39) call these justifications *rationalization tactics*—namely 'mental strategies that allow employees (and others around them) to view their corrupt acts as justified'. They identify six such strategies— denial of responsibility, denial of injury, denial of victim, social weighting, appeal to higher loyalties, and the metaphor of the ledger—which are described and illustrated in **Figure 4.7**. People in organizations tend to use these rationalizations in order to neutralize regrets and negative associations of unethical practices.

Strategy	Description	Examples
Denial of responsibility	The actors engaged in corrupt behaviours perceive that they have no other choice than to participate in such activities.	'What can I do? My arm is being twisted.' 'It is none of my business what the corporation does in overseas bribery.'
Denial of injury	The actors are convinced that no one is harmed by their actions; hence the actions are not really corrupt.	'No one was really harmed.' 'It could have been worse.'
Denial of victim	The actors counter any blame for their actions by arguing that the violated party deserved whatever happened.	'They deserved it.' 'They chose to participate.'
Social weighting	The actors assume two practices that moderate the salience of corrupt behaviour: 1. Condemn the condemner; 2. Selective social comparison.	'You have no right to criticize us.' 'Others are worse than we are.'
Appeal to higher loyalties	The actors argue that their violation of norms is due to their attempt to realize a higher-order value.	'We answered to a more important cause.' 'I would not report it because of my loyalty to my boss.'
Metaphor of the ledger	The actors argue that they are entitled to indulge in deviant behaviours because of their accrued credits (time and effort) in their jobs.	'It's all right for me to use the internet for personal reasons at work. After all, I do work overtime.'

Figure 4.7 Rationalizing unethical behaviour

Source: Republished with permission of Academy of Management, from Anand, V., Ashforth, B.E., and Joshi, M. 2004. Business as usual: the acceptance and perpetuation of corruption in organizations. *Academy of Management Executive*, 18 (2): 39–53 (Table 1, p. 41); permission conveyed through Copyright Clearance Center, Inc.

Again, one of the most important factors abetting this type of rationalizing is euphemistic language, 'which enables individuals engaging in corruption to describe their acts in ways that make them appear inoffensive' (Anand et al. 2004: 47). The authors give the example of Nazi doctors working at Auschwitz referring to execution by lethal injection as 'euthanasia' or 'preventative medicine', but it is easy to see in contemporary corporate terms such as 'corporate restructuring' (i.e. massive lay-offs), and 'facilitation payments' (i.e. bribes) that euphemistic language is prevalent in everyday business practice. In fact, these sorts of framings easily become socialized within organizations over time, thereby creating a context that repeatedly shapes ethical decision-making, as we shall now see.

? THINK THEORY

Think about the theory of rationalizing tactics in the context of your own experience— can you recognize these having been used? Can you provide specific examples of the types of language that people have used to rationalize potentially unethical behaviour?

VISIT THE
ONLINE
RESOURCE
CENTRE
for a short
response to this
feature

ETHICS ON SCREEN 4

House of Cards

Deeply cynical about human beings as well as politics and almost gleeful in its portrayal of limitless ambition.

Joanne Ostrow, *The Denver Post*

The first seasons of the US TV series *House of Cards* broke new ground as it was one of the first high-quality series released not through a regular TV channel with weekly episodes but through the online platform Netflix, with all 12 episodes being streamed at once upon release. In a world where piracy and illegal streaming of movies and TV series is rampant this delivery model was based on giving viewers a better environment for avoiding unethical behaviour, as producer and lead actor Kevin Spacey put it: 'I think we have demonstrated that we've learned what the music industry didn't—give people what they want, when they want it, in the form they want it in, at a reasonable price, and they'll more likely pay for it rather than steal it.'

Adapted from the 1990s BBC series of the same title, *House of Cards* is set in contemporary Washington and relates the political ascent of Democratic majority whip Francis Underwood (initials 'FU', played by Kevin Spacey). Together with his wife Claire (Robin Wright), who runs an NGO, we see a fascinating picture of a professional couple plotting and scheming in a web of politics, business, and civil society in the largely amoral and ruthless pursuit of their own ambitions.

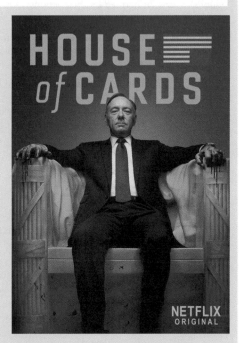

Media Rights Capital/The Kobal Collection

The world we are shown is full of conspirators, bullies, liars, bluffers, addicts, adulterers, and even murderers. In the case of Underwood all of these are even united

Context-related factors

Our second group of situational influences are context-related factors. By context, we mean the organizational context in which an employee will be working—especially the expectations and demands placed on them within the work environment that are likely to influence their perceptions of what is the morally right course of action to take. These factors appear to be especially important in shaping ethical decision-making within organizations. In **Ethics on Screen 4**, for example, the depiction of the amoral world of politics in the US capital in the TV series *House of Cards* is discussed in relation to the ethical decision-making of the main characters in the series. Just as importantly for the management of business ethics, these contextual factors are also, as we shall see, probably the main factors that can be addressed in order to *improve* ethical decision-making in the workplace.

in one character! In some ways, especially compared to its British original, this series is a vivid portrayal of how individual morality is shaped by national context: many moves and plots are driven by the rather masculine, short-term oriented North American culture and the specific nature and set-up of political institutions in Washington. Seeing Underwood and his wife working together though certainly provides little evidence of gender differences—only that when Claire threatens, curses, or insults, the chill in the viewer's spine is just that little more intense.

The Underwoods are a great example of how different levels of cognitive moral development can coexist in a person. While their engagement with the outside world is never transcending a conventional level, they have a rather sophisticated and developed sense of right and wrong when dealing with each other. Overall though, the show's most interesting angle is that it depicts the entire organizational environment in which political decisions are made in the US capital.

To begin with, the language in the series presents Underwood as a master of moral framing. One can easily Google numerous websites gathering the most famous quotes in which he provides the rationale for his dubious acts. For example, he sets up the downfall of one rival by deviously encouraging him to take the blame for Underwood's own actions. 'What a martyr craves more than anything is a sword to fall on', he suggests. 'So you sharpen the blade, hold it at the right angle, and then 3, 2, 1 . . .'. The influence of roles on ethical decision-making is also constantly explored as Underwood famously states in Season 1: 'After all, we are nothing more or less than what we choose to reveal. What I am to Claire [his wife] is not what I am to Zoe [his mistress], just as Zoe is not to me what she is to her father.'

All characters in the series follow an unwritten but powerful set of rules which highlight the corrupting influence of power and bureaucracy within the political game in Washington. Despite the apparent dubious morality, there are certain secondary, organizational virtues that no one can violate unpunished: 'The nature of promises,' Underwood explains just after being betrayed by the president's chief of staff, 'is that they remain immune to changing circumstances.' Accordingly, he seeks revenge for the disloyalty of the chief of staff after she renegades on a promise to promote him.

Overall, *House of Cards* is hugely entertaining, and from the perspective of ethical decision-making it is a rich showcase of the individual and situational factors that can influence—in this case mostly stifle—ethical decisions. The series, whose first season was aired in 2013, has won numerous awards and accolades, including four Emmies and one BAFTA.

Sources

Spacey, K. 2013. James MacTaggart Memorial Lecture, 2013 Guardian Edinburgh International Television Festival, http://www.theguardian.com/media/interactive/2013/aug/22/kevin-spacey-mactaggart-lecture-full-text.

http://www.netflix.com/houseofcards.

Systems of reward

We tend to take it for granted that people are likely to do what they are rewarded for—for example, many organizations offer commission or bonuses for salespeople in order to motivate them to achieve greater numbers of sales—yet it is easy to forget that this has implications for ethical conduct too. For example, if an organization rewards its salespeople for the number of sales they make, then those salespeople may be tempted to compromise ethical standards in their dealings with customers in order to earn more commission. This would particularly be the case if the organization did not appear to punish those salespeople who were seen to behave unethically towards their customers, for example by exaggerating a product's benefits or misleading customers about a competitor's products. Quite simply, ethical violations that go unpunished are likely to be repeated.

Similarly, adherence to ethical principles and standards stands less chance of being repeated and spread throughout a company when it goes unnoticed and unrewarded—or still worse, when it is actually punished, as we saw with the example of whistleblowing above. In fact, survey evidence suggests that something like one in five employees actually experiences some form of retaliation for reporting ethical misconduct—and as a result, around 40% who observe misconduct do not report it (Ethics Resource Center 2013). Sometimes, however, the effects of rewards and punishments may not even be direct; employees may sense the prevailing approach to business ethics in their organization by looking at who gets promoted and who does not, or who seems to get the favour of the boss and who does not, and interpret 'correct' behaviour from the experiences of their more or less fortunate colleagues.

There is considerable evidence to suggest that employees' ethical decision-making is indeed influenced by the systems of reward they see operating in the workplace. We have already seen in the previous section how Crane's (2001) research revealed that fears of marginalization and lack of progression could influence managers to avoid the explicit moral framing of problems and issues. Robert Jackall's (1988) extensive research into managers' rules for success in the workplace further reveals that what is regarded as 'right' in the workplace is often that which gets rewarded. For instance, he reports a former vice-president of a large firm saying: 'What is right in the corporation is not what is right in a man's home or in his church. *What is right in the corporation is what the guy above you wants from you.* That's what morality is in the corporation' (Jackall 1988: 6).

Tony Watson (1998) contends that managers are actually more likely to take a balanced approach, whereby pragmatic concerns and instrumental rewards are consciously interwoven with moral considerations in management decision-making. Survey work, however, has certainly tended to support a strong relationship between rewards and ethical behaviour, with the majority of studies revealing a significant correlation between rewards and sanctions and ethical and unethical behaviour (Craft 2013; Loe et al. 2000).

Authority

Authority
The exercise of hierarchical power to compel a subordinate to act in a certain way. It is a key factor in shaping ethical decisions because employees tend to follow the explicit and implicit preferences, orders, and rules of their superiors.

This leads us to also consider the issue of **authority**, which is the exercise of hierarchical power by managers on subordinates. People do not just do what gets rewarded, they do what they are told to do—or perhaps more correctly, what they *think* they are being told to do. Sometimes this can be a direct instruction from a superior to do something that the subordinate does not question because of their lower status in the hierarchy. At other times, the manager may not be directly instructing the employee to do something unethical; however, their instructions to the employee may appear to leave little option but to act in a questionable manner. For example, a university professor may ask their PhD student to grade 200 undergraduate exam scripts in two days, leaving the PhD student insufficient time to even read all of the scripts, let alone mark them competently. As a result, the student might resort to grading the scripts in an arbitrary and unfair way.

Managers can also have an influence over their subordinates' ethical behaviour by setting a good or bad example (Brown and Mitchell 2010; Mayer et al. 2013). Many of us tend to look up to our superiors to determine what passes for ethical behaviour in the workplace. Significantly, however, employees sometimes seem to perceive their superiors as lacking in ethical integrity. For example, a survey of government employees revealed that (Ethics Resource Center 2008: 9):

- Around 20% think top leadership is not held accountable for their own violations of ethics standards.

- About 25% believe that top leadership tolerates retaliation against those who report ethical misconduct.

- About 30% do not believe their leaders keep promises and commitments.

Clearly, those in authority can influence their employees' ethical decision-making simply by looking the other way when confronted with potential problems. For example, Chhabara (2008) claims that the widespread prevalence of sexual harassment in the workplaces of domestic companies in Asia is at least partly due to lack of attention by managers. Fearing any escalation in complaints and lawsuits, managers avoid instituting the kinds of sexual harassment prevention programmes that may avoid unethical behaviour in the first place. However, with surveys suggesting that the proportion of women experiencing sexual harassment is as much as 40% (China), 47% (India), or even 78% (Pakistan), lack of attention clearly does little to curb the rate of incidence (Chhabara 2008). **An Ethical Dilemma 4** provides a specific scenario where you can examine the influence of authority in relation to other individual and situational factors in a real-life scenario.

Bureaucracy

Underlying the influence of rewards, punishments, and authority is the degree of bureaucracy in business organizations. **Bureaucracy** is a type of formal organization based on rational principles and characterized by detailed rules and procedures, impersonal hierarchical relations, and a fixed division of tasks.

Based on the work of Max Weber (1947) regarding the bureaucratic form, as well as later discussions of bureaucracy in relation to morality by Robert Jackall (1988), Zygmunt Bauman (1989, 1993), and René ten Bos (1997), the bureaucratic dimension has been argued to have a number of negative effects on ethical decision-making:[8]

- **Suppression of moral autonomy.** Individual morality tends to be subjugated to the functionally specific rules and roles of the bureaucratic organization. Thus, effective bureaucracy essentially 'frees' the individual from moral reflection and decision-making since they need only to follow the prescribed rules and procedures laid down to achieve organizational goals. This can cause employees to act as 'moral robots', simply following the rules rather than thinking about why they are there or questioning their purpose.

- **Instrumental morality.** The bureaucratic dimension focuses organization members' attentions on the efficient achievement of organizational goals. Hence, morality will be made meaningful only in terms of conformity to established rules for achieving those goals—i.e. instrumentalized—rather than focusing attention on the moral substance of the goals themselves. Accordingly, ethical decision-making will centre around whether 'correct' procedures have been taken to achieve certain goals rather than whether the goals themselves are morally beneficial. Thus, loyalty rather than integrity ultimately becomes the hallmark of bureaucratic morality.

Bureaucracy
A type of formal organization based on rational principles and characterized by detailed rules and procedures, impersonal hierarchical relations, and a fixed division of tasks. It tends to prevent personal moral reflection in favour of prescribed organizational policies.

AN ETHICAL DILEMMA 4

Stuck in the middle?*

You have recently been appointed to the position of civil engineer in a small town in a developing country. You are responsible for the maintenance of the town's infrastructure, such as public buildings and roads. You are one of the youngest members of the senior management team and report directly to the director of public works. All of the members of the management team have been working for the organization for a very long time, and you feel like something of an outsider. The director of public works, the human resources director, and the CEO often have lunch together, and it is generally felt that most important organizational decisions are made over lunch.

Your position had been vacant for a long time prior to your appointment and the director of public works had assumed responsibility for a number of your current responsibilities. On your appointment, your manager asked you to check with him before implementing any major changes. He also retained the authority to approve major works.

After some time, you realized that despite having a full staff complement, a number of outside contractors were doing various jobs within the organization. When you queried this, the director simply put it down to 'rusty skills', 'a significant backlog', and 'quality of work'. However, you have been impressed with the quality of work that your staff have produced on odd maintenance jobs that you have assigned them. Recently, when you were complimenting one of your supervisors on the way he handled an emergency, he expressed his frustration at being given the 'boring, odd jobs' instead of the 'challenging' projects given to contractors.

You decided to utilize your own staff rather than contractors for the next project because you felt that you would be able to supervise the work better and ensure the right quality. You planned it meticulously and wanted to enlist the support of your manager to ensure that all went well. You prepared all of the paperwork and took it to your manager for discussion. He looked disinterested and simply asked you to leave the paperwork with him because he was preparing for a meeting.

The following week, your manager informed you that he had gone through your paperwork, and asked one of the more experienced contractors to submit a proposal for the job. He told you that he had already discussed this issue with the CEO, because he felt that this was a critical job and the contractors would complete the work within a shorter time than the internal staff. You were very upset about this and asked your manager why he had not involved you in the decision-making process. You are increasingly uncomfortable that you are expected to supervise and authorize payments for contractors whose appointment seems questionable.

*This dilemma was prepared by Nelisiwe Dlamini and has been reproduced with the author's permission.

Questions

1. What is the right thing to do in this situation from an ethical point of view? What ethical theory supports your position?

2. If you were the civil engineer, what would you *actually* do? Is your response to this question different to your response to question 1? If so, why?

3. What are the factors that influenced your decision/action? How important is the role of authority on the part of your boss?

4. Do you think that everybody who reads this dilemma will make similar decisions? Why?

- **Distancing**. Bureaucracy serves to further suppress our own morality by distancing us from the consequences of our actions—for example, a supermarket purchasing manager in London is rarely going to be faced with the effects of their supply negotiations on farm workers producing the supermarket's coffee beans in Columbia.

- **Denial of moral status**. Finally, bureaucracy has been argued to render moral objects, such as people or animals, as things, variables, or a collection of traits. Thus, employees become human 'resources' that are means to some organizational end; consumers are reduced to a collection of preferences on a marketing database; animals become units of production or output that can be processed in a factory. The point is that by dividing tasks and focusing on efficiency, the totality of individuals as moral beings is lost and they are ultimately denied true moral status.

? THINK THEORY

Think about the theory proposed here—that bureaucracy suppresses morality. Consider a bureaucratic organization that you have had personal experience of and try to relate the four effects highlighted here to that organization. Does the theory seem to have much validity in this instance?

VISIT THE ONLINE RESOURCE CENTRE for a short response to this feature

---

Work roles

As we have seen, the bureaucratic organization of work assigns people to specific specializations or tasks that represent work roles. These are patterns of behaviour expected by others from a person occupying a certain position in an organization (Buchanan and Huczynski 1997: 374). Work roles can be *functional*—for example, the role of an accountant, an engineer, or a shop assistant—or they can be *hierarchical*—the role of a director, manager, or supervisor for example. Roles can encapsulate a whole set of expectations about what to value, how to relate to others, and how to behave.

These expectations are built up during formal education, training, and through experience, and can have a strong influence on a person's behaviour. For example, think about when you are in the lecture theatre or seminar room of your university or college. Most readers of this book probably naturally adopt the role of 'student' in the classroom—listening, taking notes, asking and answering questions when prompted—and the person taking the class will probably naturally adopt the role of 'teacher'. But it would not take much for us to refuse to adopt those roles: for the students to stand up and walk out, or for the teacher to sit down and say nothing. The main reason we do not is the fact that, as a rule, we all seem to know how we are supposed to act and we stick to it fairly faithfully. We simply adopt our prescribed roles.

In the business ethics context, prescribed work roles, and the associated expectations placed on the person adopting the role, would appear to be significant influences on decision-making. Our individual morality, the values and beliefs we might normally hold, can be stifled by our adoption of the values and beliefs embedded in our work role. Perhaps the most vivid illustration of this is the Stanford prison experiment, which is the subject of **Ethics in Action 4.2**. This is about as powerful an example as you can get of how work roles can have substantial impacts on how we behave.

VISIT THE
ONLINE
RESOURCE
CENTRE
for links to
useful sources
of further
information

ETHICS IN ACTION 4.2

The Stanford Prison Experiment

The Stanford Prison Experiment, co-ordinated by Dr Philip Zimbardo, took place in 1971. The experiment frequently features in discussions about human psychology, roles, and ethical behaviour—and has achieved an enduring place in popular culture. Not only has it served as the inspiration for a BBC TV show called *The Experiment*, a German movie *Das Experiment*, as well as the 2010 US movie *The Experiment*, starring Adrien Brody and Forest Whitaker, it has also given its name to an American punk band, the Stanford Prison Experiment. So what accounts for the classic status of Zimbardo's experiment?

Zimbardo's plan was to take 24, average, healthy, middle-class, male college students and randomly assign them into one of two groups—one to play prisoners and the other to play prison guards—for a two-week period. His intention was to examine the psychology of prison life. The 'prisoners' were rounded up unexpectedly by a police squad car, blindfolded, handcuffed, and then locked in stark cells in the 'jail' in the basement of the Stanford University psychology building. While the prisoners were given smocks and nylon stocking caps to wear, the guards were given uniforms, reflector sunglasses, clubs, and handcuffs—all of which emphasized their roles, minimized their individuality, and reinforced the power differentials between the two groups. Prisoners had to refer to guards as 'Mr Correction Officer', and guards were given only minimal instructions in order to achieve their goal of 'maintaining law and order'. Although physical violence was forbidden, they were allowed to devise their own rules and ways of working.

Although planned to last two weeks, the experiment was dramatically halted after only six days. Some of the guards had begun to treat the prisoners with excessive aggression and clearly took pleasure in exercising their power and inflicting psychological cruelty. The prisoners quickly became servile, dependent, helpless, and depressed, thinking only of their own survival and their hatred of the guards. After only 36 hours, the first prisoner had to be released due to fits of rage, uncontrollable crying, and depression. More prisoners were released in the days that followed, suffering from similar symptoms.

Despite being randomly allocated to the two roles, the study's participants had almost immediately begun to think of themselves as their prisoner and guard roles. They rapidly adopted the ways of thinking and behaving associated with those roles, and the arbitrary rules of the new organizational environment into which they had been thrust were accepted as legitimate. The participants became so programmed to think of themselves as prisoners that they did not feel capable of just withdrawing from the experiment, and the researchers themselves even became so locked into their roles as prison authorities that the prisoners' deteriorating physical and mental conditions were initially interpreted as faked in order to 'con' their way out of the experiment! The distinction between the real self and the role had blurred to such an extent that nearly all aspects of the individual's thoughts, feelings, and behaviours, whether as participant or researcher, had experienced dramatic changes. Zimbardo concluded that the experiment supported the theory that individual behaviour is largely controlled by role and situation, rather than personal characteristics and traits.

Although it is clear that most workplaces are quite different to the prison environment, the Stanford experiment does show us that people very easily adopt the roles they are assigned to, and may quite readily fall into attitudes and behaviours that conflict significantly with those they have in 'normal' life. As Zimbardo himself said of the guards: 'These guys were all peaceniks. They became like Nazis.' Zimbardo later served as an expert witness in the defence of one of the prison guards at the notorious Abu Ghraib prison in Baghdad where guards had been involved in torture and degradation of prisoners in the aftermath of the 2003 invasion of Iraq. Zimbardo's subsequent book, *The Lucifer Effect: Understanding How Good People Turn Evil*, drew on similarities between his experiment and the events at Abu Ghraib to illustrate how perfectly decent individuals can be influenced by their environment to act unethically.

For more details, go to: http://www.prisonexp.org, which has a detailed description of the experiment, including a slide show and video clips. There are also links to further reading.

Sources

Brockes, E. 2001. The experiment. *Guardian*, G2, 16 October: 2–3.
Buchanan, D. and Huczynski, A. 1997. *Organizational behaviour: an introductory text*. Hemel Hempstead: Prentice Hall: 380–1.
http://www.lucifereffect.com.
http://www.prisonexp.org.

? THINK THEORY

Think about what this experiment says about roles and moral relativism. Is it reasonable to justify any kind of behaviour on the grounds that ethical evaluations may differ according to different contexts?

VISIT THE
ONLINE
RESOURCE
CENTRE
for a short
response to this
feature

While there is considerable evidence supporting a significant impact for work roles on organizational behaviour *generally*, there has been rather limited research to date that has specifically addressed the impact of roles on *ethical* decision-making and behaviour. Nonetheless, the important thing to remember is that many of us will adopt different roles in different contexts, reinforcing this idea of people having multiple ethical selves. For example, many people take on different roles when with their family compared with when they are at work, or with their friends, or in other social situations. Roles are therefore not constant traits or facets of our personality (as was the case with our individual factors), but are highly contextual influences on our decision-making and behaviour.

Organizational norms and culture

Another set of potentially powerful influences on ethical decision-making are the group norms that delineate acceptable standards of behaviour within the work community—be this at the level of a small team of workers, a department, or the entire organization. Group norms essentially express the way in which things are, or should be, done in a certain environment, and might relate to ways of acting, talking, justifying, dressing, even thinking and evaluating. Group norms may well conflict with the official rules or procedures laid down by the organization. For example, a group of office workers may agree amongst themselves that illegally pirating licensed software from work for home use is perfectly acceptable as an unofficial 'perk' of the job, even if it is officially prohibited. As such, group norms tend to be included within a more or less unofficial or informal set of characteristics, including shared values, beliefs, and behaviours that are captured by the notion of **organizational culture**.

Organizational culture
The meanings, beliefs, and common-sense knowledge that are shared among members of an organization, and which are represented in taken-for-granted assumptions, norms, and values.

While there are numerous, often conflicting definitions of what organizational culture actually is, at a basic level we can say that it represents the overall environment or climate found within the organization (or certain parts of it). Culture is further said to constitute particular meanings, beliefs, and common-sense knowledge that are shared among the members of the organization, and which are represented in taken-for-granted assumptions, norms, and values.

Organizational culture has been widely identified as a key issue in shaping ethical decision-making. Not only has it been frequently included in models of ethical decision-making (e.g. Ferrell et al. 1989), but it has also been widely examined in empirical investigations (O'Fallon and Butterfield 2005). This is not particularly surprising, for there is wide-ranging evidence, as well as strong conceptual support, for the proposition that culture and ethical decision-making are profoundly interwoven (e.g. Sinclair 1993; Dahler-Larsen 1994; Starkey 1998; Anand et al. 2004).

The organizational culture explanation of ethical decision-making suggests that as employees become socialized into particular ways of seeing, interpreting, and acting that are broadly shared in their organization, this will shape the kinds of decisions they make when confronted with ethical problems. Such cultural expectations and values can provide a strong influence on what we think of as 'right' and 'wrong'. For example, the failed US energy giant Enron was shown to have developed a culture of dishonesty that culminated in the misleading accounting that brought down the firm in 2001 (Sims and Brinkmann 2003). Similar observations held true for the reasons for the financial crisis of the late 2000s as being rooted in a culture of risk taking (Langevoort 2010). Our cultural understandings and knowledge can thus act as both facilitators and barriers to ethical reflection and behaviour.

As a consequence of such reasoning, as well as compelling survey evidence (e.g. Ethics Resource Center 2014), many authors such as Treviño and Nelson (2014) and Ferrell et al. (2014) speak of the need for an 'ethical culture' to enhance and reinforce ethical decision-making. However, as we shall see in Chapter 5 (when we move on to discuss ways of managing business ethics), there is considerable disagreement about how this should be done, or indeed whether it is even possible or desirable. Certainly, it would appear that the deliberate management of culture is an extremely challenging undertaking, and one where many of the outcomes will be unpredictable. Nonetheless, even though it may be unclear how to deal with organizational culture's influence on ethical decision-making, the very fact that there is some kind of relationship between the two would appear almost irrefutable.

National and cultural context

Finally, just as the culture of the organization or work group may influence ethical decision-making, so might the country or culture in which the individual's organization is located. This factor varies from the national and cultural characteristics discussed on pp. 143–145 under Individual influences on ethical decision-making: at that time, we were looking at the nationality of the individual making the decision; now we are considering the nation in which the decision is actually taking place, regardless of the decision-maker's nationality. As we have discussed a number of times in the book so far, to some extent different cultures still maintain different views of what is right and wrong, and these differences have significant effects on whether a moral issue is recognized, and the kind of judgements and behaviours entered into by individuals. For example, a French office manager working in the US may start to become sensitized to different perceptions of what constitutes sexual harassment compared with their colleagues back in France. Or a Danish human resource manager might consider the issue of employment conditions quite differently should they be working in Indonesia rather than at home. However, with globalization eroding some of these national cultural differences, we might expect to see shifts in the influence of this factor, perhaps with more complex effects and interactions emerging.

While some models have incorporated factors relating to the social and cultural environment (e.g. Hunt and Vitell 1986; Ferrell et al. 1989), there has been relatively little empirical research investigating the effect of this on ethical decision-making. However, several key studies suggest that the local national context does indeed have an effect on managers' ethical evaluations (Spicer et al. 2004; Bailey and Spicer 2007). For instance Bailey and Spicer (2007) demonstrate empirically that the ethical attitudes of expatriate American managers in Russia towards local business practices converge with those of Russian managers despite differences in their individual national identities.

☑ Skill check

Analysing situational influences on ethical decision-making. This is a key skill because it helps you to assess the key characteristics of a business situation that hamper or encourage ethical behaviour in business.

■ Summary

In this chapter we have discussed the various stages and influences on ethical decision-making in business, so that by now you should have a reasonably clear picture of the overall process and its most important elements. The basic model presented in the chapter provides a clear outline of how these elements fit together, although as we mentioned earlier, this model should be regarded simply as an illustration of the relationships involved, not as a definitive causal model. Having discussed both individual and situational influences on ethical decision-making, we would suggest that some individual factors—such as cognitive moral development, nationality, personal values, and integrity—are clearly influential, particularly on the moral *judgements* made by individuals. However, in terms of *recognizing* ethical problems and actually *acting* in response to them, it is situational factors that appear to be the most influential. This is important because it means that situational factors are likely to be the most promising levers for attempts to manage and improve ethical decision-making in organizations. In particular, the possibilities for addressing organizational culture as a route to managing ethics has been widely alluded to in the literature and will provide an important aspect of our discussions in Chapter 4.

Study questions

1. What is the difference between descriptive and normative ethical theories?

2. Set out the four stages in Rest's (1986) ethical decision-making process. What practical use is the model for managers seeking to understand ethical and unethical behaviour in their organizations?

3. Is the prevalence of unethical behaviour in business due to a few 'bad apples' or is it more a case of good apples in bad barrels? How would your answer differ for government or civil society organizations?

4. Describe Kohlberg's theory of cognitive moral development and critically evaluate its contribution to our understanding of ethical decision-making in organizations. What are the main implications of the theory for business leaders?

5. What are the two main types of issue-related factors in ethical decision-making? What is the significance of these factors for managers seeking to prevent ethical violations in their organizations?

6. What are the main impacts of bureaucracy on ethical decision-making? How would you suggest that a highly bureaucratic organization could enhance its employees' ethical decision-making?

Research exercise

Look at a recent business scandal that has made the headlines. Identify the main people involved in the scandal and investigate their individual characteristics. Then identify the key situational factors that may have influenced their behaviour. Which of these individual and situational factors seem to have been most important in causing the scandal? Would you have any suggestions for how to avoid such a situation recurring in the future?

Key readings

VISIT THE
ONLINE
RESOURCE
CENTRE
for links to
further key
readings

1. Banaji, M.R., Bazerman, M.H., and Chugh, D. 2003. How (un)ethical are you? *Harvard Business Review,* 81 (December): 56–65.

This is a summary of core personal characteristics of individuals that can bias ethical decision-making. Written by leading psychologists it uncovers how unethical decision-making can be the result of unconscious processes that are shaped by a number of factors in a person's upbringing, personal life, professional context or educational history. It includes details of a website where students can test themselves on how far they are exposed to these biases.

2. Anand, V., Ashforth, B.E., and Joshi, M. 2004. Business as usual: the acceptance and perpetuation of corruption in organizations. *Academy of Management Executive,* 18 (2): 39–53.

This article will help you to see why unethical practices persist in organizations, and provides a really helpful way of thinking about how people and organizations respond to corruption.

Case 4

VISIT THE
ONLINE
RESOURCE
CENTRE
for links to
useful sources
of further
information on
this case

News Corporation's phone hacking scandal: no news is good news?

This case examines the events surrounding the phone hacking scandal at the UK newspaper, the *News of the World*, which until it was closed in July 2011 was part of the News Corporation media empire. The company's attempts to portray ethical misconduct at the paper as limited to a single 'rogue reporter' are compared with evidence from other investigations that pointed to a culture of wrongdoing at the firm and a failure of compliance systems. The case thus provides an opportunity to explore the role of individual and situational factors in ethical decision-making, and to put them in the context of ethical management practices.

When the former editor of the UK newspaper the *News of the World*, Andy Coulson, was convicted in 2014 of conspiracy to intercept voicemails, it marked the final nail in the coffin for what had been the UK's most popular Sunday newspaper. Known for its combination of racy 'kiss-and-tell' stories, prodigious sports coverage, and sensationalist exposes of the rich and famous, the *News of the World* consistently outsold its nearest rival by more than 30%, and at its peak was bought by one in six people in the UK.

All that ended in 2011 when the *News of the World* was closed down in the face of a debilitating phone hacking scandal that led to most of the paper's advertisers withdrawing their business from the title. By this time, Coulson had already left the newspaper and was working as communications director for the office of the British prime minister, David Cameron. He resigned this position, as he had that of editor at the *News of the World*, stating, 'when the spokesman needs a spokesman it is time to move on'. Along with his former boss at the *News of the World*, Rebekah Brooks, and a number of other defendants he then went on to face a protracted trail at London's Old Bailey that was reportedly the most expensive in British legal history. Despite claiming for many years that he knew nothing of the illegal practices that were taking place under his editorship, and that it was the work of a single 'rogue reporter', Coulson was finally sentenced to 18 months in prison for his part in the illegal hacking of people's voicemails, while Brooks and the other defendants were cleared. But Coulson was not alone; four others had already pleaded guilty to phone hacking before the trial had even begun and numerous other journalists at the newspaper had since been arrested and were awaiting trial. It is now clear that phone hacking was anything but an isolated incident at the *News of the World*. And Coulson, as the chief prosecutor in the sentencing hearing argued, had 'utterly corrupted' the newspaper.

News Corporation's media empire

The *News of the World* was established in 1843 and at the time of its closure was operated by News International (now renamed News UK), a UK-based company with a suite of leading UK titles. This included the world renowned quality newspapers *The Times* and *The Sunday Times* as well as the *News of the World*'s sister paper the *Sun*, which for many years has been the UK's most popular daily tabloid.

News International was itself a part of another much larger global media company, News Corporation, which was headquartered in the US and included among its businesses HarperCollins Publishers, Dow Jones & Company (a financial news publisher, including the *Wall Street Journal*), and the Fox Entertainment Group (which includes the movie studios Fox Searchlight Pictures and 20th Century Fox as well as the Fox TV network). As shown in **Figure C4.1**, News Corporation has since been broken into two different companies: News Corp and 21st Century Fox.

News Corporation's media empire has long been overseen by its chairman and CEO, Rupert Murdoch, who built the company since his first forays into the newspaper business in his native Australia in the 1950s. He extended his international reach by acquiring the *News of the World* in 1969 and the *New York Post* in 1976. He then founded News Corporation in 1979 as a holding company for his various national media businesses, which rapidly swelled in the 1980s and 1990s as Murdoch moved into the film and television businesses across the world, and in the 2000s and 2010s as he extended into online and digital media.

Murdoch and his family own a large proportion of the voting shares in News Corporation (and in turn in the two demerged companies News Corp and 21st Century Fox), providing him with considerable control over the company. Members of his family have also held positions of significant influence in the business. For example, son James Murdoch is a former executive chairman of News International and today is the deputy chief operating officer of 21st Century Fox. Likewise, another son Lachlan Murdoch is on the board of both News Corp and 21st Century Fox.

As a result, many have referred to News Corporation as akin to Murdoch's personal fiefdom, and his control over the company has brought him and his family considerable

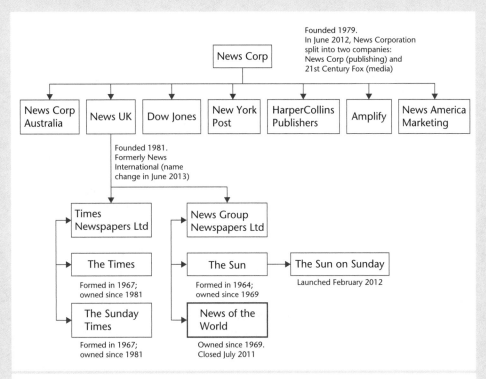

Figure C4.1 News Corp organizational structure

Source: News Corp website: http://newscorp.com/about/our-businesses/.

economic and political influence, not to mention enormous wealth. He has been courted by several generations of British politicians, mainly due to the importance of getting positive coverage in his populist newspapers, the *Sun* and the *News of the World*. In 2013, Murdoch was ranked number 33 in *Forbes'* list of the world's most powerful people and, with a personal fortune of more than $14 billion, number 78 in their 2014 list of the richest people on the planet.

The phone hacking scandal emerges

Under Murdoch's ownership, the *News of the World* became well known for breaking big stories in the UK, many of them involving sex scandals and cover-ups. Over the years, reports in the paper drove a number of top politicians to resign following revelations about hidden affairs or other sex scandals, earning the paper the epithet the 'News of the Screws'. A string of investigations into corruption, drug dealing and influence peddling by the undercover reporter Mazher Mahmood (nicknamed the 'fake sheikh' because of his typical disguise) led to exposés of everyone from sports stars to members of the royal family, eventually resulting in nearly 100 criminal prosecutions. In 2010, Mahmood won the UK's Reporter of the Year award for his undercover sting operation that led to the banning of several leading Pakistani cricketers for accepting bribes in return for match fixing.

Despite its successes, the *News of the World*'s approach to journalism stoked controversy. Its heavy reliance on 'chequebook journalism' (paying for stories) and entrapment, along with an apparent disregard for individual privacy prompted a raft of complaints from those at the receiving end of its scoops. However, bolstered by Murdoch's huge political influence, the newspaper long appeared immune to its critics. This threatened to unravel in 2006 when it emerged that some of the *News of the World*'s famous exposés might have been the result of downright illegal practices.

In 2006, Clive Goodman, the paper's royal editor (responsible for stories about the royal family), was arrested on suspicion of illegal phone hacking following a complaint from Prince William's office. The investigation arose when certain details of the royal household were published in the *News of the World* that could only have been gleaned from listening in to recorded voicemails. Goodman, along with the private investigator Glen Mulcair, were eventually found guilty of unlawfully intercepting hundreds of telephone voicemail messages received by three members of staff at Buckingham Palace. In 2007, Goodman and Mulcair were sentenced to, respectively, four and six months in prison. The paper's editor, Andy Coulson, also resigned, saying that he shouldered ultimate responsibility for the problem, despite claiming that he knew nothing about the practices that had led to the convictions. As he said later at a government inquiry, 'I have never condoned the use of phone hacking and nor do I have any recollection of incidences where phone hacking took place . . . I took full responsibility at the time for what happened but without my knowledge and resigned.'

Throughout the police investigations and trial of Goodman and Mulcaire, the *News of the World* and its parent companies claimed that phone hacking was strictly limited to one 'rogue reporter' (Goodman) working with one private detective (Mulcair). According to the company, the issues had been thoroughly investigated and no further wrongdoing was found. When Les Hinton, the News International executive chairman at the time, was asked by an MP whether the company had conducted 'a full, rigorous internal inquiry' and whether he was 'absolutely convinced that Clive Goodman was the only person who knew what was going on', he responded: 'Yes, we have and I believe he was the only person.'

Goodman was sacked by the newspaper, but soon afterwards he threatened to sue his former employers for unfair dismissal. According to a letter written by Goodman to News International, his hacking of the royal household phones was carried out with the 'full knowledge and support' of his superiors, was a common practice among journalists at the newspaper, and was 'discussed in the daily editorial conference until explicit reference to it was banned by the Editor.' He also claimed that he had been assured of keeping his job providing he did not implicate the newspaper during his trial. Fearing a formal employment tribunal, News International prevented Goodman's complaints from being aired by settling with the reporter and awarding him a substantial payment.

The scandal erupts

Following Goodman and Mulcair's imprisonment, damaging allegations continued to surface that phone hacking might be more widespread at the *News of the World* than just Goodman alone. The *Guardian* newspaper, which doggedly pursued the story over a number of years, revealed that more than a million pounds was paid out by News International in out-of-court settlements to claimants threatening to seek prosecutions. A 2010 *New York Times* article included interviews of several *News of the World* employees who described the company culture as 'a frantic, sometimes degrading atmosphere in which some reporters openly pursued hacking or other improper tactics to satisfy demanding editors.' News

International continued to stonewall. For example, in response to the *Guardian* revelations, the company issued a statement claiming: 'All of these irresponsible and unsubstantiated allegations against *News of the World* and other News International titles and its journalists are false.'

But any hope that the *News of the World* had of keeping a lid on the story ended in 2011 when the phone hacking scandal erupted over revelations, again by the *Guardian* newspaper, that reporters had secretly hacked into the voicemail of murdered schoolgirl, Milly Dowler, when she had disappeared back in 2002. For once the *News of the World*'s victim was not a public figure considered by many fair game for media intrusion, but an innocent child and her family going through a major tragedy. The furore over the company's practices sparked a massive boycott, resulting in most of the paper's advertisers withdrawing from the title. In the face of a fatal blow to its legitimacy the paper published its last ever edition in July 2011.

Although this marked the end of the *News of the World*, the phone hacking scandal continued as police investigated further allegations of wrongdoing at the company, the *Guardian* continued its investigation of the story, and the UK government initiated several inquiries, including in a wide-scale judicial public inquiry into the practices and ethics of the UK press (the Leveson Inquiry). Amid revelations that hundreds of people were likely victims of phone hacking, and a spate of arrests of former *News of the World* reporters and senior executives, News International, News Corporation, and even Rupert Murdoch himself, became the subject of intense scrutiny.

As the scandal deepened, News International admitted for the first time in 2011 that the single 'rogue reporter' claim was erroneous, but denied that a culture of wrongdoing characterised the company. In fact, senior executives claimed, the firm had a strict code of conduct with 'zero tolerance' to wrongdoing. Phone hacking was therefore confined to a small group of employees who acted without the knowledge of senior managers because of the decentralized, 'hands-off' approach to day-to-day activities by management. Most of the firm's critics remained unconvinced.

The fall and rise of News Corporation

The reputation of News International in the UK and News Corporation as Murdoch's global holding company took a severe battering due to the phone hacking scandal. The Culture, Media and Sport Committee, made up of members of Parliament and appointed by the UK's House of Commons, published a scathing report about the company in 2012, including accusations that senior executives had suffered from 'collective amnesia' and had 'misled' the Committee during earlier investigations about the extent of phone hacking at the *News of the World*. It criticized the firm's leadership for 'failing to investigate properly' when evidence emerged of wrongdoing, and 'covering-up' such wrongdoing rather than disciplining the perpetrators. As the Committee's report concluded, 'News International and its parent News Corporation exhibited willful blindness, for which the companies' directors—including Rupert Murdoch and James Murdoch—should ultimately be prepared to take responsibility'. However, in giving evidence to the committee, the Murdoch's had resolutely refused to acknowledge any such responsibility for the problems at their company. 'I do not accept ultimate responsibility,' Rupert Murdoch told the Committee, 'I hold responsible the people that I trusted to run it and the people they trusted. It is for them to pay . . . I think that frankly, I'm the best person to clean this up.'

The Leveson inquiry report, also published in 2012, recommended dramatic changes in the way the British press should be regulated in the aftermath of the phone hacking scandal. It also severely criticised News International for having 'lost its way' in relation to phone hacking and failing to take misconduct seriously. 'Most responsible corporate entities' the report concluded, 'would be appalled that employees were or could be involved in the commission of crime in order to further their business. Not so at the *News of the World*.' Moreover, the report noted a 'failure of systems of management and compliance' where 'none of the witnesses were able to identify who was responsible for ensuring compliance with an ethical approach to journalism and there was a general lack of respect for individual privacy and dignity.'

These reports, and the public hearings that accompanied them, provided the worst possible exposure for News International. The arrest of former editors of the *News of the World* Andy Coulson and Rebekah Brooks, along with more than a dozen other reporters associated with the newspaper, also presaged yet more bad publicity—their court trials during 2013 and 2014 put the story right back on the front pages just when News Corporation was looking to put the scandal behind it.

However, in many ways the company has rebounded successfully from the scandal. The *News of the World* was quickly replaced by a new Sunday tabloid from News International—the *Sun on Sunday*—which launched less than a year after the closure of its predecessor, and with a considerably lower cost structure. Successive revolts at News Corporation's AGMs demanding the ousting of Murdoch were also easily defeated, not least because of the family's huge voting block and a soaring stock price. After the split of the company in 2013, the firm's highly profitable film and television business became insulated from the scandal-prone newspaper business, leading to a huge rise in total shareholder value. As a result, despite Murdoch's self-proclaimed 'humbling' in the wake of the *News of the World* scandal, his businesses appear to be prospering even more than they did before it.

The question of who should ultimately take responsibility for the phone hacking scandal, however, remains. The imprisonment of former editor Coulson has clearly put to rest the single 'rogue reporter' defence that News International stuck to for so long, and shows that Goodman and other journalists were probably acting on the instructions of their bosses, or at the very least had their implicit approval. But how far up the organization the use of such practices was known, or should have been known, is an open question. News Corporation executives may have operated a 'don't ask, don't tell' policy as the parliamentary reports have suggested. But few would agree that the old adage 'no news is good news' is a good motto for a media business.

Questions

1. What is phone hacking and why is it considered unethical and illegal? Do you think that hacking the phones of celebrities and non-celebrities should be considered ethically equivalent?

2. Describe the 'rogue reporter' defence adopted by the *News of the World* in response to the phone hacking allegations and explain why it might be an appealing response to ethical misconduct by a company.

3. Which individual traits, if any, do you think are most likely to lend themselves to a 'rogue reporter' type of explanation?

4. What were the main situational influences that appear to have encouraged reporters at the newspaper to engage in phone hacking? How would you prioritise them?

5. Do you think that News International and its parent company News Corporation handled the phone hacking scandal well? Explain your answer.

6. What, if anything, should (a) News International, and (b) News Corporation do now to enhance their approach to ethics management?

Sources

Guardian 2011. James and Rupert Murdoch at the Culture, Media, and Sport Select Committee— full transcript. *Guardian*, 20 July 2011. http://www.theguardian.com/news/datablog/2011/jul/20/james-rupert-murdoch-full-transcript.

Guardian 2011. Phone-hacking denials: what Murdoch executives said. *Guardian*, 16 August 2011. http://www.theguardian.com/media/2011/aug/16/phone-hacking-cover-up-denials.

Guardian's phone hacking coverage: http://www.theguardian.com/media/phone-hacking.

House of Commons, Culture, Media and Sport Committee. 2012. *News International and Phone-hacking*. London: The Stationery Office Limited.

Leveson, B.H. 2012. *An inquiry into the culture, practices and ethics of the press*. London: PN The Stationery Office.

New York Times 2010. Tabloid Hack Attack on Royals, and Beyond. *New York Times*, 1 September 2010. http://www.nytimes.com/2010/09/05/magazine/05hacking-t.html?pagewanted=all&-r=0.

Notes

1. The English translations are quite misleading, as 'ethics of responsibility' ('*Verantwortungsethik*') sounds more positive than in its original German rendition, whereas 'ethics of ultimate ends' ('*Gesinnungsethik*') seems rather narrow for Weber's argument.
2. There are numerous studies that have examined this question, including: Becker and Fritzsche's (1987) study of French, German, and US managers; Lysonski and Gaidis' (1991) study of US, Danish, and New Zealand business students; Nyaw and Ng's (1994) study of Canadian, Japanese, Hong Kong, and Taiwanese business students; Jackson's (2000) study of French, German, British, Spanish, and US managers; and Jackson's (2001) ten-country study across four continents.
3. Gledhill, R. 2008. Rowan Williams says 'human greed' to blame for financial crisis. *The Times*, 15 October 2008: http://www.timesonline.co.uk; Stolberg, S.G. and Labaton, S. 2009. Obama calls Wall Street bonuses 'shameful'. *New York Times*, 29 January: http://www.nytimes.com; Anon. 2008. Hindus blame greed for current global financial crisis and suggest adopting 'spiritual economics'. *American Chronicle*, 7 October: http://www.americanchronicle.com.
4. James Rest (1986), whose depiction of the stages of ethical decision-making we presented earlier in the chapter, has been a vigorous proponent of cognitive moral development and devised a widely used measuring instrument called the Defining Issues Test. A summary of some of the vast amount of empirical work carried out can be found in Rest (1986), some of which is also presented in Goolsby and Hunt (1992).
5. *Collins English Dictionary and Thesaurus*, standard edition. 1993. Glasgow: HarperCollins: 1287.
6. See the company website for more information: http://www.pic.com.
7. http://bangladeshaccord.org.
8. Criticizing bureaucracy has been a popular pastime for organization scholars for a considerable time, and business ethics writers have also tended to offer largely negative evaluations of the effects of bureaucracy on ethical decision-making. However, for a powerful and eloquent critique of some of these ideas, see du Gay (2000).

5

Managing Business Ethics

TOOLS AND TECHNIQUES OF BUSINESS ETHICS MANAGEMENT

Having completed this chapter you should be able to:

- Explain the nature, evolution, and scope of business ethics management.
- Explain why firms increasingly manage their overall social role rather than focusing primarily on just managing the ethical behaviour of employees.
- Critically examine the role of codes of ethics in managing the ethical behaviour of employees.
- Critically examine current theory and practice regarding the management of stakeholder relationships and partnerships.
- Explain the role of social accounting, auditing, and reporting tools in assessing ethical performance.
- Understand different ways of organizing for the management of business ethics.

Key concepts and skills:

Concepts	Skills
• Business ethics management	• Implementing codes of ethics
• Code of ethics	• Prioritization of stakeholders
• Stakeholder management	• Stakeholder relationship management
• Social accounting	
• Ethical leadership	• Assessing ethical performance
	• Designing ethics programmes
	• Managing ethical culture

■ Introduction

It is being increasingly recognized by managers, policy-makers, and researchers that business ethics in the global economy is simply too important to be left merely to chance. Global corporations such as BP, News Corporation, Siemens, Walmart, and others have realized to their cost the threat that perceived ethical violations can pose to their zealously guarded reputations. Stricter regulation has also had a significant impact. For instance, the 2010 UK Bribery Act made possible the prosecution of companies engaging in bribery anywhere in the world providing they have links to the UK. In the US, the 2010 Dodd-Frank Act, among other things, mandated transparency on so-called conflict minerals, and the disclosure of payments to host governments by resource sector companies. In a similar vein, legislation in countries such as Denmark, France, Japan, Malaysia, and the UK has required large firms to report on certain social and environmental factors relating to their business, while India has instituted a requirement for all large firms to contribute 2% of their profits to CSR initiatives.

As a result, there have been numerous attempts, both theoretical and practical, to develop a more systematic and comprehensive approach to *managing* business ethics. Indeed, this has given rise to a multi-million dollar international business ethics 'industry' of ethics managers, consultants, auditors, and other experts available to advise and implement ethics management policies and programmes in corporations across the globe. This is all relatively recent. For instance, in 2005, *Business Ethics* magazine identified that corporations were 'rushing to learn ethics virtually overnight, and as they do so, a vast new industry of consultants and suppliers has emerged. The ethics industry has been born' (Hyatt 2005). In general, over the past decades we have seen a sharp rise in management positions in 'compliance', 'risk', or more generally 'corporate responsibility' which often overlap substantially with business ethics management—a topic we will pick up at the end of this chapter when talking about organizing business ethics management.

How then can companies actually manage business ethics on a day-to-day basis across the various national and cultural contexts that they may be operating in? Is it possible to control the ethical behaviour of employees so that they make the right ethical decision every time? And what kinds of management programmes are necessary to produce the level of information and impacts that various stakeholders demand? These are the kinds of questions that we will deal with in this chapter. However, in this area in particular there are as yet few definite answers, not least because many of the questions themselves have only fairly recently been addressed at any length. Indeed, much of the theory and practice covered in this chapter is at the very forefront of current business ethics debates.

■ What is business ethics management?

Before we proceed, it is necessary to first establish what exactly we mean by managing business ethics. Obviously, managing any area of business, whether it is production, marketing, accounting, human resources, or any other function, constitutes a whole range of activities covering formal and informal means of planning, implementation, and control. For our purposes though, the most relevant aspects of **business ethics management** are those that are clearly visible and directed specifically at resolving ethical problems and issues.

Business ethics management
The direct attempt to formally or informally manage ethical issues or problems through specific policies, practices, and programmes.

Typical components of business ethics management

- Mission or values statements
- Codes of ethics
- Reporting/advice channels
- Risk analysis and management
- Ethics managers, officers, and committees
- Ethics consultants
- Ethics education and training
- Stakeholder consultation and partnership
- Auditing, accounting, and reporting

Figure 5.1 Business ethics management

Business ethics management, as we shall now show, covers a whole range of different elements, each of which may be applied individually, or in combination, to address ethical issues in business.

Components of business ethics management

There are numerous management activities that could be regarded as aspects of business ethics management, some of which, such as codes of ethics, are fairly well established, while others, such as social auditing, are still in the relatively early stages of development and uptake. Without intending to be exhaustive, **Figure 5.1** sets out the main components currently in place today, at least within large multinational corporations. These are all explained briefly below. The most important of these components are described in fuller detail in the section Setting standards of ethical behaviour (p. 190) onwards, when we look in depth at managing the ethical behaviour of employees, managing stakeholder relations, and managing and assessing ethical performance.

Mission or values statements

These are general statements of corporate aims, beliefs, and values. Such statements have increasingly included social, ethical, and environmental goals of one kind or another (King et al. 2010). For example, the global social media company Facebook has the mission 'to give people the power to share and make the world more open and connected', while the Swedish furniture chain IKEA states: 'We are a values-driven company with a passion for life at home. Every product we create is our idea for making home a better place'. Virtually all large and many small- and medium-sized organizations now have a mission statement of some kind, and it is clear they are important in terms of setting out a broad vision for where the company is going. However, in terms of business ethics, they often fail to set out a very specific social purpose, and there is little evidence to suggest that they have much impact on employee behaviour (Bart 1997). Moreover, even a well-crafted, appropriate, and inspirational social mission is unlikely to be effective unless it is backed up by substantive ethics management throughout the organization.

Codes of ethics

Sometimes called codes of conduct or simply ethics policies, these are explicit outlines of what type of conduct is desired and expected of employees from an ethical point of view within a certain organization, profession, or industry. As probably the most widespread approach to managing business ethics, we shall discuss codes of ethics in more detail in Setting standards of ethical behaviour: designing and implementing codes of ethics (pp. 190–199).

Reporting/advice channels

Gathering information on ethical matters is clearly an important input into effective management. Providing employees with appropriate channels for reporting or receiving advice regarding ethical dilemmas can also be a vital means of identifying potential problems and resolving them before they escalate and/or become public. Many organizations have therefore introduced ethics hotlines or other forms of reporting channels specifically for employees to notify management of ethics abuses or problems and to seek help and guidance on solutions. UK survey evidence reported that something like 50% of large firms have instituted channels of this kind (Webley and Le Jeune 2005), although some countries such as Germany and France prohibit certain features of hotlines due to privacy restrictions. According to KPMG's integrity survey (KPMG 2013a), employees are increasingly using such mechanisms to report suspected misconduct.

Risk analysis and management

Managing and reducing risk has become one of the key components of business ethics management, not least because awareness of potential reputational and financial risks has been one of the key drivers of increased attention to business ethics in recent years. As Alejo Jose Sison (2000) suggests, the language of risk assessment has enabled business ethics to 'show its bite' by spelling out the risks that firms run by ignoring ethics, and measuring these risks in monetary terms, such as the fines, damages, and sanctions that courts can impose. This has been particularly prominent in the US, with the Foreign Corrupt Practices Act and the Sarbanes–Oxley Act providing a legal impetus for greater attention to unethical business practices such as bribery and accounting malpractice. In Europe and Asia too, such legislation is having a similar effect on the large number of non-US multinationals that are jointly listed in the US or that do business in the country.

Managing business ethics by identifying areas of risk, assessing the likelihood and scale of risks, and putting in place measures to mitigate or prevent such risks from harming the business has led to more sophisticated ways of managing business ethics, although as yet, most companies have not developed an integrated approach to risk and ethics. Perhaps inevitably, such risk management techniques tend to focus more on easily identifiable legal risks and more quantifiable ethical risks, such as those relating to pollution or product liability. However, this is an area of continual development, and a greater range of ethical problems such as human rights violations, corruption, and climate change impacts are beginning to be seen on the risk radar of major companies.

Ethics managers, officers, and committees

In some organizations, specific individuals or groups are appointed to co-ordinate and/or take responsibility for managing ethics in their organization. Designated ethics officers (under various titles) are now fairly prevalent, especially in the US where an Ethics and Compliance Officer Association (ECOA), set up in 1992, has grown to around

1,300 members, including representatives from more than half of the Fortune 100. This growth is at least partly due to the increasing emphasis on compliance in the US with the tightening of regulations that followed the Sarbanes–Oxley legislation. As one commentator put it (Reeves 2005):

> the structure of sentencing policy has driven the appointment of ethics officers and fuelled a boom in business ethics training. If an executive ends up in the dock for corporate wrongdoing, he or she will get a shorter time in the nick if they can demonstrate that they have hired an ethics officer and rolled out courses across the firm.

In Europe, Asia, and elsewhere, such positions are less common, but the ECOA now boasts members across five continents and, in countries such as the UK and France organizations such as the Institute of Business Ethics and the Cercle Européen des Déontologues (European Circle of Ethics Officers) provide membership services to ethics managers. A growing number of large corporations also now have an ethics committee, or a CSR committee, which oversees many aspects of the management of business ethics. In India, for example, a board level CSR committee is a requirement of the 2013 Companies Act for all companies larger than a certain size.

Ethics consultants

Business ethics consultants have also become a small but firmly established fixture in the marketplace, and a wide range of companies have used external consultants rather than internal executives to manage certain areas of business ethics. The initial growth in this sector was driven by environmental consultants who tended to offer specialist technical advice, but as the social and ethical agenda facing companies has developed, the consultancy market has expanded to offer a broader portfolio of services including research, project management, strategic advice, social and environmental auditing and reporting, verification, stakeholder dialogue, etc. At present, while there are numerous small ethics consultancy firms, the market is dominated by large professional service firms such as Ernst & Young, KPMG, and Deloitte, which offer management, risk, fraud, reporting, and assurance services, as well as leading niche specialists, such as Bureau Veritas, DNV-GL, Good Corporation and SustainAbility.

Ethics education and training

With greater attention being placed on business ethics, education and training in the subject has also been on the rise. Provision might be offered either in-house or externally through ethics consultants, universities and colleges, or corporate training specialists. Again, formal ethics training has tended to be more common in the US than elsewhere, with a recent survey revealing that in 2013 ethics training was being conducted at 81% of US companies, up from 74% in 2011 (Ethics Resource Center 2014). In Asia, organizations such as CSR Asia also provide a wide range of training courses to meet growing demand in the region.

Many academic writers have stressed the need for more ethics education among business people, not only in terms of providing them with the tools to solve ethical dilemmas, but also to provide them with the ability to recognize and talk about ethical problems more accurately and easily (Thorne LeClair and Ferrell 2000). Diane Kirrane (1990) thus summarizes the goals for ethics training as: (a) identifying situations where ethical decision-making is involved; (b) understanding the culture and values of the organization; and (c) evaluating the impact of the ethical decision on the organization. Some companies have developed innovative approaches to achieving this (Reuters 2009), an example being Novartis, the Swiss health-care multinational, where employees:

> 'play' there [sic] way to learning about the company's code of ethics in 'Novartis Land', an online training program offering the opportunity to interactively explore the policies and answer questions in an online dialogue-role-play setting. Employees interact online with 3D characters and have dialogues based on scenarios found within the company's corporate policies. They navigate through the dialogue, making decisions they may have to make in real life and answer a quiz style game show on company ethics.

Stakeholder consultation, dialogue, and partnership programmes

There are various means of engaging an organization's stakeholders in ethics management, from surveying them to assess their views on specific issues to including them more fully in corporate decision-making. The more advanced forms may be central activities in the promotion of corporate accountability. Just as importantly though, it is evident that if 'good' business ethics is about doing the 'right' thing, then it is essential that organizations consult with relevant stakeholders in order to determine what other constituencies regard as 'right' in the first place. Either way, stakeholder consultation, dialogue, and partnership are increasingly becoming accepted—if still relatively new—ways of managing business ethics, and since they are issues that we will return to throughout the book, they will be explained in greater detail in the section Managing stakeholder relations (pp. 199–206), when we address the more general topic of managing stakeholder relationships. In the meantime, **Ethics Online 5** discusses the rather novel phenomenon of corporations communicating with their stakeholders about corporate social responsibility issues through social media.

Auditing, accounting, and reporting

Finally, we come to a set of closely related activities that are concerned with measuring, evaluating, and communicating the organization's impacts and performance on a range of social, ethical, and environmental issues of interest to their stakeholders. Unlike most of the previous developments, these aspects of business ethics management have not been pioneered in the US but rather in Europe, with companies such as BT, the Co-operative Bank, Norsk Hydro, Traidcraft, the Body Shop, and Shell being at the forefront of innovation in this area. However, there is rapid development in this field across the globe, with KPMG's 2013 survey suggesting that 93% of the largest 250 companies worldwide now issue corporate responsibility reports, with the highest growth rates in countries such as India, Chile, Singapore, Australia and China (KPMG 2013b). According to the survey, the highest level of reporting is in the mining and utilities sectors (where 84% and 79% of companies, respectively, issue a report) while trade and retail is trailing with 62%. This global diffusion is further evident in programmes such as SA 8000 and the Global Reporting Initiative (GRI) that—as we shall discuss in more detail later—seek to provide internationally comparative standards for aspects of auditing, accounting, and reporting. Indeed, although these elements of management are still in relatively early periods of experimentation and development, they can play a crucial role in enhancing corporate accountability in the era of corporate citizenship,

ETHICS ONLINE 5

Stakeholder communication through social media

Sarah Glozer, Royal Holloway, University of London

In the last decade, 'Web 2.0' technological developments have significantly increased the speed, accessibility, and transparency of communication between organizations and stakeholders. The progressively interactive climate afforded by social media sites in particular is also changing the face of corporate social responsibility (CSR) communication. Once premised upon providing information to stakeholders, or responding to their queries, CSR communication is now evolving to actively *involve* stakeholders in the consumption and production of information on social, environmental, and ethical issues.

Arguably still a core platform for communicating CSR, websites are increasingly being complemented with a range of interactive social media tools including weblogs (e.g. food retailer Delhaize's 'Feed Tomorrow' blog), microblogs (e.g. Campbell Soup's CSR Twitter feed), content communities (e.g. Samsung's 'Responsibility in Motion' YouTube channel), and social networking sites (e.g. software company SAP's CSR Facebook page). Interaction on these platforms boils down to textual exchanges, image/video sharing and voting, with some companies even adopting 'gamification' techniques to incentivize sustainable behaviour, such as Recyclebank's link up with Foursquare to reward everyday green actions. These approaches expand the reach of CSR communications, build stakeholder engagement, and ultimately foster stronger, more personalised relationships. Research has also suggested that communicating CSR through social media can build reputational benefits, competitive advantage, and innovation opportunities.

At a broader level, CSR communications in social media environments may also generate positive social impact. Take Global Handwashing Day, supported by Unilever and Procter & Gamble. The campaign takes advantage of Facebook's 1.3 billion monthly active users to raise awareness of the importance of handwashing in preventing infections that take the lives of millions of children in developing countries each year. In 2014 alone, over 200 million people supported Global Handwashing Day, with Facebook being used to disseminate communication materials, share successes, and promote the campaign across over 100 countries.

However, with these benefits come challenges. Given the plethora of social media channels (Wikipedia suggests that there are around 350) and pace of change in online contexts, organizations face a fragmented and dynamic communicative landscape. Where previously it was largely 'controlled' by the company, CSR communication now involves a range of different actors whose only prerequisite is an internet connection. These actors may support, shape, contest and co-construct framings of CSR to both organizational benefit and detriment.

The latter can be illustrated vividly in Greenpeace UK's online activism campaign against Nestlé and its approach to palm oil sourcing. Greenpeace's campaign video targeted Nestlé's iconic Kit Kat bar with the label 'Killer' for its role in destroying the habitat of Orangutans. The video ended up garnering almost 1.5 million views, and even Nestlé's attempt to force its removal from YouTube only served to gain mainstream media attention and a new audience when it was reposted on Vimeo (an alternative video-sharing platform). Eventually, as well as addressing its palm oil sourcing strategy, Nestlé also had to rebuild the damage done to its reputation. Critical voices may also appear in social media from within the organization in the shape of disgruntled employees. In 2013, the UK music retailer HMV saw its social media manager 'live' tweeting to the outside world sensitive information about staff redundancies, placing the media spotlight on a troubled organization.

These examples show that through engaging in 'transparent' and decentralized online communication, companies face the risk of public scrutiny, scepticism, and criticism at breakneck speeds. As they continue to grapple with such crisis situations, social media sites remain littered with unanswered stakeholder questions, traces of deleted comments, 'moderated' spaces for discussion, and policies for 'online rules of engagement'. This begs the question whether social media genuinely offers free, collaborative and innovative spaces for real organization–stakeholder engagement and dialogue.

What is unquestionable, however, is the powerful role that social media plays in augmenting views of organizations, and most specifically CSR agendas. As monological (one-way) communications approaches give way to dialogical (two-way) strategies, what remains to be seen is the extent to which stakeholder communication around CSR will be shaped by social media in the years to come.

Sources
Eberle, D., Berens, G., and Li, T. (2013). The impact of interactive corporate social responsibility communication on corporate reputation. *Journal of Business Ethics*, 118 (4): 731–46.
Morsing, M. and Schultz, M. (2006). Corporate social responsibility communication: stakeholder information, response and involvement strategies. *Business Ethics: A European Review*, 15 (4): 323–38.
Campbell Soup Co CSR: https://twitter.com/CampbellCSR.
Delhaize Group blog: http://blog.delhaizegroup.com.
Global Handwashing Day: https://www.facebook.com/globalhandwashingday.
Samsung CSR: http://www.youtube.com/user/SamsungCSR.
SAP CSR: https://www.facebook.com/SAPCSR.
Recyclebank blog: https://foursquare.com/recyclebank.

as we suggested in Chapter 2. Accordingly, we will return to these developments in more detail below in the section Assessing ethical performance (pp. 206–214).

Evolution of business ethics management

Before proceeding to discuss some of the most common components in more detail, we should stress that few, if any, businesses are likely to have *all* of these tools and techniques in place, and many may not have *any* of them. This will particularly be the case with small- and medium-sized companies, which tend not to introduce the more formal elements of ethics management and reporting (Spence 1999). However, in general, the take-up of different components does appear to be increasing. For example, UK and US surveys between 2005 and 2015 tended to report escalating adoption of most, if not all, components (Webley 2008; Ethics Resource Center 2014).

Also, since 2000 there appears to have been a change in emphasis concerning the purpose of business ethics management. Whereas previously, business ethics management tended to focus primarily on *managing employee behaviour* (through codes, etc.), there has been increasing attention to developing and implementing tools and techniques associated with the *management of broader social responsibilities*. These more externally focused components have typically involved the consideration of other stakeholder demands and considerations, such as in the development of social accounting tools and techniques.

Few would argue that these kinds of external components have an ethical dimension, yet business ethics as a management practice has historically had a tendency to focus primarily on the internal aspects of the business. Nonetheless, effective business ethics management needs to take account of both aspects—the internal and the external dimensions. However, firms have tended to be slow in integrating their ethics and compliance functions with the CSR and sustainability areas of the business.

In the next three sections, we shall take a look at the three main areas where the management of business ethics might be particularly relevant:

- **Setting standards of ethical behaviour**. Here we shall mainly examine the role of ethical codes and their implementation.

- **Managing stakeholder relations**. Here we shall look mainly at how to assess stakeholders, different ways of managing them, and the benefits and problems of doing so.

- **Assessing ethical performance**. Here we shall consider the role of social accounting in contributing to the management and assessment of business ethics.

■ Setting standards of ethical behaviour: designing and implementing codes of ethics

Since the mid-1980s many organizations have made efforts to set out specific standards of appropriate ethical conduct for their employees to follow. As we shall see later in the chapter, much of this standard-setting might well be done informally or even implicitly, such as through the example set by leaders. However, most attention in business ethics theory and practice has focused on **codes of ethics**, which are voluntary statements by organizations or other bodies that set out specific rules or guidelines that the organization or its employees should follow.

Code of ethics
A voluntary statement that commits an organization, industry, or profession to specific beliefs, values, and actions and/ or that set out appropriate ethical behaviour for employees.

There are four main types of ethical codes:

- **Organizational or corporate codes of ethics**. These are specific to a single organization. Sometimes they are called codes of conduct or codes of business principles, but basically these codes seek to identify and encourage ethical behaviour at the level of the individual organization.

- **Professional codes of ethics**. Professional groups also often have their own guidelines for appropriate conduct for their members. While most traditional professions such as medicine, law, and accountancy have long-standing codes of conduct, it is now also increasingly common for other professions such as marketing, purchasing, or engineering to have their own codes.

- **Industry codes of ethics**. As well as specific professions, particular industries also sometimes have their own codes of ethics. For example, in many countries, the financial services industry will have a code of conduct for companies and/or employees operating in the industry. Similarly, at the international level, the electronics industry has developed a code of conduct 'to ensure that working conditions in the electronics industry supply chain are safe, that workers are treated with respect and dignity, and that business operations are environmentally responsible and conducted ethically'.[1] The code was developed by a number of companies engaged in the manufacture of electronics products, including Dell, Hewlett Packard, and IBM. It has since been adopted by a range of multinationals, such as Apple, Cisco, HTC, Intel, Lenovo, Microsoft, Samsung, and Sony.

- **Programme or group codes of ethics**. Finally, certain programmes, coalitions, or other sub-grouping of organizations also establish codes of ethics for those participating in specific programmes. For example, a collaboration of various business leaders from Europe, the US, and Japan resulted in the development of a global code of ethics for business called the CAUX Roundtable Principles for Business (http://www.cauxroundtable.org). Sometimes, conforming to a particular programme code is a prerequisite for using a particular label or mark of accreditation. For instance, companies wishing to use the Fairtrade Mark must meet the social, economic and environmental standards set by the international Fairtrade system (see Chapter 9 for more details).

There has been a lot of research on codes of ethics, primarily focusing on four main issues:

- Prevalence of corporate codes of ethics.
- Content of codes of ethics.
- Effectiveness of codes of ethics.
- Possibilities for global codes of ethics.

Prevalence of codes of ethics

On the first point, codes of ethics are increasingly common, with a substantial rise in their usage identified during the past decades, particularly in large and medium-sized companies. Almost all large US companies have a code, while something like 80% of large European companies and 50% of large Asian companies do (KPMG and RSM Erasmus University 2008). Evidence of their prevalence among SMEs is fairly scant, but the general indication is of a much lower figure (Spence and Lozano 2000).

Content of codes of ethics

In terms of content, codes of ethics typically address a variety of issues, many of which appear to reflect industry factors and the prevailing concerns of the general public. As the OECD (2001: 2) reports, 'environmental management and labour standards dominate other issues in code texts, but consumer protection and bribery and corruption also receive extensive attention'. Perhaps unsurprisingly, codes from the apparel industry tend to focus more than others on labour issues, while codes from the extractive industry tend to feature environmental issues more than others.

In dealing with these issues, most codes attempt to achieve one or both of the following:

- Definition of principles or standards that the organization, profession, or industry believes in or wants to uphold.
- Setting out of practical guidelines or rules for employee behaviour, either generally or in specific situations (such as accepting gifts, how customers are treated, etc.).

Figure 5.2 shows the code of ethics developed by Unilever for its business operations across the globe. As you can see, this mainly focuses on *general* principles, such as: 'Unilever believes in vigorous yet fair competition', but it also includes *specific* guidelines or rules for behaviour in areas such as bribery. For instance, the code specifies that 'any demand for, or offer of, a bribe must be rejected immediately and reported to management'.

Standard of conduct

We conduct our operations with honesty, integrity and openness, and with respect for the human rights and interests of our employees. We shall similarly respect the legitimate interests of those with whom we have relationships.

Obeying the law

Unilever companies and our employees are required to comply with the laws and regulations of the countries in which we operate.

Employees

Unilever is committed to diversity in a working environment where there is mutual trust and respect and where everyone feels responsible for the performance and reputation of our company. We will recruit, employ and promote employees on the sole basis of the qualifications and abilities needed for the work to be performed. We are committed to safe and healthy working conditions for all employees. We will not use any form of forced, compulsory or child labour. We are committed to working with employees to develop and enhance each individual's skills and capabilities. We respect the dignity of the individual and the right of employees to freedom of association. We will maintain good communications with employees through company based information and consultation procedures.

Consumers

Unilever is committed to providing branded products and services which consistently offer value in terms of price and quality, and which are safe for their intended use. Products and services will be accurately and properly labelled, advertised and communicated.

Shareholders

Unilever will conduct its operations in accordance with internationally accepted principles of good corporate governance. We will provide timely, regular and reliable information on our activities, structure, financial situation and performance to all shareholders.

Business partners

Unilever is committed to establishing mutually beneficial relations with our suppliers, customers and business partners. In our business dealings we expect our business partners to adhere to business principles consistent with our own.

Community involvement

Unilever strives to be a trusted corporate citizen and, as an integral part of society, to fulfil our responsibilities to the societies and communities in which we operate.

Public activities

Unilever companies are encouraged to promote and defend their legitimate business interests. Unilever will co-operate with governments and other organisations, both directly and through bodies such as trade associations, in the development of proposed legislation and other regulations which may affect legitimate business interests. Unilever neither supports political parties nor contributes to the funds of groups whose activities are calculated to promote party interests.

The environment

Unilever is committed to making continuous improvements in the management of our environmental impact and to the longer-term goal of developing a sustainable business. Unilever will work in partnership with others to promote environmental care, increase understanding of environmental issues and disseminate good practice.

Innovation

In our scientific innovation to meet consumer needs we will respect the concerns of our consumers and of society. We will work on the basis of sound science, applying rigorous standards of product safety.

Figure 5.2 Unilever's Code of Business Principles

Source: http://www.unilever.com. Reproduced with permission. © Unilever N.V./Unilever PLC. Unilever is a registered trademark of the Unilever group.

Competition

Unilever believes in vigorous yet fair competition and supports the development of appropriate competition laws. Unilever companies and employees will conduct their operations in accordance with the principles of fair competition and all applicable regulations.

Business integrity

Unilever does not give or receive, whether directly or indirectly, bribes or other improper advantages for business or financial gain. No employee may offer, give or receive any gift or payment which is, or may be construed as being, a bribe. Any demand for, or offer of, a bribe must be rejected immediately and reported to management. Unilever accounting records and supporting documents must accurately describe and reflect the nature of the underlying transactions. No undisclosed or unrecorded account, fund or asset will be established or maintained.

Conflicts of interests

All Unilever employees are expected to avoid personal activities and financial interests which could conflict with their responsibilities to the company. Unilever employees must not seek gain for themselves or others through misuse of their positions.

Compliance—Monitoring—Reporting

Compliance with these principles is an essential element in our business success. The Unilever Board is responsible for ensuring these principles are applied throughout Unilever. The Group Chief Executive is responsible for implementing these principles and is supported in this by the Corporate Code Committee comprising the General Counsel, the Joint Secretaries, the Chief Auditor, the SVP HR, the SVP Communications and the Corporate Code Officer, who presents quarterly reports to the Unilever Executive. Day-to-day responsibility is delegated to all senior management of the regions, categories, functions and operating companies. They are responsible for implementing these principles, if necessary through more detailed guidance tailored to local needs, and are supported in this by Regional Code Committees comprising the Regional General Counsel together with representatives from all relevant functions and categories. Assurance of compliance is given and monitored each year. Compliance with the Code is subject to review by the Board supported by the Corporate Responsibility and Reputation Committee and for financial and accounting issues the Audit Committee. Any breaches of the Code must be reported in accordance with the procedures specified by the General Counsel.

The Board of Unilever will not criticise management for any loss of business resulting from adherence to these principles and other mandatory policies and instructions. The Board of Unilever expects employees to bring to their attention, or to that of senior management, any breach or suspected breach of these principles. Provision has been made for employees to be able to report in confidence and no employee will suffer as a consequence of doing so.

In this Code the expressions 'Unilever' and 'Unilever companies' are used for convenience and mean the Unilever Group of companies comprising Unilever N.V., Unilever PLC and their respective subsidiary companies. The Board of Unilever means the Directors of Unilever N.V. and Unilever PLC.

Figure 5.2 Continued

? THINK THEORY

Think about the distinction between principles and guidelines. Can you identify further examples of each in the Unilever code. Evaluate these in terms of the degree of commitment from Unilever and the feasibility of their implementation, especially across national contexts. Do you consider the code to be a useful management tool?

VISIT THE ONLINE RESOURCE CENTRE for a short response to this feature

According to Hoffman et al. (2001: 44), to be effective, codes should address *both* of these tasks: 'rules of conduct without a general values statement lack a framework of meaning and purpose; credos without rules of conduct lack specific content'. The question of exactly how codes can actually be crafted to achieve these ends is, however, a crucial one. Cassell et al. (1997), for example, argue that while clarity is obviously important, the desire for clear prescriptions for employees in specific situations can clash with needs for flexibility and applicability to multiple and/or novel situations. As we shall discuss in more detail shortly, this is particularly pertinent in the context of multinationals where employees are likely to be exposed to new dilemmas and differing cultural expectations (Donaldson 1996). Similarly, given that many ethical dilemmas are characterized by a clash of values or by conflicting stakeholder demands, ethical codes might be expected to identify which values or groups should take precedence—yet the need to avoid offending particular stakeholder groups often results in rather generalized statements of obligation (Hosmer 1987).

Such ambiguousness has unsurprisingly led many commentators to conclude that codes of ethics are primarily a rhetorical PR device that firms can offer as evidence of ethical commitment in order to pacify critics while maintaining business as usual. Indeed, there is little empirical evidence to suggest that simply having a formal written code is either sufficient or even necessary for ensuring ethical behaviour (Kaptein and Schwartz 2008).

Effectiveness of codes of ethics

In many respects then, in terms of effectiveness it is perhaps less important what a code says than how it is developed, implemented, and followed up. A code imposed on employees without clear communication about what it is trying to achieve and why might simply cause resentment. Similarly, a code that is written, launched, and then promptly forgotten is unlikely to promote enhanced ethical decision-making. Perhaps worst of all, a code that is introduced and then seen to be breached with impunity by senior managers or other members of staff is probably never going to achieve anything apart from causing employee cynicism.

So how is it possible to get the implementation right? While there are few, if any, unequivocal answers to this question, a number of suggestions have been presented. Mark Schwartz (2004), for example, interviewed employees, managers, and ethics officers about what they felt determined the effectiveness of codes. His study suggests the following factors as the most important:

- **How the code is written**—such as its readability, the use of appropriate examples, the tone used, and the relevance and realism of the code with respect to the workplace.

- **How the code is supported**—such as does it have top management support, is it backed up with training, is it regularly reinforced?

- **How the code is enforced**—for instance, is there an anonymous reporting channel, are violations communicated to employees, and are there incentives and punishments attached to compliance and non-compliance?

The issue of enforcement is clearly crucial. Another large-scale survey of employees, for example, revealed that 'follow-through' (such as detection of violations, follow-up on notification of violations, and consistency between the policy and action) was much more important in influencing employee behaviour than simply putting a code into place (Treviño et al. 1999). This can present particular challenges to companies when senior management is found to have violated the code as they are the ones supposed to be setting the tone from the top. However, there are a number of high-profile examples of companies taking their codes of ethics sufficiently seriously to apply them even to their senior executives. The chief executives of Boeing (2005), and Hewlett-Packard (2010), and the incoming CEO of Lockheed Martin (2012) all were forced to resign because of breaches of the company's code of conduct. All of these cases involved sexual affairs with employees or contractors—a behaviour clearly defined as inappropriate in their respective codes. Apart from the Hewlett-Packard case, where the affair also included fake expense claims as part of a cover up, those CEOs' unethical actions 'did not affect the company's operational or financial performance', as Lockheed Martin put it in a press release. On the contrary, in the Boeing incident, veteran CEO Harry Stonecipher had been brought out of retirement to help restore the company's bruised reputation after a series of ethics scandals in the early 2000s, and had been successful in restoring trust and boosting the share price by 50%. However, his insistence that even minor violations of the code could not be tolerated ultimately let to his own ignominious exit.[2]

Follow-through of this nature sends an unambiguous message to employees. But how are organizations to ensure that such follow-through is established throughout its span of operations? For this to happen, it is imperative that violations are identified and procedures are put in place to deal with them. Sethi (2002) therefore suggests that codes need to be translated into a standardized and quantified audit instrument that lends itself to clear and consistent assessment, and that code compliance must be linked to managers' performance evaluation.

Although codes are widely regarded among ethics practitioners as an important component of effective business ethics management, there has been a stream of literature more critical of such codes (Clegg et al. 2007; Stansbury and Barry 2007; Painter-Morland 2010). Not only have codes been identified as questionable control mechanisms that potentially seek to exert influence over employee beliefs, values, and behaviours (Schwartz 2000; Stansbury and Barry 2007), but as we saw in Chapter 3, there is growing interest from postmodernists, feminists, and others in the possibility for codified ethical rules and principles to 'suppress' individual moral instincts, emotions, and empathy in order to ensure bureaucratic conformity and consistency. In **An Ethical Dilemma 5**, you can work through some of these issues in the context of a specific example.

Global codes of ethics

Finally, the issue of global codes of ethics has also received increasing attention from business, researchers, and others in recent years (Wieland 2014). Given the rise of multinational business, many organizations have found that codes of ethics developed for use in their home country may need to be revisited for their international operations. Are guidelines for domestic employees still relevant and applicable in overseas contexts? Can organizations devise one set of principles for all countries in which they operate?

Consider the issue of gift giving in business. This is an issue where cultural context has a distinct bearing on what might be regarded as acceptable ethical behaviour. While

AN ETHICAL DILEMMA 5

Getting explicit about the code of conduct

It is another Monday morning and after a relaxing weekend you are sitting in your office preparing your agenda for the week. As the IT manager of a small financial services company you have to prepare for your staff meeting at 10am when all of your 15 IT team members will be present. You are planning to discuss the launch of your new promotion scheme, which is due to begin at the end of the week. Fortunately, Paul, who is the main market analyst for the company, was prepared to do some extra work at home over the weekend in order to make sure the forecasts were ready for the meeting.

While sipping your first cup of coffee someone knocks at the door. It is Fred, the hardware manager. He looks a bit embarrassed, and after a little stilted small talk, he tells you that 'a problem' has come up. He has just checked-in the laptop that Paul the market analyst had taken out of the company's pool and used at home over the weekend in order to finish the forecasts you had asked for. However, when completing the routine check of the laptop, Fred tells you he noticed links to various pornography sites in the history file of the laptop's internet browser. He tells you that they must have been accessed over the weekend when Paul had the laptop—the access dates refer to the last two days, and as is usual practice, the history file was emptied after the last person had borrowed it.

There is a strict company policy prohibiting employees from making personal use of company hardware, and access to sites containing 'material of an explicit nature' is tantamount to gross misconduct and may result in the immediate termination of the employee's contract. When your hardware manager leaves the office, you take a big breath and slowly finish your coffee.

After a few minutes thinking through the problem, you ask Paul to come into your office. You have a quick chat about his work and tell him that you are really pleased with the forecasts he put together over the weekend. Then, you bring up the problem with the laptop's history file. When you tell him what has surfaced, Paul is terribly embarrassed and assures you that he has absolutely no idea how this could have happened. After some thought, though, he tells you that he did allow a friend to use the laptop a couple of times over the weekend to check his email. Although Paul says that this is the only possible explanation for the mystery files, he does not volunteer any more information about the friend involved.

As it happens, this does not make you feel much better about the situation—the company's code of conduct also prohibits use of IT equipment by anyone other than employees. The company deals with a lot of private data that no one outside the company should have access to. You remind Paul of this and he tells you that he did not realize there was any such policy. You are left wondering when the last time was that anyone did any training around the ethics policy—certainly not recently. Scratching your head, you tell Paul that you will need 24 hours to think it over, and you get on with preparing for the team meeting.

While driving home that evening, you turn the issue over and over in your head. Yes, there is a corporate policy with regard to web access and personal use of company resources. And in principle you agree with this—after all, you were part of the committee that designed the policy in the first place. A company like yours has to be able to have clarity on such issues, and there have to be controls on what the company's equipment is used for—no doubt about that. You cannot help thinking that Paul has been pretty stupid in breaking the rules—whether he visited the sites himself or not.

On the other hand, you are also having a few problems with taking this further. Given the amount of embarrassment this has caused Paul already, is this likely to be just a one-off? Does the company not need Paul's experience and expertise, especially now with the big launch a few days off? Why cause problems over a few websites, especially when the company has not been very active in communicating its ethics policy? Would it be better to keep it quiet, give him a warning, and just get on with the launch? This looks set to be a tough call.

Questions

1. What are your main ethical problems in this case?
2. Set out the possible courses of action open to you.
3. Assess these alternatives according to a utilitarian perspective and a duty-based perspective. Which is the most convincing?
4. What would you do, and why?
5. Based on your answer, what are the apparent benefits and limitations of the code of conduct in this example?

many organizations have specific guidelines precluding the offer or acceptance of gifts and hospitality as part of their business operations, in some countries, such as Japan, not only is the offering of gifts considered to be a perfectly acceptable business activity, but the refusal to accept such offerings can be regarded as offensive. Similarly, questions of equal opportunity are somewhat more equivocal in a multinational context. European or US organizations with codes of practice relating to equal opportunities may find that these run counter to cultural norms and even legal statutes overseas. For example, in many countries such as India, there is a cultural expectation that people should show preference for their close friends and family over strangers, even in business contexts such as recruitment. In many Islamic countries, the equal treatment of men and women is viewed very differently from the way it is viewed in the West, with countries such as Saudi Arabia still having major restrictions on women even entering the workforce (Murphy 2007).

According to Thomas Donaldson (1996), one of the leading writers on international business ethics, the key question for those working overseas is: when is different just different and when is different wrong? As such, the question of how multinationals should address cultural differences in drafting their ethical codes returns us to the discussion of relativist versus absolutist positions on ethics that we introduced in Chapter 3. A relativist would suggest that different codes should be developed for different contexts, while an absolutist would contend that one code can and should fit all. Donaldson's (1996) solution is to propose a middle ground between the two extremes, whereby the organization should be guided by three principles:

- Respect for core human values, which determine an absolute moral threshold.

- Respect for local traditions.

- The belief that context matters when deciding what is right and wrong.

What this means is that global codes should define minimum ethical standards according to core human values shared across countries, religions, and cultures, such as the need to respect human dignity and basic human rights. Beyond this, though, codes should also respect cultural or contextual difference in setting out appropriate behaviour in areas such as bribery or gift giving.

The search for core values or universal ethical principles as a basis for global business codes of ethics has given rise to a number of important initiatives:[3]

- In 1994, business and government leaders, theologians, and academics representing three religions—Christian, Jewish, and Islamic—devised the Interfaith Declaration: A Code of Ethics on International Business for Christians, Muslims and Jews. This sought to identify key principles shared by the three faiths that could guide international business behaviour. These principles are justice, mutual respect, stewardship, and honesty.

- Principles for Responsible Business. The CAUX Roundtable, an international network of senior business leaders from Europe, the US, and Asia, has advanced a set of 'ethical norms for acceptable businesses behaviour' across the globe. These seven principles include 'respect stakeholders beyond shareholders', 'contribute to economic, social and environmental development', and 'build trust by going beyond the letter of the law'. Originally developed in the early 1990s, the latest version of the principles was released in 2010 in response to the global financial crisis.

- In 2000, the United Nations launched the UN Global Compact, a set of ten 'universally accepted' principles concerned with human rights, labour, the environment, and anti-corruption. By 2014, more than 8,000 businesses in 145 countries around the world had signed up to the Compact. For an extended discussion of the global compact, see Ethics in Action 11.2.

☑ Skill check

Implementing codes of ethics: This is a key skill for managing business ethics as it enables managers to develop and adopt appropriate rules around ethical conduct and ensure that the code is effectively applied to business conduct.

While the necessity of developing globally acceptable and relevant principles means that such codes tend to be rather general in nature, these developments do at least show that some level of international agreement on appropriate standards of business behaviour is possible. And for multinationals, although establishing and implementing a global code of ethics represents a huge challenge, it is one that is increasingly expected in the contemporary business environment (Sethi 2002). This does not just go for those high-profile big brand companies on the high street, but also companies that are more frequently below the ethics radar. Consider, for example, the Swedish engineering group, Sandvik. The company launched its code across its global operations around 2004 with a series of two-day seminars for all of its managers in some 130 countries. With the goal of rolling out the code to the firm's entire 50,000 employees, it is clear that multinationals such as Sandvik have to invest a great deal of time, energy, and resources into introducing a global code in a meaningful way.

Ultimately, however, it is important to realize that the drive for codes of ethics, whether national or international, is never going to 'solve' the management of business ethics. As we saw in Chapter 4, there is a vast array of influences on individual decision-makers within the organization, of which a written code is but one aspect. A code can rarely do more than set out the *minimum expectations* placed on organizations and their members, and cannot be expected to be a substitute for organizational contexts supportive of ethical reflection, debate, and decision-making, or decision-makers with strong personal integrity. Moreover, while the introduction of codes of ethics primarily represents an attempt to manage employee conduct, organizations have increasingly found that the management of business ethics also requires them to manage relationships with a wide range of stakeholders, as we shall now discuss.

> **? THINK THEORY**
>
> Think about the notion of a global code of ethics from the perspective of (a) rights, and (b) postmodern perspectives on ethics. What does each contribute and can they be reconciled?

VISIT THE ONLINE RESOURCE CENTRE for a short response to this feature

■ Managing stakeholder relations

In Chapter 2 we introduced stakeholder theory as one of the key theories in the debate on the role and responsibilities of business in society. While our main concern there and in Chapter 3 was to highlight the normative basis of stakeholder theory, it is important also to acknowledge the descriptive argument that managers do indeed appear to recognize distinct stakeholder groups and manage their companies accordingly. While in some countries this is institutionalized in corporate governance, such as in the German two-tier supervisory board, even in more shareholder-focused countries many managers appear to have embraced at least some degree of recognition for stakeholder claims. One survey, for example, found that four out of five executives from global companies agreed that generating high returns for investors should be balanced with other stakeholder interests. Indian managers articulated the most positive response (90% endorsed a 'public-good' dimension) and executives based in China demonstrated the least commitment (25% said that investor returns should be the sole focus of corporate activity).[4]

The recognition that not only businesses but organizations of all kinds, including charities, schools, universities, and governments, have a range of stakeholders whose interests might need to be taken into account in making decisions has given rise to a significant body of research dealing with the management of stakeholder relations. Let us look at some of the main themes addressed in this literature.

Assessing stakeholder importance: an instrumental perspective

Stakeholder management
The process by which organizations seek to understand the interests and expectations of their stakeholders and attempt to satisfy them in a way that aligns with the core interests of the company.

Much of the **stakeholder management** literature has tended to focus on the strategic aspects of identifying which stakeholders actually matter to the organization and how they should be dealt with in order for the organization to effectively achieve its goals. Thus, Jones and Hill (2013: 380–81), in one of the leading Strategic Management textbooks, suggest that:

> **A company cannot always satisfy the claims of all stakeholders. The goals of different groups may conflict, and in practice few organizations have the resources to manage all stakeholders ... Often the company must make choices. To do so, it must identify the most important stakeholders and give highest priority to pursuing strategies that satisfy their needs.**

As Donaldson and Preston (1995) contend, it is important to distinguish this *instrumental* perspective on stakeholder theory from the *normative* perspective we developed in Chapters 2 and 3, and the *descriptive* perspective mentioned briefly above. Hill and Jones' (2013) argument is not so much that organizations have to rate the relative strength of the *ethical* claims of their various stakeholders, but rather that strategic objectives can best be realized by deciding which stakeholders are more likely to be able to *influence* the organization in some way. This is likely to be particularly important when organizations are in a position where they have to decide how to assign relative importance or priority to competing stakeholder claims.

Following a comprehensive review of the stakeholder management literature, Mitchell et al. (1997) suggest three key relationship attributes likely to determine the perceived importance or *salience* of stakeholders:

- **Power**. The perceived ability of a stakeholder to influence organizational action.
- **Legitimacy**. Whether the organization perceives the stakeholder's actions as desirable, proper, or appropriate.
- **Urgency**. The degree to which stakeholder claims are perceived to call for immediate attention.

According to Mitchell et al. (1997), managers are likely to assign greater salience to those stakeholders thought to possess greater power, legitimacy, and urgency. Thus, stakeholders thought to be in possession of only one of these attributes will be regarded as the least important and might be regarded as 'latent' stakeholders. Those in possession of two of the three attributes are moderately important and hence can be thought of as 'expectant' stakeholders. Finally, those in possession of all three attributes will be seen as the most important constituencies and hence are termed 'definitive' stakeholders. For businesses, these definitive stakeholders often require active engagement in order to develop an effective and appropriate working relationship. Indeed, a variety of different relationships might be expected to emerge between businesses and their stakeholders, as we shall now see.

☑ Skill check

Prioritization of stakeholders. A key skill for managers consists in allocating scarce resources to those stakeholders that have the strongest impact on the organization's ability to achieve its goals.

Types of stakeholder relationship

Until relatively recently, it had been generally assumed that relationships between businesses and their stakeholders tended to be somewhat antagonistic, even confrontational in nature. For example, companies might exploit consumers or downsize employees, while consumers might boycott the company's products, and employees might initiate industrial action. Similarly, suppliers can withhold credit, competitors might engage in industrial espionage, and pressure groups can employ aggressive direct action campaigns against companies.

Increasingly however, it has been recognized that there might also be a place for co-operation between stakeholders. Much of this development in broader stakeholder collaboration was pioneered in the field of environmental management, but it has since expanded to a wide range of social issues. One prominent approach, as we shall describe in more detail in Chapter 10, has been cross-sector partnerships between businesses and NGOs (Seitanidi and Crane 2014). Similarly, the Dutch covenant approach has been successful in improving firms' environmental performance by negotiating voluntary environmental agreements between government and industry bodies (Bressers et al. 2011). These extended forms of stakeholder collaboration have also emerged in other areas of business: various charities have joined with corporations in cause-related marketing campaigns; governments have worked with corporations to develop public-private partnerships for tackling social, educational, health, and transportation problems; and NGOs, trade unions, and government organizations have worked with businesses to develop initiatives aimed at improving working conditions and stamping out child labour and other human rights abuses in developing countries.

All of these developments and more will be discussed in greater detail in the second part of the book where we focus on business ethics and specific stakeholder groups. What is immediately clear, however, is that stakeholder relationships can take a variety of different forms, including everything from outright challenge and conflict right up to joint ventures.

Confrontational forms of relationship are still very much in evidence. For example, in 2014 Greenpeace launched a global campaign against the Danish toy company Lego to try and force it to end its relationship with the oil company Shell, in which Shell-branded Lego sets were sold at petrol stations. Lego initially refused to talk to Greenpeace but after a hugely successful social media campaign it eventually backed down and announced it would not renew the relationship (Vaughan 2014). Over time, however, there has clearly been a significant shift towards more collaborative types of relationship, such as stakeholder dialogue and alliances (Selsky and Parker 2005; Seitanidi and Crane 2014). **Ethics in Action 5.1** describes a typical example of a 'social partnership' that corporations and civil society organizations now often engage in.

Collaboration between stakeholders will certainly not always lead to beneficial ethical outcomes (consider, for example, the problems posed by two competitors collaborating over price setting). However, it is certainly an increasingly important tool for *managing* business ethics, primarily because closer forms of collaboration can bring to the surface stakeholder demands and interests, and thereby provide companies with a greater opportunity to satisfy their stakeholders in some way. Working directly with stakeholders can therefore mean that problems are dealt with more effectively. Moreover, by involving stakeholders more, it can be argued that a greater degree of democratic governance is introduced into corporate decision-making, thus enhancing corporate accountability.

VISIT THE
ONLINE
RESOURCE
CENTRE
for links to
useful sources
of further
information

ETHICS IN ACTION 5.1   http://www.ethicalcorp.com

NGO partnering: save the reputation?
Stephen Gardner, 3 June 2013

GlaxoSmithKline is working with Save the Children to cut infant mortality—but how far are the motives behind the initiative more than just philanthropy?

It looks like a perfect partnership. One of the world's best-known charities, Save the Children, has teamed up with pharmaceuticals giant GlaxoSmithKline. They will jointly apply their considerable weight to tackling the tragedy of infant mortality in poor countries. The overall aim is to prevent a million child deaths in Africa, Asia and Latin America, starting with pilot programmes in the Democratic Republic of Congo and Kenya.

Save the Children will provide the network and on-the-ground experience. GSK will provide products that will be trialled in difficult conditions, such as in very hot regions that lack refrigeration. Save the Children says the initiative is about solving basic problems through the application of tried and tested medicines, specifically an antiseptic that can be used to clean new-borns and prevent infection, and an anti-biotic that acts against pneumonia. The project is 'looking at the hardest-to-reach children,' says a spokesman. 'It's not about testing [new products]. It's about existing products and how they can be reformulated for difficult environments.'

In its statement on the announcement of the partnership, Save the Children points out that 'almost seven million children died in 2011 through lack of access to basic healthcare, vaccines or nutritious food.' Over its five-year duration, the partnership with GSK aims to reduce the terrible toll.

But the partnership, though its aims are laudable, has also brought to the fore concerns that Save the Children is cosying up to GSK just a little too much. In August 2012, only a few months ahead of the announcement of the scheme, Save the Children recruited a new chief operating officer, Rachel Parr. She brought to the charity considerable corporate experience, most recently as finance vice-president of GSK, where she worked for more than 20 years.

Of course, GSK could certainly use a good news story. In 2012, it settled a US health-care fraud case with a $3 billion payment—the largest in US history—and in April 2013 the UK Office of Fair Trading accused it of making underhand payments to delay the production of generic versions of a branded antidepressant.

Huge gains

The Save the Children spokesman says that to focus on this would be to miss the point. GSK's misbehaviour 'was left over from a long time ago. Now there is a huge gain that can be made for children, and that is the priority.' John Hilary, executive director of War on Want, says GSK stands to benefit by making inroads into developing countries where markets could be established, but for Save the Children the long-term benefits are less evident. For companies, 'these types of initiatives are important loss-leaders,' and 'part of a major long-term strategy for growth,' he says.

A GSK spokesperson says the company wanted to cooperate with Save the Children because there was 'a realization of what we can do and achieve together'. GSK adds: 'The size and scale of this partnership show that it is much, much more than a PR stunt.'

For War on Want, the application of pharmaceutical products as a solution to health problems in poor countries should not obscure the need to tackle underlying problems, chiefly poverty. 'We are sceptical at the prospect of these partnerships being good news for communities in the long run,' Hilary says. 'From our point of view, it is not a good model for delivery of long-term structural change.'

Sources

Ethical Corporation, Stephen Gardner, 3 June 2013, http://www.ethicalcorp.com. Reproduced with the kind permission of Ethical Corporation.

? THINK THEORY

What types of stakeholder relationships are described here? What are the benefits and limitations of these approaches for managing business ethics?

VISIT THE
ONLINE
RESOURCE
CENTRE
for a short
response to this
feature

On the reverse side, it is also clear that despite their obvious benefits for the management of business ethics, developments towards closer stakeholder relationships are not without their problems.

Problems with stakeholder collaboration

Potential problems with stakeholder collaboration can arise at a number of different levels, but can be basically summarized as follows:

1. **Resource intensity**. Stakeholder collaboration can be extremely time-consuming and expensive compared with traditional forms of corporate decision-making. Not only may firms not have sufficient resources to engage in extensive stakeholder collaboration, but by doing so they may fail to meet the short-term financial goals expected of them by shareholders. Small businesses, in particular, may typically lack the time and financial resources necessary to develop partnerships, even though they often stand to benefit significantly due to the need for external expertise and support.

2. **Culture clash**. Companies and their stakeholders often exhibit very different values and goals, and this can lead to significant clashes in beliefs and ways of working, both between and within collaborating groups (Crane 1998).

3. **Schizophrenia**. At the same time as they are collaborating on one issue or project, companies and their stakeholders may also often be in conflict over another issue or project. This development of 'multiple identities' can result in apparently schizophrenic behaviour on either or both sides, which their partners may find hard to deal with (Elkington and Fennell 2000; Crane and Livesey 2003).

ASKHAM BRYAN
COLLEGE
LEARNING RESOURCES

VISIT THE
ONLINE
RESOURCE
CENTRE
for links to
useful sources
of further
information

ETHICS ON SCREEN 5

Pink Ribbons, Inc.

A quietly effective, often emotionally searing doc.

Linda Barnard, *Toronto Star*

Pink Ribbons, Inc. is a documentary that critically examines the relationships between companies and breast cancer. It focuses on the pink ribbon campaign that has seen numerous companies raise funds and awareness for breast cancer by adopting the pink ribbon symbol in their promotions and tying sales to donations to the cause. Directed by Canadian filmmaker Léa Pool and premiered at the 2011 Toronto International Film Festival, the movie is based on the 2006 book *Pink Ribbons, Inc: Breast Cancer and the Politics of Philanthropy* by Queens University professor Samantha King.

The documentary focuses its attention on the activities of the Susan G. Komen charity (or 'Komen' for short), which first launched the Pink Ribbon campaign in the early 1990s. Komen is the largest breast cancer charity in the US and, according to its website, has donated more than $2.5 billion in breast cancer research, community health outreach, advocacy and programmes in more than 30 countries. *Pink Ribbons, Inc.* casts a critical light on many of Komen's strategies and in particular their relationship to the many large corporations with which they partner.

According to Komen's website, the organization partners with more than a hundred corporations. 'Each of them has made a positive impact on our mission to end breast cancer by taking a stand to do good while doing business,' the organization states, 'they've helped shape the face of the breast cancer movement through cause marketing, event sponsorship, community and employee engagement, and the power of volunteerism. We're fortunate to have such dedicated and caring companies supporting our organization, and we thank

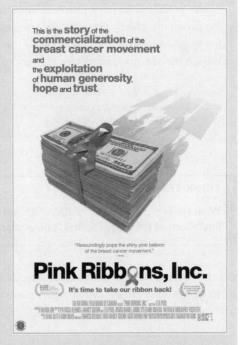

NFB/First Run Features/The Kobal Collection

4. **Co-ordination**. Even with the best intentions of all parties, there is no guarantee with stakeholder collaboration that a mutually acceptable outcome can always be reached. However, not only can consensus be elusive, but by collaborating with many different partners, organizations can face major co-ordination problems, increasing the risk of losing control of their strategic direction (Babiak and Thibault 2009).

5. **Co-optation**. Some critics have raised the question of whether, by involving themselves more closely with corporations, some stakeholder groups are effectively just being co-opted by corporations to embrace a more business-friendly agenda rather than maintaining true independence (Baur and Schmitz 2012; Dauvergne and LeBaron 2014). **Ethics on Screen 5** provides a vivid illustration of this problem.

them on behalf of the millions who've been affected by breast cancer.'

Pool's documentary, however, presents another side to the story, focusing not only on the benefits of corporate involvement with charity, but also its limits and risks. At issue are the many pharmaceutical, cosmetics, and food companies that have partnered with Komen and that use the Pink Ribbon in the marketing of their products. For such companies, their core customers are typically women, among whom breast cancer is undoubtedly a significant personal concern. And many of these companies, in particular pharmaceutical companies, have products for which breast cancer patients are a considerable target market.

The movie contends that there is a great deal of cynicism behind these commercially driven forms of business–charity relationships. The yoghurt manufacturer Yoplait, for instance, is claimed to have enthusiastically used the Pink Ribbon in its branding while selling milk products containing recombinant bovine growth hormone (rBGH), a possible cause of breast cancer. Similarly Estée Lauder and Revlon, important partners of Komen, are argued to have used a plethora of carcinogenic substances in their cosmetics. However, it is the pharmaceutical companies Astra Zeneca and Eli Lilly that are portrayed as the most blatant 'Pinkwashers': Pool contends that they not only profit from breast cancer through their respective cancer drugs, but they also produce hormones and other substances fed to farm animals that may be sources of cancer in humans.

The movie thus exposes an approach to social responsibility by firms that focuses primarily on philanthropy while failing to address their core business practices. It also highlights some of the ethical challenges faced by civil society organizations such as charities. Komen is portrayed in the documentary as having failed to attend sufficiently to the interests of its own core stakeholder group of breast cancer patients and survivors. This is partly exposed by the type of research the organization funds: only 5% is actually dedicated to the research of cancer *prevention* and *root causes*, while the lion's share is allocated to research on how to treat the disease—the latter of course being a potentially lucrative market for the very corporations that support Komen.

By interviewing patients and survivors, the movie also questions the 'shiny pink story of success' narrative promulgated by Komen that has turned breast cancer into a 'dream cause' for companies. While breast cancer is a devastating disease, Komen predominantly celebrates it as a challenge that can be beaten and turned into a collective celebration of human survival—all within an increasingly commercialized atmosphere. So although Komen, its donors, and partner companies have undoubtedly done much to fund breast cancer research that might not have been otherwise possible, Pool's documentary shows the dangers of tying commercial motives to people's suffering. As one member of a cancer support group says, 'It's like our disease is being used for people to profit and that's not okay.'

Sources

Barnard, L. 2012. Pink Ribbons, Inc. review: not so pretty in pink. *Toronto Star*, 2 February 2012.

http://ww5.komen.org.

https://www.nfb.ca/film/pink_ribbons_inc.

6. **Accountability**. While stakeholder collaboration may partially redress problems with *corporate* accountability, there are also important concerns about the accountability of stakeholder organizations themselves (Bendell 2000). Government bodies, activists, trade unions, and NGOs, for example, can also be challenged on grounds of accountability to their members or the general public. Moreover, when stakeholders such as business and government collaborate 'behind closed doors', accountability to the public may be compromised (Dahan et al. 2013).

7. **Resistance**. As a result of these and other concerns, organization members or external parties may try and resist the development of collaborative relationships, thus preventing the partners from fully achieving their goals (Selsky and Parker 2005).

■ Assessing ethical performance

As with any other form of management, the effective management of business ethics relies to some extent on being able to assess and evaluate performance. Low or disappointing performance in business ethics might call for increased attention to ethical issues and problems; high performance might indicate an effective approach to the management of business ethics. Almost immediately, however, it is possible to identify some drawbacks to this whole notion of ethical performance. What exactly is ethical performance? How can it possibly be measured? What criteria can we use to determine how good or bad an organization's ethical performance is? What level of ethical performance is expected by, or acceptable to, stakeholders? These are all vitally important questions to answer if we are to make any progress at all towards the effective management of business ethics. Unfortunately, while there are impressive developments currently taking place in this area, we are still a long way from being able to provide a comprehensive response (Burritt and Schaltegger 2010).

At present, there is a whole patchwork of initiatives that we might include within the umbrella of assessing ethical performance. These include ethical auditing, environmental accounting, and sustainability reporting, as well as various other mixtures of terminology. With such a diversity of labels in use, there are obviously problems with distinguishing between different tools, techniques, and approaches. This is not helped by the fact that, at times, the distinctions between these terms are fairly illusory and there has been much inconsistency in the way that different terms have been applied and used. While Toyota currently produces a 'sustainability report', Total produces a 'CSR report', Microsoft produces a 'citizenship report', and the Body Shop produces a 'values report'. Sometimes even the same company changes between the different labels from one year to the next!

Given this confusion, we shall refer to social accounting as the generic term which encapsulates the other tools and approaches. With its first usage dating back to the early 1970s, social accounting is also, according to Gray et al. (1997), the longest established and simplest term with which to work.

What is social accounting?

Social accounting is related to, but clearly distinct from, conventional financial accounting. The key factors that distinguish social accounting from financial accounting are:

- Its focus on issues other than (but not necessarily excluding) financial data.

- Its intended audience extending beyond (but not excluding) shareholders.

- Its status as a voluntary rather than a legally mandated practice (at least in most jurisdictions).

So what does the process of social accounting involve? Again, there are no clear answers to this question. Unlike financial accounting, there are as yet no strict formal

Social accounting
The voluntary process concerned with assessing and communicating organizational activities and impacts on social, ethical, and environmental issues relevant to stakeholders.

standards laying down the rules that determine which issues should be included, how performance on particular issues should be assessed, or on how the organization should communicate its assessments to its audience (Wood 2010). In many ways, this is not surprising. After all, while it is reasonably straightforward to calculate how much wages an organization has paid, or how many sales it might have made, this is much more difficult with social, ethical, and environmental issues. True, some of the social activities of an organization can be reasonably accurately determined, such as how much effluent might have been discharged into local rivers, or how much money has been given away to charitable causes. But even here, this does not tell us what the actual impact of these activities has been—how polluted this makes the water, and what the ultimate consequence is for fish and other life. Or what were the actual effects of company donations on their recipients and how much happiness did they cause?

Much of the data collected and reported in social accounting is therefore inevitably qualitative in nature, particularly as organizations move away from an emphasis on environmental impacts towards more integrated social or sustainability reports. For example, *The Shell Sustainability Report 2013* includes a mixture of quantitative data, such as greenhouse gas emissions, safety statistics, and gender diversity, as well as more qualitative data in the form of case studies of specific projects, quotes from various stakeholders, and outlines of key social issues and Shell's position on them.

The problem though is not only one of how to assess social impacts, but also of which impacts to *account for* in the first place. Organizations have different aims, problems, and achievements; their stakeholders have different interests and concerns; and the reasons for even engaging in social accounting at all will vary between different organizations. Inevitably, the nature and process of social accounting adopted by any organization is to some extent a function of how the particular organization sees itself and its relationship with its stakeholders (Zadek et al. 1997). As such, the practice of social accounting to date has tended to be evolutionary in nature, with organizations not only developing and refining their techniques over time, but also building in adaptation within the development cycle of a given report or audit.

Figure 5.3 provides a general framework for social accounting. This begins with *determining aims and strategy* for social accounting, where the organization will consider what the general purpose for measuring and reporting is, who the organization wants to communicate with, and what it hopes to achieve through the process. Next, the organization will likely *conduct a materiality assessment* in order to determine which particular issues are important to provide information on (or 'material') from the point of view of users. Such an analysis assesses the relative importance of various social, ethical and environmental issues to stakeholders and evaluates their relative impact on business success. **Figure 5.4** provides an example of a basic 'materiality matrix'. Plotting the range of possible issues on such a matrix gives a company a clearer sense of which issues it should be prioritizing. For example, the sports apparel company Puma identifies its most material issues in the top right quadrant which include 'responsible sourcing of raw materials', 'child and forced labour', 'water use and management', 'corruption' and 'living wage'.[5] Such an analysis is becoming a common practice in social reporting, partly because the Global Reporting Initiative reporting standards are strongly focused on the issue of materiality (see **Ethics in Action 5.2**).

Once the organization has identified its material issues, it will typically *select the performance indicators* that will be used to measure its progress in responding to such issues. It will then go about *collecting and analysing data* with respect to those indicators. This could

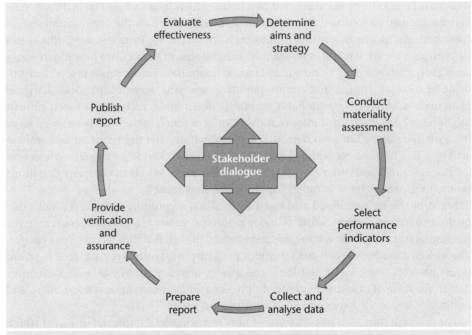

Figure 5.3 Stakeholder dialogue: social accounting process

include data from stakeholder surveys, operational data from individual business units, results of social audits of supplier factories, and other forms of hard and soft data from across the organization. The organization will then *prepare a report* (or reports), which could be either hard-copy or online communications, and as standalone reports or integrated into the firm's regular financial reporting and other corporate communications.

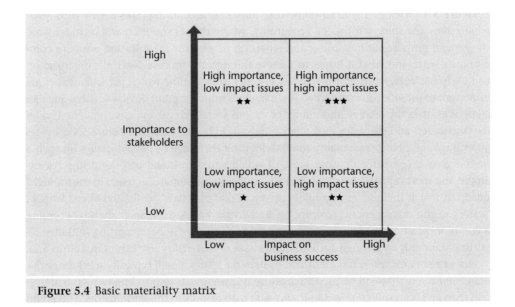

Figure 5.4 Basic materiality matrix

An important element in ensuring the information provided by the firm is credible for their intended audience is establishing some kind of *verification and assurance* of the data and analysis conducted. Although not all organizations engage in this practice during social accounting (whereas in financial accounting they are legally required to), it is widely regarded as a critical element in ensuring an organization's accountability to its stakeholders (O'Dwyer et al. 2011). Typically assurance is provided by a third-party auditor, such as one of the 'Big Four' accounting firms or a more specialist social audit consultancy. Following the *publication of the report,* many organizations will seek to determine how effective the report has been in achieving the goals set out at the beginning of the process. This might be through stakeholder consultation as well as social media and web analytics of various kinds. In fact *stakeholder dialogue* can play a role in virtually any part of the process of social accounting, whether it is setting priorities, identifying salient issues, or determining relevant indicators and data.

Figure 5.3 represents a general social accounting process, but organizations typically develop their own particular approaches. Although this has resulted in some innovative, impressive, and genuinely useful methodologies and reports, it has also led to the production of some vague, self-serving, and rather disappointing efforts that have been useful neither to stakeholders nor to the organization's management. This raises two important questions:

- Why do organizations take up social accounting in the first place?

- What makes for an effective approach to social accounting?

Why do organizations engage in social accounting?

As with many aspects of business ethics, there are both practical and moral reasons for taking up social accounting, but in essence, we can usefully reduce these to four main issues.

- **Internal and external pressure**. Pressure from competitors, industry associations, governments, shareholders, consumers, and even internal executives can all provide incentives for firms to engage in various aspects of social accounting (Solomon and Lewis 2002). For example, the burgeoning socially responsible investment industry and the development of the FTSE4Good and the Dow Jones Sustainability indices have created incentives to audit and report more fully on sustainability issues. Similarly, pressure from unions, the media, and pressure groups has prompted firms to develop social auditing practices to evaluate working conditions in their supply chains.

- **Identifying risks**. Social auditing, in particular, provides organizations with a clearer picture of what is happening in terms of their social, ethical, and environmental impacts throughout their sphere of operations. This information is critical for identifying business risks and other potential problems that can harm the organization and its stakeholders. For instance, in the absence of a thorough audit of its overseas factories, how can an organization know if it is potentially threatening the human rights of its employees or at risk of a major environmental problem?

- **Improved stakeholder management**. At the very least, social accounting provides a new channel of communication to stakeholders by which organizations might seek to improve their reputation. At a more sophisticated level, though, social accounting helps improve managerial decision making by providing critical information relevant for stakeholder management (Burritt and Schaltegger 2010). Social accounting can give organizations a clearer picture of what they are trying to achieve, what they are actually doing, and what the implications are of their business activities (Kolk 2010).

- **Enhanced accountability and transparency**. Social accounting is not just about more effective management though. As we saw in Chapter 2, the need for corporations to make evident their social role and impacts (transparency) is a key requirement for ensuring that they are answerable in some way for the consequences of their actions (accountability). Clearly by reporting on social performance, social accounting can play a significant role in this drive for enhanced accountability and transparency (Gray 1992; Zadek 1998; Owen 2005). However, there are also limitations to the approach, particularly as it currently stands. Not only is social accounting voluntary, but also without adequate standards, organizations can effectively report on anything they want. At present, companies are far more likely to consult stakeholders in an opportunistic manner in order to build consensus for what they are already doing rather than use social accounting as a means of genuinely engaging stakeholders in a two-way conversation that involves them in meaningful decision-making (Manetti 2011).

Given these reasons, there is a reasonably strong case for suggesting that corporations 'should' engage in better social accounting, and for many firms, even *some* degree of social accounting would be an improvement. The reporting element of social accounting is still almost exclusively a large firm phenomenon, with few small and medium enterprises producing stand-alone reports (Owen and O'Dwyer 2008). So there are clearly also a number of important disincentives for social accounting. These include: perceived high costs; insufficient information; inadequate information systems; lack of standards; secrecy; and an unwillingness to disclose sensitive or confidential data.

VISIT THE
ONLINE
RESOURCE
CENTRE
for a short
response to this
feature

> **? THINK THEORY**
>
> Should social accounting be advocated on a consequentialist or non-consequentialist argument? How would the two arguments differ?

What makes for 'good' social accounting?

Clearly the question of what is 'good' social accounting will depend on what the initial purpose is, and which perspective—organizational, stakeholder, or other—you are asking the question from. However, it is evident that as the development of tools and techniques has evolved and been refined over time, there is some consensus emerging about standards of quality. The following eight issues have been proposed as the key principles of quality (see Zadek et al. 1997):

- **Inclusivity**. Good social accounting will reflect the views and accounts of all principal stakeholders, and will involve two-way communication *with* them, rather than just one-way communication either *to* them or *from* them.

- **Comparability**. In order for assessment of social performance to be meaningful, social accounting should allow for comparisons across different periods, with other organizations, and relative to external standards or benchmarks.

- **Completeness**. All areas of the organization's activities should be included in the assessment, rather than just focusing on areas where a more positive impression might be realized.

- **Evolution**. In order to reflect changing stakeholder expectations, social accounting practices should also demonstrate a commitment to learning and change.

- **Management policies and systems**. To ensure effective institutionalization of the social accounting process, it should be consolidated within systems and procedures that allow it to be rigorously controlled and evaluated.

- **Disclosure**. The issue of accountability would suggest that good social accounting should involve clear disclosure of accounts and reports to all stakeholders, in a form that is appropriate to their needs.

- **External verification**. The extent to which audiences will have faith and confidence in a social account will depend to some extent on whether it has been verified as a true representation of reality by an external body trusted by that audience. The perceived independence of verifiers from the organization will also be critical in this respect.

- **Continuous improvement**. Finally, a good method of social accounting should be able to actively encourage the organization to continually improve its performance across the areas covered by the process, and to extend the process to areas currently unassessed, or assessed unsatisfactorily.

Existing evidence suggests that many of these principles are not currently integrated particularly well into most companies' social accounting procedures. As O'Dwyer and Owen (2005: 208) note: 'many academic researchers have been critical of key features of emerging practice, given its tendencies towards managerialism at the expense of accountability and transparency to stakeholder groups'. Analyses even of leading social reports suggest that while improvements are evident, significant deficiencies in some of these quality indicators persist (Belal 2002; O'Dwyer and Owen 2005; Owen and O'Dwyer 2008; Manetti 2011). Milne and Gray (2013) go so far as to claim that current practices mainly serve to reinforce business-as-usual and may even contribute to greater levels of 'un-sustainability'.

Nonetheless, the delineation of quality principles does represent an important step in a process towards developing adequate standards for social accounting—a process that is already well under way. Several important schemes are currently in place that seek to tackle specific aspects of social accounting. For example:

- **Auditing and certifying**. The social accountability standard, SA 8000, is a global workplace standard launched in 1997 that covers key labour rights such as working hours, forced labour, and discrimination, and crucially it certifies compliance through independent accredited auditors. Therefore, following inspection, production facilities can be certified as SA 8000 compliant, thus guaranteeing a widely accepted level of ethical performance. SA 8000 was developed through consultation with a broad range of stakeholders, including workers, employers, NGOs, and unions, and by 2014 had certified over 3,400 facilities in 65 countries, amounting to more than 2 million workers.[6]

- **Reporting**. The Global Reporting Initiative (GRI) is an international multi-stakeholder effort to create a common framework for reporting on the social, economic, and environmental triple bottom line of sustainability. **Ethics in Action 5.2** describes the challenges and achievements of the GRI in more detail.

VISIT THE
ONLINE
RESOURCE
CENTRE
for links to
useful sources
of further
information

ETHICS IN ACTION 5.2

The Global Reporting Initiative

At present, several thousand companies around the world report information on their economic, environmental, and social policies, practices, and performance. However, this information is often inconsistent, incomplete, and unverified. Measurement and reporting practices vary widely according to industry, location, and regulatory requirements. A generally accepted framework for reporting is therefore regarded as vital if stakeholders are to be able to gauge the social performance of organizations and make meaningful comparisons with other organizations.

The Global Reporting Initiative (GRI) was established in 1997 by the Coalition for Environmentally Responsible Economies (CERES) in partnership with the United Nations Environment Programme (UNEP). Its mission was to create just such a common framework for voluntary reporting on economic, environmental, and social performance, i.e. the 'triple bottom line' of sustainability. The GRI is an international multi-stakeholder effort, involving dialogue and collaboration between corporations, non-governmental organizations (NGOs), accountancy organizations, business associations, and other stakeholders in order to develop and implement widely applicable sustainability reporting guidelines.

Following a lengthy consultation period and extensive pilot testing in companies such as British Airways, the Body Shop, Electrolux, Norvo Nodisk, and Ford, the first GRI guidelines were released in 2000. These represented the first global framework for comprehensive sustainability reporting, and have been referred to, or followed by, thousands of companies across the globe since their release. By 2014, there were more than 6,600 organizations using the GRI guidelines in developing their reports.

The GRI guidelines have taken an enormous step in the ongoing drive towards harmonization and enhancement of reporting procedures. Clearly, though, the path to widely accepted guidelines for reporting on something as complex and multi-faceted as sustainability is likely to be a long and difficult one. The standardization sought by GRI, particularly given the impressive inclusivity of its consultation process, might easily become a recipe for dilution of standards towards the lowest common denominator.

GRI obviously recognizes the enormous challenge presented by its mission and adopts a process of continual learning and revision of its guidelines. Immediately following the release of the 2000 guidelines, the GRI initiated another extensive and wide-ranging consultation process involving hundreds of organizations and individuals, including both reporters and report users. The purpose of this was to develop the next draft of the guidelines, which were subsequently released in 2002. A similar process of consultation and feedback preceded the release of the third and fourth generation of GRI guidelines, known as G3 and G4, in 2006 and 2013 respectively. The GRI has also developed sector supplements for particular industries, national annexes for country-level information, training materials, and even the provision of specialist guidance for small- and medium-sized enterprises.

The GRI has come a long way towards its current mission 'to make sustainability reporting standard practice for all organizations'. However, the GRI has understandably had to make compromises along the way in order to engage a wide range of reporters and other stakeholders. It is notable that several vision statements of the programme have fallen by the wayside as it has progressively re-evaluated its ambitions. The GRI's original aim of elevating sustainability reporting to the status enjoyed by financial reporting and to make sustainability reporting 'as routine and credible as financial reporting in terms of comparability, rigour, and verifiability' was jettisoned as it became clear that different companies wanted to report on different things. Now, rather than focusing on a single set of metrics for all, the latest G4 version of the guidelines focus much more on 'materiality', i.e. they allow companies to 'provide only information that is critical to their business and stakeholders'.

Another earlier goal to become 'the generally accepted, broadly adopted worldwide framework for preparing, communicating, and requesting information about corporate performance' has also now been dropped. This is because a number of alternative frameworks for sustainability reporting have appeared in recent years, typically with a stronger focus on reporting primarily for investors. The most notable ones are 'integrated reporting' (promoted by the International Integrated Reporting Council), which focuses on a framework for reporting sustainability and financial data together, and the 'sustainability accounting standards' developed by the Sustainability Accounting Standards Board (SASB) which aim to 'help public corporations disclose material, decision-useful information to investors'.

GRI clearly faces challenges ahead, but it has undoubtedly met with considerable success in disseminating good practice in sustainability reporting and making the critical first steps towards greater harmonization in reporting practices. With so many organizations across the world not only using its guidelines but also having experience of actually contributing to them, the GRI will continue to shape the field of sustainability reporting for some time to come.

Sources

Baker, M. 2013. Global Reporting Initiative G4—Generation Materiality. *Ethical Corporation Magazine*, July 2013: 11–14.

Laufer, W.S. 2003. Social accountability and corporate greenwashing. *Journal of Business Ethics*, 43 (3): 253–61.

https://www.globalreporting.org/.

VISIT THE
ONLINE
RESOURCE
CENTRE
for a short
response to this
feature

> **? THINK THEORY**
>
> Think about the GRI in terms of Zadek et al.'s (1997) eight principles of quality
> in social accounting. To what extent would you say it conforms to and contributes to
> good practice?

- **Reporting assurance**. The AA1000S Assurance Standard, launched in 2002, is the first attempt to provide a coherent and robust basis for assuring a public report and its underlying processes, systems, and competencies against a concrete definition and principles of accountability and stakeholder engagement. The standard is specifically designed to be consistent with the GRI sustainability reporting guidelines.[7]

Such programmes are still being revised and refined, yet they clearly offer considerable progress in providing more effective means for assessing, and ultimately improving, the sustainability and accountability of corporations through social accounting. Moreover, the ongoing efforts of the organizations leading the development of AA1000S, GRI, and SA 8000 to integrate their different systems and approaches means that corporations are gradually being offered a range of interlocking standards for some of the many different aspects of business ethics management. As we shall now see, in the next and last main section of this chapter, there are a number of different ways of organizing these various aspects within an overall approach to business ethics management.

☑ **Skill check**

Assessing ethical performance. Using and applying the tools of social auditing and reporting is important to enable you to assess how well an organization is achieving its ethical, social, and environmental goals.

■ Organizing for business ethics management

If businesses are going to directly manage business ethics, then at some stage they are likely to face the question of how best to organize the various components and integrate them into the company in order to achieve their goals. In the US, it has become commonplace for business ethics specialists and textbooks to advocate formal ethics or compliance programmes, and such an approach has been taken up by many leading US corporations. However, due to a different regulatory environment, as well as significantly different business cultures in Europe, Asia, and elsewhere, such a formal approach to business ethics management has been much more rarely promoted or adopted outside North America. However, the increasing attention being devoted to ethics, social responsibility and sustainability across the globe suggests that a more formal approach to management is becoming more widespread and can be expected to become more so in the future.

Formal ethics programmes

According to Treviño et al. (1999), there are four main ways of approaching the formal organization of business ethics management (see **Figure 5.5**):

- **Compliance orientation**. Under this approach, the main emphasis is on preventing, detecting, and punishing violations of the law. Employees are informed of the law and are motivated to do the right thing through fear of being caught. This is based on the assumption that, regardless of their own values, the competitive environment may encourage employees to do whatever it takes to get a job done, including illegal or unethical activity (Hoffman et al. 2001).

- **Values orientation**. This approach is based on defining organizational values and encouraging employee commitment to certain ethical aspirations (Paine 1994). According to Treviño et al. (1999: 135), the values approach is 'rooted in personal self-governance' and provides the means for ethical decision-making where no particular rules are in place.

- **External orientation**. An external orientation focuses less on company values and more on satisfying external stakeholders such as customers, the community, and shareholders (Treviño et al. 1999). Here, what is regarded as right is what is expected, or at least acceptable, to key external constituencies.

- **Protection orientation**. Finally, Treviño et al. (1999) suggest that some programmes are (or at least are perceived to be) primarily oriented towards protecting top management from blame for ethical problems or legal violations. Employees and other stakeholders may see the introduction of ethics management as little more than an attempt to create legal cover for managers in case of accidents or legal infractions of some sort.

In the US, compliance approaches appear to predominate (Weaver et al. 1999), whereas in Europe and Asia, as we have seen, the emergence of ethics management has tended to be driven more by external and values-based approaches. However, the important thing to remember is that these four approaches are not mutually inconsistent, and most organizations are likely to combine two or more approaches (Weaver et al. 1999). For example, earlier in the chapter we explained that many ethical codes are based on core corporate values and principles (a values orientation), whereas the effectiveness of such

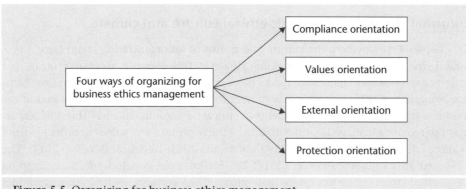

Figure 5.5 Organizing for business ethics management

codes also depended on appropriate implementation and follow-through, such as the disciplining of employees found in breach of them (compliance orientation). Similarly, rigorously policed ethical auditing processes based on stakeholder consultation and engagement might be said to combine values, external, and compliance orientations.

☑ **Skill check**

Designing ethics programmes. In order to enhance ethical behaviour in organizations managers need skills in designing programmes that comprehensively address the management of ethical issues across the organization.

Although research on the effectiveness of different approaches (and combinations of approaches) is fairly scant, Treviño et al.'s (1999) survey of over 10,000 employees in six large American companies suggests that a values orientation is the most effective single orientation for encouraging ethical behaviour, although compliance and external orientations should also, to a lesser degree, be helpful. A protection approach was found to be a clearly harmful approach. Nonetheless, regardless of their importance, these formal elements are only one aspect of business ethics management. As Treviño and Brown (2004) argue, the idea that formal ethics codes and programmes are sufficient to manage ethics is no more than a commonly held myth. As we saw in Chapter 4, many authors suggest that the broader ethical context, embedded in the culture and climate of the organization, is highly influential in shaping ethical decision-making. So, without a supportive culture, formal programmes are unlikely to significantly influence behaviour. Hence, in organizing for business ethics management, it is important to also consider the ethical culture of the organization.

? THINK THEORY

Think about the growth in business ethics management, identified earlier in the chapter, which is due to the impact of Sarbanes–Oxley legislation and other regulatory and governance reforms. Are these developments likely to initiate business ethics management that is characterized by a compliance, values, external, or protection orientation?

Informal ethics management: ethical culture and climate

In Chapter 4 we saw how the culture and norms of an organization could have a profound effect on ethical decision-making. However, this does not necessarily mean that culture can be simply changed or made 'more ethical' to support enhanced business ethics. Nonetheless, this is exactly the argument that has been commonly advocated in the business ethics literature. Improvements in ethical decision-making have been widely argued to require a managed transformation of the organization's values in order to create a 'more ethical' culture (Chen et al. 1997; Schwartz 2013; Treviño and Nelson 2014). The US-based Ethics Resource Center (2014: 22), for example, concludes from its ongoing research of ethics in the workplace that 'strong ethics cultures reduce both misconduct overall and the likelihood that a misdeed which does occur is a pervasive, ongoing issue'.

Despite the popularity of the *ethical culture change* approach, there has been limited attention focused on establishing how such a transformation might take place, why it might occur, or even if it is possible at all. As the management and organizational studies literatures have so effectively demonstrated, the deliberate management of culture is a difficult, lengthy process, which is rarely successful, except at very superficial levels.[8] Indeed, there has been precious little empirical evidence in the literature that provides wholesale support for the claim that culture can indeed be managed in the realm of ethical behaviour. Existing cultural beliefs and values about what is right and wrong tend to be very resistant to change (Anand et al. 2004; Desmond and Crane 2004).

Accordingly, the use of explicit culture change to improve corporate ethical behaviour has also been seriously questioned. Amanda Sinclair (1993: 68), for example, concludes that: 'the lessons from research are that you meddle with the organizational culture if you've got little choice, lots of resources, and lots of time—a combination of circumstances, some would argue, rare enough to render the approach irrelevant'. Peter Dahler-Larsen (1994) further contends that attempts to create 'ethical cultures' tend to reward conformity rather than the very autonomy that is crucial for a sense of morality to exist. Even the Ethics Resource Center (2014), which is one of the most strident advocates of culture change approaches, acknowledges that despite heightened attention to ethics management, only around one-fifth of US companies have a strong ethical culture—and that this has remained more or less constant between 2005 and 2015.

A somewhat different approach has therefore also been advocated that focuses more on *ethical cultural learning*. Rather than seeking conformity to a single set of values, the learning approach focuses on smaller subcultural groups within the firm and enabling employees to make their own ethical decisions. By encouraging surveillance, dialogue, and critique between these subcultural groups (and with the firm's stakeholders), 'ethical discourse and dialectic as well as conflict' can be prompted, thus bringing to the surface and challenging commonplace assumptions and behaviours (Sinclair 1993: 69). Ken Starkey (1998) thus contends that moral development in organizations requires factionalism and dissent in order to promote learning. The role of management consequently becomes one of identifying conflicting values, unleashing the moral commitment of subcultures, and from this promoting *moral imagination* rather than imposing authoritarian *ideological control* (Stansbury and Barry 2007).

Clearly both approaches have their merits and problems. The ethical culture change approach may have only limited potential to effect real change, but it is considerably more attractive to many firms who not only may desire considerable control over the culture, but may also be worried about the potentially damaging effects of bringing out moral differences through the process of ethical cultural learning. Moreover, both pose significant challenges for company leaders in shaping a more appropriate context for ethical decision-making.

☑ Skill check

Managing ethical culture. Understanding, influencing or leveraging ethical culture is a key skill for leaders in promoting and empowering ethical decision-making in organizations.

Business ethics and leadership

Whatever approach an organization might have to managing business ethics, whether it is formal or informal, compliance based or values based, minimal or extensive, the role of the organization's leaders in demonstrating **ethical leadership** is going to be significant (Ciulla 2013). Good examples are companies such as Walmart or Coca-Cola, which over the years have faced a range of ethical criticisms, but have more recently undergone major turnarounds, primarily initiated by their CEOs at the time (Doh and Quigley 2014). Similarly, the Unilever CEO Paul Polman is widely credited with instigating the company's lauded Sustainable Living Plan.

Leaders are often said to set the ethical tone in organizations. If they are perceived as being ruthless and inconsiderate in their dealings with others, or if they seem to care only about the short-term bottom line, employees are likely to get that message too. On the other hand, research has shown that the personal values of CEOs can significantly influence the degree to which their companies engage in responsible practices (Chin et al. 2013). Leaders can also play a significant role in the contextual factors, such as authority, norms, and culture, which we have shown to be key influences on ethical and unethical decision-making (Sims and Brinkmann 2002).

Unfortunately, although leadership is one of the most widely discussed and researched areas of organizational behaviour, there is considerable disagreement about even the most elemental aspects of the subject (Gini 1997). However, the main starting point is usually to delineate leadership from management. According to Kotter (1990), whereas management is about *imposing order*—through planning, organizing, budgeting, and controlling—leadership is more about *coping with change*—setting direction and vision, motivating and inspiring people, and facilitating learning. For many writers, leadership is an intrinsically moral terrain, for it is fundamentally entwined with a particular set of values or beliefs about what is the right thing to do. As Gini (1997: 325) argues:

> All leadership is value laden. All leadership, whether good or bad, is moral leadership … The point is, all leadership claims a particular point of view or philosophical package of ideas it wishes to advocate and advance. All forms of leadership try to establish the guidelines, set the tone and control the manners and morals of the constituency of which they are a part.

If one accepts this argument, then leaders clearly have a profound role in shaping the ethical decisions of their employees. However, as we saw above in relation to the management of culture, it is one thing to say that something—leadership, culture, etc.—*shapes* business ethics, but it is quite another to then suggest that one can simply *change* the culture or the leadership to ensure ethical behaviour. Nonetheless, it would appear reasonable to conclude that since leaders do appear to influence the actions of their employees, it is important to look at how best to develop ethical leadership.

If we return to our two approaches to managing for an ethical culture—*ethical culture change* and *ethical cultural learning*—it is possible to identify two very different modes of ethical leadership. Under the culture change approach, the leader's role is to articulate and personify the values and standards that the organization aspires to, and then to inspire and motivate employees to follow their lead. For example, Treviño et al. (1999) suggest that there are two pillars to developing a reputation for ethical leadership: to be perceived as a *moral person* and as a *moral manager*. For the executive to be perceived as a moral person, employees need to recognize genuine individual traits

Ethical leadership
Describes the role of senior managers in setting the ethical tone of the organization and fostering ethical behaviour among employees.

in them such as honesty and integrity. To be seen as a moral manager entails focusing the organization's attention on ethics and values and infusing the organization with principles that will guide the actions of all employees. This is a well-worn path for commentators on business ethics to go down, but it holds clear dangers if employees perceive a credibility gap between the public pronouncements of senior executives and the reality they experience according to their view 'from the trenches' (Badaracco and Webb 1995). As we saw earlier in the chapter, follow-through is often significantly more important in encouraging ethical behaviour than statements of beliefs or codes of ethics.

From the cultural learning perspective, the role of leadership is more one of participation and empowerment in order to foster moral imagination and autonomy. Thus, employees are encouraged 'to think independently, to be able to make reasoned, responsible evaluations and choices on their own; to be, in short, free moral agents' (Rosenthal and Buchholz 2000: 194). There are resonances here with those advocating both postmodern ethics and discourse ethics. Ethical behaviour is not to be promoted simply through the promulgation of specific beliefs and principles, but through facilitating personal moral engagement, dialogue, and choice (Crane et al. 2008). There are dangers here too though—such as shifting from encouraging individual choice to accepting moral relativism, or surrendering control over employees and their decisions.

Ultimately, given the controversy and debate that continues to rage in the leadership literature, there is unlikely to be any real consensus emerging in relation to ethical leadership. Clearly, though, it is an important area of business ethics management, and without top management support, most of the tools and techniques discussed in this chapter would be unlikely to contribute all that much to improving business ethics. However, there is always a slight danger of focusing too strongly on the few people at the top of the organization when many of the fundamentals of business ethics are about the day-to-day decisions that each and every one of us makes in our organizational lives.

? THINK THEORY

Think about organizations you have been part of, either as an employee or as a member of some sort. To what extent would you say that the leaders of those organizations were ethical leaders in that they promoted ethical behaviour from you or your colleagues? Which model of ethical leadership, if any, did they fit into?

VISIT THE
ONLINE
RESOURCE
CENTRE
for a short
response to this
feature

■ Summary

As this chapter has demonstrated, the area of business ethics management is evolving rapidly, and much of the literature we have covered here has been at the very forefront of contemporary business ethics theory and practice. As a result, much of what we have presented is, by its very nature, somewhat partial and inconclusive. Nonetheless, we have shown that the nature of business ethics management increasingly emphasizes an external, socially-based orientation, rather than concentrating solely on ethical codes to ensure compliance. Indeed, we have shown that the effectiveness of codes of ethics has been seriously questioned, with current thinking stressing the importance of implementation over content. We have also set out a clear picture of developments in stakeholder management, social accounting, and organizing for the management of business ethics.

At present, organizations are clearly on a learning curve regarding ethics management. While there may well be little substance behind some superficial codes of ethics or glossy social reports, this does not mean that we should denounce all business ethics management as cynical window-dressing. Each case should be assessed on its own merits. The key issue to address is how to determine what makes for best practice in each area, and how best to establish widely accepted frameworks and quality standards through which meaningful evaluations and comparisons can be made. Progress with respect to such frameworks and standards is clearly being made, although it is understandably slow. In addition, it is important to recognize that the application of these tools can only ever assist in managing business ethics, and their success or failure rests not so much on the tool itself but on the motivation for its use, the process of its development, and the manner in which it is implemented and followed up.

Study questions

1. What are the main elements of business ethics management? To what extent are they likely to be used in large versus small companies?

2. What are codes of ethics and how useful are they for the management of business ethics?

3. Set out the main types of relationship that corporations can have with their stakeholders. Are any of these types preferable? Explain your answer with reference to examples from current business practice.

4. What is social accounting and why do companies engage in it?

5. Assess the relative benefits and drawbacks of different approaches to ethics management. Would you recommend that an organization emphasized a formal or an informal approach to business ethics management?

6. Identify a well-known business leader and critically examine the case that they are an ethical leader.

Research exercise

Search on the internet for examples of two companies that produce social reports where the two companies are either:

(a) from different industries but in the same country; or

(b) from the same industry but in different countries.

1. What differences are evident between the two companies in terms of the range of issues dealt with in the reports and the depth of coverage on specific issues?

2. To what extent can these differences be explained by the country or industry differences? What other explanations might there be?

3. Assess the apparent quality of the social accounting approach utilized by each company according to Zadek et al.'s (1997) criteria.

4. How appropriate would it be for the two companies to use the same standardized approach?

Key readings

VISIT THE ONLINE RESOURCE CENTRE for links to further key readings

1. Burritt, R.L., and Schaltegger, S. 2010. Sustainability accounting and reporting: fad or trend? *Accounting, Auditing & Accountability Journal*, 23(7): 829–46.

    This is a comprehensive review of the literature on social accounting from a sustainability perspective. The analysis is particularly useful as it combines managerial and critical perspectives on a field that is often sharply divided along these lines.

2. Treviño, L.K., Hartman, L.P., and Brown, M. 2000. Moral person and moral manager: how executives develop a reputation for ethical leadership. *California Management Review*, 42 (4): 128–42.

    This article addresses the question of what it means to be an ethical leader. Featuring the results of a survey of employees, it shows the importance of different dimensions of ethical leadership. A 'must-read' for anyone hoping to develop a reputation for ethical leadership!

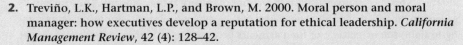

Case 5

VISIT THE ONLINE RESOURCE CENTRE for links to useful sources of further information on this case

Siemens: engineering change in anti-corruption

This case examines the Siemens bribery scandal and its repercussions for the firm's approach to the management of ethics and compliance. The case examines the circumstances that led to the firm paying the highest ever fine for a bribery settlement, and the actions Siemens subsequently took to institute an industry-leading management system to help eradicate the root causes of bribery at the firm and to guard against future violations.

Founded in Germany in 1847, Siemens is not only Europe's largest engineering company, but it also regularly counts among the top 50 companies in terms of revenue among the global Fortune 500. The engineering giant produces a wide range of goods and services, from light bulbs to power stations, and has a leading position in many of its markets, which include white goods, rail transportation systems, health-care technology, IT and financial services, to name just a few. It is a large, decentralized conglomerate operating in more than 190 countries, and employing more than 360,000 people across the globe.

Despite its impressive commercial track record, and a regular place high on various lists of most respected companies, Siemens also has one record that it is no doubt rather less proud of. In December 2008, after a long-running bribery scandal, the company settled out of court with the US authorities and was landed with a record-breaking fine of $800 million—a figure far in excess of any previous penalty imposed under the US Foreign Corrupt Practices Act. Along with fines levied in Germany and other countries, as well as a World Bank settlement in 2009, the total paid by the company rose to more than $1.7 billion, roughly 35 times larger than any previous anti-corruption settlement. However, including lawyers' and accountants' fees charged to the company during the cases, the full cost was ultimately even higher, at well above $2.5 billion in total.

The company had been investigated on multiple counts of bribery, adding up to more than $2.3 billion in alleged payments during the 1990s and early 2000s. This included allegations of $5 million paid to the son of the Bangladeshi prime minister for a mobile phone contract, $22 million to Chinese officials for a metro trains deal, and $40 million worth of payments in Argentina for a $1 billion contract to produce identity cards—just to name a few examples.

The scandal unfolds

The Siemens case started coming to light in the early 2000s when prosecutors in Germany and the US first began investigating allegations of bribery at the company. The firm and its leadership initially denied any knowledge of the payments. But with more incidents coming to light, the magnitude of the payments becoming ever higher, and trials of former company managers suggesting that bribery was common practice in the firm, this position became increasingly tenuous.

As the scandal unfolded, it became clear that bribery at Siemens was not simply a case of a few rogue managers acting alone and breaking the company rules to secure lucrative overseas contracts. Corruption looked to be endemic in the company, or, as one prosecutor put it, 'bribery was Siemens' business model'.

The various investigations and subsequent trials brought to the surface a murky picture of the payments made to public officials in a bid to win large overseas contracts for the company. Given that much of Siemens' business relies on large government contracts, often in developing countries with poor governance and a high prevalence of corruption, Siemens' managers had often found themselves in a competitive market where they and their rivals were frequently expected to bribe to secure business. According to various witness statements, Siemens' employees often simply thought that bribery was how the game was played and that they had to engage in corruption in order to win business, keep jobs secure and their company strong. Corruption appeared to be seen in rather amoral terms and as a victimless crime—if a crime at all. Furthermore, it did not exactly help that the German corporate tax code only made bribery technically illegal in the late 1990s. Until then, bribes paid in foreign countries were even tax deductible and were declared under the notorious label 'useful expenses' (in German: *nützliche Aufwendungen*).

Siemens, like most German multinationals, also tended to grant a lot of autonomy to local executives—the argument being that they dealt with complex technical products with a need for a high level of customer-specific local adaptation. The downside from an ethical perspective, however, appeared to be twofold. First, decisions about payments could be taken locally, without any real oversight or understanding from the headquarters. Second, if the leadership back home did become aware, the decentralized structure could make it difficult to implement effective ethics management across the firm's span of operations.

When the first signs of the bribery allegations surfaced in 2005, the then newly appointed CEO announced that fighting corruption would be his top priority. However, by 2007, he and the supervisory board chairman had both been forced to resign because of the ongoing stream of bribery allegations that engulfed the company. The firm then made its first appointment of an outsider as CEO, Peter Löscher, who was tasked with getting the firm back on its feet again.

Beginning the ethical turnaround

Löscher, the new CEO, needed to act fast to head off the bribery scandal, but he also faced a company with corruption apparently deeply engrained in its culture, making it particularly hard to initiate a major change in attitudes. Many Siemens employees had been with the company for their entire career, leading to densely woven webs of contacts, informal relationships, and networks, in which problems like corruption (and its cover-up) could thrive. As the trial hearings revealed, the maintenance of corruption on the scale alleged at Siemens had actually required a deep degree of loyalty from employees. One executive testified to the court that he was chosen to become the co-ordinator of the 'useful expenses' payments because his superiors trusted him and because he was a loyal worker who could be relied on not to simply direct some of the bribe money into his own pockets.

Within the first few months of his tenure, Löscher had made wholesale changes, including replacing 80% of the firm's top-tier executives, 70% of its second tier and 40% of its third tier. To ensure that auditing personnel throughout the company were competent, every member of the firm's 450 audit function was required to reapply for their jobs. Siemens also brought in a new General Counsel, appointed the co-founder of Transparency International (an international anti-corruption NGO) to serve as its compliance adviser, and agreed to co-operate with the US authorities in its investigations. The firm also initiated an amnesty for any whistleblowers with knowledge of bribery in the company (which was taken up by more than 100 staff) and spent millions on an internal investigation conducted by a US law firm. The new leadership team began spreading the message across the company that 'only clean business is Siemens business'.

Siemens institutes a new compliance infrastructure

Central to the new approach instituted by Löscher and his new management team was a much enhanced and far-reaching compliance system. The firm set up a compliance management system to oversee the prevention, detection and response to legal and ethical violations at the firm. From 86 compliance officers in 2006, the firm soon expanded to more than 500. Siemens also developed a series of anti-corruption compliance policies, tools, and communication channels, including a compliance audit department, web-based risk assessment tools for employees, and 24/7 secure reporting channels for employees and external stakeholders.

The new compliance system also involved systematic training for Siemens employees. Between 2007 and 2013, the firm completed over 300,000 compliance training sessions for staff, about a third of which were classroom based over four to eight hours, and the rest were online. The company also instituted intensive and ongoing training for compliance officers, regular training for 'sensitive functions' such as sales, and a compliance module for new employees. In 2012, compliance training was again refreshed to focus on face-to-face 'integrity dialogue' among managers and their teams. To this end, compliance officers train business unit managers, the managers train the employees who report directly to them, and they in turn train the employees that report to them.

Many of these changes were already implemented when Siemens was finally sentenced by the Department of Justice in 2008. For example, extensive compliance training had been provided to over half of the workforce by the time the fine was handed down. By

September 2008, Siemens' senior leadership has also visited 54 of the firm's highest-risk countries as part of a 'compliance roadshow' to explain to country managers and employees the importance of compliance. Indeed, Siemens' impressive efforts to institute the new compliance system along with its willingness to conduct its own independent investigation and co-operate with the Department of Justice investigators meant that the huge $800 million fine it received was actually far less than it would otherwise have been. As the Department of Justice stated, 'the reorganization and remediation efforts of Siemens have been extraordinary and have set a high standard for multi-national companies to follow.'

Although the nature of the final settlement in the US did not actually require Siemens to admit to bribery (it was only required to admit to having inadequate controls and keeping improper accounts), the firm acknowledges that it experienced 'systematic violations of anti-corruption laws and accounting regulations ... over many years'. The new Siemens' leadership made it clear that the firm needed to continue to change its ways. As the CEO, Peter Löscher, said: 'We regret what happened in the past but we have learned from it and taken appropriate measures. Siemens is now a stronger company.'

The US settlement in fact required the company to further implement and continue its compliance enhancements. This included that an independent compliance monitor assist with the continuous improvements and a review of the compliance systems between 2009 and 2012. During this time, Siemens continued to strengthen its compliance policies, tools, and training. In 2009, the board signed off a revised version of the firm's Business Conduct Guidelines, which sets out the firm's principles and rules on ethical behaviour. Additional compliance guidelines were also introduced to give more specific advice on corruption. However, in general the firm has looked to simplify essential compliance rules so as to make them easily understood across the company and more helpful to employees. This appears to be working to the extent that inquiries to the firm's 'Ask Us' compliance help desk reduced year on year from around 3,000 in 2010 to about 400 in 2013.

After the US ruling Siemens also moved to integrate compliance measures into personnel processes, such as hiring, promotions, and management bonuses. In 2012, a new comprehensive compliance risk assessment system was subsequently instituted whereby compliance risks are systematically identified, assessed, and mitigated by senior management on an annual basis.

As a result of these developments, Siemens has been widely recognized as having developed an outstanding ethics and compliance management system. Even so, it remains a work in progress to achieve a corruption-free company, especially when bribery might still be seen by some as necessary to drive business opportunities. As CEO Peter Löscher said at the time of his appointment, instilling an ethical corporate culture 'is a marathon for us, not a sprint'.

One of the biggest challenges facing Siemens is ensuring that its ethics management does not conflict with its business success. According to Löscher, 'performance with ethics—this is not a contradiction, it is a must', but if their clients still seek bribes and their competitors are willing to pay them, then Siemens may well be faced with a handicap. One way that the firm has sought to tackle this is through its anti-corruption outreach activities that go under the banner 'Collective Action'. That is, in addition to internal company changes, Siemens also started to engage its external stakeholders in anti-corruption efforts to create fairer market conditions. This began as part of a groundbreaking settlement agreed with the World Bank in 2009 following the firm's acknowledged misconduct and the bank's investigations into corruption in the awarding of contracts to Siemens subsidiaries. The settlement committed Siemens to pay $100 million over 15 years to support anti-corruption work, to co-operate to change industry practices, and work with the World Bank to fight corruption.

To comply with the settlement, Siemens launched the 'Integrity Initiative' with a budget of $100 million to support anti-corruption projects. It also took a lead in initiating project-specific and industry-wide compliance pacts to ensure fair bidding on public contracts. For example, Siemens Argentina recently concluded a compliance pact with several competitors in the field of energy transmission. In Brazil, Siemens has started to support a project aimed at creating transparency when awarding infrastructure projects connected with the soccer World Cup in 2014 and the Olympic Games in 2016. The company also seeks to increase the compliance awareness of current and future business leaders by conducting business round-table discussions and presentations, and developing learning materials for students.

Löscher is widely credited with turning around the Siemens corruption scandal and pulling the company out of its crisis. However, concerns over the firm's performance and its failure to meet the CEO's own aggressive growth targets led to his ousting in 2013. 'The clean-up man,' one newspaper ruefully observed, 'was swept aside'.

Questions

1. What were the main causes of the Siemens corruption scandal? Which, in your opinion, would be the most difficult to resolve?

2. Critically evaluate the initiatives that Siemens has implemented to address bribery problems across its operations. Are these sufficient to tackle the causes of the problems or would you suggest further action?

3. What kind of balance has Siemens struck between values and compliance-based approaches to ethics management? Do you think this is the most effective approach to corruption problems?

4. What is the relationship between corruption and business performance? Can ethics management be organized to achieve business success and high ethical integrity simultaneously, or are they contradictory goals?

5. To what extent is a fine—however high—an adequate response to Siemens' misconduct? Are settlements like that of the World Bank more or less effective in developing cleaner business?

Sources

Dietz, G. and Gillespie, N. 2012. Rebuilding trust: How Siemens atoned for its sins. *Guardian*, 26 March 2012: http://www.theguardian.com/sustainable-business/recovering-business-trust-siemens.

Dougherty, C. 2007. Chief of Siemens pledges to streamline operations. *New York Times*, 6 July 2007: http://www.nytimes.com/2007/07/06/business/06siemens.html?fta=y&_r=0.

Koehler, M. 2012. Revisiting a Foreign Corrupt Practices Act compliance defense. *Wisconsin Law Review*, 609: http://wisconsinlawreview.org/wp-content/files/13-Koehler.pdf.

Reguly, R. 2013. Siemens' Peter Loescher: The cleanup man who was swept aside. *Globe* and *Mail*, 11 October 2013: http://www.theglobeandmail.com/report-on-business/careers/careers-leadership/siemens-peter-loescher-the-cleanup-man-who-was-swept-aside/article14848291/.

Schubert, S. and Christian Miller, T. 2008. At Siemens, bribery was just a line item. *New York Times*, 20 December 2008: http://www.nytimes.com/2008/12/21/business/worldbusiness/21siemens.html.

Siemens 2013. *The Siemens Compliance System*, Munich: Siemens AG: http://www.siemens.com/about/sustainability/en/core-topics/compliance/system/index.php.

Notes

1. See the website of the Electronic Industry Citizenship Coalition (EICC): http://www.eicc.info/.
2. See Daniel, C. 2005. Boeing chief ousted for having affair. *Financial Times*, 8 March: http://www.ft.com; Done, K. 2005. Stonecipher falls victim to own code of conduct. *Financial Times*, 8 March: http://www.ft.com; Worthen, B. and Lublin, J.S. 2010. Mark Hurd Neglected to Follow H-P Code. *Wall Street Journal*, 9 August: http://www.wsj.com; Shalal-Esa, A. 2012. Incoming Lockheed CEO resigns over ethics violation. *Reuters*, 9 November: http://www.reuters.com.
3. For more information on these initiatives, there are further details on these (and other similar programmes) at the websites of the CAUX roundtable (http://www.cauxroundtable.org) and the global compact (http://www.unglobalcompact.org).
4. McKinsey & Company. 2006. The McKinsey Global Survey of Business Executives: Business and Society. *McKinsey Quarterly* (2): 33–9.
5. http://about.puma.com/en/sustainability/stakeholders/materiality-matrix.
6. http://www.saasaccreditation.org/certfacilitieslist.htm.
7. http://www.accountability.org/standards/aa1000as/index.html.
8. This has been a recurring theme in the organizational and management studies literature. See for example Ogbonna and Harris (1998).

PART B

Contextualizing Business Ethics

The Corporate Citizen and its Stakeholders

Introduction to Part B

The second part of this book looks in turn at the key individual stakeholder groups faced by the corporation—shareholders, employees, customers, suppliers, competitors, civil society, and government—and addresses business ethics within the specific context represented by each of these groups.

The structure of chapters 6–11 breaks down into five main parts reflecting some of the key themes developed in Part A of the book. So, following the introduction of each chapter there is:

- A brief explanation of how and why this particular constituency can and should be represented as a *stakeholder* for the corporation.

- An overview of the *ethical issues* and problems typically encountered in relation to this particular stakeholder, along with consideration of potential responses and solutions.

- A deepening discussion of those issues and problems in the light of *globalization*.

- An analysis of how these problems and issues can be reframed or responded to from the viewpoint of *corporate citizenship* thinking.

- An examination of the challenges thrown up by notions of *sustainability* in relation to this particular stakeholder group.

As we progress through Part B we will also continue to raise the question of how theories relating to business ethics can be applied to address the problems faced by corporations with respect to stakeholder groups. To this end, the 'Think theory' comments and questions utilized in Part A will continue to be posed at relevant points in each chapter.

6

Shareholders and Business Ethics

Having completed this chapter you should be able to:

- Describe the nature of shareholder relations to the corporation.
- Explain the rights and the duties of shareholders in the context of corporate governance.
- Explain the differences in corporate governance models in various parts of the world.
- Identify the ethical problems arising from the company–shareholder relationship.
- Critically evaluate the ethical implications of globalization for company–shareholder relations.
- Critically evaluate the roles of shareholder democracy, shareholder activism and responsible investment in promoting ethical business behaviour.
- Critically evaluate the role of sustainability indices and alternative forms of ownership in influencing corporations towards sustainability.

Key concepts and skills:

Concepts

- Corporate governance
- Executive accountability
- Insider trading
- Shareholder activism
- Socially responsible investment
- Social purpose corporations

Skills

- Analysing manager–shareholder relations
- Distinguishing between different corporate governance systems
- Applying socially responsible investment criteria

■ Introduction: reassessing the importance of shareholders as stakeholders

As we saw in Chapter 2, there are strong voices out there (for instance Milton Friedman) arguing that corporations exist, and indeed act, solely for the benefit of shareholders. The pursuit of dividends and increases in share prices to satisfy financial markets are major features of the dominant capitalist model of value creation—but have also been widely cited as crucial contributory factors influencing firms to play fast and loose with business ethics.

Even if we adhere to this narrow view of shareholder dominance, nothing has brought ethical issues more attention than the financial crisis that began in 2008. For instance, between October 2007 and October 2008 shareholders investing in companies traded on the New York Stock Exchange lost on average 40% of their investments (Nanto 2008)! As many of the reasons for this crisis have a strong ethical dimension (such as lending practices in the US mortgage industry), business ethics is now a core consideration for some investors and shareholders. Other people point to the expansion of socially responsible investment and the emergence of various indices of 'sustainable' stocks to suggest that shareholders are interested in societal good as well as their own self-interest. Whichever way you look at it, the role of shareholders is fundamental to understanding business ethics, and as such they are the first stakeholder group that we will focus on in this second part of the book.

We first discussed the role of shareholders in the corporation (albeit quite briefly) in Chapter 2. Our argument there was in favour of a broad perspective that acknowledged various constituencies with a stake in the corporation. This suggested that while shareholders clearly have a crucial stake in the corporation, this has to be understood within the range of other stakeholders, such as employees, consumers, and suppliers.

In this chapter we will investigate the finer nuances of this perspective. While maintaining support for a broad stakeholder perspective, we will examine the contention that shareholders in some way have a unique and superior claim upon the corporation. This relationship, as we shall see, confers certain crucial rights on shareholders, as well as imposing some quite important responsibilities in terms of the governance and control of corporations. By examining this relationship in some detail, we will provide the all-important context for discussing the various ethical issues that arise in shareholder relations, including insider trading, executive pay, and money laundering.

As we shall explain, both the impetus and the resolution of these issues and problems are shaped by certain national characteristics of corporate governance. We shall therefore go on to look at how shareholder relations vary quite significantly in different regional contexts. This will be combined with a further broadening of perspective to allow for a deeper understanding of the relationship between globalization and shareholder rights and responsibilities. Such issues have received a growing amount of attention due to the rapid global spread of the financial crisis in the late 2000s. We shall therefore move on to discuss the broader issues surrounding shareholder and stakeholder accountability before finally taking a look at how shareholders can use their unique position to address the question of sustainability of corporations.

■ Shareholders as stakeholders: understanding corporate governance

At the beginning of modern capitalism, and throughout the nineteenth-century industrial revolution, the common pattern of governing companies was a very simple one. At that time, industrialists, such as the Cadburys in the UK and the Thyssens in Germany, both owned and managed their companies directly. Today, except in very small businesses, owner-managers are considerably rarer. Some exceptions to this include David and Charles Koch in the US, Richard Branson and his Virgin conglomerate in the UK, and the Tata family in India. However, the common pattern in large corporations is a separation of ownership and management functions. In fact, this separation is at the heart of modern capitalism: owners no longer have a personal relationship to 'their' corporation, but rather they buy a 'share' in the corporation and expect the managers and employees of the company to run it in their (and other shareholders') interests.

The debate about the separation of ownership and control dates back at least to the 1930s and the landmark publication by Adolph Berle and Gardiner Means (1932). This debate essentially problematizes the notion of ownership when applied to corporations. In our everyday life, to own a bike or a car or even a house implies that we are able to do with our property pretty much whatever we like, and therefore can exert a considerable amount of control over it. After all, as we discussed in Chapter 2, the right to property is one of the fundamental rights of citizens. If I want to paint my bike green, ride it down the street, or even completely destroy it, then I can.

However, with regard to the ownership of corporations there are some crucial differences (see Parkinson 1993: 56–63; Monks and Minow 2011):

• **Locus of control**. The control of the owned property no longer lies in the hands of the owner. The actual control lies in the hands of the directors, the board, or another committee. Shareholders thus have at best indirect and impersonal control over their 'property'.

• **Fragmented ownership**. There are so many shareholders of a corporation that one individual could hardly consider themselves to be the owner in the same way that the plumber next door owns their own company.

• **Divided functions and interests**. Shareholders have interests that are not necessarily the same as the interests of those who control the company. Shareholders might seek profits, while managers seek growth. Furthermore, a shareholder has no real task and responsibility regarding their property apart from keeping a piece of paper that entitles them to a share in the company.

Given this somewhat modified interface between shareholders and directors of corporations we can analyse their relationship a bit more closely. Obviously the primary consideration for shareholders is the protection of their investment that, in the given context, amounts to certain specific rights (Monks and Minow 2011):

• The right to sell their stock.
• The right to vote in the general meeting.

- The right to certain information about the company.

- The right to sue the managers for (alleged) misconduct.

- Certain residual rights in case of the corporation's liquidation.

Most notably, these rights do not include the right to a certain amount of profit or dividend; this is not only subject to the effort and skill of the management but is also—even if the company is profitable—dependent on the decision of the other shareholders in the general meeting.

Managers are entrusted with the duty to run the company in the interest of shareholders. This general duty breaks down into various more specific duties (Parkinson 1993: 76–100):

- **Duty to act for the benefit of the company**. This obligation can be interpreted both in terms of short-term financial performance and long-term survival of the company. Principally, it is for the shareholders to decide at which level they want the company to perform; however, managers have a considerable amount of discretion in actually implementing this duty.

- **Duty of care and skill**. Living up to this duty implies that managers seek to achieve the most professional and effective way of running the company.

- **Duty of diligence**. This last duty is the most general one and, as a rather legally flavoured term, 'refers to the expected level of active engagement in company affairs' (Parkinson 1993: 98). Consequently, this is the broadest way of establishing pressure on managers to invest every possible effort in running the company in the most successful way.

Clearly, the duties of managers are rather broadly defined. After all, one of the main tasks of a manager is to manage the 'property' of shareholders in their interests. This involves so many things that it is hard to pin it down to concrete activities and initiatives: which strategies, which products, which international investment projects will add to the success of the corporation? These questions are already hard to tackle for an insider, let alone for a shareholder who has only a little knowledge about the internal workings of the corporation and the finer specifics of its products, markets, and competitors.

The relationship between shareholders and the company is therefore defined by relatively narrow, but well-defined, *rights for the shareholder* and far-reaching, but rather ill-defined, *duties for managers* or for the firm in general. It is no wonder that this situation has always been a delicate one and that conflicts continue to plague the relationship between managers and shareholders. Such conflicts focus on the nature of **corporate governance** (Parkinson 1993: 157). Corporate governance includes various rules, processes, and structures that enable shareholders to exercise direction and control over managers. This includes how they can influence goal definition, supervision, control, rewards, and sanctioning of management. In the narrow sense, this just focuses on shareholders and the senior executives of a corporation, but in a broader sense, it also encompasses other stakeholders that might have a legitimate role in directing and controlling managers.

Corporate governance
The rules, processes, and structures through which corporations are directed and controlled in the interests of shareholders and other stakeholders.

Corporate governance: a principal–agent relationship

At first glance, it might seem unlikely that corporate governance should bring up too many ethical issues. After all, shouldn't shareholders and senior executives want the same thing, namely a growing, profitable company? Let us look at some high-profile governance scandals to see just what some of the problems could be:

- Two weeks after taking over as CEO of Japanese electronics company Olympus in October 2011, Michael Woodford discovered that the company had hidden $1.5 billion of investment losses and illegal payments in a so-called 'tobashi' (concealment) scheme. When he exposed the problem he was immediately fired as part of a cover-up by long-standing board members. The scandal wiped out 75% of the stock market valuation of the company.[1] How was it possible that senior management could hide such an amount of losses from shareholders and persist in covering up their past mistakes?

- In 2013, the 4.6 million customers of the UK Co-operative Bank were shocked to hear that their bank, formerly owned by the Co-operative Group, had been virtually taken over by a consortium of American hedge funds. The bank was in dire financial difficulties and the only solution appeared to be to attract capital from private investors. Thus it was that a cornerstone of the co-operative movement for more than 140 years was virtually privatized. How is it possible that customers and the bank's co-operative holding company were powerless to prevent a decision that not only changed their stake in the bank but also gave rise to fears that the firm's ethical policies would change dramatically with hedge fund managers at the helm?[2]

- In 2014, General Motors faced a lawsuit from its shareholders alleging securities fraud in the way that the company had handled a recall of 2.5 million cars due to a faulty ignition switch. The company had allegedly known about the problem for more than ten years resulting in, by some estimates, up to 150 people being killed in accidents. How was it possible that General Motors could conceal the problem for such a long time from its 'owners' who suffered significant losses when the scandal finally broke in 2014?

? THINK THEORY

Think of the duties of managers to their shareholders from the perspective of ethics of duty (Kant's categorical imperative test). Apply this theoretical lens to the three incidents described above.

VISIT THE ONLINE RESOURCE CENTRE
for a short response to this feature

The essential problem here is that firm–shareholder relationships cannot be so easily framed in a contract that neatly states rights and responsibilities. As authors like Jensen and Meckling (1976) have shown, the relationship is a so-called *agency relation*. This means that the shareholder is a *principal* who contracts management as an *agent* to act in their interest within the boundary of the firm. **Figure 6.1** presents a very basic view of the relationship between manager and shareholder using this framework.

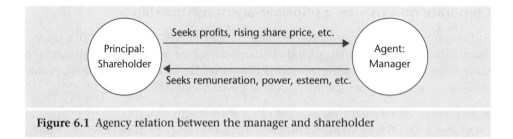

Figure 6.1 Agency relation between the manager and shareholder

Shareholders want the managers in the firm to perform a certain task for them. As a principal, they want managers to do certain things with their property. Managers as agents, on the other side, have certain interests as well, and Figure 6.1 provides some examples from a potentially long list of such interests. Agency relations, however, are special relationships due to two features that are by no means necessarily common for all other manager–stakeholder relations (Shankman 1999):

1. There is an inherent *conflict of interest* between shareholders and managers. Shareholders want profits and increases in share price, which require major effort on the part of managers, and may suggest low salaries (i.e. the more managers are paid, the lower the resulting profit for shareholders). Managers want to have high salaries and might pursue power and prestige to the detriment of shareholder value. Consider the fact that acquisitions and mergers in the most competitive financial markets such as the US, UK, and Canada typically provide no additional value to shareholders and in fact often erode shareholder value (Alexandridis et al. 2010). Why then do managers continue to create mega-mergers that put them at the head of enormous corporations? It would seem to be more to do with their own pursuit of power than their obligation to act in the interests of shareholders.

2. The principal has only limited knowledge and insight into the qualifications, actions, and goals of the agent, something economists refer to as an *informational asymmetry*. The shareholders of Olympus and GM in our examples above might have been happy with the profitability of their companies, yet they only had limited insight into what managers were actually doing and the risks this created for them.

It is the combination of these two characteristics that makes shareholder relations with managers, and the whole issue of corporate governance, so precarious. Indeed, conflicts of interest and informational asymmetry can be seen to underlie a host of ethical problems and dilemmas for either side to deal with in the area of corporate governance, as we shall see in a moment. Before we move on to the main ethical issues pertaining to shareholders, though, we need first to clarify the position of shareholders in relation to other stakeholders. Specifically, it is important to recognize that there are different models of corporate governance in different parts of the world.

☑ **Skill check**

Analysing manager–shareholder relationships. Identifying and evaluating the different roles, interests and information held by managers and shareholders is a crucial skill because it enables you to determine each party's strategic priorities.

Shareholders' relationships with other stakeholders: different frameworks of corporate governance globally

In its broadest sense, corporate governance describes how the priorities of the corporation should be determined and, ultimately, who the company is there to serve. Different models of corporate governance operate in different countries, and so the role of shareholders varies quite significantly between different countries internationally (Aguilera and Jackson 2010). For many commentators there are two broad systems of corporate governance. On the one hand, there is the *Anglo-American* model of capitalism (Aguilera et al. 2006), which is primarily a market-based form of corporate governance. On the other hand, there is a *continental European model*, sometimes also called 'Rhenish Capitalism' (Albert 1991). This model is a more network- or relationship-based form of corporate governance of which the European model is the oldest and most widely known. However, a similar approach based on relationships (rather than markets) can also be found in many countries, in particular in the developing world. **Figure 6.2** provides an overview of the relevant differences from the perspective of corporate governance.

The Anglo-American model is predominantly in evidence in the UK and the US as well as a few other countries such as Australia, Canada, and Ireland. Crucially, the Anglo-American model has also started to influence many emerging economies, particularly in Latin America and Asia (Reed 2002). The continental European model is evident throughout most of the rest of Europe, most notably France, Italy, Germany, and Spain as the largest economies on the continent. As Figure 6.2 shows, there are similarities but also important differences between these models and those in other parts of the world, such as the BRIC countries of Brazil, Russia, India, and China.

The Anglo-American model

This Anglo-American model focuses on the stock market as the central element of the system of governance. Most of the larger, publicly owned companies source their capital on the market, and in these countries shareholding is in the hands of multiple investors with the result that shares are broadly dispersed, ownership is frequently changed, and goals emphasize profitability and shareholder value (Aguilera et al. 2006; Becht and Röell 1999). With the stock market being the most important source of capital, corporations have to provide a high degree of transparency and accountability to shareholders and investors. Executives are in turn increasingly remunerated with regard to their corporation's performance on the stock market.

In this model, ethical concerns from the shareholder's perspective arise mainly around the proper functioning of market mechanisms and the market-related patterns of corporate governance. Typical ethical problems would be insider trading or manipulated accounting statements. In a broader perspective, the Anglo-American model clearly assigns a dominant role to shareholders, and consequently the major criticisms of the shareholder-oriented model of managerial capitalism discussed in Chapter 2 would apply to this approach.

The continental European model

Under this model of governance, corporations tend to be embedded in a network of a small number of large investors, among which banks play a major role. Within this network of mutually interlocking owners, the central focus is typically the long-term

	USA, UK (Anglo-American Model)	France, Germany, Italy ('Rhenish Capitalism')	Russia	India	China	Brazil
Ownership structure	Dispersed	Concentrated, interlocking pattern of ownership between banks, insurance companies, and corporations	Concentrated in either the hands of owner-managers or the wider circle of employees in joint-stock corporations	Highly concentrated; recent tendency to more dispersed ownership	Highly concentrated in state-owned companies; fairly concentrated in private enterprises	Highly concentrated ownership by family owned business groups; wave of privatization since 1990 has reduced state ownership
Ownership identity	• Individuals • Pension and mutual funds	• Banks • Corporations • State	• Owner-managers • Employees • State	• Families • Foreign investors • Banks	• State • Families • Corporations	• Family owned business groups • State
Changes in ownership	• Frequent	• Rare	• Frequent, but decreasing tendency	• Traditionally extremely rare, but recently changing	• Rare, but increasingly dynamic	• Rare • Increasing influence of foreign investors
Goals of ownership	• Shareholder value • Short term profits	• Sales, market share, headcount • Long-term ownership	• Profit for owners • Long-term ownership	• Long-term ownership • Growth of market share	• Long-term ownership • Sales, market share	• Long term ownership • Profit for owners
Board controlled by	• Executives • Shareholders	• Shareholders • Employees	• Owner-managers • Other insiders	• Owners • Other insiders	• Owners • State	• Owners/shareholders
Key stakeholders	• Shareholder	• Owners • Employees (trade unions, works councils)	• Owners • State	• Owners • Customers in overseas markets	• Owners/State • Guanxi-network of suppliers, competitors, and customers (mostly) in overseas markets	• Owners • Customers in overseas markets

Figure 6.2 Comparison of corporate governance regimes globally

preservation of influence and power. For continental European corporations, banks and their loans (rather than just the stock market) are of major importance for the purpose of sourcing capital. Next to shareholder value, the expansion of market share, retention of employees, and other goals not directly profit-oriented are important for owners. Executive pay is usually less directly performance-related, and has historically been regarded as an issue between the boards of corporations and managers, without any perceived relevance or need to disclose this to the general public. More recently, this practice has begun to change, mostly due to the increasing influence of global investors in Europe.

Perhaps most significantly from an ethical point of view, within the continental European model, stakeholders other than shareholders also play an important role, sometimes even equivalent to or above that of shareholders (Fiss and Zajac 2004). For instance, in German companies, up to half of the members of a corporation's supervisory board (which oversees the management of the firm) have to be appointed by the employees of the corporation. In contrast, in the Anglo-American model, employees typically have no say at all in the control of the firm. One could argue, therefore, that the continental model of capitalism is to some extent a European manifestation of the stakeholder theory of the firm, with corporations being expected to serve wider goals than just those of investors. From the perspective of individual shareholders, however, major ethical concerns derive from the fact that the system of ownership prefers the interests of big, mostly corporate shareholders and the interests of many other actors who have no direct ownership rights in the corporation rather than the individual investor.

Asian models

In some ways, the continental European model of governance is similar to the approach to corporate governance in Asia (Claessens and Fan 2002), which some refer to as a relationship-based approach to corporate governance (Clarke 2007). The economic structures of countries such as Korea with its large, mostly family-owned conglomerates (*chaebol*) or Japan with its mostly bank-financed *keiretsu* organizations are close to the European approach in that they do not rely predominantly on the stock market for sourcing capital and investment. The Japanese *keiretsu* model often consists of a large multinational company, such as Toyota or Hitachi, and can include their suppliers, customers, and other related firms in the supply chain.

As a result, the interests pursued by these companies are not predominantly the maximization of shareholder value, but include a host of other considerations, including securing employment, market share, and wider societal interests, such as education, social security (through lifetime employment), etc. These considerations might be especially prominent when firms are state owned, which is common in countries such as China and Taiwan. From a corporate governance perspective, the situation of minority shareholders or foreign investors in Asian models is particularly precarious as reporting, transparency, and accountability among such organizations are still fairly underdeveloped, particularly in comparison with the Anglo-American model.

As Figure 6.2 shows, the BRIC countries tend in one way or another to follow what is akin to a relationship-based approach, according to their specific economic and political heritage. In all of these countries, however, we see some degree of a shift towards more market-based mechanisms. An interesting example of how these different trends blend into each other can be found in the Indian approach to corporate governance (Sarkar and Sarkar 2000), which on the one hand is similar to the continental European model (as it is based on large block holdings of majority investors), but on the other hand also demonstrates elements characteristic of the Anglo-American approach (since many of these investors are actually companies and senior executives). This development is particularly encouraged by comparatively large numbers of foreign investors. Similar hybrid forms of governance can be found in many emerging economies such as Brazil, where it is only in the last few decades that companies have tried to attract more foreign capital and therefore adopted elements of the Anglo-American model (Rabelo and Vasconcelos 2002). The Russian case, furthermore, is interesting in particular for the phenomenon of owner-managers, often referred to as 'oligarchs', who amassed large parts of privatized former state-owned industries in the Boris Yeltsin era of the 1990s. With owners being managers at the same time, considerable conflicts of interest might obviously arise.

☑ Skill check

Distinguishing different corporate governance systems. Forms of ownership, models of risk sharing and measures of financial success differ widely across corporate governance systems and you need to be able to distinguish between them to evaluate ethical corporate behaviour.

Although it is useful to simplify corporate governance frameworks along these lines, it is important to take into account some important qualifications. First, as we have indicated, there are considerable pressures towards convergence in governance models, leading to hybrid models and shifts in the form if not always the substance of traditional governance arrangements (Yoshikawa and Rasheed 2009). For example, many of the more relationship-oriented forms of governance appear to be gradually taking on some elements of the Anglo-American model, but these are often resisted or combined with existing approaches, rather than simply replacing them. Especially since the global financial crisis of the late 2000s, the Anglo-American approach has been increasingly brought into question and it is now rarely considered (as it perhaps once was) the 'best model' of corporate governance (Aguilera and Jackson 2010). Also, different countries characterized as using the same system may actually differ quite considerably. This goes not only for the diverse countries captured by the 'continental European' umbrella, but also, as Aguilera et al. (2006) show, for the ostensibly similar approaches evident in the UK and the US, which actually differ in a number of key respects.

VISIT THE ONLINE RESOURCE CENTRE
for a short response to this feature

? THINK THEORY

Thinking of different corporate governance practices around the world in the context of moral relativism, are these just 'different' (i.e. reflecting different cultural and customary practices) or would you argue that some of them are actually more or less ethical?

■ Ethical issues in corporate governance

Corporate governance has been a business ethics topic high on the agenda of all major economies in recent years. Partly this has been the result of various scandals that have hit the headlines since the turn of the century. This started with the 'dot-com bubble' and the financial scandals, which saw the spectacular bankruptcy of companies such as Enron, Tyco, and WorldCom in the US, and shocking revelations of financial irregularities at Parmalat in Italy and Ahold in the Netherlands, amongst others. Attention later turned to the collapse of many banks and financial institutions in the financial crisis of 2008 and its aftermath. A swathe of governance scandals in Asia in the 2010s, including at Olympus, Tokyo Electric Power and Daiwo Paper in Japan, also led to suggestions of 'seemingly free-wheeling behavior—and disregard for corporate governance … among top management at some of Japan's leading companies' (Tabuchi 2011). Such phenomena have resulted in unprecedented interest in the ethical dimensions of corporate governance. In the following sections we will examine the main issues arising here, focusing specifically on those that primarily affect shareholders. **Ethics on Screen 6** provides a discussion of several of these issues in the context of the Wall Street movies and provides some interesting historical and contemporary context for the current debate.

Executive accountability and control

Looking at corporate governance, there are certain core elements that need to be present in order for the principal–agent relationship to be managed effectively. The most important element is a separate body of people that supervises and controls management on behalf of principals, namely a board of directors. It is the board to which the chief executive officer is accountable for their performance, and the board that will appoint the CEO and determine their salary. Unless the board has effective oversight and control of senior executives, the principal–agent relationship collapses. Effective corporate governance therefore relies on **executive accountability**.

In practice, the drive for executive accountability and control tends to result in a dual structure of the board of a publicly owned corporation. On the one hand, there are *executive directors* who are actually responsible for running the corporation as well as supposedly providing a link between managers and shareholders. On the other, there are *non-executive directors* who are supposed to ensure that the corporation is being run in the interests of principals, usually shareholders.

The different governance frameworks globally have important differences in the way that this board is structured and composed. There are basically two extremes. In the *Anglo-American* and *Asian* models, there is usually a single-tier board that comprises both executive and non-executive directors. In *continental Europe*, however, a two-tier board is more common. The upper tier is composed of non-executive directors and the lower tier of executive directors. The upper tier, often also called a *supervisory board*, effectively oversees the lower tier, which is more concerned with the day-to-day running of the company. As we have already said, the supervisory board commonly includes representatives of stakeholders other than just shareholders, including banks and employees. Perhaps unsurprisingly, therefore, there is considerable variability across countries in the extent to which executives are actually held accountable for the performance of their firms, for example by being fired for poor returns (Crossland and Chen 2013).

Executive accountability
The systems and processes through which senior executives can be held responsible for the performance of the firm by shareholders and other stakeholders, typically via the board of directors.

VISIT THE ONLINE RESOURCE CENTRE for links to useful sources of further information

ETHICS ON SCREEN 6

Wall Street and Wall Street: Money Never Sleeps

An upscale morality tale to entertain achievers who don't want to lose touch with their moral centers, but still have it all.

Vincent Canby, *New York Times*

The original *Wall Street* movie is one of the best-known movies to have brought the dilemmas and challenges of business ethics to mainstream Hollywood cinema. Released in 1987, it has become a classic—mostly due to its powerful storyline, great writing and directing by Oliver Stone, and an Oscar-winning performance by Michael Douglas. It is considered by many to be the ultimate 1980s business portrait, reflecting the rise of liberalized financial markets and the stock-market boom during that decade.

The core story is about a young stockbroker Bud Fox (Charlie Sheen) who in his quest for the success and glamour of a rich Wall Street banker's life falls under the spell of corporate raider Gordon Gekko (Douglas). The moral maze that Bud finds himself in focuses on a deal regarding the takeover of an airline company, which he can recommend to Gekko based on insider information gathered through his father. The latter, played by Sheen's own father Martin, is an airline mechanic and union member—and as such, highly suspicious of the dealings of his son. Ultimately, the Securities and Exchange Commission (SEC) gets wind of the deal and after being arrested, Bud ends up saving his own neck by providing evidence about Gekko's role as the true villain in the game.

Besides being a highly entertaining, funny, and intelligently scripted piece of cinematography, the film has become a classic for a number of reasons. Certainly, it is full of witty and thought-provoking dialogue. Michael Douglas delivers killer lines such as 'lunch is for wimps', 'I create nothing. I own' and 'rich' is not '$450,000 a year, but rich enough to have your own jet'. Unforgettable too is his notorious 'greed is good' speech in the film, which he makes to the shareholders of a company he wants to buy out. These scenes remind us of how closely the film is

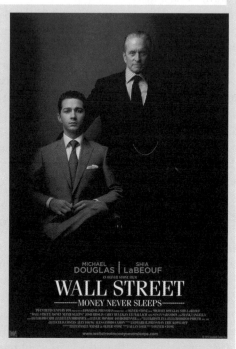

Appian Way/Paramount/The Kobal Collection

modelled on some of the real-world insider scandals on Wall Street at that time. One of those Wall Street icons, Ivan Boesky, later sentenced for insider trading, gave a nearly identical speech to a business school audience months before.

Twenty-three years later, as part of the spate of post-financial crisis movies (see also **Ethics on Screen 1 and 2**), Stone released the sequel *Wall Street: Money Never Sleeps*. The movie returns our attention to Gordon Gekko (played again by Michael Douglas), who after eight years in jail for the crimes he committed in the first movie, is back in the game, which now is the world of hedge funds and private equity. Set in the late 2000s, this time his younger, to-be-corrupted counterpart is his future son-in-law, Jacob Moore (played by Shia LaBeouf).

Gekko begins the movie as an apparently changed man, promoting his book *Is Greed Good* and warning of imminent financial collapse on the talk-show circuit. However, it soon becomes evident that he is just as sly an operator as ever, playing fast and loose with rules of corporate governance to suit his own ends, which in this case also involves reconciling with his estranged daughter. The plot involves many twists and turns as Gekko finds a way to engineer millions of dollars into his hedge fund while helping Moore to avenge the collapse of his former mentor's investment bank during the financial crisis.

While the critical acclaim of the sequel clearly falls short of the iconic status of the original *Wall Street* movie, both movies are worth viewing, not least for the different perspectives they provide on governance scandals. The first movie centres on insider trading, its very personal costs, and the emerging culture of greed in Wall Street. The sequel, in contrast, focuses less on specific acts of wrongdoing and more on the institutional problems of governance in the financial sector. Companies are wrecked and fortunes are lost at the whim of the market and the swirling of rumours rather than hard facts, while global capital flows make effective oversight next to impossible. So, taken together the two movies provide a real-life example of why cultural change on Wall Street is so difficult to achieve and how a liberalized economic system predicated on ruthless maximization of self-interest easily incentivizes actions of questionable moral status.

Sources

Canby, V. 1987. Film: Stone's Wall Street. *New York Times*, 11 December 1987.
Scott, A.O. 2010. The Pride That Went Before the Fall. *New York Times*, 23 September 2010.
http://www.rottentomatoes.com/m/wall_street.
http://www.rottentomatoes.com/m/wall_street_money_never_sleeps/.

Regardless of the structure of the board, the central ethical issue here is clearly the independence of the supervisory, non-executive board members. They will only be able to reasonably act in the principal's interest if they have no directly conflicting interests. In order to achieve this, a number of points are important (see Nader 1984; Boyd 1996):

• Non-executive directors should be largely drawn from outside the corporation.

• They should not have a personal financial interest in the corporation other than the interests of shareholders. This includes the fact that the remuneration for the non-executive director role must not significantly exceed a reasonable compensation for time and other expenses.

• They should be appointed for a limited period in order to prevent them from getting too close to the company.

• They should be competent to judge the business of the company. This would require, and to some degree allow, a limited number of insiders, such as former executives or even works council members (such as in certain parts of Europe).

• They should have sufficient resources to get information or commission research into the corporation.

• They should be appointed independently. This would be either by the shareholders directly in the annual general meeting, or through appointment by the supervisory board.

A further element of supervision comes from an independent auditor who audits the work of the executive board—normally the main aspect of their role—and also of the non-executive board. We will discuss the role of auditors and the ethical issues involved a little later.

Despite the guidelines above, the independence of non-executive directors remains a delicate issue. Often they belong to the same peer group as executive directors, or are themselves in executive roles elsewhere, or have been in such roles in the past. This means that a completely neutral and independent approach will always be quite difficult to achieve (Gordon 2002).

Executive remuneration

The financial crisis of the late 2000s brought the issue of executive pay to centre stage in an unprecedented fashion given that executives of bankrupt or failing companies continued to earn millions in salaries and billions in bonuses. 'Shameful' and 'the height of irresponsibility' were US President Obama's comments on what continued to be common practice not only in the US, but in many other countries across the globe. As **Ethics Online 6** shows, public concern about excessive executive salaries have fuelled a rise in online attention to the issue, including a slew of websites dedicated to promoting transparency about current pay levels.

The general trend towards ever-increasing executive salaries has been driven by the dominance of the shareholder value ideology. However, the key element here actually derives from an attempt to address the core of the agency problem: in order to align the interests of both parties, the perfect solution appeared to be to pay executives in the same 'currency' that matters to shareholders, namely dividends and rises in share price. The logical conclusion then is to pay executives in shares—or more commonly, in options that allow executives to buy shares on a future date. In order to make the incentives work, it would not be sufficient to pay them with just a few shares or options but to a degree that substantially impacts on their wealth. As a consequence, the US in particular has led the way in rewarding senior managers with massive stock option deals. This approach of performance-related pay has especially taken hold in the finance industry, resulting in high salaries and bonuses even for mid-level executives in financial services and banking.

In 2012 the ten top-earning CEOs in the US took home at least $100 million each, with Facebook's Mark Zuckerberg topping the list with a whopping $2.27 billion in total compensation (Rushe 2013)! At the same time, the average ratio of CEO-to-worker pay in the US had risen to more than 350 : 1, while in Europe the same ratio ranged from 28 : 1 in Poland, to 48 : 1 in Denmark, 84 : 1 in the UK, and 148 : 1 in Switzerland.[3] Meanwhile, the link between executive remuneration and stock market performance has always been somewhat tenuous (Walsh 2008).

Examples such as these unveil many of the ethical problems with executive pay in firm–shareholder relations:

- First, there is the issue of designing appropriate *performance-related pay* in a world of reinvigorated shareholder value (Koslowski 2000). In order to tackle the problem of divergent interests, most executive remuneration packages now contain a significant amount of share options to align shareholder and manager interests, but this has resulted in rocketing salary levels and uncertain effects on share prices.

- Secondly, these shifts in remuneration show the influence of *globalization* on executive pay. Since the market for executive talent is a global one, increases in one country tend to drive up pay internationally.

- Thirdly, the *influence of the board* appears to be somewhat limited and often fails to reflect shareholder (or other stakeholder) interests. Why would shareholders want to reward a CEO who had overseen a period of poor performance?

Such problems show few, if any, signs of diminishing, and indeed may be expected to occupy shareholders (not to mention the general public) for sometime yet. In Europe, the EU Commission began attempts in the mid-2010s to strengthen shareholder rights with regard to executive compensation, while Switzerland even put the topic to an unsuccessful public referendum in 2013 (Dijkhuizen 2014). What drives reform here is of course not so much the public feeling sorry for shareholders, but the fact that the pay differentials between those at the top and those at the bottom appear to be so inequitable. We shall cover this issue again in Chapter 7 when we address the question of fair pay for employees.

? THINK THEORY

Assess the pay packages of chief executives from the perspective of justice theories. Is the main objection one of distributive justice (executives get more than they deserve or are rewarded when other deserving parties are not), or procedural justice (in that the mechanism for executive remuneration is not fair)?

VISIT THE
ONLINE
RESOURCE
CENTRE
for a short
response to this
feature

Ethical aspects of mergers and acquisitions

From a societal point of view, mergers and acquisitions might be encouraged if they involve the transfer of assets to an owner who will use them more productively and thereby create more wealth. The alternative is to leave the assets in the hands of a less-effective management, with higher costs, less innovation, and other costs to society. However, there are a number of ethical issues that might arise, as many examples of unsuccessful mergers demonstrate. The central source of ethical concern in this context is that managers may pursue interests that are not congruent with the shareholders' interests. A study by KPMG of 700 mergers found that only 17% created real value for shareholder while more than half actually destroyed value (Surowiecki 2008). As a result of such failures, some companies have reversed their decisions and have begun demerging. Consider Hewlett Packard, which after having spent more than $60 billion in the previous decade on acquisitions, announced in 2014 that it would be splitting its business. Around the same time, eBay announced the sale of PayPal, representing another example of a costly, yet ultimately unsuccessful merger (Surowiecki 2014). Basically, the conflict here is around the desire for power and prestige among senior executives in driving mergers on the one hand, and the interests of shareholders in driving profit and share price on the other.

There is in particular a wealth of discussion in the American business ethics literature on this issue, mainly since the US business system strongly encourages these types of transactions—more so than is the case in tightly regulated Europe or in BRIC countries with more narrowly held stock ownership. However, with an increasing deterritorialization of financial markets, these practices have also become more common across the globe in recent years, as the example of mergers of French, German, or Swedish

VISIT THE ONLINE RESOURCE CENTRE
for links to useful sources of further information

ETHICS ONLINE 6

Tracking executive remuneration

Executive remuneration has become a highly controversial topic. Together with a growing debate on income inequality in most Western democracies the public's interest in the issue has grown considerably over recent years. Consequently, campaign groups, advocacy organizations, and governments are increasingly turning to the internet to not only draw attention to the issue but also to create higher levels of transparency.

We can identify three types of websites dealing with executive remuneration. First, we see a growing number of activist groups who use the internet to expose high salaries and provide resources to understand the problems around executive pay and income inequality. A good example of this type of activist website is the UK-based High Pay Centre which defines itself as 'an independent non-party think tank established to monitor pay at the top of the income distribution and set out a road map towards better business and economic success'. Next to a tongue-in-cheek pay counter displaying the average salary of a FTSE100 CEO since the beginning of the year (it moves pretty fast!) it provides research on the topic, video footage, and other social media relating to executive pay. Other activist websites along these lines are based in the trade union movement, such as the American Federation of Labor-Congress of Industrial Organizations (AFL-CIO), which has a section called Executive Paywatch where you can find instructive infographics about the issue. Similar websites creating transparency and providing advocacy around executive remuneration are now available in many other languages and countries, such as the German *Gehaltsreporter* ('salary reporter').

A second group of websites about executive remuneration are those initiated by governments, primarily for the purposes of disclosure rather than advocacy. In the US, transparency around executive pay has been particularly pushed by recent legislation in the Dodd–Frank Act (see also Ethics in Action 6.1), which requires companies to publish the ratio between CEO compensation and the median salary of employees. In Canada, to date, such transparency has focused only on public sector salaries, with the provinces publishing the salary of all public sector employees earning more than $100,000 per year (including, we should add, university professors). This so-called 'sunshine list' gets published every year and is subject to wide public scrutiny—not to mention being a ceaseless source of office gossip across the Canadian public sector.

A third group of web resources relating to the topic are sites, often run by advisory consultants, that not only offer transparency about typical pay levels of particular jobs but also provide advice to employees on how to best negotiate their salary, or, to employers, on how best to set their employees' salaries. Salary.com, for example, enables you to browse the going salaries for a multitude of positions across the US and Canada, providing data on upper and lower levels and the median salary, both with and without bonuses.

The issue of executive compensation is likely to stay on the public agenda for some time. The internet is proving to be a powerful resource offering much more data and insight on this often secretive issue. Ultimately, this looks set to be a boost for advancing transparency and accountability relating to one of the thorniest of ethical problems in corporate governance.

Sources
Activist websites:
http://highpaycentre.org.
http://www.aflcio.org/Corporate-Watch/Paywatch-2014.

http://www.workerscapital.org/priorities/shareholder-activism/campaigns/trends-in-global-
    executive-compensation/.
http://www.gehaltsreporter.de.
Government resources:
http://www.sec.gov/rules/proposed/2013/33-9452.pdf.
http://www.fin.gov.on.ca/en/publications/salarydisclosure/pssd/ (the 'sunshine list' for the Province
    of Ontario).
Advisory services:
http://www.salary.com.
http://www.payscale.com.

companies in the telecommunication and utility industries illustrates. In the following, we will look at the main issues that have arisen or are likely to arise.

Next to 'normal' mergers: there are particular ethical problems involved in so-called *hostile takeovers*. Here, an investor (or a group of investors) intends to purchase a majority stake in a corporation (often secretly) against the wishes of its board. Without going into a detailed philosophical debate, there are basically two lines of argument here (see De George 1999: 462–4). On the one side, it could be argued that hostile takeovers are ultimately possible only because shareholders want to sell their stock; otherwise they would keep it. On the other side, an ethical concern may arise with the remaining shareholders that do not want to sell. If the company is taken over by someone who has different ideas about the corporation—for instance, an 'asset stripper' that wants to split the company and sell off certain parts—a hostile takeover might interfere quite significantly with the property rights of those remaining shareholders.

Even relatively friendly acquisitions can create ethical challenges when they are predicated on realizing shareholder value at the expense of other stakeholders. For instance, Jack Welch, the well-known former CEO of General Electric (GE) acquired his nickname 'Neutron Jack' because he turned GE into one of the best-performing conglomerates on Wall Street through the acquisition of all sorts of corporations, and significantly *restructuring* and *downsizing* them immediately after takeover. The buildings and assets remained; only the people had to leave—similar to the effect of a neutron bomb. Very often acquisitions only target the profitable parts of the bought-up corporation, while at the same time the other parts will be liquidated. Sometimes these acquisitions even focus only on the brand value or certain patents and technologies of the bought-up firm, with the consequence that other stakeholder interests, such as those of employees or local communities, are seriously disregarded.

The role of financial markets and insider trading

There has been a remarkable silence in the literature on financial markets with regard to ethical issues (Rudolph 1999). A simple justification for this would be the following: financial markets, especially the stock market, are based on shareholders expecting a future dividend and/or a rise in share prices as a basis for their decision to buy or sell stocks. As long as the rules of the market are set fairly and everyone plays according to these rules, no ethical dilemma is to be expected. Issues such as mergers, acquisitions, or executive pay are not so much the object of ethical consideration as a simple part of the economic calculation of the shareholder: if the shareholder does not agree to the CEO's remuneration demands, they are fully entitled to sell the stock. It might be presumptuous to demand more pay, or the merger might be problematic, but ultimately the shareholder can make a fully informed decision and could sell their stock.

Behind this argument there is the assumption of a perfect market, and in particular the assumption that, ultimately, all publicly available information about the company is reflected by the stock price. However, we all know that this simple rationale of 'the stock market never lies' is only part of the truth. Sometimes, the alleged 'information efficiency' of stock markets is quite flawed, as the following issues show.

Speculative 'faith stocks'

An often-discussed problem is the speculative nature of share prices. This not only became evident in the financial crisis of the late 2000s but also during one of its predecessors, the burst of the 'dot-com' bubble in the late 1990s. Start-ups that had not made a single cent in profit but were valued at billions of dollars on the Nasdaq in New York or the Neuer Markt in Frankfurt then took this speculative element to an extreme. These stocks were not so much built on solidly calculated profit expectations, but were more like 'faith stocks' (Gordon 2002), built on little more than blind faith. Even a company such as Amazon.com, which is one of the successful survivors of that crisis, needed more than seven years to make even a dollar in profit. Even now, after twenty years in business, it still does not consistently generate profits and regularly reports quarterly losses. Yet its share price rose from $60 to $400 from 2006 to 2014 making the 'believers' in its stock rich (Stewart 2014).

In some sense, the financial crisis of the late 2000s had similar roots. The complex structured finance products that mortgage lenders and other financial institutions traded to manage the risk of sub-prime mortgages were all based on 'faith' that the real estate market would continue to rise. As long as this faith held, most actors involved thrived. When the downturn set in, however, it not only turned out that the optimism was misplaced, but also that the products were way too complex for the managers involved to foresee the likely consequences.

One problem here is that many pensioners whose funds had invested in these bonds lost large parts of their income. The ethical issue clearly lies in the fact that while stock prices always contain an element of speculation, stock markets do not always fully reveal the amount of uncertainty. This might be somewhat trivial for brokers or other stock-market professionals; however, with large institutional investors investing other people's money in these stocks, the fact that these bonds may be based entirely on speculation can be said to be close to an abuse of trust. This also questions the role of analysts and accountants (see The role of financial professionals and market intermediaries, pp. 249–251) who, among others, are responsible for ensuring *informed* transactions on the stock market.

High-frequency trading

With the rise of electronic trading and an ever-increasing speed of data processing, a new area of ethical concern has arisen around what is often referred to as 'high-frequency trading' (HFT) (Lewis 2014). Brokers using HFT buy financial assets and only hold them for microseconds to benefit from minimal changes in the value of the assets before selling them. There are two main problems with this practice (Davis et al. 2013). First, depending on the hardware of the company and its cable connection to the electronic stock exchanges, some players in the market have their information microseconds before competitors and thus might be said to have an unfair advantage. The other problem is that all of those trades are executed through electronic algorithms and since most actors in the market use very similar algorithms, the risk of market crashes is quite substantial. So, for instance, a short but dramatic 'flash crash' of the Dow Jones Index by more than 1,000 points within a few minutes in May 2010 is blamed on such an effect of HFT. It is exacerbated by the fact that HFT only generates substantial benefits when the size of the investment is very high. HFT is currently under scrutiny by many regulators.

Insider trading

Insider trading occurs when securities are bought or sold on the basis of material *non-public* information (Moore 1990). Although it therefore shares with HFT a problem of some traders benefiting from an unfair advantage, it is a much longer-standing problem that has been a feature of stock markets for more than a century. The point is that executives of a corporation and other insiders know the company well, and so might easily know about events that are likely to have a significant impact on the company's share price well in advance of other potential traders. Consequently, insiders are privileged over other players in the market in terms of knowledge, a privilege that they could take advantage of to reap a questionable profit.

Insider trading
A financial market transaction based on information that is not publicly available to all other market participants.

In the long run, insider trading can undermine investors' trust in the market (Carroll and Buchholtz 2012: 105)—a problem that has led many stock markets to forbid the practice. However, concerns around insider training persist, and certainly the US courts have pursued insider trading cases with great vigour in recent years. For instance, the high-profile case of hedge fund owner Raj Rajaratnam and former managing director of McKinsey, Rajat Gupta, led to both men being arrested for insider trading and prison sentences of 11 years and two years, respectively.

The ethical assessment of insider trading tends to rely on one or more of the following four arguments (Moore 1990):

- **Fairness.** There are inequalities in the access to relevant information about companies, leading to a situation where one party has an unfair advantage over the other. Moore (1990) argues that this is the weakest but most common argument that tends to be used against insider trading.

- **Misappropriation of property**. Insider traders use valuable information that is essentially the property of the firm involved, and to which they have no right of access. According to Moore (1990), this has become a common basis for legal cases involving insider trading.

- **Harm to investors and the market**. Insider traders might benefit to the cost of 'ordinary' investors, making the market riskier and threatening confidence in the market.

- **Undermining of fiduciary relationship**. The relationships of trust and dependence among shareholders and corporate managers (and employees) are based on managers acting in the interests of shareholders, yet insider trading is fuelled by self-interest on the part of insiders rather than obligation to their 'principal'. Moore (1990) argues that this is the strongest argument against insider trading.

VISIT THE
ONLINE
RESOURCE
CENTRE
for a short
response to this
feature

> **? THINK THEORY**
>
> How do these four arguments correspond to the traditional ethical theories set out in Chapter 3?

Whichever way we look at it, the central problem here seems to lie in the question of where to define the boundaries. After all, every investor tries to receive as much knowledge about a company as possible and analysts of major investment banks would by no means necessarily treat their knowledge as publicly available. A particular problem has arisen from the aforementioned fact that many companies remunerate their executives with stock options or shares. These people may use their inside knowledge of the company to decide when to exercise their options or sell their shares (and, arguably, it could be irrational to expect them to do otherwise). As a result, such 'acceptable' incentives are difficult to distinguish from 'unacceptable' insider trading. **An Ethical Dilemma 6** presents a typical situation where the boundaries of insider trading might be very difficult to draw clearly.

AN ETHICAL DILEMMA 6

Who cares whose shares?

It has become something of an institution to go out drinking with your friends on Friday nights, especially since you started working for PharmChemCo (PCC) five years ago and began pulling in a big salary. The company is one of the biggest pharmaceutical and chemical companies in the world, and working there has brought you career success and a very healthy bank balance. It has also turned you into quite a successful player in the stock market. Since you were promoted to regional marketing director for the North East, PCC has paid a large chunk of your bonuses in stock options. Even with a dipping market, this has proved to be an extremely lucrative package, given your success in meeting sales targets and, of course, shrewd investment over the last two-and-a-half years.

This particular Friday night, however, you are not feeling so great. Yes, you have an expensive cocktail in your hand; yes, you have some of your best mates with you, all very much up for a big night out; and yes, Freddie, your best friend from college, will be arriving any minute. However, the last week in the office has been a nightmare. A special meeting had been called by one of the vice-presidents for all of the senior managers. At the meeting, it was announced that scientists in a leading research lab at SFW University in the US had discovered some potentially lethal side-effects associated with one PCC's best-selling herbicides. The report had been confidential to the board of PCC, but an article containing the research was going to be published in *Big Science* magazine on Thursday next week. The purpose of the meeting was to inform everybody and to discuss potential strategies to tackle the problem. Consequently, you were urged to stay absolutely silent about the research findings, particularly as the likelihood was that this would turn out to be a major news story.

Knowing about this makes you uneasy now. It is pretty certain that this information will have a major effect on the share price of PCC as court cases in the US with huge damages are a certainty. Digesting the news in your office after lunch, you had already decided to sell your shares in PCC first thing on Monday—as it is almost certain that the value of your stocks will not be the same in the foreseeable future once this news is out. However, you are certain that Freddie, your friend from college, is also going to be badly affected by the news once it gets out. He is now an account manager for a major investment bank. And not only has he invested heavily in PCC shares himself, he has also advised many of his clients—among them managers of major funds—to invest in PCC.

You are quite uneasy about what to do. Freddie is your best friend, and you want to help him. You know he will hear the news soon anyway and maybe, given his contacts, even before it is published next Thursday. But if you tell him now, you are certain that he will sell his own shares (which you really would not mind), but as he is measured by the performance of his advice to his clients, you can be pretty certain that he will also advise his clients to sell. The effect on the share price before the publication of the article could be substantial.

Questions

1. What are the main ethical issues in this case?

2. Who are the main stakeholders here, and how would you compare the relative importance of their stakes?

3. Explain what you would ultimately decide and why.

4. Is there an ethical difference between acting yourself on the information you were given and passing this information on to Freddie? Is there an ethical difference between Freddie acting on the information for himself and him giving advice to his clients?

The role of financial professionals and market intermediaries

One of the main institutions to bridge the asymmetric distribution of information between shareholders and corporate actors is that of financial professionals and market intermediaries. The two single most important types of actors here are *accounting firms* and *credit-rating agencies* (CRAs). The task of these organizations is to provide a 'true and fair view'—as they say in accounting—of a company's financial situation or a judgement of the trustworthiness of an investment opportunity. While the 'big three' major CRAs (Fitch Ratings, Moody's Investors Service, and Standard & Poor's Financial Services) are a global oligopoly, even across the range of accounting, audit, assurance, and other advisory functions of the main accounting firms, the big four of Deloitte, Ernst & Young, KPMG, and PwC also have an effective oligopoly at least in terms of providing audit services to large firms.

With shareholder value orientation becoming more and more popular over the last few years, the nature of the accounting profession has undergone substantial changes (Mellahi and Wood 2002). Rather than certifying the quality of published accounts, today's audits focus a great deal not only on statements of past periods but also on the future potential of the corporation. This process, sometimes pejoratively termed 'creative accounting', mirrors the demands of a major group of addressees of corporate state-ments, namely investors. However, the risk inherent in this process is evident: the discre-tionary element of auditing existing figures is already quite significant; this is even more the case for projections based on these figures. To take up the expression used above, the ethical challenge for audit firms lies in the fine line between presenting a share as a 'faith stock' or repackaging what one would normally simply call a dud or a 'lemon' (Gordon 2002: 1236).

Issues of a similar nature have occurred with CRAs, which are seen by some experts as one of the main culprits in the financial crisis of the late 2000s (Scalet and Kelly 2012). The primary role of the CRA is to provide a credible assessment of financial products so that investors have a better idea about what a fair price for the product would be and what the risks associated with that product are. From that perspective, CRAs are a pivotal element in the largely deregulated infrastructure of global financial markets. The main question then is whether the assessment of the CRA is trustworthy. For many, this is all but proven: since all three of the main CRAs rated the majority of the 'toxic' mortgage-based securities that caused the financial crisis as 'triple A', the best possible rating (Bahena 2009), 'it is beyond argument that ratings agencies did a horrendous job evaluating mortgage-tied securities before the financial crisis hit' (*The Economist* 2013). Even Lehman Brothers had at least an 'A' rating from all three agencies up to the very day before it collapsed (Evans and Salas 2009).

It is therefore no wonder that accounting firms and CRAs increasingly find themselves in the ethical spotlight. Ballwieser and Clemm (1999) identify five main problematic aspects of the financial intermediary's job:

- **Power and influence in markets**. Just how much market power intermediaries wield became especially evident in the financial crisis in 2008. The bankruptcy of American International Group (AIG) and its subsequent bailout by the US Treasury were precipi-tated by the fact that CRAs substantially downgraded AIG's double A rating. As many of AIG's contracts with other banks were predicated on this rating, the company sud-denly had to hand back many collaterals to their partners—but was not able to come up with the necessary cash (Evans and Salas 2009). The power of CRAs can even have a political dimension as they also rate government-issued bonds. This became a deli-cate political issue for the British and French governments in 2013 when various CRAs downgraded both countries due to high levels of governmental debt following slow economic growth.

- **Conflict of interest**. Intermediaries necessarily get a very close insight into the work-ings of the companies they evaluate. It is only natural then that they use this insight to develop an extra source of income by providing consultancy and other business services to their clients. The crucial problem, however, is that this additional involve-ment with their clients risks the necessary neutrality of the auditor. The same problem exists with CRAs since 98% of ratings are paid for by the issuers of financial products—not the investors in whose interest the ratings should be conducted. Consequently, CRAs have strong incentives to provide good ratings to their clients in order to secure business and prevent them from switching to a competing CRA to get 'better' results.

In many cases, CRAs even 'consult' their clients about how to structure and design a financial product only to give them the 'promised' ranking once the advice is taken (Bahena 2009). Such conflicts of interest in company–supplier relationships are discussed in more detail in Chapter 9.

- **Long-term relationships with clients**. Financial intermediaries and their individual representatives enter a position of confidentiality with their clients and therefore the tendency is to look for long-term relationships. Although this is restricted by the accounting laws of some countries, the general problem persists. Having such a confidential position of trust with clients often creates long-term personal relationships that can threaten independence.

- **Oversight and controls**. CRAs, such as Moody's or Standard & Poor's, and many accounting firms, such as KPMG and PwC, are large multinational companies. The bigger the firm is, the more economies of scale it can realize in terms of staff training, standardization of auditing procedures, and rating tools, and the better it can specialize in different tasks. However, the more a firm grows, the harder it may become to maintain oversight and controls over standards of diligence. Standardized procedures of auditing may also diminish the diligence of the individual auditor, who might lose the personal sense of responsibility for the task. This distancing effect of bureaucracy was something we first discussed in Chapter 4 (Bureaucracy, pp. 167–169).

- **Competition between firms**. With intensifying competition between financial intermediaries, there is an inherent danger that firms will sacrifice public interest in the quest to beat the competition. Corners may be cut to reduce costs, greater emphasis may be placed on assessments that put the client in a positive light, and overall there may be less diligence in their core audit and evaluation functions.

? THINK THEORY

Explain the ethical dilemmas and conflicts for accounting firms and CRAs by applying the theoretical framework of situational influences on ethical decision-making discussed in Chapter 4.

VISIT THE
ONLINE
RESOURCE
CENTRE
for a short
response to this
feature

The ethics of private equity and hedge funds

The broad ethical concerns we have discussed already around issues of transparency and shareholder control have been exacerbated through the rise of *private equity* (PE) firms and *hedge funds* (HFs). PE firms usually invest money from institutional investors and wealthy individuals to reach a majority stake in a public company. After then taking the company private, PE firms may seek to restructure the firm with the goal of generating more cash and achieving the highest possible value for the company (or the parts of it) when it is refloated (Cumming and Johan 2013). For example, after Burger King was bought by 3G Capital, a Brazilian private equity firm, in 2010, its number of employees was reduced from nearly 40,000 to less than 3,000 in a quest to reverse its financial decline. When 3G took the firm public again in 2012, its stock market valuation grew almost 100% in two years (Leonard 2014).

There are a host of ethical issues raised with PE (see Nielsen 2008). The most general concern is that in most jurisdictions, once the company is taken private, there are no longer many obligations for providing public information about the company. While this entails ethical problems in itself, there are also other concerns around their lack of consideration for other stakeholders, most notably employees and earlier investors.

Hedge funds are one specific form of PE firm—initially for investing in complex structured financial products for 'hedging' risks from other investments, but now operating in a diverse array of financial investments. They too have raised a number of specific ethical concerns, most notably around their 'emblematic' opacity (Donaldson 2008). Transparency issues are particularly pronounced with HFs since these highly specialized funds are structured in such a way that they do not have to report to regulators in the same way as other investment firms, and they do not even fully disclose their strategies to their own investors. Despite fairly good returns—and fairy-tale salaries for their managers—HFs have become notorious because of their high risks, unusually low taxes, huge fees for investors, and an obvious potential for misleading potential investors about their performance (Donaldson 2008). It has also been suggested that their lack of transparency has a broader social cost because it hides systemic risk (Donaldson 2008). Some commentators have identified them as playing a key role in bringing about the financial crisis of the late 2000s. Moreover, their influence in restructuring many companies at the expense of jobs and employees continues to raise criticism as the controversy around Mitt Romney's role at Bain Capital during his presidential campaign showed in 2012 (Taibbi 2012).

■ Shareholders and globalization

Globalization has had a crucial impact on the role of shareholders, the nature of their ownership, and the scope of their activities. With global equity and finance markets being probably the most globalized markets, the consequences of this reformed role for shareholders have become increasingly visible. We might think of shareholders becoming players in the global arena in four different ways:

- Shareholders might become *directly* involved abroad by buying shares of companies in other countries. Typically, this would mean, for example, that French or Spanish investors would buy shares at the London Stock Exchange for a UK company.

- Shareholders might be involved *indirectly* by buying shares in a domestic (or international) company that operates globally by selling goods and services worldwide. Even the shareholders of a corporation such as Porsche, which avowedly wants to remain a 'German' company (by refusing to invest anywhere other than at home), are nevertheless involved in the globalization process given that the corporation has the majority of its sales abroad. This aspect has particular consequences for many European or Asian countries where the capital markets are still very nationally focused.

- Similar to this indirect involvement, but more pronounced, is the role of shareholders in explicitly *multinational corporations* (MNCs). Investing in such companies makes shareholders indirect players in global capital markets, especially if these companies are heavily involved in foreign direct investment activities in other countries.

- Finally, shareholders may become *direct players* in international capital markets by investing in funds that explicitly direct their money to global capital markets. Significant players in this category are the so-called 'sovereign wealth funds' which we will discuss in more detail later.

This differentiation helps us to recognize the particular effects of globalization on the ethical issues confronting firm relationships with shareholders. The first two instances involve stakeholders as actors in certain well-defined national capital markets. The ethical issues of corporate governance as discussed above are therefore similarly relevant for these instances. The two latter cases, however, are special since they involve shareholders in the context of global financial markets. We would define these markets along the following lines:

> Global financial markets are the total of all physical and virtual (electronic) places where financial titles in the broadest sense (capital, shares, currency, options, etc.) are traded worldwide.

If we just recall our definition of globalization in Chapter 1, global financial markets can perhaps be presently regarded as the most globalized markets since they are the least dependent on a certain territorial basis. The main factors leading to globalization that we mentioned in Chapter 1 are clearly at play here: *technological* advances mean that via electronic trading, financial markets today are confined neither to certain locations nor to certain time slots (Parker 1998: 267–72); the key *political* development is the high degree of deregulation of financial markets, which makes it possible to talk about one global market rather than many individual places of financial trade.

From an ethical point of view, these developments raise some serious issues, among the most important of which are the following:

- **Governance and control**. Global markets raise the problem that no national government is entitled to govern them (Becker and Westbrook 1998). With regard to financial markets, this means that the allocation of a fundamentally important resource for modern industrialized economies takes place without any serious normative rules other than the 'laws' of supply and demand (Koch 2000: 189–209). This might not sound too much of a problem, but such a lack of governance and control becomes immediately clear if we look at the sometimes negative consequences of global financial market transactions. The most recent example of this is certainly the financial crisis of the late 2000s. What initially started in the US very quickly became a global problem for many international banks since many of the mortgage-based securities were traded globally and assets based on these investments came under pressure all over the world. The spectacular effect of these rapid movements of capital around the globe became most visible in Iceland—a country that initially attracted large numbers of investors in the mid-2000s. When the rapid devaluation of mortgage-based securities occurred (in which many of the Icelandic banks were heavily invested), it caused the country to undergo one of the most severe financial crises ever experienced by a single economy.

- **National security and protectionism**. A specific governance issue has recently arisen with a particular group of investors often referred to as *sovereign wealth funds*. These are government-owned funds of countries that invest their budget surpluses—three-quarters of which comes from oil and gas revenues—in capital markets worldwide. Among the countries with large funds, apart from Norway ($893 billion), none is governed by a liberal democracy. These include funds held by the United Arab Emirates ($773 billion), Saudi Arabia ($757 billion), Kuwait ($548 billion), and Singapore ($320 billion).[4] What if these funds invest in companies in North America or Europe for motives beyond the simple maximization of their value? This became a subject of debate in the US when a Dubai-based investor was interested in buying a company that—among other things—owned strategic assets such as the ports of New York and New Jersey. Similar concerns were raised when capital from sovereign wealth funds was used in the rescue of many banks in Europe and North America after 2008, giving those funds some degree of strategic control over major financial institutions. One of the potential results of the rise of these funds might be new forms of protectionism, by which governments in the West might want to avoid countries such as China or Venezuela gaining control of key industries, such as banking, telecommunications, energy, and utilities.

- **International speculation**. Global financial markets encourage speculation. This is not an ethical problem as such, and in fact, speculation is one of the key principles underlying why financial markets exist in the first place. However, speculative movement of capital may have quite significant impacts on real-life situations. In the UK many people still remember 'Black Wednesday' in 1992, where the plans of the UK government to realign the currency rate of the pound to the European Currency System were undermined by speculative trading on both sides of the Atlantic. The result was serious damage to the government finances which, by some accounts, cost every British citizen £12, and contributed to the end of the Conservative government (McGrew 1997). Many activists have pointed out, however, that large speculative movements of financial assets can have particularly detrimental effects on the poor in developing economies (Birchfield and Freyberg-Inan 2005). A much-touted route for reform is via financial transaction taxes, sometimes labelled a 'Tobin tax' or a 'Robin Hood tax' that levy a charge on all or some financial market trades. Several European countries, including Italy, Finland, and France, have already instituted some form of financial transaction tax, and in 2012 the European Parliament approved a EU Financial Transaction Tax which would see 11 member states instituting a harmonized tax (expected to be about 0.1%) on trades in equities and certain derivatives by 2016.

- **Unfair competition with developing countries**. A number of economic crises in developing countries during the 1990s, such as in Mexico, Brazil, or most notably East Asia, were mainly triggered by speculative moves of capital out of the country. Investors are attracted to invest in developing countries during boom phases, but when they turn to bust, rapid capital withdrawal can have disastrous effects for local economies and people. One of the main problems here is that while global financial markets are strongly deregulated and thus capital can flow easily in and out of the countries, this is not the case for the markets for goods and services (Hauskrecht 1999).

This debate has been exacerbated by recent practices of investment firms in food commodity markets. It is estimated that around 60% of purchases on the Chicago wheat exchange are speculative, with the effect of globally rising prices for food staples (up from 12% in 1996). Goldman Sachs allegedly earned $400 million in 2012 from speculating on food commodities, while the World Bank argues that in 2010, 44 million people were pushed into poverty due to speculation-induced rising food prices (Doane 2013).

- **Space for illegal transactions**. As these markets are not fully controlled by national governments, they can easily be used for transactions that would be illegal in most countries. Terrorism, money laundering, international drug trafficking, and the illegal trade of weapons are all substantially aided by global financial markets in their present shape. The problem of tax evasion and fraud through international capital flows to so-called 'tax-havens', such as Luxembourg, the Channel Islands, or the Cayman Islands has also risen to prominence in recent years. However, there are clearly major obstacles to reform in this arena, given the persistence of national idiosyncrasies in culture and regulation. For example, secrecy has been a major ingredient in the success of Switzerland or Luxembourg as global banking hubs, and so implementing tougher global rules about the identity and origin of deposits in banks potentially threatens the very basis of the finance industry in these countries.

Reforming corporate governance around the globe

With the rise of global financial markets and the subsequent spread of Anglo-American forms of more market-oriented corporate governance, we have seen a flurry of attempts to reform this aspect of economic life in most countries in the world (see **Ethics in Action 6.1** for an overview). Often these reforms follow corporate scandals, as was the case of the Sarbanes–Oxley Act in the US in 2002 or the Dodd–Frank Act, again in the US, in 2010. These have led to significant changes in the governance practices of corporate America. In contrast to many reforms discussed further in this section, these are mandatory pieces of legislation attempting to reform corporate governance through the improvement of internal controls and external reporting mechanisms—the main focus being the avoidance of criminal misconduct. Given that many European and Asian companies have substantial business activities in the US, both Acts have had palpable knock-on effects on the rest of the world as well as in the US (Webb 2006; Bafilemba et al. 2014).

In Europe and many other parts of the world, probably the main way that reform has been addressed is through the definition and implementation of new corporate governance codes. The European Corporate Governance Institute lists more than 400 national corporate governance codes, principles and recommendations that have been introduced since 1998, including 35 in the UK alone.[5] Governance reform has very much spread across the world, including to countries with a relatively small number of listed companies, including Albania, Bosnia and Herzegovina, Croatia, Estonia, Kazakhstan, Malta, Philippines, Qatar, and Yemen. Despite such proliferation, some codes such as South Africa's 1994 'King Report on Corporate Governance in South Africa' (the 'King Code') and its revisions in 2002 and 2009 have been influential as a template for corporate

VISIT THE
ONLINE
RESOURCE
CENTRE
for links to
useful sources
of further
information

ETHICS IN ACTION 6.1   http://www.ethicalcorp.com

Banking regulations struggle to avert the next financial crisis

Stephen Gardner, 13 October 2014

Ethical CORPORATION

The past five years have brought a wave of new financial regulation. In the US, the monolithic Dodd–Frank Wall Street Reform and Consumer Protection Act was signed into law in 2010. It is intended as a catch-all: 848 pages covering financial-system oversight, bank capital requirements, executive pay, investor protection and many other issues, plus a range of miscellaneous regulations thrown in—including disclosure rules for conflict minerals and provisions on the safety of coal mines.

The EU, meanwhile, has taken a piecemeal approach. More than 50 post-crisis laws on the financial system have been proposed by Brussels. About two-thirds of these have been finalized. Broadly speaking, the EU laws cover the same ground as Dodd–Frank, but there are some significant differences between what the EU and US have adopted.

There is a view that the EU has been less decisive than the US in imposing tough rules on banks. Kenneth Haar, a researcher with watchdog Corporate Europe Observatory, says: 'The EU rules have generally been adopted later than the corresponding US rules, and have generally been weaker. The result can be seen in the statistics. The biggest European banks are weaker than the Wall Street banks.'

In particular, US banks quickly repaid money that the US government sunk into them to keep them afloat during the crisis. The US government has even made a $40 billion profit so far, according to the Bailout Tracker maintained by ProPublica, a non-profit investigative journalism group.

In Europe, by contrast, progress has been much slower. In the UK, for example, taxpayers still own about 80% of Royal Bank of Scotland, with no indication of when the value of its shares will rise enough to pay back its bailout. In the Netherlands, ABN Amro remains in government hands, while ING expects to finish repaying its bailout in mid-2015.

Different, but the same

Despite differences in approach, the banking regulations adopted in the EU and US have broadly similar aims. The objective is to make banks more robust in case of crisis, to improve supervision by regulators so that any risks coming down the tracks can be identified and dealt with earlier, and to have a framework in place so that any banks that fail go bust in an orderly way.

In the first area—bank robustness—both the US and EU are implementing an international standard known as Basel III. Under this, banks are required to hold at all times capital equivalent to 8% of their assets, adjusted for the riskiness of those assets, in order to have a cushion with which to absorb unexpected losses. The 8% level is the same as earlier international standards, but Basel III requires the composition of the 8% cushion to be of higher quality.

Robert Priester, deputy chief executive for regulatory policy at the European Banking Federation, says it is in this area that 'Europe's banks had the most catching up to do. So far banks have been moaning and groaning, but it was necessary.' One controversial issue in Europe is the 'leverage ratio' under Basel III. Banks must also now have enough assets that can be easily sold to meet a 30-day liquidity crisis. However, setting money aside for possible liquidity crises means that 'this money cannot be used for other purposes' such as lending to businesses that want to invest, Priester says.

When things go wrong

Another aspect of the bank regulation reform is crisis planning—what should be done if banks still get into trouble. During the financial crisis, some banks did go bust, most famously US investment bank Lehman Brothers. In Iceland, the big three banks all failed over the course of three days in October 2008. But in Europe in general, governments responded by stepping in to protect depositors, at great cost to taxpayers.

The implicit government guarantees also encouraged moral hazard in some of the banks at the heart of the crisis. This was most starkly illustrated by tapes leaked in Ireland of conversations between senior executives of Anglo Irish Bank, which was nationalised in 2009. The tapes revealed that the executives did not initially disclose the extent of the bank's problems to the Irish government for fear that the required bailout would be considered too big to be politically acceptable. By initially asking for a smaller amount of money, the executives guessed—correctly—that the government would then not be able to renege on its commitment to support the bank when the full details of the funding black hole were made public.

In the US, Dodd–Frank has ruled out future bank bailouts. Instead, the newly created Federal Deposit Insurance Corporation will act as the receiver of failed banks, and will seek to protect depositors and pay off creditors. But ultimately, if the money is not there, everyone will take a loss.

Compared with the US, the EU was also late to adopt rules in this area. In spring 2014, it finalised the Bank Recovery and Resolution Directive, a set of rules on winding down failed banks that are similar to those under Dodd–Frank. For a bank in trouble, Priester says, the directive gives powers of 'escalating interference and insertion into the bank's management', and this should mean that in most cases, struggling banks can be turned around before they fail.

The measures should 'reassure the taxpayer that they are not in future the first line of defence' Priester adds. 'Banks should be able to go bust.'

Risky trading and salary caps

The reconstructed regulatory framework for banks has further facets. In the US, for example, Dodd–Frank introduced the Volcker rule, named after former US Federal Reserve chairman Paul Volcker. This is a general ban on proprietary trading by banks—in other words, high-risk trading in pursuit of high profits.

Such a ban is contentious in Europe, however, and the EU has not yet followed suit, though the walling off of trading from retail banking activities is under consideration. Robert Priester argues that proprietary trading is a relatively small part of the activities of European banks, and that to limit it could undermine the development of capital markets, which in Europe are smaller than in the US.

The EU has, however, capped bonuses paid to bank executives. In April 2013, the European Parliament approved a law that limits bonuses to 100% of salary, or 200% with shareholder approval. In the US, the rule under Dodd–Frank is more concerned with disclosure—that banks should publish details of the average pay of their staff, and the ratio of the CEO's pay to the average level.

A July 2014 report by consultants Mercer found that most EU banks were seeking shareholder approval for 200% of salary bonuses, or were increasing base salaries of executives to compensate for lower bonuses. And to get around the rules, 55% of EU banks were planning to pay cash 'allowances' in addition to bonuses and salaries to top staff. This was 'guaranteed cash with no variable link to performance, which is far from satisfactory' according to Mercer head of talent Mark Quinn.

Priester says that in the past bonuses 'were excessive' but caps cause problems. One concern is that banks lose out to hedge funds for the top talent. But banks can also suffer in other ways. Some, says Priester, are 'struggling to get the type of employees they need for IT', including experts in preventing fraud and cybercrime—they also potentially can lose out because of bonus caps.

Sources

Ethical Corporation, Stephen Gardner, 13 October 2014, http://www.ethicalcorp.com. Reproduced with the kind permission of Ethical Corporation.

VISIT THE
ONLINE
RESOURCE
CENTRE
for a short
response to this
feature

? THINK THEORY

Think about banking reform from the perspective of the intersecting domains of law and ethics introduced in Chapter 1. Can such reforms effectively shift ethical issues in banking from the grey area of business ethics into the black-and-white certainties of law?

governance for the entire continent (Andreasson 2011). Subsequently, we have seen the emergence of new governance codes in at least 15 countries on the African continent since 2000.

The idea of codes is to prescribe 'best practice' standards for corporations so as to help ensure that certain minimal standards of corporate behaviour are met. Typical issues dealt with in codes of corporate governance are:

- Size and structure of the board.

- Independence of supervisory or non-executive directors.

- Frequency of supervisory body meetings.

- Rights and influence of employees in corporate governance.

- Disclosure of executive remuneration.

- General meeting participation and proxy voting.

- Role of other supervising and auditing bodies.

The legal basis and the power of these codes vary significantly: while governments and the general public would ideally like to make codes legally binding, industry tends to adopt a more cautious stance. On the one hand, the general implementation and enforcement of codes is desirable; on the other hand, extra regulation makes business more inflexible and extends bureaucracy and 'red tape'. In practice, most of these codes have been voluntary, while some have implemented mandatory frameworks for disclosure that follow the rule 'comply or explain'.

Although corporate governance codes are now an established element of most developed economies, their role is still therefore somewhat ambivalent. In developing countries, for example, the advantages gained by reform towards more market-oriented Anglo-American style governance—such as attracting foreign investment, increasing competitiveness, and reducing corruption—have to be balanced against the threats of 'crowding out' indigenous businesses through the influx of foreign companies and the shift towards a more globally homogeneous shareholder-oriented governance model (Reed 2002). This debate becomes even more pronounced as the financial crisis of the late 2000s has raised serious concerns about the viability of the 'tarnished' Anglo-American model of capitalism (Whitley 2009). As Ethics in Action 6.1 describes, we have definitely seen in most Western economies a deeper involvement of the state, be it as direct owner or more active regulator, both of which point to the expectation of slightly more regulated markets for capital, and through this also for corporate control and governance (Cappelli 2009).

Islamic finance

A somewhat different perspective on the role of financial markets is provided by Islamic finance. Islamic finance is concerned with providing financial products and services that are *sharia* compliant. It therefore seeks to incorporate distinct faith-based ethical principles into finance for the purpose of enhancing social welfare (Uppal and Mangla 2014). Specifically, the key differences between Islamic finance and conventional finance are its:

- prohibition on charging and paying interest (*riba*) in financial transactions;

- prohibition on uncertain and speculative transactions (*gharar*);

- requirement for profit, equity and risk sharing in investments;

- prohibition on investment in sinful (*haram*) activities, including pornography, gambling, alcohol;

- requirement for all financial products to be backed by a tangible asset (because money has no value in itself).

These requirements mean that Islamic finance will take a slightly different approach compared to conventional investments. For example, in an Islamic mortgage a bank would not lend money to an individual to buy a property. Instead, it would buy the property itself and then either sell it to the customer at a higher price which is paid in instalments or provide a rent-to-own arrangement to the customer until that person owns the property outright (*The Economist* 2014a). This provides certainty to both parties (there are no variable interest rates involved) and ensures that the lender has an equity stake in the property and shares in the risk in case of default or market fluctuations.

The Islamic banking and finance industry has grown rapidly in the last two decades, with Ernst & Young estimating that it grew at 18% between 2009 and 2013 (*The Economist* 2014a). It is heavily concentrated in Iran, with Indonesia, Malaysia, Turkey, and the Gulf States also accounting for substantial proportions of the total market. It has also generated widespread interest in the West, especially in London which is reportedly the biggest centre of Islamic finance outside the Islamic world (Hooper 2013). Western-based banks such as Barclays, Citi, Deutsche Bank, Lloyds and UBS all offer Islamic accounts and/or have Islamic banking units and even non-Muslim customers have at times been attracted to Islamic financial services companies.

Islamic finance has received considerable attention in the context of the global financial crisis, and debates about the merits or otherwise of alternative modes of investment. Indeed, Islamic banks demonstrated greater stability during the financial crisis of the late 2000s (Hasan and Dridi 2010) and have been heralded by some as a way of reducing systemic risk and moving towards more 'ethical banking' (El-Din 2014). However, the sector remains controversial. Uppal and Mangla (2014) suggest that many ostensibly sharia-compliant banking practices 'fall far short of the ideals of Islamic finance' and effectively charge interest under another name, while customers are provided 'with an equal or a more risky product and at a higher transaction cost'. Crucially, as with most global financial market practices, Islamic finance lacks a global regulator to rule on whether practices are genuinely compliant. This gives rise to periodic disputes and challenges to the legitimacy of the industry, especially as it grows in size and influence. However, the Islamic Financial Services Board based in Malaysia has emerged as a global standard-setter for the industry, and provides some degree of harmonization in how Islamic finance institutions are regulated.

VISIT THE ONLINE RESOURCE CENTRE
for a short response to this feature

> **? THINK THEORY**
>
> Think about the system of Islamic finance from the perspective of non-consequentialist ethics. What advantages and disadvantages do religiously based rules have compared to secular codes of governance?

■ Shareholders as citizens of the corporation

In Chapter 1 we briefly mentioned the fact that globalization weakens national governments, while at the same time MNCs are becoming increasingly powerful. This idea was developed in Chapter 2 with the broader notion of the firm as a *political actor* replacing some of government's role in governing citizenship. We also discussed the growing demand for transparency and accountability to the general public that results from this gradual shift in the role of corporations. In this section, we take up these ideas and explore whether the constituency of shareholders could at least be a starting point to regain some control over corporations. The idea is to show that shareholders have a particularly powerful position from which to hold the company accountable on a variety of issues that involve the governance of citizenship.

Shareholder democracy

The notion of shareholder democracy is a commonly discussed topic in corporate governance (Parkinson 1993: 160–6). The basic idea behind the term is that a shareholder of a company is entitled to have a say in corporate decisions. Analogous to the political realm, shareholder democracy describes a community of people that have an important stake in the company and are therefore able to influence it in some way. The idea here is that in comparison with other stakeholders, shareholders, by means of their property rights, have a legally protected claim on the corporation.

Given the vast number of shares in dispersed ownership forms of governance, the influence of the single shareholder is rather small; however, with institutional investors, or other large shareholders, the situation looks considerably different. For example in the 2010s, activist investors contributed to the ousting of two successive CEOs at Yahoo as well Steve Ballmer as the CEO of Microsoft, among other high-profile casualties. Both firms subsequently saw their stock rise, giving shareholders a sizeable payoff for their trouble (*The Economist* 2014b). Nevertheless, the actual ways of influencing the board of the corporation and the institutions of proxy differ across the globe. Furthermore, since the crucial occasion where shareholders vote is the annual meeting, their power is mainly focused retrospectively. They may or may not approve of the company's activities during the last year, whereas their influence on *future* plans is somewhat limited. This is because in most cases management will be reluctant to publish too much about their plans in advance.

Clearly though, these limitations and qualifications do not exclude corporations from being *accountable* to their shareholders. You may remember that we suggested in Chapter 2 that corporate accountability 'refers to whether a corporation is answerable in some way for the consequences of its actions'. Corporations and their managers are then (at least in principle) answerable to their shareholders, mainly through the AGM, but also through the shareholders' representatives on the board of directors. In empowering shareholders to exert power over the corporation, a crucial role also falls to the annual report and quarterly guidance given to investors. These are the main vehicles through which shareholders learn about 'their' company, and are the main resources they have by which to make decisions regarding how they will vote at AGMs.

Now this is all well and good, and our discussion would probably end there if our interest was just in corporations being accountable for their financial performance. However, our concern is more with whether shareholders can be a force for wider *social* accountability and performance. For this, we need to consider three further issues.

- **Scope of activities**. It is one thing to say that corporations need to answer for their financial performance, but it is quite another to suggest that they need to also be accountable for all sorts of other ethical decisions and social and environmental impacts. Are shareholders interested in such issues or do they just look for a decent return on their money?

- **Adequate information**. This leads on to the second issue, namely that if shareholders are to decide on the ethical performance of the corporation, they have to be provided

Shareholder activism	Socially responsible investment
Single-issue focus	Multiple-issue focus
Active role in corporate governance	Passive role in corporate governance
Seeks engagement with management	Avoids engagement with management
Seeks publicity	Avoids publicity

Figure 6.3 Two approaches to 'ethical' shareholding

Source: Derived from Sparkes, R. 2001. Ethical investment: whose ethics, whose investment? *Business Ethics: A European Review*, 10 (3): 194–205.

with adequate information on such issues. This is where *social accounting* comes in (see Chapter 5, What is social accounting?), since it usually results in the production of a social report or sustainability report of some kind. This can be used by shareholders for making informed decisions, just as the annual report can. Therefore, this instrument can play an important role in empowering investors to exert their 'democratic' rights over the corporation.

- **Mechanism for change**. Finally, we have to think about the mechanism for change that shareholders can use in order to communicate their ethical choices and influence the corporations that they own stock in. One way of doing this is for family owners of corporations to use their powerful positions to encourage attention to business ethics. However, in situations characterized by a division of ownership and control, the role of shareholders broadly falls into two categories: *shareholder activism* and *socially responsible investment* (Sparkes 2001). In the following, we will look at both approaches to supposedly 'ethical' shareholding, an overview of which is provided in **Figure 6.3**.

Shareholder activism

Normally, investors exercise their rights to speak at the AGM and engage with management to encourage firms to address issues of financial performance and other typical shareholder concerns. However, these rights also open up the opportunity to voice concerns about social, ethical, and environmental issues too, and in particular governance considerations such as executive pay, as discussed earlier. Some activist investors will do this behind close doors through direct engagement with senior leaders of the company, while others may look to get broad media attention for these issues by 'disrupting' the annual general meeting from its usual course of action. In this situation, what we typically have is a stakeholder group (such as an NGO) that adopts the role of a shareholder, but does so in a way that potentially provides it with greater leverage. These activities are

Shareholder activism
The attempt to use shareholder rights to actively change the practices and policies of a corporation.

typically referred to as **shareholder activism**.

Shareholder activism has been taking place for decades, most notably in the US, where shareholder resolutions have addressed a range of social issues over the years, including product safety, labour issues, and climate change (Goranova and Ryan 2013; O' Rourke 2003). In 2013, a record number of 417 shareholder resolutions on social and environmental issues were filed in the US, up from 365 in 2012.[6] In many other countries, however, it can be quite difficult to raise issues at the AGM since this would need the involvement of larger institutional investors (Taylor 2000: 174). However, there are examples of shareholder activism in other parts of the globe in more recent years. For example, in 2014 protestors from the Boycott Divestment Sanctions South Africa group bought shares in popular South African high street retailer Woolworths in order to put pressure on management to stop sourcing products from Israel in the face of conflict in the Middle East.[7] Embedded in larger campaigns, direct engagement with managers, the filing of shareholder resolutions, talking at annual meetings, or even filing law suits as a shareholder can be very effective ways of making corporations change their behaviour—or at least of informing a broader range of constituencies (especially other shareholders) about critical ethical issues.

On the downside, in buying shares of a corporation, the particular shareholder group gets involved with 'the enemy' and in the long run there might be certain integrity problems. Furthermore, for activists, shareholder resolutions are costly and resource intensive, and can impact negatively upon their other campaign tactics (O'Rourke 2003).

Socially responsible investment

The second main mechanism, **socially responsible investment** (SRI, or also known as 'responsible investment' or 'ethical investment'), is further removed from the corporation and certainly less active than confronting managers head-on at AGMs. Over the past decades a large and rapidly growing body of shareholders has emerged who specifically include environmental, social and governance (ESG) concerns (as they are known in the investment community) in their investment decisions. In many respects, the US is the leading country here, with a market volume in 2012 of some $3.74 trillion in socially responsible investment, although Europe (with a market volume in 2013 of €237.9 billion) has shown remarkable growth in recent years.[8] The most recent development in the SRI world, however, is the growing interest among investors in emerging markets. Here, issues such as climate change, deforestation, and relations with indigenous people among others have been increasingly seen as material to investment decisions, although good governance tops the list of ESG concerns in emerging markets among the SRI community (EIRIS 2012).

In contrast to shareholder activism, socially responsible investors do not directly use their investment to make companies listen to their concerns and subsequently change their behaviour. Rather, they look for a profitable investment that at the same time complies with certain non-financial criteria or goals. These criteria can either be negative or positive, i.e. investors can choose to exclude certain companies with undesired features from their investments (negative screening) or actively include companies with certain desired features (positive screening). **Figure 6.4** provides an overview of the most common issues for both types of criteria.

Socially responsible investment (SRI) An investment decision that combines the search for financial returns with the achievement of social, ethical, and environmental goals.

? THINK THEORY

How could the ethical theories set out in Chapter 3 help an investment fund manager to determine positive and negative criteria? Take an example from Figure 6.4 and make your case by using one or more normative ethical theories.

VISIT THE ONLINE RESOURCE CENTRE for a short response to this feature

Negative criteria

- Abortion, birth control
- Alcoholic beverages production and retail
- Animal rights violation
- Child labour
- Companies producing or trading with oppressive regimes
- Environmentally hazardous products or processes
- Gambling
- Genetic engineering
- Nuclear power
- Poor employment practices
- Pornography
- Tobacco products
- Weapons

Positive criteria

- Conservation and environmental protection
- Environmental performance
- Equal opportunities and ethical employment practices
- Green technologies
- Inner city renovation and community development programmes
- Public transportation

Figure 6.4 Examples of positive and negative criteria for socially responsible investment

In addition to the normative motivations for SRI, some commentators (and indeed investors) have also argued that choosing according to ethical criteria makes sense from an economic perspective too. The risks of public boycott of products or the risk linked to environmental impacts can influence the performance of shares, making ostensibly 'ethical' companies potentially less risky investments. For example, supporters of the fossil fuel divestment movement argue that there is an economic logic as well as a moral imperative to sell stocks in coal and oil companies because of their exposure to the risks of future climate change action (Lovins 2015). In a similar vein, the potential market success of ethical products might make a socially responsible investment into a very profitable one. The example of the electric car manufacturer Tesla is just one recent case of the spectacular success some green investments can have. By the time the company reached a market capitalization of $20 billion in 2013 its share price had gone up 390% in a single year and Tesla was worth more than competitors such as Mazda, Suzuki, or Fiat—despite making little more than 20,000 cars a year (Farzad 2013).

Among SRI funds there are two broad types (Mackenzie 1998). *Market-led funds* are funds that choose the companies to invest in following the indication of the market. These gather data about the social and ethical performance of corporations from various research agencies. Among the most reputed institutions here is the London-based Ethical Investment Research Service (EIRIS), which provides regular research on over 3,000 companies against various criteria, organized into four clusters—social, environmental, governance, and 'other areas concern' such as weapons, gambling and pornography (www.eiris.org). The market is not to everyone's tastes. For example, **Figure 6.5** lists the company stocks most commonly held by SRI funds in emerging markets, and these might

Position	Company	Industry
1.	Samsung Electronics (*South Korea*)	Electronics
2.	Taiwan Semiconductor (*Taiwan*)	Electronics
3.	China Mobile (*China*)	Telecommunications
4.	Industrial & Commercial Bank of China (*China*)	Financial services
5.	America Movil (*Mexico*)	Telecommunications
6.	Petrobras (*Brazil*)	Oil and gas
7.	Gazprom (*Russia*)	Oil and gas
8.	CNOOC (*China*)	Oil and gas
9.	China Construction Bank (*China*)	Financial services
10.	Vale (*Brazil*)	Mining

Figure 6.5 Top ten stocks held in SRI funds invested in companies in emerging markets 2012

Source: Derived from EIRIS. 2012. *Evolving markets: what's driving ESG in emerging economies?* London: EIRIS. Reproduced with permission.

not necessarily feature in everyone's list of 'ethical' companies. Among them are several oil and gas companies and a high proportion of Chinese companies despite the various human rights issues associated with the country.

In contrast to market-led funds, *deliberative funds* base their portfolio decisions on their own ethical criteria. This involves more research and forces the fund's management to regularly assess companies and practices. The difference in practice is that deliberative funds provide investors with detailed ethical criteria, whereas market-based funds just provide a list of companies regarded as ethical by the market.

In practice, the choice of the right criteria and companies is not always clear-cut (Cowton 1999b; Sparkes 2001; Entine 2003). So, for instance, many electronics companies may well produce components for household appliances as well as military technology. Some investors would also object to investing in bank stocks because banks fund industries across the board, including probably a number of companies that do not comply with the ethical norms of investors. These processes involve fund management in constant updating of their criteria and company research, encouraging a more flexible and less bureaucratic approach over time (Cowton 1999).

SRI is quite a striking example of what we referred to at the beginning of this section as 'shareholder democracy'. By allocating their investment to corporations that comply with certain ethical standards, investors not only have some influence on the company's policy, but they also set incentives for other companies to review their policies. That is, analysts and investment firms even beyond the SRI niche increasingly question companies on their ESG performance. An example of this 'mainstreaming' is the growing number of efforts by banks and other large investors to include ESG criteria in investment decisions regarding large infrastructure projects, such as dams and pipelines in the developing world (Goff 2006). Examples include the 'Sustainability Framework' of the International Finance Corporation (the private sector arm of the World Bank) and the 'Equator Principles', a set of guidelines for commercial banks.[9] The latest development

Principle 1: We will incorporate ESG issues into investment analysis and decision-making processes.

Principle 2: We will be active owners and incorporate ESG issues into our ownership policies and practices.

Principle 3: We will seek appropriate disclosure on ESG issues by the entities in which we invest.

Principle 4: We will promote acceptance and implementation of the Principles within the investment industry.

Principle 5: We will work together to enhance our effectiveness in implementing the Principles.

Principle 6: We will each report on our activities and progress towards implementing the Principles.

Figure 6.6 Principles of responsible investment
Source: http://www.unpri.org.

in this arena is the United Nations 'Principles for Responsible Investment',[10] which were launched in 2005 and now boast more than 1,300 signatories from the global investment industry. They contain six basic principles committing signatories to the integration of ESG issues into investment decisions and ownership practices, as well as promoting the principles and reporting on progress (see **Figure 6.6**).

Despite the undoubted importance of these initiatives, the jury remains out on the real impact of SRI on the actual social performance of companies. While evidence suggests that SRI screens do indeed help investors to reduce their risk (Lee et al. 2010) and numerous examples point to companies responding to demands from their investors, there is little clear evidence that overall ESG performance improves as a result of SRI (Wagemans et al. 2013). This is because the percentage of SRI compared to conventional investment is tiny, and SRI funds rarely co-operate to influence companies so they have little real leverage (Wagemans et al. 2013). Also, as Peter Frankental (2006) from Amnesty International argues, in practice fund managers are still predominantly concerned with financial performance rather than ESG issues and so only when an ESG issue such as human rights threatens the former are companies actually willing to change their practices. More systematically, David Vogel (2005: 37–8) has summarized the main concerns regarding the contemporary SRI movement:

• **Quality of information**. Most of the information on social and ethical performance, on which funds base their decisions, is based on data provided by the companies themselves. While this in itself may not be a major problem, the main concern is that the sources, ways of verifying, and comparability of the data is rather heterogeneous, unregulated, and unstandardized. This makes the data somewhat questionable as a base of sound investment decision.

• **Dubious criteria**. Looking at the criteria that SRI funds use (see Figure 6.4), some of them often reflect very specific ideological or political views. As Vogel argues, many ethical fund managers might actually enjoy a glass of wine, but during the working day they treat the companies who sell it to them as 'irresponsible'. In a similar vein, not everybody will find companies using genetic engineering to treat diseases or companies providing the technology for legitimate national defence purposes as 'socially irresponsible' *per se*.

- **Too inclusive**. Citing a study of 600 SRI funds, Vogel points at the fact that 90% of the Fortune 500 companies are held by at least one SRI fund. Not only were notorious companies such as Enron held by SRI funds, but so too were many of the overleveraged banks and mortgage houses that were involved in the financial crisis of the late 2000s. Companies such as Fanny Mae, AIG, Bank of America, and Citigroup were all involved in rather irresponsible approaches to risk management and lending practices, yet remained a major part of SRI portfolios (Entine 2008).

- **Strong emphasis on returns**. Usually, fund managers in the SRI industry screen companies in terms of performance first, and then select among the good performers due to their social, ethical, or environmental criteria. A company that deliberately invests in a long-term strategy, for instance in green technology, and focuses on the achievement of ethical criteria at the expense of short-term profitability would therefore not stand a chance of being included in most SRI portfolios. So some of the more socially responsible companies may never make it onto the list of responsible companies in the world of SRI.

☑ **Skill check**

Applying socially responsible investment criteria. To navigate the fast-growing world of SRI, a good understanding of positive and negative criteria and how they impact ESG performance is a key skill.

■ Shareholding for sustainability

With shareholders having the potential to use their power and ownership rights to encourage companies to live up to their role as corporate citizens, they might be said to contribute to one of the major goals of business ethics: the triple bottom line of environmental, economic, and social sustainability. In this last section, we will look at two selected aspects where shareholders become directly involved in contributing to sustainable corporate behaviour. The first area is closely linked to our discussion in the previous section and looks to shareholders aligning their investment decisions to the criterion of sustainability. While this first approach uses the market to achieve sustainability, the second approach focuses on corporate structure and will look at alternative ways of linking ownership, work, and community involvement.

Sustainability indices

Since the late 1990s there have been several attempts to construct share indices that rate corporations according to their performance towards the broader goal of sustainability. The more long-standing tradition emerges from the US, where the Dow Jones Sustainability Indices (DJSI) have become the leading family of indices in this respect since their inception in 1999 (Knoepfel 2001; Cerin and Dobers 2001a, 2001b; Barkawi 2002). Subsequent developments in Europe led to the launch in October 2001 of the 'FTSE4Good' in London. This includes a family of indices that embrace companies that meet certain social, environmental, and ethical standards (Oulton 2006).

Since 1990 we have witnessed the launch of numerous other indices many of which either compete head-on with DJSI and FTSE4Good (such as the MSCI and STOXX sustainability indices) or focus on particular country markets or different investor interests (Louche and Lydenberg 2006). For example, countries as diverse as Canada, Egypt, Mexico, Taiwan, Switzerland, and South Africa all now have sustainability indices tailored to companies and ESG issues relevant to their specific contexts. In addition, particular sectors have their own sustainability indices to rank member companies in terms of their ESG performance. One prominent group of these are 'Cleantech Indices' that specifically include companies employing clean, environmentally friendly technology solutions.

As the DJSI continues to be the most well-known sustainability index, it is worth spending a little more time exploring its characteristics in order to better understand how these tools work. The DJSI follows a 'best-in-class approach', comprising those companies identified as the sustainability leaders in each industry. Companies are assessed in line with general and industry-specific criteria, which means that they are compared against their peers and ranked accordingly. The companies accepted into the index are assessed according to 'financially relevant economic, environmental and social factors that are relevant to the companies' financial success, but that are under-researched in conventional financial analysis.'[11] These include:

- **Environmental factors**. For example eco-design, environmental management systems, executive commitment to environmental issues, climate change mitigation.

- **Economic factors**. For example risk management, quality and knowledge management, supply-chain management, corporate governance mechanisms, anti-corruption policies.

- **Social factors**. For example employment policies, management development, stakeholder dialogue, affirmative action and human rights policies, supply chain standards, social reporting.

The data that form the basis for the judgements are based on questionnaires, submitted documentation, corporate policies, and reports, combined with a 'media and stakeholder analysis' which monitors publicly available information 'to identify companies' involvement and response to environmental, economic and social crisis situations that may have a damaging effect on their reputation and core business'.

The DJSI is now in fact a family of indices that focus on different markets and regions, including specific indices for emerging markets and the Asia-Pacific region as well as Europe and North America. Its flagship, Dow Jones Sustainability World Index, however, seeks to identify industry leaders in sustainability across the globe. In 2014 it comprised the top 10% of the best social and environmental performers among the world's largest 2,500 companies, spread over 59 industries and 41 countries.[12]

According to its proponents, by focusing on sustainability, the index identifies those companies with future-oriented and innovative management. At the time of its 15-year anniversary in 2014, only 16 companies had remained in the DJSI world index since its inception, almost half of which were German firms, including Bayer, BMW, and Siemens.[13] Interestingly, since its inception, the DJSI has slightly outperformed the mainstream Dow Jones Index, although it should be noted that financial robustness also forms an important part of the DJSI.

There are, however, a number of criticisms of the index, some of which focus on the technicalities of the index and some of which concentrate on the ethical credentials of the companies chosen.

- The biggest criticism is that the data on which a company is accepted into the index depends largely on data provided by the corporation itself. Although the data are analysed by the Swiss investment analytics firm, RobecoSAM, and verified by an independent auditor, the assessment is basically an inside-out provision of data.

- This coincides with criticisms over the questionable criteria used by the index. Some critics have asked how it could be that corporations with massive ethical credibility problems, such as large oil companies, are included in the index. Similarly, the entry of the cigarette manufacturer, British American Tobacco, into the index in 2002 was greeted with considerable controversy. The index does not, however, exclude on the basis of industry. Despite the obvious problems for sustainability of the tobacco industry (as well as armaments, alcohol, energy, and others), the DJSI argues that industry leaders should be identified and rewarded in order to stimulate progress towards sustainability. Other indices, such as the FTSE4Good, use negative criteria; for instance, currently the tobacco industry is excluded from it.

- The sustainability assessment focuses mainly on management processes rather than on the actual sustainability of the company or its products. Evidence of policies and management tools features more prominently than concrete emission data or resource consumption figures. Again, DJSI argues that the index does not identify sustainable companies, but those making progress towards addressing the issues.

Overall, then, the DJSI has to be regarded as an important step in linking investors' interests in financial performance with the broader goal of sustainability. However, the development towards sustainable investment ratings is still relatively recent and the emergence of competing indices for different investor needs suggests progress towards more sophisticated investment tools over time. Nonetheless, while criticisms that it is simply a case of 'greenwashing' without any substantial performance implications are probably a little overwrought, developments such as the DJSI are never likely to be sufficient to encourage firms towards fully sustainable practice. Indeed, another rather more fundamental way of addressing sustainability from the perspective of shareholders is to completely rethink the whole notion of corporate ownership.

Rethinking sustainable corporate ownership: alternative models of ownership?

For some advocates of sustainability thinking, one of the crucial limitations of corporations that are effectively 'owned' by shareholders is that whatever their attention to other stakeholders, the ownership model simply precludes an entirely just allocation of rewards. In passing, we have already discussed some alternative forms of ownership of corporations, but in the following we will detail four specific alternatives—state-owned firms, family-owned firms, co-operatives, and social purpose corporations.

State-owned firms

First, we may think of governments owning corporations, which in many developed countries has often been the case with postal and telecommunication services, utilities, or health care. Although privatization has brought many of these into private hands, in the aftermath of the financial crisis of the late 2000s, government ownership has resurfaced again in a number of countries, in particular in the banking and automotive industries. In some respects, the 'bailout' of banks and car companies by governments was due to the fact that a potential failure of these companies would hurt too many other stakeholders beyond shareholders, in particular employees, suppliers, and local communities. It is interesting to see that many commentators are cautiously optimistic about this ownership approach (Wong 2009), partly because government bureaucrats are hardly able to do a worse job at governing these companies than the managers who ran them into trouble in the first place. **Case 6** provides an overview how in one 'industry' different forms of ownership can have a massive impact on the success of organizations.

State ownership also still thrives in other parts of the world. French and German governments, for instance, still own controlling stakes in Renault and Volkswagen, not to mention countries such as China, where the 'state-owned enterprise' (SOE) is still the dominant pattern of economic organization. However, it is not clear whether governmental ownership is automatically a step to higher ethical standards or a more inclusive approach for all stakeholders. On the opposite side of the coin, corruption, inefficiencies, and rent-seeking are often dominant traits in government involvement (Wong 2004).

Family-owned firms

Another alternative ownership model of course is *family ownership*. The main feature of this approach from an ethical perspective would be that families often have longer-term goals for their companies rather than short-term profit maximization. That said, it is not a given that families will automatically show more concern for other stakeholders. Nonetheless, many family-owned companies have shown quite a significant commitment to philanthropy and social responsibility, a prime example being the Tata Group in India, which has been majority owned by members of the Tata family since 1868 (Elankumaran et al. 2005).

Co-operatives

A common hybrid form of ownership is the co-operative model. These are businesses that are owned neither by investors nor by their managers but which are owned and democratically controlled by their workers or their customers. Co-operatives are not set up to make profit but to meet the needs of their members. The reasons for founding co-operatives therefore can be quite different. For example, consider the following cases:

• Retail co-operatives are set up to meet retailing needs: for example, in remote parts of Sweden, consumers founded the Kooperativa Forbundet to provide them with shopping facilities. Crédit Mutuel, nowadays the number five bank in France, was initially founded to supply its members with capital.

1. Voluntary and open membership

2. Democratic member control

3. Economic participation of members

4. Autonomy and independence

5. Education, training of the membership, staff, and general public

6. Co-operation among co-operatives

7. Concern for community

Figure 6.7 Principles of co-operation

Source: International Cooperative Alliance, http://www.ica.coop/.

- Producer co-operatives are set up to meet production needs: for example, many agricultural co-operatives, today most notably in developing countries, were founded to share tools, supplies, and know-how.

- Purchasing co-operatives are set up to meet buying needs: for example, the German Dachdeckereinkaufis a co-operative of small companies in the roof-laying industry that use co-operation to increase purchasing power.

Figure 6.7 provides an overview of the internationally agreed principles of co-operation upon which all co-operatives are based. As this shows, co-operatives are based on the principles of voluntary membership, democratic control through the members, and concern for the community, which suggests some in-built advantages in terms of addressing sustainability challenges.

Worldwide, there are some 750,000 co-operatives, with 760 million members in 100 countries. In many countries, large proportions of the population are members of at least one co-operative. For example, about 15% of the Spanish population are members of co-operatives, while nearly 30% of Malaysians, 40% of Canadians, and 40% of Norwegians are.[14] As **Ethics in Action 6.2** demonstrates, the standing of co-operatives appears to have been strengthened in recent years as people look to alternatives to the system of capital financing and ownership that gave rise to the financial crisis.

Co-operatives are common in countries with a more collectivist tradition, most notably southern Europe and in parts of Asia and Latin America (Thomas 2004). One of the most well-known examples of a co-operative is the Spanish Mondragon Corporación Cooperativa based in the Basque region of Spain (see Cheney 1995). It was founded in 1956 by five engineers and a catholic priest after having been built up over 15 years prior to that date. Today the co-operative is one of Spain's largest business groups and consists of around 250 companies, about half of them also co-operatives, employing some 75,000 people. It includes large companies such as the Eroski supermarket chain as well as smaller companies in the manufacturing and finance sectors, and a training and education arm. Each co-operative has its own general assembly meetings where all workers have the same vote and decide on the corporate policies. In addition, each company has a vote in the general assembly of the Mondragon co-operative as a whole. The co-operative has remained highly profitable, with some of the highest worker productivity in the country. Notably, in stark contrast to the wide disparities in salaries between regular workers and senior executives that we identified earlier in the chapter,

VISIT THE
ONLINE
RESOURCE
CENTRE
for links to
useful sources
of further
information

ETHICS IN ACTION 6.2   http://www.ethicalcorp.com

Alternative ownership structures—stronger together

Stephen Gardner, 5 February 2013

The economic crisis has been a tale of woe and disaster. In some economies though, one sector has proved remarkably resilient in the face of economic strife. Alternatively structured businesses, including co-operatives and mutuals, have prospered during the crisis.

According to trade body Co-operatives UK, between 2008 and 2011, while the UK economy as a whole shrank by 1.7%, the 'co-operative economy' grew by an amazing 19.6%. In the same period, the number of co-operatives increased from 4,820 to 5,933. Even in the countries worst affected by rising unemployment and economic contraction, co-operatives have held their own. According to a review carried out by the European Confederation of Workers' Co-operatives, co-operatives in countries such as Italy and Spain are in a 'healthy, almost defiant, state'. Although the number of workers' co-operatives in Spain declined by 2.5% in 2011, they fared better than standard businesses, 14.7% of which closed down. Italian social co-operatives (which provide social services) took on 4.5% more employees in 2010.

John Lewis Partnership

The John Lewis Partnership is Britain's largest employee-owned business. It is famous for motivating its 81,000 staff, which it calls partners, by sharing its profits with them. This is no small measure: in the year to the end of January 2012—a year the company called 'difficult'—John Lewis made a profit of £353.8 million and paid £165.2 million of that to its workers, equating to a 14% salary boost for each employee.

The partnership's structure dates back to 1928 when John Spedan Lewis took control of his father's Oxford Street shop. Lewis took the view that excessive profits were potentially destabilising to society—'it is all wrong to have millionaires before you have ceased to have slums,' as he put it.

As well as sharing profits, Lewis set up a structure to promote employee involvement in the management of the company. In practice, this means that employees can participate in branch councils, divisional councils and, ultimately, a partnership council, which can appoint some directors and influence the company's direction. The partnership council can also, in principle, dismiss the chairman—effectively, the chief executive—though this has never happened.

John Lewis Partnership's Neil Spring says: 'All of these forms of engagement have increased productivity.' Staff at John Lewis department stores, and at the supermarket chain Waitrose, which the partnership owns, are more loyal, and the business has been consistently profitable, and has proved resilient during the economic downturn. Its first-half 2012 profits jumped by 60% compared with the previous year—meaning the next staff bonus it is likely to comfortably beat that 14%.

The John Lewis Partnership also prioritises sustainability. Spring says this is 'more driven from the centre rather than coming up from the shop floor,' though, 'the nature of the business being employee-owned encourages us to take a long-term view'. It has the reputation of selling quality, responsibly-sourced goods. Waitrose is regularly ranked, alongside Marks & Spencer, as the most sustainable supermarket for seafood, for example.

Case study: Bath & West Community Energy

Bath & West Community Energy (BWCE) is a UK 'BenCom', a community benefit society—a particular type of co-operative. It was set up to develop and install low-carbon energy generation projects. Its first investments have been in solar power, with solar arrays at a business park in Wiltshire, and on the roofs of local schools.

BWCE crowdsources the money to pay for these projects by selling shares at £1 a piece (minimum investment £500). Each investor becomes a member of the society with one vote. Members elect the board and have a say in other key society decisions. Such is the interest in the scheme, says BWCE's Peter Andrews, that at the first annual general meeting, two-thirds of the members turned up—a level of engagement most co-operatives can only dream of.

The interest is down to two factors. First, the scheme appeals to those who want to see something done about climate change. The schools that have lent their roofs to BWCE get free electricity, and any surplus money from selling electricity is ploughed into a community fund that supports low-carbon projects.

Second, BWCE aims to offers a 7% return to its investors. The UK government's feed-in tariff for solar electricity generation means a guaranteed price until 2032. Unsurprisingly, in a time of below-inflation interest rates on bank savings, the first BWCE share offer quickly raised £750,000 from 200 members. There is a 'backlog of potential investors,' Andrews says.

The approach has been effective in getting clean energy projects off the ground, though so far in a limited way—the local schools meet about a third of their energy needs via BWCE's solar panels. Andrews believes the co-operative model can be replicated and scaled up. It is 'an archaic structure, but one which is coming back into fashion and we find very useful'.

BWCE is looking into further solar projects, and at wind and hydro power generation. 'We hope to build on that,' Andrews says, speculating that one day co-operative renewable energy provision could be 'as big as E.ON'. While he is of course half joking, there is no reason why renewables should not be funded like this and such projects can easily be scaled up.

Sources

Ethical Corporation, Stephen Gardner, 5 February 2013, http://www.ethicalcorp.com. Reproduced with the kind permission of Ethical Corporation.

VISIT THE
ONLINE
RESOURCE
CENTRE
for a short
response to this
feature

> **? THINK THEORY**
>
> Think about the nature of different ownership structures in terms of their ability to achieve the triple bottom line of sustainability. Are co-operatives more suited to address specific elements (economic, social, or environmental performance) than others, or are they well positioned to tackle all of them simultaneously?

Mondragon limits its top-paid workers to earning no more than 6.5 times the lowest-paid (Wolff 2012).

The contribution to sustainability of co-operatives like Mondragon is striking:

- **Economic sustainability**. The principle of solidarity between the different parts of the organization means that they mutually support each other in years of economic downturn in one industry. This leads to long-term survival and growth of the co-operative as a whole. Furthermore, the workers will always have an interest in the long-term survival of the corporation as they personally own it.

- **Social sustainability**. Tremendous job security, embeddedness in the local communities and active support for social projects such as education, housing, and drug prevention make Mondragon an active supporter of a socially stable and supportive environment. With workplace democracy as the guiding principle, the individual worker enjoys relatively high protection of the rights that we will discuss in detail in Chapter 7.

- **Environmental sustainability**. Although the literature is not too explicit about this aspect, it is clear that with local ownership of the corporation, the group of people who would be directly affected by polluted air, water, or soil is at the same time the very constituency to decide about these issues. This at least ensures attention to environmentally friendly working conditions and production processes.

However successful Mondragon has been in the past, it nevertheless faces some challenges in the age of globalization. The typical cultural fabric of the Basque region has increasingly eroded over the years, and the co-operative faces growing international competition that means it needs to develop more market orientation. However, there remains considerable optimism that Mondragon and other co-operatives will continue to be successful examples of a 'third way' in corporate governance that directly addresses sustainability challenges.

Social purpose corporations

Co-operatives have been around at least since the industrial revolution. A more recent innovation in the ownership and governance of firms has come in the form of new models of incorporation for corporations that explicitly require them to pursue a social mission. Although, as we have seen throughout the book so far, many conventional corporations may well look to combine profit and purpose through their CSR or sustainability practices, **social purpose corporations** are distinctive in that they have their social goals written into their articles of incorporation.

Many countries have introduced new legal forms into their corporate law in order to accommodate the rise of social purpose corporations. These include the UK's 'Community

Social purpose corporation
A type of corporation that is legally required to pursue a social purpose in addition to its commercial goals.

Interest Company', the 'Community Contribution Company' in Canada, Italy's 'Sociali Impresa', and Belgium's 'Social Purpose Company'. Probably the best-known version, however, is the 'Benefit Corporation' form that has been introduced in many states across the US. The new legislation creates a whole new category for incorporation whereby such firms *must* do the following:

- Pursue a general public benefit (or a specific public benefit) in addition to profit.

- Consider the effect of their decisions on shareholders, employees, suppliers, customers, community, and environment (i.e. a full range of stakeholders).

- Produce an annual benefit report detailing their performance in relation to their proposed public benefit against a third-party standard.

One of the main reasons for the introduction of new legal forms like that of the benefit corporation is that it legally protects the firm from being forced by its shareholders into acting solely in their financial interests. In this sense it preserves the social purpose of the firm regardless of who actually owns the firm. As Yvon Chouinard the founder of the Patagonia outdoor apparel company said on re-registering his company as a Benefit Corporation in 2012: 'Benefit Corporation legislation creates the legal framework to enable mission-driven companies like Patagonia to stay mission-driven through succession, capital raises, and even changes in ownership, by institutionalizing the values, culture, processes, and high standards put in place by founding entrepreneurs.'[15]

To date, companies choosing to incorporate as social purpose corporations have tended to be small and medium-sized firms explicitly founded to advance a social purpose. As we will see in Chapter 10 (Social enterprise, pp. 473–475), some have even started off in the non-profit world as 'social enterprises' before incorporating as independent for-profit companies. For such purpose-driven companies, the advantages of having a legal form that enables them to make a long-term, inviolable commitment to sustainability goals are clear. However, it remains to be seen how attractive such forms will be to larger and multinational firms or even medium-sized firms looking to access larger amounts of capital for growth. Will there be enough socially responsible investors out there willing to invest in firms that can, if they choose, legally elect to place sustainability goals above their investors' financial interests? The introduction of new legal forms for social purpose corporations is an exciting development, but as *The Economist* (2012) notes, they will ultimately be 'tested in the market'.

■ Summary

In business ethics texts, shareholders are normally a somewhat neglected species. This is perhaps not surprising given that since they are prioritized in virtually all other areas of management education and practice, business ethics is usually considered the area where a counterpoint can be developed. However, our view is that since they are such an important corporate constituency, it is simply inappropriate to sideline them in this way. This chapter has therefore tried to achieve a more balanced view of shareholders, and thereby afford them at least equal status with the other stakeholders discussed in the second part of the book.

We started by looking at the peculiarity of the principal–agent relation that defines the relationship between managers and shareholders, and provides the basis for our understanding of corporate governance. We showed here how divergent interests and an unequal distribution of information between the two parties effectively institutionalize some fundamental ethical conflicts in governance. This led us to examine the different models of governance evident across the globe, followed by the various ethical issues pertinent to shareholder relations, such as executive control, remuneration, insider trading, etc. Furthermore, the peculiar situation of shareholders also shone through in the three main issues that reframed the contemporary challenge for ethical business—globalization, citizenship, and sustainability.

Globalization, we have shown, has thrown up new challenges in the governance of international financial markets and has driven a range of reforms in corporate governance across the globe. We also discovered that shareholder democracy enables investors to use their critical role in the supply of capital to influence corporations to behave more ethically. Finally, we showed how shareholders could also play a role in driving corporations towards enhanced sustainability by using the tools of sustainability indices as well as through more unconventional patterns of ownership.

Study questions

1. Why is the ownership of corporations different from that of other forms of 'property'? What implications does this have for the nature of shareholder rights?

2. Define corporate governance. What are the main ethical problems that arise in the area of corporate governance?

3. 'Executive pay is not an ethical issue—it is just a question of paying people a market rate.' Critically evaluate this statement using examples from contemporary business practice.

4. In this chapter we have mentioned a number of times the financial crisis of the late 2000s. In your view, what are the main reasons from an ethical perspective for the occurrence of this crisis? Also, what potential solutions would you see to prevent such problems occurring again?

5. Define insider trading. What are the main ethical arguments against insider trading?

6. Compare the effectiveness of SRI and shareholder activism in ensuring ethical conduct in corporations.

Research exercise

Go to the university library or check on the internet to do some research on the nature of corporate governance in your home country. You might find details in a corporate governance or corporate finance textbook, or on a website dealing with national governance codes or governance reform.

1. Set out as clearly as you can the system of corporate governance that operates in your home country.

2. To what extent is the system you have set out in accordance with the Anglo-American or the continental European governance model? How would you explain any differences?

3. What priority does this system appear to afford to different stakeholders?

4. Do you think that the governance system in your country provides a fair basis for corporate activity?

Key readings

VISIT THE ONLINE RESOURCE CENTRE for links to further key readings

1. **Aguilera, R.V. and Jackson, G. 2010. Comparative and international corporate governance.** *Academy of Management Annals*, 4(1): 485–556.

    Although somewhat lengthy, this review article provides a superb overview of different corporate governance regimes globally. It not only provides a structured and well-referenced summary of the debate but also explains historically the background of the different institutional arrangements around the purpose and responsibilities of corporate ownership. The article is an excellent basis for further understanding how and why corporate governance differs between countries.

2. **Donaldson, T. 2008. Hedge fund ethics.** *Business Ethics Quarterly*, 18(3): 405–16.

    This article provides an interesting and very readable account of some of the key ethical issues involved in corporation–shareholder relations by focusing on one particularly controversial form of financial institution, the hedge fund. It highlights the critical role of transparency in effective governance, and suggests possible routes for ethical reform of hedge funds through regulation and self-regulation. This latter discussion provides a good introduction to some of the debates to be covered in Chapter 11 of this book.

Case 6

VISIT THE ONLINE RESOURCE CENTRE for links to useful sources of further information on this case

Corporate governance of professional football clubs: for profit or for glory?

This case describes the corporate governance issues that have arisen in European football clubs. The ethical issues associated with the shifting ownership and investment landscape of modern football are discussed and alternative forms of ownership of football clubs are identified. The case provides an opportunity to understand the tensions between ownership, shareholding, and stakeholding in a unique industry context.

When Manchester City were crowned champions of the English Premier League in 2014, their Argentinian manager, Manuel Pellegrini remarked, 'I manage a great group of players and a great institution. [It's a] very special group.' But City's 'special group' had only been made possible by the huge influx of cash from owner Sheikh Mansour bin Zayed al Nahyan and his Abu Dhabi Investment Group, which had invested more than €1 billion in the club since taking over in 2008. City's new-found riches transformed the club from mid-table obscurity to champions, turning the tables on their long-time overachieving neighbours, Manchester United. Unsurprisingly, United's fans voiced their disapproval; but disquiet with City's turnaround went far beyond their Manchester rivals. As *Forbes* magazine remarked, 'Manchester City will not be popular champions with many, because ultimately they bought the title.' In fact, only days after claiming the title, City were landed with a record €60 million fine from UEFA (the European football governing body) for breaching financial fair play regulations, having racked up hundreds of millions of pounds in losses over the past few years in their search for glory. With wealthy backers seemingly intent on spending their way to victory, whatever the costs, Manchester City's story crystallized the transformation in European football from a community sport to a multi-billion dollar international industry with serious corporate governance problems.

The changing face of the football 'industry'

The commercialization of football has been a significant trend since the 1980s—and one that has transformed almost beyond recognition the way the sport is organized, controlled, marketed, and financed. Long gone are the days when football players in Europe's top leagues would earn wages not much different from the supporters in the stands. Today, the elite clubs pay their stars millions of dollars a year in salary, which is then further increased with image rights and endorsements. In 2013, football's top earner Cristiano Ronaldo raked in some $80 million in total earnings, placing him at number 30 in *Forbes'* annual list of the world's most powerful celebrities.

One of the key changes, of course, has come from the growth of commercial television in the game. This has led not only to vast increases in income for the clubs themselves, but also to a larger, global audience for the teams and their players. It is now commonplace to find fans of Europe's top clubs, such as Manchester United, Real Madrid, or AC Milan, in Africa, Asia, and Latin America. Parallel to these huge TV revenues, opportunities for generating revenue from merchandising club paraphernalia and advertising contracts have increasingly helped to fill the clubs' coffers. In 2013, Ronaldo's club Real Madrid was named as Europe's richest club with a revenue of €519 million, followed by Barcelona (€483 million), Bayern Munich (€431 million), and Manchester United (€424 million).

Another major change has been the trend towards new ownership and investment models for football clubs, particularly among the English Premiership elite. Starting in the 1990s, many UK clubs began listing their stock in order to source new investment, such that by the mid-1990s, 27 clubs had listed on the stock exchange. However, football clubs quickly fell out of favour with shareholders because of their meagre return on investment, especially with escalating player salaries eating into profitability. In fact, since 2006/07, wage costs have consumed 83% of Premier League clubs' revenue growth. By 2012, therefore, only three British teams remained publicly listed.

In the place of public ownerships models, many clubs have been taken back into private ownership, typically by wealthy individuals and private investment companies. For instance, Manchester United, is majority owned by Malcolm Glazer via his Red Football parent company, having delisted the club from the stock exchange in 2005. Similarly, Chelsea is owned by parent company Fordstam Limited, which is controlled by Roman Abramovich, the Russian oligarch. Private ownership has often been accompanied by huge accumulation of debt to finance the initial purchase of clubs and sustain growth. In 2012, Chelsea had net debts of £878 million and Manchester United owed some £366 million. The total net debt held by English Premier League clubs was a whopping £2.4 billion.

A similar pattern, albeit with some variations, has taken hold across many of Europe's biggest clubs. **Table C6.1** describes the ownership structure of some of Europe's top clubs by revenue, most of which exhibit very narrowly held ownership. The big difference comes in Spain where the country's two footballing giants, FC Barcelona and Real Madrid are both owned by supporters associations.

Governance challenges

With these developments towards commercialization and private capital investment, significant challenges confront the football 'industry'. With roots in what was a simple local institution for fans and communities, many football clubs have struggled to enter the world of professional business. Not only in the UK but all over Europe, clubs have been beset by financial problems.

Spectacular bankruptcies, such as the one at Rangers in Scotland in 2012, which saw the club liquidated and eventually admitted into the fourth tier of the Scottish league as a new company, are one obvious manifestation of these problems. By 2012, there had in fact been 92 instances of insolvency at clubs competing in the top five divisions in England since the formation of the Premier League in 1992. In Italy, 103 professional clubs from the four top divisions collapsed between 2002 and 2012, while more than 20 Spanish clubs went into bankruptcy protection in the 2010s alone.

More generally, across Europe many football clubs have struggled to generate profitability despite increasing revenues. The German Bundesliga League and the English Premier League have been the only 'big five' leagues in Europe (the others being Italy, Spain and France) to even generate an operating profit, before financing and player trading is taken into account. Once they are included, the picture has looked even bleaker. For instance, the net losses of the 20 Premier League clubs run to several hundred million annually (approximately £245 million in 2012) and only eight Premier League clubs made a net profit in 2012. The Bundesliga, however, has succeeded in remaining the most profitable in Europe mainly because of regulations from the German football authorities that exercise greater control over the ownership and financial models of clubs. First, clubs are limited in terms of how much they can spend on wages relative to revenues; and second, external ownership of German clubs is restricted, which prevents wealthy foreign owners from pushing up costs and debt loading.

Beyond Germany, UEFA (the European governing body) has also sought to bolster the financial management of European football clubs. UEFA's Financial Fair Play regulations, which were first applied in the 2011/12 season, aim to encourage clubs to build for long-term success using sound financial management. They were brought in to stop what UEFA general secretary Gianni Infantino referred to as 'greed, reckless spending, and financial insanity' within European football. The main requirements of the regulations are that any club qualifying for a UEFA competition must:

- Prove that they do not have overdue payables towards other clubs, players, and tax authorities throughout the season.

- Break even (starting in the 2013/14 season). Clubs can only spend up to €5 million more than they earn each year. This limit can be exceeded by up to €45 million (2013–15) or €30 million (for the following three seasons) if it is entirely covered by a direct contribution from the club owner(s) or a related party.

Club	2015 Revenue* (million $)	2015 Value* (million $)	Ownership	Country (owner)	Description of ownership
Real Madrid	746	3,260	Registered Association	Spain	Owned by supporters who elect the club's president who has operating control over the club. The club president cannot invest money into the club and can only spend what the club earns. It is not possible to purchase shares in the club, only membership. Members form an assembly of delegates which is the highest governing body of the club.
Manchester United	703	3,100	Public Corporation, majority ownership by Malcolm Glazer via Red Football parent company	US (Malcolm Glazer); UK (Red Football company)	Taken over in 2003 by Malcolm Glazer, delisted from stock exchange in 2005 with full ownership by Malcolm Glazer via his Red Football parent company. Purchased through loans held by Red Football, some of which were later sold to hedge funds. In 2012, shares were sold on the NYSE.
Bayern Munich	661	2,350	Joint stock company—run by FC Bayern München AG (spin-off company)	Germany	Stock is not listed on public stock exchange, but is privately owned; 81% of FC Bayern München AG is owned by the club, FC Bayern München e.V. (registered club), 9.1% is owned by Adidas, 9.1% is owned by Audi.
FC Barcelona	657	3,160	Registered Association	Spain	Same as Real Madrid.
Paris Saint-Germain	643	634	Qatar Investment Authority (full owner in 2012)	Qatar	QIA was founded in 2005 to manage the oil and gas surpluses by the government of Qatar. In 2011, QIA became the majority shareholder of PSG (70%). In late 2012, QIA completed the buyout and became the sole shareholder of PSG. QIS invested $340 million in the club afterwards. For the 2011–14 period, PSG spent a record €364 million.

Manchester City	562	Fully owned by Sheikh Mansour (Mansour bin Zayed Al Nahyan), since 2008)	United Arab Emirates (Sheikh Mansour)	Sheikh Mansour is deputy prime minister of the United Arab Emirates, minister of presidential affairs, and member of the ruling family of Abu Dhabi (son of first president of UAE). Owner of the privately held Abu Dhabi United Group (ADUG), an investment company that acquired Manchester City and has overseen the club since. (Personal wealth of £20 billion, family wealth over £1 trillion.)
Chelsea	526	Chelsea FC plc is owned by parent company Fordstam Limited, which is controlled by Roman Abramovich	Russia (Roman Abramovich); UK (Fordstam Limited)	Funded by Abramovich via interest free soft loans channelled through his holding company Fordstam Limited.
Arsenal	487	Parent company, Arsenal Holdings plc, is a non-quoted public limited company	US (Stan Kroenke); and Russia/UK (Usmanov and Moshiri)	Parent company, Arsenal Holdings plc, has 62,219 shares that are traded infrequently on PLUS, a specialist market. Largest shareholder is Stan Kroenke, owner of Kroenke Sports Enterprises (67% in 2015). Red & White holdings, co-owned by Alisher Usmanov and Farhad Moshiri, owns 30% (2015).
Juventus	379	Owned by Edoardo Agnelli family (since 1923)	Italy (Agnelli family)	Edoardo Agnelli, Fiat owner, gained control of the club in 1923. The club has remained under the ownership of the Agnelli family since then. Andrea Agnelli, grandson of Edoardo, is current president of Juventus.
AC Milan	339	Subsidiary of Fininvest Group, controlled by Silvio Berlusconi's family	Italy (Silvio Berlusconi)	Fininvest is a holding company that includes football, TV and film businesses. It is controlled by the family of Silvio Berlusconi, the former prime minister of Italy, and managed by his daughter.

Table C6.1 Ownership structure of top European football clubs

Source: Forbes http://www.forbes.com/soccer-valuations/ Value is based on past transactions, market value, debt, and stadium.

Clubs not meeting these requirements face a range of sanctions including fines, points deductions and even disqualification. Manchester City's punishment in 2014, for example, not only landed them a hefty fine but also restricted the number of players they could register for the following season's Champions League—thereby inflicting a significant blow to their hopes for success in the competition.

UEFA's regulations have not only hit the big clubs bankrolled by sheikhs and oligarchs. As of 2013, a total of 76 clubs were being investigated because of failed break-even calculations for 2012. However, since the regulations only apply to clubs entering European competitions, they have also prompted similar moves to regulate domestically. The Football League, for example, which represents the lower tiers in England, announced the agreement of a Financial Fair Play framework including a break-even rule and a protocol limiting total spending on player wages to a proportion of club turnover.

The role of fans

Another major governance challenge facing European football concerns the role of fans in the running of football clubs. After all, at the end of the day, clubs depend on their fans for their livelihood, as either spectators, TV audiences, or consumers of merchandise. Also, football fans are unlike typical consumers in that they rarely if ever switch allegiance and so are 'brand loyal' often for their entire lives, regardless of the varying fortunes of their team. This means that they might be seen as one of the most important stakeholders in the club and could be expected to have a significant say in the running of its affairs.

In recent years, several initiatives have been taken to address fans' interests more directly, as two examples from the UK illustrate. A government-funded initiative, Supporters Direct, was initiated in 2000 to encourage the creation of supporters' trusts, which organize collective shareholding for fans in their clubs. The aim of these trusts is 'to bring about responsible, democratic representation at spectator sports clubs, and so help promote the highest standards of governance, accountability and embed those clubs deeper into their communities'. The trusts have grown in popularity amongst supporters, with many clubs now having one, but in only a handful of small teams have the trusts directly assumed ownership of the clubs.

Another initiative by the clubs themselves has been the Football in the Community scheme. This involves the clubs in various social projects, generally targeted at embedding the club in the local community and addressing social exclusion, unemployment, or antisocial behaviour in the immediate vicinity of the clubs. Corporate social responsibility programmes have become more widespread in the world of football, especially amongst large clubs, where teams such as Arsenal and Chelsea now have initiatives, reports, and websites dedicated to social responsibility. Even smaller clubs, such as Charlton and Brentford, have initiated a host of award-winning community schemes, often in partnership with fans, the police, and local councils.

While these philanthropic initiatives appear laudable, the tension about the core purpose of a football club remains: is it just another business that can 'give back' to the community some of its commercial success, or is the actual primary purpose of clubs to provide value to fans? Perhaps the most striking alternative is illustrated by clubs such as Real Madrid and FC Barcelona, which are member-owned, democratic, not-for-profit organizations. Here, the club leadership is accountable to the people who watch and pay, and the primary rationale for the club is to play football. Members at Barcelona, for example, can vote on the election of the club's president and the governing board, and have a right to participate in key decisions.

Barcelona and Real Madrid are both hugely successful teams that have dominated the Spanish league for decades, as well as recording a string of European successes. It is hardly surprising, therefore, that they have attracted an avid membership, as well as recording Europe's highest annual revenues, demonstrating that it is not necessary to have either a wealthy oil sheikh or stock market financing to be financially viable at the top of the game. Indeed, by 2013, after a period of football domination in Europe, Barcelona could probably lay claim to being the club with the most official members in the world—some 222,000. Nonetheless, the domination of Real and Barcelona in Spain has often come at the expense of Spain's other teams who have rarely been able to exercise the kind of economic muscle necessary to challenge for the Spanish title and compete with the European elite.

Back in the UK, governance issues have remained high on the agenda in the wake of financial problems among various clubs, a failure to nurture domestic talent (leading to poor showings of the national team in international tournaments), and an ongoing unease about the source of funds flowing into the game. A Parliamentary Football Group proposed a number of recommendations to enhance governance in the 'industry', including an enhanced 'fit and proper persons test' which was adopted by the Premier League in 2009 in order to exclude unscrupulous club owners and directors.

In the case of Manchester City, Sheikh Mansour passed the test, but not without criticism from NGOs such as Human Rights Watch, which denounced Abu Dhabi (the country that he, as deputy prime minister, and his family run) as a repressive 'black hole' for human rights. Still, his predecessor would have fared even worse. Thaksin Shinawatra, the former prime minister of Thailand who bought the club in 2007 before selling it for a €150 million profit little more than a year later, is currently on the run having been sentenced to two years imprisonment in his native Thailand. As a convicted criminal he almost certainly would have failed the fit and proper persons test. However, despite being dismissed from his position as honorary club president by the new owners because of his conviction, Shinawatra remains popular amongst City fans for rescuing them financially and starting them on the path to glory. Football fans, it seems, may want their clubs governed better, but not if it means missing out on silverware at the end of the season.

Questions

1. Set out the main stakeholders of football clubs. Describe their 'stake' in the organization and assess the legitimacy of their interests.

2. What are the key governance issues that each of these stakeholder groups might have?

3. The case describes a number of approaches that offer potential solutions to the governance issues raised. Set out these approaches and evaluate their likely effectiveness in dealing with governance challenges in football clubs.

4. Ultimately, who 'should' own football clubs and what should their priorities be in managing the enterprise?

Sources

Brown, A. and Supporters Direct 2012. *The Heart of the Game: Why supporters are vital to improving governance in football*. Supporters Direct Europe: www.substance.coop/node/664.

Conn, D. 2103. Abu Dhabi accused of 'using Manchester City to launder image'. *Guardian*, 30 July 2013: www.theguardian.com/football/2013/jul/30/manchester-city-human-rights-accusations.

Conway, D. 2014. UEFA investigates 76 clubs over Financial Fair Play. BBC, 28 February 2014: http://www.bbc.com/sport/0/football/26390770.

Macguire, E. 2014. Manchester City crowned champions on EPL final day. CNN, 12 May 2014: http://edition.cnn.com/2014/05/11/sport/football/manchester-city-premiership-winners/.

Supporters Direct website: http://www.supporters-direct.org.

Szymanski, S. 2012. Manchester City buy the Premier League Championship. *Forbes*, 13 May 2012: http://www.forbes.com/sites/stefanszymanski/2012/05/13/manchester-city-buy-the-premier-league-championship/.

Taylor, D. 2009. City dump Thaksin from president's role. *Guardian*, 11 February 2009: http://www.theguardian.com/football/2009/feb/10/manchester-city-thaksin-sacked.

The Economist 2012. IPOs in football: If at first you don't succeed. *The Economist*, 12 July, 2012: IR www.economist.com/blogs/gametheory/2012/07/ipos-football-0.

Walters, G. and Chadwick, S. 2009. Corporate citizenship in football: delivering strategic benefits through stakeholder engagement. *Management Decision*, 47 (1): 51–66.

Notes

1. http://www.businessinsider.com/michael-woodford-exposure-olypus-scandal-2014-3.
2. http://www.theguardian.com/business/2013/nov/04/co-op-group-rescue-activist-hedge-funds.
3. https://hbr.org/2014/09/ceos-get-paid-too-much-according-to-pretty-much-everyone-in-the-world/.
4. http://www.swfinstitute.org/fund-rankings/.
5. http://www.ecgi.org/codes/index.php.
6. http://www.sustainablebrands.com/news_and_views/stakeholder_trends_insights/jennifer_elks/record_number_social_environmental_sharehol.
7. http://www.iol.co.za/business/companies/woolworths-agm-disrupted-by-protest-1.1786657#.VHYN8_1xspE.
8. Data and trends sourced from the Forum for Sustainable and Responsible Investment (USSIF) http://www.alfi.lu/sites/alfi.lu/files/files/Press/Press%20releases/European-responsible-Investing-Fund-Survey-2013-final-web.pdf.
9. See http://www.ifc.org; http://www.equator-principles.com.
10. See http://www.unpri.org.
11. http://www.sustainability-indices.com.
12. *Ibid*.
13. http://www.sustainability-indices.com/images/140911-djsi-review-2014-en-vdef.pdf.
14. http://ica.coop.
15. http://www.patagonia.com/us/patagonia.go?assetid=68413.

Employees and Business Ethics

Having completed this chapter you should be able to:

- Explain the specific role of employees as a stakeholder.
- Describe the main employee rights and duties.
- Critically evaluate the ethical issues raised by globalization for managing employees in different national and cultural contexts.
- Explain the role of good corporate citizenship in managing human rights.
- Identify the implications for sustainability of firms' relationships with employees.

Key concepts and skills:

Concepts	Skills
• Employee rights	• Managing diversity
• Employee duties	• Enabling employee participation
• Discrimination	• Setting fair wages
• Employee privacy	• Managing human rights
• Employee participation	
• Work–life balance	

■ Introduction

Dealing with employees is probably the area where all of us at some stage are most likely to encounter ethical issues and dilemmas. Whether it is a question of fair wages and conditions, sexual harassment in the workplace, or simply taking advantage of company resources for personal use—employee-related ethical problems are unavoidable for most contemporary managers. Such problems can run from the everyday questions of how to treat disabled workers appropriately to fundamental questions of human rights.

In a certain sense, one could argue that ethical issues with regard to employees have been a consideration for corporations long before the topic of 'business ethics' was even on the agenda of higher education, let alone of corporations. When we look to the first wave of the industrial revolution in the nineteenth century, the fair and proper treatment of employees was a controversial issue right from the outset. Famous writers, such as Charles Dickens in his novel *Hard Times*, explored the exploitation and poor working conditions of the masses during this era. In a more positive vein, this period also saw various examples of industrialists setting an example by looking after their workers' housing, health care, and diet, just to name a few examples (Cannon 1994: 7–29). As some have argued, this paternalistic involvement of employers with the working and living conditions of their employees was often motivated by what we referred to earlier as 'enlightened' self-interest: only if workers live in halfway decent living circumstances are they likely to be productive and committed to the firm's economic success (Fitzgerald 1999).

One could in fact argue that the major political divide of the twentieth century— between capitalism on the one hand and socialism or communism on the other— originally focused on the function of employees in the working process. Karl Marx, Lenin, and even Mao developed their ideas ostensibly with the improvement of workers' living conditions in mind. On a smaller scale, the political agendas of traditional 'labour', 'socialist', or 'social democratic' parties were targeted at changing legislation, implementing a so-called 'welfare state', and providing the masses with an entitlement to decent working conditions. By the end of the last century, however, with socialism and communism in retreat, and even most left-wing governments under heavy budget pressures to cut back on the welfare state and reduce regulation, ethical issues in employment had regained their position on the business ethics agenda.

These days, however, such issues are treated somewhat differently than in the past. Crucially, there are still problems similar to those faced by workers in the nineteenth century, albeit less so in industrialized countries, but certainly in developing countries. MNCs from the global North are confronted with issues such as the protection of workers' human rights in their factories in Bangladesh, China, or Cambodia, while in their own countries a variety of different ethical questions for MNCs arise from the usage of new technologies such as the internet, and the introduction of new work environments such as call centres (Fleming and Sturdy 2011). A crucial development here seems to be that fewer and fewer issues are directly addressed through governmental legislation compared with a hundred, or even 50, years ago. Increasingly, we witness a growing tendency to leave the solution of these issues to corporations themselves. Consequently, the discussion of ethical issues in firm–employee relations is a matter of growing interest and concern.

■ Employees as stakeholders

Like shareholders, employees take on a peculiar role among stakeholders as they are closely integrated into the firm. Whereas shareholders basically 'own' a share of the corporation, employees actually constitute the firm. They are perhaps the most important production factor or 'resource' of the corporation, they represent the company towards most other stakeholders, and act in the name of the corporation towards them. This essential contribution, as well as the fact that employees benefit from the existence of their employers and are quite clearly affected by the success or otherwise of their company, are widely regarded as giving employees some kind of definite stake in the organization.

? | THINK THEORY

In Chapter 2 we discussed different models of the firm, notably the managerial view and the stakeholder view. The managerial view puts shareholders' interests first, while the stakeholder perspective would consider other groups' interests as legitimate as well. Try to construct an ethical argument in favour of employees as legitimate (or even dominant) stakeholders of the firm.

VISIT THE ONLINE RESOURCE CENTRE for a short response to this feature

Referring back to our definition of stakeholders in Chapter 2, both the legal and the economic side of the relationship between employees and the corporation are worthy of examination. On the *legal* level, there is normally some sort of contract between the corporation that stipulates the rights and duties of the two parties. This legal relationship, furthermore, is quite strongly embedded in a rather dense network of legislation that provides a legally codified solution to a large number of issues between companies and employees, such as minimum wages, working conditions, and due process. Although there are certainly, to a varying degree, a fair number of legal rules pertinent to all other stakeholder relationships, the relation between corporations and employees is peculiar in that it has traditionally been the subject of governmental regulation in most countries from the very beginning of the industrial revolution onwards.

This characteristic has strong implications also for the *economic* aspect of firm–stakeholder relationships. The relationship between firms and employees is characterized by certain externalities on both sides—by which we mean that there are costs to each that are not included in the employment contract. These hidden costs can lead to situations of 'asset specificity'—that is, employees 'invest' time and effort in developing 'assets' specific to a particular employer, and vice versa. Such costs of specificity can create what we call a *moral hazard* for both parties, opening up a wide range of ethical issues. Examples from the perspective of the employee include investing in a new job by moving to a new town, which might involve things like leaving behind friends and family, finding new schools for your children, etc. Another aspect is hidden in the familiar English synonym of 'making a living' for having a job. Much of our waking life is committed to our job. As a result, it is often the place where friends and social relationships are made and where the human need for self-actualization is met. All of this results in a considerable amount of dependence from an employee on their employer.

Employers, on the other hand, also face similar elements of moral hazard from their employees. A spectacular example is the spate of 'rogue traders' in recent years that have caused enormous damage for the banks that employed them (see **Ethics in Action 4.1**). As this shows, companies do not have complete control of their employees, and can sometimes find out only later whether they actually do their job properly. Especially in finance, IT, and other knowledge-intensive industries, employees have considerable power due to their specialized knowledge. Employers face the risk that some of their most valuable 'assets' might remain underused or even be poached by a competitor.

As mentioned above, many of these moral hazards in the employer–employee relationship have been subject to legislation. Since the moral hazard is normally greater for the employee (because they are the more dependent and weaker party), most of this legislation focuses around workers' rights. However, as we have discussed in Chapter 1, there are clear limits to the legal trajectory in settling ethical issues. Furthermore, the nature of the relationship between employer and employee often makes the sheer application of existing law (and the exploitation or otherwise of legal loopholes) an object of ethical considerations. Remember, in Chapter 2 we discussed 'legal responsibility' as one of the four key elements of corporate social responsibility. In this chapter, therefore, we will look at the issues involved in the relationships of the company to the stakeholder group of employees.

■ Ethical issues in the firm–employee relation

Management of human 'resources'—an ethical problem between rights and duties

Employees are, in principle, managed by the human resources department—a term which already indicates a first problem from an ethical perspective. As it is, the term 'human resource management' (HRM) and its implications have been the subject of some debate in business ethics (Hart 1993; Torrington 1993; Barrett 1999; Greenwood 2002). If we recall Kantian theory, the second maxim requires us to treat humanity 'always as an end and never as a means only'. HRM, however, does exactly this: we as humans are constituted as an important *resource*, and in most cases the most costly resource as well. Consequently, employees are subject to a strict managerial rationale of minimizing costs and maximizing the efficiency of the 'resource'. In fact, one could argue that the core ethical dilemma in HRM lies in the fact that people in the firm, under economic criteria, are nothing more than a resource, next to and often competing with other resources, most notably new technology or cheaper resources from overseas.

Ultimately, though, the management of human 'resources' implies more than just the application of economic criteria. In other words, human beings within the firm are, of course, a means to an end as they are employed to perform certain functions. However, from an ethical perspective, they should not be treated as a means *only*, and it is this restriction that makes all the difference in terms of business ethics. This distinction becomes fairly visible when looking at the gap between the rhetoric of HRM policies and the reality often hidden behind it. Some common examples are given in **Figure 7.1**.

Rhetoric	Reality
'New working patterns'.	Part-time instead of full-time jobs.
'Flexibility'.	Management can do what it wants.
'Empowerment'.	Making someone else take the risk and responsibility.
'Training and development'.	Manipulation.
'Recognizing the contribution of the individual'.	Undermining the trade union and collective bargaining.
'Teamworking'.	Reducing the individual's discretion.

Figure 7.1 Rhetoric and reality in HRM

Source: Based on Legge (1998).

Employee rights
Entitlements of workers with respect to their employer, based on a general understanding of human rights and often codified in employment law.

According to Kantian thinking, it is human dignity that forbids treating employees as a means only, and it is this duty that constitutes the main ethical boundary for the management of employees. As we argued earlier, Kantian duties have their equivalent in the rights of the individual. Human beings deserve respect and are entitled to certain basic rights. It is therefore no surprise that the central ethical issues in HRM can be framed around the issues of **employee rights** (workers' entitlements with respect to their employer) and **employee duties** (workers' obligations to their employers) (van Gerwen 1994; Rowan 2000).

Employee duties
Obligations of workers towards their employer, based on individual contracts and wider employment laws.

> **? THINK THEORY**
>
> Think about what it means to talk about employees in terms of 'human resources'. Compare Kant's theory with the feminist approach to business ethics in relation to human resource management. Do you think the term HRM is adequately chosen? What are the implications of this terminology from both perspectives?

VISIT THE ONLINE RESOURCE CENTRE
for a short response to this feature

Figure 7.2 provides a selection of the most important rights and duties and the main ethical problems commonly associated with them in the day-to-day reality of business. We should stress that these rights and duties are all more or less directly deduced either from the general notion of human rights, or are in some way or other codified in various employment and contract laws. The codification of workers' rights is particularly advanced in Europe (Poole 2013) so that corporations in most cases should simply have to obey the existing law in the country. From this perspective, the density of codified employee rights would suggest little necessity for ethical reasoning in firm–employee relations. As discussed in Chapter 1 though, there is a widening 'grey area' of ethical issues beyond those covered by the law, and employee rights is one of the most prominent parts of this zone.

This prominence is chiefly due to globalization and its effect on the ability and willingness of nation states to regulate and enforce the protection of employees. Consequently, we have seen a massive surge in business involvement in ethical issues in HRM, mostly under the broader labels of 'labour standards' and 'business and

Employee rights	Issues involved
Right to freedom from discrimination.	• Equal opportunities. • Affirmative action. • Reverse discrimination. • Sexual and racial harassment.
Right to privacy.	• Health and drug testing. • Electronic privacy and data protection.
Right to due process.	• Promotion. • Firing. • Disciplinary proceedings.
Right to participation and association.	• Organization of workers in works councils and trade unions. • Participation in the company's decisions.
Right to healthy and safe working conditions.	• Working conditions. • Work–life balance. • Presenteeism. • Occupational health and safety.
Right to fair wages.	• Pay. • Industrial action. • New forms of work.
Right to freedom of conscience and speech.	• Whistleblowing.
Right to work.	• Fair treatment in the interview. • Non-discriminatory rules for recruitment.

Employee duties	Issues involved
Duty to comply with labour contract.	• Acceptable level of performance. • Work quality. • Loyalty to the firm.
Duty to comply with the law.	• Bribery.
Duty to respect the employer's property.	• Working time. • Unauthorized use of company resources for private purposes. • Fraud, theft, embezzlement.

Figure 7.2 Rights and duties of employees

human rights' (Sullivan 2003; United Nations 2008). Almost all of the rights of employees that are set out in Figure 7.2 are derived from a more fundamental human right as enshrined in the Universal Declaration of Human Rights (UDHR).[1] The UDHR is considered to be probably the broadest common baseline on basic human entitlements globally, and is accepted across diverse culture and religions. It is therefore no surprise that global companies have begun to align their employment policies more with human rights. This has led to a number of global codes of conduct for firms and industries that govern the treatment of workers. Most of these are based on the various labour standards of the International Labour Organization (ILO), which are 'legal instruments drawn up by the ILO's constituents (governments, employers and workers) and setting out basic principles and rights at work'.[2]

In the following sections, we shall therefore discuss each of the eight employee rights set out in the top half of Figure 7.2, before proceeding to examine the three main employee duties to the firm that are depicted in the bottom half of the figure.

Discrimination

Workplace discrimination occurs when employees receive preferential (or less preferential) treatment on the grounds of some enduring human characteristic that is not directly related to their qualifications or performance in the job.[3] The most common of these characteristics are race, gender, age, religion, disability, and nationality. However, any factor that is unrelated to merit might be used to discriminate against employees, including marital status, physical appearance, sexual orientation, or even gender reassignment. Accordingly, many organizations are now having to come to terms with the fact that their employees increasingly come from a range of different religious, racial, national, and cultural groups, making the whole issue of *managing diversity* a prominent feature of contemporary business discourse.

Workplace discrimination
When decisions are made on the basis of an enduring human characteristic, other than merit, that is irrelevant to the effective performance of the job in question.

Discrimination in essence is a violation of the second principle of Rawls' *Theory of Justice*, as outlined in Chapter 3, that 'social and economic inequalities are to be arranged so that they are attached to offices and positions open to all under conditions of fair equality of opportunity'. There are inequalities between individuals, but the reasons for choosing one person over another should be based on qualifications that in principle could be fulfilled by anyone. Making gender or race a criterion for a particular position would exclude certain people right from the start, and would clearly constitute an act of discrimination. However, determining whether a factor such as one's appearance, ethnic background, or marital status is related to one's job performance is sometimes not as clear as we might suppose.

Consider the example of the owner of an Indian supermarket in Rotterdam who is looking for a manager who speaks Hindi or Urdu fluently, who has a reasonable knowledge of Indian culture, and knowledge of current consumer preferences in the Dutch Asian products market. Although one might reasonably consider that this would mean that it would be perfectly acceptable to advertise specifically for an Indian manager, this would in fact be discriminatory. Certainly, these criteria might be *most likely* met by a certain ethnic group, but it is in principle possible for *all* potential applicants to attain these qualifications, and so they should have equal opportunity to apply. In many countries, for example, it is illegal to specify a preferred gender or ethnicity for applicants for a vacant position.

Although the most overt forms of discrimination have now been addressed reasonably successfully through regulation, problems of this nature persist. For instance, the clothes retailer Abercrombie & Fitch lost a lawsuit filed by a female employee of its London flagship store. The 22-year-old woman, who wore an arm prosthesis that she covered by wearing a cardigan, was removed from working on the shop floor as her dress style allegedly violated the 'good looks' policy of the company. The reason she won the case, however, was not that she was treated differently but that the company did not make an exception from their policy to take account of her disability (Topping 2009).

In fact, issues of disability, as well as other concerns such as age discrimination, are among the most recent diversity issues in developed countries. The first of these includes some unique issues, in that the physical environment and systems of the company itself might prove to be discriminatory for disabled employees (and disabled visitors for that matter). The location of stairs can impair the ability of the physically disabled to do their job; the use of hard-to-read signs and documents can negatively impact those with sight disability or dyslexia; and failure to incorporate induction loop technology can seriously impede those with hearing impairment. Employees across the world with health problems such as HIV/AIDS have also faced considerable discrimination and harassment from their colleagues and bosses.

In the case of age discrimination, workers both old and young have suffered. For example, the trade union Amicus reported a number of cases in the UK where companies had laid off staff between the ages of 45 to 49 because pension rights make it far more costly to lay off workers beyond the age of 50. Some companies even run the risk of an employment tribunal, given that the fine for unfair dismissal can be considerably cheaper than paying redundancies for older workers (Wylie and Ball 2006).

Another as yet unresolved issue is gender discrimination. Women still, on average, receive lower wages for the same jobs as their male equivalents. Women are also still severely under-represented in top management positions, despite success lower down the ranks and often outperforming men educationally. **Figure 7.3** sets out some statistics from the UK of the proportion of women on boards. This demonstrates that although women are still under-represented (with 21% of board seats), significant progress is being made in tackling discrimination in the boardroom. However, this picture varies dramatically across different countries, with Norway leading with 40% of boardroom seats held by women, compared to 17% in the US, 14% in Germany, 8% in China, 5% in India, and 2% in Japan (as of 2014).[4]

The point is that despite decades of anti-discrimination legislation, many forms of discrimination are deeply embedded in business. Consider the case of the investment bank Morgan Stanley, which in 2004 agreed to a settlement for $54 million after a female employee took the firm to court in the US over accusations of unequal pay and unequal career opportunities. Among other things, the allegation was that key client meetings were held in strip clubs and female employees were barred from these venues.[5] Sometimes this is referred to as *institutional discrimination*, namely that the very culture of the organization is prejudiced against certain groups.

	2000	2004	2008	2014
Female held directorships (in % of total directorships)	69 (5.8%)	110 (9.7%)	131 (11.7%)	231 (20.7%)
Female executive directors	11	17	17	20
Female non-executive directors	60	93	114	211
Companies with 2 women directors	14	19	39	79
Companies with no women directors	42	31	22	2

Figure 7.3 Women in top management positions. Female directors in FTSE 100 companies 2000–2014.

(FTSE 100: largest 100 companies on the Financial Times Stock Exchange Index)

Sources: Sealy, R., Singh, V., and Vinnicombe, S. *The Female FTSE Report 2007*, International Centre for Women Leaders, Cranfield School of Management; Sealy, R., Vinnicombe, S., and Singh, V. *The Female FTSE Report 2008*, International Centre for Women Leaders, Cranfield School of Management. Vinnicombe, S., Dolder, E., and Turner, C. *The Female FTSE Board Report 2014*, International Centre for Women Leaders, Cranfield School of Management.

For example, one could suggest that in a company where there was an informal understanding amongst the staff that in order to get on they had to stay late at the office and work far in excess of 'normal' office hours, certain groups, such as single parents (who might be unable to commit such time over and above their contractual obligations), would face an institutionalized barrier to progression. Goldman Sachs, for example, faced a class action lawsuit in 2014 that included all female employees from the preceding 12 years because of alleged systematic gender discrimination (Kolhatkar 2014).

VISIT THE ONLINE RESOURCE CENTRE for a short response to this feature

---

? THINK THEORY

Although we have suggested that employees have a *right* to be free from discrimination, it is clear that it still occurs. Is this just because employers have not recognized that discrimination is wrong, or is it possible to establish a defence of discrimination from the perspective of other ethical theories? Which theory provides the most convincing defence?

Sexual and racial harassment

As well as discrimination occurring in the areas of promotion, pay, and job opportunities, diversity considerations also have to take account of physical, verbal, and emotional harassment. In the case of sexual harassment, a problem might even be that certain sexual favours are requested for promotion or other rewards that would normally be a result of successful work. 'Mild' forms of harassment would be jokes or comments about a person's gender, race, sexual orientation, etc., that could lead to significant effects on working relations.

Harassment is difficult to detect and prevent, mainly because the line between harassment on the one hand and 'office romance', 'joking', or other forms of personal interaction are blurred, especially when communication crosses over into social media and other online communications such as Facebook posts or text messages (Mainiero and Jones 2013). Factors such as context, culture, timing, and frequency all might shape whether a particular set of behaviours are viewed as harassment or acceptable workplace interaction. Essentially, workplace harassment is a psychological construct that occurs when it is unwanted and appraised by the recipient as offensive or threatening rather than meeting any specific objective criteria (McDonald 2012). However, legal definitions of harassment tend to focus on whether harassment creates a 'hostile work environment' or takes place in a context of threats involving employment-related decisions such as pay, promotion and termination (Mainiero and Jones 2013). Companies have therefore increasingly introduced policies and diversity programmes in order to tackle these issues and to delineate more clearly the borders of harassment (Crain and Heischmidt 1995). However, research consistently demonstrates that individuals who experience workplace harassment often do not make formal complaints despite suffering 'significant psychological, health- and job-related consequences' (McDonald 2012: 1).

Equal opportunities and affirmative action

So how should organizations respond to problems of unfair discrimination? In one sense, they could simply look to legislation to tackle the problem, particularly as many industrialized countries have a reasonably well-established legal framework of anti-discriminatory laws and statutes. However, as we have already seen, even the existence of clearly specified laws has not prevented discrimination from occurring. Moreover, most legal approaches do not specify exactly how discrimination should be avoided, leaving many decisions open to the discretion of management. As a result, many companies have sought to tackle discrimination through the introduction of so-called equal opportunity or affirmative action programmes. These programmes establish policies and procedures that aim to avoid discrimination, and may even go so far as to attempt to redress inequity in the workforce.

The most basic and conservative approach is usually referred to as an *equal opportunity programme*. These have been widely introduced in business, and it is now common to see job adverts and company websites proclaiming that an organization is an 'equal opportunity employer'. Of course, many countries legally require that companies are equal opportunity employers, but the label is usually intended to signify that the organization has gone beyond the normal expectations.

Equal opportunity programmes mainly involve the introduction of procedures that ensure that employees and prospective employees are dealt with equally and fairly. For example, one way of ensuring equal opportunity to jobs is by ensuring that they are advertised in such a way that all potential applicants can reasonably learn of the vacancy and apply—as opposed to, say, simply selecting someone through informal channels. Similarly, by setting out specific criteria for jobs, and ensuring that interview panels use structured assessment of candidates against those criteria, factors unrelated to the job such as gender or race can be excluded from the formal appraisal of candidates. As such, equal opportunities programmes are generally targeted at ensuring that *procedural justice* is promoted, i.e. the key issue is ensuring that the procedures are fair to all.

Some equal opportunities programmes go further than merely introducing non-discriminatory procedures. Often referred to as *affirmative action* (AA) programmes, these approaches deliberately attempt to target those who might be currently under-represented in the workforce, for instance by trying to increase the proportion of women, disabled, or racial minorities in senior management positions. Four main areas of affirmative action can be distinguished (De George 1999: 431–5):

- **Recruitment policies**. In order to enhance the proportion of under-represented groups, AA programmes might look at actively recruiting these groups, for example by deliberately targeting job ads in media with a wide circulation amongst under-represented groups, or dispatching outreach recruitment staff to areas or schools where under-represented groups might predominate. The French car manufacturer Peugeot SA, for example, introduced a system of online application that allows for 'anonymous CVs' as a basis for recruitment decisions in order to encourage the employment of a more diverse workforce (Lokiec 2008). In the UK, employers displaying the government-initiated 'Two Ticks' disability symbol guarantee a job interview to all applicants with a disability who meet the minimum criteria for a job vacancy.

- **Fair job criteria**. Discrimination can often surface in an ostensibly 'objective' form through the definition of job criteria in such a fashion that they automatically make the job beyond the reach of a great number of potential applicants. In many cases, these job criteria might not necessarily be crucial to the achievement of the job role, yet they disadvantage certain parts of the population more than others. For example, those from low income or immigrant communities may not have had the same educational opportunities as others. This will often mean that regardless of intelligence, experience, or ability to do the job, they may be less likely to have the formal qualifications required by potential employers. Similarly, given that it is usually mothers rather than fathers who most frequently take on childcare and other household roles, inflexibility in employees' working times can discriminate against women. Ensuring that job criteria are fair to all is often a major task for AA programmes to tackle.

- **Training programmes for discriminated minorities**. Even following the revision of job criteria to ensure greater fairness, it is very possible that they will still include certain special skills, qualifications, and experience that particular under-represented groups are simply unlikely, from a statistical point of view, to have. This might be because of discrimination earlier in life, historical or cultural precedents, or just the plain realities of certain groups' socio-economic situation. In principle, ethnic Algerians might be accepted by a French *Grand Ecole* (elite university), but in practice, the social situation of these families does not encourage the children to pursue such an academic option compared with certain other groups in French society. Not all possible remedies here are within the company's scope of action—no one is expecting them to eradicate discrimination throughout the whole of society—but targeted pre-recruitment training programmes for under-represented groups can boost their eligibility for vacant positions.

- **Promotion to senior positions**. Women and ethnic minorities are severely under-represented on boards of directors. For instance, in the US, ethnic and racial minorities make up only 10% of corporate directors despite representing 35% of the population, while these minorities occupy only 3.4% of board seats in Canada despite representing over 19% of the population (Dhir 2015). The fact that senior management positions in virtually all industries in Europe and North America are dominated by white males might also be tackled by specific leadership training for women and minorities once they are already within the organization. For example, Deloitte operates a 'Mass Career Customization' programme that specifically targets women to deal with the work–life balance issues that are normally the biggest obstacle to progress up the ranks of seniority.[6] Similarly—although not uncontroversially—Apple, Facebook and other Silicon Valley companies offer financial support to their female employees to freeze their eggs so that they can delay motherhood to a phase when they have already achieved career progression (Henderson 2014).

Reverse discrimination

Affirmative action targets the remediation of long-standing discriminatory tendencies in the workplace: people of a certain gender, sexual orientation, or ethnic background become the subject of policies or regulations that provide supposedly fairer conditions for these groups. In many cases, this does not simply intend to provide equal opportunities for these groups, but AA in many cases focuses on the correcting of past injustices by, for instance, attempting to enhance the percentage of women in executive positions. One of the best-known examples of this approach in recent years has been the Black

Economic Empowerment (BEE) laws in South Africa that seek to install a fairer represen-tation of black workers after apartheid (Juggernath et al. 2013). However, one common side-effect of such robust attempts at affirmative action is that at some point AA can itself be deemed discriminatory because it disadvantages those thought to already be in an 'ad-vantaged' position. In some countries, it is deemed acceptable to 'tip the scales' to favour under-represented groups if candidates are thought to be equal on all other criteria. For example, if you are a white, Canadian man applying for a job in a Canadian university, the employment ad might inform you that in the case of equal qualification, a female aboriginal or racial minority applicant will be preferred.

This situation is taken a step further if minorities are preferred to mainstream candi-dates when the minority candidate is *less qualified* for the job or promotion. For instance, some countries allow for certain jobs to be subject to quotas that specify that a propor-tion of a certain minority group must be selected for interview, or even for the job itself, regardless of whether they are less qualified than over-represented groups. Norway, for example, requires that 40% of board positions are reserved for women, which explains its significantly higher female representation than other countries, although similar gender quotas have subsequently been introduced in Belgium, Iceland, Italy, the Netherlands, and Spain.[7] In these cases, non-minorities suffer *reverse discrimination* exactly because AA policies prefer certain minorities.

The justification of 'reverse discrimination' is somewhat ambiguous. On the one hand, companies could argue that women or ethnic minorities have been discrimi-nated against for such a long time and are so badly under-represented that it is time to reverse this development, and consequently they deserve preferential treatment. This argument could be based on the notion of *retributive justice*—i.e. that past injustices have to be 'paid for'. On the other hand, there is the problem that the individual ap-plicant, say a white male, is not responsible for the misconduct of his race or gender on previous occasions and so should not be made responsible by being the subject of reverse discrimination.

More defensible are arguments based on *distributive justice*—i.e. that rewards such as job and pay should be allocated fairly among all groups (Beauchamp 1997). These arguments tend to be underlined by the observation that many male executives have been promoted not necessarily because of their objective qualifications but because of their membership in 'old boys networks' or similar groups. Even objective 'merit' can be difficult to determine when certain roles and industries have been dominated for so long by certain genders or races. Women and racial minorities, it might be argued, require role models in professions they have been excluded from, and those profes-sions in turn might need to acquire new ideas about what a 'normal' professional would look or sound like. How many of us, for instance, automatically assume that a company director will be a white man in his fifties or sixties, rather than, say, a young black man or a woman? For most advocates of reverse discrimination, then, cultural arguments such as these suggest that fair outcomes rather than fair procedures should be paramount.

Opponents of reverse discrimination tend to marshal a number of fairly compelling arguments criticizing the practice, not least the basic notion that discrimination is wrong *per se* and that procedural justice should be paramount. Moreover, it can be argued that someone promoted on the basis of their gender or colour may well be discredited amongst their peers, and if they are not the best person for the job, this can even harm business efficiency (Pojman 1997). Heilman (1997) has further shown that decisions made on the basis of race, gender, or any other characteristic unrelated to merit can actually serve to promote stereotyping and reinforce existing prejudices. Burke and Black (1997) go so far as to suggest that reverse discrimination can prompt a 'male backlash' against the perceived injustice.

For reasons such as these, stronger forms of reverse discrimination tend to be illegal in many countries. For example, while it may be acceptable for companies to have 'targets' or 'aims' relating to how many women or minorities they would like in certain roles or levels, they may be prevented from having an explicit quota that has to be fulfilled.

Ultimately then, addressing discrimination in all of its forms and with all of its side-effects has become a key new area of management, which increasingly is referred to as managing diversity (Barak 2013; Kirton and Greene 2010). Rather than discriminating on the basis of gender, race, ethnicity or sexual orientation, the notion of diversity is driven by the ethical values of fairness and justice and focused on embracing difference as a potential strength. That is, diversity management is often driven by the enlightened self-interest of corporations that understand that diverse organizations can tap into a richer pool of knowledge and experience among its workforce—which can make a company more productive and more attractive to different customers. In the global context it is important to understand though that any particular emphasis on diversity management differs significantly from place to place: while, for instance, in India religion might be a challenge for managing diversity (Rao 2012), in the US the embrace of diverse sexual identities appears to be one of the main contemporary challenges (Bell et al. 2011). This is particularly challenging for multinational companies since they have to calibrate a universal commitment to diversity in close consideration of local circumstances.

☑ Skill check

Managing diversity. The ability to attract, accommodate and nurture a diverse workforce is seen as increasingly important in a global, multicultural business environment. Rather than discriminating on the basis of personal characteristics, those skilled in diversity management see them as a source of business success.

Employee privacy

Let us begin this next section with a short test. Answer each of the following questions True or False:

1. I feel sure there is only one true religion.

2. My soul sometimes leaves my body.

3. I believe in the second coming of Christ.

4. I wish I were not bothered by thoughts of sex.

5. I am very strongly attracted to members of my own sex.

6. I have never indulged in any unusual sexual practices.

You may be relieved to know that we are not going to ask you to announce your answers to these questions in class! However, these are actual questions from a pre-employment test administered by Dayton Hudson Corporation for the position of security guard at one of its Target stores in California in 1989 (Boatright 2012). The company eventually conceded in court that asking such intimate questions constituted an invasion of privacy, but the prospect of companies invading employees' privacy has become an increasingly pressing issue in the contemporary workplace. The escalation in health, drug, alcohol, and even genetic testing of employees, coupled with the possibilities for more and better surveillance through advances in information and communication technologies (West and Bowman 2015), has meant that **employee privacy**—i.e. a worker's ability to control information about them and how it is used and shared—has never been so much under threat.

The fundamental right to privacy consists of an individual's entitlement to control information about themself, and to control situations where such information could be gleaned (Cranford 1998). According to Michele Simms (1994), there are four different types of privacy that we might want to protect:

Employee privacy
An individual employee's ability to control information about themself, and the circumstances under which that information is shared inside and outside the workplace.

- **Physical privacy**. Physical inaccessibility to others and the right to 'one's own space'. For example, organizations that place surveillance cameras in employees' private rest areas might be said to compromise physical privacy.

- **Social privacy**. Freedom to behave in our private life in whichever way we choose. For instance, some employers will threaten social privacy by suggesting that employees should not bring their firm into disrepute by behaving in an 'unacceptable', 'immoral', or illegal way during their social lives. For example, in 2014 the CEO of Centerplate, a US-based food services company, was forced to resign following a much-publicized incident in which he was caught on video abusing a dog in an elevator.[8]

- **Informational privacy**. Determining how, when, and to what extent private data about us are released to others. This can be breached, for example, when employers hire private security firms to investigate employees without due cause, or when employees' social media use outside the workplace is monitored by their employers (West and Bowman 2015).

- **Psychological privacy**. Controlling emotional and cognitive inputs and outputs, and not being compelled to share private thoughts and feelings. For instance, psychological privacy is threatened when retailers introduce programmes aimed at making sure employers smile and appear happy in front of customers. Cathay Pacific Airways flight attendants, for example, threatened 'work-to-rule' industrial action in 2012 that would include 'not smiling at passengers'.[9]

Obviously, not all social interactions or information about ourselves can be deemed private. Employers have a right to know about our qualifications and work experience, just as they have a right to know if we have had a meeting with one of the company's clients. The key issue is whether certain aspects of our life are *relevant* to the relationship we have with our employer (Simms 1994). Let us take a look at this question in the main areas where employee privacy appears to be challenged.

> **? THINK THEORY**
>
> Think about the surveillance of employees' email and internet use by their employers from a perspective of rights and justice. Which rights on both sides are involved and what would be a fair balance in addressing these issues?

VISIT THE ONLINE RESOURCE CENTRE for a short response to this feature

Health and drug testing

In 2011, the Toronto Transport Commission (TTC), which operates the buses, trams, and subway in Canada's largest city, announced that it would institute random drug testing for the majority of its 10,000 employees, including drivers, maintenance workers, supervisors, and even executives. Although the TTC argued the measure would improve public safety, by 2015 the programme was still on hold and the transit workers' union had threatened legal action, accusing the TTC of violating employees' right to privacy. Indeed, the Canadian Human Rights Commission has asserted that 'random drug tests cannot be shown to be reasonably necessary to accomplish the goal of ensuring that workers are not impaired by drugs while on the job' and therefore deems them a violation of the Canadian Human Rights Act *except* where they refer to 'safety-sesitive' positions (as would be the case with transit drivers).[10]

Health and drug testing is quite a contested issue in business ethics. The central objection is that such tests make available far more information on the employee than the employer actually needs. Des Jardins and Duska (1997) highlight three main aspects here.

- **Potential to do harm**. There are only a few jobs where information on health and drug use is really vitally important for the safety of the job or for the protection of customers. An AIDS test might conceivably make sense for a nurse or a chef, but it is certainly not an issue for a software specialist or a lorry driver. The key issue for Des Jardins and Duska is whether the job involves *a clear and present danger to do harm*.

- **Causes of employee's performance**. Employers are well within their rights to determine whether their employees are performing at a satisfactory level and to take action if they are not. However, the employer does not necessarily have a right to know about all of the personal factors influencing the employee's performance. Suppose we are depressed, or suffering from bereavement, or have just stayed up drinking too much the night before—this may affect our performance, but then again it may not. It would be quite difficult to accept that we should reveal this information on arriving at the office in the morning unless there is a clear, ongoing problem with our performance. Indeed, it has been shown that many employer-related factors are likely to have a greater impact on performance than drug and alcohol use, including bad working conditions, excessive workloads and work-related stress (Joseph Rowntree Foundation 2004).

- **Level of performance**. Finally, Des Jardins and Duska further claim that an employer is only entitled to an *acceptable* level of performance from their employees, not their *optimal* performance. Most drug, alcohol, and health tests aim to identify factors that potentially might prevent the employee from functioning in the most optimal fashion. Again, the key issue is whether we are performing at an acceptable level in the first place, not whether we could be made to perform better.

Despite these criticisms, such tests have become increasingly common in the modern workplace, particularly in the US. The particular cultural context of the US may help to explain this, in particular the strong legalistic approach that makes employers vulnerable to litigation from customers and others employees if members of staff are found to have put them at risk when unfit for work due to sickness, drugs, or alcohol. However, testing programmes are most certainly on the rise in Europe, Asia, and Australasia, occasioned perhaps by the global spread of US business practices (Eaglesham 2000). Nonetheless, despite these developments, probably the biggest threat to employee privacy at present comes from the increasing use of electronic surveillance.

Electronic privacy and data protection

Surveillance and control of workers has a long legacy in management practice. However, the rise of electronic communication, social media, the internet and in general the escalation in usage of new technologies in business has added a new dimension to the issue of privacy (Ottensmeyer and Heroux 1991; West and Bowman 2015).

First, there is the fact that the computer as a work tool enables new forms of surveillance. The computer makes possible a detailed overview of the time and pace of work carried out, particularly since every strike of the keyboard can now be monitored easily. This means that the employer is not only in a position to judge the result of the employee's work, but they can also trace in every detail the process of its coming into existence. Similarly, many 'eavesdropping employers' now routinely place cameras and other recording devices in work areas to monitor employees (Ciocchetti 2011). While this might be justified to assess performance or to prevent thefts and other misdemeanours, it is clearly an entry into the physical privacy of employees, particularly when it intrudes on ostensibly private areas such as changing rooms, bathrooms, and staffrooms. It remains a highly contested issue as to how far this breach of privacy is legitimate.

This control does not only extend to the work process, but it pertains also to the usage of employees' time for private reasons, such as when using email, the internet, or social media. This includes fairly straightforward issues such as the downloading of pornography, but also extends to all sorts of other usage of communication technologies for private purposes. Should companies be allowed to monitor and check their employees' email or their private conversations on the phone? With regard to conventional mail, there are extensive regulations in place safeguarding privacy, which are simply not applicable to email in the same way. Meanwhile most companies have established codes of conduct that at least provide the employee with some knowledge of the boundaries to privacy established by the firm. However, globally, there are different standards in legislation that determine the extent to which privacy could be restricted in these areas. In the US, for example, employees have considerably less regulatory protection of their electronic privacy compared with their European and Canadian counterparts (Lasprogata et al. 2004).

While the abuse of company time is a perfectly legitimate complaint of companies, we might ask whether policing to prevent or identify such an abuse legitimates such a far-reaching incursion into workers' privacy. As with drug and alcohol tests, the invasion of privacy here is often based on the threat of *potential* harm to the company rather than *actual* harm. However, the harm to both employees and the firm itself can be very real when implementing such extensive surveillance (West and Bowman 2015). After all, for employees such as call centre operatives, who spend most of their work time on the telephone, not only is almost everything they say during the day open to surveillance, but employers often also enforce a way of talking and behaving to clients that potentially threatens psychological privacy as well. In the long run, employers may also suffer by eroding trust within the organization and failing to capitalize on employee discretion.

Finally, the issue of privacy occurs in situations where data are saved and processed electronically (De George 1999: 346–53). The relationship between an employee and the company's doctor is one of privacy, and if the doctor enters the data of the employee into their computer system, this is not a breach of patient–doctor confidentiality. But as soon as this database is linked with the company's other systems, the employee's privacy will clearly be broken. The problem here is that it might not be a problem if companies are in possession of their client's or employee's data *per se*. The problem occurs where, for instance, the phone company is taken over by the credit card company and both clients' databases are matched: such an operation suddenly provides access to a wide range of information posing a far more potent breach of privacy. This issue is exacerbated by social networking sites, such as Facebook, Instagram, Twitter, Renren, and Weibo where the lines between private and public employee data are often ambiguous. **An Ethical Dilemma 7** provides an opportunity to explore how this can pose an ethical problem for many current and future employees in today's business world.

With advances in information and communication technologies accelerating at an unprecedented rate, we might expect threats to privacy such as these to intensify. However, legislation is often relatively slow to catch up with these changes, and since employee surveillance is so ingrained in management, managers often do not even recognize privacy as an ethical issue (Ottensmeyer and Heroux 1991). Therefore, we might at the very least question whether 'spying' on employees is counterproductive to fostering trust and integrity in the workplace.

? THINK THEORY

Think about electronic surveillance in terms of utilitarianism. What are the costs and benefits involved? Is this likely to offer a reasonable justification for incursions into employee privacy?

VISIT THE ONLINE RESOURCE CENTRE for a short response to this feature

Due process and lay-offs

As anyone who has ever worked in kitchens, bars, and restaurants will be able to vouch, many employees are constantly at risk of arbitrarily losing their jobs for relatively minor indiscretions, personality clashes, or simply because their face 'does not fit'. The right to due process though has a long history in working practices and can be deduced from the notion of procedural justice. As we saw with discrimination, this form of justice requires the application of rules and procedures to people in a consistent and even-handed way, avoiding arbitrary decision-making, and without discrimination on bases other than merit (Chryssides and Kaler 1996: 45). Promotion, disciplinary proceedings, and firing are the most common processes where the right to due process is particularly important.

The case of firing and redundancies is especially challenging in this respect, most notably because firms often downsize to remain competitive and increase shareholder value (Jung 2014). For example in the aftermath of the financial crisis of 2008, 10.2 million

AN ETHICAL DILEMMA 7

Off your face on Facebook?

You are the human resource manager of AllCure Pharmaceuticals. It is a busy time and the guys in the product approval department have called you because they desperately need to hire a new team member to assist them with the clinical trials of what could become the next blockbuster drug for the company. You get started and within a week you have managed to get three well-qualified applicants for the job. The interviews went well and there are two really good applicants. Both are women, recent college graduates, and you find it hard to decide among them.

The clinical trials that the new hire will work on are very important. They require a very reliable, meticulous work attitude, but also good social skills to manage the different relations between the clinics, the approving authorities, and various departments in the company. A colleague suggests you check the two finalists out on various social networking sites to see how suitable they seem. Later in the day, you login to Facebook, and yes, one of them is there! Surfing through her posts and photos you see a very sociable, obviously well-travelled individual.

The other candidate is a bit more difficult to locate. This is too bad, as she already has some work experience and on paper is the slightly better candidate of the two. Her details are only available to friends, but browsing through her list of some 800 friends, you find that one of your current interns is actually on her list. You call in your intern, who it turns out briefly met this second candidate on a course they took together at college years ago, and together you take a look at the Facebook page of the second candidate. Doing so, you make some interesting discoveries: not only do you find a number of photos of her taking her shirt off at parties, but there are plenty of pictures of her apparently engaged in heavy alcohol use and even two pictures where she is undoubtedly taking illegal drugs.

You thank your intern for her help and sit back in your chair wondering what to do. You are worried about hiring someone who is too much into partying, and possibly even illegal activity, especially for a job that requires sensitive and conscientious work. Plus, you can just imagine what the reaction of patients, coworkers or even more importantly, the officials at the regulating bodies might say if the pictures became public. 'Hey, have you heard about the AllCure girl' you can imagine them saying, 'you really have to see these pictures …'.

Questions

1. What are the main ethical issues in this case?
2. What are the main ethical arguments for and against the use of social network sites for potential employers in this situation?
3. Think of how you use Facebook or similar sites. Does this case influence the way you might use these sites in the future?
4. How would you finally decide as the human resource manager in this situation?

Source

Based on Du, W. 2007. Job candidates getting tripped up by Facebook. 14 August 2007: http://www.msnbc.msn.com/id/20202935/from/ET/.

employees in Europe had lost their jobs by 2013 (ILO 2013). This development is particularly severe in information technology and business services, where European companies are currently offshoring jobs at a rate of 130,000 per year.[11] In many countries, the legal framework provides some codification of employee and employer rights in these circumstances—but even where they do, some industries and countries tend not to respect these as fully as others. Therefore, a number of ethical considerations arise in the process of downsizing.

- **Involvement**. A first important area is the information policy of the corporation (Hopkins and Hopkins 1999). It can be contended that employees have a *right to know* well ahead of the actual point of redundancy that their job is on the line. This issue of timing is closely connected to the method of announcement. **Ethics on Screen 7** caricatures an approach to laying-off employees which is often a dire reality: unless there are legal constraints such as in some European countries, many employees only learn about being laid off when it is already a fait accompli. Furthermore, it is sometimes contended that employees have a right to know about the causes for the downsizing, as this will provide them with the possibility of judging the fairness of the downsizing process (Hopkins and Hopkins 1999).

- **Remuneration**. A second important area is the compensation package of redundancy payments and other benefits employees receive when laid off (Hopkins and Hopkins 1999). These typically should include enough money to bridge the time necessary for finding a new job. Some firms tend to have quite a generous approach to these issues, and many also provide social schemes for redundant workers including early retirement options for those workers whose chances of finding another job are lower due to advanced age.

With increasing moves towards restructuring and flexibilization, however, the needs of employees in lay-off situations have moved beyond merely involvement and remuneration to retraining and re-integration into the workforce. Over the past decades, many employees have increasingly been exposed to the need for *occupational transitions*—i.e. having to find work in completely new industries rather than just switching employers. This has obviously meant that employees have experienced escalating insecurity, while also facing greater challenges in developing their employability (Kieselbach and Mader 2002).

Such developments have potentially raised new expectations on corporations, particularly in respect to developing 'outplacement' strategies to help employees find work following lay-offs. In the Netherlands, for example, most companies offer employability training, and restructuring is often supported with career counselling; in Belgium and Italy, companies are legally obliged to offer outplacement counselling in the case of lay-offs (Kieselbach and Mader 2002). Although in other countries, such as Spain and the UK, employment is primarily regarded as an individual or governmental responsibility, there is clearly a case for suggesting that some form of outplacement process might be a 'fairer' approach to lay-offs.

VISIT THE ONLINE RESOURCE CENTRE for a short response to this feature

> **? THINK THEORY**
>
> Think about outplacement strategies from the perspective of justice and fairness. See if you can set outplacement in the context of Rawls' theory of justice.

ETHICS ON SCREEN 7

Up in the Air

A defining movie for these perilous times. The firing scenes only hurt when you laugh.

Peter Travers, *Rolling Stone*

Jason Reitman's Oscar-nominated movie *Up in the Air* follows the fortunes of corporate downsizer Ryan Bingham, played by George Clooney. Bingham's job is essentially to fire people. He works for Career Transitions Corporation, where he makes a living travelling from one workplace to the next, informing people that they have lost their jobs. In 2009, when the movie was released, this was a highly topical theme as much of the world was sunk in the Great Recession following the financial crisis of the late 2000s. The US in particular had experienced a swathe of lay-offs across the country and Reitman expertly tuned into the mood of the times, even to the extent of using non-actors who had recently been fired to act out some of the firing scenes in the movie.

Clooney's character Bingham is depicted as an expert at firing people. And with downsizing the order of the day in the recessionary US, his company is getting lots of business hiring him out to employers who would rather not do the unpleasant task themselves. He criss-crosses the country, racking up endless air miles, in a rootless existence that sees him living out of hotels and airport lounges for 322 days a year. Bingham sees his work and lifestyle not as a burden though but as freedom from all the things—relationships and possessions—that can tie you down. Relishing the perks of his elite frequent flyer status, his most pressing goal is to join the ultra exclusive club of flyers with ten million points. Along the way, he even sidelines as a motivational speaker extolling the freedoms of travelling light through life. 'The slower we move,' his maxim goes, 'the faster we die.'

Bingham carries his philosophy into his firing strategy. Rather than offer remorse to his unfortunate victims he presents the terminations as an opportunity to throw off their baggage and follow their dreams. 'Anybody who ever built an empire or changed the world sat where you are right now—and it's because

Paramount Pictures/The Kobal Collection

they sat there that they were able to do it,' he tells one disgruntled worker. 'How much did they first pay you to give up on your dreams?' he asks another long-term manager dismayed by the impending loss of his livelihood.

In changing economic times, though, even Bingham's job is not secure. His carefully engineered world is suddenly threatened by his firm's plan to replace in-person lay-offs with videoconference calls in order to cut costs. Virtual layoffs will make travelling consultants like Bingham 'irrelevant' according to his boss. The idea is the brainchild of the freshly graduated new hire Natalie (played by Anna Kendrick), who argues that Bingham's approach is inefficient and should be replaced with a more technological solution. Bingham retorts that Natalie has no experience of the firing process and clearly does not know how best to deal with people facing termination. Much to his dismay, Bingham's boss decides to send him on the road for one last trip, but with Natalie in tow to learn the ropes.

As they travel across the country together Bingham and his upstart sidekick begin to reassess their assumptions. While Natalie discovers the difficulties in managing the trauma of downsizing, Bingham starts to reconsider his disavowal of personal attachments. Eventually, after they are brought back to the head office to implement the new system, Natalie decides to quit when one of the people she fired commits suicide. Bingham meanwhile tries to kick-start his

personal life but discovers it is not so easy to suddenly start building real relationships after a lifetime as an executive frequent flyer.

As a comedy, the movie deals with its serious themes in a light-hearted way, but it still manages to shine a light on the despair brought about by downsizing, as well as the alienation engendered by the corporate lifestyle. Reitman also shows that the way you conduct layoffs matters. For all the fake optimism of Bingham's motivational approach to firing people, he does, as the *New Yorker* magazine put it, retain some principles—'the least you can offer, when you're destroying a human being, is to do it face to face.'

Sources

Lane, A. 2009. Nowhere Man. *New Yorker*, 7 December 2009: http://www.newyorker.com/magazine/2009/12/07/nowhere-man-2.

Travers, P. 2009. Up in the Air. *Rolling Stone*, 14 December 2009: http://www.rollingstone.com/movies/reviews/up-in-the-air-20091214.

Employee participation and association

The recognition that employees might be more than just human 'resources' in the production process has given rise to the claim that employees should also have a certain degree of influence on their tasks, their job environments, and their company's goals—i.e. a right to **employee participation**. There are a number of ethical justifications for this claim (see Cludts 1999; Claydon 2000). Apart from references to human rights, some grounding can be derived from Kant's thinking. Specifically, participation implies that people are not treated only as a means to another's end. Employees have their own goals and their own view of which ends should be served, and so they have some rights to determine the modalities of their involvement in the corporation. Other justifications can be based on egoism, namely that an employee can only freely pursue their own interests or desires with some degree of participation at the workplace.

Questions over the right to participation are controversial though, not least because such a right often clashes with management's duty to determine how best to protect the interests of owners. However, the key issue at a practical level now is not so much whether employees should have a right to participate in decisions, but rather to what degree this should take place. There are two main areas to which a right to participation extends (Kaler 1999a).

Financial participation allows employees a share in the ownership or income of the corporation. Initiatives predicated on partly remunerating executives with stocks or stock options in order to align incentives with shareholders, as discussed in Chapter 6, have looked to work in this direction. However, many start-ups, especially in the technology industry, have also offered equity in their firms to a wide range of employees at different seniorities since it involves no upfront cash outlay (which is particularly attractive for new firms) but can provide a substantial incentive to talented employees who might

Employee participation
Practices that give employees some influence in how the workplace is organized, managed, and governed.

otherwise be out of the firm's pay range. Successful Silicon Valley technology companies have over the years made legions of engineers rich, a feat replicated by the Chinese e-commerce giant Alibaba when it went public in 2014, creating thousands of millionaires among its current and former employees, from executives to receptionists (Jacobs and Gough 2014).

Operational participation occurs at a more practical level and can include a number of different dimensions:

- **Delegation**. Employees can be delegated control over a range of decisions relevant to their jobs. Efforts of this kind have often been labelled as 'job enrichment' or 'job enlargement' schemes and have been practised successfully, for instance, in the automotive industry. Several European companies, such as Volvo and Porsche, have in part stopped their line production and reorganized their workforce in semi-autonomous teams. In this way, many decisions about how to actually manufacture a car have been taken away from the formal control of managers and put into the sphere of the individual employee (Woywode 2002).

- **Information**. Employees can also participate by receiving information about crucial decisions that have an effect on their work. This especially concerns information about the performance of the corporation, the security of jobs and pensions, etc. This form of participation is in many respects wider than just participation through delegation since it may also pertain to issues that are not directly necessary for the fulfilment of the employee's own immediate task.

- **Consultation**. In some contexts, employees may have the opportunity to express their views on potential decisions planned by the employer. This form of participation is stronger still, since it opens up the opportunity to actually influence the decision taken by the employer.

- **Co-determination**. Here employees have a full and codified right to determine major decisions in the company. This is the strongest form of participation and would include decisions about the strategic future of the corporation, such as mergers or diversification into new markets (Ferner and Hyman 1998).

In a global context, there is still quite some variety with regard to the degree of participation allocated to employees. Whereas employees in the US, for instance, mostly find out online or through the grapevine if their jobs are on the line, Swedish or French companies usually cannot take measures regarding redundancies without detailed communication, consultation, and agreement with employees. In many such countries there is an extensive body of legislation that focuses on the representation of the workforce. Consequently, employees do not practise many of these participatory rights directly but through their representatives in works councils, trade unions, or other bodies.

☑ **Skill check**

Enabling employee participation. Providing the means for employees to participate in the organization, management, and governance of the firm is an important skill that helps respect the dignity of employees and secure their commitment.

Given the important role for works councils and trade unions in facilitating the right to participation, we must also consider here the underlying question of whether employees have a 'right' to join together in such organizations. This is usually framed in terms of a *right to association*. The crucial factor here is that without a right to associate, employees often lack an effective form of representation of their interests to employers, leaving them in a far weaker position than management in bargaining over pay and conditions. Still, even where rights to associate are legally protected, companies may seek to obstruct or avoid them. For example, Royle (2005) vividly illustrates how, in the fast-food industry, companies with a strong 'anti-union' stance, such as McDonald's, have been able to tame, neutralize, or subvert systems of employee representation, especially at a workplace level. In Germany, for instance, he argues that the company has 'been fighting the establishment of German work's councils for over 30 years' (p. 48). **Figure 7.4** provides an overview of how membership in trade unions has developed over the last four decades. The figures not only reflect different legal frameworks and traditions in industrial relations—for example, if we compare the US to Canada, Finland, or Australia—but also shows that the general trend in union membership is on the decline in most countries (with the exception of Finland).

Despite this decline in the importance of unions, the underlying rights to participate and associate still remain crucial issues for corporations, especially when moving to countries where the legislative framework is different from at home. The motivation, however, does not only have to come from concerns about compliance with legislation or issues of fairness and equity. Participation has also been identified as a means to enhance worker efficiency, especially when jobs ask for flexibility and creativity on behalf of the employee (Collier and Esteban 1999). Ultimately, though, the rights to participation and association within a company follows a similar line of argument to that concerning participation of citizens in the political process (Ellerman 1999). Corporations have power over one of the most important areas of an employee's life, namely their economic survival. Consequently, the principles of a democratic society necessarily ask

	Union density in % 1980	Union density in % 2010	Change in union density in % 1980–2010
Australia	49	19	−30
Canada	34	30	−4
Finland	69	70	+1
Germany	35	19	−16
Japan	31	19	−13
New Zealand	69	21	−48
United Kingdom	51	28	−23
United States	22	11	−11

Figure 7.4 Union density (percentage of union members as a proportion of the total workforce) in selected countries

Source: Based on Schnabel (2013).

for some rights to participation in the firm, usually through a representative body of some kind such as a trade union or a works council. Trade unions, however, also play an important role in other employee rights, including those of due process, fair wages, and as we shall now see, working conditions (Preuss et al. 2014).

Working conditions

The right to healthy and safe working conditions has been one of the very first ethical concerns for employees, right from the early part of the industrial revolution. Novelists such as Charles Dickens and various social reformers such as Robert Owen, who pioneered the co-operative movement, sought to shed light on the appalling conditions faced by those working in mines, factories, and mills at the time. Consequently, a considerable number of issues concerned with working conditions were initially addressed as far back as the early nineteenth century, either by way of legislation (such as Bismarck's social laws in Germany) or by voluntary initiatives of paternalistic, often religiously motivated entrepreneurs (Fitzgerald 1999).

Today most industrialized countries have implemented a dense network of health, safety, and environmental (HSE) regulation that companies have to abide by. Consequently, such issues are either already regulated by existing laws or become an object of court proceedings, rather than necessarily being ethical issues that have to be resolved within the boundaries of the firm. The main issue, however, often becomes the *enforcement and implementation of existing regulation*. In practice, some companies may cut corners on health and safety through negligence or in contempt of regulators. Similarly, many of these regulations, such as wearing a safety helmet or ear plugs, may be disliked by workers themselves. This imposes a responsibility on employers to actually 'police' workers' compliance with regulations. A common example is the signs, typically found in the bathrooms of pubs and restaurants, which instruct members of staff to wash their hands (or 'wash your hands NOW!') after using the toilet. HSE requirements may also become a more pressing issue in developing countries, where corporations may not be forced by the law to heed tight standards. However, many of these issues, as mentioned earlier, actually occur in the operations of companies' suppliers rather than their own, and as such will be discussed in more detail in Chapter 9.

However advanced protection measures and HSE regulation might be, there will always be certain jobs that include a high risk to health and life. Working on an oil rig, doing research in nuclear technology, or working as a stunt person in action films are all inextricably linked to certain hazards. As a general rule, one could adopt the *principle of informed consent*: no worker should be exposed to risks without precise information about what those risks actually are. Consequently, any damage to the worker's health is the result of their deliberate decisions—perhaps to effectively 'trade' exposure to health risks for the higher compensation that is often linked to such jobs.

HSE issues also become increasingly relevant in the context of new risks, most commonly in the form of *new diseases* and *new technologies*. In fact, some diseases even owe their name to the companies where they first occurred, such as 'Pseudo-Krupp', a lung disease first discovered among workers and neighbours of the German steel mill 'Krupp'. New technologies can pose a particular challenge when the health risks to workers may not be known about at the time they are first introduced. For instance, when asbestos was first developed for use as a fire retardant, nobody was aware of its inherent health risks. Given that asbestosis—the debilitating, often fatal condition caused by exposure to asbestos—can take up to 20 or 30 years to surface after exposure, enormous numbers of production and installation workers handling the substance were placed at serious health risk (Treviño and Nelson 2014). The long-term health consequences of extended computer work are also only now beginning to emerge. The dilemma for corporations lies in the fact that the more sophisticated certain technologies are, such as genetic engineering, the greater their potential benefits but also the greater their potential risks. The principle of informed consent that we mentioned earlier can only partially be applied because the very nature of those risks lies in the fact that the potential consequences, let alone their likelihood, are simply not known. Some therefore suggest the necessity for something more akin to the *precautionary principle* that acknowledging scientific uncertainty about many processes and impacts imposes the burden of proof of harmlessness on those introducing a technology.

Work–life balance

We briefly discussed the threat of unemployment above. However, many workers face exactly the opposite problem, namely the increasing incursion of working hours into their social life. There has been a growing pressure for longer hours in (and travelling to) the workplace. This is notable amongst both professionals, such as doctors or accountants, and low-paid workers in unskilled jobs, where people may voluntarily work excessive hours in order to meet bare minimum standards of living. These problems are even more pronounced in developing countries, as with the dormitory labour system in China, where many workers from rural areas leave their families and move to work in factories and live in dormitories under pretty dismal conditions (Smith and Pun 2006).

Clearly, a 'healthy' balance between work and non-work activities—or **work–life balance**—is difficult to maintain (Kalliath and Brough 2008). Parents may face difficulty with childcare and/or hardly see their children, couples may face the delicate task of maintaining a long-distance or weekend relationship, and many employees might find that their life is completely absorbed by work without any time or energy left to maintain or build up meaningful social relationships (Simpson 1998; Collier 2001). In the following, we will discuss two of the most pressing issues in work–life balance, namely:

Work–life balance
An employee's preferred ratio between work-related and non-work related activities.

- Excessive working hours and presenteeism.
- Flexible working patterns.

Excessive working hours and presenteeism

An increasing threat to employee health and well-being that is receiving considerable attention is excessive work hours. In particular, excessive hours are thought to impact on the employee's overall state of physical and mental health. For example, one survey found that 84% of managers claimed to work in excess of their official working hours, with the average being between 50 and 60 hours a week (Simpson 2000).

'*Presenteeism*', as in the phenomenon of being at work when you should be at home due to illness or even just at rest and recreation (Cooper 1996), is a common cultural force in many organizations. The implicit assumption is that only those putting in long hours will be rewarded with career progression and other company rewards. Presenteeism appears to especially affect the middle and upper levels of management, and in particular it is likely to disadvantage women's career progression since they tend to have more responsibilities for child care, etc., at home (Simpson 1998).

A specific form of presenteeism is connected to the use of smartphones, tablets, and other mobile devices that have further eroded the boundaries between working time and private time. Essentially, most professionals are, like their devices, in 'always-on' mode. However, there have been some attempts to address this (de Castella 2014). Consider, for example, the 2014 agreement in France between trade unions and the employer's federation in the technology and consulting industry that gave employees the explicit right to switch off work email after leaving the office. Since 2011, Volkswagen has blocked employees' email accounts from half an hour after their shifts end until half an hour before they start again. A number of legislative initiatives in Europe are also under discussion in order to establish rules around work emailing after hours.

Flexible working patterns

Changes in working patterns have also led to more 'flexibility' in working arrangements. Greater flexibility can enhance opportunities for women and other disadvantaged groups, but it can also have a major downside for those marginalized from 'standard' work and working conditions. As Karen Legge (1998) suggests in Figure 7.1, flexibility can just be another way of saying that management can do what it wants.

Recent years have seen the emergence of a large constituency of workers in 'non-standard' work relationships, including part-time work, temporary work, self-employment, and teleworking (Stanworth 2000). The legal status of such workers on the 'periphery' of the organization is often less secure than that of those at the 'core', giving rise to the potential for poorer working conditions, increased insecurity, lower pay, exclusion from training and other employment benefits, as well as a whole raft of other possible disadvantages. 'Precarious work' as it is sometimes known, involves a shifting of risk from employers to employees and has increasingly spread from industrialized countries to Asia and elsewhere (Kalleberg and Hewison 2013).

These problems are particularly acute in low-skill service industries such as retailing, the hospitality industry, industrial cleaning, and in call centres—areas that have actually seen some of the greatest growth in jobs in recent years (Cederström and Fleming 2012). Such workers are often expected to work 'unsocial' hours, with working hours often being unpredictable and changed at short notice. Royle (2005: 46), for instance, claims that fast-food companies in Europe commonly insist that workers clock off during quiet times and are even 'persuaded to compete in all-night cleaning "parties"'. Work intensification in such service industries is common, as are significant levels of surveillance and control. Perhaps the ultimate in flexible working patterns though is exemplified by some retailers that have used 'zero-hours' contracts. These guarantee no minimum hours, no stable level of earnings, and prevent workers from planning even the basic elements of their lives (Stanworth 2000). A steep rise in the use of such contracts in the wake of the financial crisis across Europe led to calls for reform. In the UK, where the number of people on zero hours contracts was estimated to be in excess of 1.4 million, a ban on the use of exclusivity clauses to prevent workers from seeking other employment while on such contracts was introduced in 2014.[12]

Of course there are good arguments why flexibility can boost competitiveness and provide for a strong economy (Hayman 2009), as well as providing new opportunities for women and other groups traditionally excluded from 'standard' working patterns due to home responsibilities, etc. (Robinson 2005). However, the problem comes when flexibility erodes basic protections for employee rights, and/or where one group of workers on part-time, temporary, or otherwise 'flexible' contracts is treated unfairly compared with the core workforce.

The ethical problems here are quite difficult to resolve. From the individual's perspective, any demands for better work–life balance may ultimately be counterproductive to their career aspirations or even a danger to their job security. Furthermore, some jobs, especially where they involve a high level of specialized skill, are not easily reducible or sharable. Nonetheless, some companies have also discovered that employees with poor work–life balance might not be as effective in the long run, and that different work patterns might need to be encouraged. We will come back to some of the solutions when we discuss more sustainable working places later on.

Fair wages

As with most rights in this section, the right to a fair wage is to some extent protected through regulation in many countries. This certainly applies to lower incomes—for example, with the establishment of a statutory minimum wage, which is by now common in many countries. However, our assessment of what is a 'fair' wage becomes more complex when we compare wage levels of those at the bottom of the organizational hierarchy with those at the top.

The starting point for determining fair wages is the *expectations* placed on the employee and their *performance* towards goals, measured by hours worked, prior training, risks involved, responsibility for assets, meeting of targets, etc. However, jobs are valued very differently in some employment markets compared to others. Consider the market for elite football players—in 2014, FC Barcelona player Lionel Messi was reportedly the best-paid soccer star with an annual income of €20 million, followed by Real Madrid's Gareth Bale (€19 million) and Cristiano Ronaldo (€17 million). While one would certainly concede that being a professional footballer can be hard and disciplined work at times, this also applies to mining workers who are paid a fraction of Messi's salary. Similar discussions about excessive compensation for executives came up when the US president suggested salary caps for CEOs of companies who had received governmental funding in the aftermath of the stock-market collapse of 2008. Athletes and CEOs are both examples where the measure for assigning compensation is related to the consequences of the employee's activities on relevant markets: if we put Messi's or Ronaldo's salary in relation to what their club earns from television and other media deals, one could potentially argue that their salary is acceptable. Similarly, some CEOs earn so much money because they get paid in relation to how the stock market values their company, and what the prevailing labour market for CEOs dictates is a 'reasonable' sum (see Chapter 6, Executive remuneration, pp. 242–243, for more discussion on the ethics of executive pay).

Conversely, looking at the bottom of the pay scale we witness in many countries a widening debate around the notion of a 'living wage' as a yardstick for minimum wages. **Ethics in Action 7.1** tells the story of how this debate recently unfolded in Cambodia around a statutory minimum wage. However, such considerations are not confined to the developing world: in 2014 we saw what many commentators labelled a new phase in industrial action among fast-food workers across the US with attention focusing on establishing genuine living wages as a minimum (Finnegan 2014). For instance, while fast-food workers in New York were paid $7.25/hour (the statutory

**VISIT THE
ONLINE
RESOURCE
CENTRE**
for links to
useful sources
of further
information

ETHICS IN ACTION 7.1   http://www.ethicalcorp.com

Cambodia's wage protests: fashion brands support garment workers

Ethical CORPORATION

Paul French, 9 October 2014

While garment workers' minimum wages are rising in many Asian economies, in Cambodia, unusually, it is Western brands that are responding to public pressure, not the government.

Several Asian countries are raising minimum wages in what appears to be a response to pressure from civic and worker organisations. Taiwan's Ministry of Labour, after long-term pressure from civic groups, has announced that it will raise the minimum wage by 'about 4%' in 2015. This means the monthly wage will rise to about $668 and that the minimum hourly wage will be about $4. The rise is more than double Taiwan's expected inflation rate this year. On the Chinese mainland, minimum wages vary from province to province and city to city but are generally on the increase— major production centres such as Hangzhou and Wenzhou have raised their minimum wages by about 12%. Vietnam, Thailand and Indonesia are also raising their minimum wage rates.

The clearest victory for worker protests is the news that Cambodian textile workers have persuaded major international fashion brands to agree to a minimum wage of nearly double the current rate to $177 a month.

Cambodia has been the country where militant action has been most pronounced recently and where changes are being forced by worker activism and an aversion to bad publicity by brands. Thousands of textile workers, mainly women, have taken to the streets of Phnom Penh over the past year or so calling for higher wages as increasing numbers of Western fashion brands move production to the country, looking to partially escape fast rising wages and costs in China.

Workers in orange T-shirts have been protesting in their lunch hours and the government became so concerned it called out the army several times. However, now the brands themselves have reached a settlement with the workers—Next, New Look, C&A, H&M, Inditex (owner of Zara, Massimo Dutti, and other brands), and Primark have all joined the settlement and informed the Cambodian government and the local Garment Manufacturers Association.

The Cambodian 'solution' is interesting in that, unlike the government-mandated minimum wage hikes in other Asian countries, in Phnom Penh the agreement is between workers' organisations and the brands themselves, effectively circumventing the government and, hopefully, forcing the government to raise the minimum wage overall at some point. In a letter to the government, and Prime Minister Hun Sen, the brands argue that the central authority should take steps itself to raise the minimum wage across the board and engage with unions. So far the government has failed to do this, and continues to call out the troops to quash protests.

Cambodia has become a crucial centre in the minimum wage debate across Asia because of the government's intransigent stance and the fact that, although it is one of the top 20 clothing producers in the world, Cambodia has among the lowest minimum monthly wages in the industry, according to the International Labour Organization (ILO).

The Coalition of Cambodian Apparel Workers Democratic Union (CCAWDU) is pushing ahead with more activism, despite rallies of workers—invariably peaceful and led by women textile workers—attracting soldiers armed with loaded rifles. The CCAWDU claims rallies have been held at more than 200 factories across the country.

There will be planned negotiations between the government, unions and factories in early October 2014 to set the 2015 minimum wage for the industry as a whole. It is to be hoped that the government will opt to follow the lead of the brands in raising wages and not to respond with troops again. A crackdown on striking garment workers in January this year left at least four people dead with many activists and union leaders still in detention or placed under court supervision banning them from joining any further meetings and/or public gatherings.

Since enacting economic reforms and moving away from a planned economy in the 1990s, Cambodia has been intent on integrating itself into both the regional Asean and World Trade Organization trading systems. The textiles sector, which employs close to 700,000 workers and earned the country about $5.5 billion in garments exports last year, has been keen to support this push.

The actions by the major brands show they are concerned about the ethical situation in Cambodia and will bear this in mind when deciding where to place orders, where to source their goods from, and where to employ their people in future. Forcing confrontation and sending in troops against seamstresses does not seem a great way to raise Cambodia's attractiveness as a sourcing location or a centre for ethical textiles production.

Sources

Ethical Corporation, Paul French, 9 October 2014, http://www.ethicalcorp.com. Reproduced with the kind permission of Ethical Corporation.

? THINK THEORY

Think about the Cambodian solution to increasing the minimum wage for workers from the perspective of the supply and demand for labour. Does the fact that Cambodian workers had to take to the streets to force an increase in the minimum wage suggest that the labour market was not functioning correctly to set a fair wage, or is it evidence that labour markets do indeed eventually find a suitable level without government intervention?

VISIT THE ONLINE RESOURCE CENTRE for a short response to this feature

minimum wage) in 2014, it has been estimated that a full-time worker would need at least $22.66/hour to survive in the city. The 'fight for 15' saw workers at McDonald's, Burger King, Wendy's, and other fast-food companies go on strike to try and raise the minimum wage to $15/hour.

With such huge disparities evident between the top and bottom earners in society, widening attention has been paid to the problem of *income inequality*, namely the distribution of income across society from the highest to the lowest earners. Income inequality has greatly increased in most countries, irrespective of their level of development (United Nations 2005; Freeman 2011). In China, income inequality has rapidly escalated so that today the richest 10% of households earn around 60% of total income, while in the US, the share of national income going to the richest 1% of Americans has doubled from 10% to 20% since 1980.[13] For corporations, this represents something of a challenge. On the one hand, they are increasingly looking to cut labour costs (especially among the rank and file), while on the other hand they have to compete for talent among the senior ranks of executives, and there are often few alternatives to paying the market rate. One potential solution has been for some business leaders, such as Howard Schultz of Starbucks, to lobby for increases in the minimum wage.[14] Another approach has been to extend stock options so that more employees can benefit from the company's success.

Another area of increasing ethical contestation is employee benefits, most notably health insurance and pension plans, where many employees have faced substantial cuts in recent years. Consider that in 1985 almost all Fortune 100 companies in the US offered a traditional defined benefit pension plan, whereas by 2012 that number was down to just 11 companies (Geisel 2012). One main reason for this is that in times of economic downturn many companies consider their employees' pensions as a legitimate source of capital to cover other losses. In the area of health care, especially in countries without public health care, similar ethical issues have arrived. Most notably, these issues have arisen in the US or in some developing countries, where health insurance is typically paid by employers rather than guaranteed by the public welfare system. This makes employees highly dependent on the company and may easily lead to a situation where employees are willing to put up with many demands just so that they do not lose their health coverage. This represents a clear moral hazard, as we discussed in the early part of this chapter.

☑ Skill check

Setting fair wages. Determining what is a fair wage is a key skill that involves assessment of the supply and demand for specific skills and qualifications as well as an understanding of relative pay distributions and reasonable minimum living wages.

Freedom of conscience and freedom of speech in the workplace

Normally, the right to freedom of conscience and speech is guaranteed by governments, and so individuals can usually count on the government to protect these rights. However, within the boundaries of the firm, there might also occur situations where these rights, especially the freedom of speech, might face certain restrictions. This is the case with regard to, for example, speaking about 'confidential' matters regarding to the firm's R&D, marketing, or accounting plans that might be of interest for competitors, shareholders, or other stakeholders. In almost all cases, this restriction of the freedom of speech is unproblematic since most rational employees would find it in their own best interest to comply with company policy, and there is little reason to suggest that most corporate decisions need to be made public.

However, there are some cases where such restrictions could be regarded as a restriction of employee's rights. Imagine, for example, that a manager asks you to take part in activities that are of contestable moral status, such as some 'creative accounting' for the organization. The problem for you is that you cannot ask third parties outside of the organization for help in this situation without risking serious embarrassment, disruption, and even possibly financial harm to your company. As we said in Chapter 4, if employees decide to inform third parties about alleged malpractice within the firm, this behaviour is normally called 'whistleblowing' (see Personal integrity, pp. 150–155). The main problem for employees with whistleblowing is the fact that it involves a considerable risk for them. As they violate the confidentiality that would normally be part of their duty of loyalty towards the firm, they put their job and thus their economic security at risk. This risk can be very high, and even if the allegations are true, the individual worker might find themselves in a critical situation until any whistleblowing activity is finally vindicated. Various regulatory efforts have been undertaken in a number of countries to secure the whistleblower's position, at least when there are issues of public interest at stake. These include efforts of self-regulation where companies work out a code of practice for whistleblowing, up to formal regulation such as the UK's Public Interest Disclosure at Work Act 1998.

The right to work

Established in the Declaration of Human Rights and more recently in the European Charter of Human Rights, the right to work has been codified as a fundamental entitlement of human beings. As such, the right to work is derived from other basic human rights (De George 1999: 359–65), namely: it is linked to the *right to life*, since work normally provides the basis for subsistence; and it reflects the *right to human respect*, as the ability to create goods and services by working represents a major source for self-respect for human beings.

In the context of modern economies, however, there has been considerable debate whether a right to work automatically translates into a right to employment (van Gerwen 1994). On a macroeconomic level, one might argue that governments have the responsibility to create economic conditions that protect the right of every citizen to work. Nevertheless, as demonstrated by the efforts of the Obama administration and other governments in the course of 2009 to protect banks and car companies, governments in most capitalist economies will only be able to *directly* provide this right in the public sector, whereas most jobs are provided in the private sector where the government has, at best, an *indirect* influence on the realization of the right. So does this mean that individuals have a right to demand employment from corporations, since they are the ones who directly provide jobs?

The answer from an ethical perspective would be to ask if this right of the employee collides with the rights of the employer, and most notably the shareholders of the company. Employing and paying people a salary is only possible if the company is able to sell a reasonable amount of goods and services. If this condition is not fulfilled, a one-sided focus on the right to work would clearly violate the right to own property, and the right to free engagement in markets. Therefore, the right to work in a business context cannot mean that every individual has a right to be employed.

Is the right to work completely irrelevant? Certainly not; but rather than granting everybody employment, the right to work should result in the claim that every individual should be able to expect the same equal conditions in exerting this right. Consequently, the right to work mainly results in equal and fair conditions in hiring and firing.

Relevant duties of employees in a business context

So far in this chapter we have focused exclusively on employee rights. However, these rights also need to be considered in the context of a set of duties that are expected of employees (van Gerwen 1994). You might wonder therefore why we have given so much attention to employees' rights here. However, in the context of business ethics, the main focus has to be on the rights of employees, as these are more endangered than the rights of employers, primarily because employees are more dependent on the employer and face a greater risk of sacrificing or bargaining away their rights in order to secure or keep a job. Consequently, even when talking about employee duties, our main focus will be the consequences of those duties for employers.

The most important duties of employees include the duty to comply with the labour contract and the duty to respect the employer's property. Among these duties are the obligation to provide an acceptable level of performance, make appropriate use of working time and company resources, and to refrain from illegal activities such as fraud, theft, and embezzlement. As research in employee theft has shown, the propensity of employees to commit crimes is highly dependent on the organizational climate in the organization (Gross-Schaefer et al. 2000). This leads to an important question when discussing employees' duties: what is the employer's responsibility with regard to ensuring that employees live up to their duties? Normally these duties are codified in the employment contract and other legal frameworks. Ethically delicate issues arise when looking at how the employer will enforce these duties and monitor employee compliance. Is the employer allowed to check emails and phone calls? Should they be allowed to monitor which websites employees are accessing? What measures are allowed to control working time and work quality? Most of these kinds of issues ultimately touch on the employee's right to privacy, which we discussed earlier on in this chapter, but **Ethics in Action 7.2** illustrates the challenges of enforcing employee compliance with their duties in the context of social media, which represents a particularly difficult arena for monitoring and control.

There are some very specific areas where corporations are actually responsible for ensuring that their employees live up to a particular duty. This is particularly the case with the duty to comply with the law since this duty often asks for some 'help' from the side of the employer. In Ethics in Action 4.1 we discussed the example of the British 'rogue trader' Kweku Adoboli at UBS. Many people argued that it was his employer's responsibility to put effective mechanisms in place that would have prevented him from his speculative deals. Similar issues occur, for instance, in the area of bribery: winning a contract by bribes not only benefits the individual employee but ultimately the corporation as well. Consequently, corporations might, on one hand, provide a context that to some extent encourages behaviour that is of dubious legality, and on the other hand they might be expected to ensure that employees fulfil their legal obligations.

The most common tools for corporations to take up this responsibility are codes of conduct and employee training (Gordon and Miyake 2001; Somers 2001). In establishing such a code, corporations have to make sure that employees know about corporate policy with regard to the legal framework of their operations. However, such codes, and other forms of documenting and establishing policy, do not necessarily ensure that employees actually comply with their duties. From a corporate perspective though, the main point is often to document that they have done everything they can to prevent illegality. In practice, many of these codes of conduct are more symbolic 'red tape' than they are real substance, and have been shown to have had mixed results on the actual ethical and legal behaviour of employees (Higgs-Kleyn and Kapelianis 1999). For further discussion on such codes and their impact, you might want to review Chapter 5 (Setting standards of ethical behaviour: designing and implementing codes of ethics, pp. 190–199).

■ Employing people worldwide: the ethical challenges of globalization

Globalization of business practices has had a significant impact on the question of the ethical treatment of employees. The move towards international expansion, and global supply chains, has resulted in many companies operating subsidiaries or sourcing products from 'low-wage' countries in the developing world. While the simple explanation for this is obviously the lower costs associated with production in these countries, these 'favourable' conditions for companies are often accompanied by questionable working conditions for workers: low wages, high risks for health and safety, inhumane working conditions, just to name a few.

This, however, is part of a broader question about the universality of employee rights. Issues such as discrimination, fair treatment, acceptable working conditions, fair wages, and the necessity for freedom of speech are interpreted and made meaningful in different ways in different cultures. For example, a conception of racial, sexual, or religious discrimination in Iceland might be different from that in Italy, India, Israel, or Indonesia. Similarly, freedom of speech might be conceived differently in Mexico than in Myanmar. In the following, we will look at some of the underlying issues involved here, namely:

• National culture and moral values.

• The race to the bottom.

• Migrant labour and illegal immigration.

National culture and moral values

As we discussed in Chapter 4, there is a connection between national cultures and moral values across the globe. At that stage we introduced the Hofstede (1980, 1994) model with its five dimensions characterizing different cultural values: individualism/collectivism, power distance, masculinity/femininity, uncertainty avoidance, and long-term/short-term orientation. These dimensions implicitly focus on some of the key aspects underpinning the moral values than govern employer–employee relations. For example, consider the dimension of individualism/collectivism, which represents the degree to

VISIT THE
ONLINE
RESOURCE
CENTRE
for links to
useful sources
of further
information

ETHICS IN ACTION 7.2   http://www.ethicalcorp.com

Social media challenges: do employees tweet your values?

Sabrina Basran, 21 February 2012

Ethical CORPORATION

In recent years the attention of the business world has been drawn to the potential and pitfalls of social media. The benefits of social media for corporate communications are well known; less familiar is how to deal with the ethical challenges it can create for organizations.

Recent headlines demonstrate the risks involved, including: 'Cyber bullying more harmful'; 'Online monitoring of job candidates raises disturbing questions'; and 'Third of firms forced to discipline workers over social media tweets and updates'. Two ethical challenges that this (relatively) new technology creates arise firstly from its use as a marketing tool and secondly from employees' personal use of social media.

The speed and potential global reach of social media make it an effective medium through which companies market themselves and their products and services, but it can also heighten ethical risks. Whichever form marketing takes, companies and their employees have a duty to market responsibly. Employees using social media this way should be wary of misleading consumers with positive product reviews or endorsements. This can be avoided if employees declare that they are representing or have an interest in the company.

Values are values

Organizations can mitigate the ethical risks by encouraging employees to recognise that, just as with any other form of communication, they should apply the company's ethical values when using social media. Failure to do so can have serious consequences.

One example is the case of Nestlé in 2011when an employee who was managing content on the company's Facebook fan page posted offensive comments in response to negative remarks by the public. The employee's behaviour violated the company's business principle of integrity and their commitment to 'avoid any conduct that could damage or risk Nestlé or its reputation' and provoked a consumer backlash. By acting irresponsibly when using social media on behalf of the company, the employee undermined Nestlé's commitment to ethical practice and exposed it to an integrity risk.

Employees' personal use of social media can also create ethical challenges for business. It can be more problematic to identify and deal with dilemmas in this context than if an employee is acting irresponsibly whilst representing the company, as in the Nestlé case.

Cyber-bullying crisis?

Cyber-bullying of colleagues through a personal social media account provides an increasingly common example. Recent surveys cite one in ten UK workers believe that workplace cyber-bullying is a problem and a fifth of employers have had to discipline staff for posting nasty comments about a colleague online.

Such bullying behaviour poses a serious concern for employers, but it is questionable whether companies have any right to interfere with employees' personal activities. Just as it is difficult for companies to manage employees' behaviour outside the workplace, it is difficult to manage employees' personal use of social media.

Some companies reserve the right to monitor employees' social media profiles as a way of addressing this. Arguably, if employees' personal activities are having an impact on their colleagues and by extension, an impact on their employer, it is justifiable for the company to intervene. Yet monitoring employees' personal use of social media raises questions around individuals' right to privacy and freedom of expression.

Personal opinions

These ethical challenges arise because social media blurs the boundaries between personal and work life. When personal opinions expressed through social media refer to a company or its employees, it is unclear what control, if any, the company then has over comments communicated in this way and what action it can or should take. The situation is further complicated when not taking action conflicts with the company's values or business principles. For example, by not tackling workplace cyberbullying an employer is failing in its duty of care to employees.

This suggests a need for companies to develop guidance for employees on appropriate use of social media. A social media policy needs to be consistent with the company's code of ethics and will overlap with other policies around communication, use of company assets and confidentiality of information.

The policy should also set out the company's position on employees' personal use of social media, for example stating that employees are not judged for personal activities or opinions as long as they are within the law, not offensive to others or the company, and do not refer to the company or work life.

In 2012, a case of constructive dismissal was awarded against BG Group. John Flexman, a former HR manager at the company, was called to an internal disciplinary hearing for inappropriate social media use after posting his CV on LinkedIn and registering his interest in 'career opportunities'. BG Group contended Flexman's actions violated company policy on conflicts of interest. He was also alleged to have made negative remarks and disclosed confidential information about the company in his CV.

Policy clarity

This case demonstrates that guidance in itself is not sufficient for an organization to address the ethical challenges of social media. Guidance needs to be regularly reviewed and effectively communicated, more so than with other policy areas because of the rapid development of social media. Engaging in dialogue with employees can also help ensure the policy's content is fair and understood and acceptable to both parties.

Social media has created new opportunities and new challenges for companies. As this technology continues to develop, it is likely business will face additional concerns.

If an organization has clear ethical values, which are communicated well at all levels of the organization, it can be confident that it is future-proofing against further technological developments.

By being aware of the ethical challenges and knowing how to deal with these effectively, companies can continue to live up to their ethical values whilst using social media to its full advantage.

Sources

Ethical Corporation, Sabrina Basran, 21 February 2012, http://www.ethicalcorp.com. Reproduced with the kind permission of Ethical Corporation.

VISIT THE
ONLINE
RESOURCE
CENTRE
for a short
response to this
feature

? THINK THEORY

Think about the duties that employees have towards their firms. Should these extend to their use of social media outside of the office as well as when they are acting on behalf of their employers?

which people think of themselves as independent autonomous actors or acting for the good of the group. Individualist cultures will tend to regard it as more acceptable for each worker to be individually responsible to their employer, whereas collectivist cultures will tend to emphasize the necessity of association and collective participation. Similarly, in collectivist societies, a person's ability to work well with others and make collaborative decisions might be just as much prized as educational and professional qualifications. As Treviño and Nelson (2014) suggest, this might mean that in a collectivist culture the extent to which an applicant and their family are known, trusted, and liked by the employer will be considered an important qualification, whereas in individualist countries such 'nepotism' may be considered to be biased and discriminatory.

The point is that different cultures will view employee rights and responsibilities differently. This means that managers dealing with employees overseas, or even critics of business who look to business practices overseas, need to first understand the cultural basis of morality in that country. Of course, this then begs the question as to whether it is fair to treat people differently, and to what we in the developed world might regard as a 'lower' standard, just because they happen to live in Lagos and not in Lisbon. Do Vietnamese employees not have the same needs for health protection as workers in Venice? This raises the problem of relativism versus absolutism.

VISIT THE
ONLINE
RESOURCE
CENTRE
for a short
response to this
feature

? THINK THEORY

We have just looked at one of Hofstede's six dimensions and its implications for understanding employee–employer relations. Think about the other five dimensions, and set out how each may affect one's view of employee rights and duties. Go back to Chapter 4 (National and cultural characteristics, pp. 143–145) if you need to review Hofstede's theory.

Absolutism versus relativism

We first discussed the issue of absolutism versus relativism in Chapter 3. Absolutism, we suggested, represented the idea that if an ethical principle were to be considered valid, it had to be applicable anywhere. Relativism, by contrast, suggests that no one view of ethics can be said to be right since it must always be relative to the historical, social, and cultural context. We contended in Chapter 3 that both extremes of ethical absolutism and relativism do not give a sufficient answer to the different conditions evident in countries across the globe.

- *Relativists* would finish the argument quite easily by dismissing the necessity for moral judgement from the West about foreign cultural contexts. If Pakistani culture is permissive of a 14-hour working day, or harassment of women, who are we to judge by imposing our Western standards? Relativism ultimately would deny any ethical problem around exploitation and poor working conditions as long as such conditions comply with the standards of the respective country or culture.

- At the other end of the spectrum, *absolutists* would say that if our moral standards are right, they are right everywhere around the globe. Consequently, companies should respect employee rights equally, wherever it is that they are actually contracted to work.

Obviously, these two sides are never likely to reach a common solution. Therefore, if we are to find a practical way forward, we need to look at this a little differently, and a little more carefully. Far from having reached a consensus, the debate has nevertheless highlighted some yardsticks that might be useful for establishing guidelines for behaviour (Donaldson 1996).

The most general rule would be to start with *human rights* as a basic compass for providing direction (Frankental 2002). The Universal Declaration of Human Rights, ratified in 1948 through the UN, is the most widely accepted set of principles pertaining to the rights of others. If a certain practice violates human rights, there is fairly broad acceptance that it is ethically wrong and unacceptable.

Beyond considerations of human rights, ethical considerations circle around the fact that differences in the treatment of employees on a global scale are not necessarily ethically wrong *per se*, but depend on the relative *economic development* of the country in which the practice is taking place. The basic ethical question then is to ask whether the differences in wages and labour conditions are due to the stage of economic development of the developing country (Donaldson 1989: 101–6). For example, one could argue that today's Pakistan is at a stage of economic development similar to many European countries just after the end of World War II. Therefore it is ethically fair to have longer working hours in today's Pakistan since back in the 1950s and 1960s most European countries still had a 48-hour week.

The 'race to the bottom'

Apart from adapting or not adapting to *existing* employment standards in foreign cultures, Scherer and Smid (2000) among others argue that MNCs also play a role in *changing* standards in those countries. Globalization clearly enables corporations to have a fairly broad range of choice for the location of plants and offices. This has meant that when you pick up the phone in London and dial the customer service department of your bank, you could just as well be connected to an operative in Dublin or Delhi,

Manchester or Mumbai. Consequently, developing countries compete against each other to attract the foreign investment represented by such relocation decisions.

Many critics of globalization have contended that among the key factors in this competition for investment are the costs incurred by MNCs through environmental regulation, taxes, and tariffs, social welfare for employees, and health and safety regulations. As a result, large investors may well choose the country that offers the most 'preferable' conditions, which often means the lowest level of regulation and social provision for employees. This competition therefore can lead to a 'downward spiral' of protection, or what is often called a 'race to the bottom' in environmental and social standards (Rudra 2008). MNCs in particular have been accused of being the key actors in propelling this race (Spar and Yoffie 1999).

The logic here is straightforward and compelling, and there is some convincing evidence that countries do indeed compete on the basis of reduced labour market standards to attract foreign direct investment (Olney 2013). Not surprisingly, though, it has also been hotly contested, not least because of the political and ethical ramifications of such an argument. Those advocating unfettered free trade tend to see the 'race to the bottom' argument as not only fallacious, but opposed in principle to free trade and deregulated global markets. Moreover, as **Ethics Online 7** illustrates, the idea that companies can force or encourage countries to lower their protections of employee rights is increasingly challenged by the ample supply of information about the treatment of employees across the world that is being made available through online platforms. The more activists, consumers, and others who know about the reality of labour conditions overseas, the less prospect there is for companies to take advantage of them.

VISIT THE ONLINE RESOURCE CENTRE
for links to useful sources of further information

ETHICS ONLINE 7

Enabling activism around labour conditions in global supply chains

The potential of the internet to provide more transparency about working conditions in the developing world has been manifest for a while. It was really the factory collapse of the Rana Plaza building in Bangladesh in 2013 which took this feature to a new level: the pictures of clothes with Western brands in the rubble of the building, together with photos of the victims on Twitter, Facebook, or Instagram, made clear once and for all that what happens in Bangladesh no longer stays in Bangladesh.

Next to this general effect of the internet and social media on enhancing transparency of corporate behaviour in remote places there is a growing community of online activists who take advantage of the new technological opportunities to campaign for better labour conditions worldwide. Next to NGOs, such as Amnesty International or the Clean Clothes Campaign, who all have a web presence, there is a host of dedicated websites just focusing on labour and human rights in global supply chains. That said, many of the classic NGOs, such as the Fair Labor Association, now also provide detailed resources for local and global campaigners, such as tracking charts with a summary of past audits of suppliers all over the world. Others provide maps about past and ongoing strikes and in-depth legal advice on Chinese labour law (China Labour Bulletin). Some websites focus on specific constituencies, such as Labourstart, which does extensive reporting but also offers a broad selection of Tweets all around the subject, specifically as a resource for journalists. Buy Sweat Free focuses on government procurement and provides information, but also a reporting tool for governments who want to source their supplies responsibly.

While most websites are set up by NGOs and campaign groups focusing on single issues, some websites are backed by trade unions (e.g. China Labour Bulletin), and others are even supported by development agencies of Western governments (e.g. Open Development Cambodia).

But the use of those websites is by no means confined to developing countries. The current industrial action in the US relating to minimum wages for fast-food workers is to a large part co-ordinated and supported by Strikefastfood.org. The website serves as an information platform on industrial action across all states and, together with a Twitter handle and a Facebook page, it attempts to build and strengthen a community of workers engaged in the campaign for a minimum wage across the entire US.

There are a number of portals whose campaign and mobilization is exclusively online. Here it turns out that labour issues are part of multi-issue campaigns, such as Behind The Brands, which also looks at food quality and environmental issues. A particular section of this part of the movement focuses on serving as a platform where users can vote for awards.

These include positive awards, such as 'The Bobs', a website where annually the best online activism campaign in the world gets voted for by users (hosted by Deutsche Welle, the German, government-run, international broadcasting station). On the negative side, websites such as the Public Eye Award annually invite voting on the most irresponsible and egregious corporate practices.

Finally, the Rana Plaza disaster in Bangladesh 2013 not only exemplified the power of the web in communicating irresponsible corporate practices; the case also unfolds into showcasing the potential of online services in addressing some of these issues. Rana Plaza Arrangement is a website where victims of the disaster can register their claims for compensation. It was set up as a multi-sector partnership including local government and industry, NGOs, trade unions, and three global brands involved in the disaster: the Spanish department store chain El Corte Inglés, the Canadian supermarket chain Loblaw, and the Irish clothes retailer Primark. This type of website demonstrates that the strength and leverage of online communication not only lies in providing information about otherwise easy to cover up practices; it also showcases that the internet provides access to otherwise marginalized and neglected communities in the context of labour conditions in global supply chains.

Sources

Websites focused on:

- Information (developing country focus)
  http://www.clb.org.hk/en/.
  http://www.globallabourrights.org.
  http://www.labourstart.org.
  http://www.opendevelopmentcambodia.net.
  https://chinastrikes.crowdmap.com.
  http://www.laborrights.org
  http://buysweatfree.org/faq.
  http://www.antislavery.org/english/campaigns/free_campaigns_resources.aspx.
  http://www.fairlabor.org/transparency/tracking-charts.
- Information (developed country focus, e.g. US)
  http://strikefastfood.org.
  http://www.uniondemocracy.org/.
- Naming and shaming campaigns
  https://thebobs.com/english/.
  http://www.behindthebrands.org/en.
  https://www.facebook.com/nationalconsumersleague/app_208195102528120.
  http://publiceye.ch.
- Victim compensation
  http://www.ranaplaza-arrangement.org.

This debate also leads to a broader potential responsibility for MNCs in the context of globalization. Rather than being concerned with ethical standards solely within the premises of their own company, MNCs, as perhaps the most powerful actors in such countries, are also in a position to assume a key role in building up so-called 'background institutions' (Spar and Yoffie 1999; Scherer and Smid 2000). This includes institutions such as trade unions, health and safety standards, and various other rules, regulations, and standards that help to protect workers' rights. Nien-hê Hsieh (2009), for instance, contends that MNEs have a duty to avoid causing harm and that this carries with it a responsibility to promote minimally just social and political institutions in countries in which they operate should such institutions be lacking.

Migrant labour and illegal immigration

A more recent phenomenon of globalization has been the growing mobility of workers globally (Wickramasekara 2008; Binford 2009). This can typically occur in the form of South-to-North immigration, such as the influx of immigrants from Latin America to the US or from Africa into the European Union. But it also occurs in many other regions globally, such as in Southern Africa or the United Arab Emirates, the latter drawing a large workforce from Pakistan, India, and Bangladesh. Migrant labour can also be a phenomenon attracted by certain industries, such as the mining industry which often operates in geographic locations where there is no immediate workforce to recruit (Jeschke 2007).

Ethical issues around this phenomenon are manifold. To start with, migrant labour often puts corporations in a position to provide a host of social infrastructure, such as housing, transport, health care, or education, in place. As migrant workers often come from poor countries, they are frequently willing to accept working conditions and salary levels that would normally be considered unacceptable. A key issue, however, is that these workers often enter countries illegally. In many places it is against the law to employ migrant workers, however much businesses or even whole sectors may rely on such a pool of workers. All of these factors make migrant workers particularly vulnerable to exploitation and it is no surprise to learn that migrant labourers often end up in working conditions akin to modern-day slavery (Crane 2013b). **Case 7** at the end of this chapter explores some of these challenges around migrant labour in more detail.

The US-based clothing company American Apparel, which we discussed in Case 2 (pp. 80–84) has taken a particularly interesting approach to migrant labour. Having eschewed the more common approach of outsourcing its production and stitching to overseas contractors, the company focuses production in-house in its downtown Los Angeles facilities, where it makes extensive use of the city's pool of largely Hispanic migrant labour. Notably, the company offers its workforce generous working conditions, including decent wages, health care, subsidized lunches, English language classes, and employment security, that stand in stark contrast to conditions in most overseas contractors. Perhaps most unusual though is the company's active engagement in promoting progressive immigration reform in the US with its 'Legalize LA' campaign.[15]

■ The corporate citizen and employee relations

As we have discussed in some detail earlier in the chapter, ethical issues in employee relations are primarily framed in terms of a collection of rights. As such, these issues have a close relationship to the notion of corporate citizenship: corporations govern a great deal of the social and civil rights of citizens via the workplace. They need to protect privacy of information, provide humane working conditions, ensure fair wages, and allocate sufficient pensions and health benefits. Looking across the globe, however, we discover that the extent to which corporations take over this role, as well as the degree to which corporations are held accountable for the governance of these rights, varies considerably.

A first aspect here is how far different legal and governance systems in various countries push companies to respect the rights of their employees. As we have discussed in Chapter 6, there are some quite substantial differences between the various regional approaches to corporate governance. Arguably, the area where legal frameworks are strongest is continental Europe, often referred to as 'Rhenish Capitalism', following the French author Michel Albert (1991). This alludes to the fact that the heartland of this approach lies particularly in those countries bordering the River Rhine: France, Germany, the Netherlands, Switzerland, Austria, but in a broader sense also the Scandinavian countries and Italy, Spain, and Portugal. The main difference in the context of this chapter is that capitalism in continental Europe has tended to take into account the interests of employees to a greater degree than the Anglo-Saxon model (which includes the UK, the US, and to some degree Australia, Canada, and Ireland). This has given rise to a variety of legal, educational, and financial institutions that focus particularly on the rights of employees.

The key concept in this context is the idea of *co-determination*, which describes the relationship between labour (employees) and capital (shareholders) in Europe, namely that both parties have an equal say in governing the company (Ferner and Hyman 1998). In Germany and France, in particular, this has resulted in a very strong legal position for workers, works councils, and trade unions. So, for instance, in German companies in the metal industry, half of the supervisory board consists of employee representatives, and the executive board member for personnel has to be appointed by the workers directly. Consequently, the employees and their rights tend to be far better protected than in the Anglo-American model, where shareholders are regarded as the most important group.

Beyond the developed world context, it is fair to argue that generally the level of regulation (or at least enforcement of regulation) protecting employees is rather low in developing countries. Hence, many of the issues discussed here fall into the realm of voluntary 'good citizenship' from corporations which, as we discussed in Chapter 2, often assigns to companies a role in respecting, protecting, and implementing basic human rights in the workplace. That said, however, we see that in many emerging economies, governments have, over time, tended to strengthen the protection and implementation of employees' legal rights. A prime example here is perhaps China, which for a long time has made headlines for the fairly poor labour standards prevailing in much of its industrial system. In 2008, though, the Chinese government implemented a new Labour Contract Law which represented a sea change in its approach to these issues by better protecting workers rights, for instance by committing all employers to providing employment contracts (Wang et al. 2009). While there are still clear possibilities for circumventing such regulation, it has been seen to have had a significant impact on worker protection—albeit by also increasing costs for firms (Adams 2008). A revision of the law implemented in 2013 looked to close some of the remaining loopholes by preventing abuse of temporary agency workers who had been recruited in droves by Chinese companies as a means to avoid costly labour benefits.[16]

Managing international human rights

These regional differences and shifts in legal protections over time make it difficult for corporations to determine the scope of their responsibilities for protecting employee rights, especially in relation to the government responsibility for doing so. We discussed the notion and relevance of human rights for business ethics back in Chapter 3; one of the most concrete manifestations of how embedded in business strategy human rights are becoming is the work by the UN and its former special representative on business and human rights, John Ruggie. Following extensive consultation and research, Ruggie (2008) developed a framework for understanding business responsibilities in the area of human rights. This framework of 'protect, respect and remedy' offers an important starting point for delineating corporate and governmental responsibilities in this controversial area:

- **Protect**. Under international law, states have a duty to protect against human rights abuses by non-state actors, such as corporations. This might be when such abuses have affected people within the state's jurisdiction or, in some circumstances, when the corporation is within the jurisdiction of the state even if the abuse happens overseas (for example in the case of the Swedish government protecting against abuse by a Swedish company in another country).

- **Respect**. Corporations have a responsibility to respect human rights in that they are expected to obey laws on human rights even if these are not enforced, and should respect the relevant international principles of human rights even if national law is absent. Firms are therefore required to undertake due diligence in identifying areas where there are potential threats to human rights and managing these risks accordingly with tools such as impact assessments and performance tracking.

- **Remedy**. Finally, given that disputes over human rights impacts are inevitable, firms and governments need to put in place formal grievance procedures and systems for investigation and punishment of abuses.

The three principles were adopted by the United Nations Human Rights Council in 2011[17] (since then called the 'UN Guiding Principles on Business and Human Rights', UNGP) and have been picked up subsequently by the governments of more than 30 countries, from Canada to Germany to Qatar, as a policy template for responsible business behaviour.[18] For companies exposed to human rights challenges the framework offers some important clarifications about the different responsibilities of business and government for protecting employees' (and other stakeholders') rights. Much work still needs to be done, but the UNGP have become a standard reference point for firms seeking to tackle human rights issues across their span of operations (Balch 2013).

☑ **Skill check**

Managing human rights. This is a key skill for managers in situations where governments do not adequately protect human rights and corporations have to manage their risks of violating various rights.

■ Towards sustainable employment

In this chapter we have talked a great deal about respecting and guaranteeing employee rights in the workplace. On the one hand this inevitably suggests certain tensions when we think in terms of sustainability. Sometimes protection of wages and conditions for workers may have to be sacrificed to encourage sustainable economic development and maintain employment. Expansion of environmentally damaging industries such as the airline industry can often be seen to be good for job creation. Looking at it this way: there usually have to be some sacrifices or trade-offs between protecting employees and promoting various aspects of sustainability.

On the other hand it is also possible to discern certain links with the intention to protect employee rights and the notion of sustainability. Only if we are gainfully employed in useful work, and feel respected as human beings, are we actively contributing to long-term sustainability in the *economic* sense. A workplace that puts us under stress, or where we are treated unfairly will have long-term effects on our lifestyle, health, and well-being. This aspect is closely linked to the *social* dimension of sustainability: organizations should treat the community of workers in a way that stabilizes social relationships and supports employees to maintain meaningful social relationships with their families, neighbours, and friends. Sustainability, finally, is also an issue here in the *ecological* sense. The modern corporation has in many ways created workplaces that are ecologically unsustainable. Employing fewer and fewer people in a highly mechanized and energy-intensive technological environment, while at the same time making no use at all of something like 10–15% of the potential workforce, could be seen as a major waste of material and energy.

In this section we shall look at three main ways in which these problems and tensions have been addressed, both in theory and in practice:

- Re-humanized workplaces.
- Wider employment.
- Green jobs.

Re-humanized workplaces

The 'alienation' of the individual worker in the era of industrialized mass production has been discussed at least since the time of Karl Marx. The suggestion is that the impact of technology, rationalized work processes, and the division of labour has meant that many employees simply repeat the same monotonous and stupefying actions over and over again, resulting in there being little real meaning, satisfaction, or involvement in their work (Braverman 1974; Schumacher 1974). Whether in factories, fast-food restaurants, or call centres, much employment has been reduced to a series of meaningless 'McJobs' subject to intense management control, and with little chance of real engagement or job satisfaction. Even a shift towards more 'white collar' work in offices can be argued to have created a legion of cubicle dwellers, tirelessly tapping away at computers rather than enjoying active, creative, meaningful work (Cederström and Fleming 2012).

Therefore, although our 'rational' ways of organizing work can, and have, brought us tremendous efficiencies and material wealth, they have also created the prospect of a dehumanized and de-skilled workplace. The relationship between technology and the quality of working life is, however, actually a complex one (Connell et al. 2014). The impacts on the workplace are at the very least contingent on a variety of factors, including work organization, managerial motivation, and employee involvement (Wallace 1989). The point is that meaningful work is clearly not available to all, representing another form of injustice that we need to be aware of, beyond simple distribution of benefits (Sayer 2009).

There have been numerous attempts over the years to re-humanize the workplace in some way, for example by 'empowering' the employee (Lee and Koh 2001). This might include 'job enlargement' (giving employees a wider range of tasks to do) and 'job enrichment' (giving employees a larger scope for deciding how to organize their work). Many of these ideas attempt a completely different pattern of production. Rather than huge assembly lines, the idea is to create smaller-scale units where workers can be engaged in more creative and meaningful work, utilizing 'human-centred' technology (Schumacher 1974). Some car manufacturers (most notably the Swedish firms Saab and Volvo) have experimented with replacing the production line with small, partly autonomous, team-based working groups. Again, though, the success of such schemes has been contested, suggesting that the 'humanized' approach might be more appropriate and effective in some cultures (e.g. Scandinavia) than others (Sandberg 1995). More recently, the idea of 'greening the workplace' has prompted firms to consider a range of initiatives intended to promote human health and sustainability at work. This includes resource and waste reduction programmes, as well as incentives for using bicycles and public transportation, use of non-toxic cleaners, and providing healthy, locally produced, or organic food in staff canteens.[19]

Wider employment

The mechanization of work has led to the situation where a large proportion of unemployed people has become a normality in many countries, threatening not only the right to work, but the social fabric of communities. It has been argued that efforts by politicians to change job markets or reinvigorate their economies will only ever partly solve the problem, since the increasing level of mechanization and computerization of working processes has meant that we simply do not require as many workers to provide the population with its needs (Gorz 1975). Authors such as Jeremy Rifkin (1995) have even gone so far as to suggest that new technologies herald the 'end of work'.

From a sustainability perspective, the problem is essentially one of ensuring that meaningful work is available to all. Modern employment patterns have tended to create a cleavage between those who have the highly skilled jobs that require long hours of work for high returns, and those who are reduced to unemployment or at best a succession of low-skilled, poorly paid, temporary jobs. In recent years, there have been a number of interesting efforts to tackle this problem of creating a society of 'haves' and 'have-nots'. One attempt from the French government was the introduction of a 35-hour week. By legally reducing the working time for the individual, the idea was that organizations would be forced to employ more people to maintain the same level of output. Attractive as the idea may have been to some, it nevertheless had an ambiguous effect. For certain industries, the number of workers employed clearly rose, while in others the relative increase in the cost of labour prompted a tendency to replace labour with technology (Milner 2002).

This debate got a new boost with the concept of the '21-hour week' developed by the UK-based think tank, the New Economics Foundation (NEF 2010). It proposes a radical new approach to distributing work in society and suggests a model where everyone works just 21 hours a week. The core argument is that such a reduction of the core working time would not just distribute work more equally; most importantly, it would free up people's life to pursue other currently neglected tasks, such as preparing more of one's own food, caring for children and the elderly, more time for civic engagement, to name just a few examples. Far from a utopian ideal, the report also provides a number of examples where this approach has already gained traction: for instance, the state government of Utah in the US in 2008 introduced the four-day week for its employees. The benefits were not only a boost in productivity and job satisfaction; it also resulted in a 20% reduction of gasoline consumption and greenhouse gas release through cutting commuting.

Green jobs

In the context of the economic downturn of the late 2000s and the debate on how to restructure the economy in a more sustainable fashion, many politicians and business leaders focused on the idea of creating more 'green jobs' (Gopal 2009). One aspect of these green jobs is of course that they are in industries producing environmentally friendly products (such as hybrid cars or solar panels) and services (such as recycling or car sharing). Another aspect of this movement towards green jobs is that the job itself, the workplace, the way labour is organized, become more environmentally sustainable (Forstater 2006; Gnuschke 2008).

Companies have taken a number of approaches to achieve the goal of a greener workplace. Incentivizing car pooling, introducing the paperless office, reducing business travel by using videoconferencing, increasing recycling, moving into low energy use office space are just some examples of the types of initiatives organizations have explored to green the workplace. Another widely advocated solution is home-based teleworking. Although as we discussed previously this can be used as an excuse for poorer working conditions, teleworking can also, for example, help those with families to carry out their jobs while at the same time being able to look after children and fulfil other important family roles (Sullivan and Lewis 2001). Apart from the *social* benefits for the employee that teleworking can potentially bring, there may also be *economic* benefits for the company and even *ecological* advantages too. For instance, rather than commuting into work and adding to road congestion and air pollution, teleworkers are likely to use far fewer resources by staying at home and communicating remotely.

? THINK THEORY

To what extent is the role of the company in providing a sustainable workplace an expression of the extended view of corporate citizenship? What are the specific areas where corporations are replacing traditional features of the welfare state here?

VISIT THE
ONLINE
RESOURCE
CENTRE
for a short
response to this
feature

■ Summary

In this chapter we have discussed the specific stake that employees hold in their organizations, and suggested that although this stake is partially regulated by the employment contract, employees are also exposed to further moral hazards as a result of the employee–employer relationship. We have discussed how deep the involvement of corporations with employees' rights can be. Nearly the entire spectrum of human rights is touched upon by the modern corporation, including issues of discrimination, privacy, fair wages, working conditions, participation, association, due process, and freedom of speech.

The corporate responsibility for protection and facilitation of these rights is particularly complex and contestable in a global context since it involves dealing with employees whose expectations and protections for rights may differ considerably. Indeed, we explained that the governmental role in issuing legislation to protect employees' rights has to some extent retracted. With the removal of such certainties, corporations would appear to have gained a good deal more flexibility with respect to employee relations. This has its downside in that corporations are left with a far larger amount of discretion regarding the protection of employee rights, making ethical decision-making far more complex and challenging—and more ripe for abuse.

We also explained how corporations in different parts of the globe face different regulatory environments, making it sometimes easier, sometimes more difficult, to live up to ethical obligations towards employees. While some of the issues, such as human rights or the role of trade unions, are more long-standing, we also discussed recent challenges such as illegal immigration and migrant labour. We also explored how the corporate role in relation to employees quite often puts corporations in a position very similar to that occupied by governments in relation to their citizens. This role is also visible in our discussion of challenges emerging from the call for more sustainable workplaces. This aspect is sure to be of increasing ethical interest for firms and their employees in the future.

Study questions

1. What rights do employees have in a business context? To what extent are employee rights protected by:

   (a) The employment contract?

   (b) Legislation?

2. Do firms have an ethical obligation to increase diversity in the workplace? Provide arguments for and against, providing examples where relevant.

3. What is reverse discrimination? What are the main ethical arguments for and against reverse discrimination?

4. What are the four main types of privacy that employees might expect? Provide examples where each type of privacy might potentially be violated in a business context.

5. To what extent is it possible to accept that a Western multinational corporation will offer lower standards of wages and conditions in less-developed countries? What implications does your answer have for the proposition that when in Rome we should do as the Romans do?

6. What responsibility should employers have for ensuring that their employees maintain an appropriate work–life balance? Set out some practical steps that employers could take to improve work–life balance and ensure a sustainable workplace environment for employees.

Research exercise

The apparel industry has faced a range of criticisms over the years for its unethical labour practices. Choose a company that you have recently bought clothes from and conduct some research on its labour practices, past and present. You should start with the company's own website but also look further afield such as at NGO websites, media reports and elsewhere.

1. What ethical issues or problems has the firm faced with respect to employees? Are there specific employee rights that appear to be most at risk of violation?

2. Explain why you think these issues have arisen. Be as specific as you can as to the likely causes.

3. How has the firm gone about dealing with these problems? Detail the specific practices as well as what you think its overall strategy to labour rights might be.

4. In which ways is the protection or violation of employee rights likely to impact upon the financial success of the firm?

5. How would you advise the company to go forward with its labour rights strategy?

Key readings

VISIT THE ONLINE RESOURCE CENTRE for links to further key readings

1. Ruggie, J. 2008. Protect, respect and remedy: a framework for business and human rights. *Innovations* (Spring): 189–212.

   This publicly available paper from the UN provides a helpful introduction to the problems of allocating responsibilities between business and government in the area of human rights. It offers a clear description of the increasingly influential 'protect, respect and remedy' framework that has been developed by Ruggie and promoted by the UN.

2. West, J.P., and Bowman, J.S. 2015. Electronic surveillance at work: an ethical analysis. *Administration & Society*, forthcoming. doi: 10.1177/0095399714556502.

   This article explores the changes in employee privacy resulting from the rise of electronic technologies in the workplace. It lays out the main issues and provides an ethical evaluation of both the arguments in favour of surveillance as well as their drawbacks. The article also provides some useful recommendation for practice and for future research into the issue.

VISIT THE
ONLINE
RESOURCE
CENTRE
for links to
useful sources
of further
information on
this case

Case 7

The expendables: migrant labour in the global workforce

This case discusses the ethical challenges involved in employing migrant labour across a number of regional contexts. It provides an insight into the vulnerabilities of migrant workers, and the poor working conditions that they often encounter, sometimes giving rise to slave-like conditions. The case provides an opportunity to examine the issues of employee rights discussed in Chapter 7, as well as offering a deeper look at the conditions giving rise to violations of these rights.

Millions of workers across the world migrate to new countries, regions or cities in order to make a better life for themselves and their families. Whether it is Polish workers moving to the UK, Mexicans to the US, or Indians to Bahrain, migrants have become a major part of the global economy. However, migrant workers are also typically the most vulnerable members of the modern workforce. They are far from home, often with limited language skills, scant financial resources, poor support, and sometimes questionable legal status. As a result, migrant workers are at a particularly high risk of encountering poor working conditions, exploitation, and human rights violations of various kinds. In addition, they typically face discrimination and have few resources available to bargain for better conditions or to ensure the protection of their rights. For their employers, these conditions may make migrant workers an attractive, low-cost labour force, but it also injects considerable ethical risks into the global economy that are difficult to manage.

Migrant workers in Europe

With its colonial ties to much of the developing world and its close proximity to Central and Eastern Europe and Africa, Western Europe has long been a major destination for migrant workers. The expansion of the European Union since 2004 to include Central and Eastern European countries gave rise to significant movements of people across the continent looking for better opportunities. For example, in 2001 there were approximately 60,000 Poles living in the UK, but following Poland's accession to the EU in 2004, that number had risen tenfold to almost 600,000 by 2011. In total, the UK experienced a net migration of some 2.5 million people during the first decade of the 2000s. More broadly, between 3.5 million and 4 million people migrated to and between the EU member states every year during the same time period. Some 10% of the European population who had migrated there were born outside the EU.

The vast majority of migrant workers in Europe are fully documented and legal, although depending on their countries of origin and destination they may experience some restrictions on their access to particular forms of employment and welfare support. For example, people from more recent EU accession countries, Bulgaria and Romania, experienced strict rules on the kind of jobs they could take and the benefits they could claim in a number of EU states from the time that their countries joined the EU in 2007 until 2014 when the restrictions were lifted. A similar arrangement was put in place in a number of destination countries when Croatia joined the EU in 2013.

Europe has also been a common destination for illegal immigrants, although the numbers entering the EU illegally have been far smaller than those migrating legally. Typically, there might be tens of thousands illegal arrivals per year into the continent, most commonly arriving from North Africa into the Central Mediterranean. A peak influx of around 140,000 was recorded in 2011 following conflict during the Arab Spring, and a further spike followed the Syrian civil war in the mid-2010s.

In the face of such growth in all kinds of migration across Europe, it has become a hot political issue in most Western European and Scandinavian countries, giving rise to a steep increase in popularity of anti-immigrant political parties and policies. As such, the plight of migrant workers in Europe is quite challenging. Overall, they fare considerably worse than their native-born counterparts in the workplace. According to official EC statistics, first-generation migrants experience considerably lower levels of labour market participation, higher levels of unemployment, and a higher rate of over-qualification (i.e. being skilled or educated beyond what is necessary to do the job) compared with native borns. However, far worse conditions are typically experienced by those living or working illegally in the EU or those with strict limitations on the jobs open to them. For instance, it was estimated that in 2012 there were 880,000 people in forced labour in the European Union, the majority being EU citizens who had migrated from one member state to another. Domestic work, agriculture, manufacturing, and construction have been identified as the industries most likely to experience forced labour among migrants in Europe.

The exploitation of migrant workers in the EU is often connected to the way in which they enter the country, irrespective of whether they enter legally or illegally. Recruitment agents and middlemen operating in the workers' countries of origin may use various forms of deception or coercion to recruit workers with the promise of sometimes non-existent jobs in their destination country. Workers often borrow large amounts of money to pay recruiters for arranging transport and travel documents and a fee for securing a job in the expectation of future returns. However, if the job they finally receive upon arrival does not enable them to repay the loan, let alone to further support their family and community at home, they sometimes become trapped by huge debts and have insufficient funds to return home. These debts may be further exacerbated through inflated charges for basic accommodation and food, which are in turn deducted from their salary. In extreme cases this can land migrant workers in debt bondage to their employer or recruiter.

Consider, for example, the case of Noble Foods, one of the UK's largest suppliers of premium and free-range eggs to high street retailers including McDonald's, Sainsbury's, and Marks and Spencer. In 2012, it was revealed that 30 Lithuanian workers employed by a temporary labour provider to work at farms contracted to Noble Foods 'were subjected to slave-like conditions and controlled through the use of violence'. Despite being able to work legally in the EU, the labour provider was found to have charged the workers excessive recruitment fees, deducted £40 a week from workers' wages to live in a damp house infested with bedbugs and fleas, charged workers high amounts for transportation from worksite to worksite, and sometimes stopped paying them entirely, forcing workers into a situation of debt bondage. The workers also described being kept under control by enforcers using physical and verbal abuse, including being beaten, punched, given black eyes and broken ribs, and then beaten again if they complained. An investigation from the government agency responsible for licensing the recruitment firm found that 'workers suffered exploitation so extreme that [we] had to order the firm to stop supplying workers to farms and food factories immediately' and called the case 'one of the worse cases of exploitation [we have] ever uncovered in the food supply chain.'

Migrant workers in the Middle East

Although Europe has seen a surge in migrant workers since the turn of the century, in other parts of the world migrants make up a much larger proportion of the workforce. Nowhere is this more evident than in the Middle East, and the Persian Gulf in particular. Taken together, the Gulf states of Bahrain, Kuwait, Qatar, Saudi Arabia, and the UAE are the largest recipients of temporary migrant workers in the world, constituting almost 43% of their population in 2010. In some Gulf states, such as Qatar and the UAE, more than 80% of the population consists of non-nationals, the majority of whom are contract workers.

Most of the foreign workers in the Middle East are Asian—the major countries of origin being Bangladesh, India, Indonesia, Pakistan, Philippines, and Sri Lanka. Two-thirds of migrant workers are men, the majority of whom are engaged in low-skill occupations in production, construction, and service sectors. Women, meanwhile, have typically been employed in domestic service.

Abuses of foreign workers in the Middle East have been documented for many years, but the issue made international headlines in the mid-2010s following reports of hundreds of foreign worker deaths and reputed conditions of 'modern-day slavery' in the construction boom generated when Qatar was awarded the right to host the 2022 FIFA World Cup. Over a two-year period almost a thousand construction workers from India and Nepal were recorded as having died, with Nepalese workers dying at the rate of one a day in the summer of 2013 because of extreme temperatures, enforced 12-hour working days, and limited access to water. Evidence emerged of workers routinely having their documents confiscated, pay being withheld for months, inadequate safety standards, and squalid labour camps with overflowing sewage and inadequate running water. Conditions were so bad, according to the International Trade Union Confederation (ITUC), that the Qatar World Cup construction would 'leave 4,000 migrant workers dead' before the tournament kicked off in 2022.

Migrant workers are critical for the Qatar economy but have long been plagued by limited rights and freedoms. There are 1.4 million migrant workers in Qatar, representing 94% of the country's entire labour force and approximately 85% of the population. However, the average migrant worker makes about $300 a month, compared to the average national salary of $2,140 a month and gross national income per capita of $80,000. So, while revenues from oil and natural gas have enabled Qatar to attain the highest GDP per capita in the world, the majority of its foreign workforce continues to experience low salaries and poor working conditions.

The plight of migrant workers in Qatar is exacerbated by the state-run 'kafala' sponsorship system, which also operates is Saudi Arabia and a number of other Gulf states. Under the kafala system, workers must have an in-country sponsor (typically their employer) who is responsible for their legal status. Workers are therefore unable to change jobs or leave the country without their sponsor's permission, making them highly dependent on their employer, and giving them limited means of seeking redress when faced with exploitation.Moreover, certain categories of workers in Qatar are excluded from labour law protections and only Qatari workers are allowed to form or join trade unions.

Following revelations of systematic abuse of migrant workers in the construction industry in Qatar, organizations such as Amnesty International, the ILO, the ITUC, and the UN all called for Qatar to repeal or revise its labour laws in order to provide better protections for foreign workers. Companies involved in the construction sector were also urged to take action and institute more effective due diligence policies and procedures to prevent labour exploitation, including among subcontractors and suppliers where much of the abuse was found to occur. Following a severe ruling by the ILO, the ITUC stated that companies were 'on notice that doing business with Qatar goes against international laws. Until Qatar brings its laws in line with international norms, companies face the reputational and legal risks of using forced labour in Qatar.'

In the face of such major international pressure, the Qatari authorities finally announced substantial reforms to their labour laws in 2014. This included a strengthening of laws related to recruitment agency fees, mandatory requirements for firms to pay workers by electronic bank transfer rather than arbitrary cash payments, an end to foreign workers needing their employer's permission to leave the country or change jobs, and a commitment to phase out the kafala system. However, critics remained unconvinced, arguing that the plans included few specifics or a timeline for change. According to Amnesty International, it was a 'missed opportunity' that fell 'far short of the fundamental changes needed to address systemic abuses against migrant workers'.

Migrant workers in China

Migrant workers are not always intent on crossing national boundaries. China, for example, is home to more than 250 million domestic migrant workers who have been drawn from rural areas to cities in search of higher incomes and an escape from poverty. By 2014, the rural migrant worker population represented about a third of the total workforce.

Chinese rural migrant workers have been crucial to China's economic growth, fuelling the supply of low-cost labour for the country's booming export economy. Internal migrants are typically young, poorly educated, generally healthy, and highly mobile. Short-term employment sectors, including manufacturing, construction, and social services industries, account for over 60% of such migrants.

As with cross-border migrants in Europe and the Middle East, domestic migrants in China also face major inequalities. Local urban workers tend to predominate in the primary labour market (which offers high salaries, stable employment and good working conditions), while rural migrants have mainly been employed in the secondary labour market (characterised by lower salaries, insecure employment and poor conditions of work). Rural migrants are particularly disadvantaged by the hukou system—rules that keep rural residents from obtaining jobs in the formal sector, and that prevent them from obtaining many of the same services as urban residents, including health and unemployment insurance, pensions, free education for children, and subsidized housing. This has not only led to continued income disparity between urban and rural populations, but also to the mistreatment of migrants. Discrimination or harassment from employers and co-workers is common.

A further problem with migrant workers in China concerns the fate of their families. Studies have reported that there are more than 60 million 'left-behind children' who parents have been forced to abandon in the home village when moving to the city. These children face a number of challenges and often struggle with emotional and developmental problems. On the other hand, the 30 million children who have been able to migrate with their parents have faced their own problems, mainly due to the lack of time and financial means on the part of their parents to provide a decent upbringing.

The plight of migrant workers in China was brought into sharp relief in the West by a spate of worker suicides at Foxconn plants in Southern China in 2010 where products for Apple, Hewlett Packard, and other technology brands are produced. China also experienced a surge in labour protests by migrant workers seeking better pay and conditions, threatening the Chinese authorities' vision of a harmonious society.

Such problems have not gone unnoticed. While companies have sought to address poor labour conditions and discrimination with codes of conduct and supplier training, the Chinese government has instituted various labour market reforms, including attempts to reform the hukou system. To date, these have met with some success, but deeper change has been difficult to achieve due to the complex nature of the current system and problems with enforcement given the entrenched nature of rural discrimination in the country.

Questions

1. What are migrant workers and what role do they play in the global economy?

2. Should migrant workers have the same employment rights as native-born workers? To what extent do you think they actually experience equality of rights in Europe, the Middle East, and China?

3. What are the main causes of vulnerability among migrant workers that give rise to exploitation in the workplace? Can you account for any similarities or differences across different regions?

4. What role should (a) governments, and (b) companies take in protecting migrant workers from exploitation? Do you have any suggestions as to how the two can work together to address such problems?

5. What long-term strategies do you suggest for companies looking to deal with the exploitation of migrant workers in their supply chains?

Sources

Amnesty International 2013. The Dark Side of Migration. Spotlight on Qatar's construction sector ahead of the World Cup. November 2013: http://www.europarl.europa.eu/document/activities/cont/201402/20140206ATT78948/20140206ATT78948EN.pdf.

Center for Child Rights and Corporate Social Responsibility 2013. They are also parents. A study on migrant workers with left-behind children in China. CCR CSR, August 2013: http://resourcecentre.savethechildren.se/sites/default/files/documents/they_are_also_parents_-_a_study_on_migrant_workers_in_china_ccr_csr_english.pdf.

Council on Foreign Relations 2009. China's Internal Migrants. 14 May 2009: http://www.cfr.org/china/chinas-internal-migrants/p12943.

Eurostat 2011. Migrants in Europe, A statistical portrait of the first and second generation. Eurostat. http://ec.europa.eu/dgs/home-affairs/what-we-do/policies/pdf/migrants_in_europe_eurostat_2011_en.pdf.

Gibson, C. 2014. Qatar promises to reform labour laws after outcry over 'World Cup slaves'. *Guardian*, 14 May 2014: http://www.theguardian.com/world/2014/may/14/qatar-admits-deaths-in-migrant-workers.

GLA 2012. Gangmasters Licensing Authority Annual Reports and Accounts, 1 April 2011 to 31 March 2012. Available online: http://www.official-documents.gov.uk/document/hc1213/hc01/0165/0165.pdf.

ILO 2012. ILO 2012 Global Estimate of Forced Labor, http://www.ilo.org/wcmsp5/groups/public/---ed_norm/---declaration/documents/publication/wcms_181921.pdf.

ITUC 2011. Trade unions and NGOs joining forces to combat forced labour and trafficking in Europe. ITUC, February 2011: http://www.ituc-csi.org/IMG/pdf/Forced_labour_EN_FINAL.pdf.

ITUC 2014. New ruling from UN on forced labour is a warning to companies doing business with Qatar. ITUC, 31 March 2014: < http://www.ituc-csi.org/new-ruling-from-un-on-forced>.

Lawrence, F. 2012. Workers who collected freedom food chickens 'were trafficked and beaten'. *Guardian*, 29 October 2012: www.theguardian.com/law/2012/oct/29/workers-chickens-allegedly-trafficked-beaten.

Migration Policy Institute 2013. Labor Migration in the United Arab Emirates: Challenges and Responses. 18 September 2013: http://www.migrationpolicy.org/article/labor-migration-united-arab-emirates-challenges-and-responses.

National Bureau of Statistics of China 2014. Statistical Communiqué of the People's Republic of China on the 2013 National Economic and Social Development. 24 February 2014: http://www.stats.gov.cn/english/PressRelease/201402/t20140224_515103.html.

Pattisson, P. 2013. Revealed: Qatar's World Cup 'slaves'. *Guardian*, 25 September 2013: http://www.theguardian.com/world/2013/sep/25/revealed-qatars-world-cup-slaves.

Notes

1. For more details on the UN Declaration of Human Rights, see http://www.un.org.
2. Full details on these codes (or protocols, as the ILO calls them) can be found at http://www.ilo.org.
3. The word 'discrimination' in the proper sense just means 'to make distinctions'. However, in the context of employment issues, people nearly always talk of 'discrimination' when in fact they mean 'unfair' or 'unjust discrimination'. For simplicity reasons, we use the term in this normative sense as well.
4. http://www.catalyst.org/knowledge/women-boards.
5. Business Legal Reports 2004. Morgan Stanley settles landmark discrimination case for $54m. http://compensation.blr.com/Compensation-news/Discrimination/Equal-Pay-Comparable-Worth/Morgan-Stanley-Settles-Landmark-Discrimination-Cas/#, 13 July 2004.
6. http://www.deloitte.com.
7. http://www.economist.com/blogs/economist-explains/2014/03/economist-explains-14.
8. http://www.theglobeandmail.com/report-on-business/international-business/us-business/centerplate-ceo-steps-down-after-dog-abuse-incident-in-vancouver/article20297029/
9. http://www.telegraph.co.uk/finance/newsbysector/retailandconsumer/leisure/9737387/Cathay-Pacific-crews-threaten-no-smile-strike.html.
10. Kalinowski, T. 2011. TTC approves random drug testing. *The Star*, 19 October 2011: http://www.thestar.com/news/city_hall/2011/10/19/ttc_approves_random_drug_testing.html. Kalinowski, T. 2015. TTC drug and alcohol testing program on hold. *The Star*, 26 March 2015: http://www.thestar.com/news/gta/transportation/2015/03/26/ttc-still-hasnt-implemented-random-drug-and-alcohol-testing.html. Canadian Human Rights Commission's Policy on Alcohol and Drug Testing, Revised October 2009: http://www.chrc-ccdp.gc.ca/sites/default/files/padt_pdda_eng_2.pdf.
11. http://www.cnbc.com/id/100975246.
12. http://www.bbc.com/news/business-27996448.
13. See 'For richer, for poorer'. *The Economist*, 13 October 2012: http://www.economist.com/node/21564414; and 'To each, not according to his needs'. *The Economist*, 15 December 2012: http://www.economist.com/news/finance-and-economics/21568423-new-survey-illuminates-extent-chinese-income-inequality-each-not.
14. http://dailysignal.com/2014/06/20/starbucks-ceo-minimum-wage-hike-right-thing-despite-traumatic-effects-small-business/.
15. http://www.americanapparel.net/contact/legalizela/.
16. http://www.clb.org.hk/en/content/china-curbs-its-enthusiasm-new-labour-contract-law.
17. http://business-humanrights.org/en/un-guiding-principles.
18. http://business-humanrights.org/en/un-guiding-principles/latest-news-on-ungps.
19. David Suzuki Foundation. 2009. 'David Sukuki at Work': http://www.davidsuzuki.org/publications/downloads/2009/dsaw_toolkit_web.pdf.

8

Consumers and Business Ethics

Having completed this chapter you should be able to:

- Explain the stake that consumers have in corporations.
- Describe the ethical issues and problems faced in business–consumer relations.
- Critically evaluate the impact of globalization on responsibilities towards consumers.
- Analyse the arguments for more responsible marketing practices.
- Explain the role of ethical consumption in effecting positive social change through corporations.
- Identify the challenges posed by sustainable consumption.

Key concepts and skills:

Concepts

- Consumer rights
- Consumer deception
- Consumer vulnerability
- Consumerism
- Ethical consumption
- Sustainable consumption
- Sharing economy

Skills

- Determining the ethical limits of marketing communication
- Analysing the ethics of pricing strategies
- Determining consumer vulnerability
- Applying the consumer sovereignty test

■ Introduction

Consumers are obviously one of the most important stakeholders for any organization, since without the support of customers of some sort, such as through the demand for or purchase of goods and services, most organizations would be unlikely to survive for very long. By consumers, though, we do not just mean the end consumers who ultimately buy finished products in the shops. All of the organizations that purchase or otherwise contract for the provision of goods and services from other organizations can be regarded as customers. A university, for example, is just as much a consumer as you are, in that it buys furniture, stationery, books, journals, cleaning services, and various other products and services in order to go about its business of providing teaching and research. It has also become increasingly common for people to refer to departments serviced in some way by other departments within the *same* organization as internal customers. Hence, whilst our main focus will be on private individual consumers such as you, we will also at times refer to the broader category that includes the whole chain of internal and external constituencies that receive goods or services through exchange.

Given the importance of consumer support for the ongoing success of an organization, it is no surprise that being ethical in dealing with consumers is generally regarded as one of the most crucial areas of business ethics. Moreover, since consumers are primarily outside the organization, ethical problems in this area are often some of the most visible and most difficult to hide of ethical violations. This can lead to potentially damaging public relations problems, media exposés, and other threats to the reputation of the corporation that might be more easily avoided in the context of employees, shareholders, and other stakeholders.

In this chapter we shall examine the challenges faced by corporations in dealing ethically with consumers in the global economy. The main corporate functions responsible for dealing with consumers are sales and marketing, and it is evident that these professions have long been subjected to a great deal of ethical criticism. Many writers on marketing ethics have highlighted the lack of public trust in the advertising, public relations, and sales professions (e.g. Laczniak and Murphy 1993; Assael 1995; Larsson 2007), and marketing has long been perceived as among the least ethical of business functions (Baumhart 1961; Tsalikis and Fritzsche 1989).

However, although ethics does not appear to have traditionally been a central concern of marketing professionals and academics, there is some evidence of moral considerations entering marketing thought for as long as marketing has existed as a distinct field in its own right (Desmond 1998). After all, it does not take someone with an MBA to work out that there are likely to be certain benefits in having customers that feel they have been treated honestly and ethically, rather than just feeling like they have been cynically ripped off. More recently, though, there has been a surge in interest from the public, practitioners, and academics alike regarding ethical marketing, ethical consumption, and the like. As we shall see, this has led to a fascinating yet still unresolved debate about the nature of ethical marketing, and in particular about the role of consumers in shaping the social impact of corporations through their purchase decisions. In order to address such questions, though, we first have to establish the nature and scope of the stakeholder role played by consumers.

■ Consumers as stakeholders

It is by now largely commonplace to hear the argument that businesses are best served by treating their customers well. Indeed, this is essentially one of the core tenets of business strategy—that organizations succeed by outperforming their competitors in providing superior value to their customers. Those companies that prosper in the marketplace are those that pay close and continuous attention to satisfying their customers. Indeed, in many ways, it is hard to argue against the logic of this argument. Of course, an organization will seek to satisfy its customers, for if it does not then those customers will defect to competitors, thus resulting in loss of sales, and ultimately, profitability.

However, one might also ask why, if the interests of producers and consumers are so closely aligned, the abuse of ethics relating to consumers continues to hit the headlines and the reputation of the marketing and sales professions remains so poor. For example, within the last decade, there have been numerous examples of firms being accused of treating their customers in a questionable manner:

- Multinational drug companies have been accused of exploiting the sick and poor by maintaining high prices for lifesaving pharmaceuticals and preventing the sale of cheaper generic drugs.

- Fast-food and soft-drinks companies have been condemned for targeting children with unhealthy, high sugar, low nutrition products.

- Banks and credit card companies have put their customers, and even their own businesses, at risk of financial ruin by offering easy credit to people already in serious debt.

- Mobile phone companies have been condemned for having restrictive contracts and overcharging their customers with expensive call rates.

- Technology companies have raised concerns about consumer privacy by tracking people's web use and making it available to advertisers and even governments.

- Schools have been criticized for offering pupils a diet of cheap processed food at lunchtimes rather than serving appropriately nutritional meals.

These are just a few of the many examples that are regularly revealed by the media and by consumer groups and other 'watchdog' organizations. Clearly, such incidents are cause for concern, but what does this tell us about the nature of the stake held by consumers? The first point to make here is that we must question whether the satisfaction of consumer stakeholders is necessarily always consistent with the best interests of the firm. Whilst such an assumption of aligned interests may well be legitimate in some contexts, or where certain conditions are met, there may also be situations where the interests of buyers and sellers *diverge* (Smith 1995).

We shall examine some of these contexts and conditions as we proceed through the chapter, but at the most basic level, the co-alignment of interests between the two groups depends on the availability of alternative choices that the consumer might reasonably be able to switch to. Secondly, in the absence of a clear mutual interest in all contexts, we also need a normative conception of the stake held by consumers in order to determine what constitutes unethical behaviour towards them. Typically, this normative basis has been established on notions of **consumer rights**. Given the notion of rights that

Consumer rights
Inalienable entitlements to fair treatment when entering into exchanges with sellers.

was introduced in Chapter 3, consumer rights rest upon the assumption that consumer dignity should be respected, and that sellers have a duty to treat consumers as ends in themselves, and not only as means to the end of the seller.

What constitutes *fair treatment* is, however, open to considerable debate. In the past, consumers were adjudged to have few if any clear rights in this respect, and the legal framework for market exchange was largely predicated on the notion of *caveat emptor*, or 'buyer beware' (Smith 1995). Under *caveat emptor*, the consumer's sole right was to veto purchase and decide not to purchase something (Boatright 2012). The burden for protecting the consumer's interest, should they have wanted to go ahead with purchase, therefore lay with the consumer, not with the party making the sale. So, under the rule of buyer beware, providing producers abided by the law, it was the consumer's responsibility to show due diligence in avoiding questionable products. If they were subsequently harmed or dissatisfied with a product or service, it was regarded as their own fault.

The limits of *caveat emptor*

During the latter part of the twentieth century, this notion of *caveat emptor* was gradually eroded by changing societal expectations and the introduction of consumer protection laws in most developed countries (Smith 1995). Consequently, protection of various consumer rights, such as the right to safe and efficacious products (i.e. effective in doing what they are supposed to do) and the right to truthful measurements and labelling, is now enshrined in UN guidelines as well as in EU regulations and various national laws. **Figure 8.1**, for example, shows the main objectives and principles of the UN Guidelines on Consumer Protection, which set out the consumer needs that governments are expected to meet. As we have restated a number of times in this book though, business ethics often begins where the law ends. So it is frequently in the context of the more ill-defined or questionable rights of consumers, and those that are not legally protected, that the most important ethical questions arise.

For example, we might reasonably suggest that consumers have a right to truthful information about products, and legislation usually prohibits the deliberate falsification of product information on packaging and in advertisements. However, certain claims made by manufacturers and advertisers might not be factually untrue, but may end up misleading consumers about potential benefits.

Consider that in many countries, claims that a food product is 'low fat' are permissible providing the product is lower in fat than an alternative, such as a competing product or another of the company's product line. This means that even a product with 80% fat can be labelled 'low fat' providing there is an alternative with 85% fat. For customers seeking a healthy diet, the 'low fat' product may seem attractive, but it might not actually provide the genuinely healthy benefits suggested by the labelling. Indeed, evidence suggests that low-fat labels lead people, especially those who are already overweight, to actually increase their calorie intake (Wansink and Chandon 2006). So we might reasonably question whether the consumer purchasing such a product has been treated fairly by the seller. It is in such grey areas of consumers' rights that questionable marketing practices arise. In the following section we will review the most common and controversial of these ethical problems and issues.

Before we go on to discuss these practices, it is important to mention at this stage that the stake consumers hold in corporations does not only provide them with certain rights, but also entrusts them with certain responsibilities. At one level, we can think of this just in terms of the expectations we might have for consumers themselves to

Objectives

Taking into account the interests and needs of consumers in all countries, particularly those in developing countries; recognizing that consumers often face imbalances in economic terms, educational levels and bargaining power; and bearing in mind that consumers should have the right of access to non-hazardous products, as well as the right to promote just, equitable and sustainable economic and social development and environmental protection, these guidelines for consumer protection have the following objectives:

(a) To assist countries in achieving or maintaining adequate protection for their population as consumers.
(b) To facilitate production and distribution patterns responsive to the needs and desires of consumers.
(c) To encourage high levels of ethical conduct for those engaged in the production and distribution of goods and services to consumers.
(d) To assist countries in curbing abusive business practices by all enterprises at the national and international levels which adversely affect consumers.
(e) To facilitate the development of independent consumer groups.
(f) To further international cooperation in the field of consumer protection.
(g) To encourage the development of market conditions which provide consumers with greater choice at lower prices.
(h) To promote sustainable consumption.

General principles

Governments should develop or maintain a strong consumer protection policy, taking into account the guidelines set out below and relevant international agreements. In so doing, each Government should set its own priorities for the protection of consumers in accordance with the economic, social and environmental circumstances of the country and the needs of its population, bearing in mind the costs and benefits of proposed measures.

The legitimate needs which the guidelines are intended to meet are the following:

(a) The protection of consumers from hazards to their health and safety.
(b) The promotion and protection of the economic interests of consumers.
(c) Access of consumers to adequate information to enable them to make informed choices according to individual wishes and needs.
(d) Consumer education, including education on the environmental, social, and economic impacts of consumer choice.
(e) Availability of effective consumer redress.
(f) Freedom to form consumer and other relevant groups or organizations and the opportunity of such organizations to present their views in decision-making processes affecting them.
(g) The promotion of sustainable consumption patterns.

Figure 8.1 UN Guidelines on Consumer Protection

Source: United Nations 2003. *United Nations Guidelines for Consumer Protection* (as expanded in 1999). New York: United Nations Department of Economic and Social Affairs: 2–3. http://www.un.org.

act ethically in dealing with the producers of products. Customers might sometimes be in a position where they can take an unfair advantage of those who supply them with products, particularly if we think about the situation where customers are actually other firms. For instance, powerful retailers may exert excessive pressure on their suppliers in order to squeeze the lowest possible prices out of them for their products. Even at the level of individual consumers, certain expectations are placed on us to desist from lying, stealing, or otherwise acting unethically in our dealings with retailers, insurance companies, and other companies. For instance, illegal file sharing on the internet has prompted record companies to combat music downloaders, for instance through legal proceedings against individual consumers, and via new arrangements with internet service providers. One case resulted in a man being given a five-year prison term and a fine of $1.5 million for file sharing movies, music, and games online (Kerr 2013).

At a different level though, and probably more importantly, various writers have also suggested that certain responsibilities are placed on us as consumers for controlling corporations in some way, or for avoiding environmental problems, through our purchase decisions. If we do not like the way that Apple treats the workers in its supply chain, or the way that ExxonMobil has responded to global warming, is it not also up to us to make a stand and avoid buying their products in order to get the message across? If we really want to achieve sustainability, do we not have to accept certain curbs on our own personal consumption? These are vital questions in the context of corporate citizenship and sustainability, and we will discuss these problems in more depth towards the end of the chapter.

■ Ethical issues, marketing, and the consumer

The question of dealing ethically with consumers crosses a wide range of issues and problems. Generally speaking, these fall within one of the three main areas of marketing activity, as summarized in **Figure 8.2**. We shall look at each of these in turn, and explore the different perspectives typically applied to such problems in order to reach some kind of ethical decision or resolution.

Ethical issues in marketing management

Most ethical issues concerning business–consumer relations refer to the main tools of marketing management, commonly known as the 'marketing mix'—product policies, marketing communications, pricing approaches, and distribution practices.

Ethical issues in product policy
At the most basic level, consumers have a right to—and in most countries, organizations are legally obliged to supply—products and services that are safe, efficacious, and fit for the purpose for which they are intended. In many respects, it is in both the buyer's and the seller's interests that this is the case, since a producer of shoddy or unsafe products is generally unlikely to prosper in a competitive marketplace. Indeed, the vast majority of exchanges are conducted to the entire satisfaction of both parties. However, many everyday products that are bought or used can potentially harm, injure, or even kill people, especially if they are used improperly. This goes not only for products such as alcohol and cigarettes, but also for cars, bicycles, tools, medicines, public transport, investment services, catering services—in fact almost no area of consumption is free from at least the potential to inflict some form of physical, emotional, financial, or psychological harm upon consumers. The questions that arise are:

- What lengths should the producers of goods and services go to in order to make them safe for the consumer's use?

- To what extent are producers responsible for the consequences of the consumer's use of their products?

Area of marketing		Some common ethical problems	Main rights involved
Marketing management	Product policy	Product safety Fitness for purpose	Right to safe and efficacious products
	Marketing communications	Deception Misleading claims Intrusiveness Promotion of materialism Creation of artificial wants Perpetuating dissatisfaction Reinforcing stereotypes	Right to honest and fair communications Right to privacy
	Pricing	Excessive pricing Price fixing Predatory pricing Deceptive pricing	Right to fair prices
	Distribution	Buyer–seller relationships Gifts and bribes Slotting fees	Right to engage in markets Right to make a free choice
Marketing strategy		Targeting vulnerable consumers Consumer exclusion	Right to be free from discrimination Right to basic freedoms and amenities
Market research		Privacy issues	Right to privacy

Figure 8.2 Ethical issues, marketing, and the consumer

One way to look at this is to argue that manufacturers ought to exercise *due care* in ensuring that all reasonable steps are taken to ensure that their products are free from defects and safe to use (Boatright 2012). The question of what exactly constitutes due care is of course rather difficult to define, but this assessment tends to rest on some notion of negligence and whether the manufacturer has knowingly, or even unwittingly, been negligent in their efforts to ensure consumer protection. Such presumptions go well beyond the moral minimum typically presented by the notion of *caveat emptor*. Rather, here the suggestion is that it is the producer's responsibility to ensure that products are fit and safe for use, and if they are not, then producers are liable for any adverse consequences caused by the use of these products.

Ultimately though, safety is also a function of the consumer and their actions and precautions. Providing a producer has exercised due care in ensuring consumers are protected under expected conditions (or perhaps even extreme or emergency situations), and has informed them of the risks, consumers themselves must take some responsibility for acting hazardously or misusing the product. For example, surely we cannot blame a manufacturer of ice cream if a consumer eats so many tubs in one go that they make themselves sick from over-consuming the product (providing at least that such practices have not been advocated by the firm in its advertising).

If we think about the example of cars, we can see that the consumer's right to a safe product is not an *unlimited right*. Whilst they might certainly expect that a manufacturer has ensured that the vehicle meets 'reasonable' safety standards, any given cars could obviously have been made safer yet—though at some cost, and in all likelihood with some compromise on other features such as performance or styling. Because these improvements are possible, it does not mean that consumers have a right to them. However, firms marketing inherently risky products (such as tobacco or unhealthy food), or products that are especially prone to misuse (such as alcohol), might still exercise responsibility in ensuring that consumers properly understand the risks involved in consuming their products.

Ethical issues in marketing communications

In all of the areas of business ethics pertaining to marketing and consumption, probably no other issue has been discussed in so much depth and for so long as has advertising. Advertising, though, is just one aspect of marketing communications, and whilst much less attention has been afforded to other aspects, ethical problems and issues also arise in respect to personal selling, sales promotion, direct marketing, public relations, and other means of communicating to consumers.

Criticisms of these practices have been extensive and varied, but can be usefully broken down into two levels: individual and social. At the level of the individual consumer, critics have been mainly concerned with the use of *misleading or deceptive practices* that seek to create false beliefs about specific products or companies in the consumer's mind, primarily in order to increase the propensity to purchase. At the social level, the main concern is with the *aggregate social and cultural impacts* of marketing communications on everyday life, in particular their role in promoting materialism and reifying consumption.

Looking first at misleading and deceptive practices affecting individual consumers, marketing communications are typically said to fulfil two main functions:

• to *inform* consumers about goods and services; and

• to *persuade* consumers to actually go ahead and purchase products.

If such communications were just about providing consumers with information, then it could be suggested that the question of misleading practices is essentially one of assessing whether a particular claim is factually true or not. However, this perspective suffers from a number of shortcomings, most notably that:

• marketing (along with much human communication) does not only deal with straightforward declarative sentences of literal fact; and

• it is possible to mislead even when making statements of fact (De George 1999: 278).

The first shortcoming is evident if we think about some typical advertisements. Consider, for example, the ad campaign for the soft drink Red Bull which claims 'Red Bull gives you wings'. Obviously, the advertiser is not claiming that by drinking Red Bull the consumer will literally sprout a pair of wings, simply that the high-caffeine drink can give you a bit of an energy boost. Similarly, the 'global warming ready' slogan used by the Italian clothing company Diesel in its controversial Life's a Beach ad campaign launched in 2007 was not meant to deceive us that Diesel clothes would literally prepare us for climate change, but was rather meant as an ironic statement about their cool summer collection. Such claims are not misleading because we do not expect them to be telling us a literal truth.

The second shortcoming of this perspective is clear if we look at some cases where manufacturers have been criticized for making factually true yet somewhat misleading claims. For example, when firms claim that only 'natural' flavourings and colours are used in a product, this may veil the true provenance of the additives used. For example, Eric Schlosser's (2001) book *Fast Food Nation* calls attention to the very unnatural processes that sometimes lurk behind the all-natural claims. One example he gives is of cochineal extract (also known as carmine or carminic acid, or simply hidden by the phrase 'colour added') which:

> is made from the desiccated bodies of female *Dactylopius coccus* Costa, a small insect harvested mainly in Peru and the Canary Islands. The bug feeds on red cactus berries, and colour from the berries accumulates in the females and their unhatched larvae. The insects are collected, dried, and ground into a pigment. It takes about 70,000 of them to produce a pound of carmine, which is used to make processed foods look pink, red, or purple.

Carmine has been used in many food products, including fruit drinks, frozen fruit bars, sweets, and fruit fillings—yet few customers (including vegetarians!) would have any idea where the products got their colour from. Starbucks was forced to remove it from its Strawberry & Crème Frappuccino, while Danone has long used it in its strawberry and other flavoured yoghurts (Tepper 2013).

The situation is not so clear-cut that we can simply limit our discussion to factual truth. The persuasive nature of most marketing communications means that we expect them to exaggerate, overclaim, boast, and make playful, if sometimes outlandish, allusions—and indeed we often enjoy them for these very same reasons (Levitt 1970). When Volvo uses the slogan 'Volvo. For Life', we are not evaluating this as a factual statement that a Volvo really lasts a lifetime, but as a typically exaggerated claim that seeks to convince us of the superior quality of the company's products.

It is important to recognize that persuasion in itself is not inherently wrong. We all attempt to persuade people to do or believe certain things at various times: your lecturer might try and persuade you about the benefits of reading your Crane and Matten, *Business Ethics* text; your friends might try and persuade you to forget about studying and join them for a night of drinking and partying. The problem comes when persuasion involves deception of some sort.

Consumer deception is somewhat difficult to define in this respect, but it is largely concerned with acts whereby companies deliberately create false impressions on the part of consumers to satisfy their own ends. It is one thing to make something appealing—after all, much marketing communications activity, such as public relations and advertising, is intended to show organizations and their goods and services in the best possible light. However, when this involves creating or taking advantage of a belief that is actually *untrue*, then we start to move into the field of deception. As Boatright (2012) suggests, deception occurs when the ability of people to make rational consumer choices is interfered with by marketing communications that rely on false beliefs.

For example, if your lecturer chose to persuade you to read Crane and Matten's book by suggesting that by doing so you would automatically get better marks in the end of semester examination, then we might consider that they had attempted to create a false belief in your mind. If a person of reasonable intelligence would be likely to believe the claim, then it could be suggested that this might impair your rational judgement about whether to read the book and thus would constitute an act of deception. However, it is important to recognize that deception is not just about telling lies, or even just about verbal claims. Consumers can also be deceived by advertisements that appear to intimate that using a certain product will make them more attractive, more popular, or more successful. They might similarly be deceived by slogans that give a false impression of a product's qualities. For example, in 2014, L'Oréal agreed to a settlement with the Federal Trade Commission in the US over claims made in the advertising of its 'Youth Code' skincare product that it can generate 'youth benefits' by targeting the user's genes.[1] By focusing on consumers' ability to make rational choices as a result of their exposure to marketing communications, we are essentially concerned with consumers' rights to make independent decisions free from undue influence or coercion. The new area of neuro marketing has provided companies with powerful new tools, but as **Ethics in Action 8.1** shows, these tools also expose this controversial fault line between persuasion and manipulation from an ethical perspective.

Potential violations of such rights occur fairly frequently in the field of marketing communications, not least because the line that needs to be drawn between honest persuasion and outright deception becomes somewhat hazy where certain practices are concerned. For instance, some manufacturers have chosen to veil price increases by making small, unannounced reductions in package sizes whilst keeping prices constant, thus creating the impression that prices have remained stable. Should we expect them to issue us with announcements of any size changes, or given that weights and volumes have to be legally identified on packaging anyway, is it not up to us as consumers to check sizes? **Ethical Dilemma 8** presents another typical situation where questions of deception might arise.

Practices such as these are usually perfectly legal, particularly as the advertising industry continues to push for self-regulation rather than governmental regulation of its members. The European Advertising Standards Alliance (EASA), for example, brings together self-regulatory organizations and advertising industry representatives throughout Europe to promote self-regulation and to set and apply ethical rules and guidelines for good practice.[2] In the US, however, consumers often turn to the courts to sue corporations for perceived infringements. For instance, in 2014 Red Bull agreed to a $13 million settlement because the above-mentioned claim that its beverage 'gives you wings' was

Consumer deception
When a marketing communication either creates, or takes advantage of, a false belief that substantially interferes with rational consumer decision-making.

VISIT THE ONLINE RESOURCE CENTRE
for links to useful sources of further information

ETHICS IN ACTION 8.1   http://www.ethicalcorp.com

Marketing—the ethics of emotions from a can
Mallen Baker, 2 May 2013

Marketers discovered many years ago that devices such as focus groups have major limitations. They do not always deliver the truth, and in the early days nobody knew whether this was because subjects knowingly lied or simply knew less about their own preferences than they imagined.

But new tools have given us great understanding and insights. In particular, neuro-marketing—where brain scans give us information about what is really going on in a customer's mind—has shown just how subtle the process of persuasion can really be. For instance, we discovered just how highly connected our sense of smell is to our memories, and how powerful invoking memories can be in persuading people to buy. So, increasingly, though you may not have realised it you walk through a sensory feast where stores pump aromas into the air hoping to quietly seduce you into making that additional purchase. This is invisible marketing.

That smell of chargrilled beef that gets you buying the burger in that fast-food restaurant whereas you came in hoping to buy salad? It came out of a can. The freshly baked bread smell in the supermarket that entices you to feel more hungry and buy more stuff? Most such supermarkets no longer have a genuine on-site bakery. So where does that smell come from?

Is it ethical? Sure. But it is a step into the grey. Invisible influence. Tweaking sensory experiences to provoke an unconscious reaction designed to favour the marketer. It is that slippery aromatic slope. By the way, you know that lovely smell of coffee you get when you break the wrapper on a jar of premium instant coffee? Totally made up. Instant coffee does not smell. I was gutted when I discovered that. I love that smell.

But it goes further, much further. We know that we are creatures of habit. So marketers now create or co-opt rituals that will give us the habit of doing what they want us to—buying their product. They have also discovered that the reaction in the brain we have when we see a powerful brand is almost identical to the reaction in the brain of a religious person when contemplating the highest spiritual experience. And you can bet that some brands exploit the heck out of that.

Suddenly, we have tools to know consumers better than they know themselves. The smokers may have answered 'yes' to the question about whether warning messages on packs of cigarettes made them less likely to smoke, but the brain scans showed that the opposite was true—the messages actually triggered their craving for a smoke.

And we discovered that our view of ourselves as predominantly rational beings responding to choices was wrong. Brain scanning has shown that our emotions impact our decision-making time after time—and the factors that trigger those emotions are automatic processes, not deliberate thinking—and can be manipulated.

Let's take this to another level. Suppose marketers were able to use this technology to identify what were the real barriers to people behaving sustainably. Supposing they were able to come up with the concepts that would enable politicians to persuade people to accept some of the necessary, but tough, policies in the future to give us a hope of a better world. Since, to date, we have routinely failed to achieve this, it would be of interest, would it not? It would be an ethical use of marketing that we would celebrate. And we are already intrigued by the possibilities.

Let me change the proposition just a little: supposing these techniques could be used instead to pull the little levers in people's minds to get them to acquiesce to authority under all circumstances. And by routine exploitation of these mind tricks, a government could do what it wanted without fear of backlash among the population. That would be bad, right? I mean nightmarishly George Orwell-style bad. But the only difference is one of intent.

So the question is an open one. At what point does marketing become unethical, if it is able to use our mechanical responses to stimuli to manipulate what we do? And if we want to use such techniques to promote sustainable behaviour change, does that make any difference to the ethics of manipulation?

Sources

Ethical Corporation, Mallen Baker, 2 May 2013, http://www.ethicalcorp.com. Reproduced with the kind permission of Ethical Corporation.

? THINK THEORY

In light of the normative ethical theories discussed in Chapter 3, how can we evaluate the use of the neuroscience-based marketing techniques discussed above?

VISIT THE ONLINE RESOURCE CENTRE for a short response to this feature

---

judged 'deceptive and fraudulent' in court (Culzac 2014). Ultimately, any assessment of consumer deception will depend critically on what degree of interference in consumers' rational decision-making we decide is acceptable, how well consumers can delineate between fact and fiction, and whether by getting this wrong they will be significantly harmed. After all, as Boatright (2012: 226) contends: 'claims in life insurance advertising, for example, ought to be held to a higher standard than those for chewing gum'.

The second level at which criticisms of marketing communications have been raised concerns their social and cultural impact on society. For instance, the UK self-regulatory body, the Advertising Standards Authority (ASA), suggests that advertisements should be 'legal, decent, honest and truthful' in that they:

- Must not contain anything that is likely to cause serious or widespread offence.

- Must not cause fear or distress without justifiable reason.

- Must contain nothing that is likely to condone or encourage violence or antisocial behaviour.

- Must not condone or encourage an unsafe practice.

- Must not encourage consumers to drink and drive.[3]

Most of the complaints received by the ASA refer to advertisements that have caused offence, such as those featuring nudity or shocking images of one sort or another. A 2014

AN ETHICAL DILEMMA 8

A fitting approach to shoe selling?

You are the manager of an independent high street shoe store, specializing in fashionable shoes for men and women. Your staff comprises a small team of eight salespeople who all take part in selling shoes, checking and maintaining stock, and processing sales and orders. You run a pretty successful operation, but there is intense competition from major shoe-store chains as well as one or two other independent stores in the city where you are located. To motivate your staff, a couple of years ago you introduced an incentive scheme that gives employees 5% commission on everything they sell. This has worked pretty well—the store has maintained profitability and the employees are all fairly well paid.

You have recently hired a new salesperson, Lola, who has made quite an impact on sales. She not only seems to be enjoying a great deal of success selling shoes, but she has also proved to be popular with everyone in the store, including the customers. Since she has arrived, though, Lola has also been giving you some cause for concern. Although no one has complained about her, you have noticed that, at times, some of her successful sales techniques do not always involve her being completely truthful.

For example, on one occasion last week you noticed that she was serving a customer who was plainly unsure whether to purchase a particular pair of shoes. Lola obviously thought the shoes suited the woman, but to create a little more urgency, she said that the model the woman was interested in was the last pair in stock and that she did not think the store would be able to get any more for another month. However, you knew for certain that there were at least five or six pairs in the stockroom, and that reordering when they were sold out should only take a week. Still, the customer eventually decided to buy the shoes, and once she had made the decision she seemed delighted with them.

Then yesterday, Lola was serving a man who obviously wanted a particular pair of shoes that he had seen in the window. She asked him his size (which was 43) but when she got to the storeroom she discovered that there was only a 42 and a 44 in stock. She asked you if you knew whether there was a 43 anywhere but you had to tell her no—you had sold the last pair yourself only the day before. Undeterred, Lola picked up both the 42 and the 44 and took the shoes back out to the man. Giving him the 42 first, she said to him that the company did not sell 'odd' sizes and they only came in 42 and 44. The customer tried on the 42, but obviously found them too small. While he was doing this though, Lola took out the 44 and carefully placed an additional insole in the bottom of the shoe. 'Give this a go,' she said handing the shoes to the man, 'this should do the trick'. To his delight, they fitted fine and he said he would take them. At this point, Lola mentioned that because the manufacturer did not do 'odd' sizes, she had put insoles into the shoes, which would cost an additional €3. Still pleased with the shoes, the man said fine and paid for both the shoes and the insoles.

You were unsure what to do about the situation. Although the customers seemed pleased with their purchases, Lola was clearly lying to them. Would there be any long-term repercussions of such practices? And what would the rest of the team think about it? Would they start copying Lola's successful sales techniques?

Questions

1. What are the arguments for and against Lola's actions?

2. Do you think such practices are common in sales situations? What would you think if you were a co-worker or a customer of Lola's?

3. To what extent do you think your incentive scheme has contributed to Lola's actions?

4. How would you approach this situation as Lola's manager?

advertisement from the Irish bookmaker Paddy Power, for example, became the ASA's most complained about non-broadcast advert ever in the UK because of its offensive references to the murder trial of Olympic athlete Oscar Pistorius. The advert proclaimed 'it's Oscar time', 'money back if he walks' and 'we will refund all losing bets on the Oscar Pistorius trial if he is found not guilty'.

The argument about social and cultural impacts, however, also concerns the aggregate impact of marketing communications in society rather than just being specifically focused on particular campaigns or techniques. There are a number of strands to this argument, but the main objections appear to be that marketing communications:

- **Are intrusive and unavoidable**. We are exposed to hundreds of adverts every day, on the television and radio, in newspapers and magazines, on the internet, in stores, on billboards, on the side of buses, at concerts, on tickets and programmes, on athletes and footballers, to the extent that almost no public space is free from the reach of corporate branding, sponsorship, or promotion. In her bestselling book about the ubiquity of branding, *No Logo*, Naomi Klein (2000) highlighted the increasing incursion of brands into previously unbranded space including schools, towns, streets, politics, even people (think, for example, about the popularity of brand logos as templates for tattoos).

- **Create artificial wants**. The persuasive nature of advertising has long been argued to make us want things that we do not particularly need (e.g. Packard 1957). The economist John Kenneth Galbraith was perhaps the most popular advocate of this argument, suggesting that firms generate artificial wants in order to create demand for their products (Galbraith 1974). For example, one might question whether we really felt a need for products such as personal computers, mobile phones, or cars that talk to us before companies developed the technology and set out to create a demand for them. The problem here, though, is in defining what are 'real' wants and needs and what are 'artificial' or 'false' ones. Jean Baudrillard (1997), for example, condemns Galbraith's 'moralizing idealism' and his depiction of the individual as a passive victim of the system, suggesting instead that the consumer is an active participant seeking to satisfy very real needs for social identity and differentiation through consumption.

- **Reinforce consumerism and materialism**. More broadly then, the saturation of everyday life under a deluge of marketing communications has been argued to generate and perpetuate an ideology of materialism in society, and to institute in our culture an identification of consumption with happiness (Pollay 1986). Cultural studies authors, as well as the popular press, now commonly depict modern Western society as being a 'consumer society', where not only is consumption the principal site of meaning and identity, but it also increasingly dominates other arenas of life such as politics, education, health, and personal relations (e.g. Featherstone 1991; Baudrillard 1997). Thus, emotional or psychological ills that might threaten our self identity, such as a broken relationship, depression, or low self-esteem, might be more readily addressed through 'compensatory consumption' than other more traditional channels (Woodruffe 1997; Kim and Rucker 2012). As Smart (2010: 4) argues, Western-style **consumerism** has also increasingly spread to other countries, especially China and India, making it 'the most persuasive and pervasive globally extensive form of cultural life, one to which more and more people around the world continue to aspire.'

Consumerism
An attitude that makes consumption the centre of meaning and identity construction.

- **Create insecurity and perpetual dissatisfaction**. Ashamed of your mobile phone? Embarrassed by your cheap brand of coffee? Guilty that your baby is not clothed in the most advanced (and expensive) diapers? Worried that your feminine sanitary products will let you down? These are all typical worries and insecurities that ad campaigns identify and perpetuate in order to enhance demand. Hence, critics of advertising have further contended that by presenting glorified, often unattainable images of 'the good life' for us to aspire to, marketing communications create (and indeed rely on creating) constant dissatisfaction with our lives and institute a pervading sense of insecurity and inadequacy (Pollay 1986).

- **Perpetuate social stereotypes**. Finally, marketing communications have also been argued to spread socially undesirable stereotypes of certain categories of person and lifestyle (see Pollay 1986), such that women are always either housewives or sex objects; health, beauty, and happiness are only possible with 'perfect' body shapes; 'nuclear' families become associated with 'normality'; and racial minorities, the disabled, and gay and lesbian people become excluded from the picture of 'normal' life. Whilst the usual defence to this argument is that marketers reflect the social norms of target audiences (Greyser 1972), it is clear that it is in companies' own interest to depict images desired by their customers. For example, Unilever's commercials for its best-selling skin whitener 'Fair & Lovely' have caused a great deal of controversy in some countries because they suggest that fairer skinned women can find better husbands and jobs than those with darker skins. While women's groups have criticized the advertisements as 'demeaning', 'racist', and 'discriminatory', the company has pointed to research showing that women want to use whiteners because fair skin is seen as an aspirational step up the social and economic ladder (Luce and Merchant 2003; Karnani 2007).

Such criticisms have been common since at least the 1970s. Nonetheless, many social commentators also contend that, as a society, we have never been so informed and educated about the role of advertising, promotion, and branding as we are today, and that it provides us with much-needed enjoyment and escapism (Holbrook 1987). Accordingly, it would appear that consumers are now much more media literate and less likely to be the 'victims' of marketing communications than when these criticisms were first raised. To some extent, the wider ethical case against marketing communication as a social phenomenon is fairly difficult to uphold, not least because many of the criticisms often essentially boil down to criticisms of capitalism (Phillips 1997). This is not to deny that these problems with marketing communications are significant; more that if we accept capitalism, we must also to some extent accept these problems.

? THINK THEORY

Think about the question of whether marketers should be responsible for the aggregate consequences of their actions. Which ethical theories do you think would typically be used to argue either for or against this proposition?

VISIT THE
ONLINE
RESOURCE
CENTRE
for a short
response to this
feature

☑ Skill check

Determining the ethical limits of marketing communication. Understanding what constitutes a misleading or deceptive practice, and a positive or negative social or cultural impact, is essential for determining the ethics of marketing communications.

Ethical issues in pricing

It is perhaps unsurprising that issues of pricing are often among the criticisms levelled at companies, for it is in pricing that we most clearly see the potential for the interests of producers and consumers to diverge. While consumers may desire to exchange the goods and services they require for as little cost as possible, producers are likely to want to maximize the amount of revenue they can extract from the consumer. Pricing issues are thus central to the notion of a fair exchange between the two parties, and the *right to a fair price* might typically be regarded as one of the key rights of consumers as stakeholders.

The concept of a fair price is open to a number of different views, but typically is thought of as the result of a mutual agreement by the buyer and seller under competitive conditions. Thus, under neoclassical economics, prices should be set at the market equilibrium, where marginal cost equals marginal revenue. However, the assumption here is that buyers and sellers can leave the market at any time, and that there are a number of competing offerings in the market. Problems of fairness arise then when prevailing market conditions allow companies to exploit an advantageous market position, such as a monopoly, or where consumers are unable to leave the market, perhaps because they have an irrevocable need for a product, such as for housing, food, or medicine.

In most countries, there are regulatory agencies in place to police market distortions of this kind. In Europe, for instance, organizations, such as the Bundeskartellamt (Federal Cartel Office) in Germany and the Autoriteit Consument and Markt (Authority for Consumers and Markets) in the Netherlands, provide national protection, while the Directorate-General for Competition of the European Commission deals with pan-European issues. In Japan, a Fair Trade Commission deals with such issues, and in China enforcement is handled through the Ministry of Commerce. However, ethical problems still arise in different countries, either because the distortions are opaque, or because market conditions fail to explain the perceived unfairness of prices.

There are four main types of pricing practices where ethical problems are likely to arise:

- **Excessive pricing**. Sometimes known as *price gouging*, the idea of an 'excessive' price rests on the assumption that the fair price for goods and services has been exceeded. While this may well be due to prevailing market conditions, as discussed above, the perceived fairness of a price may also depend on other factors, such as the relative costs of the producer, or the price charged to other consumers. For example, our readers will certainly be familiar with debates around the pricing of university textbooks. **Figure 8.3** shows that prices of educational books in the US have risen almost four times more than average consumer prices since 1978. It appears that such pricing is possible because the end consumer of college textbooks, the student, ultimately has little choice as to which book to buy as this decision is taken by the instructor who puts the book on the syllabus, often irrespective of the price actually charged.

- **Price fixing**. The problem of excessive pricing is probably most difficult to address when, rather than being the actions of one single firm, it occurs as a result of collusion between competing firms to fix prices above the market rate. This is illegal in Europe, the US, and most other parts of the world, but difficulties in detection and conviction mean that many instances of price fixing go unnoticed. However, the last few years have seen an intensification of investigations into price fixing. For example, Apple was engaged in a long-running court case in the US in the 2010s regarding an alleged agreement it made with five of the largest American publishing houses to prevent e-books from being sold at less than $14.99 (Vaara 2014).

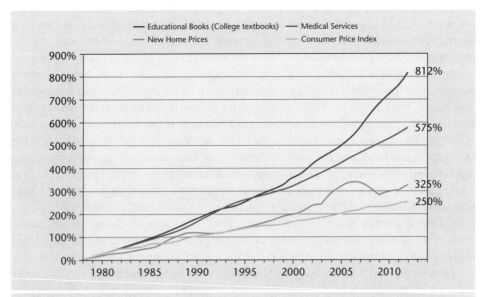

Figure 8.3 Per cent changes since 1978 for educational books, medical services, new home prices, and consumer price index in the US

Source: Perry, M.J. 2012. The college textbook bubble and how the 'open educational resources' movement is going up against the textbook cartel. American Enterprise Institute Ideas Blog, 24 December 2012, http://www.aei.org. Reproduced with permission.

- **Predatory pricing**. A further problem of anticompetitive practice can occur when a firm adopts the opposite course of action, and rather than charging *above* market rate, sets a price significantly *below* the market rate in order to force out competition. Known as predatory pricing, this practice allows firms with a size or other advantage to use their power to eliminate competitors from the market so that more favourable market conditions can be exploited. The above-mentioned case involving Apple in fact also involved allegations of predatory pricing. That is, Apple's agreement with e-book publishers was a response to Amazon's practice of selling e-books from the same five publishers for $9.99, which was often below their wholesale prices. As a result, Amazon with its Kindle reader had a market share of 99% of the e-book market by the time Apple attempted to enter the market with its iPad in 2010. Arguably, Apple had engaged in price fixing as a result of Amazon's strategy of predatory pricing (Auletta 2012)!

- **Deceptive pricing**. Finally, unfair pricing can also occur when firms price in such a way that the true cost to consumers is deliberately obscured. For example, in 2014 low-cost air carrier Southwest Airlines was fined by the US authorities for advertising cut-price flights that were not actually available on its website at the advertised price.[4] Other airlines, too, have been found advertising prices that were only available for a small percentage of flights, with substantial booking restrictions, and with no acknowledgement of the additional taxes and fees that would be levied, thereby deceiving consumers into thinking prices were lower than they actually were. Given that advertised prices represent a claim on the part of producers, deceptive pricing can be assessed in the same way as deception in marketing communications.

Clearly the issue of pricing is crucial when it comes to assessing and protecting the relative rights and responsibilities of consumers and companies. As we can see here, much of the activity associated with ethical practice in this area actually also concerns the relationships between firms and their competitors. We shall examine this in more depth in Chapter 9.

☑ Skill check

Analysing the ethics of pricing strategies. This is a key skill as it enables decision-makers to determine whether prices might be judged to be unfair—i.e. excessive, fixed, predatory or deceptive.

? THINK THEORY

Fairness in pricing will obviously depend on how we define fairness. One way we can do this is by using Rawls' theory of justice (see Chapter 3, The problem of justice, pp. 109–112). How would the practices outlined here be assessed according to this theory?

VISIT THE
ONLINE
RESOURCE
CENTRE
for a short
response to this
feature

Ethical issues in channels of distribution

In the final area of marketing management, channels of distribution, we are concerned with the ethical issues and problems that occur in the relationships between manufacturers and the firms that deliver their products to market, such as wholesalers, logistics firms, and retailers. This is often referred to as the *product supply chain*. Most of Chapter 9 is devoted to such relationships between firms and their suppliers, so here we will just mention that ethical problems clearly arise in this context—for example, when retailers demand 'slotting fees' from manufacturers in order to stock their products, or when assessing the environmental impact of different logistics systems.

Ethical issues in marketing strategy

Marketing strategy is primarily concerned with the decisions of market selection and targeting. The targeting of markets is central to marketing theory and practice, and the choice of specific groups of consumers (or market segments) to target has been carefully refined over the years by companies eager to focus their efforts on 'attractive' segments, characterized by factors such as high profitability, low competition, or strong potential for growth. As marketers have become more adept at targeting specific groups of consumers—and even sometimes individual consumers—important criticisms have emerged. In particular, critics tend to be concerned over potential violations of the consumer's *right to fair treatment*. This violation can happen in two main ways:

Consumer vulnerability
The state of being unable to make an informed, reasoned decision about a product purchase.

- **Consumer vulnerability**. Some target markets are composed of consumers who are deemed 'vulnerable' in some way, such as children, the elderly, the poor, or the sick, and marketers may unfairly take advantage of this vulnerability to exploit consumers.

- **Consumer exclusion**. Certain groups of consumers may be discriminated against and excluded from being able to gain access to products that are necessary for them to achieve a reasonable quality of life.

Targeting vulnerable consumers

If we begin with the targeting of vulnerable consumers, it is evident that this concern rests largely on this perceived right to fair treatment for consumers, which imposes certain duties on sellers. Specifically, arguments criticizing unfair targeting practices are based on the degree of *vulnerability of the target*, and on the *perceived harmfulness of the product* to those consumers (Smith and Cooper-Martin 1997).

Vulnerability of the target is somewhat difficult to determine here, and to some extent will be contextually defined. Clearly, though, there is a case for saying that some consumers are less capable than others of making an informed, reasoned decision about whether to purchase a product. There are a number of reasons why consumers might be vulnerable, such as because they:

- Lack sufficient education or information to use products safely or to fully understand the consequences of their actions.

- Are easily confused or manipulated due to old age or senility.

- Are in exceptional physical or emotional need due to illness, bereavement, or some other unfortunate circumstance.

- Lack the necessary income to competently maintain a reasonable quality for life for themselves and their dependants.

- Are too young to make competent independent decisions.

Consumer vulnerability is often said to give rise to a *duty of care* on the part of sellers. Where it is possible for a seller to exploit the vulnerability of a potential customer—for example, where a pharmaceutical company might be in a position to charge an excessively high price for life-saving medications, or an insurance salesperson might be able to exploit the financial illiteracy of a potential investor by misrepresenting the terms and conditions of an investment—it can be argued that the seller has an inherent duty to act in such a way as to respect the interests of the consumer in addition to the interests of themselves and their company.

For example, one of the main groups typically agreed to be vulnerable in some way are young children. A child of four or five might reasonably be said to lack the cognitive skills necessary to make entirely rational choices. Therefore, it is perhaps not surprising that the direct targeting of young children, especially for toys, has been the subject of much criticism over the years (Crane and Kazmi 2010). It is not so much that the children themselves purchase the products targeted at them, but that advertisers seek to encourage and take advantage of the 'pester power' that children have over their parents. Practices such as daytime television advertising for toys, as well as merchandising tie-ups with children's movies and computer games like *Star Wars* and *Frozen*, might be said to take advantage of young children, who are highly impressionable, incapable of distinguishing the persuasive intent of advertising, and cannot understand the usual limitations of family purchasing budgets. The development of commercially sponsored websites containing games, promotions, and contests designed for children (often with brands as an integral element of the game as a game piece, prize, or secret treasure) has raised further concerns about the blurring of advertising and entertainment directed at children (Moore 2004). While one could maintain that it is the responsibility of parents as the ultimate purchasers to resist the pestering of their children, this does not detract from the criticism that by directly targeting a vulnerable group, advertisers might be guilty of violating consumer rights through deliberate manipulation and treating children only as means to their own ends (De George 1999: 283).

Still there is the difficulty here in deciding at what age children can be legitimately regarded as able to make a rational, informed decision. Although there is considerable controversy over research results, it is apparent that even very young children tend to recognize and recall advertising very well, but it would appear that they do not have a good understanding of its persuasive intent until they are around eight years old (Gunter et al. 2005)—but even then they may not invoke that understanding when forming judgements (Moore 2004). Many countries have actually introduced legislation restricting marketing to children, although these restrictions vary enormously between countries. For example, all advertising to children under 12 is illegal in Norway and Sweden, whereas many other countries just prohibit certain types of advertising. In the UK, for instance, food high in fat, salt and sugar cannot be advertised in or around

VISIT THE ONLINE RESOURCE CENTRE for links to useful sources of further information

ETHICS ON SCREEN 8

Fed Up

Fed Up has a fire in its belly to change things.

Peter Travers, *Rolling Stone*

Over the last decade-and-a-half we have seen a spate of movies focusing on the ethics of companies in the food industry. Ever since Morgan Spurlock underwent the experiment of surviving on McDonald's food for a month in *Supersize Me*, feature films such as *Fast Food Nation* and a spate of documentaries (*Food Inc.*, *End of the Line*, *Black Gold*, *GMO-OMG*, and others) have scrutinized various aspects of the industry.

Many of these movies have looked at the impacts of our Western system of food production and consumption and explored, for instance, labour practices in supply chains, environmental impacts of fish and meat production, or the general unsustainability of the modern food industry. *Fed Up*, directed by Stephanie Soechtig, focuses on the consumer interface and the way in which corporations shape consumer behaviour towards food.

The film makes its case by taking stock of the obesity 'pandemic' in the US. While in 1980 there were zero cases of childhood type 2 diabetes the number rose to almost 60,000 by 2010. Experts tell us that over 95% of all Americans will be overweight or obese within the next two decades, and that by 2050 one out of every three Americans will have diabetes.

Fed Up makes a powerful case by zooming in on the most vulnerable consumers: children. Roughly a fifth of 2–19-year-olds are currently obese. It is argued in the movie that this is not the result of lack of exercise or too much time in front of the computer or TV, but children's inability to resist sugary foods. Today, 80% of food items sold in America have added sugar. The experts cited in the film argue that sugar—and in particular the heavily processed sugars used by the food industry as food additives—has an addictive potential similar to cocaine or nicotine. And it is this addictive function that leads the movie to making the claim that today's food industry is copying the

FROM **LAURIE DAVID** PRODUCER OF **AN INCONVENIENT TRUTH** AND **KATIE COURIC**

Before you take another bite...

FED UP

It's time to get real about food.

IN THEATERS MAY 9

Atlas Films/The Kobal Collection

strategies used by the tobacco industry some 40 years ago. The sugar industry and its powerful lobby in Washington, it is suggested, have secured massive subsidies while preventing any meaningful regulation. The movie thus argues that obesity is ultimately funded by the government, and it assigns a damning role to regulators in this context.

Despite its sober content the movie is a rather entertaining watch. Narrated and co-produced by celebrity news anchor Katie Couric, its case studies of obese 12-year-olds, and an array of experts from Michael Pollan to Bill Clinton, make it highly accessible. Most importantly, it gets the viewer thinking about the role of companies in influencing our diet, and in particular through exploiting their most vulnerable customers. Unsurprisingly then, it has become 'the film that the food industry doesn't want you to see' as one critic put it, generating some fierce criticism on industry-backed forums such as http://www.foodinsight.org.

Sources

Nicholson, A. 2014. Is Sugar the New Cigarettes? Fed Up, a New Sundance Film, Thinks So. *Village Voice*, 21 January 2014: http://blogs.villagevoice.com/runninscared/2014/01/fed-up-sugar-documentary.php.

Rosen, C. 2014 'Fed Up' Poster: New Look at the Movie the Food Industry Doesn't Want You to See. *Huffington Post*, 10 April 2014: http://www.huffingtonpost.com/2014/04/10/fed-up-poster_n_5127876.html.

Smith-Edge, M. and Raymond, M. 2014. Correcting the 'Fed Up' Record. Food Insight, 13 May 2014: http://www.foodinsight.org/FedUp-review.

Travers, P. 2014. Fed Up. *Rolling Stone*, 8 May 2014: http://www.rollingstone.com/movies/reviews/fed-up-20140508.

http://fedupmovie.com.

television programmes specifically geared to children under the age of 16, while in Iran there is a ban on soft-drink advertising on television. France, meanwhile, requires that all advertising of processed food to children must be accompanied by a message on the principles of dietary education, such as 'For your health, eat at least five fruits and vegetables a day'.

As this suggests, the debate about advertising to children has been particularly pronounced in the context of food. Concerns about escalating obesity and other health problems among children have prompted considerable debate about marketing food and drink products to children. **Ethics on Screen 8**, for example, provides an overview of the movie *Fed Up* which roundly criticizes the food industry for deliberately targeting children with high-sugar products.

Such challenges have led to an escalation in *industry self-regulation*. By this, we mean efforts by food companies to establish their own controls over how, when and where they market to children. Indeed, in a comprehensive review of regulatory efforts across more than 50 countries, Hawkes and Lobstein (2011) showed that efforts to curb food advertising to children have initially focused on self-regulation from business rather than new government restrictions. One prominent example is the initiative of UNESDA, the European soft-drinks industry body, which includes Coca-Cola and PepsiCo. This commits companies to refrain from advertising soft drinks to children under the age of 12 across all print, TV, and digital media and has achieved a level of about 95–100% compliance among its members.[5] However, there is growing evidence about the limited effectiveness of many self-regulatory initiatives (Roberts et al. 2014).

The issue of the perceived harmfulness of the product is also a critical one in assessing the ethics of particular targeting approaches. Although there is evidence of a general social unease with the targeting of vulnerable groups, whatever the harmfulness of the product, it is perhaps unsurprising that much of the literature dealing with ethics and targeting has focused on products with a clear and present potential to do harm, such as cigarettes and alcohol (Smith and Cooper-Martin 1997). By focusing on such products, the ethical arguments shift somewhat from a focus on rights and duties towards a greater focus on consequences. Hence, the issue is less that taking advantage of consumer vulnerability is wrong in and of itself, but that it is primarily wrong only if the consumer might be expected to suffer in some way. For instance, the issue of selling sub-prime mortgages really came to prominence in the wake of the financial crisis in 2008. The devastating consequence of people losing their homes brought to the fore questions about the ethics of targeting home purchasers who could not really afford the mortgages they were being sold.

☑ **Skill check**

Determining consumer vulnerability. Being able to assess whether a particular group of consumers is vulnerable in some way enables better decision-making about ethical target marketing.

Consumer exclusion

Some criticisms of marketing strategy focus not on who *is* targeted but on who *is not* included in the target market. In some cases, this can lead to accidental or even deliberate exclusion of certain groups of consumers from accessing particular goods and services that might be deemed necessary for them to maintain a reasonable quality of life, thus exacerbating social exclusion and other problems. This problem has come to particular prominence in recent years with widespread debates around, for example, financial exclusion of poor families, lack of access to affordable water and other amenities in undeveloped regions, and the exclusion of low-income neighbourhoods from access to fresh and healthy food. As Kempson and Whyley (1999) show, exclusion can take a variety of forms, including:

- **Access exclusion**—where lack of appropriate distribution outlets and channels may prevent people from accessing essential goods and services such as postal and health services, utilities, and food.

- **Condition exclusion**—where restrictive conditions on product offerings such as financial service products may prevent certain groups from being able to qualify for purchasing them.

- **Price exclusion**—where the price of a product is simply too high for consumers to be able to purchase it in sufficient quantities for a reasonable standard of living.

- **Marketing exclusion**—where firms deliberately exclude certain groups from their target marketing and sales activities.

- **Self-exclusion**—where people may decide that there is little point applying for or trying to access a product because they believe they would be refused, either due to previous negative experiences or because of a belief that 'they do not accept people who live round here'.

In the case of financial products, evidence suggests that in countries such as the US something like 28% of the population, or about 88 million people, are either unbanked (they have no checking or savings account) or under-banked (they have some relationship with payday lenders or other unregulated financial providers; Glinska 2014). At least some of this is due to the spread of the practice of 'redlining', whereby particular areas in towns and cities where the populace predominantly have low incomes and very poor credit ratings are denied access to financial products, primarily through marketing- and -condition exclusion. By effectively drawing a red line around particular geographi- cal no-go zones, critics charge that companies can be said either to be discriminating against consumers (by judging them on their residential location rather than individual merit) or to be treating them unfairly by preventing them from participating in normal market activity. This practice can be particularly problematic when consumers are subse- quently forced to enter into arrangements with unscrupulous, sometimes illegal, substi- tute providers of these products, such as loan sharks and unregistered moneylenders. In the huge Dharavi slum in Mumbai, for example, the cost of credit is over 50 times more than in a rich neighbourhood of the city, whilst potable water is almost 40 times more expensive (Prahalad and Hammond 2002).

Ethical issues in market research

The final area where we need to examine the rights of consumers is in relation to market research. The main issue here is one of the possible threats posed to rights to **consumer privacy**. Market research involves the systematic collection and analysis of enormous amounts of data pertaining to individual consumers, including much information that consumers may not know that researchers have in their possession, and much that they might not wish to have shared with a third party. Surveys suggest that most consum- ers are concerned about the type, accuracy, and deployment of information held about them, but it appears that many are also unaware of the regulations in place to pro- tect them, and make only limited use of strategies to avoid infringement of privacy (Dommeyer and Gross 2003).

Consumer privacy
The right of a consumer to control what information companies can collect about them and how it is stored, used, and shared.

Many of the most pressing issues of consumer privacy are related to dangers posed by digital data, social media, and online privacy. The combination of technological innova- tion and cultural change have enabled marketers to collect unprecedented quantities of 'big data' about almost every aspect of our lives, from what we like to do and where we go, to who our friends are and what we think of them. Hence (Milne and Culnan 2004: 16):

> disclosing information to an online organization requires a degree of trust because of information asymmetries that limit the consumer's knowledge about the organiza- tion's information practices and whether their personal information may be used in ways that could result in harm to the consumer, or lead to unwanted future solicita- tions, credit card theft, or even a hijacking of one's online identity.

Questions about how technology giants such as Facebook or Google should be allowed to use and commercialize their users' data is an ongoing ethical—and often legal— debate. In 2015, for instance, the largest-ever class action suit in Europe was opened in an Austrian court against Facebook, challenging many of its practices for infringing consumer privacy.[6]

Another major area of pressing concern is the use of *genetic testing* results by insurance companies. Whilst there are various advantages to the emergence of tests that can predict the likelihood of an individual's genetic predisposition to certain conditions and illnesses, there are fears that insurance companies might use the information to increase premiums or deny cover altogether for those with high susceptibility. Whilst one might argue that such information is private, particularly if it might be used to create a 'genetic underclass' unable to obtain health or life cover, it can also be argued that premiums are 'fairest' when based on the best available information. The case for such 'genetic discrimination' has yet to be fully resolved, and in the UK, for example, the government has an agreement with the Association of British Insurers to maintain a moratorium on the use of predictive genetic tests results in assessing applications for life insurance policies until 2019.[7]

■ Globalization and consumers: the ethical challenges of the global marketplace

Convergence in consumer needs across different countries has been widely identified as one of the key drivers of globalization in business, not least because brands such as Coca-Cola, McDonald's, Microsoft, Sony, and Toyota among others have been able to expand into multiple international markets, often necessitating little if any adaptation in their products to local tastes and preferences.

At one level, these developments have clearly extended many of the issues identified in the previous section to an international context, and indeed have made a number of the problems more acute. The problem of 'acceptable' levels of safety, for example, is accentuated where the lack of even basic products and services might mean that even partially defective products may be better than none. This controversy flared up around the Tata Nano, a low-cost automobile targeted at developing-country markets. The car failed European standards for crash safety, but in the Indian context, where the motorcycle or other, even less safer forms of transport are the next-best options, the Tata Nano still represents a major improvement in road safety (Olterman and McClanahan 2014).

At another level, globalization has also brought with it a new set of problems and issues relevant to consumer stakeholders (Witkowski 2005). Broadly speaking, these expanded, reframed, and/or new issues can be explained in relation to three main considerations:

- Different standards of consumer protection.
- Exporting consumerism and cultural homogenization.
- The role of markets in addressing poverty and development.

Different standards of consumer protection

As we saw at the beginning of the chapter, international organizations such as the UN recognize a set of global rights for consumers. However, the fact remains that the level of protection offered to consumers varies considerably across the globe, in terms of both government regulation and the standards offered by companies. Globalization therefore offers firms the opportunity to exploit these differences, especially where the provision of higher standards of protection, such as may be offered in developed countries, may be seen as an added cost burden that can be avoided in developing countries.

A good example is provided by the global tobacco industry. With markets in decline in most developed countries, tobacco firms have increasingly looked to developing countries for continued growth. Restrictions on the marketing of tobacco in Africa, Asia, and Latin America have frequently been less stringent than in North America and parts of Europe, giving companies more opportunity for concerted marketing campaigns direct to customers. Sales of cigarettes in developing countries have therefore escalated enormously, with China now representing the largest market globally for tobacco sales. In fact, consumption in China in 2014 was greater than that in the next 29 top cigarette consuming countries combined. Other major markets now include emerging economies such as Russia, Indonesia, India, Turkey, and Vietnam among the top ten global consumers of cigarettes.[8]

Unsurprisingly, tobacco companies have been increasingly criticized for targeting cigarettes at customers in developing countries, especially as such customers might have less knowledge of health problems, be more susceptible to inducements to purchase (such as free gifts), and less likely to be protected through regulations on advertising (Brodwin 2013). A major response to this situation emerged with the development of the World Health Organization Framework Convention on Tobacco Control (FCTC), which went into force in 2005. This commits signatory countries to a range of measures designed to reduce tobacco demand and supply, including a ban on tobacco advertising, promotion, and sponsorship. As of 2015, 180 countries had signed up to the framework, making it one of the most widely embraced treaties in UN history.[9] Such a concerted international response is rare, however, and for products such as food and drink, medicines, and automotives, substantial differences persist across countries.

Exporting and cultural homogenization

A second problem associated with the drive by companies to expand into new international markets with brands already successful at home is that they frequently come up against the accusation that they are not only exporting products, but are also ultimately exporting a whole set of cultural values. A prominent focus of debate here is the potential for mass marketing of global products and brands to contribute to the erosion of local cultures and the expansion of *cultural homogenization* (Baughn and Buchanan 2001; Witkowski 2005). While colonialism and global trade have long provided a context for cultural exchange or imposition, the unprecedented international success of global brands has led to increasing concerns over rising standardization and uniformity (Klein 2000). There are few high streets in the cities of Europe, Asia, or North America now without the ubiquitous McDonald's, KFC, or Starbucks outlets, or where the shops do not stock the same global products, such as the Apple iPhone, Diesel jeans, Heineken beer, or L'Oréal cosmetics. Even in the entertainment and media industries, Hollywood movies, recording artists such as Beyoncé, and even sports stars like Cristiano Ronaldo or Maria Sharapova have become global brands that have driven out interest in local cultural products. In their defence, of course, global marketers point to the fact that they have never forced consumers to buy their products, and that their success is simply based on giving people what they want. However, as we shall examine in more detail in Chapter 9, some have argued that the tactics of many such multinationals include the deliberate and aggressive removal of incumbent domestic rivals.

Whatever the intentions behind international marketing efforts, the drive for global dominance has meant an intensification of marketing activity in countries once largely immune to mass marketing activities. Expansion in global communications technologies such as satellite TV and the internet has meant that the promotion and glorification of consumerist lifestyles now takes place not just within national borders but on a global scale (Sklair 1991). The increasing predominance of consumerist ideologies in emerging and transitional economies such as China and the countries of central Europe has therefore raised considerable debate, particularly around the role of advertising in promoting consumerism (e.g. Zhao and Belk 2008).

These developments raise a number of complex ethical problems, particularly at a time when Western modes of consumption are increasingly subject to criticism due to their role in fostering socially and environmentally undesirable consequences. By promoting products and brands that are beyond the purchasing possibilities of the majority of consumers in developing countries, are multinationals simply reproducing dissatisfaction on an even greater scale than previously possible? Should emerging economies be 'protected' from potentially making the same mistakes or do they also have a right to the same 'opportunities' in terms of raising consumption levels? Are indigenous patterns of consumption in less-developed countries inherently better, fairer, or more sustainable than Western patterns, or are they even more inequitable and destructive? Whose responsibility is it, if anyone's, to police consumption activities?

We talked earlier in the context of safety standards about the Tata Nano car which brought many of these ethical questions to the surface. By targeting a price of 1 lakh or 100,000 rupees (approx. €1,500), the so-called 'People's Car' utilized cost-saving innovations to offer millions of Indians a once unimaginable opportunity for car ownership. On the one side, advocates argued that the fuel-efficient car would revolutionize mobility, drive economic growth, and offer a safer and more environmentally friendly alternative to motor rickshaws and other common forms of transport in developing countries. On the other hand, critics have argued that the Nano's likely impact on an already expanding car market in developing countries could be socially and environmentally disastrous and bring countries like India to gridlock.

VISIT THE ONLINE RESOURCE CENTRE for a short response to this feature

> **? THINK THEORY**
>
> Compare arguments based on consequences with arguments based on rights and justice in assessing the impact of a product such as the Tata Nano in India. What recommendations do you think proponents of these theories would have for responsible marketing practice in such a context?

The role of markets in addressing poverty and development

Finally, as the Tata Nano example suggests, globalization also raises the prospect of firms potentially targeting their products at a much wider, but far poorer, market of low-income consumers in developing countries. This issue has received considerable impetus in recent years with the introduction of the *bottom of the pyramid* concept (Kolk et al. 2014). Developed mainly by C.K. Prahalad and his colleagues, this idea essentially urges multinationals to tap into the 'fortune at the bottom of the pyramid' of economic development by offering innovative products and services to the world's poorest people in Africa, Asia, and Latin America. As Prahalad and Hammond (2002: 48) put it:

> By stimulating commerce and development at the bottom of the economic pyramid, MNCs could radically improve the lives of billions of people and help bring into being a more stable, less dangerous world. Achieving this goal does not require multinationals to spearhead global social development initiatives for charitable purposes. They need only act in their own self-interest, for there are enormous business benefits to be gained by entering developing markets.

In the global marketplace, this idea has gained significant attention and there is clearly a case to be made for advancing poverty reduction by developing what the United Nations Development Programme (UNDP) calls 'inclusive markets' in less-developed countries and regions. Examples of successful initiatives include the provision of microcredit services for poor entrepreneurs in the informal sector in Brazil by Banco Real (owned by the Spanish multinational bank, Santander), the launch of a high nutrition yoghurt product for poor children in rural Bangladesh by the French food company Danone, and the development of a low-cost laptop for schoolchildren in developing countries by the American microchip manufacturer Intel.

Despite garnering considerable enthusiasm, the bottom of the pyramid concept has also met with some important criticism. For example, Aneel Karnani (2007) has identified what he terms the 'mirage' of marketing to the bottom of the pyramid, suggesting that the profit opportunities are actually quite limited, and that firms looking to tackle poverty should focus on the poor primarily as producers rather than as consumers. As he contends, 'the only way to alleviate poverty is to raise the real income of the poor' (2007: 91). Certainly, there are few examples of firms actually generating anything like the 'fortune' that Prahalad promises, leading us to conclude that the drive towards more inclusive markets in developing countries probably relies as much on social purpose and corporate responsibility as it does on naked profit motivation—a point underscored by the relatively high proportion of non-profit social enterprises that have flourished in this niche (Karnani 2007). **Case 8** explores this phenomenon in more detail in the context of microfinance.

■ Consumers and corporate citizenship: consumer sovereignty and the politics of purchasing

We said at the beginning of this chapter that changing expectations and improved protection of consumer rights had moved us away from the traditional conception of *caveat emptor* or buyer beware. More now is expected of firms in terms of how they treat their customers. But what exactly would constitute truly ethical marketing in this sense? According to Craig Smith (1995), the most effective way to answer this question is by drawing on the notion of *consumer sovereignty*.

Consumer sovereignty

Consumer sovereignty is a key concept within neoclassical economics. It essentially suggests that under perfect competition, consumers drive the market; they express their needs and desires as a demand, which firms subsequently respond to by supplying them with the goods and services that they require. This gives rise to the idea that the customer is king—or, to put it another way, that consumers are sovereign in the market.

Real markets, however, are rarely characterized by perfect competition: consumers may not know enough about competing offerings to find out exactly where they can get the best deals (what economists call informational asymmetries); there may be very few competitors in some markets, thus limiting consumer choice; some firms may be able to take advantage of monopolistic positions to exploit consumers with high prices; and so on. Hence, in practice, there are clearly some limitations to the power and sovereignty of consumers. In many situations, they simply cannot exercise informed choice.

These limitations in making informed choices are an ethical problem on two counts. First, it may well mean that individual transactions will be unfair in some way to certain consumers. And secondly, that without consumer sovereignty, the economic system itself does not work efficiently and allocate resources fairly (see Smith 2014). In basic terms, this would imply that the economy serves business interests rather than those of consumers. By the same token, then, enhanced consumer sovereignty would therefore shift the balance of power *away* from business and *towards* the consumer. It is for this reason that Smith (1995) argues that consumer sovereignty represents a suitable ideal for marketing ethics to aspire to, and to be evaluated against. According to this argument, the greater the degree of sovereignty in a specific exchange or market, the more ethical the transaction should be regarded as. But how is consumer sovereignty to be assessed? For this, Smith (1995) proposes the consumer sovereignty test (CST).

According to Smith (1995), consumer sovereignty is comprised of three factors:

- **Consumer capability**. The degree of freedom from limitations in rational decision-making enjoyed by the consumer, for example, from vulnerability or coercion.

- **Information**. The availability and quality of relevant data pertaining to a purchase decision.

- **Choice**. The extent of the opportunity available to freely switch to another supplier.

The CST therefore is a test of the extent to which consumers are capable, informed, and free to choose when confronted with a potential purchase situation. If sovereignty is substantially restricted—say if the consumer's capability is reduced through vulnerability, or the option of switching is precluded due to high switching costs—then we might suggest that any exchange that happens may well be, at the very least, open to ethical question.

How exactly one defines what is an adequate level of sovereignty is of course rather hard to define. Sovereignty is a relative, rather than an absolute, concept. However, some of the ways in which adequacy can be established for each factor in the CST are presented in **Figure 8.4**, along with a summary of the main elements of the CST.

	Dimension	Definition	Sample criteria for establishing adequacy
Consumer Sovereignty Test	**Consumer capability**	Freedom from limitations in rational decision-making	Vulnerability factors, e.g. age, education, health
	Information	Availability and quality of relevant data	Quantity, comparability and complexity of information; degree of bias or deception
	Choice	Opportunity for switching	Number of competitors and level of competition; switching costs

Figure 8.4 Consumer sovereignty test
Source: Derived from Smith (1995).

Ultimately, as with many business ethics tools, the CST cannot really be expected to tell us exactly where consumers have been treated unethically. However, it does provide us with a relatively simple and practical framework with which to identify possible ethics violations, and even to suggest potential areas for remediation. This is particularly important from the corporate citizenship perspective. If, as we have argued, corporations, just as much as governments and other social actors, have come to be responsible for protecting consumers' rights, then they need clear ways of assessing ethical situations. Nonetheless, as Smith (1995) suggests, the application of the CST by managers not only requires some kind of moral impulse or conscience on their part, but also leaves consumers relying on the marketer's paternalism for their protection.

☑ **Skill check**

Applying the consumer sovereignty test. Using the consumer sovereignty test effectively helps to identify whether a marketing transaction is likely to be regarded as ethical.

Ethical consumption

While forms of **ethical consumption** of one sort or another have been around for centuries, the phenomenon has risen to considerable prominence in the early 1990s. Ethical consumption covers a range of different activities, including boycotting certain companies in response to a poor social, ethical, or environmental record, buying non-animal-tested products, avoiding products made by sweatshop or child labour, choosing fair trade or organic products, reusing or recycling products, etc. It is difficult to sum up the full range of activities that could potentially be included under the umbrella of ethical consumption, but at its core is the desire to make certain consumption choices due to personal moral beliefs and values.

What makes a consumption decision driven by moral beliefs different from one that is not is open to debate, but arguably one of the key characteristics here is that the decision is about considering others—i.e. ethical consumption is about decisions beyond self-interest. The main form of ethical consumption we are concerned with here is where the consumer's personal moral beliefs and values refer to the specific actions of businesses, such as a decision to deliberately boycott Shell over its Arctic exploration, or a decision to deliberately seek out detergents low in bleach because of environmental considerations.

There is much evidence to suggest that many consumers do indeed include ethical considerations in their evaluations of businesses and the products they sell. For example, one UK survey suggested that spending on ethical goods and services grew by 9% in 2013 while the UK economy overall only grew 1.9%.[10] Although few consumers have been found to be completely consistent in their selection of ethical features over the alternatives (Auger et al. 2006), such findings do imply that ethical consumerism can no longer be dismissed as simply a few disparate pockets of extremists. Taken together, the ethical market in the UK is now said to be worth something like £78 billion, which represents an increasing proportion of overall market spend.[11] Much of this growth has come from 'ethical finance' products such as ethical investments, which we explored in

Ethical consumption
The conscious and deliberate choice to base consumption choices on personal moral beliefs and values.

some detail in Chapter 6 (Socially responsible investment, pp. 263–267). Other major areas of growth include electric, hybrid, and more fuel-efficient cars (up 78% in 2013) and green electricity tariffs (up 58%). Similar findings have appeared across much of the rest of the world. According to a 2012 survey of nearly 28,000 online consumers in 56 markets by the market researchers Nielsen, over 66% of consumers around the world say they prefer to buy products and services from companies that have implemented programmes to give back to society and support environmental sustainability.[12]

Such findings obviously have significant implications for businesses—although survey results of this kind have to be treated with caution, given that respondents tend to provide socially desirable answers that do not necessarily closely match their purchasing behaviour (Auger and Devinney 2007). Nonetheless, there seems little doubt that a small but significant proportion of purchases are influenced by ethical considerations—and that this occurs across the globe, from Europe to North America to Asia (Devinney et al. 2010).

Ethical consumers have therefore been increasingly seen as playing an important role in prompting businesses to address ethics more enthusiastically, either through marketing specifically ethical products, or through developing a more ethical approach to business in general (Crane 2001). As such, firms can adopt either an *ethical niche* orientation or a *mainstream* orientation to the ethical market (Crane 2013a). While the former is concerned with offering specialist ethical products to a committed minority, the latter involves firms in integrating ethical considerations into conventional product offerings for broader market segments.

If we draw the connection here with consumer sovereignty, what this means is that consumers to some extent can act as a social control on business (Smith 2014). If consumers demand improved business ethics through the market, then business might be expected to listen and respond. Hence, the consumer is effectively using their purchases as 'votes' to support or criticize certain business practices rather than using the ballot box to vote for political solutions through government and regulation. Dickinson and Carsky (2005: 36) refer to this as *consumer citizenship*. This, as we initially mentioned in Chapter 2, is significant for the notion of corporate citizenship since the corporation may then act as a form of conduit for the exercise of consumers' political entitlements and aspirations as a citizen.

In many Western democracies, such political consumerism has become one of the most widespread forms of political participation, second only to voting (Copeland 2014). That is, apathy towards conventional politics has taken hold in many European countries, the US, and elsewhere, particularly among young people, while consumer activism appears to be on the increase. As Noreena Hertz (2001a: 190) contends:

> instead of showing up at the voting booth to register their demands and wants, people are turning to corporations. The most effective way to be political today is not to cast your vote at the ballot box but to do so at the supermarket or at a shareholder's meeting. Why? Because corporations respond.

Consider the issue of depleting fish stocks. We typically think that such resource conservation issues are a matter for governments to resolve through national and international fisheries agreements, etc. However, with the advent of certified sustainable fish in the marketplace, consumers can encourage and reward firms for tackling the problem, rather than by making a political choice at the ballot box. In Hertz's words, such issues have undergone a 'silent takeover' by corporations, with consumers using the lever of the all-important corporate reputation to effect social change. These developments take ethical consumption away from merely being a way for consumers to assuage their consciences, towards active participation in making social and political choices.

In the absence of better ways to make their views heard, ethical consumption is certainly a positive phenomenon. However, it does have its downside. For example:

- However socially responsible they may be, the motives of corporations will always be primarily financial rather than moral. Hence, their attention to social concerns will always be driven by market appeal. Minority interests or unattractive causes are likely to be ignored or pushed aside.

- Market choices are predicated on an ability and willingness to pay. If consumers decide they no longer want to pay extra for these ethical 'accessories', or if they can no longer afford them, will they just be dropped?

- If purchases are 'votes', then the rich get far more voting power than the poor. The market is hardly democratic in the same way that elections are.

For all its benefits, then, ethical consumption is never going to be an adequate replacement for political action—even if political action appears to be falling out of favour as ethical consumption becomes more mainstream. It does, however, show us that consumers are now important actors in the regulation and shaping of business ethics—and that whether we like it or not, corporations are increasingly becoming a preferred channel through which moral choices can be expressed. And if the value of ethical consumption is subject to challenge, the question of sustainability contests the whole practice of consumption itself.

■ Sustainable consumption

As we noted earlier in the chapter, it is now commonplace to refer to the contemporary world as a consumer society. Not only are levels of consumption ever-increasing, but we increasingly define ourselves by what and how we consume; we use consumption as a site for social, cultural, and, as we saw above, political activity; and consumption of products and services increasingly pervades new areas of our lives, such as the movement away from active participation in sporting activities to consumption of sports products such as TV programmes, computer games, and replica shirts, or the replacement of home cooking with pre-packaged 'ready meals' while watching a cooking show on TV.

Consumption is ultimately the reason why anything gets produced. Without doubt, the massive growth in consumption in the latter part of the twentieth century and the beginning of the twenty-first century has placed enormous strains on the natural environment. After all, the consumer society is built on two very problematic assumptions: that consumption can continue to increase because there are no finite resource limits, and that the by-products and wastes created by consumption can be disposed off indefinitely. Hence, it is not unreasonable to suggest that high (and ever increasing) levels of consumption pose enormous barriers to the development of sustainable business (Kilbourne et al. 1997; Schaefer and Crane 2005)—and that consumers can be held responsible for much of the social and environmental degradation that their spiralling demands for products and services inevitably seem to bring (Heiskanen and Pantzar 1997). This is particularly true in the developed world, where consumption is, on average, about 32 times more per person than in the developing world (Diamond 2008). The UN expects the world's resource consumption to triple by 2050—a highly unsustainable scenario unless humanity were to find a way to 'decouple' economic growth and resource consumption (UNEP 2011). Sustainable consumption is one important approach to contribute to this goal.

What is sustainable consumption?

While current levels of consumption may indeed be unsustainable, the question of how to move towards a more sustainable form of consumption is a vexed one, but also a vital one. As we saw at the beginning of the chapter, even the UN now regards the promotion of sustainable consumption as a basic element of consumer protection (see Figure 8.1). So what would constitute a sustainable level of consumption? One reasonable definition that is used by the European Environment Agency and a number of other organizations comes from the 1994 Oslo Symposium, which states that **sustainable consumption** is 'the use of goods and services that respond to basic needs and bring a better quality of life, while minimising the use of natural resources, toxic materials and emissions of waste and pollutants over the life-cycle, so as not to jeopardise the needs of future generations'. As this shows, sustainable consumption is not just about the point of consumption but also about a product's impact across its entire life cycle from extraction to disposal.

Sustainable consumption
Consumer behaviour that enhances quality of life and minimizes or eliminates social and environmental harms throughout a product's life cycle.

Although such definitions do not specify any given level of consumption to be sustainable, it would be a mistake to assume that people can, or will, readily give up current levels of consumption, given that it is widely regarded as an enjoyable, liberatory, and expressive activity in modern society (Borgmann 2000). Indeed, the whole notion of ensuring that the satisfaction of needs does not compromise the satisfaction of future generations' needs is extremely problematic if the 'needs' satisfied by contemporary consumption are those of sustaining our self-image, our identity, and even our social relationships and culture (Schaefer and Crane 2005).

Rogene Buchholz (1998) suggests that a move towards more sustainable consumption therefore needs to be seen in the light of changes in the ethics governing our societies (see **Figure 8.5**). Returning to the work of Max Weber, Buchholz argues that the Protestant ethic of self-discipline and moral sense of duty that held sway during the establishment of market systems in much of Europe encouraged people to engage in productive labour for the pursuit of gain, but to desist from immediate pleasure in order to accumulate capital and wealth (ostensibly for the glory of God). However, the advancement of secularization, and in particular the ethic of consumerism that has gradually replaced these traditional values, have served to promote instant gratification and hedonism, and have downgraded the value of saving and durability.

Ethic	Imposes limits to	Promotes
Protestant ethic	Consumption	Investment in productive capacity
Consumerism ethic	Saving	Instant gratification and consumption
Environmental ethic	Consumption	Alternative meanings of growth and investment in the environment

Figure 8.5 Changing social ethics and consumption
Source: Derived from Buchholz (1998).

To move towards sustainability, Buchholz suggests, we need a new environmental ethic that again provides moral limits to consumption. Of course, reducing consumption is problematic, both politically and practically, for it also has serious implications for employment, income, investment, and other aspects crucial to economic well-being and growth. The culture of consumption is deeply embedded in the dominant organizing framework of modern societies—a framework which is beneficial to, and sustained by, powerful social, economic, and political actors (Kilbourne et al. 1997; Schaefer and Crane 2005). However, as we said in Chapter 7, by redirecting growth towards more socially beneficial ends—such as environmental products, green jobs, clean technologies, etc.—growth *could* still occur. This idea of the need to decouple the economic consumption that fuels growth from the material resource consumption that negatively impacts the environment has indeed been a position commonly taken by governments and corporations despite limited evidence to date of its feasibility (Jackson 2014).

Ultimately then, the real challenge of sustainable consumption is to introduce alternative meanings of growth into society so that we can learn to cultivate deeper non-material sources of fulfilment. You do not need us to tell you that this is an immense challenge in the consumer culture of the twenty-first century. Such changes in values can only ever happen gradually, and usually imperceptibly. In terms of real actions to promote more sustainable consumption on a day-to-day level, we need to look at the more practical solutions that are emerging from businesses, government, and consumers.

? THINK THEORY

Think about the challenge of sustainable consumption from a consequentialist point of view. This is the main approach to justifying increased consumption, but can it also provide the basis for moving towards a more sustainable level of consumption?

VISIT THE
ONLINE
RESOURCE
CENTRE
for a short
response to this
feature

Steps towards sustainable consumption

On a practical level, there is much that business, government, and consumers *can* do to seek more sustainable modes of consumption. **Ethics Online 8** provides an illustration of some of the practical tools available to individual consumers and businesses to measure and modify their consumption choices with respect to environmental impacts. As yet, however, progress towards more sustainable consumption has been slow, though signs of change are emerging, primarily in the areas of producing environmentally responsible products, product recapture, service replacements for products, product sharing, and reducing demand.

Producing environmentally responsible products

Perhaps the most obvious way for firms to respond to the challenge of sustainable consumption is to develop and market products that impact less harmfully on the environment. This has been an area of activity for some 25 years or so, and has led to the development of a vast array of products, including recycled and unbleached paper, 'green' detergents, low-energy light bulbs, non-toxic toys, and energy-efficient appliances. Even the car market has begun to see genuine innovations towards more environmentally responsible products. Toyota started this trend with its Prius in the late 1990s,

VISIT THE
ONLINE
RESOURCE
CENTRE
for links to
useful sources
of further
information

▲ **ETHICS ONLINE** 8

Tracking sustainable consumption

The debate on changing consumption behaviour has become ever more animated. Most notably, heightened awareness on climate change has made it increasingly evident that major changes to our carbon footprint require more fundamental changes in the way we consume. Few would disagree that we need to move towards more sustainable consumption patterns, but most of us are not exactly sure who really needs to change, by how much, and how. In recent years though a number of online tools and indices have been launched which help us to track how our consumption choices impact on the environment, and how we can improve our decisions.

Take Zerofootprint. It provides a free online tool for people to measure and manage their carbon footprint that is especially targeted at young people and schools. Or National Geographic, which provides a free online tool for consumers to measure their broader environmental impact with its Greendex system, developed in collaboration with Globescan, the international polling firm. The Greendex project also provides a rating of consumers across 18 different countries that illustrates which countries have the most environmentally responsible consumers. In the 2014 results, for example, the top three rated countries were India, China, and South Korea while bottom of the list were Japan, Canada and America.

Most tracking tools also include advice and guidance on how to improve your consumption practices. The footprint calculator of WWF, for instance, provides the user with an idea how many planets would be needed if everybody had the same lifestyle as them

and then offers them the chance to sign up to the Footprint Challenge to reduce their impact. Similarly, Slavery Footprint, which allows users to calculate, based on basic consumption data, how many slaves currently work for them around the world invites users to take action through the associated online Action Center and Free World mobile apps.

These developments are part of a broader move to provide new tools for consumers on the go to make more informed sustainability decisions. For instance, Social Impact App uses the current location of a consumer and provides a customized list of the closest fair trade coffee shops, B Corps and other sustainable consumption outlets. Choco-locate does the same by finding the closest fair trade chocolate shop. Services such as ThisFish enable consumers to track where each fish in the store has come from, including who it was caught by and where, simply by keying in a code on their smartphone. Likewise Ethical Bean, one of Canada's first B Corps, provides an app that scans the QR code on its coffee bags and then provides the consumer with detailed information about where the coffee was grown and who picked it, and cupping, scoring, and roasting information.

Increasingly companies are being offered tracking services to enhance their sustainability impact. Zerofootprint, for example, has commercialized tracking software for businesses eager to track and incentivize more sustainable decisions among employees and consumers. Similarly, the makers of the Slavery Footprint app, Made In A Free World, market software to businesses to help them assess and manage the risks of forced labour in their supply chains.

Sources

http://www.socialimpactapp.com/.
http://www.ethicalbean.com/coffee/app/.
http://choco-locate.com.
http://slaveryfootprint.org.
http://madeinafreeworld.com.
http://environment.nationalgeographic.com/environment/greendex/.
http://footprint.wwf.org.uk.
http://calc.zerofootprint.net.
http://thisfish.info.

which boasts a hybrid petrol and electric motor. As a result, it has low emissions, high fuel efficiency, and is about 90% recyclable—making it one of Japan's most popular cars and one of Toyota's top-selling lines. More recently, electric cars have grown in popularity. In 2014 US sales of electric cars doubled compared to 2012 to some 120,000 units, while in the UK the January 2015 sales of electric cars were up 300% compared to the year before.[13] Competition is also escalating from emerging economies such as India and China, where companies are seeking to be global leaders in electric vehicles by leapfrogging existing petrol-based technologies.[14]

Developing new products is a key element of any movement towards sustainable consumption, but consumers also have to want to use them. Green product development should therefore be seen within a broader context of *sustainable marketing*, whereby firms develop and promote sustainable solutions for consumers. A key element of sustainable marketing is the development of appropriate *eco-labels* that communicate to consumers a product's environmental features.

Eco-labels are important because, as we saw above, consumer sovereignty demands that consumers have appropriate information with which to make informed choices between competing offerings. However, a survey of products in the US, Canada, UK, and Australia revealed that although environmental claims and information were becoming significantly more common, most of them committed at least one 'sin' of greenwashing— namely 'the act of misleading consumers regarding the environmental practices of a company or the environmental benefits of a product or service' (Terrachoice 2009). Eco-labels, therefore, need to act as a trusted guarantee that a product genuinely delivers the environmental benefits that it claims. Effective and successful eco-labels tend to be operated or verified by independent third parties (rather than simply being a company's self-declared stamp of greenness); they should be easy to recognize and understand, comparable, and focused on criteria that matter to consumers. **Ethics in Action 8.2** highlights some of the issues around eco-labels in the context of one the fastest-growing segments of sustainable consumption, organic food.

More broadly, progress towards sustainability will also require a willingness to change markets as well as changing products (Peattie and Crane 2005). Hence, rather than just considering the introduction of new products and labels, attention is beginning to focus more on *product service systems*, i.e. constellations of products, services, supporting networks, and infrastructure that provide benefits to consumers in ways that impact less on the environment (Mont 2004). These include product-recapture systems, service replacements for products, product sharing, and other innovative ways of re-engineering markets.

Product recapture

Current business systems of production tend to operate on a linear model where materials are used to make products, which are then consumed and disposed of (see **Figure 8.6**). And that is the last that we see of them. However, moving towards a circular use of resources—ensuring that so-called 'waste' is recaptured and brought back into productive use—not only minimizes waste, but means that less 'virgin' material is needed at source (Fuller 1999). Reconstructing products in this way (by recycling, refurbishing, or re-manufacturing) can also help to bring prices down because the cost of material inputs is often lower (Pearce 2009). As we shall see in Chapter 9, this often relies on close collaboration between businesses to be truly effective, but product recapture can also be introduced

VISIT THE
ONLINE
RESOURCE
CENTRE
for links to
useful sources
of further
information

ETHICS IN ACTION 8.2

http://www.ethicalcorp.com

Organic food—what is an 'organic' label really worth?

Jon Entine, 12 July 2013

Consumers are willing to pay a premium for organic products, but the realities can mean you get little more than a psychological boost for your buck. Supermarkets in North America and Europe are overflowing with organic-labelled fruit, vegetables, eggs, and meats. More than 80 countries have organic standards and products carry one or more of 200 seals, logos, and certification claims.

But are consumers able to make informed choices? What is the real ethical impact of 'buying organic'? The answers are murkier than you might think. Ecolabels represent an ecological, ethical ingredient or sustainability claim. The US, Canada, the European Union, and Japan have comprehensive organic standards overseen by governments. Many nations have a '100% organic' label. But the devil is in the detail, and the details can be devilish indeed.

In the US, the Department of Agriculture label has numerous levels—headed by the 100% designation USDA Organic seal. The US government also allows the word 'organic' on products that contain 95% organic ingredients. But they could contain monosodium glutamate, a flavour-enhancing natural ingredient, or carrageenan, a seaweed substance that thickens food. Both ingredients are an anathema to organic-favouring foodies, who believe that they pose health dangers even though government scientists have cleared them as perfectly harmless.

So, how reliable are organic labels? For one thing, conventional and genetically modified seeds are known to occasionally mix with organic supplies. But in-depth field testing to ensure compliance on this is a rarity. Typically, certification requires only that operations must have a system plan and compliance records. Some organic labels are more rigorous than others. To earn the EU's new organic label, farmers and processors must follow a strict set of standards, including the requirement that 95% of the product's agricultural ingredients have been organically produced and certified as such. Some member countries have their own organic labels in addition to the EU-wide regime.

The organic industry in North America and Europe is now estimated to be worth a combined €40 billion a year. According to the European commission, those regions comprise 90% of global organic consumption.

Of course, with success comes temptation; the organic industry is no different from any other. In 2009, for example, American retailer Target was nabbed for falsely advertising soymilk as organic. Two years earlier the USDA considered pulling the organic certification from Target's dairy supplier—and the US's largest—Aurora Dairy, which supplies mega-organic company Horizon, for selling non-organic milk marketed as organic for more than four years. In early 2013, German authorities said they had identified more than 200 farms suspected of selling premium priced eggs as organic free range that actually were laid by hens kept in pens. While strict rules exist in many countries for meat, egg, and dairy farms claiming to be organic, unresolved issues about the ethical treatment of animals remain contentious.

Italy has emerged as fraud central. In April 2013, in an operation dubbed Green War, prosecutors in Pesaro identified 23 suspected members of a counterfeiting ring. The fraudsters apparently set up a dozen shell companies across Europe, issuing fake organic certificates for conventional foodstuffs. In previous fraud cases, conventional goods were brought into the EU and then relabelled. Now, say prosecutors, products are stamped 'organic' in the Ukraine or Moldova and fraudulently certified on site.

China has emerged as a nettlesome challenge. It has moved aggressively into the organic market, exporting canned tomatoes, milk, and dried fruit and tea. But its certifying system is less than reliable. Banned toxic pesticides and other chemicals have shown up on several occasions.

Next to issues of labelling and auditing, there remain some inherent trade-offs with organic food. Although organic farming may be environmentally benign when producing small quantities for regional markets, it is precarious on a large scale. In 2008, the USDA conducted the Organic Production Survey, the largest ever study of organic farming yields. In line with previous research, the survey found that it takes one-and-a-half to two times as much land in the US to grow food organically as it does to grow food by conventional methods. This production shortfall puts pressure on global farmers to grow more to make up the difference. In the developing world, that can mean burning down forests to turn the land into farmland, a process that emits a tremendous amount of carbon dioxide into the atmosphere and harms the water cycle and species that live in forests. In other words, although organic farming might require the use of fewer manufactured pesticides, its broader impact can be environmentally problematic.

Sources

Ethical Corporation, Jon Entine, 12 July 2013, http://www.ethicalcorp.com. Reproduced with the kind permission of Ethical Corporation.

? THINK THEORY

Think about the problems of organic food certification in terms of the consumer sovereignty test. Do consumers have full information, capability, and choice in making organic food choices?

VISIT THE
ONLINE
RESOURCE
CENTRE
for a short
response to this
feature

within a single company. The challenge for companies is to design for recycling, reuse, and repair and to establish channels that facilitate the flow of product recapture.

Such considerations have been brought into sharp focus by extended producer responsibility legislation that has been introduced in various countries. Probably the best known is the EC Directive on Waste Electrical and Electronic Equipment (WEEE), which came into force in 2004 and was revised in 2012. This aims to minimize the impacts of electrical and electronic equipment on the environment by making producers directly responsible

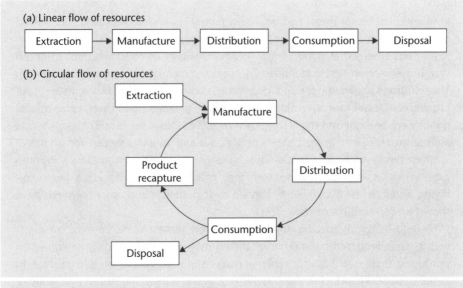

Figure 8.6 From a linear to a circular flow of resources

for financing most of the activities involved in taking back and recycling electrical and electronic equipment, at no cost to the consumer. At least 25 US states have also introduced electronics take back legislation to tackle the growing problem of e-waste.[15]

Service replacements for products

If this thinking is taken a little further, there is no reason for the consumer to own the product in the first place. After all, what we are often seeking when we buy products is their performance—the ability to wash clothes for example—not necessarily the ownership of the physical product itself—a washing machine. By replacing the sale of the product with an agreement to provide an ongoing service, firms can substantially reduce the amount of material goods being produced, as well as managing emissions and energy inputs more efficiently (Rothenberg 2007). What we have seen in recent years then are companies experimenting with forms of product leasing, where the company maintains ownership, but conducts servicing, replacement of worn parts, upgrading of obsolete elements, and ultimately replacement and/or redistribution.

The 'servicizing' approach has been most common in industrial contexts—for example, Xerox typically rents and leases most of its commercial photocopiers—mainly because customers are larger and easier to service (Rothenberg 2007). During the 2010s, Philips has experimented with servicizing in its commercial lighting business—that is, the company now sells lighting as a service where customers only pay for the light, and the company takes care of the technology risk and the investment by taking the equipment back when it is appropriate to recycle or upgrade the materials for reuse.[16] However, such changes can also be challenging. One servicing pioneer, the carpet manufacturer Interface, ran into problems when it discovered that tax and accounting rules favoured sales over leasing, and that most of its customers operated very different budgets for purchasing and leasing—meaning that it had to deal with different people from those it was used to dealing with (Esty and Winston 2009).

Product sharing

Another similar way of reducing consumption is for products to be shared by groups of consumers, thereby getting more use out of the same resources. This way of increasing eco-efficiency has been fairly successful in certain parts of Europe, such as Germany and the Netherlands, with products such as cars, washing machines, and certain tools being found to be particularly suitable for sharing (Schrader 1999). Although inconvenience is a major disadvantage, studies suggest that consumers welcome the savings in storage space, money, and the hassle of repairs and maintenance—not to mention benefiting the environment.

One area where this idea has particularly caught on is in car sharing, which now is available in more than a thousand cities across the globe.[17] Since many of these services are co-ordinated and managed on the internet we have seen the rise of what is often referred to as the '**sharing economy**'. Whether it is renting a spare bedroom on Airbnb, a spare driveway on JustPark, a prom dress from Rent The Runway, a neighbour's car through RelayRides, booking a taxi ride on Uber, or even just giving away unwanted stuff on Yerdle—around a quarter of US, UK, or Canadian consumers engage in these services, easily accessed by apps on their smartphones (Ufford 2015). The upshot of this new sector is indeed that it reduces the consumption of material goods since it enhances the utilization of existing products.

> **Sharing economy**
> An economic system built around the sharing of human and physical resources.

On the other hand, such a peer-to-peer marketplace is also not unproblematic. First, in order to be comfortable sharing your car or your home with strangers there is a strong demand for trust and new forms of identity verification—with some rather problematic implications for data privacy. More critical from an ethical perspective though is the fact that the sharing economy provides people with jobs that are generally lower paid, lack insurance and other social protections (Reich 2015). It is therefore very much an open question whether this new sector—as much as it contributes to ecological sustainability—can over time develop into a market or workplace that is also sustainable from the social perspective.

Reducing demand

Ultimately, the challenge of sustainability can only really be met if society accepts that people simply have to buy less stuff. It does not take much intelligence to work out that this idea tends not to be too popular with business—nor for that matter with customers or governments! However, there are some areas where deliberate reduction of demand has been actively encouraged. For example, in 2008 China instituted a complete ban on free plastic bags in order to reduce pollution—and within a year it had saved an equivalent of 1.6 million tonnes of oil (Watts 2009). Where excessive consumption can even mar consumer enjoyment and threaten business—such as in the tourism industry—demand reduction can be particularly pertinent.

Demand reduction can also come from consumers themselves. As a slightly different form of ethical consumption (as described earlier in the chapter), consumers choosing to go down the route of 'voluntary simplicity' or 'downshifting' go beyond registering their approval or disapproval of certain companies or practices and actively attempt to consume less overall. Indeed, as Shaw and Newholm's (2001) study of voluntary simplifiers makes clear, some degree of reflection on restraint is almost inevitable once consumers begin to take ethical stances on consumption. Instead of buying a shirt guaranteed to be sweatshop free, why not do without completely? Just as car sharing might seem more sustainable than owning your own, the decision to cut down on making journeys altogether, or replacing them with walking or biking, probably represents a yet more sustainable option. For many people, such decisions may often be taking things just a step too far. But if modern society is to tackle sustainability seriously, we may just find that reducing consumption is simply a bitter pill that has to be swallowed.

■ Summary

In this chapter we have discussed the specific stake held by consumers and outlined some of the main rights of consumers, including rights to safe products, honest and truthful communications, fair prices, fair treatment, and privacy. That firms still sometimes fail to respect these rights suggests that the interests of producers and consumers are not always seen by firms to be as aligned as stakeholder theory might imply. These problems simply would not occur if firms really saw their own interests to be best served by looking after their consumers' interests. Of course, in many of the problems and examples we have traced in this chapter, there are quite complex ethical arguments at stake. And doing the right thing by customers and potential customers may not always seem particularly attractive when one thinks that they are, for most companies, the single source of revenue to keep the business going. Still, consumers appear to be demanding better treatment, and we suggested that tools such as the consumer sovereignty test might at least provide some guidance on what should constitute ethical practice.

What we have also shown in this chapter, though, is that as the expectations placed on business have grown so too have the possibilities for consumers to assume certain responsibilities in the control of business. The rise of ethical consumption places consumers in the role of policing companies, and even exercising their political rights as citizens through corporations. Notwithstanding the problems and dangers of such a situation, the challenge of sustainability pushes this yet further. In the consumer society that we currently live in, it appears that consumers might be expected to shoulder increased responsibilities, as well as being afforded certain rights.

Study questions

1. 'Of course, corporations should avoid treating their customers in an unethical manner. After all, in the long run, unethical behaviour towards customers only serves to harm firms' own interests.' Critically evaluate this statement with reference to examples from the following:

   (a) Mobile phone companies.

   (b) Holiday companies.

   (c) Chemical companies.

   How does your answer differ for each type of company? Explain your answer.

2. What is deception in marketing communications? Give examples of marketing practices that you believe are deceptive.

3. Set out and explain the four main pricing practices where ethical problems are likely to arise.

4. How is it possible to determine consumer vulnerability? Whose responsibility is it to prevent exploitation of vulnerable consumers? Explain, using examples from contemporary business practice.

5. What are the arguments for and against firms extending their marketing strategies to poor consumers in developing countries? Should firms have a responsibility to serve those at the bottom of the pyramid?

6. What is the difference between ethical and sustainable consumption—and how should firms respond to either challenge?

Research exercise

Food companies have often been accused of targeting children with adverts for unhealthy products such as fast food, confectionery, and snacks. Your task is to determine the extent of such targeting, and its appropriateness.

1. Review the websites of three major food companies serving these markets in your country (for example, one fast food, one confectionery, and one snacks), and collect examples of communications to customers.

2. Record three hours of TV programming on Saturday morning and note the details of all the adverts—the product, the advertiser, and the target.

3. Assess the extent of advertising of 'unhealthy food' to children based on this evidence—is it more or less than other products? Are children targeted more than adults?

4. Analyse the way that children are communicated to in these marketing communications. To what extent are advertisers taking advantage of the vulnerability of children?

Key readings

VISIT THE ONLINE RESOURCE CENTRE for links to further key readings

1. **Smith**, N.C. 1995. **Marketing strategies for the ethics era.** *Sloan Management Review*, 36 (4): 85–97.

   This is an easy-to-read article that explores a number of interesting cases in order to take a close look at changes in expectations about marketing ethics. It then presents a powerful way of thinking about what should constitute an ethical exchange in today's marketplace.

2. **Prahalad**, C.K. and Hammond, A. 2002. **Serving the world's poor, profitably.** *Harvard Business Review*, 80 (9): 48–57.

   A ground-breaking article offering a new perspective on marketing to the world's poorest people. It does not really deal with all of the ethical issues involved, but it provides a great introduction to the debates about the role of corporations in poverty reduction and social inclusion.

VISIT THE
ONLINE
RESOURCE
CENTRE
for links to
useful sources
of further
information on
this case

Case 8

Targeting the poor with microfinance: hype or hope for poverty reduction?

This case discusses the phenomenon of microfinance, whereby small-scale financial services are targeted directly at poor consumers in developing countries that have been excluded from the mainstream banking sector. It explains the different forms and providers of microfinance, the challenges faced in using microfinance as a strategy for addressing poverty, and raises questions over the rates of interest charged to borrowers. The case provides an opportunity to explore questions of consumer exclusion, fair pricing, and 'bottom of the pyramid' marketing strategies.

Microfinance refers to the range of financial services targeted directly at poor customers who are normally unable to access traditional banking services. The reasons for the exclusion of the poor from mainstream banking are many. They include their lack of formal employment, little access to collateral for loans, a perceived lack of creditworthiness, limited banking infrastructure in poor areas, and the unwillingness of banks to service small-ticket financial services (because of the high cost ratio involved). According to most reliable estimates, somewhere in the region of 2.5 billion people lack access to formal banking services.

Microfinance seeks to open the doors to poor consumers by developing financial services specially suited to their circumstances. The types of services offered range from small-scale loans (often referred to as 'microcredit'), to savings vehicles, insurance services, and money transfer services. It is microcredit, though, that has garnered the most attention to date, not least because lending services have been the longest and most well-developed form of microfinance.

Pioneered in Bangladesh in the 1970s by the Grameen Bank and its founder, Muhammad Yunus (who together won the 2006 Nobel Peace Prize), microcredit can work in a number of ways. The main characteristic, however, is that it is not based on collateral, or even necessarily on any legally enforceable contracts, but rather on a system of 'group lending'. That is, rather than covering the lender's risk with assets of the borrower and/or the threat of legal proceedings, borrowers are formed into small groups where they either monitor one another through mutual trust or are required to guarantee each other's loans. Repayment is typically organized into instalments with relatively short spacing (often weekly or semi-weekly), the amounts lent are relatively modest (averaging around €100, hence the 'micro' label), and services are often targeted predominantly at women in order to address gender inequality issues.

Despite the scepticism of traditional lenders, microcredit has proved to be an extremely successful lending model. By 2009, there were estimated to be some 3,500 microcredit institutions, lending to over 150 million customers who otherwise would have been unable to access financial services—or forced to rely on unscrupulous moneylenders in the informal economy. This number has rocketed in recent years, with China alone now accounting for more than 7,000 microcredit companies, having tripled in number from 2010 to 2013.

The default rates for microcredit loans, on average, have been considerably lower than for conventional loans. Globally, microcredit repayment rates average around 97%, according to the Microfinance Information Exchange which records data on more than 2,000 microfinance institutions, serving some 94 million borrowers across the developing world. Grameen Bank, for example, boasts a loan recovery rate of 96.7% across more than 8 million borrowers—96% of whom are women.

Microcredit institutions have also managed to generate good returns from lending to the poor, with an average rate of return of around 6% per year. The best performers can generate two or three times that amount. For instance, the Mexican microfinance institution, Compartamos, reported a return on assets of 13–18% for the five-year period 2008–12, and profit margins of 30–42%.

Beyond microcredit, microfinance providers have increasingly offered a wide array of other services. As well as savings and loans, some microfinance institutions also offer education on financial issues and even social services. In recent years, attention has focused particularly on the introduction of innovative services provided through new information and communication technologies. In 2007, for instance, Vodafone's Kenyan subsidiary Safaricom Kenya launched a mobile banking service, M-Pesa, enabling money transfers based on text messaging. In a country where only 40% of the 44 million residents have a bank account (around 8–10 million people), M-Pesa has far outstripped this number, with some 18 million users in 2014. The system allows customers to use mobile phones like debit cards, so that they can transfer money between virtual accounts. This enables users to make a range of financial transactions, including the withdrawal and deposit of cash with registered outlets, paying for goods, and even repaying microcredit loans—all simply by sending a text message.

Building a path to poverty reduction?

In many respects the development of microfinance is clearly a success story. Microfinance has been particularly successful in Asia (which accounts for more than 50% of all borrowers), with countries such as India, Bangladesh, and Indonesia among the largest national markets. Latin America and Africa have also increasingly embraced microfinance practices, and even developed countries such as the US have a small number of providers.

Such financial inclusion has enabled those towards the bottom of the economic pyramid to participate more fully in the formal economy, to develop financial literacy and independence, evade the risks and uncertainty of informal saving and lending, and build credit histories that can in turn lead to further accumulation of assets. Some evidence also suggests that microfinance has led to greater consumption (which in turn drives local economic growth), and by extension, can provide greater opportunities for education of borrowers and their families. Although the evidence supporting such claims remains somewhat inconclusive, it does appear fairly certain that if nothing else, microfinance has helped borrowers to smooth their consumption levels so that they are less vulnerable to seasonal variations, such as the vagaries of crop success or failure, or to personal emergencies and natural disasters.

Another impact frequently claimed for microfinance is that it has a positive effect on alleviating poverty. Indeed, for many of its advocates, poverty reduction is essentially the *raison d'être* of microfinance. This is because many microfinance institutions specifically target small-scale microbusinesses, offering financial and other support to create self-employment opportunities for the poor. That is, rather than providing funds for consumption, microfinance is often directed towards small business start-ups to fuel income generation. These businesses include: cottage industries such as weaving, crafts, embroidery, and jewellery making; microretail businesses such as street stalls, kiosks, and small shops; agricultural and farming businesses; and a range of small-scale trading operations. By supporting the establishment of these businesses, microfinance providers offer their clients the opportunity to help themselves rather than rely on charity or government handouts. It views the poor as empowered producers rather than exploited workers or passive consumers.

To date, though, despite the claims of its many enthusiastic supporters, the evidence on the impact of microfinance on poverty alleviation is limited. In part this is simply due to the relative youth of the industry, as well as the very real problem of providing any definitive correlations given the range of variables involved in determining poverty levels. Despite numerous case studies of successful initiatives, hard empirical evidence is lacking, and where researchers have managed to conduct appropriate studies, the results have often been contradictory. However, one of the most extensive reviews by David Roodman who gathered data over three years from hundreds of lenders and borrowers in microfinance institutions to research his 2012 book *Due Diligence: An Impertinent Inquiry Into Microfinance,* concluded that 'on current evidence, the best estimate of the average impact of microcredit on the poverty of clients is zero.'

At best, the existing evidence seems to suggest that, on average, microfinance reduces vulnerability and dependence among client groups, even if it does not necessarily make them richer. And certainly many small businesses supported by microcredit have thrived, even at times bringing new and much-needed new goods and services to poor areas. A good example is provided by the Grameen 'telephone-ladies' who use Grameen Bank loans to buy mobile phones and offer phone services in Bangladeshi villages previously without accessible telecommunications. The project has enabled hundreds of thousands of telephone-ladies to start businesses, many of which have proved to be profitable.

Some critics though, such as Aneel Karnani, a professor at the University of Michigan, have raised a more fundamental criticism of microfinance and its impacts on poverty reduction. According to Karnani and other critics, microfinance can actually hinder efforts to reduce poverty because it diverts attention and resources away from other more proven ways of promoting economic development such as the creation of employment through small and medium-sized enterprises (as opposed to microbusinesses and self-employment). As he argues:

> rather than giving microloans of $200 each to 500 women so that each can buy a sewing machine and set up a microenterprise manufacturing garments, it is much better to lend $100,000 to an entrepreneur with managerial capabilities and business acumen and help her to set up a garment manufacturing business employing 500 people ... Microcredit, at best, does not help to reduce poverty, and probably makes the situation worse by hindering more effective approaches to poverty reduction.

One need only look to China to see how poverty reduction can also be achieved through supporting the introduction of larger-scale industry.

Amongst the supporters of microfinance, such views are contested, not least because the innovativeness of the model means it has the potential to offer a more organic, inclusive, bottom-up approach to poverty alleviation than traditional models. That said, even the most ardent supporters recognize that more work needs to be done to refine the model, and to evaluate where it can and cannot have a material effect on poverty.

Balancing the books

Another challenge facing microfinance is its underlying business model, and the degree to which microfinance institutions can (or should) balance business success with explicit social goals. At one end are microfinance organizations operated by civil society organizations, or those directly funded by government or charities, which put a premium on poverty reduction and other social goals. At the other extreme are commercial banks, which have increasingly entered the microfinance market as a result of the model's proven results in generating returns and keeping default rates down—as well as its relative immunity to the recent global financial turmoil.

Approximately one-third of all microcredit borrowers are now served by non-profit institutions whereas up to two-thirds are actually served by commercial financial institutions. Commercial microfinance institutions are more likely to involve larger loans, fewer women customers, lower costs per dollar lent, higher costs per borrower, and greater profitability.

Among the banks involved in microfinance major multinationals such as Standard Chartered, HSBC, and Deutsche Bank have rubbed shoulders with numerous smaller, local players. The big banks typically operate microfinance as a niche offering among their broader portfolio of products and services, and emphasize the need for it to demonstrate its commercial viability. To date, commercial banks have tended to fluctuate in their interest in microfinance, depending on the financial results they have generated. However, in India domestic banks are required by law to set aside 40% of their reservable funds for the 'priority sector', which includes microfinance and financing of 'small-scale industries'.

In between the two extremes of non-profits and big banks is a large swathe of dedicated microfinance institutions, ranging from those, like Grameen, that are set up with a distinct social mission, to those, like Compartamos in Mexico, that have a more explicit commercial orientation—but all seek to operate on a secure financial footing. Wherever they might fall on this continuum, the aim of almost all microfinance institutions is to marry pro-poor business models with some degree of economic viability. The problem comes with determining how the right balance should be reached. Providing financial services to the poor may not be as risky as once thought, but it remains expensive because of the large numbers of small transactions that need to be processed and the considerable resources that need to go into developing education and outreach services. For this reason, a number of microfinance organizations continue to rely on donors.

However, among those like Grameen and Compartamos that have proved they can become sustainable without additional funding, there remain unresolved questions about what kind of pricing model they should adopt. When Compartamos, one of the largest microfinance institutions in Latin America, held an initial public offering (IPO) of its stock in 2007, the sale was oversubscribed by 13 times, and the bank's valuation shot to $1.6 billion, making millions for its owners. The bank's financial success, however, rested on an aggressive business development strategy that had seen the company reap high profits from its microcredit business. At the time of the stock offering, Compartamos' borrowers were paying interest rates of more than 90%, a quarter of which went straight into profit. Whilst this certainly demonstrated once and for all that microfinance had the clear potential to attract the private investment necessary to expand rapidly and service more clients, critics suggested that the bank's practices were tantamount to 'microloan-sharking'. The levying of high interest rates on the poor, the argument went, was against the very purpose of the movement: microfinance companies were supposed to be social businesses, not cynical moneylenders. 'Microfinance', one commentator noted at the time, 'has lost its innocence'.

The tensions in commercial microfinance have if anything intensified since that time. SKS, the largest microfinance company in India, became the country's first microfinance IPO in 2010. The offering attracted leading investment groups, such as Morgan Stanley and JP Morgan, and like Compartamos was substantially oversubscribed. The company valuation reached $1.5 billion, and five weeks after trading began the share price had risen by 42%. However, the company, and commercial microfinance companies in general, were soon mired in controversy regarding their role in a spate of 200 suicides in rural Andhra Pradesh, the country's microlending hub. Evidence emerged that many of the suicides were by defaulting borrowers who had experienced forceful collection of loans, public shaming, and communal harassment from other borrowers, including orchestrated sit-ins outside their homes. Police jailed microfinance employees, including dozens from SKS. Among the charges was abetment to suicide, essentially driving people to kill themselves, a crime under Indian law. According to a *Wall Street Journal* report, one woman drank pesticide and died a day after an SKS loan agent told her to prostitute her daughters to pay off her debt, while another SKS debt collector told a delinquent borrower to drown herself in a pond if she wanted her loan waived. The next day, she did. Investigations suggested that SKS employees had overlooked its basic lending principles in a quest to diversify their client base and thereby appeal more to investors.

The Indian authorities quickly clamped down on the lending practices of microfinance companies. Other suggestions to prevent exploitation by microlenders have included Muhammad Yunus' advocacy of a legal cap on interest rates. To date, though, the legal route has not been widely followed, although government pressure, market dynamics, and company priorities have led to a substantial variation in interest rates across countries and companies. The global average is currently around 30%, which is considerably higher than for conventional lending. This, most commentators agree, can be justified to some extent by the higher costs involved in servicing small loans. Nonetheless, many lenders charge considerably more than this, with some lenders in Africa, Latin America, and the Caribbean imposing rates of up to 80–90%.

Perhaps, though, given the aim of many in the microfinance community to prove its commercial credentials, the high interest rates should not come as too much of a surprise. As one leading figure in the industry remarked, 'To attract the money they need, microfinance institutions have to play by the rules of the market. Those rules often have messy results.'

Questions

1. Consider the market for financial services in developing countries in terms of consumer exclusion. What forms of financial exclusion are being practised by mainstream financial institutions, and how legitimate is this practice?

2. In what ways might microfinance improve the lives of poor consumers?

3. To what extent is microfinance likely to have a significant impact on poverty alleviation? Where, in your opinion, should governments, civil society, and business be focusing their attention in addressing poverty?

4. Are microcredit lenders justified in charging high rates of interest to poor borrowers? What exactly is a fair price in this context?

5. Consider the role of ownership structure on microfinance practices. Are for-profits more likely to exploit consumers than non-profits, or is private capital an essential means for expanding financial inclusion?

Sources

Associated Press 2012. SKS Under Spotlight in Suicides. *Wall Street Journal,* 24 February 2012: http://online.wsj.com/news/articles/SB10001424052970203918304577242602296683134.

Convergences 2013. *Microfinance Barometer 2013* (4th edn.). Paris: Convergences. http://www.citi.com/citi/microfinance/data/2013a_barometer.pdf.

Chen, G., Rasmussen, S., Reille, X., and Rozas, D. 2010. Indian microfinance goes public: the SKS initial public offering. *GCAP Focus Note No. 65*, September 2010: http://www.cgap.org/sites/default/files/CGAP-Focus-Note-Indian-Microfinance-Goes-Public-The-SKS-Initial-Public-Offering-Sep-2010.pdf.

Cull, R., Demirgüç-Kunt, A., and Morduch, J. 2009. Microfinance meets the market. *Journal of Economic Perspectives*, 23 (1): 167–92.

Karnani, A. and Santos, F. 2009. Is microfinance helping to reduce poverty? *Ethical Corporation*, 11 August: http://www.ethicalcorp.com.

Lewis, J.C. 2007. What would Leland Stanford do? An editorial commentary submitted to the microfinance community about the Compartamos IPO. *Microcredit Summit E-News*, 5 (1), July 2007: http://www.microcreditsummit.org.

Microcapital 2013. Microcapital brief: People's Bank of China (PBC) Reports Growth of Microcredit Sector in Country, 15 August 2013: http://www.microcapital.org/microcapital-brief-peoples-bank-of-china-pbc-reports-growth-of-microcredit-sector-in-country/.

Rosenberg, R., Gaul, S., Ford, S., and Tomilova, O. 2013. Microcredit Interest Rates and Their Determinants 2004–2011. *CGAP/KFW/MIX*: http://www.mixmarket.org/sites/default/files/microcredit_interest_rates_and_their_determinants_2004-2011.pdf.

Von Stauffenberg, D. 2007. Remarks by Damian von Stauffenberg, Executive Director, MicroRate. *Microcredit Summit E-News*, 5 (1), July: http://www.microcreditsummit.org.

http://www.mixmarket.org.

http://www.safaricom.co.ke.

Notes

1. http://www.ftc.gov/news-events/press-releases/2014/06/loreal-settles-ftc-charges-alleging-deceptive-advertising-anti.

2. For more information, see http://www.easa-alliance.org.

3. See UK Code of Non-broadcast Advertising, Sales Promotion and Direct Marketing (CAP Code) at http://www.cap.org.uk/Advertising-Codes/Non-Broadcast.aspx.

4. http://www.bbc.com/news/business-27628481.

5. For more information, see the UNESDA website at http://www.unesda.eu.

6. http://europe-v-facebook.org/.

7. http://www.phgfoundation.org/news/16536.

8. For data on global tobacco consumption, see http://www.tobaccoatlas.org.

9. http://www.who.int/fctc/signatories_parties/en/.

10. Ethical Consumer. 2014. *Ethical Consumer Markets Report.* Manchester: Ethical Consumer. http://www.ethicalconsumer.org/portals/0/downloads/ethical_consumer_markets_report_2014.pdf.

11. *Ibid.*

12. http://www.nielsen.com/us/en/insights/news/2012/the-global-socially-conscious-consumer.html.
13. http://www.businessgreen.com/bg/news/2394293/electric-car-sales-accelerate-into-2015; http://insideevs.com.
14. http://www.statista.com.
15. http://www.electronicstakeback.com/wp-content/uploads/Compare_state_laws_chart.pdf.
16. http://www.mckinsey.com/insights/sustainability/toward_a_circular_economy_philips_ceo_frans_van_houten.
17. For an overview see the World Car Sharing Consortium: http://www.ecoplan.org/carshare/cs_index.htm.

9

Suppliers, Competitors, and Business Ethics

Having completed this chapter you should be able to:

- Explain the specific role of suppliers and competitors as stakeholders.
- Describe the ethical issues and problems that arise in an organization's dealings with its suppliers and competitors.
- Critically evaluate the ethical challenges of global business networks.
- Explain the role of corporations in influencing the social and environmental choices of suppliers and competitors through their business relationships.
- Identify the implications for sustainability of firms' relationships with suppliers and competitors.

Key concepts and skills:

Concepts	Skills
• Industrial network	• Identifying and preventing personal inducements
• Conflict of interest	• Distinguishing intelligence gathering from industrial espionage
• Ethical sourcing	• Designing business–business regulation
• Fair trade	
• Circular economy	

■ Introduction

The relationships between different firms—as opposed to relationships between a firm and its non-business stakeholders—have probably been among the most commonly overlooked aspects of business ethics. This is perhaps not so surprising when we stop to consider that ethical problems in dealing with consumers, employees, pressure groups, or the local community tend to be quite public and visible, and frequently enjoy the spotlight of media attention. Ethical problems between businesses, however, tend to stay relatively hidden from public view, and violations of one sort or another are rather less easy to uncover and scrutinize when they do not emerge from behind the screen of the business world. More recently, though, responsibility issues in the supply chain have come more to the fore, due in part to revelations of poor social and environmental conditions in supplier factories, as well as recognition that ethical reputations depend as much on what happens in an organization's business partners as it does within the organization itself. **Ethics on Screen 9** illustrates the trend towards revealing ethical issues in firms' supply chains in documentary films.

In this chapter we shall examine these inter-organizational relationships in the context of two types of businesses—suppliers and competitors. The issue of other businesses that are customers is something that we dealt with in Chapter 8. What, though, of an organization's behaviour or responsibilities towards those who supply it with the goods and services necessary to conduct its day-to-day business? There are clearly many of these suppliers, whether they are providing raw materials for making products, stationery for the office, cleaning services for the plant, or consultancy services to help improve competitiveness—just to name a few examples. Contracts between businesses and their suppliers often involve substantial sums of money, which can even mean the difference between business survival and failure. Hence there is always the possibility for relationships with suppliers to give rise to ethical problems, for instance when procurement staff are offered bribes or kickbacks to encourage them to select a particular supplier. Likewise, we have already seen that relationships between competitors in the same industry can lead to ethical problems if consumers get short-changed—for example, because of collusion over pricing. Such anticompetitive practices are only half the story though. Some of the main ethical problems that arise in relationships with competitors are a result of arch-rivals employing 'dirty tricks' tactics in order to outdo one another.

What will soon become clear as we go through this chapter is that the relationships between businesses can raise ethical problems both by being too adversarial as well as by being too cosy. Ultimately, though, whatever the nature of a specific relationship between two businesses, our interests in business ethics among suppliers and competitors are best framed in a somewhat broader context that takes account of the network of relationships and interdependencies that constitute the business community. It is, after all, membership in this wider community that not only helps to give credence to a notion of the corporation as a citizen of some sort, but also serves as a launch pad to explore the possibilities of addressing sustainability through business–business relationships. It is also, as we shall now see, the basis for defining other businesses such as suppliers and competitors as organizational stakeholders.

■ Suppliers and competitors as stakeholders

Models of organizational stakeholders, from Freeman's (1984) original formulation onwards, have tended to vary somewhat in their definitions of what constitutes a stakeholder and which constituencies should be included or excluded. Many conceptualizations even discriminate between primary (mainly economic) stakeholders and secondary (non-economic) stakeholders (see Carroll and Buchholtz 2012: 67–9). All formulations, however, tend to include suppliers and most, if not all, tend to exclude competitors (Spence et al. 2001). Although there are very good reasons for this, in our view, such a distinction is not entirely useful or appropriate. Let us briefly look at some of the arguments.

Suppliers as stakeholders

In Chapter 2 we used Evan and Freeman's (1993) definition as a way of clarifying what a stakeholder is. A stakeholder of a corporation is an individual or a group that either is *harmed by or benefits from the corporation* or whose *rights can be violated*, or *have to be respected*, by the corporation.

It is clear without much further argument that suppliers are stakeholders—they can benefit from the success of the corporation by receiving orders for products and services and they can be harmed by losing orders. Similarly, we might easily suggest that suppliers have certain rights that might need to be respected by corporations, such as the right to a contract, to a fair deal, or to some level of fair treatment or loyalty. Indeed, organizations and their suppliers can be seen to be *mutually dependent* on each other for their own success: just as suppliers rely on their customers for the orders which keep them in business, the purchasing firms rely on their suppliers to provide them with the products and services they need to carry on their operations. Nonetheless, as we saw with consumers in Chapter 8, saying that organizations and their suppliers are interdependent does not necessarily imply that their interests are always convergent. For example, whilst the buying company may wish to reduce costs by sourcing cheaper products, the supplier will usually seek to obtain the best possible deal and maximize revenue. We shall examine a number of such problems in the next section (Ethical issues and suppliers, pp. 393–402).

Competitors as stakeholders

Competitors, on the other hand, are rarely referred to as stakeholders—certainly not in academic treatments of business ethics, nor, it would seem, in most business communications by corporations and their leaders. As Spence et al. (2001) suggest, competitors are very much the 'forgotten stakeholders'. Why? Well, competitors are, to begin with, typically seen as being in an ongoing, zero-sum battle with each other (i.e. a situation where whatever is gained by one side is lost by the other) for customers, resources, and other rewards. Why should organizations accord their competitors any specific ethical claim when these are the very businesses that they are vying with for such rewards? What rights could, say, Samsung possibly have in its competition for customers with Apple?

This is not actually as simple, or as redundant, a question as it might at first seem. Samsung certainly has a number of *legal rights* that are more or less protected by national

VISIT THE ONLINE RESOURCE CENTRE for links to useful sources of further information

ETHICS ON SCREEN 9

Revealing the supply chain

A growing genre of documentary films shaking up the business world.

Jacob Edelman, Associated Press

Illumine Group/Two Moons/Production/Screen Media Films/The Kobal Collection

Sitting in the local café, scrolling through the news on our phones over a sandwich and coffee, or checking out the latest fashions in the mall, few of us would spare much thought to the provenance of the products we are using. But step into the cinema, or browse through Netflix, and it soon becomes clear that the components in our phones, the coffee beans in our cappuccinos, the food on our plates, and the clothes on our backs all have a story behind them. Over the past decade a swathe of feature documentaries have been released that seek to reveal the hidden supply chains of global business. Such films show us the social, environmental and very human costs that are often hidden in the everyday products we use.

The food industry has probably been the most popular subject for revealing documentaries about product supply chains. Consider *Black Gold*, a 2007 film that lifts the lid on the global coffee industry. It shows us where coffee beans come from, and who the winners and losers are along the length of the global supply chain. In particular, it seeks to demonstrate how trade in the world's most popular drink operates to enrich a few large multinational food and beverage companies whilst impoverishing farmers in the global south.

Another critically acclaimed documentary, *Food Inc.*, also takes aim at big business. The wide-ranging film delves into the industrial production of meat, grains, and vegetables making the case that the modern food industry is socially and environmentally unsustainable. More recently, *Food Chains*, a 2014 film about Florida tomato pickers, focuses more on the human costs of food supply. Targeting large buyers of produce like fast food and supermarkets, the film argues that they 'have drained revenue from their supply chain leaving farmworkers in poverty and forced to work under subhuman conditions'. More positively though, the film also trains its eye on a grassroots labour organization that is trying to tackle exploitation in the tomato fields with their Fair Food programme. Under the heading 'Take Action', the film's website provides opportunities to support the programme by joining protests, sharing facts, and 'turn the film from a movie into a movement'.

The hidden costs of business on animals have also become a major theme of contemporary documentaries. *The Cove*, a winner of the 2010 Oscar best documentary feature, used underwater microphones and high-definition cameras disguised as rocks to reveal for the first time the brutal dolphin slaughter that happens off the coast of Japan. It also traced the supply chain to show how dolphin meat containing dangerously high levels of mercury eventually finds its way onto Japanese supermarket shelves often without the knowledge of the general public.

The mistreatment of animals is a theme taken up by *The Ghosts in Our Machine*. It follows the animal rights photographer Jo-Anne

McArthur as she documents the misery inflicted on animals for the purpose of the food, entertainment, fashion, and other industries. Like most of the supply-chain exposés presented here, it is unapologetically activist in its orientation, but as the director Liz Marshall says, it does not take the usual path of identifying specific culprits: 'It's not a finger-wagging movie that's outing farmers or big corporations. Rather, it's a film that says that we are complicit in a flawed system, and we can all make a difference.'

Blood in the Mobile meanwhile certainly does take aim at specific companies. Exposing the brutal conditions in mines for metals and minerals run by armed groups in the Democratic Republic of Congo, it seeks to make the case that mobile phone companies are complicit in the labour, environmental, and human rights abuses that are customary in such contexts. As some critics have noted, however, although the film reveals deplorable conditions in the DRC mines, the supply-chain connections linking them to mobile companies are less convincing.

Finally, the supply chains of clothing and textiles form the basis for the 2014 documentary *Cotton Road*. Described simply as 'a documentary film about a global supply chain', it tells the stories of workers' lives in the cotton supply chain from farms in the US to factories in China. As with most of the films discussed above, it does not stop at producing a film though. The website also provides advice on how to use your new-found knowledge of the supply chain to get involved and make a difference. It offers a comprehensive discussion guide and provides advice on how to join Fashion Revolution Day or host a 'screen and swap' party with friends to promote more sustainable clothing choices.

As these examples demonstrate, the hidden supply chain of everyday products has become a common theme for documentary makers. It should be remembered though that although such films claim to educate, most also tend to take a strong position on the issue to create a compelling narrative. In reality they are mostly about persuading rather than simply informing or providing a balanced view. This is why they also increasingly connect their movies with a broader movement seeking to effect change. Almost all supply chain exposés complement their movies with websites, enabling the audience to dig deeper into the issues and take action to try and address the problems raised. As such, they should be seen as vehicles of activism as much as they are simple providers of greater transparency.

Given the strident message in many of these films, it is perhaps unsurprising that many of them do indeed invoke responses. *Black Gold*, for example, had special screenings at 10 Downing Street in the UK, the UN in New York, and the EU in Brussels, and it prompted a PR offensive from Starbucks, one of its main targets in the film. *The Cove*'s success, meanwhile, led to a surge of foreign protesters at the Japanese dolphin hunt, but also threats of lawsuits after it stirred huge controversy in Japan. As one critic of the Oscar-winning movie commented:

> As a piece of propaganda, *The Cove* is brilliant; as a story of ingenuity and triumph over what seems like senseless brutality, it is exceptionally well-told; but as a conscientious overview of a complex and deeply fraught, layered issue, it invokes the same phrase as even the most well-intentioned, impassioned activist docs: Buyer beware.

Sources

Hawkes, R. 2014. The Ghosts in Our Machine: 'It's not a finger-wagging movie outing farmers'. *Telegraph*, 16 July 2014: http://www.telegraph.co.uk/culture/film/film-news/10970934/The-Ghosts-in-Our-Machine-Its-not-a-finger-wagging-movie-outing-farmers.html.

Orange, M. 2009. In Theaters: The Cove. *Movieline*, 30 July 2009: http://movieline.com/2009/07/30/in-theaters-the-cove/.

http://blackgoldmovie.com.

http://www.bloodinthemobile.org.

http://www.cottonroadmovie.com.

http://www.foodchainsfilm.com.

http://www.takepart.com/foodinc.

http://www.thecovemovie.com.

http://www.theghostsinourmachine.com.

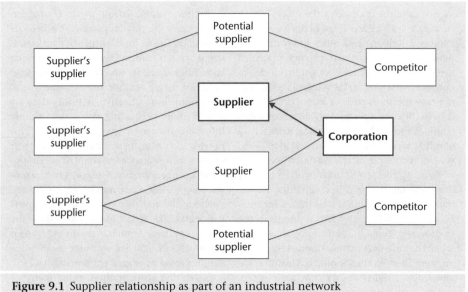

Figure 9.1 Supplier relationship as part of an industrial network

and international trade agreements that Apple must respect. These include the right to freely enter and leave the market, the right to set their own prices free from influence or coercion, and the right to inform potential customers about their products. For instance, it would be illegal for Samsung to try and influence the price that Apple sets for its tablets and smartphones.

It is a relatively short step from these legal rights to claim that a competitor also has some form of *moral claims* on an organization which go beyond those codified in law— for example, some form of right to privacy, or a right to 'fair play'. Certainly, few would contend that the mere fact of a competitive situation bestows upon an organization carte blanche to act in any way it chooses in order to beat its competitors, including lying, deception, poaching staff, and other such questionable practices that we shall examine as we proceed through the chapter—not to mention outright illegal activities such as theft and extortion.

In addition to these claims, if we look at the first condition of being a stakeholder given above, there is little doubt that competitors most certainly can be *harmed by* or *benefit from* the organization (Spence et al. 2001). Competitors can experience a loss or gain of market share as a result of the actions of their rivals, they can experience a change in trading conditions (for example, their suppliers might switch to a competitor offering higher prices), or they can face changes in the perception of their industry as a result of the behaviour of their competitors (Barnett and King 2008).

To sum up then, businesses should not be seen as isolated islands of economic activity, but as businesses operating within a web of other businesses, bound by mutual interests and interlinked flows of resources and rewards. This suggests that firms are probably best understood as part of an industrial network, rather than just as part of a simple exchange between two parties (Easton 1992; Håkansson and Snehota 2006). An illustration of such a network is shown in **Figure 9.1**, with the focal relationship between a corporation and its supplier highlighted and put into context with other relationships amongst competing companies, suppliers, and their suppliers.

According to the **industrial network** model, notable decisions about how the firm deals with any single other firm (such as one of its suppliers) can have a significant effect on numerous other members of the business network, including other suppliers, potential suppliers, and competitors. Whilst the ethical obligations that the firm has to these other network members might vary, this does not deny the fact that they all have some form of stake in the decisions made—and may act upon that stake in ways that are of consequence to the organization.

These interrelationships give rise to a number of potential ethical problems. In the following two sections we shall look at the specific issues that arise with respect to dealings with suppliers and competitors before moving on to examine the impact of globalization on the ethics of these business relationships.

Industrial network
A group of businesses bound by mutual interests and interlinked flows of resources and rewards.

■ Ethical issues and suppliers

On reading a typical contemporary text on supplier management, one might wonder how ethical problems could possibly arise in relationships with suppliers. Close relationships have been widely touted as an effective business strategy for improving performance and achieving win-win solutions for organizations and their suppliers (Cao and Zhang 2011). Thus, firms have continued to increasingly move away from traditional adversarial relationships with suppliers (based upon short-termist, transactional arrangements with large numbers of supply firms) towards more partnership-based approaches that emphasize long-term relationships with core supply firms based upon mutual trust and collaboration (Daugherty 2011).

The attention afforded to partnership sourcing is significant for our understanding of business ethics because it very much reinforces the notion of suppliers as stakeholders in the firm. In fact, though, the partnership approach is certainly not representative of all, or probably even the majority, of business–supplier relationships. Evidence suggests that whilst many progressive firms have indeed moved towards more collaborative approaches, much so-called 'partnership' sourcing actually involves problematic power relations and troublesome intra-firm tensions (New 1998; Hingley 2005). This 'dark side' of close relationships (Anderson and Jap 2005), as we shall see, can quite easily reveal a number of ethical issues.

It is also important to recognize that regardless of the overall approach to firm–supplier relations that is adopted by an organization, the individuals who actually conduct these relationships—namely the procurement and sales staff—are often confronted with a whole host of ethical dilemmas on a day-to-day level. This can include the giving and acceptance of gifts, bribes, hospitality, and other potential inducements, as well as the use of questionable tactics in business-to-business negotiations. We shall be examining these issues as we proceed through this section, but before we do, it might be helpful to work through **An Ethical Dilemma 9,** which presents some typical ethical problems occurring in supplier relations.

AN ETHICAL DILEMMA 9

A beautiful deal?

You work as a purchasing manager for a large European retailing company that is in the process of revamping its line of own-label cosmetics. This line is important to your business, and as your company has expanded, own-label cosmetics have gradually occupied an increasingly prominent role in the product mix in stores.

Your existing supplier of own-label products, Beauty To Go, has supplied your company for ten years and over two-thirds of its business is accounted for by your company's orders. You have a good relationship with the account manager who, like yourself, has been in her role for a number of years, and has become a good friend.

As you are considering how to proceed with the revamp, a competing supplier, Real Cosmetics, contacts you offering virtually identical products to Beauty To Go, with what appear to be equivalent supply arrangements, but at a slightly lower price per unit. Over a year this would work out to approximately €200,000 savings—not a huge sum for your company, but quite a substantial saving of about 2% on your costs. In addition, Real Cosmetics also highlights in its sales pitch that it goes well beyond the industry standard for non-animal testing of the products' ingredients—again, a significant improvement over what Beauty To Go has been offering you.

Questions

1. What are the ethical issues at stake in this situation?
2. Which ethical theories do you think might be of help in deciding an appropriate course of action?
3. What are the main considerations that these theories raise?
4. How would you proceed in this situation?

Misuse of power

The issue of power in buyer–supplier relationships has received much attention over the years, not least because the relative power of the two parties can be extremely influential in determining industry profitability (Porter 2008). Clearly, though, imbalances in power can also lead to the emergence of ethical problems, particularly when any imbalance is misused to create unfair terms and conditions for one or the other party.

One useful way of looking at the relative power of buyers and sellers is using *resource dependence theory* (Pfeffer and Salancik 1978). According to this theory, power derives from the degree of dependence that each actor has on the other's resources. This dependence is a function of how scarce an organization's resources are—i.e. the level of *resource scarcity*—and how useful they are to the other party—i.e. the *resource utility* (Cox et al. 2000). Therefore, the buyer is likely to be able to wield considerable power over the supplier when:

- the supplier's resources are relatively plentiful and not highly important to the buyer; and/or

- the buyer's resources are relatively scarce and highly important to the supplier.

This situation has been a major feature of the relationship between major European supermarkets and their suppliers. With a handful of very large supermarket chains dominating each national market—such as Aldi and Metro in Germany, Carrefour and Intermarché in France, and Tesco, Sainsbury's, and Asda in the UK—their resources, in terms of purchase potential and access to markets, have become relatively scarce but extremely important for food suppliers. At the same time, the suppliers' resources have become less scarce and important to the supermarkets, since they increasingly source on a global basis from a vast array of suppliers and manage to stock an impressive range of products which, except in a very few cases, would hardly suffer from the removal of one supplier's products. It is perhaps not surprising, then, that Europe's supermarkets have often been criticized for abusing their power over suppliers. For instance, in 2014, the European Commission called for action to improve protection for small food producers against unfair trading practices from supermarkets, including the establishment of Europe-wide principles of good practice and minimum standards of enforcement.[1]

Such practices can be criticized from a *deontological* perspective—in that those with power might be said to have a duty not to abuse it. More interesting, however, is a *consequentialist* position: the problems caused by abuse of supply-chain power are not just of consequence to the weaker partner. Using the example of the suppliers of UK clothing retailers, Jones and Pollitt (1998) show that an opportunistic abuse of power by retailers can lead to reductions in quality, lack of investment, lack of innovation, and even job losses and industry decline. In this case, the overexposure to risk may result in an underperformance of suppliers. Ultimately, excessive abuse of power may eventually even harm the powerful partner, particularly if their supplier relations become so dysfunctional as to jeopardize product quality and industry growth—thereby reducing long-term profitability.

Given such a set of possible negative outcomes, one might wonder why abuse of power would ever happen. Jones and Pollitt (1998) suggest that:

- In the short term, there may well be profit advantages to be gained by exercising excess power.

- Many firms will view the situation from a relatively narrow perspective and fail to see the broader cumulative industry effects that may ultimately harm them.

However, abuse of market power may also be somewhat more subtle and far less destructive at the macro level than envisaged by Jones and Pollitt (1998). Although market conditions can disadvantage suppliers, purchasing firms may choose to exploit their power differentials in some areas of business—for example by forcing down prices—but offer support and investment in others—for example by contributing market knowledge, financial support, and other management resources. This more variegated picture may well offer a more realistic picture of some industries (Ogbonna and Wilkinson 1996; Bloom and Perry 2001), but it makes any conclusive ethical evaluation difficult. Whilst individual actions may seem unethical, when put in the context of a longer-term interaction, the action may be more acceptable.

The question of loyalty

Related to the issue of power is the question of loyalty. The fair treatment expected by suppliers can be viewed in terms of a given deal struck between the two parties, but as we have just intimated, where those parties have been involved in a long series of exchanges over some time, we might also include further considerations. In particular, one might start to consider whether such an arrangement also confers some kind of expectation for loyalty on the part of the organizations. After all, if a company has been reliably supplying another for many years, should this not entitle them to some kind of stability and commitment from their partner in terms of ongoing orders and support? From an ethical point of view, though, does it make sense to suggest that firms have some kind of moral obligation of loyalty to their suppliers—and if so, how do we determine which suppliers can legitimately expect loyalty, and what exactly does an obligation of loyalty entail?

Loyalty is one of the virtues often prized in business, but loyalty to suppliers does not easily fit with an economic view of the firm that stresses the importance of free competition in order to achieve the most beneficial outcomes. According to this view, if a retailer such as Carrefour is 'encumbered' by loyalty from selecting new suppliers that offer higher quality or lower costs, then the retailer will become less competitive and its final consumers will have to face higher prices and/or poorer-quality products.

It is possible to question these assumptions on several grounds:

- First, loyalty does not necessarily imply slavish acceptance of any conditions offered by the supplier. It can perhaps be better interpreted as the establishment of a long-term commitment, from which the two partners can potentially seek mutually beneficial outcomes. So rather than accepting a poorer deal from its supplier, the firm might work with its supplier to ensure that it remains as competitive as its rivals.

- Secondly, a long-term commitment can provide the opportunity to take advantage of reduced transaction costs through less switching of suppliers and contracts, as well as enabling more complex and customized ways of working together that benefit both partners, but are not easily replicable by other industry players (Artz 1999).

These arguments can be used to construct a fairly robust defence of intra-organizational loyalty from a consequentialist point of view, provided the area of business involved is one in which benefits can accrue through longer-term working relationships. General Motors, the US automotive company, for example, announced plans in 2014 to build longer-term relationships with its core suppliers in order to develop the kind of innovations in safety and fuel economy that it had identified as increasingly necessary for competitive success (Colias 2014).

Some industries, however, appear to rely almost exclusively on short-term transactional supplier relationships. This is particularly the case where the products being exchanged are commodities with little potential for adding value through the supply arrangement, such as basic manufacturing components or simple foodstuffs like rice and sugar. In this case, the ethical case for loyalty to suppliers might have to rely on deontological or virtue-based reasoning. The issue of supplier loyalty becomes considerably more complex, however, when we look at the potential for conflicts of interest to arise between the different parties.

VISIT THE
ONLINE
RESOURCE
CENTRE
for a short
response to this
feature

? THINK THEORY

How would you apply deontological reasoning to the question of supplier loyalty? Does this offer, in conjunction with the consequentialist argument above, a sufficient rationale for judging the actions of companies such General Motors to be ethical or unethical?

Conflicts of interest

Conflicts of interest are critical factors in causing various ethical problems, not just in relation to suppliers. However, procurement and supply-chain management are areas where conflict of interest is particularly likely to surface (Handfield and Baumer 2006). A **conflict of interest** occurs when someone 'has a private or personal interest sufficient to appear to influence the objective exercise of their official duties, e.g. as a public official, employee or professional' (MacDonald et al. 2002). So a conflict of interest always involves a breach of an explicit obligation to act in another's interest (Boatright 2012: 101).

In a business-to-business context, a conflict of interest can arise in two main ways:

- **Conflict of professional and organizational interests**. When a firm is hired as a supplier of professional services of one sort or another its official duties are to act in its client's interest. However, the supplier firm may experience a conflict with obligations to look after its own financial interests. For example, an audit firm may help to cover up financial irregularities on the part of its client in order to gain more work from the client. Accounting firms, marketing agencies, law firms, and investment bankers are all organizations that might face conflicts of interest of this sort (Boatright 2012). In Chapter 6 (The role of financial professionals and market intermediaries, pp. 249–251), we also described how rating agencies, as suppliers of financial information to investors, experience conflicts of interest because they are dependent on income from investment providers.

- **Conflict of personal and organizational interests**. Sometimes, an individual employee's interests may conflict with those of their employer. For example, the procurement and sales staff of two trading companies have obligations to act in the best interests of their respective firms (i.e. their 'official duties' are to their organizations) but these obligations may at times clash with the employees' personal interests, if for example the salesperson offers the procurement manager hospitality or gifts to encourage them to seal a deal that is not the best one possible for their company.

The types of personal, professional, and organizational interests that might be at stake here can vary considerably, but those that tend to garner most attention are those involving money, gifts, hospitality, favours, and other kinds of financial inducements. However, it is not always easy to distinguish between a friendly gift and an outright bribe in business-to-business situations, so it is worth spending a little more time investigating how exactly personal inducements can be distinguished.

Conflict of interest
Where a person's or organization's obligation to act in the interests of another is interfered with by a competing interest that may obstruct the fulfilment of that obligation.

Distinguishing personal inducements

Gifts, gratuities, hospitality, bribes, kickbacks, bungs, sweeteners—there is seemingly no end to the variety of terms that are used to describe the official and unofficial 'perks' that procurement staff might be offered in the course of their interactions with salespeople. Some of these offers might be innocent and quite genuine expressions of gratitude; some might be part and parcel of maintaining a strong buyer–seller relationship. Some, however, will simply be inducements to get business that would not otherwise have been earned by more legitimate means. The offering of personal inducements is regularly identified by procurement staff as one of the main ethical issues confronting their profession (Cooper et al. 2000), but many questions remain unanswered about where to draw the line between acceptable and unacceptable practice in offering hospitality to buyers (Oakley and Bush 2012).

The key issue here is that gifts and hospitality often involve procurement staff in a *conflict of interest* between their own personal gain and the best interests of their firm (Fisher 2007). As employees of the firm, purchasers are expected to fulfil an obligation to act in the firm's interest—namely getting the best deal, whether in terms of price, quality, support services, or whatever else best achieves the company's goals. When a purchaser receives a personal benefit from the seller—such as a bottle of whisky, a trip to a sports event, or an envelope stuffed with money—the problem is that the purchaser may be swayed to make a decision that does not fulfil this obligation to their employer.

Of course, many of us could probably quite easily rationalize that the gift did not affect our decision, particularly if it was unsolicited or it was received after the actual transaction took place. How could one be influenced by something that had not even happened when the decision was made? There are a number of ways of looking at this.

- One is to consider the **intention of the gift-giver**. If their intention is to gain an additional advantage (as opposed to merely offering thanks for a job well done), then we might question the action.

- Another way is to look at the **impact on the receiver**. If their evaluation of the gift-giver is enhanced after receiving the gift, then again we might start to raise some doubts about its ethicality. This is pertinent even when the gift is received after a deal has been concluded, since it might be seen to prejudice future evaluations.

- Finally, we might focus on the **perception of other parties**. If a competing supplier might interpret the giving of the gift as a deliberate bribe, then again we should probably question the action.

The raising of the issue of perception by others is significant here because it suggests that the resolution of ethical dilemmas does not just depend on those who are directly involved in them. Bribery in particular is a problem that, when its occurrence is perceived by others, can erode trust and reinforce a culture of dishonesty. For instance, imagine if you heard that your class professor had received a Christmas present of an expensive bottle of cognac from one of your class members. Regardless of the intention of the student, or its impact on the professor, if the student received high grades in the course then you might well start questioning the integrity of your professor, and even maybe consider the possibility of purchasing a small gift yourself!

As we saw in Chapter 4, once a culture of dishonesty has been created, the prevailing ethic in the workplace can be difficult to dislodge and can be profoundly influential on subsequent behaviour. Indeed, the procurement function is widely regarded (by other company personnel and outsiders) to be largely unconcerned with ethics and very commercially minded (Drumwright 1994). The procurement environment seems to suffer more than most other organizational functions in relation to the conditions that might foster ethical abuse. As Badenhorst (1994: 741) has argued:

> The purchasing environment creates a climate which promotes unethical behaviour ... Often sales representatives have little concern for ethical behaviour, and purchasers are tempted to obtain some personal gain from a transaction, often with the approval of the representative's employer. The management often encourages its sales representatives to act in a manner which they would find entirely unacceptable in their purchasing department. These double standards create a climate of dishonesty in a company, and tempt everyone, especially the purchaser.

In an attempt to counter this, many large organizations have a formal procurement code of ethics in place, and guidelines for appropriate behaviour on issues such as gifts and hospitality are provided by professional bodies such as the Chartered Institute of Procurement and Supply (see **Figure 9.2**). This explicitly states that members of the institute should refrain from accepting any inducements or gifts except those of nominal value that are declared to their employer, and should not allow offers of hospitality to influence (or appear to influence) their business decisions.

The fact remains though that some industries are more prone to problems of personal inducements than others. For example, the pharmaceutical industry has long provided a wide range of expensive gifts to doctors who might prescribe their drugs, including holidays, meals, free travel, and tickets to sporting events. In the US alone, this activity runs into billions of dollars a year in expenditure by pharmaceutical companies (Oakley and Bush 2012). There have been a variety of attempts to tackle this problem. For instance, in the US, the pharmaceutical industry instituted a voluntary set of guidelines in 2008 that prohibited the donation of branded promotional items to doctors, while the Indian government imposed a self-regulatory code on the industry that effectively banned most forms of gifts and inducements from 2015 (Mukherjee 2014). Sceptics meanwhile criticized the initiatives for their voluntary nature and the ease with which companies could evade the restrictions.

☑ Skill check

Identifying and preventing personal inducements. Developing the skills for identifying when gifts and hospitality constitute personal inducements, and instituting appropriate controls to prevent them, enables managers to avoid corruption.

As a member of The Chartered Institute of Purchasing & Supply, I will:

Enhance and protect the standing of the profession, by:

- never engaging in conduct, either professional or personal, which would bring the profession or the Chartered Institute of Purchasing & Supply into disrepute
- not accepting inducements or gifts (other than any declared gifts of nominal value which have been sanctioned by my employer)
- not allowing offers of hospitality or those with vested interests to influence, or be perceived to influence, my business decisions
- being aware that my behaviour outside my professional life may have an effect on how I am perceived as a professional

Maintain the highest standard of integrity in all business relationships, by:

- rejecting any business practice which might reasonably be deemed improper
- never using my authority or position for my own financial gain
- declaring to my line manager any personal interest that might affect, or be seen by others to affect, my impartiality in decision making
- ensuring that the information I give in the course of my work is accurate and not misleading
- never breaching the confidentiality of information I receive in a professional capacity
- striving for genuine, fair and transparent competition
- being truthful about my skills, experience and qualifications

Promote the eradication of unethical business practices, by:

- fostering awareness of human rights, fraud and corruption issues in all my business relationships
- responsibly managing any business relationships where unethical practices may come to light, and taking appropriate action to report and remedy them
- undertaking due diligence on appropriate supplier relationships in relation to forced labour (modern slavery) and other human rights abuses, fraud and corruption
- continually developing my knowledge of forced labour (modern slavery), human rights, fraud and corruption issues, and applying this in my professional life

Enhance the proficiency and stature of the profession, by:

- continually developing and applying knowledge to increase my personal skills and those of the organisation I work for
- fostering the highest standards of professional competence amongst those for whom I am responsible
- optimising the responsible use of resources which I have influence over for the benefit of my organisation

Ensure full compliance with laws and regulations, by:

- adhering to the laws of the countries in which I practise, and in countries where there is no relevant law in place I will apply the standards inherent in this Code
- fulfilling agreed contractual obligations
- following CIPS guidance on professional practice

Figure 9.2 Chartered Institute of Procurement and Supply's Code of Professional Ethics

Source: http://www.cips.org/en/aboutcips/CIPS-Code-of-Conduct/.

Ethics in negotiation

Finally, any discussion of ethics in supplier relationships is not complete without addressing the issue of business–supplier negotiation. As we said at the start of this section, many commentators have identified a shift away from adversarial supplier relationships towards something closer to a partnership model, suggesting that negotiation might be less subject to questionable ethics than in the past. Although to some extent this may well be true, the whole process of negotiation between buyer and supplier inevitably raises some ethical tensions, given that the situation itself is often characterized as one of two combatants coming together to do battle (Badenhorst 1994). As Reitz et al. (1998) suggest, to many people ethics and negotiation are like oil and water: they just do not mix. To illustrate their point, they list ten popular negotiating tactics, all of which they contend can be challenged on ethical grounds:

- Lies—about something material to the negotiation.
- Puffery—i.e. exaggerating the value of something.
- Deception—including misleading promises or threats and misstatements of facts.
- Weakening the opponent—by directly undermining the strengths or alliances of the opponent.
- Strengthening one's own position—for example, by means not available to the opponent.
- Non-disclosure—deliberately withholding pertinent information that would be of benefit to the opponent.
- Information exploitation—misusing information provided by the opponent in ways not intended by them.
- Change of mind—engaging in behaviours contrary to previous statements or positions.
- Distraction—deliberately attempting to lure opponents into ignoring information or alternatives that might benefit them.
- Maximization—exploiting a situation to one's own fullest possible benefit without concern for the effects on the other.

According to Reitz et al. (1998), although there are certain risks in doing so, a more ethical approach to negotiation can, and should, steer clear of such tactics. This is not only because it is the right thing to do, but also because such practices can incur costs on the negotiator. Specifically, these costs are:

- **Rigid negotiating.** Unethical tactics can draw negotiators into a narrow view of the tactics available to them, especially if they are perceived as having been successful in the past. However, in longer-term relationships, a more flexible and open approach may help to yield more advantageous win-win solutions.
- **Damaged relationships.** Customers and suppliers rarely cease to rely on each other once a deal has been negotiated. Even when the negotiation is a single event, implementation of the deal may be marred as a result of perceived ethical infractions. Where negotiations are part of a longer-term cycle, the costs of unethical negotiation may

mount, as negotiators turn into embittered enemies rather than mutually supportive partners.

- **Sullied reputation**. Unethical negotiation can have a negative influence on the individual's or their company's image, making future bargaining more troublesome.
- **Lost opportunities**. Unethical negotiation not only undermines the negotiators' capabilities to reach mutually beneficial win-win agreements, but it also tends to prevent any progressive discussions which could bring new, profitable issues to the table.

Whilst this undoubtedly presents an overly positive perspective on ethics in negotiation between buyers and sellers, it is useful in helping us to view negotiation not so much as a zero-sum game, but as a chance to build towards a more mutually beneficial relationship. Firms' dealings with their suppliers do not always have to be characterized as a tussle between warring combatants. Somewhat more challenging, however, is the idea that this can also be true of their relationships with their competitors. Let us now look at this in more detail.

■ Ethical issues and competitors

As we have already mentioned, whilst there is some disagreement in the literature as to whether competitors are actually legitimate stakeholders in an organization, there does seem to be a reasonable case for suggesting that we can expect a certain level of ethical behaviour between competitors. Of course, this certainly does not preclude active, or even quite aggressive, competitive behaviour between rivals. In fact, as we saw in Chapter 8 (and shall elucidate on below), the deliberate avoidance of competitive behaviour is itself a cause for ethical concern should consumers and other stakeholders be disadvantaged as a result.

The point is that there appears to be a need to establish some kind of parameters regarding the limits to competition at either end of the scale. This means that ethical issues in dealing with competitors can relate to two distinct problems:

- **Overly aggressive competition**—where a company goes beyond acceptable behaviour in its direct relationship with a competitor, thereby harming the competitor in a way that is unethical.
- **Insufficient competition**—where the actions of one or more companies act to restrict competition in a market, thereby harming consumers in a way that is unethical.

In the following, we shall examine the main issues and dilemmas that arise in both areas.

Problems of overly aggressive competition

In a competitive global marketplace, firms are expected to act aggressively in trying to secure a competitive advantage against their competitors. However, sometimes this behaviour goes beyond the ethical boundaries of acceptable competitive behaviour—for instance, when competitors engage in spying, dirty tricks, and anticompetitive practices.

Intelligence gathering and industrial espionage

All organizations collect and make use of some kind of information about their competitors. Just as a university or college will typically investigate the courses offered by its main competitors, so too will companies take a keen interest in the products, policies, and processes undertaken by their rivals. Indeed, such intelligence-gathering activities are very much a standard aspect of conventional market research and competitor benchmarking, and make for effective competitive behaviour. As Andrew Crane (2005) suggests, though, ethical questions arise when one or more of the following are deemed to have occurred:

- The *tactics* used to secure information about competitors are questionable since they appear to go beyond what might be deemed acceptable, ethical, or legal business practice.

- The *nature* of the information sought can itself be regarded as in some way private or confidential.

- The *purposes* for which the information is to be used are against the public interest.

Questionable tactics may take many forms, from the clearly illegal, such as breaking and entering a competitor's offices to steal information and installing tapping devices, to rather more grey areas. These grey areas include eavesdropping, searching through a competitor's rubbish, hacking, hiring private detectives, covert surveillance through spy cameras or electronic 'spyware', misrepresenting oneself by posing as a potential customer or employer, pressuring competitors' employees to reveal sensitive information about their operations—or even simply being accidently exposed to sensitive data by misdirected faxes or emails (Hallaq and Steinhorst 1994; Crane and Spence 2008). **Figure 9.3** provides examples of some common grey areas encountered by competitive intelligence professionals—and what they deem to be an appropriate response.

Some of these tactics are doubtful from an ethical point of view primarily because they violate a duty to be honest and truthful in business dealings and might easily be criticized from the perspective of deontological precepts such as the 'golden rule'—do unto others as you would have them do unto you—or Kant's categorical imperative test. Moreover, once such methods become accepted into business practice—or to use Kant's words, they become 'universal law'—all firms tend to lose out: (a) because the industry is likely to suffer from a loss of trust, and (b) because it becomes necessary for all industry players to commit resources to institute procedures guarding against the loss of trade secrets to unscrupulous competitors. As Boatright (2012: 99) argues, 'companies that routinely cross ethical boundaries in gaining competitor intelligence can scarcely expect others to respect their own trade secrets and confidential business information.'

Private or confidential information may refer to any kind of information that the organization feels should not be freely available to outsiders and that therefore should have some kind of moral or legal protection. While in principle this seems quite reasonable, it is rather more difficult to establish a corporation's right to privacy than it is an individual's—and certainly, the enforcement of privacy is considerably trickier. Specifically:

- Corporations are to some extent 'boundary-less'—they have fewer clear boundaries to define the private 'corporate space' compared with private individuals.

- Corporations consist of, and deal with, multiple individuals, making control of information difficult.

How do you match up to professional competitive intelligence gatherers? Here are two scenarios that were put to experienced industry insiders to explore their perspectives on the ethics of different tactics for generating competitive intelligence.

An eavesdropping scenario

You are a competitive intelligence professional seated on a long-haul airplane. Your neighbour opens a document that is entitled 'Marketing Strategy for Product X,' which is directly competitive with one of your firm's major products. After reading a few pages, he gets up to go to the bathroom on the plane. You have four options for your next action.

- **Option A**: I will take the copy of the marketing plan and hide it in my bag. When he returns and asks me if I saw his report, I'll tell him I don't know what he's talking about.

- **Option B**: While he's gone, I'll just take notes on the key elements of the competitor's strategy. Then I'll return the document to the exact place he left it and won't say anything.

- **Option C**: While he's gone, I will ask the flight attendant to find me a new seat on the plane. I will just move to a new seat to avoid the risk of potential unethical behaviour.

- **Option D**: I won't look at the document while he's gone. When he returns, I'll advise him that I work for a competing firm, and tell him that if he chooses to keep reading, it is at his own risk that he does so.

What would you do in this situation? Most industry professionals suggested that they would select Option D. When presented at a competitive intelligence industry conference, the majority of respondents (60%) selected this option, which is typically regarded as appropriate professional conduct. Only 1% selected Option A, the outright theft. However, a full 30% selected Option B, which, from an ethical and a legal point of view, should be considered highly questionable.

A misrepresentation scenario

You are attending a trade show. You take off the badge that identifies you as a competitor, and you then approach a booth at the exhibition. You tell the representative you have an interest in the product.
   In your assessment, is this behaviour either:

- **Option A:** Normal competitive intelligence gathering practice

- **Option B:** Ethical, but aggressive competitive intelligence gathering practice

- **Option C:** Unethical competitive intelligence gathering practice

- **Option D:** Illegal competitive intelligence gathering practice?

If industry insiders are anything to go by, your response to this may have reflected your country of origin. In a survey of more than 100 competitive intelligence professionals in the US and Europe, most North Americans thought this action was either unethical (48%) or illegal (44%), probably reflecting the strict legal enforcement of industrial espionage in the US. Europeans, in contrast, saw the action as either aggressive (39%) or unethical (55%), but only 6% viewed it as illegal.

Figure 9.3 Ethics in the grey areas of competitive intelligence

Sources: Fuld, L.M. 2006. Cultural effects on legal and ethical competitive intelligence. In D. Fehringer and B. Hohhof, *Competitive Intelligence Ethics: Navigating the Gray Zone*, Alexandria, VA: Competitive Intelligence Foundation: 51–55; Sapia-Bosch, A. and Tancer, R.S. 1998. 'Navigating through the Legal/ Ethical Grey Zone: What Would You do?' *CI Magazine*, vol. 1 (1), April–June: 1–13.

- Much corporate activity takes place in public and quasi-public spaces such as shops, offices, hospitals, colleges, etc., and via shared infrastructure such as roads, railways, seas, telephone lines, fibre-optic cables, etc. These are easily and usually quite legitimately observed, infiltrated, or tracked.

However, even if it is difficult to fully ascribe a right to privacy to corporations, it is relatively more straightforward to suggest that certain information that corporations have is a form of property and is thus subject to *property rights* (Boatright 2012). This particularly tends to apply to trade secrets, patents, copyrights, and trademarks—all of which are to some extent legally enforceable *intellectual property* that is said to belong to the organization.

Intellectual property rights can be assigned to many intangible forms of property, including product formulations, theories, inventions, software, music, formulae, recipes, processing techniques, designs, and so on. The development of such 'information' frequently involves organizations in millions of dollars of investment in R&D costs. Unsurprisingly, corporations often go to great lengths and invest substantial resources in trying to keep this information secret from their competitors, so that they may reap the rewards of their investment. However, with improvements in information and communication technologies, the ease of replication of digital information, as well as the refinement of 'reverse-engineering' techniques (where competitors' products are stripped down and analysed in order to copy them), the unauthorized accessing and exploitation of intellectual property has been on the rise. China, in particular, has become a major source of intellectual property theft, with the US government estimating that China is behind some 50–80% of all intellectual property theft cases across the world, costing the US economy alone around $300 billion every year (Ovsey 2014).

Public interest issues can arise when the information gleaned through espionage is put to purposes such as anticompetitive behaviour, including the deliberate removal or ruin of competitors, price hikes, or entrenchment of a monopoly position. Public interest issues may also arise when intelligence germane to national or international security or domestic economic performance is secured. With corporations involved in designing, producing, and servicing military hardware and software, governmental data storage, and other security-related products and services, the accessing of company data by competitors (especially from overseas), or even foreign governmental agencies can lead to threats to the public interest.

Unsurprisingly, public interest issues usually rest on *consequentialist* reasoning, namely that the action can be said to cause an overall aggregate reduction in happiness for affected members of society. Should competition be reduced as a result of industrial espionage, then the public may suffer because of increased prices and lower innovation over the long term. Spying related to military or other sensitive information may harm the public through increased exposure to risks of various kinds. For instance, the US government has reported that among the spate of cyber intrusions from China in recent years, 'more than 40 Pentagon weapons programmes and nearly 30 other defence technologies have been compromised' (Tucker 2014).

☑ Skill check

Distinguishing intelligence gathering from industrial espionage. All companies collect information about their rivals, so it is important to be able to apply the above guidelines to recognize when acceptable practice has crossed the line into industrial espionage.

'Dirty tricks'

Overly intense competition can also lead to questionable tactics beyond just stealing secrets and spying on competitors. A more generic term often used in the business world to describe the range of morally dubious practices that competitors occasionally turn to in order to outdo their rivals is 'dirty tricks'. In addition to industrial espionage, dirty tricks can include various tactics, among them:

- **Negative advertising:** where the firm deliberately sets out to publicly criticize their competitors, their products, or any product or performance claims the competitor may have made.

- **Stealing customers:** where a rival's customers are specifically approached in order to encourage them to switch suppliers, often using underhand methods such as misrepresentation, providing false information, bribery, or impersonating the competitor's staff.

- **Predatory pricing:** as we saw in Chapter 8, this involves the deliberate setting of prices below cost in order to initiate a price war and force weaker competitors out of the market.

- **Sabotage:** this can take many forms, but basically involves direct interference in a competitor's business in order to obstruct, slow down, or otherwise derail their plans.

While some of these tactics may seem a little extreme, they are not all that uncommon in contemporary business practice. For example, Virgin Atlantic and British Airways have been locked in an intense, long-running competitive rivalry stemming from BA's campaign of dirty tricks in the 1990s (Topham 2014). More recently, the international ride-sharing firm Uber has been accused of a range of dirty tricks against its competitors, including poaching drivers and posing as customers of its rivals and then cancelling rides in order to tie up the drivers' availability and push customers over to Uber (Frizell 2014). One of Uber's competitors, Lyft, reported that Uber employees had ordered and cancelled more than 5,000 rides with the firm. Indeed, new technologies have expanded the range of potential techniques available for dirty tricks. Malware, such as internet viruses, worms, and Trojan Horses, have all been used by firms to sabotage their competitors' systems or to divert customers from their intended website onto a competitor's.

Anticompetitive behaviour

Putting rival firms out of business can be about more than just intense competition between two industry rivals. In many cases, the stakes are considerably higher, since the action can signal an attempt to deliberately restrict competition in an industry in order to reap longer-term profitability. As we argued in Chapter 8, such anticompetitive practices usually contravene competition law, which is in place to ensure fair competition and protect consumers and other firms from monopolistic behaviour. However, such charges can be extremely difficult to prove.

One case that did lead to a major victory for regulators, however, came in 2009 when Intel, the microchip manufacturer, was handed a record fine of more than €1 billion by the European Commission for offering hidden rebates to retailers if they sold only Intel products. Despite holding a substantially dominant position (80% of the market), it was Intel's abuse of this position in restricting competition that the EC criticized, not the monopolistic position itself. As the Competition Commissioner said at the time of the announcement, 'Intel has harmed millions of European consumers by deliberately acting to keep competitors out of the market for computer chips for many years'.[2] Another tech giant, Google, was investigated in the 2010s for anticompetitive practices in the US, Europe, Canada, and India with respect to potential abuse of its dominant position in search and related advertising services. Although the company was cleared in the US of demoting its rivals in its search results, the company risked a forced 'unbundling' of its search and other businesses in Europe or a fine of as much as $6 billion from the European Commission.[3]

Problems of insufficient competition

Anticompetitive behaviour can obviously also hurt consumers, particularly when it results in companies being able to abuse their dominance in a market to exploit customers through higher prices. Sometimes, though, ethical problems arise here not so much because rivals are overly competitive with each other, but because competition is reduced by rivals being insufficiently competitive with each other. Most of such behaviours are precluded by competition law, but the problems of determining when firms have colluded can be difficult to determine.

Collusion and cartels

At the other end of the scale from such intense rivalry is where select groups of competitors band together in a cartel or trading group to fix prices and other trading arrangements for their own mutual benefit. Again, we briefly discussed this issue of collusion in Chapter 8 (Ethical issues in pricing, pp. 353–355), since it mainly results in a potential threat to consumer interests.

■ Globalization, suppliers, and competitors: the ethical challenges of global business networks

Deterritorialization of the corporate value chain can be identified as an important influence contributing to the process of globalization. George Yip (1995), for example, identifies the key forces driving globalization in business to be: convergence of markets, global competition, cost advantages, and government influence.

The *convergence of markets* has meant that firms have increasingly sold their products across the world, thereby bringing them into direct competition with firms in, and from, different countries. This move towards *global competition* means that competitors may now hail from cultures with different understandings and expectations of business and of the nature of competition. Moreover, the impact of foreign competition in many countries might well have significant effects on the local economy.

The potential for *cost advantages* overseas has involved business in a fundamental restructuring of supply chains in the pursuit of lower-cost sites for production.

This has seen vast numbers of multinational corporations shifting the sourcing and production of their products, components, and labour to less-developed countries—a move that has been expedited by *government influence* in these countries. Again, this has involved corporations in business relationships with organizations operating under a different set of cultural practices and assumptions, and where standards of working practices, and health, safety, and environmental protection may differ markedly from at home.

What we have seen is a dramatic reshaping of ethical considerations and problems when dealing with suppliers and competitors in a global, as opposed to a purely locally-based, business network. This reshaping brings to the fore four main considerations:

- Different ways of doing business.
- Impacts on indigenous businesses.
- Differing labour and environmental standards.
- Extended chain of responsibility.

Different ways of doing business

By coming into contact with overseas suppliers and competitors, corporate managers are often confronted with very different ways of thinking about and evaluating business ethics. As we have already seen in earlier chapters dealing with employees and consumers, it is clear that certain practices which may be morally questionable at home might be seen as perfectly legitimate in a different cultural environment, just as some practices that are perfectly acceptable in one's own country may raise questions overseas. For example, Jerold Muskin (2000) suggests that for *competitors*, differences in national culture and law give rise to different notions of *intellectual property*. Whilst European, and even more so US, companies might expect the granting of exclusive rights to any novel technologies they develop, in Asia innovation is often seen as a public good to be used for the advance of technology by all.

In the main, though, different ways of doing business are primarily important for corporations' dealings with their *suppliers*, particularly in relation to *gift giving*, *bribery*, and *corruption*. Different countries tend to exhibit differing attitudes towards the appropriateness of gift giving between customers and suppliers. As we saw in Chapter 1, in Chinese cultures the widespread practice of *guanxi*—namely, 'a system of personal connections that carry long-term social obligations'—places considerable emphasis on the desirability and acceptability of reciprocal favours and gift giving to develop and maintain relationships (Millington et al. 2005: 255). This establishes different cultural expectations around gift giving in buyer–seller relationships. Whilst a European purchasing officer might easily interpret the gift as an attempt at bribery rather than simple courtesy, if they refused to accept the gift they might risk causing offence, thus harming the business relationship and jeopardizing the deal.

Thomas Donaldson (1996) suggests that as Western firms have become more familiar with such traditions, they have increasingly tolerated gift-giving practices and even applied different limits on gift giving and receiving in countries such as China and Japan. This, he argues, is not so much a matter of *ethical relativism* (which he claims, as we have, is a highly problematic approach to business ethics), but is simply a matter of respect for local tradition.

Going back to our ways of distinguishing personal inducements (see Distinguishing personal inducements, pp. 398–400), if the act is without an *intent* to gain undeserved favour, if it does not have the *effect* of doing so, and if it is not *perceived* as doing so, then it should be regarded as acceptable when consistent with a broader social norm. This is especially the case when the norm also dictates that the giving is an *exchange*. There is a significant difference between a buyer and a seller exchanging gifts, and a salesperson simply offering the buyer a long line of presents with the expectation that the reciprocity would come in the form of extra business rather than a gift in return.

The main problem here is that people all too often regard this kind of respect for tradition as a signal that all local customs should be accepted and adapted to, regardless of their ethical implications. If we accept gifts from suppliers, then why should we blanch at taking or giving bribes to oil the wheels of business? The issue of corruption is a major problem in many countries. However, evidence suggests that managers in such cultures often draw a clear distinction between gift giving within a culturally accepted framework, such as *guanxi*, which is designed to build business relationships, and illicit payments that serve the purpose of lining people's pockets at the expense of their organization (Millington et al. 2005).

The problem is not simply with those accepting bribes, but also with those willing to pay them. For example, the *Bribe Payers Index*, produced by the not-for-profit organization Transparency International, provides an illuminating picture of the propensity for bribe paying by multinationals from various countries. The index, based on responses from more than 3,000 senior business executives in 30 countries, shows that companies based in large emerging economies such as Russia and China are widely seen as likely to use bribery to gain business abroad. At the other end of the scale, Dutch, Belgian, and Swiss companies are seen as the least likely to bribe, although it should be noted that no country has a perfect score (see **Figure 9.4**). The survey on which the index is based also shows that firms in the public works, construction, utilities, and real-estate sectors are seen to be more likely to engage in bribery than others (see **Figure 9.5**).

Why is bribery so endemic to international business? The answer to some extent seems to be that multinational businesses promulgate the practice because it is 'normal', 'expected', or 'customary' in the host country. Unless we are going to slip into relativism though, this does not condone the practice. Just to say something is 'normal' does not imply that it is 'right'. Forty-one states across the world have now signed up to the OECD Anti-Bribery Convention. The convention is aimed at stamping out corruption in international business, and the broad range of signatories suggests a gathering international consensus over the undesirability of corruption, and a commitment to dealing with it. Nonetheless, enforcement of the convention remains a challenge for most states, with one recent report suggesting that there was little or no enforcement in 22 of the signatory countries and limited enforcement in eight.[4] This has led some countries (most prominently the US with the Foreign Corrupt Practices Act, and now also the UK since passing the Bribery Act 2010) to prosecute firms for overseas bribery, providing they have some commercial link to the home country.

In fact, for the individual manager, the question is not always one of whether bribery is right or wrong, but whether doing business in certain countries is even *possible* without

Rank	Country	Score
1	Netherlands	8.8
1	Switzerland	8.8
3	Belgium	8.7
4	Germany	8.6
4	Japan	8.6
6	Australia	8.5
6	Canada	8.5
8	United Kingdom	8.3
10	USA	8.1
13	South Korea	7.9
14	Brazil	7.7
15	Italy	7.6
15	Malaysia	7.6
19	India	7.5
19	Taiwan	7.5
19	Turkey	7.5
22	Saudi Arabia	7.4
26	Mexico	7.0
27	China	6.5
28	Russia	6.1

Figure 9.4 Bribe paying by multinational companies abroad according to selected country of origin

Countries are scored on a scale of 0–10, where a maximum score of 10 corresponds with the view that companies from that country *never* bribe abroad and a 0 corresponds with the view that they *always* do.

Source: Adapted from 2011 Bribe Payers Index. Copyright 2011 Transparency International: the global coalition against corruption. Used with permission. For more information, visit http://www. transparency.org.

such practices. Regardless of whether an individual firm has a code prohibiting bribery, or whether one's country has signed up to the OECD convention, if a reasonable level of business cannot go ahead without bribery, how is the individual going to proceed? Many multinational staff seem to be caught between the ethical commitments of their code and the realities of everyday business. One way that some firms have responded to this problem is to amend their codes of conduct so that employees are not penalized for any loss of business due to avoidance of bribery. For instance, if you go back to Unilever's code of business principles in Figure 5.2 (p. 192), this categorically suggests that 'the Board of Unilever will not criticize management for any loss of business resulting from adherence to these principles'.

Business Sector	Score
Public works contracts and construction	5.3
Utilities	6.1
Real estate/property development	6.1
Oil and gas	6.2
Mining	6.3
Power generation and transmission	6.4
Pharmaceutical and health care	6.4
Heavy manufacturing	6.5
Fisheries	6.6
Arms, defence, and military	6.6

Figure 9.5 Top ten sectors perceived as most likely to engage in bribery

Sectors are scored on a scale of 0–10, where a maximum score of 10 corresponds with the view that companies in that sector *never* bribe and a 0 corresponds with the view that they *always* do.

Source: Adapted from 2011 Bribe Payers Index. Copyright 2011 Transparency International: the global coalition against corruption. Used with permission. For more information, visit http://www.transparency.org.

Impacts on indigenous businesses

The role of multinationals in corruption is often one of perpetuating existing problems. However, they can often bring new problems too. The size, power, and political influence of multinationals often means that they enjoy considerable cost and other advantages compared with local competitors. As Jennifer Spencer (2008: 341) suggests, multinationals 'can harm indigenous firms by posing strong competition in product, labour, and financial markets and by offering employment alternatives to individuals who would otherwise found their own business'. This can mean that the exposure to the competition of a major multinational such as Starbucks, IKEA, Microsoft, or Monsanto can 'crowd out' local enterprises and severely threaten the business of indigenous competitors (Klein 2000).

Of course, the introduction of more and better competition can often be a force for innovation, better products, lower prices, and economic growth. Multinationals can build value-enhancing partnerships with local firms, expose local entrepreneurs to new practices, and contribute to the human capital of local workers (Spencer 2008). This is why international organizations such as the WTO promote global trade, and why even humanitarian organizations such as the UN promote the desirability of market development for underdeveloped countries. However, such competition can also result in the matching of unequal rivals, where the ultimate consequence can be the elimination of local competition, and as we saw in Chapter 8, a homogenization of the high street.

The key point here is that multinationals may often be able to negotiate far more attractive trading arrangements than their weaker indigenous competitors; they may bring specialized management knowledge, economies of scale, advanced technology, powerful brands, and a host of other advantages (Dawar and Frost 1999). Similarly, they may be able to force local suppliers into accepting terms and conditions that barely keep them in business. There are clearly issues of fairness to be considered here, as well as questions of whether local competitors should be protected in some way—particularly if multinationals themselves are benefiting from certain protections. For example, the interests of large multinationals are often promoted by their own national governments (because their success is vital to economic growth), and even by host governments overseas (since the influx of jobs and investment can be highly beneficial).

This problem of unfair competition from multinationals is a particular cause for concern when it threatens the viability of an entire local industry as this can lead to more fundamental social and economic decay. For example, the so-called 'banana war' (between the EU and the Caribbean on one side and the US and Latin American countries on the other) was the World Trade Organization's longest-running dispute, running from 1991 until 2012. The clash was a result of European attempts to protect small-scale Caribbean banana growers against cheaper imports from US multinationals, such as Dole foods, Del Monte, and Chiquita International. Many Caribbean countries had been reliant on the banana industry, but with costs up to double those of Latin American-based producers, the sustainability of the Caribbean industry was dependent on a special trading relationship it had built with former colonial powers in the EU that exempted Caribbean imports from the restrictions and tariffs on Latin American bananas. Latin American countries, partly driven by lobbying from American multinationals, lodged a series of complaints against the EU's 'discriminatory' system with the WTO. Over the course of the dispute, the US imposed sanctions on certain European imports, with the EU eventually agreeing to phase out its tariffs.[5]

? THINK THEORY

To what extent is it appropriate to protect local businesses from 'unfair' competition from multinationals? Consider this situation from the perspectives of theories of justice and utilitarianism.

Differing labour and environmental standards

As firms from industrialized countries have increasingly sourced through global supply chains, probably the most prominent ethical problem to have come under the spotlight is the labour and environmental conditions under which their suppliers operate. You may remember that back in Chapter 7 we looked at the 'race to the bottom' occasioned by the demand by multinationals for lower-cost production in developing countries such as China, Indonesia, Vietnam, India, and Bangladesh. This raises substantial ethical problems for companies that source their products in lower-cost countries, for it is often the case that lower costs are accompanied by poorer labour conditions, less environmental protection, and lower attention to health and safety protection. These, as we have already mentioned a number of times in the book so far, can, and frequently have, led to human rights and other abuses.

The number of high-profile media exposés of such incidents since the beginning of the 1990s has been phenomenal. Clothing and sportswear producers were initially the most affected, with accusations of sweatshop conditions being launched at various brands over the years including Disney, Gap, H&M, and Nike. Such problems have hardly receded since the 1990s though, with a report from the International Textile Garment and Leather Workers' Federation in 2011 naming no less than 60 high street brands involved in 'widespread violations and abuses of workers' rights' across the 83 Asian factories that it investigated. Such violations, the report concludes 'continue to be the norm in the industry'.[6] The electronics industry has also very much been in the spotlight, with Apple in particular targeted for persistent labour violations in its supply chain.[7]

Typically, this debate has mainly centred on pay, working conditions, and child labour. The fundamental conventions of the International Labour Organization (ILO) however (which are probably the most widely recognized and influential agreements on labour rights), also refer to broader issues such as freedom of association, equality, and forced labour, etc. Many companies have discovered (or their critics have discovered for them) that in their suppliers' factories, workers have been paid below a living wage, subjected to physical and verbal abuse, worked compulsory overtime, failed to have statutory rights to time off recognized, and faced a range of other violations of basic labour rights.

We have seen in Chapter 3 that different ethical theories provide a range of arguments for and against such labour practices. However, these conditions have been seen as all the more inequitable because of the startling comparison that they make with the prices paid by consumers in Europe and the US for the products they make, as well as the pay and conditions earned by staff in the company's head office—in particular, the stellar remuneration packages of the companies' CEOs. For example, one widely quoted statistic is that while ex-Disney CEO Michael Eisner was earning $9,783 an hour in the 1990s, a Haitian worker sewing Disney pyjamas earned just 28 cents an hour. This means it would have taken a Haitian worker 16.8 years to earn what Eisner had earned in one hour (Klein 2000: 352). Such disparities are alarming, and to many appear unjustifiable when the total costs of labour in producing clothes, for example, typically only amount to something like 1% of the final retail price (compared with 25% for brand profit, overheads, and promotion) (Robins and Humphrey 2000).

? THINK THEORY

In Chapter 7 we discussed Thomas Donaldson's argument that many problems of poor wages and conditions were problems of relative development rather than simply differences in ethics (Absolutism versus relativism, p. 321). How would you compare Donaldson's argument with that of the justice-based argument above?

VISIT THE ONLINE RESOURCE CENTRE for a short response to this feature

---

Different environmental and health and safety standards in suppliers' countries can also provide a loophole through which firms can potentially secure lower-cost supplies by bypassing the stringent standards in their country of origin. For example, the recycling of 'end-of-life' electronic waste (see Chapter 8, Product recapture, pp. 373–376) has increasingly been outsourced to developing countries in Asia and Africa. Despite international laws banning the export of hazardous waste to developing countries, the combination of spiralling amounts of waste, lax regulation, and a thriving and lucrative informal economy in countries such as China, India, Ghana, and Nigeria has led to a growing problem of unregulated reprocessing, where the release of lead, mercury, and other dangerous chemicals poses serious threats to human and environmental health. Millions of tonnes of electronic waste are illegally shipped by companies in the developed world to unscrupulous processors in developing countries, with Interpol reporting that almost one in three shipping containers leaving the EU that were checked by its agents contained illegal e-waste (Vidal 2013). The problem of 'digital cemeteries' of e-waste has therefore become a major ethical issue for manufacturers and recyclers alike. In 2009, the US computer producer Dell was the first major technology company to ban exports of its e-waste to developing countries, while more recently it has helped to establish formal e-waste recycling programmes in some of the worst hit areas in order to ensure safer handling of hazardous materials (Clancy 2013).

Extended chain of responsibility

Ultimately, the implication of these shifts towards global supply and competition is that individual firms are faced with an *extended chain of responsibility*. Where once it may have been perfectly acceptable to argue that the ethics of a firm's suppliers, or a firm's impact on its competitors, was simply none of its business, this idea has been gradually swept away since the beginning of the 1990s (see for example Emmelhainz and Adams 1999). The different social and economic conditions present in other countries, as well as the sheer inequalities brought to the surface by international trade, have meant that the relatively level playing field constituted by national business has been replaced with the sloping and bumpy playing surface of globalization.

What we see now is that relations with other businesses are no longer only conducted within a national community with legislation and broadly agreed rules of the game that are considered to be fair to all. Hence, corporations have to consider their ethical responsibilities much more broadly, not least because pressure groups have discovered that the best way to focus attention on practices and conditions in anonymous factories in far-off places is not to target the factory itself, but to target the big brand multinational which sources its products from it. Supply chains are now widely seen as key sources of reputation risk. This does not mean that a firm's responsibility through its supply chain is boundaryless, but it does mean that firms are expected to take moral responsibility for actions in their supply chain that they can realistically influence (Amaeshi et al. 2008). **Ethics in Action 9.1** shows that these shifts have affected a wide range of businesses, both big and small, across various sectors. As we shall now see, this has led to the supply chain being increasingly used as a conduit for ethics management and regulation.

■ The corporate citizen in business-to-business relationships: ethical sourcing and fair trade

We stated in Chapter 2 that one of the most crucial areas where corporations enter the realm of citizenship and begin to take over the role of governments is in the regulation and control of other businesses. This can be mainly seen to happen through the supply chain, via a process known as ethical sourcing.

VISIT THE
ONLINE
RESOURCE
CENTRE
for links to
useful sources
of further
information

ETHICS IN ACTION 9.1   http://www.ethicalcorp.com

Engagement—help your suppliers become better businesses

Stephen Gardner, 4 October 2012

Products are no longer manufactured in one place and sold in another. Rather, manufactured goods, especially complex products such as computers or cars, are collaborative efforts, involving numerous companies and countries. An iPod, for example, is often described as being made by Chinese mega-supplier Foxconn. But Foxconn is better described as an assembler. The iPod hard drive is Japanese-designed, but manufactured in Thailand or another Asian country. The microcontroller is a British, Korean, or US model, but made at a Taiwanese or other Asian plant. The display screen, processors, and battery are contributed by various other east Asian suppliers.

For multi-product corporations, the situation is even more complicated. Wal-Mart counts about 60,000 suppliers. Tesco has some 6,000 in Britain alone. IBM's network is made up of 28,000 suppliers spread across 90 countries. Unilever has a solid claim to the biggest supply network, with 160,000 companies providing it with goods and services.

Such networks involve a trade-off. Globalization means companies can cut costs: outsourcing production or assembly to locations that are far cheaper than their home markets. But responsibility for the product cannot be outsourced. The close interconnection between developed country brands and their developing nation suppliers creates leverage for consumers, governments, and campaigners, who want to ensure that branded products are not tainted by human rights violations or environmental crimes in vulnerable countries.

Thomas Derry, chief executive officer of the Arizona-based Institute for Supply Management, says companies should pay attention to this risk. If problems arise, such as allegations of mistreatment of workers in supplier facilities, it will be the brands at the end of the chain that are 'seen as the critical responsible party'.

Standards high

Leading companies have taken on board the message. Jörgen Karlsson, who oversees the supply chain for telecommunications equipment and services giant Ericsson, says it is 'of utmost importance that our suppliers comply with the same strict requirements as we place on ourselves. High standards in areas such as working conditions, environmental management and anti-corruption must always be expected, regardless of country, category or size of supplier.'

In most cases, suppliers buy in to the argument that 'compliance with high ethical and sustainability standards is not only good from a humanitarian and environmental point of view, but also makes perfect business sense,' Karlsson says. 'Better working conditions lead to increased employee loyalty, reduced sick leave and lower accident rates. Reduced electricity consumption means lower energy costs. Compliance with the strictest anti-corruption standards earns respect from customers.' Where Ericsson does ask a supplier to take corrective action, it is generally done on time and as agreed, Karlsson adds.

Paving the way

In the globalized world, smaller companies can also have supply chains that stretch across continents. The risks can be as big as they are for the multinationals. Marshalls is a British company with about 2,300 employees that produces stone paving. It used to source granite, limestone, and sandstone from Western Europe, but because of diminishing supplies it has, over the past decade, switched to quarries in Asia: China for granite, China and Vietnam for limestone, and India for sandstone.

The transition to new sources has thrown up a number of ethical challenges, from child labour in India to use of prison labour in Vietnam, says Marshalls marketing director Chris Harrop. Marshalls has learned, he says, that auditing has limited value. Companies must 'concentrate on capacity and implementation in partnership with suppliers and workers'.

This means finding solutions, rather than simply proscribing certain behaviours. Marshalls found that children commonly worked in quarries in India alongside their families because limited schooling was available to them, and they were needed to contribute to the family's income.

In response, Marshalls worked with a local non-profit group, Hadoti Hast Shilp Sansthan, in Rajasthan where the Indian quarries are located, to set up schools, and provide a safety net through health checks and insurance for labourers. The basic aim was to improve standards in the quarries. 'There is a financial argument,' says Harrop. The cost of accidents harms the business, and 'workers who are tired are not producing quality work'.

Marshalls monitors conditions in its source quarries, but believes that 'audit with a stick encourages audit fraud'. Marshalls local staff in Rajasthan visit sites regularly, but if shortcomings are found, they negotiate with, rather than censure, quarry owners. 'It's about showing them the benefits [of sustainability] rather than the loss that could accrue,' Harrop says.

Marshalls' experience suggests a number of recommendations for companies facing similar supply chain issues. The first step for avoiding problems is to select suppliers that can be trusted. This might entail organizational change at head office, if the emphasis has traditionally been only on the financial relationship with suppliers. Harrop also recommends 'collapsing supply into fewer suppliers and rewarding good suppliers [so that] their businesses grow as we grow'.

Ultimately, suppliers have the same constraints as the companies they sell to. Sustainable thinking will become necessary because of resource limits, and because costs will be passed up the chain if efficiency is lacking, reducing the competitiveness of the brand whose label is on the final product. For any company, resisting new ideas is 'not a good winning strategy,' says Thomas Derry of the Institute for

Supply Management. Companies must work ever more closely with their suppliers, to 'enhance the performance of both'.

Fire traps

The appalling Karachi garment-factory fire of 11 September 2012, which killed 264 people—Pakistan's worst factory blaze to date—was a grim reminder that in many developing countries, health and safety controls are weak, and that laws that are in place might not be enforced.

The Karachi fire—and another fire on the same day at a Lahore shoe factory, where 25 people died—recalled a conflagration in Bangladesh in December 2010 at a factory making clothes for Tommy Hilfiger and other brands. An investigation into that fire by US news network ABC apparently caught Hilfiger himself unawares. He told ABC that his company 'will never manufacture clothes in any of those factories again,' and claimed to be the 'gold standard' for health and safety.

A humiliating climb-down followed, with Hilfiger admitting that his branded clothing was still being made in Bangladesh. Parent company Phillips-Van Heusen, which owns Hilfiger's clothing line, conceded that inspections had failed to pick up problems at the factory, such as locked fire exits and barred windows, which made it impossible for workers to escape the blaze. Hilfiger subsequently pledged up to $2 million to improve fire safety at factories making his clothes.

Sean Ansett, of sustainability consultants At Stake Advisors, says the episode highlights a number of issues with modern supply networks. At supplier facilities, as a minimum there should be 'compliance with national laws; that is absolutely a fair expectation,' he says. He adds, however, that although many countries have the right laws in place, 'there is a lack of capacity to enforce those laws. Companies have become the default labour inspectorates due to these challenges on the ground.'

As Hilfiger learned, lack of awareness about weak points in the supply chain is a reputational risk. Brands 'definitely have responsibility for how their products are manufactured, but that is a shared responsibility [with suppliers],' Ansett says. 'Smart companies are already looking at strategies to address these issues.'

Sources

Ethical Corporation, Stephen Gardner, 4 October 2012, http://www.ethicalcorp.com. Reproduced with the kind permission of Ethical Corporation.

VISIT THE ONLINE RESOURCE CENTRE for a short response to this feature

? THINK THEORY

Think about the examples here in terms of an extended chain of responsibility. Should large and small firms alike be expected to consider what happens in their supply chain as part of their corporate responsibility?

Ethical sourcing

Ethical sourcing
The inclusion of explicit social, ethical, and/or environmental criteria into supply-chain management policies, procedures, and programmes.

Ethical sourcing (also known as ethical trade or responsible supply-chain management) occurs when a supply-chain member introduces social and environmental criteria into its purchase decisions in order to support certain practices and/or suppliers. Much like ethical consumption that we discussed in Chapter 8, ethical sourcing represents the idea that firms (rather than individual consumers) use their buying power to influence the practices of those they purchase from.

Many large companies now include some kind of criteria of this kind in their procurement policies and agreements (Hughes 2005). One of the forerunners of this practice was the UK home hardware retailer B&Q which, since 1991, has required all of its suppliers to provide information on environment performance as part of its Supplier Environmental Audit. Since this time, various firms across industries as diverse as apparel, cars, cosmetics, food, and technology have introduced supplier codes of conduct intended to prevent environmental, labour and human rights abuses in their supply chains. **Ethics Online 9** discusses some of the online resources that have emerged to help firms deal with such responsibility issues in the supply chain.

The centrepiece of many ethical sourcing programmes tends to be some kind of social audit process designed to ensure compliance with the firm's sourcing guidelines in supplier factories, farms, and other production units. The practice of designing, implementing and enforcing a code of ethics was discussed in detail in Chapter 5 (Setting standards of ethical behaviour: designing and implementing codes of ethics, pp. 190–199), where we were mainly concerned with managing ethics internally. We saw that there were four types of codes, any of which might be used in ethical sourcing, namely corporate codes (such as Apple's Supplier Code of Conduct), a professional code (such as the Chartered Institute of Procurement and Supply's code of conduct shown in **Figure 9.2**), industry codes (such as the Electronics Industry Code of Conduct that 'sets standards on social, environmental and ethical issues in the electronics industry supply chain'),[8] or a programme code (such as the Ethical Trading Initiative base code—see Chapter 10). However, it is important to recognize that when the process of managing ethical codes is extended to the supply chain, it becomes even more difficult to implement effectively because the firm does not have direct oversight or control over what is happening in its suppliers' workplaces. In particular, many firms have struggled with providing effective *traceability* in their supply chains—that is, their supply chains are so long and complex that they do not know with any certainty where all their raw materials come from. So although many companies have been relatively quick to introduce supplier codes of conduct, the implementation of effective monitoring and enforcement has proved to be more problematic (Emmelhainz and Adams 1999).

Clearly, the mere inclusion of ethical sourcing criteria in supply-chain management is no guarantee that they will improve supplier behaviour. However, studies have shown that supply-chain pressure has been a key factor in prompting suppliers to seek various social and environmental certifications of one sort or another, even when they are not necessarily perceived as intrinsically valuable. These include accreditations such as the staff training and development award Investors in People (Ram 2000) and the environmental quality standard ISO 14001 (Delmas and Montiel 2009).

For example, in the early 2000s all of the American 'big three' carmakers—Ford, GM, and Chrysler—requested their suppliers to adopt ISO 14001 accreditation—although

▲ **ETHICS ONLINE** 9

Practical resources for managing supply-chain ethics

VISIT THE ONLINE RESOURCE CENTRE
for links to useful sources of further information

For most companies, the challenge of tackling ethics in the supply chain is a daunting task. It is one thing to manage business ethics internally, but where do you start in dealing with all your suppliers, and their suppliers, and so on? Even companies with lots of experience in one area of supply chain ethics may lack expertise in important new areas such as supply chain sustainability. Suppliers too need help in developing ethical relationships with their corporate customers.

Increasing demands for improved supply chain ethics have led to the emergence of numerous online practical resources to help managers get to grips with some of these challenges. The Portal for Responsible Supply Chain Management, for example, was developed by a consortium of businesses and support organizations including Hewlett Packard, Titan, Volkswagen, and L'Oréal to provide hands-on tools and information to both producers and buyers. The site features advice on the key steps in developing responsible supply chain management from either side of the exchange relationship and includes various resources in the form of company guidelines, sourcing standards, and other reference materials.

Another site with lots of practical advice and guidance is provided by Business and the Community under their Marketplace programme on responsible supply chains. A notable feature of this site is the interesting assortment of case studies of successful company initiatives from British American Tobacco's work with tobacco growers, the office equipment company Ricoh's green procurement initiative, and Sainsbury's programme to develop sustainable fish sourcing for its UK supermarket business.

Of course, if you are a manager looking for practical help with supply chain ethics then you are probably already convinced that your company needs to take the issue seriously. But what about other people in the organization—the marketing, purchasing, or operations staff who remain uncommitted to ethical practices—or the suppliers or customers that will need to come on board to make any new initiatives successful? The Ethical Trading Initiative site provides resources for managers facing these challenges, with fact sheets, leaflets, DVDs, and video clips that lay out the case for ethical trade, and how to secure buy-in from key stakeholders. The site also offers access to codes of conduct, workbooks, guidelines, and other useful materials for practitioners.

Another major challenge faced by companies in implementing ethical sourcing is finding out credible information on the practices of current or potential suppliers, and of course the time and expense involved in auditing and monitoring them. Sedex, the Supplier Ethical Data Exchange, is a non-profit organization that enables firms to share such information through a secure, confidential online portal. Sedex also provides a valuable service to suppliers because it enables them to complete one self-assessment questionnaire that they can then share with multiple purchasing companies rather than going through the process of individual assessments one by one.

Online resources such as these offer managers—and students of business ethics—plenty of insight into the practicalities of ethical supply chain management. And for those looking for further support and assistance, they also offer consultancy, membership, advisory services, and conferences along with the freely available materials. After all, the organizations behind the websites are also potential suppliers (and we might hope ethical ones) of business services for the corporate community.

Sources
Business in the Community: http://www.bitc.org.uk.
Ethical Trading Initiative: http://www.ethicaltrade.org.
Portal for Responsible Supply Chain Management: http://www.csr-supplychain.gr/en/.
Sedex: http://www.sedexglobal.com.

▼

only about 25% actually did so before the deadline set by the companies. As Delmas and Montiel (2009) demonstrate, the willingness of suppliers to comply with or resist such initiatives is strongly determined by the type of relationship they have with the companies that purchase from them. Specifically, those suppliers with a high dependence on their customers are more likely to comply (because their assets cannot easily be deployed in supplying other firms), as are those that are relatively new entrants to the industry (because they need to build up their reputation). For suppliers, the public act of gaining ethical certification can therefore act as a way of reducing *information asymmetries* between themselves and potential buyers (King et al. 2005).

Ethical sourcing as business-to-business regulation

In the absence of specific or sufficient legislation in suppliers' countries, or more usually where there is simply weak enforcement of existing legislation, this kind of supply-chain pressure can be the most effective form of regulation for these companies. Although this is not regulation in the formal sense of ensuring compliance with government legislation, the pressure exerted by powerful corporate customers to comply with ethical sourcing guidelines and criteria does constitute some form of a regulatory intervention in the supply chain (Hughes 2001, 2005; Cashore 2002; Locke and Romis 2007). The threat of losing business or being delisted by a major customer can act as a powerful force for change, particularly when the threat is shown to be more than just an idle one. In particular, when *competitors* within an industry collaborate to introduce ethical guidelines for suppliers, it is often difficult for suppliers to avoid compliance.

This kind of pressure on suppliers can effect further change through the supply chain, and even in the wider business network. This is because not only are suppliers' own suppliers often involved in any progress towards compliance with ethical sourcing guidelines (and in turn *their* suppliers, and so on), but competing suppliers also have a chance to gain business if they have the right ethical policies or accreditations. Hence, a purchasing 'multiplier effect' can be set in motion which has the potential to achieve social change more quickly and more thoroughly than any other single activity that a particular firm could undertake (Preuss 2005).

The success of ethical sourcing initiatives, however, depends on a number of factors. As Sarah Roberts (2003) explains, this includes the power of buyers and suppliers, the reputational vulnerability of network members, the diffuseness of the supply base, and the length of the supply chain between the corporate buyer and the companies where the ethical issues are most pronounced. This, she suggests, explains why ethical sourcing initiatives in the forestry products and apparel industries have been more successful than those in the confectionery industry.

Another factor to consider is whether ethical sourcing is attempted by individual firms alone, or whether whole groups of competing firms join together in a coalition to address the problem. Such industry alliances can take a number of forms, from setting up supplier codes of conduct, to systems of supplier auditing and evaluation. Frequently, they also involve civil society organizations or government agencies as advisers or even managers of the programme. We shall be looking at some examples of these types of multi-actor initiatives in Chapters 10 and 11, but in the meantime let us consider the types of strategies that firms or alliances might use in ethical sourcing.

Strategies of business-to-business regulation

There are essentially three main ways in which firms can effect ethical sourcing through the supply chain (see Winstanley et al. 2002; Frenkel and Scott 2002; Locke and Romis 2007):

• **Compliance**. The compliance strategy involves the setting of clear standards for suppliers (e.g. a code of conduct), coupled with a means for assessing compliance with those standards (such as a social audit). Failure to meet standards in the short to medium term will result in disengagement by the company in order to do business elsewhere. The toy company Mattel's 'zero tolerance' policy on violations of its supplier code of conduct is illustrative of this approach (Iwata 2006). The compliance approach 'is characterized by global firm domination: the global firm develops and introduces the code, communicates its importance, and is responsible for its enforcement' (Frenkel and Scott 2002: 33).

• **Collaboration**. The collaboration strategy also involves setting standards and compliance procedures, but tends to rely on longer-term 'aims', together with incremental 'targets', in order to foster a step-by-step approach to improving standards. Here, the firm is likely to engage with its suppliers to achieve improvements, utilizing a collaborative approach based on partnership (though not power equality) (Frenkel and Scott 2002). The German sporting goods company Adidas is an example of a company that emphasizes this kind of collaborative, engagement type of approach (Frenkel and Scott 2002).

• **Development**. The development strategy may still include elements of a compliance or collaboration approach, but there is much more focus on ensuring that workers understand their rights and are provided with training to improve their capabilities and future prospects. For example, Apple trained 1.5 million supply-chain workers on their rights in 2013, and provided free college classes in language skills, computing, and other subjects to nearly 300,000 such workers.[9] Supplier firms too may be aided by the purchasing firm, for example with technical and organizational assistance and investments in productivity that boost profits and therefore reduce the likelihood of suppliers exploiting workers.

Most firms and industries have tended to begin with a compliance strategy because it involves clear rules and signals to suppliers and external audiences that the firm is serious about rooting out its problems. For example, **Ethics in Action 9.2** discusses how technology companies have gone about trying to ensure that electronic products are 'conflict free'—that is, produced without any minerals mined by armed groups in the Democratic Republic of Congo.

Compliance-based approaches, however, have not met with unqualified success. Investigations by academics, journalists and campaign groups have frequently uncovered widespread violations in factories that have been recently audited. Either the audits were poor quality or there had been a deliberate attempt to deceive on the part of the factories. As a *New York Times* report concluded 'the inspections are often so superficial that they omit the most fundamental workplace safeguards like fire escapes. And even when inspectors are tough, factory managers find ways to trick them and hide serious violations, like child labor or locked exit doors' (Clifford and Greenhouse 2013). In fact,

VISIT THE
ONLINE
RESOURCE
CENTRE
for links to
useful sources
of further
information

ETHICS IN ACTION 9.2   http://www.ethicalcorp.com

Conflict free minerals—tainted goods

Sam Phipps, 10 September 2014

Gary Niekerk, Intel's director of corporate responsibility, admits that the computer chip-maker was shocked into action on conflict minerals about five years ago when NGOs questioned whether it was sourcing raw materials from war-torn Democratic Republic of Congo (DRC).

'We asked our suppliers, do you know where you're procuring this stuff from? We didn't get much response—very little information came back. Then we were at a top-level meeting and our chief operating officer at the time, Brian Krzanich, who is now our CEO, said: I want this stuff out of our supply chain. Make it happen.'

Easier said than done, when Intel has about 16,000 suppliers worldwide. It was decided the simplest way to go about it was to visit the smelters—Intel staff have since been to 86 of them in 21 countries, travelling more than 250,000 miles. 'We were the first electronics company to visit a smelter. The thinking was that if we could get a smelter verified as conflict free, then we could get all our suppliers to use just those smelters.'

Today Intel, and the wider US industry, has made considerable progress, with recent legislation starting to underpin corporate efforts. The rationale is that trade in the minerals is a lucrative source of funding for armed groups in DRC, where an estimated 5 million people have died, rape is widespread as a weapon of war and child soldiers are regularly recruited.

Regulation

In the US, Congress has taken steps to try to stem the trade. As of this year, the Dodd-Frank Act requires all Securities & Exchange Commission registered companies to report annually if their products contain any gold, tin, tantalum or tungsten. The SEC estimates the ruling will affect about 6,000 companies in the US and abroad. These are not just in the electronics industry but range from automotive to aerospace, clothing (tin in zips, for instance), healthcare and jewellery.

Companies must determine if the minerals may have originated in DRC or adjoining countries. If so, they must trace the supply chain via due diligence and potentially include an independent audit. A form must conclude whether a company has determined the source to be 'DRC Conflict Free,' 'Not DRC Conflict Free' or, for the next two years, 'DRC Conflict Undeterminable' (four years for smaller reporting companies). This last category would not require an audit.

Yet there is clearly a long way to go in cleaning up the complex supply chains of the four major conflict minerals. After the June 2014 deadline for filing the first SEC reports, Sophia Pickles, a campaigner for Global Witness, said: 'While some firms have made strong submissions, most reports filed to date don't include enough information to show that companies are doing credible checks on their supply chains.'

In January 2014 Intel announced the world's first conflict-free microprocessor, an achievement that Niekerk says started as an 'internal goal' that became public. 'The vast majority of our consumer products, laptops or tablets etc, are now conflict free, though we still have others that we are working on.'

Julie Schindall, director of communications and stakeholder engagement at the Electronic Industry Citizenship Coalition (EICC), based in the US, says a growing number of companies at various levels in the supply chain now see a conflict-free minerals strategy as a core part of their business growth. 'Some publicise it and others don't. The supply chain is so long and intricate that even with the biggest and most progressive companies, it is not something that happens overnight but can take several years,' she says.

'Our whole programme began in 2008 and we've gone from two validated conflict free smelters in 2012 to about 100, so it has picked up a lot of momentum. But there's much more to do. One of the main challenges is that nobody knows how many smelters are out there.' The tipping point, Schindall argues, will be when the whole minerals industry works together, including smelters and refiners, and it becomes not just an ethical but a business imperative.

What proportion of the global supply of the four minerals is located in DRC mines? About 20% of the world's tantalum, Niekerk says, 'but as you go to tin, gold and tungsten they drop off to a small percentage. With gold, for instance, it's about 2%.' This means, at least with the last three minerals, that on a basis of simple probability, they are unlikely to be sourced from DRC in the vast majority of supply to various industries.

Buyer pressure

'It's more a question of how to set up a system to validate that because if you say there's only a 2% chance of us being indirectly involved in the murder and rape of millions of people—well, of course people want a zero chance and to feel confident about that,' Niekerk says. The likes of Apple, Dell, and Hewlett-Packard are highly active in their sourcing strategy, according to Niekerk. 'I know because they ask us to verify our materials are conflict free when they buy our microprocessors to put in their products.'

Another challenge is that the metals industry is constantly changing, Schindall says. 'The situation on the ground in the Great Lakes region of DRC is evolving all the time, so understanding what conflict free means is not static.'

Nor is the problem only related to DRC sourced minerals. The US Department of Commerce struggled to draw up a definitive list of all known conflict-processing facilities worldwide by January 2013, which it was required to do under the Dodd-Frank Act.

The Department of Commerce identified 278 conflict mineral smelters and 82 of these were in China. Under EICC auspices, Intel and other companies ask smelters to undergo a voluntary audit that will qualify them as conflict free. To help towards cost, Intel has paid $400,000 into a fund for early adopters. Typically the audit will cost 'multiple thousands,' perhaps up to $20,000, Niekerk says.

Most tungsten is used to make drilling bits for heavy-duty mining and other applications, so the EICC is urging companies in those sectors to join the campaign of gentle persuasion of smelters. In the case of China, for instance, a major tungsten producer, Niekerk is not surprised that this is sometimes a challenge.

'Imagine us saying, we want to look through your books, your shipment manifest, your inventories. Nobody likes an audit, and what happens if you fail? But we respect confidentiality and only publicise the ones that pass. Still, if the tables were turned and it was Chinese companies coming to US smelters, we'd probably see similar reluctance.'

Ultimately, an audit is only a 'snapshot in time' that will need frequent revisiting, Niekerk argues. On the plus side, the Dodd-Frank Act and impending EU legislation will strengthen the case for more transparency on this issue around the world.

The European Commission has proposed a draft regulation setting up a system of self-certification for importers of tin, tantalum, tungsten and gold that choose to import responsibly into the EU, which is one of the world's biggest markets for the minerals. Importers would have to exercise due diligence in line with OECD guidance, and the EU aims to publish an annual list of 'responsible smelters and refiners'.

Sources

Ethical Corporation, Sam Phipps, 10 September 2014, http://www.ethicalcorp.com. Reproduced with the kind permission of Ethical Corporation.

VISIT THE
ONLINE
RESOURCE
CENTRE
for a short
response to this
feature

? THINK THEORY

Think about conflict free minerals from the perspective of different strategies of ethical sourcing. Which approach or approaches would you say have been attempted by the electronics industry and what are their prospects for success?

deception of auditors appears to be widespread, with one study of Chinese toy suppliers, for instance, finding that even among the best-performing suppliers, deception of auditors was common, including the forging of documents, hiding of some workers, coaching employees about what to say to inspectors and even paying them to say the right things (Egels-Zandén 2007).

Problems such as these have led many to question the effectiveness of the compliance strategy for business-to-business regulation through the supply chain. The evidence appears to suggest that despite major efforts to implement effective social audits since the 1990s, worker rights have improved in a few areas but overall little has changed (Egels-Zandén 2014; Egels-Zandén and Lindholm 2015). As a result, many have advocated for a more collaborative or developmental strategy, built on partnership rather than control (Frenkel and Scott 2002; Locke and Romis 2007). One area where these types of collaborative and developmental approaches have been successfully introduced is in the fair trade industry.

☑ **Skill check**

Designing business–business regulation. Determining the most appropriate strategy for business–business regulation enables you to implement a co-ordinated approach to business ethics across firms.

Fair trade

So far we have discussed ethical sourcing as a form of regulation through the supply chain. This tends to give the impression that ethical sourcing is always a way of controlling suppliers. However, in some cases ethical sourcing can actually be more developmental, where suppliers that are seen to be socially beneficial in some way are protected, rewarded, and assisted in achieving development goals (Blowfield 1999; Hughes 2005). For example, the Body Shop has for many years operated a 'Community Fair Trade' programme, which seeks to assist small-scale, indigenous communities in enhancing their standard of living through supposedly 'fair' contracts to supply product ingredients to the company.

Approaches to ethical sourcing that focus on equitable trade arrangements, small-scale producers, and supplier empowerment are usually referred to as *fair trade*. As Smith and Barrientos (2005) suggest, the two types of approach—ethical sourcing and **fair trade**—have traditionally been quite different. Ethical sourcing has mainly been driven and implemented by big brand multinationals, whilst fair trade has been more relational in approach and led by alternative trading organizations. Although there has been growing convergence of the two approaches (Smith and Barrientos 2005), fair trade retains a distinctive flavour, or what some refer to as an 'ethical value-added' to conventional trading arrangements (McMurtry 2009). That is, fair trade is a system aimed at offering 'the most disadvantaged producers in developing countries the opportunity to move out of poverty through creating market access under beneficial rather than exploitative terms. The objective is to empower producers to develop their own business and wider communities through international trade' (Nicholls and Opal 2005: 6).

The point is that many of the growers of everyday products such as coffee, tea, rice, and fruit live in poverty and are faced with poor working conditions, exploitation, and limited health, safety, and environmental protection. At the heart of this problem are international commodity markets, which often set prices that fail to provide the growers even with a living wage. The aim of the fair trade movement is to foster the protection and empowerment of growers, as well as to encourage community development by guaranteeing minimum prices and conditions (Brown 1993; Nicholls and Opal 2005). This is achieved through the application, monitoring, and enforcement of a fair trade supply agreement and code of conduct, verified by an independent social auditing system. Common international standards are set by Fairtrade International, while auditing and certification is conducted by its sister organization FLOCERT. National bodies such as the Fairtrade Foundation (in the UK), Max Havelaar (in much of Europe), Reilun Kaupan (in Finland), or Fair Trade USA (in the US) promote the fair trade system in their respective countries.[10] Products sourced and produced according

Fair trade
A system of exchange based on guaranteeing producers in development countries a living wage, decent working conditions, and opportunities for community development.

to the strict Fairtrade conditions are permitted to use the 'FAIRTRADE Mark', a logo that indicates to consumers that growers have received a fair price and been afforded decent conditions and community support.

The systems put in place by fair trade organizations ensure that whatever price the market may allocate to goods such as cocoa and tea, the growers involved are guaranteed a minimum price by the purchaser. And, if market prices exceed this minimum, fair trade farmers receive a premium in order to finance development goals. As a result, growers are not only prevented from sinking into poverty at the whim of commodity markets, but can also plan and implement community initiatives. **Figure 9.6** provides an illustration from the cocoa market of how the guaranteed price offered by Fairtrade has compared with market prices over time. Many growers involved in the fair trade system also organize into local co-ops in order to ensure that the benefits are shared appropriately and so that community development can be promoted.

The fair trade movement initially operated through charitable organizations such as Oxfam, and alternative trade organizations (ATOs) such as Traidcraft. For many years now, fair trade products have also been sold through mainstream supermarkets, and other high street stores such as the Body Shop have introduced their own operations outside of the established international framework for fair trade accreditation. Since the 1990s, within the established fair trade movement there has been a move away from its charity-supported background towards more mainstream corporate involvement

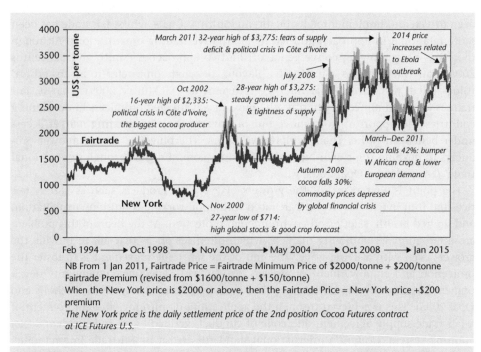

Figure 9.6 The cocoa market 1994–2015: comparison of Fairtrade and New York prices

Source: © Fairtrade Foundation. Reproduced with permission.

(Doherty et al. 2013). This has given rise to the emergence of private sector for-profit fair trade companies, such as Divine Chocolate, which markets chocolate products in the UK and the US, as well as the incorporation of fair trade products into mainstream companies such as high street retailers and major food brands like Cadbury and Nestlé. This greater commercialization has been accompanied by a steady growth in penetration of fair trade products. For example, global Fairtrade retail sales grew by 14% in 2013, totalling an estimated €5.7 billion (Smithers 2014).

Such successes can also have their drawbacks. The increasing commercialization of the fair trade movement risks potential co-optation by business, dilution of its ethical standards, and possible reputational damage to the fair trade movement (Doherty et al. 2013). The need to recruit employees with mainstream business skills and experience (rather than just commitment to fair trade values) also poses challenges for maintaining the ethical culture of fair trade firms (Davies and Crane 2010).

Perhaps the most important question though, is whether the continued success of fair trade is providing a positive force for change for the growers it is intended to help. While some critics suggest that fair trade's focus on guaranteed prices provides a disincentive to improve productivity that ultimately hinders rather than helps farmers (Porter and Kramer 2011), others point to the inequities that are created by guaranteeing higher prices for some farmers while excluding others (Booth and Whetstone 2007). In the face of such criticisms, the fair trade movement itself commissions regular impact assessments from independent research organizations that have demonstrated considerable benefits to farmers and their workers. For example, a 2014 impact assessment of small Brazilian producers of certified oranges (to be used in fair trade orange juice) showed that fair trade accelerated economic growth and created higher income for the majority of producers, improved their quality of life, and helped to keep them in business while many non-certified producers failed (Schiesari and Beat Grüninger 2014).

> **? THINK THEORY**
>
> Fair trade is presented as a fairer means of doing business—benefits are distributed more equally and basic rights are protected. However, some critics have argued that such schemes might be deemed unethical. What arguments might there be against fair trade practices, and which theoretical bases do you think they are derived from?

VISIT THE ONLINE RESOURCE CENTRE for a short response to this feature

■ Sustainability and business relationships: towards industrial ecosystems?

Finally, we need to look at the corporation's relationships with other companies in the context of sustainability. What does it mean to think of a sustainable supply chain, or more broadly, a sustainable business community? We shall look at three key levels here: sustaining the supply chain; turning supply chains into supply loops; and building industrial ecosystems.

Sustaining the supply chain

As we have just seen, approaches such as fair trade are one way in which notions of sustainability can be addressed through business–business relationships. The mixture of economic, social, and environmental goals associated with fair trade programmes are very much within the spirit of sustainability thinking and are concerned with more than just the fairness of exchange relationships in a narrow economic sense. They also emphasize the importance of sustaining suppliers and the communities and environments where they are located. Indeed, it is increasingly recognized that one of the critical best practices in sustainable supply-chain management is a focus on *supply-chain continuity*—that is, ensuring the stability and capability of one's suppliers at every level in the supply chain (Pagell and Wu 2009). Firms that ignore threats to the continuity of their supply chain risk being unable to develop effective sustainability initiatives since these are heavily reliant on the actions and investments of supply-chain members. For example, what would it mean to be a sustainable hamburger restaurant if the social, economic, and environmental stability of cattle farming could not be assured?

Sustaining the supply chain requires firms to engage in a variety of initiatives, from training and financing of suppliers to enable them to switch over to more sustainable production methods, to investing in local community development. More broadly, investments in supply-chain continuity are also critical for developing greater linkages among the various firms in the supply chain—and even for turning such chains into more sustainable 'closed loop' systems.

Turning supply chains into supply loops

As we proposed in Chapter 1, sustainability encourages us to think about the long-term maintenance of systems, raising issues of resource efficiency, pollution prevention, and waste minimization. In Chapter 8 we introduced the notion of product recapture—i.e. bringing 'waste' products back into the supply chain as resources—as a way of developing more sustainable consumption. As we suggested, such a development shifts our thinking about supply relationships away from a linear view towards a more circular perspective. If wastes are to be recaptured and brought back into productive use, we need to think not of supply chains, but of supply loops that create a circular flow of resources (we illustrated this in **Figure 8.6** in Chapter 8).

Circular economy
A way of organizing economic activity based on returning all resources involved in the production of goods and services back into productive use with the goal of eliminating waste and reducing material inputs.

Replacing supply chains with supply loops is not just about recapturing products sold to end consumers though. Every activity that a firm engages in produces wastes or by-products that can be captured and potentially reused in a way that makes them productive again. For example, waste carbon dioxide, the major gas contributing to climate change, can be captured at source and used as a resource in applications such as rooftop greenhouses that produce crops.[11] These developments have given rise to the idea of the **circular economy**, i.e. a way of organizing economic activity built upon the idea of supply loops which ensure that the resources that go into production, rather than eventually becoming waste, ultimately become inputs into new products. The design principles behind the circular economy have been a part of sustainability thinking for decades but the concept has gained considerable popularity since the turn of the century. It was incorporated into Chinese government policy in 2008, and has been vigorously promoted to and with the global businesses community through the launch of the Ellen MacArthur Foundation in 2010.

To their proponents, such closed-loop, circular models have been promoted as not only waste reducing, but even eliminating the very concept of waste (Lovins et al. 1999). Moreover, although typically seen as an additional cost burden on firms (e.g. as a result of product take-back legislation), they have also been shown to be important potential sources of value recovery (Guide and Wassenhove 2006). That is, rather than disposing of 'used' resources, organizations can transform waste into valuable materials that can be deployed productively. One report, conducted by McKinsey for the Ellen MacArthur Foundation, estimated that 'a subset of the EU manufacturing sector could realize net materials cost savings worth up to $630 billion p.a.' by using circular economy models.[12]

Closing supply loops to increase resource efficiency and minimize waste places a considerably larger burden on inter-firm relationships than is the case with more traditional linear modes of supply. Effective stewardship of a product requires attention throughout its entire lifecycle, thus necessitating active collaboration between value-chain participants (Roy and Whelan 1992). To achieve ongoing product recapture, reuse, recycling, and re-manufacture, firms have to communicate, exchange information, develop joint proposals, co-design, and conclude stable exchange relationships. In many instances, firms have to seek out, develop, and institutionalize new markets for recaptured components. For example, Nike's 'Reuse-A-Shoe' programme turns used sports shoes into 'Nike grind', a material used by surfacing companies in sports surfaces such as gym flooring, basketball courts, and soccer fields, as well as product components like the zipper pull on some Nike jackets. Since the early 1990s some 28 million shoes have been collected as part of the initiative.[13]

Industrial ecosystems

Supply loops and the circular economy begin to shift our way of conceiving organizations away from an atomistic view, where each organization is seen as a separate entity with its own inputs and outputs, towards a more system-oriented view, where groups of firms are seen as interdependent entities that share resources and produce a shared environmental burden. Sustainability urges us to take such thinking still further though. Taken beyond the context of a single product supply and recapture loop, we can begin to also conceive of wider communities of organizations bound by interdependence of all kinds of resources and wastes. These are called *industrial ecosystems* (Allenby 1993).

According to Paul Shrivastava (1995), the concept of industrial ecosystems parallels that of natural ecosystems: just as natural ecosystems comprise a balanced network of interdependent organisms and their environments, which feed off each other and give and take resources off each other to maintain equilibrium and survive, so too can businesses use each other's waste and by-products to minimize the use of natural resources.

The network of companies in Kalundborg in Denmark has been widely identified as one the best examples of the concept of an industrial ecosystem (see **Figure 9.7**). At its heart it consists of a power plant, an enzyme plant, a refinery, a chemical plant, a cement plant, a wallboard plant, and some farms. These different companies all use one

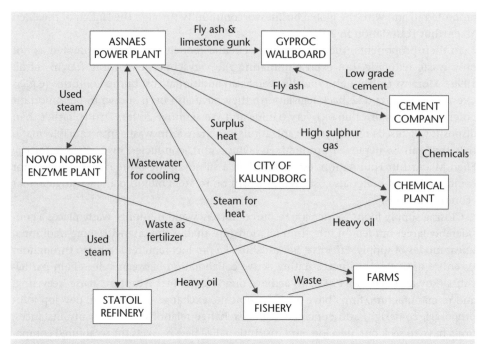

Figure 9.7 Kalundborg industrial ecosystem

Source: Republished with permission of Academy of Management, from Shrivastava, P. 1995. Ecocentric management for a risk society. *Academy of Management Review*, 20 (1): 118–137; permission conveyed through Copyright Clearance Center, Inc.

another's wastes and by-products as raw materials, co-ordinating their use of energy, water, raw materials, and waste management. For example, instead of simply dumping its wastes, the power plant sells its used steam to the enzyme plant and refinery, hands over its waste ash to the cement factory, and sells its surplus heat to the city for domestic heating. It also warms a fishery—which in turn provides its waste to local farms as fertilizer. Additional fertilizer comes from the enzyme plant's waste.

Industrial ecosystems such as the one in Kalundborg are relatively rare, but a number of similar examples have gradually emerged, often without any deliberate formal planning or organization. Examples of such 'self-organizing' networks include the city of Jyväskylä in Finland, the network clustered around the Guitang Group sugar refinery in China, and the mineral-processing area of Kwinana, Australia (Chertow 2007). One of the most complex and diverse examples yet uncovered is the industrial recycling network in the Austrian province of Styria, which includes a network of exchanges among over 50 facilities.

More formal, planned projects have also been developed, often to be found in so-called 'eco-parks' or even 'eco-cities'. This includes initiatives in the US, Europe, and Asia—although to date these have met with mixed success (Chertow 2007). Some of the most high-profile and ambitious of these projects are in China. One of the more successful to date is Tianjin Eco-City, which welcomed its first residents in 2012 and is projected to be the world's largest eco-city.[14] However, many others, such as the much heralded Dongtan in Shanghai, have so far failed to get past the planning stage. In general though

China as a whole is gradually moving 'from rhetoric to implementation' in building its circular economy at various regional and municipal levels (Su et al. 2013).

Whether industrial ecosystems will ever become more than an interesting, perhaps even utopian, vision of how industry could be organized remains to be seen. Much will no doubt rest on how local and national governments go about supporting, encouraging, and planning such initiatives. However, with the general shift towards more collaborative business activity identified at the outset of this chapter, and the drive for more climate-friendly approaches intensifying, closed-loop business models of various levels of complexity will undoubtedly become an increasingly important, if challenging, component of the industrial mix of the future.

■ Summary

In this chapter we have discussed the stake held by other companies in a corporation, focusing on both suppliers and the somewhat more contestable role of competitors. Our argument was that there were certainly issues of an ethical nature that arose in both groups of companies that went well beyond the legal protections of fair competition. These included: misuse of power, loyalty, conflicts of interest, bribery, and negotiation with suppliers; and intelligence gathering, industrial espionage, dirty tricks, anticompetitive behaviour, and abuse of a dominant position in the context of competitors. Globalization appears to have substantially increased the scope of these problems, suggesting expanded responsibilities for corporations over the span of their operations.

Despite these problems, developments in our understanding of the relationships between businesses appear to increasingly emphasize the importance of interdependence and co-operation. This is both in terms of our descriptive understandings (how businesses *do* relate) and our normative assessments (how they *should* relate). Nonetheless, ethical problems persist, and we are left to wonder if all parties can ever benefit equally from business interdependence. Many of the apparent problems are mainly raised simply by the highly competitive nature of contemporary industries and markets, particularly when the basic rules of the game do not favour all companies equally. Hence, it would appear that in the global economy there will always be winners and losers—and justice, even within the so-called business 'community', can be elusive. Indeed, as the scope of business operations expands, the ethical problems actually become more wide-ranging and complex, and so the stakes inevitably increase.

That said, business relationships are also increasingly seen as one of the main levers for effecting greater attention to social and environmental problems. In this chapter, we have mainly looked at intra-organizational pressure through the supply chain, but such self-regulation from business can also happen amongst competitors. The point is that government is certainly not the only source of business regulation, and that much informal and formal control actually takes place within the business community itself. As we shall see in Chapter 10, we should not even stop there. In addition to government and business, we also need to think about another sector involved in business regulation, namely pressure groups, or what have become known as 'third sector' or 'civil society' organizations.

Study questions

1. Compare the case for (a) suppliers, and (b) competitors to be regarded as stakeholders of a corporation. How convincing are the arguments proposing that each group is a legitimate stakeholder?

2. What is a conflict of interest? Outline the conflicts of interest that might typically arise in firm–supplier relations.

3. Should firms accept gifts from overseas suppliers? How can a firm ensure that its relationships with suppliers are strictly ethical if gift giving is allowed?

4. 'Competition between rival firms is like a battle. You play to win and anything goes.' Critically assess this statement in the context of Western multinationals competing with domestic firms in developing countries.

5. What is ethical sourcing? What factors are likely to influence the success of ethical sourcing in changing supplier practices?

6. Explain the following:

    (a) Closed-loop supply chains.

    (b) Industrial ecosystems.

7. What are the main differences between the two concepts and why are they considered to be important components of the circular economy?

Research exercise

Select a high street retailer of food, clothes, or electronics and conduct some research on their ethical sourcing practices so that you can answer the following questions:

1. Describe the supply-chain infrastructure that the firm uses—for example, does it have few or many suppliers, where are they based, etc.?

2. How would you describe your selected company's approach to ethical sourcing—for example, is there an overall strategy in place, what are the different components of the system, and how far down the supply chain does the initiative go?

3. What other organizations, if any, does the firm work with in managing its ethical sourcing programme? Can you explain why these organizations are involved?

4. To what extent does the firm report on the outcomes of its ethical sourcing initiatives?

Key readings

VISIT THE
ONLINE
RESOURCE
CENTRE
for a short
response to this
feature

1. Jones, I.W. and Pollitt, M.G. 1998. Ethical and unethical competition: establishing the rules of engagement. *Long Range Planning*, 31 (5): 703–10.

    This is one of the few articles that considers ethical issues with respect to both suppliers and competitors—and does so within an economic framework that illuminates the crucial competitive elements in inter-firm relationships. Although they are now a little dated, the use of short case studies of different industries helps to show why certain ethical and unethical practices might be more or less likely to arise in particular contexts.

2. **Doherty, B., Davies, I.A., and Tranchell, S. 2013. Where now for fair trade?** *Business History*, 55 (2): 161–89.

   Fair trade has been transformed since its emergence in the 1960s. This article from leading experts and practitioners in the fair trade movement provides an excellent overview of these changes and in particular of the challenges associated with its ongoing shift towards more mainstream business.

Case 9

VISIT THE ONLINE RESOURCE CENTRE
for links to useful sources of further information on this case

Uzbek cotton: a new spin on responsible sourcing?

This case describes the controversy surrounding the use of cotton sourced from Uzbekistan by high street clothing brands and retailers. It sets out the allegations of poor working conditions in the industry, most notably around child and forced labour, and traces the subsequent response by major companies. It offers an opportunity to examine the challenges of using responsible sourcing to protect human rights, specifically in the context of complex global supply chains in the clothing industry.

Most clothing brands and retailers have become accustomed to dealing with problems of child labour in their supply chains. Codes of conduct banning the most unsavoury sweatshop practices, regular factory audits, and other measures are now largely standard practice in the industry. But these initiatives usually just start and finish at the gates of the factories making the clothes. What about the raw materials, such as cotton, which are used to make the clothes in the first place?

Cotton is the indispensable element in most of the clothes we wear. Shirts, T-shirts, jeans, dresses, underwear—you name it, cotton goes into it. However, the question of who grows that cotton, and under what kind of conditions they work, is rarely one that we think too much about. But all that began to change when revelations started emerging in the 2000s that Uzbekistan, currently the world's fourth-largest cotton exporter, made extensive use of forced and child labour in harvesting its annual cotton crop. With the media and civil society organizations exposing how classrooms were emptied across the country every year to pick the harvest, major clothing brands had a major ethical problem on their hands. Efforts by many companies to boycott Uzbek cotton have gone some way in dealing with the issue, but significant problems remain in protesting those at risk of human rights violations and ensuring the integrity of their supply chains.

The Uzbek cotton industry

The Central Asian Republic of Uzbekistan, a former part of the Soviet Union, is one of five countries dominating global cotton exports, the others being the US, India, Australia, and Brazil. Uzbekistan is widely regarded as being an oppressive regime, led by President Islam Karimov, who has been in power since 1991. The country has limited media freedoms, low levels of democracy, high corruption, and a poor record of human rights violations. The Uzbek government rigidly controls cotton production, using a Soviet-style quota system. This involves compulsory state purchase, and various forms of pressure to ensure that targets are met.

According to the Environmental Justice Foundation, 'cotton production in the Central Asian Republic of Uzbekistan represents one of the most exploitative enterprises in the world'. Due to the low, centrally set prices paid to farmers for their quota, a large proportion of the profits generated by cotton exports is retained by regional governors and the state. Cotton farmers typically suffer due to low pay and poor working conditions. Reports from the foreign media and NGOs have identified a range of human rights violations in the industry, the most serious of which concern the use of forced and child labour.

Child labour accusations

According to many independent observers, child labour has long been rife in the Uzbek cotton industry, and it has been actively condoned and even facilitated by the state. Due to underinvestment in technology, and unlike most other countries, some 90% of Uzbek cotton is harvested by hand rather than by machine. The need for labour during the cotton harvest is so acute, and cost pressures from regional governors are so severe, that much of the harvesting has typically been carried out by children or young adults who are forced to work in the cotton fields.

Reports have suggested that during the harvesting season (typically from September to November), schools have been closed and tens of thousands of children compulsorily transported to the fields to help with the harvest. Younger children would typically be returned home by bus or truck every day, but older children would often spend the season living in barrack-style accommodation in local farm or school buildings, sometimes without water or electricity. During this time, child cotton workers could miss up to three months of school, usually toiling all day at strenuous manual work. The children would be poorly paid (around 40 cents a day), and have to pay for their own food and transport, sometimes even leaving them with next to nothing for their work after deductions have been made.

This desultory picture of the Uzbek cotton industry was first exposed in detail in a comprehensive 2005 report from the Environmental Justice Foundation. Running to some 45 pages, the report, *White Gold: The True Cost of Cotton*, set the child labour allegations within the broader context of the authoritarian nature of the Uzbek regime and the complex cotton trading system. In addition to child labour and other human rights abuses, the report also detailed a swathe of environmental problems associated with the cotton industry in Uzbekistan. Concluding that 'cotton production in Uzbekistan occurs within a framework of systematic exploitation, human rights violations, and environmental destruction', the report argued that, 'clothing manufacturers and retailers have an obligation to look beyond the "sweatshops" and into the cotton fields ... Corporate enterprises must make a critical assessment of their role in driving the problems ... and demonstrate that their supply chain does not exacerbate the chronic situation within Uzbekistan.'

At first, the response from the international business community was muted. As the executive director of the Environmental Justice Foundation put it: 'EJF has been repeatedly told, "we can't tell where the cotton comes from, our supply chain is too complicated and so we can't boycott Uzbek cotton, even if we wanted to". Case closed, so to speak.' To some extent the corporations had a point. Because of the complexity of international supply chains, the provenance of the cotton used in any particular garment is very difficult to determine. Countries such as Uzbekistan sell their cotton to international commodities-trading companies, who then sell it on to a chain of processors, manufacturers, and stitchers, before it arrives as a complete garment on the shelves of retailers. The commodity nature of cotton means that a final product will typically consist of cotton from a variety of sources. So, whilst clothes usually feature a label stating where the product was made, the source of its raw materials usually remains invisible to buyers.

Companies take action

As the pressure on firms mounted, the message started to change. The Finnish clothing design company, Marimekko, and the Estonian textile producer, Krenholm, both announced a boycott of Uzbek cotton in November 2007. By 2008, a string of clothing brands and retailers had signed up to the boycott, including the UK retailers Asda, Tesco, and Marks & Spencer, the Swedish chain H&M, and the US brands Gap and Levi's. Suddenly the impossible was possible.

The boycott marked a major victory for campaigners. More importantly, it prompted a major turnaround in Uzbekistan. In 2008, the government announced that it would ban children under 16 from picking cotton, it signed ILO conventions committing the country to stop using child labor, and instituted a National Plan of Action to aimed at meeting the ILO commitments.

Despite the progress being made in Uzbekistan's policies around child labour, the picture on the ground appeared to be improving little. A 2010 University of London report, for example, found that forced child labour was still widely used in Uzbekistan and argued that problems had if anything worsened since the country had ratified the ILO conventions. The corporate boycott therefore intensified in 2011 when the NGO, Responsible Sourcing Network, launched the Cotton Pledge. The purpose of the pledge was to consolidate the boycott activity and provide a clearer and more public commitment from companies sourcing cotton. It stated:

> As a signatory to this pledge, we are stating our firm opposition to the use of child forced labour in the harvest of Uzbek cotton. We commit to not knowingly source Uzbek cotton for the manufacturing of any of our products until the Government of Uzbekistan ends the practice of forced child and adult labour in its cotton sector. Until the elimination of this practice is independently verified by the International Labour Organization, we will maintain this pledge.

Initially signed by 50 companies, the pledge now numbers more than 150 companies, including firms as diverse as American Apparel, Adidas, Burberry, Gucci, IKEA, Lululemon, Pottery Barn, and Zara. The pledge had a major impact on Uzbek cotton exports with the annual Uzbek International Cotton and Textile Fair for the first time beginning to register no direct sales to a Western buyer. Uzbekistan's prime minister responded by ordering that schoolchildren should not to be sent to pick cotton, with subsequent NGO reports indicating a significant decline in the use of young children from 2012 onwards.

Despite the appearance of progress, it soon became clear that the Uzbekistan government had simply shifted the demographics of forced labour in the cotton harvest. Rather than young children, the government had begun conscripting older children (aged 15–18), university students, and adults, including employees of state organizations—teachers, doctors, and nurses—to work in the fields. The cotton pledge was therefore expanded in 2013 to include forced adult labour, and pressure on the Uzbek authorities continued anew. The same year, another partial victory was recorded when, after years of refusals, Uzbekistan finally allowed the International Labour Organization access to monitor the harvest, as specified under the cotton pledge. However, only a limited monitoring mission was permitted, with a mandate limited to child labour and not adult forced labour.

While the situation in Uzbekistan appears to be gradually improving as a result of pressure from Western companies, progress has been slow in the face of a recalcitrant Uzbek government. Moreover, important questions remain about the likely impact on the lives of forced labourers in Uzbekistan and the long-term implications of the boycott.

One major problem is that the Western boycott appears to have pushed the Uzbeks to target other markets less concerned about their exploitative labour practices. Indeed, despite the ban by large Western companies, Uzbekistan has continued to expand its other markets for exported cotton, particularly in Asia and Russia. Actual cotton exports have remained relatively constant since the boycott, with Bangladesh, China, and South Korea now being the major markets for Uzbek cotton. The growing importance of these export markets has given the Uzbek authorities good cause to resist changes in labour conditions. While Western brands and their consumers might feel better about boycotting Uzbek cotton, it has clearly not, as yet, ended forced labour.

Another upshot of this, of course, is that it actually remains very challenging for boycotting companies to ensure with any certainty that their products are free of Uzbek cotton because it might enter the supply chain elsewhere. When spinning mills produce yarn they often mix cotton from a number of different sources, and few companies have sufficient traceability in their supply chain to know the exact source of every bale of cotton used. Cotton from Uzbekistan can enter the supply chain via the brands' major manufacturing hubs in Asia. For most companies, even those who have signed up to the cotton pledge, this means that their public statements on the issue are understandably guarded, with most unwilling to offer any cast iron guarantees that their cotton is entirely free of forced or child labour. Typically, they suggest, like the Walt Disney Company does, that they have 'no knowledge' of Uzbek cotton being used in their products, and that they ask suppliers to make 'their best efforts' not to include Uzbek sources. Efforts are underway to improve traceability in the cotton supply chain but at present, as one supply chain compliance expert noted: 'no one can really guarantee that a product has not been produced without any ILO convention violations'.

Questions

1. Who are the main actors in the cotton supply chain and what stages are involved in transforming cotton from an agricultural crop to a finished product for consumers?

2. Describe the approach adopted by Western brands to deal with human rights violations in the Uzbek cotton supply chain.

3. To what extent has this approach been successful so far? In your opinion, what accounts for this success or failure?

4. Should Western companies consider further action to help protect Uzbek cotton workers, or have they already effectively discharged their ethical responsibility by instituting a boycott of Uzbek cotton? What other alternatives are open to them?

5. If you were working for a group dedicated to eradicating child and forced labour, what would your strategy be for the cotton industry?

Sources

Agrochart 2013. Uzbekistan: Cotton and Products Update. November 2013: http://www. agrochart.com/en/news/news/291113/uzbekistan-cotton-and-products-update-nov-2013/.

Centre of Contemporary Central Asia and the Caucasus 2010. What has changed? Progress in eliminating the use of forced child labour in the cotton harvest of Uzbekistan and Tajikistan. London: University of London. https://www.soas.ac.uk/cccac/centres-publications/.

Environmental Justice Foundation 2005. *White gold: the true cost of cotton*. London: Environmental Justice Foundation.

Mathiason, N. 2009. Uzbekistan forced to stop child labour. *Observer*, 24 May: http://www. theguardian.com/business/2009/may/24/retail-ethicalbusiness.

Trent, S. 2008. Spinning a line—why the trail of cotton from Uzbekistan needs to be clearer. *Ethical Corporation*, 4 February 2008: http://www.ethicalcorp.com/content/spinning-line—why-trail-cotton-uzbekistan-needs-be-clearer.

USDA Foreign Agricultural Service 2013. Uzbekistan-Republic of, Cotton and Products Annual Report. GAIN Report UZ1302, 1 April 2013: http://gain.fas.usda.gov/Recent%20GAIN%20 Publications/Cotton%20and%20Products%20Annual_Tashkent_Uzbekistan%20-%20 Republic%20of_01.04.2013.pdf.

Uzbek-German Forum for Human Rights and Cotton Campaign 2012. Review of the 2012 Cotton Harvest in Uzbekistan, 20 December 2012: http://www.cottoncampaign.org/ uploads/3/9/4/7/39474145/review2012_cottonharvestuzbekistan.pdf.

Webb, T. 2008. Corporate action on Uzbeki white gold. *Ethical Corporation*, 5 March 2008: http:// www.ethicalcorp.com/supply-chains/special-report-cotton-supply-chains-corporate-action-uzbeki-white-gold.

http://www.sourcingnetwork.org

Notes

1. European Commission (2014). Protect small food suppliers from industry giants, says EU, 23/07/2014: http://europe-diplomatic.eu/protect-small-food-suppliers-from-industry-giants-says/?lang=en.

2. BBC. 2009. EU slaps a record fine on Intel. *BBC News*, 13 May: http://www.bbc.co.uk/news; Nuttall, C. and Tait, N. 2009. Intel looks beyond EU litigation. *The Financial Times*, 13 May: http://www.ft.com.

3. Sandoval, L. (2014). India launches antitrust probe against Google after alleged anticompetitive practices, *Tech Times*, 14 May 2014: http://www.techtimes.com/articles/6984/20140514/india-launches-antitrust-probe-against-google-after-alleged-anticompetitive-practices.htm; De Looper, C. (2014). EU threatens Google with $6B fine as anti-competitive investigation expands, *Tech Times*, 23 September 2014: http://www.techtimes.com/articles/16320/20140923/eu-threatens-google-6b-fine-anti-competitive-investigation-expands.htm; Hartley, M. (2013). Google Inc facing heat from Competition Bureau over alleged anti-competitive behavior, *Financial* Post, 13 December 2013: http://business.financialpost.com/2013/12/13/google-inc-abusive-competition-bureau/?__lsa = 369b-ebec.

4. See Heimann, F., Földes, A., and Báthory, G. 2014. Exporting Corruption. Progress Report 2014: Enforcement of the OECD Convention on Combating Foreign Bribery. Berlin: Transparency International. Available at http://www.transparency.org.

5. BBC. 2012. Banana war ends after 20 years, *BBC News*, 8 November 2012: http://www.bbc.com/ news/business-20263308.

6. http://www.thejournal.ie/60-big-name-brands-continuing-to-use-sweatshop-labour-130318-May2011/.

7. http://www.cbc.ca/news/business/apple-on-defence-after-bbc-exposé-of-working-conditions-in-its-factories-1.2879208.

8. http://www.eiccoalition.org/standards/code-of-conduct/.

9. https://www.apple.com/ca/supplier-responsibility/empowering-workers/.
10. 'Fairtrade' (one word, capital F) relates exclusively to the work of Fairtrade International and its partners. 'Fair Trade' or 'fair trade' relates to the wider movement of organizations working to promote fairer trade policy and practice and includes fairly traded products that do not carry the FAIRTRADE Mark.
11. http://www.ellenmacarthurfoundation.org/business/featured-articles/point-of-view-treating-emissions-as-resources-by-braungart-mulhall.
12. http://www.ellenmacarthurfoundation.org/business/reports/ce2012#.
13. See http://www.nike.com/us/en_us/c/better-world/reuse-a-shoe.
14. http://www.bbc.com/future/story/20120503-sustainable-cities-on-the-rise.

Civil Society and Business Ethics

Having completed this chapter you should be able to:

■ Explain the role played by various types of civil society organizations as stakeholders of corporations, both directly and indirectly.

■ Conduct an ethical analysis of the tactics used by civil society organizations towards corporations to achieve their purposes.

■ Critically evaluate the impacts of globalization on the nature and extent of the role played by civil society towards corporations.

■ Explain the different relationships between business and civil society and their impact on corporate responsibility.

■ Explain the role of civil society in providing for enhanced corporate sustainability.

Key concepts and skills:

Concepts	Skills
• Civil society organization (CSO)	• Distinguishing types of CSO
• Social licence to operate	• Identifying CSO stakes
• Boycott	• Analysing CSO tactics
• CSO accountability	• Evaluating business–CSO collaborations
• Employee volunteering	
• Social enterprise	
• Civil regulation	

■ Introduction

So far in Part B of this book, we have looked at business ethics in relation to the corporation's four main economic stakeholders—i.e. those vital constituencies that provide firms with the resources they need merely to exist. Shareholders supply capital, employees provide labour, consumers provide income, and suppliers provide the materials necessary to produce products and services. In this chapter and in Chapter 11 we shall broaden our scope to consider other stakeholders outside the immediate economic realm of the corporation—in this chapter, civil society, and in the next, government. These constituencies, as we shall see, also have important stakes in the corporation, and various ethical problems and issues can arise in the corporation's dealings with such actors.

To some readers, though, the notion of civil society might be unfamiliar. Although civil society as a concept has long been in use, it has only returned to popular use since the 1990s. Previous to this resurgence, social and political theorists tended to model a two-sector world, comprising the market or economic sector (business) and the state sector (government). Therefore, it was assumed that issues such as social welfare and environmental protection would be looked after either through labour and product markets, state provision, or else corporate philanthropy. More recently, though, considerable attention has focused on the role of other types of organizations such as pressure groups, charities, non-government organizations (NGOs), local community groups, religious organizations, etc., in attending to these issues. There are a number of reasons to explain this renewed attention, including a failure of the state or the market to ensure effective provision of social welfare, and scepticism among certain sectors of the public that the traditional two-sector institutions actively listened to and served their interests (see Beck 1992).

This has opened up space to consider a third type of institutional actor in society, namely what has become known as civil society. As such, civil society is often said to comprise a *third sector* after the market and the state. This is illustrated in **Figure 10.1**.

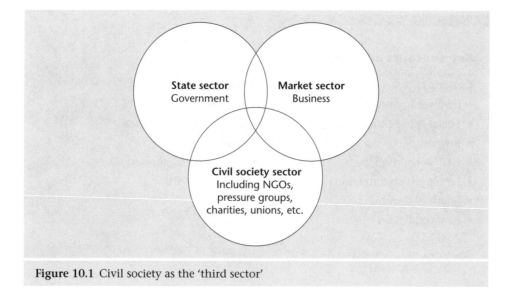

Figure 10.1 Civil society as the 'third sector'

As a third sector, civil society is usually regarded as a counterbalance to the state (and more recently also to business), guarding against the abuse of power and ensuring that the people's best interests are served (Reece 2001). Hence, the supposed role of civil society is to ensure a degree of social and political pluralism that provides for a more civilized society. More recently, as a response to globalization, it has become popular to talk of *global civil society*, as many of the issues dealt with in this context are indeed transcending the scope of just national communities, as we will explore later in this chapter (e.g. Dryzek 2012).

Civil society is made concrete and meaningful for corporations through specific **civil society organizations** (CSOs). Only very rarely do corporations actually deal with individual citizens who are not their workers or customers. It is therefore CSOs as the tangible manifestation of civil society that we shall mainly be concerned with in this chapter. However, there is considerable confusion, contradiction, and overlap in the definition of CSOs and related organizational types such as NGOs, non-profit organizations, pressure groups, and the like (McIntosh and Thomas 2002; Yaziji and Doh 2009). We shall use CSO as an umbrella term for the different types of organization that might be considered to be civil society actors. Although NGOs tend to be the most visible actors in the literature dealing with business and civil society, organizations such as labour unions, consumer associations, religious groups, community groups, etc., are also important CSOs, yet are typically not thought of as NGOs.

Essentially, then, we are using the term 'CSO' to describe all of these voluntary, non-profit bodies outside of business and government that represent a particular group or cause which brings them into contact with corporations. Clearly, there are any number of interests, causes, and goals that CSOs might be involved with, from environmental protection, to animal rights, social welfare, urban regeneration, child protection, development, famine relief, or health promotion—all of which could easily pertain to business ethics in some way.

Many of the larger international CSOs are at least as well known as large multinational corporations: the Red Cross, Greenpeace, Friends of the Earth, WWF, Amnesty International, and Oxfam are just some of the most widely recognized civil society organizations. However, although many of us may be aware of little more than a handful of the major CSO actors, the number and scope of CSOs is actually quite staggering. Given such a heterogeneous collection of organizational types, getting accurate estimates of the number of CSOs in operation is extremely difficult, but the consensus amongst most experts is that the number is huge and growing (Yaziji and Doh 2009). For example, in the US alone, there are now around 2.3 million non-profit organizations, India has something like 2 million, while even in the UK there are some 160,000 registered charities.

CSOs such as these can range from local neighbourhood associations and religious groups to powerful national-level lobbying organizations. Overall, estimations of the scale of civil society activity in different countries suggest that CSOs account for something like an average of 5% of national GDP (Salamon et al. 2007). The proportion of national employment accounted for by CSOs can range from less than 1% in countries such as Mexico and Poland to more than 10% in the Netherlands, Canada, Belgium, and Ireland (Hall et al. 2005). Globally, there has also been an explosion of international CSOs working across borders on issues as diverse as climate protection, international development, and human rights (Turner 2010).

Civil society organization
A type of organization that is neither a business nor government institution, and which is involved in the promotion of societal interests, causes, and/or goals.

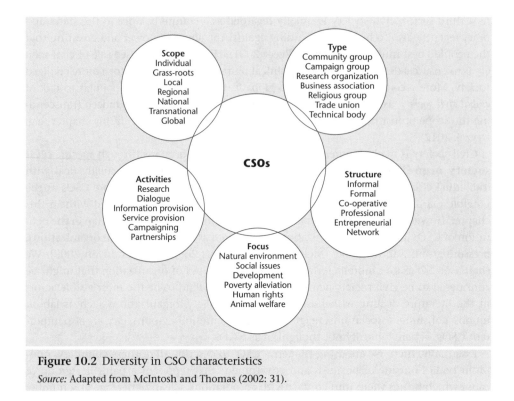

Figure 10.2 Diversity in CSO characteristics
Source: Adapted from McIntosh and Thomas (2002: 31).

It is evident, then, that there is an enormous heterogeneity and diversity amongst these millions of CSOs. Not only might they be different in terms of the issues they focus on and their scope of operations, but they also take different forms and structures and are involved in a varied mixture of activities. **Figure 10.2** illustrates this breadth of diversity in more detail.

In this chapter we shall examine the relationships that CSOs have with corporations, exploring the specific stake that they have and the ways in which they seek to influence corporate action. Whether through media campaigns, boycotts, or actively working together with corporations and governments, it is clear that now, perhaps more than ever, CSOs have a vital role to play in enhancing and ensuring ethical behaviour in business. Indeed, as we shall see as the chapter progresses, the global reach of many CSOs, coupled with their successes in working with businesses and governments, has meant that they are now often seen as an integral part of the global governance regime that shapes and regulates corporate practice.

■ Civil society organizations as stakeholders

It is clear that CSOs of one sort or another have long been involved in the activities of corporations. Whether it is receiving corporate donations, organizing employee resistance to labour practices, leading consumer boycotts of particular products, or more violent action, such as firebombing animal-testing laboratories, various CSOs have over the years been very much involved in the business ethics field. In recent years, this has escalated enormously. As Yaziji and Doh (2009: 16) state, the 'growth in the number, power and influence of NGOs represents one of the most important societal developments in the past twenty years, in terms of how the dynamics of public debates and government policies concerning corporate behaviour are changing'.

In many respects though, the stake held by CSOs is quite different from that held by other stakeholder groups. Employees, consumers, and shareholders, for example, all contribute something directly to the corporation in the form of labour, income, or capital. Likewise, as we shall see in Chapter 11, governments provide corporations with a licence to operate in a particular territory. CSOs, on the other hand, only very rarely contribute any resources directly to corporations. Hence, while consumers are able to retract their purchases from an oil company seeking to expand its operations in Antarctica, a CSO does not really have anything tangible to retract, since it does not directly contribute to the company in the first place. However, this is not to say that the CSO is not a stakeholder in this situation. As an organization with a mission, for example to protect the environment on behalf of its members, the CSO certainly might have a stake in the decision contemplated by the company. And as an actor organizing a consumer boycott against the company, the CSO has an important role to play on behalf of the consumers who wish to participate in the boycott.

Looking at it this way, the stake held by CSOs is largely one of *representing the interests of individual stakeholders*. By organizing together into a CSO, individual stakeholders of whatever kind can gain greater voice and influence than they have alone. If a local resident of Heathrow or Frankfurt wanted to voice their concern about the development of a new runway, they would have little effect alone. However, by joining a local association, or even a national or international lobby group dedicated to preventing air and noise pollution from air traffic, they would be much more likely to have their views heard. Similarly, we can also see this illustrated by trade unions and other labour organizations: they represent the interests of individual employee stakeholders, both inside the workplace and on the political stage.

If we look at the oil company–CSO situation another way, though, a slightly different form of representation effected by CSOs becomes evident. Rather than its members, or the wider public, the CSO could be argued to be representing the environment itself. As a non-human entity, the environment clearly cannot speak for itself—and therefore CSOs step in essentially as proxy stakeholders. A similar case can be made for animal welfare CSOs such as the RSPCA (Royal Society for the Prevention of Cruelty to Animals) or PETA (People for the Ethical Treatment of Animals). Hence, another potential CSO role is *representing the interests of non-human stakeholders*.

? THINK THEORY

Think about the stakes of non-human stakeholders such as animals or the environment from the perspective of utilitarianism. Would a non-human stake be given a lower valuation in cost-benefit analysis than a human stake? Think through this problem in the context of animal testing or the building of a new road in an area of high biodiversity.

VISIT THE ONLINE RESOURCE CENTRE for a short response to this feature

Whichever of these two ways of conceptualizing the stakeholder role of CSOs is relevant, it is clear that the stake of CSOs is *indirect* and *representative*. CSOs are mainly delineated as stakeholders on the grounds that they represent some broader, if less tangible, constituency of civil society itself. Corporations tend not to deal with civil society as a group of innumerable individual citizens, but as a more discrete collection of representative CSOs. As such, CSOs form part of the **social licence to operate** for companies. By this, we mean that CSOs shape the extent to which a company 'is seen as having the ongoing approval and broad acceptance of society to conduct its activities' (Prno and Slocombe 2012: 346).

Social licence to operate
The ongoing approval and acceptance of a company's activities by society, especially among local communities and civil society.

The literature on pressure groups suggests that, depending on who exactly they are representing, CSOs tend to fall into two main types—*sectional groups* and *promotional groups* (see Smith 2015; Whawell 1998). Some of the key differences between these types are summarized in **Figure 10.3**:

- **Sectional groups**. These include trade unions, professional associations, student bodies, neighbourhood groups, parent associations, etc. They are member-based and primarily seek to represent the interests of their members (i.e. a particular 'section' of society). The membership of sectional CSOs is only open to those fulfilling certain objective criteria that put them within the specific section to be represented, for example that they are part of a particular workplace, profession, or geographical region. The CSO will above all else pursue the self-interest of this membership.

- **Promotional groups**. These in contrast are focused on promoting specific causes or issues. Environmental groups, anti-smoking groups, and pro-life groups are all examples of promotional CSOs. These organizations represent those with a common ideology or shared attitudes about an issue. Membership is usually open to all, although only those with similar subjective viewpoints are effectively represented. These groups are less concerned with the self-interest of their members and more focused on seeking to achieve wider social aims.

Traditionally, sectional groups have been said to enjoy insider status, while promotional groups have largely been outsiders (Smith 2015). What this means is that because

	Sectional groups	Promotional groups
Membership	Closed	Open
Represent	Specific section of society	Issues or causes
Aims	Self-interest	Social goals
Traditional status	Insider	Outsider
Main approach	Consultation	Argument
Pressure exerted through	Threat of withdrawal	Mass media publicity

Figure 10.3 Different types of CSOs

sectional groups are regarded as the legitimate representative of a specific, identifiable constituency—say electricians, farmers, Muslims, or students—their views are actively solicited (or at least readily accepted as legitimate) on issues relevant to the constituency. For example, if the government were developing agricultural policies, then it would typically engage in some kind of consultation with farming unions.

Promotional groups, however, have tended to have less access to governmental or corporate policy-making. Since they do not represent a readily identifiable constituency, it is not obvious who exactly they are speaking for. As a result, promotional groups have usually needed to mobilize mass public opinion before they are heard or involved in any kind of decision-making. For this reason, promotional groups need to be very active and visible in the promotion of the issues they are concerned with (hence the label promotional group). This has typically involved them in articulating vigorous arguments, demonstrations, and/or provocative media stunts in order to get their message across. One need only think of Greenpeace's dramatic confrontations over the years with its adversaries in the whaling, oil, and nuclear industries to see the importance of a provocative and media-friendly argument to many promotional groups.

More recently, the various successes of promotional CSOs such as Greenpeace, Amnesty, WWF, Friends of the Earth, etc., in establishing themselves as credible and legitimate contributors to major social and environmental debates in society have given them much more of an insider status than they were once afforded (Grant 2004). Annual surveys that measure the public's trust in different institutions consistently report that NGOs enjoy considerably more trust than business or governments across the globe.[2] Although survey evidence of this type—based on the opinions of relatively small samples of key informants—does not provide conclusive evidence, the favourability and trust apparently enjoyed by CSOs gives a clear indication that they demand attention from corporations with respect to business ethics.

To begin with, this attention was typically only gained through conflict—that is, CSOs exert pressure on companies through strikes, boycotts, demonstrations, media campaigns, etc., in order to achieve their ends. While this is particularly true of promotional groups, it is also often the case with sectional groups, such as unions, whose most potent weapon is the threat of disruption and withdrawal. More recently, though, as the insider status of CSOs has expanded to include previous adversaries of corporations, we have also seen a greater propensity to engage in a more consensual and collaborative approach in business–CSO relationships (Crane and Seitanidi 2014)—a point we first introduced in Chapter 5 and one that we shall develop further later on in this chapter.

☑ Skill check

Distinguishing types of CSOs. Determining whether a CSO is a sectional or promotional group is an important skill to acquire because it helps you to determine the CSO's likely approach to corporations.

It is clear, then, that in many ways, CSOs have become just as much an accepted part of the debate over business ethics as other more conventional 'economic' or 'primary' stakeholders. Although their claim is often an indirect one, since it is a claim to represent individual stakeholders or even causes themselves, it would be hard to refute the argument that CSOs are legitimate claimants of stakeholder status—albeit less clear-cut ones. Indeed, questions of exactly *which* CSOs are legitimate stakeholders of a corporation, and *how* exactly they should go about claiming or exercising their stake, are certainly not straightforward. As we shall now see, such questions are in fact at the root of a bundle of interrelated ethical problems and issues that underlie the emergence of CSOs as significant stakeholders in the corporation.

■ Ethical issues and CSOs

In Chapter 1 we showed that despite their mission to address societal issues, CSOs are not immune from ethical problems. Those working in civil society appear to observe similar types of misconduct, and at similar intensities, as those in business and government.[3] But beyond these normal ethical problems, what of the specific problems in CSO relationships with business? Given the growing importance of CSOs to the business ethics field, it is perhaps surprising that only limited attention has yet been paid in the literature to these ethical issues surrounding corporate engagement. However, there are a number of significant issues that arise from the somewhat less tangible stake held by CSOs. Chief among these are the decisions by corporations about which CSOs might be recognized as worthy of attention, the tactics used by CSOs to gain attention, and the degree to which CSOs are genuinely representative of, and accountable to, their intended beneficiaries.

Recognizing CSO stakes

If we take any given corporation—say, BP—it is fairly straightforward to objectively determine who its consumers, suppliers, employees, shareholders, and competitors are. Once we acknowledge that inclusion within any of these groups confers some kind of stake in the company, it is a short step to identifying BP's main stakeholders. With civil society stakeholders, however, this question is considerably more muddied. With BP's diverse interests in the energy sector, it is possible to think of hundreds, probably even thousands, of CSOs that might potentially claim a stake in the company's activities. From Azerbaijan farmers to UK transport organizations, Saharan desert communities, or fishing community groups in the US, BP has been involved in debates about its operations with an extensive array of CSOs across the globe. But how does a company such as BP determine which of these groups are legitimate stakeholders and which are not? And who is to determine legitimacy here? Just because, hypothetically speaking, BP may decide that a radical Inuit land rights group has no legitimate cause to pursue regarding the company's drilling operations in Alaska, does this necessarily mean that it is not a stakeholder?

These are taxing problems to resolve, but they go to the heart of what it means to be a stakeholder. If we look back to Chapter 5 (Managing stakeholder relations, pp. 199–206), when we discussed how corporations might manage their stakeholders, we suggested that one way of assessing which stakeholders were worthy of attention was the *instrumental* approach. Here, the relative salience of stakeholders is assessed according to, for example, their power, influence, and urgency (Mitchell et al. 1997). However, we also suggested that such an approach ignores the fact that even though some stakeholders might lack much salience to the corporation, they might reasonably claim to have an ethical right to be involved in a particular decision or process (Hummels 1998).

What this comes down to is that in any given company (or any other organization for that matter), the definition of 'who our stakeholders are' is not simply a matter of objective observation. Rather, this decision is influenced by the *subjective interpretations* of managers and their value judgements of what constitutes a legitimate claim (Fineman and Clarke 1996). This issue is particularly pronounced in the case of promotional CSOs, since they cannot usually call on any specific constituency as the source of their inherent rights to claim stakeholder status. Of course, many of these groups tend to 'self-declare' themselves as stakeholders in a particular issue (Wheeler et al. 2002). This they accomplish by issuing statements, launching campaigns, or initiating some kind of action towards the corporation. For example, in 2010, the American home improvements retailer, Home Depot, suddenly found itself the subject of a boycott by the anti-gay organization, the American Family Association (AFA). The AFA self-declared as a stakeholder to protest at the firm for being 'a constant and a vocal supporter of the gay agenda' by supporting gay pride parades and promoting inclusionary policies at the firm. The boycott was eventually called off in 2013 with the Home Depot having 'consistently ignored the campaign' and reporting that it had not changed its policies or practices.[4]

As the Home Depot case illustrates, self-declaring does not necessarily lead to *stakeholder recognition*. Firms may ignore particular CSOs that they deem to be illegitimate or lacking the power to affect their business (Mitchell et al. 1997) as well as those perceived as too difficult to engage with (Wheeler et al. 2002). Extractive companies, for example, often face criticism for failing to engage sufficiently with relevant local community organizations and other CSOs (Hilson 2012).

So the question remains: which CSOs should corporations recognize as legitimate stakeholders? On the one side, there is certainly a case for arguing that companies cannot be expected to listen and engage with every organization that decides to take issue with their policies. Simon Zadek (2001: 156), for example, reports the following discussion with one exasperated British utility manager:

> As a water utility we are a major landowner. We have been approached by representatives from the anti-hunting league and asked to stop renting out a parcel of land for use by sports-hunters. To be honest, we don't particularly have a corporate view on hunting, and do not particularly want to have one. Where does this all end? If there is a church but no mosque on our land, will we eventually have to have a view on God?

However, even though many CSOs and their demands may seem peripheral, illegitimate, or just simply unrelated to the corporate sphere of activity, this does not mean they can merely be ignored. As soon as a CSO starts to direct its attentions towards a corporation, the stakes begin to rise, and the potential impact on the corporation and its reputation becomes more hazardous. While ignoring ostensibly 'irrelevant' CSOs and hoping they will go away may be a typical corporate response to such 'irritants', it may have detrimental long-term consequences. Zadek (2001: 163), therefore, goes so far as to say that 'it is simply not really the company's choice who is and is not a stakeholder'. Clearly, as he suggests, the boundaries defining which CSOs can reasonably be defined as stakeholders are permeable and evolving, rather than concrete and fixed.

Certainly, though, managers have to make important decisions about how to best respond to CSO demands for inclusion, and where to draw the boundaries of their responsibilities to such groups (Zadek 2001). After all, there is usually only a limited allocation of time and resources available for managing relations with CSOs. Firms are therefore more likely to recognize and respond to CSOs that are known, trusted, and not too critical. Typically, they will distinguish between campaigners who are regarded as 'reasonable' and those deemed 'unreasonable', and between those who are thought to have 'sound' or supposedly 'suspect' intentions in raising an issue (Fineman and Clarke 1996).

Normative stakeholder theory is not at its most helpful in determining specific boundaries of responsibility to civil society groups (Banerjee 2000). Although it may help us to identify that most affected groups have *some* claim on the firm, the nature of this claim is difficult to determine very precisely. Ultimately, though, there would seem a reasonable case to be made for at least listening to all those who feel they have a stake in the firm—even the critics—as it can raise awareness of potential problems, help to define priorities, and aid in setting out more informed visions of the future. In addition, the moral legitimacy of CSOs is probably best evaluated in terms of *how* they go about engaging with corporations—i.e. whether they adopt ethical procedures—rather than simply in terms of the legitimacy of the cause or group that they are representing (Baur and Palazzo 2011).

Of course, simply talking to CSOs is not always going to provide a sufficient level of involvement, but it represents a good place to start. Hart and Sharma (2004: 7) go further to suggest that corporations should 'systematically identify, explore, and integrate the views of stakeholders "on the fringe"—the poor, weak, isolated, non-legitimate, and even non-human—for the express purpose of managing disruptive change and building imagination about future competitive business models'. While this type of strategic reorientation would pose quite a challenge for most corporations, it certainly suggests that there appear to be both normative and instrumental arguments to support an acknowledgement of at least a limited stake in the company for such fringe groups. **An Ethical Dilemma 10** gives you the opportunity to think about and apply some of these ideas in a specific situation.

AN ETHICAL DILEMMA 10

Where's the beef?

As the public affairs manager of U-Buy, the country's leading supermarket chain, things have been fairly busy this year. Still, having successfully dealt with the media response to the company's plans to close a number of unprofitable rural branches, you feel that the latest incident should not be causing you quite as much trouble as it is.

It all started when you received an email from Gay Men for Equality (GAME), an activist group in the US. Although you had never even heard of GAME before, the group wrote to you asking about your company's position on BigBeef Corporation, a large US food company that supplies much of your processed meat products. Thinking it a strange request, but having no idea of any problems that GAME might be concerned about, you replied by saying simply that U-Buy had always enjoyed a good commercial relationship with BigBeef.

Thinking that this would be the last you would hear of GAME, you were surprised to receive a much more stridently worded reply the next day that asked why U-Buy was supporting a company that had recently been convicted after a string of accusations about discrimination against gay employees, and whose chief executive Buck Leghorn was an outspoken critic of the gay and lesbian equality movement.

You decided to do some research on the accusations, and it appeared that GAME was pretty accurate in its claims about BigBeef and Leghorn. And from the press coverage in the US, it looked like BigBeef was not going to back down on this matter. GAME had been campaigning for some time against BigBeef but had yet to get any response from the company.

Although you could have done without the association between discrimination and U-Buy, this was BigBeef's business, and you felt it did not have much to do with your company. In the meantime, though, you had started receiving several emails a day from GAME demanding a response, so you decided to write to them again. This time you reiterated that U-Buy had always enjoyed a good working relationship with BigBeef, but added that U-Buy deplored discrimination of any kind and itself actively complied with all relevant legislation.

GAME refused to be pacified by your response and started intensifying its demands, urging U-Buy to call for a complete apology and change of policy at BigBeef or to cease trading with them. When you got this email from GAME you almost laughed, thinking what a crazy suggestion this seemed to be. What did this have to do with you and U-Buy? It was not your fault that BigBeef had been prosecuted. And it certainly was not up to you what their chief executive Buck Leghorn decided to pronounce upon in the media.

Still, you thought you would mention the problem to the head of purchasing and let her know what was happening. When you did so, she made it extremely clear that there was no way she was willing to risk the good relations that U-Buy had with BigBeef. The company was one of U-Buy's most important suppliers, and the company had a lot of influence in the global food industry. 'This will soon blow over,' she told you, 'just lie low and do not say anything that will get us into trouble.'

Despite the head of purchasing's forecast, GAME's campaign seemed to be gaining ground, and the national press had got hold of the story. It looked like GAME had turned its attention to U-Buy to try and leverage its position as the country's top retailer to force through changes at BigBeef. And to your dismay, it now appeared that a local chapter of GAME had even been set up specifically to target U-Buy—it was said to be planning a demonstration outside your flagship store in the capital. Things were certainly escalating to a level that needed dealing with. You did not want to risk threatening U-Buy's good relations with your powerful American supplier, but at the same time you did not want to be associated with discrimination, however indirectly. You could just see the placards now: 'U-Buy supports gay harassment' or some such thing. How come this minor little problem was causing you such a major headache?

Questions

1. Which are the legitimate stakeholders in this situation? Give reasons why you think they are legitimate and establish some kind of priority ranking.

2. How would you proceed in this situation?

3. How would you try to prevent similar problems from occurring in the future?

> ☑ **Skill check**
>
> **Identifying CSO stakes**. Being able to determine why firms might recognize and respond to particular CSOs is a key skill in understanding business–CSO relations. This is rarely an objective exercise but one dependent on the subjective interpretation of CSO stakes.

CSO tactics

Obviously CSOs are not passive actors in the process through which corporations decide whether they are a legitimate stakeholder in a situation or issue. CSOs are frequently very active in promoting their causes and in seeking corporate recognition, engagement, and response. However, some of the tactics used by CSOs to do this can be challenged on ethical grounds (Whawell 1998). Is it acceptable, for example, for animal rights activists to break into animal-testing labs to release animals, or even to threaten the staff of testing companies? Is it possible to defend the occupation of oil platforms, the vandalism of fast-food restaurants, or the deliberate destruction of GM crops? **Ethics on Screen 10** discusses one especially controversial CSO as featured in the documentary 'F*ck for Forest'.

There is, in fact, a whole range of tactics that CSOs might call on in seeking to achieve their aims. There are *indirect* forms of action, such as provision of data, research reports, and policy briefings, as well as more *direct* forms of action, namely violent direct action and non-violent direct action.

Indirect action

At the most basic level, indirect action will tend to involve research and communication about the issues of relevance to the organization. For promotional groups in particular, the need to compete for public attention and approval often requires that they first establish a sound basis of research in order to develop credible arguments. Sometimes, though, the need to raise interest and convince a sceptical or apathetic public can lead CSOs into potential misrepresentation and overclaiming on the basis of their evidence. One area where CSOs have typically been open to ethical criticism is therefore in relation to the *provision of misleading information* (Whawell 1998). For example, in 2009, a row ensued after the London-based tribal people CSO, Survival International, was accused of 'bullying' and providing 'grossly incorrect' information in its campaign to halt the construction of a resort on the Andaman Islands by the Barefoot Group. Survival's accusation that the company was potentially going to be responsible for 'genocide' of the Jarawa people of the Andamans prompted some of Barefoot's fellow 'responsible travel' companies to mount a concerted counter-attack challenging the irresponsibility of NGO campaigners. The provocative campaign, however, proved successful with the Indian government imposing a ban on tourism activities in the area in 2012.[5]

Overall, although there is growing attention to CSO duties to be honest and truthful in their communications, the provision of misleading information does not seem to be as much of an ethical problem for CSOs as it does for corporations (see Chapter 8). As we have already said, many CSOs have been extremely successful in establishing themselves as credible and authoritative institutions, and as a whole are more trusted sources of information than corporations. More marginal CSOs involved in anti-business communication, as well as other clearly partisan civil society actors, may not of course enjoy the same degree of overall trust from the public. However, their specific slant is usually reasonably well understood, with the result that their information is often seen more as subjective interpretation than objective fact.

Violent direct action

Violent direct action is usually illegal, although as Smith (2015) notes, it frequently generates the most publicity. Because of the publicity it generates, violent action also raises awareness of the issues that the CSO is promoting very quickly. For example, when the 1999 anti-globalization protests at Seattle degenerated into street riots (known as the 'Battle of Seattle') the issue of anti-globalization was assured front-page coverage across much of the world. Similarly, the often violent campaign against animal cruelty at Huntingdon Life Sciences led by SHAC (Stop Huntingdon Animal Cruelty) resulted in extensive media publicity and a series of damaging setbacks for the company, its suppliers, customers, and investors. Nonetheless, a string of arrests involving SHAC's leadership led to the end of the campaign in 2014 (Peachey 2014).

Despite their intentions to support a cause, it is difficult to condone the more violent protest by CSOs—although the destruction of property and violence towards people would seem to be on somewhat different moral planes. For one thing, such actions can hardly be deemed 'civil', even though civil behaviour is regarded as a prerequisite for the moral legitimacy of CSOs (Baur and Palazzo 2011). Perhaps in the interests of attempting to create a more civil society in the long run (for example, one where animals are not used for tests of cosmetic ingredients), we could begin to see a defence of violent action on consequentialist grounds. However, the perceived illegitimacy of such tactics by the public, government, and business tends to make them largely unsuccessful at gaining CSO members access to decision-makers and the decision-making process—which is often a major goal of such campaigns. Overall, violent direct action remains an important, if highly controversial, tactic for CSOs. We would suggest that it seems to be particularly attractive for those who are (or who feel they are) largely excluded from any other means of engagement with decision-makers, and who feel that their ends justify their means. In a liberal, pluralistic society, though, such means have to be severely questioned.

? THINK THEORY

Think about violent direct action by CSOs in terms of consequentialism and non-consequentialism. Which is most important for the legitimacy of CSOs—that they achieve civil consequences or that they adopt civil procedures in doing so?

VISIT THE
ONLINE
RESOURCE
CENTRE
for links to
useful sources
of further
information

ETHICS ON SCREEN 10

F*ck for Forest

Exposes the ethical and moral jungle of modern society, where it's not necessarily straightforward to gauge what's right and wrong.

Steve Rose, *Guardian*

The NGO sector contains a lot of diversity, but who knew there was an eco-porn activist niche? It is this undoubted novelty that makes *F*ck for Forest*, the 2012 documentary by the Polish director Michal Marczak about the eponymous, self-proclaimed 'erotic, non-profit ecological organization', such a fascinating subject for a documentary. But while the movie may appeal to some simply for the spectacle of seeing the erotic activists at work and play, it also asks some important questions about the methods used by NGOs to generate funding, and the relationships they have with their supposed beneficiaries. Selling home-made pornography to save the rainforests is, as the movie shows, riddled with moral ambiguity.

The Berlin-based organization FFF that is the focus of the movie was originally set up in Norway in the mid-2000s, with start-up funding from the Norwegian government. Following legal problems FFF relocated to Germany, which is where Marczak catches up with them as they go about their bizarre charity work. The group combines a philosophy of sexual liberation, eco-hippy idealism, and direct action. It essentially operates by making amateur pornography featuring either its members or willing volunteers and then selling it on the internet to support its eco causes.

With a $15 monthly subscription for members to access its pictures and videos the group claims to have generated around €250,000 which it has used to fund environmental and community work in Brazil, Costa Rica, Ecuador, Mexico, and Slovakia. This includes buying up land in the rainforest and protecting it, funding replanting, and supporting conservation work. However, because of its controversial methods, many NGOs, including the WWF and others, have refused donations from the group, wishing to avoid any links with the pornography industry.

Against Gravity/Kinomaton/The Kobal Collection

As Marczak's film shows, however, the group itself is hardly typical of the adult industry. 'My first impression was, who the hell would ever watch this?' Marczak says.

And even if they would, who would pay for it? It's really vulgar and its very … hairy. Nobody shaves their armpits, and it's really badly lit. But I noticed that the people mostly seem happy in it. There are moments when they just left camera on for little while after they've finished and you see genuine emotion in people, like you hardly ever see in porn films.

Indeed, the organization promotes a 'love manifest' extolling the virtues of natural sexuality and sexual pleasure. As it says on the organization's website, 'sex is often shown to attract us to buy all kind of bullshit products and ideas, so why not for a good cause? We think it is important to show a more liberal relationship to our bodies, as a contrast to the suppressed world we live in.'

The first half of the documentary follows the group around Berlin as they engage in their free love activism and fundraising exploits. As such, it gives a unique insight into their unusual approach to raising money and their countercultural philosophy. In the second half, the movie turns more serious when it follows FFF as it travels to the Amazon rainforest and meets with a Peruvian tribe to help them buy their own land. Marczak shows the clash of cultures in stark terms—the locals are deeply skeptical of FFF and its plans, and roundly disapprove of its

rampant sexuality and eco-porn methods of fundraising. FFF, for its part, struggle to find a way to help its supposed beneficiaries, and instead encounter a tribe that does not live up to its idealistic vision of indigenous people whose 'basic philosophy and spirituality is nature connected'.

Perhaps unsurprisingly, FFF objected to its depiction in the film, and in particular to the way that Marczak allegedly staged various elements and tricked them into the meeting with the Peruvian tribe. Although as self-proclaimed supporters of freedom of expression FFF contended that despite all this 'he should be allowed to show the sides he wished', it made its views clear on the situation. 'FFF is a group of idealistic expressionists,' it wrote in its online response to the movie, 'Michal Marzak is a money and fame loving movie maker.'

Sources
Rose, S. 2013. The eco-sex activists who want to save the world. *Guardian*, 11 April 2013: http://www.theguardian.com/film/2013/apr/11/green-sex-activists-documentary.
http://www.fuckforforest.com.
http://www.fuckforforestmovie.com.

Non-violent direct action

Non-violent direct action is a far more common approach for CSOs to use against corporations. With the rise of the internet and social media, it has become far easier for CSOs to organize campaigns and other forms of activism aimed at corporations. **Ethics Online 10** discusses anti-corporate social media campaigns by Greenpeace as an illustration of the ways in which online activism can be incorporated into broader protest movements.

Non-violent direct action, whether online or on the ground, can take a variety of forms including:

- Demonstrations and marches.

- Protests.

- Letter, email, or social media campaigns.

- Boycotts.

- Occupations.

- Non-violent sabotage and disruption.

- Stunts.

- Picketing.

Sometimes these may cross the line into illegality, such as when climate change activists trespass on private land to protest about oil exploration or pipeline projects. For example, in 2013 armed Russian authorities arrested 30 Greenpeace activists and seized

VISIT THE
ONLINE
RESOURCE
CENTRE
for links to
useful sources
of further
information

ETHICS ONLINE 10

Online activism through social media

Civil society activism against companies used to be primarily a matter of letter writing and the occasional *in situ* protest, whether outside stores, at AGMs, around oil fields, or wherever most publicity could be generated. Although protests, occupations and sit-ins remain very much a part in the arsenal of civil society activists, the main battleground is now online, and in particular through social media.

Greenpeace has probably been the most effective exponent of anti-corporate social media activism in recent years. One of its biggest social media successes was its 2010 campaign that forced the giant food company Nestlé to implement sustainable sourcing of palm oil. The NGO released a spoof Kit Kat ad on YouTube that went viral garnering nearly 1.5 million views and prompted over 200,000 emails, hundreds of phone calls, and countless Facebook comments.

Greenpeace then turned its attention to social media companies themselves, in particular Facebook. Its 'Unfriend Coal' campaign cleverly used Facebook to raise awareness of the energy sources that Facebook itself was using to power its data centres. Featuring a logo that used the iconic Facebook thumbs up (and thumbs down), as well as a cheeky video that remixed the popular movie *The Social Network* about the company, the campaign also went viral, garnering a record-breaking 80,000 comments on a single Facebook post on the campaign's page in just one day. Various protests, stunts, and activist photos and videos followed from the campaign's supporters across the world. Facebook soon announced its intention to build a new renewable-powered data centre in Sweden and to source 25% renewable energy overall in powering its operations.

More recently, Greenpeace scored another major success with its 2014 campaign aimed at forcing Lego to cancel its partnership with the oil company Shell. The organization's 'Everything is NOT Awesome' video (a spoof of the theme for the hugely popular Lego

movie released the same year) reached some 6 million views and was the most viewed in Greenpeace's history. Meanwhile, a series of protests with Lego characters outside Shell garages and other landmarks kept social media buzzing for months. Lego subsequently announced it would not be renewing its 50-year partnership with the oil giant, which Greenpeace hailed as 'fantastic news for LEGO fans and Arctic defenders everywhere. And it's a huge blow to Shell's strategy of partnering with beloved brands to clean up its dirty image as an Arctic oil driller'.

What is notable about how Greenpeace has become a leader amongst CSOs in leveraging the power of social media is that it has been adroit at getting people to go beyond simple 'clicktivism'. While its campaigns may start by getting people to simply watch, like, and share content, it also designs its campaigns to provide follow-up education about the issues and to encourage deeper participation through email campaigns, off-line protests, and even user-generated content creation. The CSO has also been effective in fitting its social media campaigns into a broader strategy of social change that involves direct dialogue with companies, developing new solutions, and tackling issues at a policy level.

Of course, Greenpeace has been far from alone among CSOs in taking to social media to confront companies. Twitter campaigns using provocative hashtags, swamping corporate Facebook pages with debate about sensitive ethical issues, and using social media to co-ordinate different civil society groups to give them more collective voice have all been used to considerable effect over the past decade or so by a swathe of CSOs. At the same time, however, most campaigns hardly get off the ground and few achieve the social media Holy Grail of going viral.

As one commentator put it:

that leaves companies with the tricky conundrum of when, and indeed whether, to respond. Careful judgment is required on both counts. Act too quickly, and a company can give too much weight to an unsubstantiated complaint. Leave it too long and an online campaign can snowball out into the street and onto the shop-front. As online campaigners become more interactive, the impulse is on companies to keep pace.

Sources
Balch, O. 2009. Campaigns 2.0. *Ethical Corporation*, May 2009, 18–21.
Polisano, E. 2014. Greenpeace: how our campaign ended the Lego-Shell partnership. *Guardian*, 10 October 2014: http://www.theguardian.com/voluntary-sector-network/2014/oct/10/greenpeace-lego-shell-climate-change-arctic-oil.
Greenpeace: http://www.greenpeace.org.

their ship after they attempted to occupy a Russian oil rig in the Arctic. In the main, though, direct action of this sort tends to remain quite legal. As a result, there are fewer ethical problems arising with non-violent direct action. However, supposedly non-violent actions can lead to intimidation, and can even tacitly encourage action that is more violent. Moreover, tactics such as boycotts can also raise some concerns, and sometimes the very choice of companies to target can be a point of contention. We will not go into detail on all of the non-violent direct action tactics open to CSOs, but it seems worthwhile to focus a little more attention on boycotts since they are such an important part of the CSO 'tool box'.

Boycotts

Boycotts are probably the most commonly recognized, and most widely used, form of non-violent direct action. Research suggests that something like 30% of people claim to have boycotted, or are willing to boycott, a product for ethical reasons.[6] As such, they represent an organized form of *ethical consumption*—a subject we first discussed in Chapter 8. However, boycotts are a very specific form of ethical consumption. That is, while ethical consumption is often an individual activity or choice that may involve decisions to purchase some products and not others, a boycott is a co-ordinated endeavour among a group of consumers to refrain from making specific purchases. Its goals may be to directly influence corporate policy, or to achieve other objectives through *collective action* (Smith 2015).

    CSOs are usually the parties co-ordinating boycotts of corporations and products. Some CSOs, in fact, even come into existence simply to organize boycott activity, such as the *Boycott Divestment and Sanctions (BDS)* movement, a coalition of Palestinian organizations that boycott Israeli products and companies operating in Israel. CSO boycotts have targeted numerous companies over the years, with the *Ethical Consumer* website typically listing some 50–100 active boycott actions at any given time. **Figure 10.4** describes some more well-known boycotts that have occurred over the years.

    The question of *which companies should be targeted* (and the reasons why) is a critical ethical choice for CSOs. For a start, many campaigns focus on particularly visible or vulnerable corporate brands, even if they are not the worst offenders with respect to the issue concerned. For example, in 2014 Greenpeace's Save the Arctic campaign successfully forced Lego to terminate its relationship with Shell (which was distributing Shell-branded Lego toys at its petrol stations), even though Lego itself was not directly involved

Boycott
A co-ordinated attempt to achieve certain objectives by urging individual consumers to refrain from making selected purchases in the marketplace due to perceived deficiencies in social, ethical, and/or environmental performance.

Target company	CSO Organizer	Dates	Main issues	Outcomes
ExxonMobil (Esso)	Greenpeace, Friends of the Earth, People and Planet	2001–04	Anti climate change position, including active lobbying against Kyoto global warming treaty; lack of investment in renewable energy	Raised awareness and brought (unsuccessful) shareholder resolutions to the AGM. ExxonMobil has since shifted to a more accommodating climate change position
Triumph International	Burma Campaign	2001–02	Manufacturing operations in Burma	Announced withdrawal from the country in 2002
KFC	People for the Ethical Treatment of Animals (PETA)	2003	Cruelty towards chickens in the KFC supply chain	Some improvements in practices. Campaign called off in Canada due to new animal welfare plan but continues in US, UK, and several other countries
PG Tips Tea	Captive Animals' Protection Society (CAPS)	2004	Use of performing chimpanzees in advertisements – claimed to reduce animals to ridicule, and to involve taking young chimps from their mothers, and potential physical punishment	Removed advertisements featuring the chimpanzees in 2004, having used the image for 45 years. Now uses animated animals
Body Shop	Naturewatch	2006	Sale of Body Shop to L'Oréal. Main issues involved L'Oréal's use of animal testing	A Naturewatch press release claimed that the Body Shop had lost millions in revenue in just one year due to the campaign. No change in policy at L'Oréal
BP	Public Citizen, Democracy for America	2012	Deepwater Horizon oil spill	More than 70 0,000 people follow the Boycott BP Facebook page and protests occur at many BP petrol stations but little impact of boycott on the company since most stations are franchise owned
Chick-fil-A	Student Unions, gay rights organizations, and city mayors	2012	Anti same-sex marriage position including funding of anti-gay organizations and public opposition to gay marriage by the company president	Several cities announce restrictions on Chick-fil-A restaurant expansion plans, and funding for anti-gay organizations phased out. However, counter campaign 'Chick-fil-A appreciation day' also a success and overall sales continued increasing
SodaStream	BDS National Committee	2013	SodaStream products are made in a factory in an Israeli settlement in occupied Palestinian territory in the West Bank	SodaStream products dropped by some US and UK retailers, and flagship UK store forced to close due to picketing. Announced plans to close factory in 2014

Figure 10.4 Some well-known boycotts

Sources: http://www.caft.org.uk; http://www.ethicalconsumer.org; http://www.greenpeace.org.uk; http://www.naturewatch.org; http://www.captiveanimals.org; http://www.bdsmovement.net.

in Arctic drilling. Some might question whether such targeting is fair or whether only the worst, or most direct offenders, should be attacked in this way.

Debate about the ethics of targeting specific firms also arises when the values and causes that CSOs promote are themselves controversial. For example, boycotts of companies operating in Israel are always controversial given the contentious politics of the Middle East. This became front-page news in 2014 when the American actress Scarlett Johansson signed up to be SodaStream's global brand ambassador despite the firm being the subject of a boycott over its factory in an Israeli settlement in the occupied West Bank. The move culminated in Johansson resigning from her position as a global ambassador for Oxfam (which supports the boycott of firms and products from Israeli settlements) along with an announcement of her support for SodaStream as 'a company that is not only committed to the environment but to building a bridge to peace between Israel and Palestine, supporting neighbors working alongside each other, receiving equal pay, equal benefits and equal rights' (Kershner 2014).

? THINK THEORY

Think about the arguments for and against the boycotting of companies operating in occupied territory in the West Bank. Which ethical theories would you say these arguments primarily rely on?

VISIT THE ONLINE RESOURCE CENTRE for a short response to this feature

---

Of course, for some CSOs such high-profile controversy is exactly the purpose of calling a boycott—they want to raise awareness of the issues involved rather than necessarily expecting the company to change its behaviour. Indeed, as Friedman (1999) suggests, CSOs might actually have four different purposes for boycotts:

- **Instrumental boycotts** aim to force the target to change a specific policy. Goals may be very clear, such as the repudiation of the challenged policy, the introduction of better conditions, etc.

- **Catalytic boycotts** seek to raise awareness about the company's actions and policies. The boycott itself is more of a means to generate publicity, either for the CSO or for a broader campaign of action against the company.

- **Expressive boycotts** are more general forms of protest that effectively just communicate a general displeasure about the target company. This form tends to be characterized by more vague goals, since their focus is more on the CSO and consumers registering their disapproval.

- **Punitive boycotts** seek to punish the target company for its actions. Therefore, rather than communicating displeasure, the boycotters actively seek to cause the firm harm, usually by aiming for significant erosions of sales.

? THINK THEORY

Investigate the boycotts in Figure 10.4 and categorize them in terms of instrumental, catalytic, expressive, and punitive boycotts. What explains the difference in objectives for CSOs?

VISIT THE ONLINE RESOURCE CENTRE for a short response to this feature

Regardless of the purpose of a boycott, it is often the extent and intensity of consumer participation that determines whether such goals are met. Clearly, a number of factors can affect whether consumers join and maintain boycotts, including the degree of effort involved in switching to an alternative, the appeal of the boycotted product to the consumer, social pressure, and the likelihood of success (Sen et al. 2001). In practice, though, many more boycotts are called than are successful, and many are never even brought to the notice of the general public. This of course starts to raise the question of which constituencies exactly are CSOs supposed to be representing—and perhaps more importantly, in what way are they answerable to those whose interests they are supposed to be advancing? These are essentially questions of CSO accountability, the last of our main ethical issues confronting business relations with CSOs.

☑ Skill check

Analysing CSO tactics. CSOs may deploy a range of tactics to achieve their goals. Analysing these tactics is important in terms of defining what the CSO is looking to achieve and whether it is adopting an ethical approach in doing so.

CSO accountability

CSO accountability
The principles, processes, and mechanisms through which stakeholders hold CSOs responsible for their performance.

In recent years the issue of **CSO accountability** has been raised with increasing regularity (Baur and Schmitz 2012; O'Dwyer et al. 2015). This is perhaps not surprising when one considers that they have often been the parties most vociferously questioning the accountability of corporations. We might reasonably expect critics of corporate accountability to 'have their own house in order' first (Hilhorst 2002).

Indeed, it is interesting to note that questions about CSO accountability have largely mirrored the same questions that have been raised in relation to corporations. For example, who exactly is an organization such as Greenpeace supposed to be serving? Are the interests of its managers aligned with those of its principal constituents? To what extent and to whom are Greenpeace responsible for the consequences of their actions? We have asked almost exactly the same questions in discussing issues of corporate responsibility and accountability in Chapter 2, and issues of ownership, control, and governance in Chapter 6. This suggests that we can conceptualize CSO managers as 'agents' for a broader collective of civil society 'principals' in the same way as we do for corporate managers and shareholders (see Doh and Teegen 2002). Likewise, we can model CSOs as representative of different stakeholder interests just as we can with corporations (e.g. Hilhorst 2002).

Specifically, CSO stakeholders might be said to include:

- Beneficiaries.
- Donors.
- Members.
- Employees.
- Governmental organizations.
- Other CSOs.
- General public (especially those who support their ideals).

Significantly, though, there is also clearly a case for saying that CSOs represent some notion of *civil society itself*—a largely indefinable stakeholder, but one that is nonetheless central to the notion of the third sector. Interestingly, a growing number of organizations very similar to CSOs have been initiated since the 1990s, with *business* itself as a main stakeholder, examples being the World Business Council for Sustainable Development (WBCSD), the Global Business Coalition on HIV/AIDS (GBC), and the Global Climate Coalition (GCC). In contrast to real grassroots organizations, these are sometimes dubbed 'astroturf NGOs' (Gray et al. 2006), as they pick up typical issues of CSOs, but address them from the rather narrow angle of business interests.

Given such a range of stakeholders, issues of accountability and responsibility in CSOs are clearly quite complex. Different stakeholders might have different expectations of CSO performance, and of how that performance is reported. Similarly, different stakeholders might have very different expectations about how much say they should have in the affairs of the organization. While we might, as the general public, support the work of Oxfam in providing famine relief, we do not expect to have much meaningful input into how it goes about providing this. Perhaps our interest in this respect grows if we donate significant sums of money to the organization, but even so, we would generally be less concerned about how it spent our money than the intended beneficiaries would be.

Unsurprisingly then, it is the accountability of CSOs to their *supposed beneficiaries* that tends to raise the most debate. A number of problems are evident here, including:

- CSOs in developed countries purporting to represent the interests of those in developing countries sometimes impose their own agendas on local people without adequately understanding their situations and needs.

- The involvement of beneficiaries in agenda setting, defining priorities, and making strategic decisions is often limited.

- The need for financial support and other resources can focus CSOs' interests on donors' priorities ('upward accountability') rather than those of their intended beneficiaries ('downward accountability').

- CSO performance measures are often devised without input from beneficiaries and are frequently not communicated to them in a meaningful way.

- Beneficiaries typically lack effective mechanisms to voice approval or disapproval of CSO performance, or to seek redress when CSO interventions go wrong.

In some ways, it would appear that many CSOs have been equally as inattentive to certain issues of accountability and democracy as many corporations have. Given their largely positive impact on society, as well as their values-based stance, it could be argued, though, that perhaps the issue of accountability is less crucial in respect of CSOs. Indeed, *formal accountability* (in the form of public accounts and performance metrics) might be said to be less important for CSOs than a more *informal accountability* based on the more complex and closer ties between CSOs and their stakeholders (Gray et al. 2006). However, given the growing importance of their role in society in general, as well as their involvement in business specifically, the question of CSO accountability is only really likely to gain in significance.

Some of the largest international NGOs, including Oxfam, Amnesty International, and Greenpeace, have responded to these challenges with an 'Accountability Charter'

1. Respect for Human Rights
We commit to respecting and promoting human rights as expressed in the Universal Declaration of Human Rights.

2. Independence
We seek to be both politically and financially independent.

3. Transparency
We commit to transparency and honesty regarding our mission, structures, policies, and activities.

4. Good Governance
We commit to effective governance that ensures we act in accordance with stated values and agreed procedures and our programmes achieve outcomes that are consistent with our mission.

5. Responsible Advocacy
We commit to ensuring that our advocacy is consistent with our mission, grounded in our work, based on evidence and advances defined public interests.

6. Participation
We commit to working in genuine partnership with local communities, NGOs and other organizations which aim for sustainable development in response to local needs. We commit to the empowerment and inclusive participation of people whose lives are affected by our initiatives.

7. Diversity/Inclusion
We commit to valuing, respecting and encouraging diversity, and seek to be impartial and non-discriminatory in all our activities.

8. Environmental Responsibility
We commit to minimizing the environmental impact of our operations and programme work wherever possible, balancing it with necessities to fulfil our mandate and financial affordability.

9. Ethical Fundraising
We commit to ensuring that all donations further our mission. We respect the rights of donors and the dignity of people affected by our fundraising activities.

10. Professional Management
We commit to effective, ethical management, and continuous improvement in the quality of our work.

Figure 10.5 Accountability charter for international NGOs
Source: http://www.ingoaccountabilitycharter.org.

intended to serve as a code of conduct for NGOs on the international stage (Russell 2006). The charter defines ten key principles (see **Figure 10.5**) which members are required to report on annually. These reports are then evaluated in an independent review panel to ensure that members adhere to their commitments. However, with only 20 members as of the mid-2010s, it remains to be seen how far the charter will make inroads into the millions of CSOs across the globe.[7]

For corporations, the main questions around CSO accountability are: (a) how they should assess the legitimacy of any CSO contribution to the debate about business ethics; and (b) what this means in terms of how they should respond to particular CSO challenges. At one extreme, they could choose to play CSOs at their own game and refuse to take seriously the views of unelected, unaccountable ideologues. At the other, they could seek to work together to develop enhanced mechanisms of governance and accountability for both types of organizations. The reality, however, is likely to be somewhere in the middle—with all of the ambiguity and ambivalence that such a situation brings.

> **? THINK THEORY**
>
> Think about the relevance of stakeholder theory for CSOs compared with corporations. In which aspects is it more or less relevant or applicable for either category of organization?

VISIT THE
ONLINE
RESOURCE
CENTRE
for a short
response to this
feature

■ Globalization and civil society organizations

Globalization has brought two significant changes to CSOs that are relevant for our understanding of business ethics. First, globalization has brought multinationals into confrontation with an extended community of CSOs, including a whole new set of local CSOs in other countries that they did not have to deal with before. Second, we have also seen CSOs themselves increasingly globalize in terms of scale and/or scope. Clearly, it is not only corporations that organize across borders, and CSOs have often been extremely effective at galvanizing a transnational community of constituents to support their campaigns aimed at corporations. Let us look at each of these in a little more detail.

Engagement with overseas CSOs

For corporations acting solely within the domestic sphere, the notion of civil society tends to be quite naturally framed simply in terms of national or even regional constituencies. Just as an Italian corporation, such as the construction giant Salini Impregilo, might typically have been mainly involved in dealing with Italian labour and environmental groups (such as Italia Nostra), so might an Indian corporation such as Tata Tea, the largest tea company in the subcontinent, typically have dealt with just Indian CSOs. However, the increasingly deterritorialized nature of business activity inevitably puts corporations with international operations into a number of different civil societies across the globe. Multinationals are therefore confronted with a whole new set of unfamiliar CSOs in overseas countries.

For example, BP's involvement in extracting, refining, and transporting oil in hundreds of projects around the globe exposes the company to the attention of various local environmental and community groups in each of the countries involved. These can amount to hundreds of different groups, not just of local origin but also local subsidiaries of global CSOs, such as Save the Children, the Refugee Council, etc.

It should be noted here that in countries like India, the CSO population is huge, while in others, such as China, the local CSO population is more limited. Indeed, CSOs hardly existed in China prior to the mid-1990s, since which time their number has escalated quite rapidly. There are now some half a million registered CSOs and a further 1.5 million unregistered organizations, many of which are illegal under Chinese law but are increasingly tolerated by the authorities (*The Economist* 2014c). **Ethics in Action 10.1** discusses some of these different international contexts for local civil society and the challenges they pose for multinational companies.

Many developing and transitional economies tend to lack a strong and institutionalized civil society, with international CSOs often taking up the slack. On the one hand, a lack of local CSOs can be a plus for corporations in that it means they can either engage

**VISIT THE
ONLINE
RESOURCE
CENTRE**
for links to
useful sources
of further
information

ETHICS IN ACTION 10.1   http://www.ethicalcorp.com

Emerging market campaigners—
ground-level activism

Eric Marx, 7 March 2013

Region by region, in emerging economies around the world, local and international NGOs interact with their corporate counterparts in many and distinct ways. What can companies do to find the best way to develop relationships on the one hand, and keep themselves out of the firing line on the other?

'The biggest challenge—even for companies that want to do the right thing—is in getting the right local partners,' says Pinaki Roy, a community development consultant in India who helped guide the country's Global Reporting Initiative secretariat in the early 2000s. The way to find those partners is to assemble an address book of low-key respectable organizations that are not necessarily tied to overseas funding. These can often be found through international NGOs but also through educational institutions and legal associations. Supply chain auditors such as Rainforest Alliance aggregate local NGO groups in their country programmes, while development NGOs such as Oxfam are respected for having deep and longstanding relations with local communities around the world.

Though conditions vary greatly according to country and region, local stakeholder engagement can be effective. It takes effort and perseverance, and it is process based.

Latin America—sophisticated civil society

International conservation groups and an increasingly sophisticated network of local organizations in Latin America operate in an array of sectors as diverse as agriculture, fishing, carbon, and water. The Rainforest Alliance, for one, aims to transform practices at the farm level. It has long been an active player in Latin America, where it has developed social and environmental standards for coffee, cocoa, and bananas.

Tensie Whelan, president of the Rainforest Alliance, says her organization's community outreach work tries to discover and adjudicate land tenure conflicts, and not just act as a rubber stamp authorising local projects in exchange for community consent. 'We pull together community complaints and concerns and we look at it in terms of substantiating whether [they amount to] one person's bone to pick versus backed-up group consensus,' Whelan says. 'We rely on community feedback, we talk to local NGOs and say "this is what we heard" and "how do you respond to that?"' If problems are indeed serious enough, action will be taken—including withholding certification of projects when appropriate.

India—civil society writ large

In India, where there is no shortage of NGO representation—some estimate NGOs number more than 3 million—part of the problem lies in navigating a civil society that is highly politicised and fractured. And the government gives little deference to matters such as free, prior and informed consent, and this puts companies in a quandary, says Daniel Taghioff, an India-based consultant specialising in land rights conflicts. 'Essentially a company's core interest in making a profit is very aligned with state priorities,' says Taghioff, 'but their corporate responsibility priorities are going to pull them towards people who are very much in a position of resistance to the state.'

In India there is often great inequality of wealth between rural and urban areas, which results in deep mistrust between local communities and central administrations, says Pinaki Roy. 'Even if you go for Indian entities, there is no guarantee that the organization which is headquartered nationally in Delhi, Bombay or Bangalore will have the ability to get a wholehearted engagement from the communities that are going to be affected.'

Local partners must be chosen with great care. Often an NGO that is funded at the local level will be owned by politically powerful people based outside that local community, and NGOs can themselves become untrusted brands. 'The challenge,' Roy says, 'is that many communities feel they should be talking to the government, not to the companies.'

Activist diversity in Africa

African countries often defy easy generalization. Each has its own history and civil society structure alongside a plethora of Western aid agencies, many of which contract out their projects to NGOs that end up working in a service delivery capacity. Oxfam, Conservation International and The Nature Conservancy (TNC) are examples of the groups now fulfilling these roles. Farmer advocacy groups and thinktanks are in abundance, as are organizations focused on health-care issues.

African NGOs offer capacity and tremendous focus at the community level, but often do not have the long-term monitoring and evaluation systems in place. 'That can be challenging to corporates,' says Matt Brown, the Africa conservation director for TNC.

Since 2006, TNC has worked in Africa mainly by focusing its attention on grasslands protection in the central and eastern portions of the continent. In northern Tanzania it has secured wildlife corridors and traditional land uses for pastoralists and hunter-gatherers, while actively working as a convener of external and local NGO groups on matters of healthcare delivery in and around Lake Tanganyika, a biodiversity hotspot located in the country's western region.

Though it currently has eight projects in various stages of development, TNC has yet to enter into any large corporate partnerships. Smart mining in collaboration with the government is one possible route forwards, as is work to secure land rights in transport corridors now coming through the region. For corporate partnerships to work in Africa, Brown says TNC has to choose its projects carefully. 'The goal is to build participatory processes that create trust and on-the-ground results,' he says.

Chinese control

China's controlled economy is a challenging environment for NGO activity. Domestic programmes in China are closely monitored, but since 2011 the government has allowed limited registration of NGOs. These groups do not receive money from foreign donors. They are tightly controlled but nevertheless are indicative of a growing liberalization helped to a large extent by a communications explosion and the increased use of social media in China.

Activist, campaigning organizations do not exist in the traditional sense, but if citizens present the facts to the right people, pressure can be brought to bear, says Li Lin, WWF's deputy country representative in China. Lin cites one recent example in Shifang, southwest China, where protests against a multi-million-dollar copper plant led to riots and the temporary cessation of all construction work. Fears about the impact of development on the environment and public health are engaging a growing sector of the population, particularly the young. From a company perspective, 'the community can come to you from different angles,' says Lin. 'Identify the community leaders, and talk to them to see what their concerns are,' he counsels.

Sources

Ethical Corporation, Eric Marx, 7 March 2013, http://www.ethicalcorp.com. Reproduced with the kind permission of Ethical Corporation.

VISIT THE ONLINE RESOURCE CENTRE for a short response to this feature

? THINK THEORY
Think about the idea that CSOs overseas are stakeholders in a business. How can companies effectively recognize the right CSOs as their stakeholders in an overseas context?

with more-familiar international organizations, or even conduct their business relatively unhindered by CSO activism. On the other hand, international groups may lack legitimate representation of local communities, and the absence of an effective third sector can reinforce welfare and democracy deficits in countries where corporations would benefit from greater societal governance. Indeed, Valente and Crane (2010) suggest that some companies have developed a 'support strategy' in developing countries that involves the active promotion of well-managed civil society organizations.

Globalization of CSOs

Just as corporations have become increasingly global in scope over the past few decades, so too has civil society. Now, rather than just engaging with multiple local civil societies, some corporations are also faced with something more akin to a *global civil society*. Talk of a global civil society to describe such developments first began to spread in the 1990s and has now become fairly commonplace in social and political debates (Dryzek 2012). Its most obvious manifestation is in giant international NGOs such as WWF, Greenpeace, and Friends of the Earth, as well as international union bodies such as the International Confederation of Free Trade Unions (ICFTU). However, many social movements and anti-corporate campaigns are also global in scope. Consider the Occupy movement, which since 2011 has sought to highlight the problem of income inequality. Although it started receiving attention with the Occupy Wall Street protest in New York, its impact was multiplied by the formation of hundreds of other Occupy protests across more than 80 different countries.

This position as global institutions, on a similar deterritorialized basis as corporations, potentially brings with it new roles and responsibilities for CSOs. Most notably it offers the opportunity to address global business ethics issues on a wider scale than previously possible. For instance, WWF's commitment to water conservation led to the striking of a major global partnership with Coca-Cola. As part of the initiative, slated to run until 2020, WWF and Coke are tackling the conservation of 11 of the world's most critical freshwater river basins spanning Asia, Africa, and the Americas as well as improving Coke's own water efficiency.[8] Only a global CSO such as WWF could conceivably engage in such a far-reaching international partnership with a multinational brand like Coke.

A slightly different picture emerges if we look at the global reach of smaller, more localized CSOs. Often, CSOs in developing countries are rather local, under-resourced and in an unequal position to Western multinationals. However, based on a study of a number of resource extraction projects across four continents, Banerjee (2011) identifies the 'translocal' nature of CSOs in a global context. That is, 'local' CSOs in a world of global communication, media, and business networks increasingly link up with CSOs in other countries (often in the global north), which in turn empowers local players to critically engage with transnational companies whose activities are a source of concern. Globalization thus not only affects global CSOs, but also transforms the reach and impact of small local players.

In addition, given that most regulation of business activity was formerly in the province of local and national governments, the movement of both corporations and CSOs (but less so governments) to a global level means that CSOs might be expected to take on some of these responsibilities that were formerly held by government. As we have said a number of times, business ethics tends to begin where the law ends. And with a dearth of global laws, global CSOs have found themselves involved in (and at times have pushed themselves into) the process whereby global regulation of business is debated, decided, and implemented (Doh and Teegen 2002, 2003). As we shall discuss in more detail in the next section, this potentially has significant implications for our understanding of corporate citizenship (CC) with respect to civil society.

? THINK THEORY

Think about the theory of moral relativism in the context of global CSOs. Could there be a case for arguing that to be accountable to their local beneficiaries, CSOs have to adopt some level of relativism, or can they maintain a one-size-fits-all form of moral universalism?

VISIT THE
ONLINE
RESOURCE
CENTRE
for a short
response to this
feature

■ Corporate citizenship and civil society: charity, collaboration, enterprise, or regulation?

So far in this chapter we have mainly discussed corporate and civil society actors as though they were dedicated adversaries in a perpetual state of conflict. However, recognition by firms that 'good' citizenship might entail a positive response to civil society challenges has for some time now brought them into more constructive contact with civil actors. Traditionally, this has mainly centred on *charitable giving* and other philanthropic acts intended to benefit community groups and other civil actors. More recently, though, we have also witnessed an increasing incidence of more intensive *business–CSO collaboration*, seeking to provide more partnership-based solutions to social and environmental problems (Seitanidi and Crane 2014). At times, CSOs have even eschewed partnership with corporations and developed their own businesses, namely *social enterprises*. Finally, looking at the nature and purpose of CSO involvement in the business sector, CSOs might even go beyond collaborating with business to actually forming some kind of '*civil regulation*' of corporate action (Zadek 2001).

These tighter interrelationships should come as no surprise, particularly when we stop to think about the implications of talking about citizenship in the context of corporations. After all, civil society is typically thought of as an important arena where individual citizens can express and pursue their particular values and interests. Whether we think of corporations as fellow citizens in this society or as governors of citizenship for individuals, corporations must almost inevitably at some time become involved in civil society. In this section, we will look at these ways in which corporations and civil society have become more tightly interrelated, and consider the question of what role CSOs can play in making corporations more responsible and accountable within society.

Charity and community involvement

The main starting point for a consideration of business involvement in civil society is inevitably charitable giving and other forms of corporate philanthropy and community involvement. Corporations have long been involved in philanthropic behaviour towards local communities, charities, the arts, and various other aspects of civil society. Based on the notion of 'putting something back', many large corporations have now set up separate units or corporate foundations to strategically manage philanthropic activities—or 'social investments', as they are often referred to—on a global scale (Kotler and Lee 2005). For instance, the foundation of the mobile phone company Vodafone co-ordinates more than 28 local national foundations, as well as a global Vodafone Group Foundation. Since 1991, it has invested more than £800 million in social projects in the communities in which Vodafone operates, with a particular emphasis on mobile technology solutions to social problems.[9]

Employee volunteering
The giving of time or skills by company employees to a civil society organization during a planned activity endorsed, arranged, or funded by their employer.

Employees are also often involved in philanthropy schemes with CSOs, such as through **employee volunteering**. Although volunteering for charities has traditionally been part of a citizen's private civil engagement, companies have increasingly offered their employees the opportunity to volunteer on company time. By enabling employees to commit their time and efforts to social initiatives in this way, firms and their workers may be able to achieve a number of aims, including (Peloza and Hassay 2006; Muthuri et al. 2009; Rodell 2013):

• Making a meaningful social contribution.

• Compensating for lack of meaning in workers' jobs.

• Contributing to skills development among workers.

• Increasing employee morale and teamwork.

• Better job performance and employee retention.

- Enhancing the firm's reputation.
- Building 'social capital' within the community.

Despite these benefits, 'passive' forms of company support for employee volunteering (such as unpaid leave and provision of access to company facilities) are far more common than 'active' forms (such as paid leave and formal integration with training and development programmes) (Basil et al. 2009). This suggests that, despite its prevalence, many firms have yet to deploy a strategic or proactive approach to employee involvement, but rather rely on employees to take the initiative.

Many firms tend to regard employee involvement and charitable donations and the like as the mainstay of their 'corporate citizenship' programmes, and clearly some corporations have made significant contributions to civic life through such activities. On average, large US companies tend to donate approximately 1% of pre-tax profit to charity, with education and health organizations being the most popular destinations for corporate giving.[10] The scale and form of corporate giving, however, varies significantly between companies and between different regions. In general, US firms tend to exhibit the highest levels of corporate giving. European firms have tended to lag behind those from the US, but typically outstrip donations from Asian firms (Brammer and Pavelin 2005; Muller and Whiteman 2009). Such differences reflect distinct institutional contexts in different parts of the globe, including different tax regimes, variations in state investment in social welfare, and divergent norms and expectations around charitable giving.

Authors such as Friedman (1970) initially criticized charitable giving for effectively stealing from shareholders. More recently, attention has turned to *strategic philanthropy* (Liket and Maas 2015) and *cause-related marketing* (Robinson et al. 2012; Vanhamme et al. 2012) as ways of aligning charitable giving with firm self-interest. Under such initiatives, firms select suitable recipients of funding not so much according to need, but according to their potential for improving the firm's competitive context, enhancing its reputation, and other instrumental ends (Porter and Kramer 2006). Considering that among the largest donors of cash within US companies are Wal-Mart, Chevron, Goldman Sachs, and ExxonMobil, which have all been in the firing line for unethical and even illegal practices, such strategic forms of charitable giving seem to be thriving.[11] Although this is a logical response to doubts about the business value of community involvement, it does suggest certain limitations to philanthropy as a means of satisfying broader civic roles and responsibilities. It may benefit communities and civil society, but it does not usually allow them much voice in shaping corporate action, potentially leading to exploitation rather than empowerment (Muthuri 2008). Essentially, according to our depiction of different modes of stakeholder engagement in Chapter 5, this is a form of *one-way support* from business to civil society.

Business–CSO collaboration

In addition to these one-way philanthropic gestures, closer and more interactive relations between civil society and corporations have also risen to prominence in recent years. This move towards business–CSO collaboration has included dialogue between business and civil society actors, such as when major regeneration or construction projects are planned, and strategic alliances between business and civil partners on matters such as supply-chain management and certification. These developments have included various civil society actors, including environmental NGOs such as WWF, aid charities such as Oxfam, labour organizations such as the ILO (International Labour Organization), and various local and community groups. Some examples involving multinational companies and CSOs are described in **Figure 10.6**.

While reliable figures on the number of collaborations between CSOs and corporations are not readily available, there is general agreement that their incidence and scope has increased quite dramatically since the mid-1990s (Seitanidi and Crane 2014). There is also considerable evidence to suggest that the *degree of interaction* between commercial and civil organizations has intensified—from basic 'transactional' approaches to more 'integrative' relationships (Austin 2000). It is often suggested that CSOs are moving from being passive recipients of corporate philanthropy, or 'brand-for-hire' endorsers of existing company products, to more strategic roles in developing corporate policies and sharing resources and capabilities in order to contribute to joint value creation (Austin and Seitanidi 2012). Brugmann and Prahalad (2007) demonstrate that business and CSOs may even go so far as to co-create new businesses together—an issue that we will explore in more depth in the following section on 'social enterprise'.

Given the history of boycotts, strikes, occupations, protests, and other conflicts, businesses and CSOs might seem at first to be rather strange, and somewhat uneasy, bedfellows. However, there are a number of reasons why they have sought to work more closely together, which can largely be explained in terms of the relative resources that each party depends on the other for (den Hond et al. 2015). For companies, these reasons include a commitment to solving social problems they cannot tackle alone, an interest in leveraging CSO trust and credibility, a need to head off negative publicity, and the potential for introducing new thinking and skills into the organization. For CSOs, the reasons include a need for better resources, improved access to markets and consumers, disenchantment with governments in helping them achieve their objectives, and access to corporate supply chains. **Ethics in Action 10.2** provides some examples of how such benefits have arisen in specific examples of business–CSO partnerships.

In many respects, such collaborations appear to be very welcome, and in general have been afforded a very positive response in the academic and business press (Laasonen et al. 2012). We can see in such developments the potential for greater discussion, debate, and reflection on business ethics by the different partners. This raises the prospect of those from different sectors gaining greater understanding of the different facets of problems and learning to engage with competing, even conflicting, perspectives in order to build mutually acceptable solutions. Clearly, this has strong resonance with a *discourse ethics* approach to resolving ethical problems (Scherer and Palazzo 2011). However, as we shall now see, the value of this approach will depend on a number of other factors.

VISIT THE
ONLINE
RESOURCE
CENTRE
for a short
response to this
feature

? THINK THEORY

Think about business–CSO collaboration from the perspective of discourse ethics. What should the conditions of such collaborations be from this theoretical perspective?

Name of initiative	Country	Main CSOs involved	Main corporations involved	Launch	Aims and objectives
Marine Stewardship Council (MSC)	International	Originally developed by WWF-UK, now MSC is an independent CSO in itself	Unilever (at outset), now thousands of retailers, suppliers, and restaurants globally	1997	Establishment of standards and independent certification for sustainable fishing
Ethical Trading Initiative (ETI)	UK/International	16 NGOs & 3 trade unions	50+ companies, incl. Burberry, Fyffes, Gap, Jaeger, Monsoon, Tesco	1998	To define best practice in ethical trade and enable firms to implement labour standards in international supply chains
Sustainable Coffee	US/International	The Rainforest Alliance	Kraft Foods	2003	To bring certified sustainable coffee beans into Kraft's mainstream brands, including Carte Noir, Tassimo, and coffee supplied to McDonald's restaurants
International Business & Poverty Reduction	Indonesia	Oxfam	Unilever	2004	Research programme to explore the nature of Unilever's Indonesia business and its impacts on people living in poverty
HSBC Climate Partnership	International	The Climate Group, Earthwatch Institute, Smithsonian Tropical Research Institute, WWF	HSBC	2007	To combat climate change through programmes in education, research, conservation, and engagement with business, government, and communities
Green Works	US	Sierra Club	Clorox	2008	Endorsement of 'green' line of cleaning products
Aqueduct Alliance	International	World Resources Institute	Founded by GE and Goldman Sachs, expanded to 10+ companies	2011	Development of global water risk mapping tools to help companies, investors, and governments better understand water risks and opportunities
Accord on Building & Fire Safety in Bangladesh	Bangladesh/International	Two global trade unions, eight Bangladesh trade unions, and four NGOs	Almost 200 apparel brands, retailers, and importers from over 20 countries	2013	To build a safer Bangladeshi garment industry based on independent inspection programme, funding for remediation, and worker empowerment

Figure 10.6 Some examples of business–CSO collaboration

ETHICS IN ACTION 10.2   http://www.ethicalcorp.com

Partners in sustainability
Stephen Gardner, 2 February 2012

Strategically driven business-type partnerships between companies and non-governmental organizations are on the rise. Recent research from C&E Advisory, a sustainability consultancy, found an increase of 10% in such partnerships over the preceding 12 months, while other types of partnerships declined.

Business-type partnerships are defined as NGOs and companies working together to improve corporate practices, or for social business development—partnerships for greater corporate responsibility, in other words. They contrast with other partnerships, such as cause-related marketing, simple endorsement or sponsorships.

Two recent examples illustrate the trend. First, American NGO ForestEthics has worked with banana giant Chiquita to eliminate from its vast transportation fleet fuel derived from Canadian tar sands. Tar sands produce 'the dirtiest oil on Earth,' the campaigners say, and it was pushing Chiquita to join other companies pledging to steer clear of it. The company has now put in place a policy to work with ForestEthics to trace its fuel supplies back to source, and sever links with tar sands crude refineries.

Second, Greenpeace and Facebook have agreed to collaborate on a project to switch the social network's data centres to renewable energy. The agreement comes in the wake of a two-year campaign to persuade Facebook to 'unfriend coal', during which Greenpeace mobilized 700,000 supporters to message, poke and generally pressurize Facebook into changing its ways.

The campaigns both focused on single, high-profile companies with emblematic value. ForestEthics director Aaron Sanger says that creating such examples can motivate other companies. 'It is important for all companies to follow leadership examples, especially if the leader and the follower are in the same sector. This helps competitors keep pace,' he says.

Now for the big boys

ForestEthics now has Wal-Mart and US supermarket giant Safeway in its sights. Both 'burn an enormous amount of gasoline and diesel to move their products in huge trucks all over North America,' Sanger says. Persuading them to change their ways could have a real impact on demand for tar-sands-derived fuel. 'Because of the corporate sector's public influence and buying power, when large brands take action on environmental or social problems in their footprint, they can help to bring about practical solutions,' Sanger adds.

Mauricio Lazala, deputy director of NGO the Business & Human Rights Resource Centre, says such partnerships are 'not necessarily a natural collaboration'. He says such initiatives 'require extra efforts on behalf of both the NGOs and the companies' because of their different cultures and objectives. There are also risks. Some NGOs might 'consider that a partnership would undermine the credibility of any subsequent campaigning they undertake in relation to that company or sector,' and due diligence is necessary.

But companies and NGOs recognize that each has assets that can produce benefits when combined in partnership, and ultimately both have the same objective, which is to operate effectively within sustainable constraints. Business-type partnerships can be 'win-win,' Sanger says. ForestEthics wants companies to 'adopt a model of continuous improvement' in ethical terms. 'As long as the company continues to make adequate progress, we will support that progress; and as long as the company insists on continuing destructive activities, we will work to change them.'

Sources

Ethical Corporation, Stephen Gardner, 2 February 2012, http://www.ethicalcorp.com. Reproduced with the kind permission of Ethical Corporation.

? THINK THEORY

Think about the costs and benefits for the CSOs and companies involved in these partnerships, not just from the point of view of the partners but also society more broadly. What does this kind of utilitarian analysis tell you about the ethical desirability of cross-sector collaboration?

VISIT THE ONLINE RESOURCE CENTRE for a short response to this feature

Limitations of business–CSO collaboration

Despite their clear potential for effectively addressing social, ethical, and environmental problems, it is important to recognize that business–CSO collaboration also has a number of possible problems or limitations. Foremost among these are potential power imbalances between the partners, unequal distribution of benefits, and the prospect for co-optation of CSOs by business.

The question of *power imbalance* is a crucial one in addressing the potential for partnerships to bring benefits to the two parties. Typically, one would expect business partners to be considerably more powerful than CSOs in terms of size, capital, political influence, and other key power resources. However, such a perspective tends to overlook the important power that CSOs wield in terms of specific knowledge, communications expertise, and public credibility (Arts 2002). Certainly, though, where large companies and relatively more dependent CSOs work together, there is a danger that the relative influence of the two parties will be skewed towards corporate interests, and rewards may be unevenly shared. Thus, despite the good intentions of both parties, the rhetoric of 'partnerships' might often mask somewhat more traditional and asymmetric relations between the two sectors (Seitanidi and Ryan 2007). Dauvergne and LeBaron (2014) suggest in fact that rather than just masking or exploiting power imbalances, partnerships may actually reinforce these imbalances by corporatizing activism and limiting CSOs to market-based solutions. In addition, it has been argued that business–CSO alliances might favour the interests of companies and CSOs in developing countries over those in less-developed countries (Bendell and Murphy 2000).

We might also look to the *distribution of the benefits* of partnerships. Darcy Ashman (2001), for example, suggests that the benefits of many CSO–business partnerships are garnered more by the partners than they are by the constituencies they are supposed to be aiding. Examining ten cases of collaboration in Brazil, India, and South Africa, Ashman (2001) reveals that although both businesses and CSOs tended to reap benefits in terms of improved public images, better external relations, gains in resources, and organizational capacity-building, the development impacts on community beneficiaries were less predictable and considerably less emphatic. In fact, though, relatively little attention has actually been paid to assessing the real impacts of partnerships on the social problems and communities they are supposed to be benefiting, not least because of the major conceptual, methodological, and practical problems involved in conducting such impact assessments (Van Tulder et al. 2015).

Finally, another key risk in business–CSO collaboration is the prospect it raises of *corporations co-opting CSO partners*. This is a particular concern, since it threatens the independence that makes the civil sector such an important balance to corporate (and government) power. Through working with business, CSOs lay themselves open to the accusation of 'sleeping with the enemy' and thereby forfeiting some of their legitimacy and public credibility (Herlin 2013). This, in fact, is part of a broader ethical problem of *CSO independence* that requires further elaboration.

CSO independence

For the relationships between CSOs and businesses to function effectively, whether those relationships are adversarial or collaborative, it requires that the parties remain independent of one another. On the one hand, CSOs are unlikely to be able to occupy the moral high ground and pose a credible challenge to corporate abuses unless they are, and are seen to be, sufficiently distant from their corporate adversaries. On the other hand, if CSOs become too closely involved in working with corporations, they might lose the public credibility that made them attractive partners for business in the first place. For example, the decision by the US environmental group, the Sierra Club, to endorse the 'Green Works' range of Clorox cleaning products in 2008 prompted accusations that the CSO had 'sold out'—especially since few of the NGO's members had been consulted prior to striking the deal. However, the partnership was not renewed in 2014 after a period of declining sales for the brand led to a major marketing overhaul aimed at appealing more to mainstream consumers.[12]

In many ways, though, the issue of CSO independence goes yet deeper. If we return to our earlier categorization of civil society as the 'third sector', the idea that CSOs provide social and political pluralism in order to create and sustain a civilized society is clearly compromised if the third sector loses its independence from the other sectors (market and government). The very purpose of CSOs as representatives of the diversity of interests in society is potentially weakened once they begin to lose their unique position outside of the market sector. This is particularly problematic in a society where the power of corporations and of the market is so substantial that working with them can often be the most effective way of achieving real change. As many CSOs have found, if you want to improve the working conditions of workers in developing countries, or prevent the destruction of tropical rainforests, the best way to do so is to leverage the purchasing power of corporations in the West. But what happens when the former 'poacher' becomes the 'gamekeeper' (Zadek 2001: 80)?

There is clearly a certain degree of ambivalence here. While CSOs might want to harness the power of the market (usually through corporations) to achieve social ends, the market can be seen to 'contaminate' the primarily moral orientation of the civil sector (Eikenberry and Kluver 2004). As Kaler (2000) suggests, the power of many campaigning groups to tap into public opinion and influence business is in itself derived from the avowedly moral stance that they take—and in particular, their ability to relate to people as moral agents rather than just as consumers. The ethical challenge for CSOs, then, is to retain their distinctly moral orientation, while making a positive and constructive contribution to business practice—a delicate balance by any standards.

Thus far, most CSOs appear to have been relatively successful at doing this. Sometimes they will do so by setting up a separate 'business' unit within the organization, such as Amnesty International's Business Group, or by forming specific task forces charged with developing business relations, while the rest of the organization gets on with its usual campaigning role. Clearly, though, such a development involves CSOs (and, for that matter, corporations) in a certain degree of schizophrenia, i.e. they often need to be both friends and foes to corporations, sometimes even at the same time (Elkington and Fennell 2000; Crane and Livesey 2003). Perhaps the most fundamental problem here, though, is one of *CSO accountability*, a problem that we discussed in some depth earlier in the chapter. After all, the proposition that CSOs should remain to some extent independent of corporations is based on an assumption that they have a specific task to fulfil on behalf of a certain constituency—and that this task is compromised by a loss of independence. This issue is even more pronounced when CSOs do not merely partner with business, but actually transform into a business, as we shall now see.

☑ Skill check

Evaluating business–CSO collaboration. Collaborations between business and CSOs offer considerable benefits along with important limitations. The ability to identify and evaluate these costs and benefits is critical for determining whether or how such collaborations should go ahead.

Social enterprise

The escalating number of CSO alliances with businesses suggests an increased attention in the sector to using market-based solutions to address social problems. Indeed, the growing influence of business strategies and tools within civil society is undeniable (Eikenberry and Kluver 2004). One facet of this has been the more business-like approach to philanthropy that is evident in the emergence of *venture philanthropy* and *impact investment*. These use financial investment techniques and clear impact metrics to guide grant making and social investments (Moody 2008). Bodies such as the Bill and Melinda Gates Foundation or Google.org, the social venture arm of the Google company, are good examples of this, given their focus on social return on investment, active engagement with grantees, commitment to innovation and technology, and belief in the power of business ideas to address major problems such as poverty, global health problems, climate change, and education.

Beyond the changing landscape of philanthropy, civil society has also incorporated business methods into the very fabric of new organizational forms. The emergence of **social enterprise** as a distinct model of CSO has been a significant development within civil society since the 1990s (Defourny and Nyssens 2006). A social enterprise seeks to take elements of a business enterprise and of a CSO in the same organization—i.e. it forms a kind of 'hybrid organization' that is distinguished by its 'pursuit of the dual mission of financial sustainability and social purpose' (Doherty et al. 2014).

Social enterprise
A hybrid form of organization that pursues a clear social purpose through commercial trade.

As a relatively new phenomenon, the definition of social enterprise (also known as 'social entrepreneurship' or 'social business') remains rather fuzzy, but several key characteristics distinguish social enterprises from either traditional CSOs or from business enterprises. These are summarized in **Figure 10.7**. As the table shows, social enterprises occupy something of a middle ground between a conventional business and a civil society organization (whether promotional or sectional). Some elements they share with the former (such as the production and trade of goods and services for a profit) while others they share with the latter (such as having a distinct social purpose).

Social enterprise originally emerged from the civil society sector, primarily as a way for non-profit organizations to diversify their funding and become more self-sufficient. For instance, the founders of the children's education and development charity, Free the Children, set up the social enterprise, Me to We, to market ethical clothing and educational products as a way of creating a sustainable funding stream for the charity.[13] As the idea has spread, stand-alone social enterprises have emerged with fewer connections to traditional charities, some of which have been registered as regular companies, while others have looked to register under new legal categories such as those discussed in Chapter 6 (Social purpose corporations, pp. 274–275) including community interest companies (in the

	Social Enterprise	Civil society organization	Corporation
Aims	Social and economic value creation	Social value creation	Economic value creation
Role of profit	Profit earning; limits on profit distribution	Non-profit making	Profit maximising
Activities	Production and trade of social goods and services	Production of social goods and services, campaigning, advocacy, research, grant-giving, etc.	Production and trade of goods and services
Funding	Self-funding (at least partially)	Grants, donations, or membership dues	Self-funding
Governance	Based on participation and democracy amongst stakeholders	Based on participation and democracy amongst stakeholders	Based on accountability to providers of capital

Figure 10.7 Key differences between social enterprise, CSOs, and corporations
Sources: Dees (1998); Defourny and Nyssens (2006); Nicholls (2006).

UK) and benefit corporations (in the US). As such, the phenomenon has been met with considerable attention and enthusiasm (Nicholls 2006). Well-known examples include the fair trade confectionary company Divine Chocolate, the UK-based Big Issue company which sells magazines to support the homeless, the microfinance organization Grameen Bank, and the Aravind Eye Hospital in India that provides eye surgery to low-income patients. In many cases, social enterprise has been associated with bottom-of-the-pyramid strategies for addressing poverty that we first introduced in Chapter 8.[14]

Social enterprises can bring a number of benefits to civil society, including the development of more sustainable and diverse funding streams, the introduction of innovative solutions to social problems, greater efficiency and better targeting of services to client needs. However, their novel form also throws up some particular ethical challenges, mainly because of the various tensions that arise in combining divergent economic/social goals, values, norms, and identities (Smith et al. 2013). Some of the most important of these are the following (see Dees 1998; Eikenberry and Kluver 2004; Foster and Bradach 2005):

- **Compromise of social mission**. The demands of the commercial marketplace can place stress on the social goals and purpose of the organization, leading to 'mission drift' away from its founding mission.

- **Moral legitimacy**. As we showed earlier in the chapter, civil society tends to be afforded greater trust than business. Therefore, the more business-like that social enterprises become, the less moral legitimacy they may hold for key stakeholders.

- **Escalation of risk**. Given their role in critical social arenas such as health, education, housing, and poverty, CSOs typically operate in a context of quite highly managed risk. Social enterprise, however, tends to emphasize greater risk-taking and innovation, which can pose threats to both essential services and clients.

- **Prioritization of profitable markets**. The need to secure sustainable sources of revenue encourages social enterprises to focus on potentially profitable social goods and services, where clients are willing to pay, rather than unprofitable areas where clients might be more needy.

Such risks pose important challenges for managers in social enterprises. Given that in many countries, social enterprises do not even have explicit legal recognition as a distinct social form, institutional pressures may well encourage them towards being increasingly understood and practised in more narrow commercial and revenue-generation terms (Dart 2004). However, in being aware of the potential pitfalls, social entrepreneurs can at least steer clear of the major dangers and press for broader institutional change. Indeed, civil society has increasingly taken a stronger role in the regulation of commercial enterprise, as we shall now see.

Civil regulation

In Chapter 9 we saw how some regulation of business could be achieved outside government. At that juncture, we looked mainly at self-regulation by business, corporations 'policing' their suppliers, and even competitors regulating each other through industry partnerships and programmes. As we have already seen in the current chapter, civil society can also be a source of regulation of corporations. Whether through protests and boycotts or various forms of collaboration, CSOs increasingly appear to have the power to shape, influence, or curb business practice. Some authors refer to this as **civil regulation** (e.g. Bendell 2000; Zadek 2001; Vogel 2008; Williams et al. 2011). As Williams et al. (2011) suggest, civil regulation refers to 'arrangements that allow for the involvement of civil society organizations in pressing corporations to deliver improvements in social and environmental standards'.

Civil regulation
Arrangements whereby civil society organizations play a role in defining and enforcing social and environmental standards for business.

Civil regulation, then, goes somewhat further than just the *relations* that CSOs have with business. Rather, we also have to look at the *outcomes* of these processes. Sometimes these outcomes are company or project specific, sometimes they have more lasting impact. For example, it is evident that many of these conflicts and collaborations have led to the establishment of codes of conduct or standards intended to govern corporate action. Such codes clearly encompass aspects of norm creation and enforcement that are more institutionalized and lasting than say a single change in corporate policy made as a result of boycott action. The point is that business collaboration with civil society can sometimes help to build social and political structures that effectively change the rules for whole groups of business actors, or even entire industries. Returning to **Figure 10.6**, we can see that the Marine Stewardship Council, the Ethical Trading Initiative and the Bangladesh Accord, among others, have all had the effect of instituting this kind of civil regulation at both the national and the global level.

The *Ethical Trading Initiative* (ETI), for example, commits its members to adopting its code of practice on workplace standards, and requires that members report on their performance against its provisions. **Figure 10.8** presents the core activities of the initiative and shows how it includes a mixture of rule definition, awareness raising, provision of resources and tools to enable effective operation, and a method for ensuring compliance with its rules. These activities essentially act as regulatory forces on member organizations, since failure to abide by them would, at least in principle, lead to companies being thrown out of the initiative. While this is rare, Levi Strauss was suspended from the ETI in 2007 for refusing to sign up to a principle guaranteeing workers a 'living wage' (Butler 2007).

Probably the main drawback of this and other examples of civil regulation is their voluntary nature. Whereas state regulation is obligatory and usually includes some form of punishment for non-compliance (such as a fine), civil regulation relies on the voluntary commitments of companies. Many companies will not choose to join, and even among those that do, there is always the option to leave if their priorities change. For example, in 2009, the UK retailer Boots pulled out of the ETI due to a change in strategy regarding its approach to ethical sourcing—but it vehemently denied that the move was in any way related to its transfer of ownership into private equity (Mathiason 2009). Although some form of censure is available for civil actors in these kinds of circumstances—they can publicize the incidents, create bad publicity, and even initiate protests, boycotts, and other forms of direct action—this constitutes a relatively 'soft' form of regulation compared to traditional government modes.

Despite such limitations, civil society has certainly taken an increasingly important role in forming codes of practice and even some more formal elements of rule setting and regulation (Zadek 2001). As we intimated in the previous section on globalization, given the apparent absence of effective global government, this is especially the case with transnational regulations, such as those dealing with environmental management

We define best practice in ethical trade

All corporate members of ETI agree to adopt the ETI Base Code of labour practice, which is based on the standards of the International Labour Organisation (ILO). We work out the most effective steps companies can take to implement the Base Code in their supply chains. We learn by doing, and by sharing our experience. Our projects and working groups develop and try out new ideas, often piloting these approaches on the ground in sourcing countries. By taking part in these groups as well as in roundtable discussions, our members collectively establish good practice in ethical trade. We then develop training and resources to capture this learning, providing practical tools to help companies to put their ethical trade policies into effect.

We help workers to help themselves

Codes of labour practice can, and should, help create space for workers to bargain with management through trade unions. In several countries around the world we are supporting initiatives that raise workers' awareness of their rights and helping create work cultures where workers can confidently negotiate with management about the issues that concern them. We also broker resolutions where there are major breaches of trade union rights by companies that supply our members.

We build strategic alliances that make a difference

Finding effective and sustainable solutions to workers' issues requires joint action between companies, suppliers, trade unions, NGOs and governments. We build alliances in key sourcing countries and internationally, to address problems that occur not only in individual workplaces, but also affect entire countries and industries.

We persuade and influence key players

Retailers and brands are responsible for using their buying power to influence their suppliers' employment practices. Governments, employers, trade unions, consumers and the media also have a distinct and vital role. We raise awareness of how everyone can play a part in protecting workers' rights and work closely with governments and international labour agencies to influence policy and legislation.

We drive improvements in member companies' performance

In today's global economy, all companies have issues in their supply chains. By joining ETI, a company is acknowledging these issues and making a commitment to tackling them. Our member companies report annually on their efforts and the results they are achieving at farm or factory level.

We expect them to improve their ethical trade performance over time, and have a robust disciplinary procedure for companies that fail to make sufficient progress or to honour their membership obligations.

Figure 10.8 Core activities of the Ethical Trading Initiative

Source: Ethical Trading Initiative, 'What We Do': http://www.ethicaltrade.org. Reproduced with permission.

or labour conditions. In contrast, at the national level civil regulation is much more rooted to state policies and the law, where CSOs are more likely to work with rather than in place of governments (Williams et al. 2011). Although the business literature has been fairly slow to acknowledge this development, even here the growing influence of civil society in the institutional arrangements facing international business has been recognized (e.g. Doh and Teegen 2002; Dahan et al. 2006). Certainly, CSOs can now at least be considered to be part of the group of actors shaping the rules, norms, and practices of international business—assigning them a place in what writers in the politics literature tend to call systems or regimes of 'global governance' (e.g. Bernstein and Cashore 2007; Vogel 2008). We shall examine the implications of this further in Chapter 11 when we move on to discuss more generally the role of government and regulation in shaping the context of business ethics.

The key point to take away from this section is that civil society can act as a conduit through which individual citizens can exert some kind of leverage on, or gain a form of participation in, corporate decision-making and action. When we speak of corporate citizenship in its fullest sense, the idea that corporations are increasingly involved in governing various citizens' rights suggests that those citizens might need a way of registering their desires and wishes in some way. Voting and consumer choices are two avenues; participation in civil society is another. As we shall see in the final section, this issue of participation also has important ramifications for notions of sustainability.

■ Civil society, business, and sustainability

Civil society has been at the forefront of the development of sustainability theory and practice. This is hardly surprising when we consider that each of the three elements of sustainability—social, environmental, and economic—have been typical foci for CSOs of various kinds, from humanitarian NGOs (social issues), to development agencies (economic and social issues), and environmental activists (environmental issues). Moreover, many environmental and other CSOs are now actually dedicating themselves to advancing the cause of sustainability itself (rather than focusing on specific issues), often through engagement with business among other stakeholders. For example, the mission of Rainforest Alliance is to 'to conserve biodiversity and ensure sustainable livelihoods by transforming land-use practices, business practices and consumer behavior.'[15]

It is, then, the representative nature of the stake held by CSOs that makes them so integral to sustainability in business. At best, corporations can only really claim to represent economic interests. However, progress towards sustainability requires that a wider set of interests are also represented and incorporated in business decisions. Certainly, government is one actor that can do this, but given the retraction of the state and the growth in civil society influence, CSOs also increasingly fulfil this role for social, environmental—and to a lesser extent, economic—interests. As we saw with some of our examples of business–CSO collaboration in the previous section, diverse social, environmental, and economic interests can be brought together to develop solutions that are more balanced on the sustainability scorecard. Of course, it is contestable whether business has to necessarily work *with* civil society to achieve sustainable solutions, but at the very least civil actors have a role to play in encouraging business to take notice of and address particular dimensions of sustainability.

The problem here, though, is that because CSOs are advancing particular interests, they cannot necessarily be expected to agree on what actions are likely to be the most appropriate for corporations to take. Sustainability remains contested in most, if not all, areas where corporations might be expected to act. Hence, if corporations are serious about addressing sustainability, one principal challenge is inevitably going to be how best to balance the *competing interests* of different civil actors. At another level, even once the competing interests of civil society have been taken into account, corporations are still left with the problem of deciding the extent of community and NGO *participation* in decision-making. Finally, some argue that the importance of civil society to sustainable business is so great that companies should not simply resign themselves to the existence of CSOs, but should actively seek to *sustain civil society* through their actions.

Balancing competing interests

Civil society is made up of a wide variety of disparate actors, each of which may be promoting single issues that comprise different aspects of sustainability. While some, such as Amnesty International, will primarily advocate social issues, others, such as the WWF, will promote environmental issues, and others, such as business associations, will promote economic interests. This means that sustainable business needs to take account of such competing interests simultaneously—representing a major challenge for any organization. For example, in recent years, civil interests have clashed in a number of key industries—the energy industry, aviation, agriculture, and tourism—being just some of the examples. If we look to one particularly interesting example, the renewable energy industry, we can see how some of these competing interests might play out.

The energy industry has been the scene of contestation between civil groups for many years, involving a range of issues around oil extraction, power-station location, nuclear power, and more recently, renewable energy generation such as wind, wave, and solar power. If we take the example of wind power, a number of competing civil interests are evident. Many governments and national and international environmental NGOs, for example, actively promote investment in wind-power technologies because they offer clean renewable energy. Similarly, local governments, development agencies, farming groups, and landowners have generally been supportive of wind-farm development because of the financial rewards, jobs, and investment that they bring. However, some local environmental organizations, community groups, conservation groups, and tourism promoters have opposed the erection of wind turbines, arguing that they despoil the countryside and disrupt bird and wildlife. In this sense, wind farms have become a battle of 'green v green' (Lynas 2008).

In some parts of the world this has led to wind farm developments arousing much controversy, and many of them have been blocked. In the UK, for example, campaigns have led to a substantial proportion of proposed projects being refused permission, and until the 2010s, relatively few had in fact been built. As a result, in 2014 just 9% of the UK's electricity came from wind power, compared with about one-third of electricity generation in Denmark, and 20% in Spain, Portugal, and Ireland.[16] Significantly, Denmark appears to have avoided planning protests by developing wind power through a modest step-by-step approach that initially saw four out of five Danish turbines being erected by individuals on their own land rather than in large concentrated wind farms (Houlder 1999).

The debate about wind farms and other renewable energy sources looks set to continue, especially with governments across the world struggling to meet their commitments to reducing climate change emissions, and increasingly concerned about 'energy security' because of their reliance on sources from the Middle East, Central Asia, Africa, and other relatively unstable parts of the globe.

VISIT THE
ONLINE
RESOURCE
CENTRE
for a short
response to this
feature

> **? THINK THEORY**
>
> Think about the triple bottom line of sustainability and set out the various stakeholders that represent the different interests involved in wind power. Is it possible to determine which of the elements of sustainability are deemed more legitimate (or are the most strongly represented) by the stakeholders involved?

Fostering participation and democracy

As the wind-generation industry shows, the range of interests represented by different civil actors often puts them at odds with each other, especially when different facets of the triple bottom line of sustainability are at issue. We have focused here on an 'upstream' activity—i.e. resource extraction and utilization—since it is often here where different interests are most evident, and where local communities in particular tend to be involved. However, we could easily have also referred to the various other areas where different civil actors have fought over specific business issues, including plant closures, gene technology applications, retail park or housing developments, road building, mining, and dam construction.

In some ways, though, the key issue for sustainability in business–civil society relations is not so much that civil groups agree, but that they are able to actively *participate* in decisions that affect them. Many authors writing about sustainability in business stress the need for greater democracy in corporations through community participation. As Bendell (2000) contends: 'organizations ... that affect you and your community, especially when they affect the material foundations of your self-determination, must be able to be influenced by you and your community ... What are required are new forms of democratic governance so that people can determine their own futures in a sustainable environment.' CSOs clearly have a crucial role to play in enabling individuals to participate, at least in some way, in the corporate decisions that affect them. This issue is particularly important for those groups or interests that might typically not have any other voice in corporate decision-making. The natural environment, non-human species, and future generations are all sustainability stakeholders that need CSOs to represent their interests.

Although evidence suggests that corporations tend to limit the degree of participation that civil groups and other stakeholders can exercise—often concentrating more on simply managing them rather than involving them—this does at least provide a *possible* mechanism for participation, although certainly not a guaranteed one (Manetti 2011). However, while arguments about the accountability and representativeness of CSOs themselves are likely to persist, their role in bringing a plurality of interests to bear on corporations undoubtedly makes them important actors in democratizing the evolving sustainability agenda.

Sustaining civil society

As we can see then, in one way or another, whether as irritant or inspiration, CSOs play a vital role in encouraging business towards more sustainable practice. Sometimes this is played out in direct business–CSO relationships, sometimes via their work influencing government regulation of business, and sometimes simply through demonstrating how sustainability can be achieved through social enterprise. Therefore, for companies serious about sustainability, the health and vitality of civil society are crucial.

A flourishing civil society is something that corporate managers in most developed countries take for granted. Therefore their role in ensuring that CSOs prosper is likely to require the typical forms of charity, volunteering, and collaboration that we discussed above. However, in developing and transitional economies, the situation can be very different. As we discussed before, countries such as China have a much less developed civil society, and this situation is replicated across numerous other contexts, including Russia, Eastern Europe, the Middle East, and Central Asia. In these contexts, corporations may find that they need to develop capacity amongst local NGOs to deal with sustainability issues. For example, Sekem, an Egyptian agricultural company that promotes sustainable development, helped to create the Egyptian Biodynamic Association, a CSO that promotes the organic-agriculture movement among the country's farmers and provides them with research and training (Valente and Crane 2010). Similarly, the mining companies AngloGold Ashanti and Anvil Mining have worked with the international NGO Pact to build local community capacity among informal groups and small civil organizations in the conflict ridden Democratic Republic of Congo (Kolk and Lenfant 2012).

This kind of high engagement with the sustaining of civil society itself may seem like a step too far for most companies. However, the importance of a strong civil society, as well as other 'countervailing forces' to business—such as government and the media—should not be underestimated in attempts to tackle sustainability challenges. By their very nature, sustainability problems are complex and multidimensional, often requiring change across a number of arenas. Without an active and effective civil society, corporate sustainability initiatives may lack the legitimacy and impact necessary to develop meaningful solutions.

■ Summary

In this chapter we have discussed the role that civil society plays in business ethics. We have taken a fairly broad definition of what constitutes civil society in order to include the whole gamut of organizations outside business and government that are relevant for corporations to deal with. These CSOs have been shown to have a somewhat different stake in the corporation compared with the other stakeholders we have looked at so far. Specifically, the representational nature of CSO stakes makes their claim rather more indirect than for other constituencies.

In examining the ethical issues arising in business–CSO relationships and the attempts by business to deal more responsibly with civil society, we have charted a gradual shift in the nature of these relationships. Business and civil society have moved from a solely confrontational engagement to a more complex, multifaceted relationship that still involves confrontation but also includes charitable giving, collaboration, social enterprise, and aspects of civil regulation. Regardless of the nature of this interaction, though, we argued that for citizens, local communities, and other groups typically excluded from the decision processes of business, CSOs can act as important conduits through which their interests can be expressed and advanced within business. Although civil groups themselves may not even always agree with each other, the contribution they make to engendering a pluralistic context for business decision-making and action appears to be vital to our understanding of business ethics.

Study questions

1. What are civil society organizations, and what relevance do they have for business ethics?

2. Select one civil society organizations that you have some knowledge of. Who or what does this organization purport to represent—does this make it a promotional or a sectional group? In what ways is the organization accountable to its various stakeholders?

3. 'It is simply not really the company's choice who is and is not a stakeholder' (Zadek 2001: 163). Evaluate this statement in the context of civil society organizations as stakeholders of business.

4. What is a social enterprise? What are the main opportunities and challenges faced by social enterprises in achieving social outcomes?

5. Explain the concept of civil regulation. How appropriate is this term for describing the nature of civil society activities towards companies?

6. What role do civil society organizations play in enhancing business sustainability?

Research exercise

Select a CSO with which you are familiar and conduct some research on its main activities with and/or against business.

1. What are the main tactics and approaches used by the CSO in its relations with business?

2. Would you say its approach has shifted at all over time? Explain your answer.

3. How effective and ethical do you think the CSO's approach has been?

VISIT THE
ONLINE
RESOURCE
CENTRE
for links to
further key
readings

Key readings

1. **Baur, D. and Palazzo, G. 2011. The moral legitimacy of NGOs as partners of corporations.** *Business Ethics Quarterly*, 21 (4): 579–604.

    This article provides a closer look at the important question of how we can judge the moral legitimacy of CSOs when they partner with corporations. It offers a framework for assessing the special stake held by CSOs as well as a set of criteria for determining CSO moral legitimacy based on how exactly they interact with companies.

2. **Doherty, B., Haugh, H., and Lyon, F. 2014. Social enterprises as hybrid organizations: A review and research agenda.** *International Journal of Management Reviews*, 16 (4): 417–36.

    The literature on social enterprises has expanded rapidly since the turn of the century. This article provides an excellent overview of the research to date, focusing particularly on the issues emerging from the 'hybrid' nature of social enterprises in pursuing simultaneous social and economic goals.

Case 10

From conflict to collaboration? Greenpeace's Greenfreeze campaign

This case examines Greenpeace's attempts to develop a solutions-oriented approach to introducing more sustainable technologies in the refrigerants industry. The case details the NGO's initial collaboration with the former East German manufacturer Foron to develop the 'climate-friendly' Greenfreeze refrigerant, and its subsequent negotiations with companies to diffuse the technology across the globe. The case provides the opportunity to examine the approaches open to civil society organizations in attempting to influence corporate policy, and in particular their roles and responsibilities in shaping the rules and norms of global business practice.

VISIT THE ONLINE RESOURCE CENTRE for links to useful sources of further information on this case

In January 2014, the Coca-Cola Company installed its one millionth HFC-free 'climate friendly' cooler, marking a major milestone in the company's effort to phase out the use of HFC refrigerants in its coolers and vending machines across the world. In making the switch from HFCs, the company looked set to prevent the emission of more than 50 million tonnes of carbon dioxide over the next ten years, an amount equivalent to the annual emissions of more than 10 million passenger vehicles.

Twenty years earlier, no one at Coca-Cola or at any of the major players in the refrigeration industry were considering alternatives to HFCs. In fact, if anything, HFCs were considered the environmentally friendly alternative to CFCs (which contributed to ozone depletion) and HCFCs (which also contributed to ozone depletion, but to a lesser degree). However, the campaigning pressure group Greenpeace had other ideas. Over two decades, the civil society organization worked to get its alternative clean refrigerant, 'Greenfreeze', commercialized and then diffused throughout the global refrigeration industry as an alternative to the existing climate-damaging refrigerants that dominated the market. Remarkably, in an industry dominated by big corporations, it was a civil society organization best known for its occupations and protests that proved the commercial viability of a clean alternative and which ultimately helped to develop the new markets and technologies that set the scene for Coca-Cola's transformation.

The emergence of Greenfreeze

Greenfreeze is a refrigerant, i.e. a type of coolant used in fridges, freezers, air conditioners, and other types of cooling appliances. It was first developed by scientists at the Dortmund Institute of Hygiene in Germany in 1989. At that time, most of the refrigeration industry was starting to move from refrigerants using CFCs to HCFCs and HFCs, which contributed less to ozone depletion. However, all of these alternatives, regardless of their impact on the ozone, contributed significantly to climate change. In fact, some HFC gases are up to 11,000 times more harmful to the climate than carbon dioxide, the most widely known greenhouse gas. However, although Greenfreeze succeeded in avoiding both of the main environmental problems of existing refrigerants (and their supposed replacements), the refrigeration industry took almost no notice of the new technology, and the Dortmund project was abandoned.

It was at this point that Greenpeace became involved in the story. The organization is probably best known for its dramatic campaigning activities on the high seas—saving whales, attempting to block nuclear tests, and storming oil platforms, among other things. But in 1992, when Greenpeace entered the Greenfreeze story, it decided to take a different approach to its usual confrontational, protest-based methods. Seeing the significant potential of the new technology, it decided to take it upon itself to champion hydrocarbons to refrigerator manufacturers. So, it was Greenpeace that gave Greenfreeze its distinctive name, and it was Greenpeace that attempted to resurrect the stalled development programme of the new technology.

The task of converting the refrigeration industry was, however, a daunting one. Most of the industry infrastructure, including the manufacturers and their suppliers, was set up for the existing refrigerants and so the major players refused to 'leapfrog' to an entirely new technology. Moreover, the powerful chemical industry, which supplied refrigerants to the fridge and air-conditioner manufacturers, was actively pushing HFCs as the replacement of choice for CFCs. Chemical manufacturers had little interest in developing Greenfreeze commercially since the mixture could not be patented (because it consisted of two common gases) and the technology was free.

In the end, only the former East German manufacturer, Foron Household Appliances, was willing to experiment with the new technology. Like many former East German firms after reunification, Foron was close to bankruptcy, but agreed to work with the Greenfreeze technology as a last resort. In May 1992, Greenpeace secured an arrangement between Foron and the Dortmund Institute, and commissioned ten prototype greenfreeze refrigerators. Before work could be completed though, the German authorities announced that Foron would be liquidated. Greenpeace and Foron rapidly organized a press conference, and almost overnight produced the first Greenfreeze fridge to present at the conference. Greenpeace also launched a grassroots campaign to persuade consumers and the media, and at the last moment Foron was saved and secured additional funding to keep going.

Overcoming barriers

Having overcome its first initial barrier, Greenpeace was to face many more in the years to come. At first, even its own staff posed a threat and the organization faced an internal revolt over the collaboration with Foron. Endorsing any kind of company was a significant departure from Greenpeace's usual confrontational style, and it was viewed by many inside the organization as a 'sell-out'. One member referred to the response as a 'bloody internal battle', not least because Greenfreeze represented the first main attempt by Greenpeace to leverage the market to try and create positive change in an industry.

The main resistance, however, came from the chemical and refrigerator industries. At first they launched press and communications campaigns, warning manufacturers and retailers that the technology was unproven, unfeasible, inefficient, and potentially dangerous—'a potential bomb' no less! However, Greenpeace's publicity machine generated over 70,000 advance orders from consumers, and eventually the claims against Greenfreeze were dropped as Greenpeace successively managed to persuade the government and scientists to test (successfully) for product safety. By the end of 1992 Greenfreeze was certified by the German safety standards authority, and the following February Foron's 'Green Cooler' fridge, using Greenfreeze technology, was awarded the prestigious 'Blue Angel' eco-label.

By 1994, all German manufacturers declared that they would abandon HCFCs and HFCs for Greenfreeze. Greenpeace, of course, heralded this as a major success, but for Foron, the wider adoption meant that the company rapidly lost its competitive advantage. The Greenfreeze technology was available free to anyone (and even Greenpeace received no financial remuneration or royalty for developing the product), so as the more sophisticated rivals adopted the new technology, Foron's precarious financial position and lack of marketing clout left it in a weak market position. The company eventually declared bankruptcy in 1996, and its refrigerator division was purchased by the Dutch firm ATAG.

Greenpeace, meanwhile, took its Greenfreeze campaign into the rest of Europe and ultimately worldwide. As it did so, most manufacturers initially resisted the technology, but with some smart manoeuvring from the civil society organization, most eventually switched. Greenpeace had quickly discovered that its leverage was greatest when it targeted the big brands using refrigeration technology rather than the manufacturers, whose business tended not to deal with the end consumer very often. A milestone in the campaign involved the 2000 Sydney Olympic Games, where Greenpeace targeted the Games' sponsors, including Coca-Cola and McDonald's, branding them 'dirty Olympic sponsors'. The organization even set up a website, CokeSpotlight, and released postcards and badges aping the style of the famous 'Enjoy Coca-Cola' slogan, with the acerbic 'Enjoy Climate Change'. Before long Coca-Cola announced a new refrigeration policy that would see all of its fridges and dispensing machines converted to Greenfreeze.

Similarly, McDonald's responded to the campaign, and in 2003 it opened its first HFC-free restaurant in Denmark. The next major milestone came in 2004 when Unilever, a leading producer of frozen food and ice cream, joined Coca-Cola and McDonald's in launching the Refrigerants Naturally! initiative, the main objective of which was to phase out HFCs in point-of-sale cooling equipment. Unilever has since placed over a million cooling units using climate-friendly refrigerants in every country in which it operates. Not content with this, Greenpeace moved on to targeting major retail brands such as Tesco, Sainsbury's, and Iceland in the UK, all of which eventually made commitments to phase out HFCs.

Greenfreeze goes global ... almost

In the rest of the world, too, Greenpeace was active in promoting Greenfreeze. Developing countries had posed a particular problem since Western multinationals were using their older CFC- and HCFC-based technologies in countries such as China and India. However, in China, Greenpeace played a pivotal role in 'matchmaking' governmental agencies and international donors (such as the World Bank, the German Ministry for Development Aid, and the US Environmental Protection Agency) with key international and local manufacturers. By 2008, Greenfreeze had become the dominant technology in China with a market share of 75%. Although progress in other developing countries was also initially hampered by various factors, including technical challenges, industry resistance, and government inertia, the technology has now been adopted in most major developing countries, including Argentina, Brazil, Indonesia, and India. Indeed, by 2013, over 700 million of the world's refrigerators employed Greenfreeze technology, which represents 40% of global production each year. Through a smart mix of government lobbying, media pressure, consumer activism, and behind-the-scenes dialogue, Greenpeace had succeeded in getting the technology adopted by virtually all of the leading manufacturers in Europe, Japan, China, Australia, India, and South America—almost everywhere in fact except North America.

The continued resistance of North American producers to make the switch to climate-friendly refrigerants remained the last major hurdle for Greenpeace. As one of the world's largest emitters of greenhouse gases, the US represents a key battleground for climate-change campaigners, yet even with major food and beverage manufacturers beginning to switch to alternative refrigerators, US manufacturers continued to stall. Ironically, one of the main problems was the obstacle posed by the Environmental Protection Agency's (EPA) approval process for green alternatives. US manufacturers were clearly reluctant to navigate through the necessary bureaucracy to try and secure EPA approval for the new technology.

In the late 2000s, things started to change at last. Through their relationship with Coca-Cola in Refrigerants Naturally! Greenpeace had the opportunity to engage with the Consumer Goods Forum (CGF), a global network of major consumer goods companies. Following a speech by Greenpeace's 'Solutions' director at the 2010 CGF conference, the members committed to phasing out HFCs by 2015, which meant that most of the largest consumer goods companies in the world, including huge players like Wal-Mart, now had a stake in ensuring that climate-friendly alternatives were available globally.

Greenpeace also worked with Ben & Jerry's, the ice cream company owned by another Refrigerants Naturally! partner, Unilever, to test out the US's first Greenfreeze-cooled freezers in two of its scoop shops as part of a trial approved by the EPA. General Electric followed by announcing its intention to bring Greenfreeze-style refrigerators to the US for the first time. The two companies then made representations to the EPA, which finally announced approval for some climate friendly refrigerants in a limited number of applications (including household refrigerators) in 2011. But in the face of continued resistance, it was not until 2014, more than 20 years after the launch of Greenfreeze, that the EPA expanded its list of approved clean refrigerants and enabled their use in larger-scale, commercial applications as well as air conditioning machines and vending machines. Finally, Greenpeace looked on the cusp of achieving more widespread diffusion in the holdout US market. And Coca-Cola could at last put one of its climate-friendly vending machines in its own Atlanta headquarters.

Questions

1. Set out the tactics used by Greenpeace in the Greenfreeze campaign. Can you discern an overall strategy used by the organization?

2. To what extent would you say that Greenpeace had changed from a conflict-based approach to a more collaborative mode of engagement?

3. Who are Greenpeace's stakeholders in this case? What responsibilities, if any, would you say they had to these stakeholders?

4. How would you assess Greenpeace's relative advantages in pursuing the Greenfreeze campaign compared to a company attempting to diffuse an innovation?

5. In what ways, and in which industries (if any), is the notion of a 'civil regulator' a useful way of describing Greenpeace's role in this case? Elaborate on your answer by looking at the way the campaign was carried out in different parts of the world.

Sources

Environmental Protection Agency 2014. EPA proposes approval of new climate-friendly refrigerants. EPA Press release: http://yosemite.epa.gov/opa/admpress.nsf/0/54F2D8CBA76572A 285257D04004E2F5D.

Murray, S. 2005. Campaigners use peace as a weapon—partnerships: pressure groups need activists who can do deals with the enemy. *Financial Times*, 5 May: 4.

Stafford, E.R. and Hartman, C.L. 2001. Greenpeace's 'greenfreeze campaign': hurdling competitive forces in the diffusion of environmental technology innovation. In K. Green, P. Groenewegen, and P.S. Hofman (eds.), *Ahead of the curve*, 107–31. Dordrecht: Kluwer.

Stafford, E.R. and Hartman, C.L. 2014. NGO-initiated sustainable entrepreneurship and social partnerships: Greenpeace's 'solutions' campaign for natural refrigerants in North America. In M.M. Seitanidi and A. Crane, *Social partnerships and responsible business*, London: Routledge: 164–90.

Stafford, E.R., Hartman, C.L. and Liang, Y. 2003. Forces driving environmental innovation diffusion in China: the case of Greenfreeze. *Business Horizons*, 46 (2), March-April: 47–56.

Stafford, E.R., Polonsky, M.J., and Hartman, C.L. 2000. Environmental NGO-business collaboration and strategic bridging: a case analysis of the Greenpeace-Foron alliance. *Business Strategy and the Environment*, 9: 122–35.

http://www.greenpeace.org.

http://www.refrigerantsnaturally.com.

Notes

1. US data is for 2012, see Katie L. Roeger, Amy S. Blackwood, and Sarah L. Pettijohn, *The Nonprofit Almanac 2012* (Washington DC: Urban Institute Press, 2012). India data is for 2014, see http://qz.com/182757/india-has-2-million-non-profits-and-thats-not-a-lot/. UK data is for 2014, see Charity Commission's 'Recent charity register statistics' at http://www.gov.uk/government/statistics/charity-register-statistics.

2. Two regular surveys that report these findings are the Edelman Trust Barometer (http://www.edelman.com/insights/intellectual-property/2015-edelman-trust-barometer/) and the Globescan Radar (http://www.globescan.com/expertise/trends/globescan-radar.html).

3. See Ethics Resource Center (2008), *2007 national nonprofit ethics survey: an inside view of nonprofit sector ethics*, Arlington, VA: Ethics Resource Center.

4. See Siegel, R.P. (2013). Anti-gay group ends boycott against Home Depot, claiming victory where none exists. Triple Pundit, 16 September 2013: http://www.triplepundit.com/2013/09/anti-gay-group-ends-boycott-against-home-depot-claiming-victory/.

5. For details of the Survival International campaign, go to: http://www.survival-international.org/about/barefoot. For details of the anti-NGO campaign, see http://www.theblueyonder.com/blog/2009/06/irresponsible-ngo-campaign.html.

6. For example, the Co-operative Bank, The Ethical Consumerism Report 2005 (http://www.co-operativebank.co.uk) reported that 28% of UK consumers had claimed to have boycotted at least one product in the past year, while a 2005 international online opinion poll on 15,500 consumers in 17 countries conducted by GMI Poll (http://www.gmi-mr.com) reported that 36% of consumers worldwide were boycotting products.

7. For more details on the charter, see: http://www.ingoaccountabilitycharter.org.

8. For more information, see: http://www.worldwildlife.org/partnerships/coca-cola.

9. See Vodafone Foundation webpages: http://www.vodafone.com/content/index/about/foundation.html. Data reported in: http://www.forbes.com/sites/rahimkanani/2014/07/09/vodafone-foundation-chief-talks-mobile-technology-and-social-impact/.

10. Data sourced from: CECP 2014, Giving in Numbers: 2014 Edition: http://cecp.co/research/benchmarking-reports/giving-in-numbers.html.

11. Corporate giving data sourced from: https://doublethedonation.com/blog/2014/08/top-10-companies-that-donated-to-charity/.

12. Entine 2008 Sell-out at the Sierra Club. *Ethical Corporation*, September, p66. Levere, J.L. 2013. In an overhaul, Clorox aims to get Green Works out of its niche. *New York Times*, 21 April 2013: http://www.nytimes.com/2013/04/22/business/media/cloroxs-green-works-aims-to-get-out-of-the-niche.html?_r=0.

13. For details on Me to We, see http://www.metowe.com. More information on Free the Children can be found at http://www.freethechildren.com.

14. For examples and case study descriptions of poverty-related social enterprise, see Brugmann and Prahalad (2007) and Seelos and Mair (2005).

15. See Rainforest Alliance website: http://www.rainforest-alliance.org/about.

16. UK data, see http://reneweconomy.com.au/2015/u-k-germany-smash-wind-power-records-17562. European data, see: http://www.bbc.com/news/science-environment-25623400.

11

Government, Regulation, and Business Ethics

Having completed this chapter you should be able to:

- Explain the specific stake that governments have in corporations by outlining the double agency that governments assume.
- Describe the ethical issues and problems faced in business–government relations.
- Critically evaluate the shifts in these issues and problems in the context of globalization.
- Critically evaluate the changing role of business and CSOs in the regulatory process.
- Explain the role of governmental regulation in achieving potentially sustainable solutions.

Key concepts and skills:

Concepts	Skills
• Imperative regulation	• Distinguishing the dual stakes of governments
• Private regulation	• Analysing the ethical limits of modes of business–government influence
• Lobbying	
• Corruption	• Distinguishing forms of business regulation in a global context
• Global governance	

■ Introduction

With the growth in corporate attempts to influence government policy through lobbying, political donations, and even bribery, the issue of business relations with government has increasingly become a key facet of business ethics. Is it acceptable for corporations to use their considerable power to shape government policy? Is the government jeopardizing its role in protecting the public interest when politicians sit on the board of corporations? Should powerful business interest groups such as the oil industry or the food industry actively contribute to the development of regulation that is supposed to ensure they operate in society's best interest? These are all crucial questions for business ethics when looking at relationships with governments. And as we shall see, they represent some of the most pressing problems confronting us in an era of globalization, where the lack of a 'global government' makes the 'policing' of multinational corporations increasingly problematic.

In this chapter we will analyse in more depth some of these ideas that have been bubbling up throughout the book—the increasingly political role taken up by corporations, the involvement of private actors in the regulation of business ethics, the weakening of the state in protecting our social, political, and civil rights, etc.—as well as examining some new (but related) issues that arise when looking at the business–government relation, such as corporate lobbying and party financing. Government has a crucial role to play in establishing the 'rules of the game' by which we judge business ethics. However, as we shall see in this chapter, in the era of globalization, the traditional boundaries between business and government have blurred to such an extent that defining these rules has become a matter of ethical concern in itself.

■ Government as a stakeholder

Government is frequently presented as a major stakeholder in business, but before we proceed to specify the nature of this stake, it is important that we define a few terms a little more precisely.

Defining government, laws, and regulation

We have actually come across government several times already in this book. For a start, government is involved in issuing laws regulating business practice. Back in Chapter 1, for example, when we made our initial definition of business ethics, we pointed out that business ethics tended to begin where the law ended. This would suggest that government takes on the role of setting at least the baseline of acceptable practice in business. As we shall see shortly, the government also effectively provides business with a 'licence to operate' in its jurisdiction.

When talking about 'the government' in this context, though, we have to be aware that we are actually talking about a whole group of different actors, institutions, and processes. In democratic societies, the government would include all legislative and executive bodies that act on the basis of parliamentary consent. Furthermore, the incorporation of those functions pertains to various levels: it would start with the legislative bodies at the *transnational level*, such as the United Nations or the European

Commission; it would then include the *national government*, but also in many cases *regional governments*, such as the Welsh Assembly or the government of a Canadian Province; finally, it would also relate to *local or municipal authorities*. In short, government consists of a variety of institutions and actors at different levels that share a common power to issue and enforce laws. By laws, you should remember that in the context of business ethics, we are basically concerned with the codification of what society deems are appropriate and inappropriate actions. Laws serve as a codification into explicit rules of the social consensus about what a society regards as right and wrong.[1]

Looking specifically at laws codifying right and wrong *business* practices, it is important to recognize that the law is only one aspect of the broader area of regulation of business. Although laws are of some relevance to business ethics, it is the role of regulation that it is most vital to understand. This is because it is regulation more generally, rather than the law specifically, which tends to operate in the *grey areas* of business ethics. After all, once we have a clear legal ruling on certain business practices, they are no longer really matters of business ethics. But those that are still open to other forms of non-legally binding regulation certainly are. So what exactly do we mean by regulation here?

Regulation is all about the *rules* governing business behaviour. It includes laws and acts, but also pertains to other forms of formal or informal *rule-making and enforcement*. This includes broader governmental policies, concepts, goals, and strategies, all of which ultimately enable or restrict the activities of business actors. For example, in the UK there are specific laws dealing with issues of discrimination in the workplace, including the Sex Discrimination Act 1975 and the Race Relations Act 1976. In addition to these legally binding rules, though, there are also other *regulatory instruments* that are intended to encourage compliance with non-discrimination through non-legally binding (hence 'weaker') modes of influence. For instance, until the introduction of the Employment Equality (Age) Regulations in 2006, anti-ageism in the UK was tackled by a voluntary code rather than by a specific law. Not all regulation is therefore enforced through the law; sometimes it operates by creating norms that define 'acceptable' behaviour, but which essentially only operate through social enforcement or encouragement.

Originally, most regulation would be issued and enforced by governmental bodies in the narrow sense such as parliament, ministries, and public authorities. However, if we look at the way many financial markets are regulated, we find that the majority of rules that govern actors in these markets are not in fact issued by the government at all, but by a *private* body, such as the Financial Conduct Authority in London or the Securities and Exchange Commission in New York. In a similar vein, in Chapters 9 and 10 we raised the prospect of corporations and civil society organizations becoming involved in regulatory activity. Later in this chapter we will discuss in more detail the role of *private actors* in regulatory processes. To begin with though, it is important to clearly state that regulation is no longer the solitary prerogative of the government: it can be delegated to other parties.

These two clarifications—that regulation is about certain types of rules, and that it operates through governmental and non-governmental actors—lead us to an understanding of regulation at two levels. On the one hand, there is government regulation that is backed up by the sanction mechanisms of police, military, courts, and parliaments—all of

Imperative regulation
Rules that are issued by governmental actors and other delegated authorities to constrain, enable, or encourage particular business behaviours. It includes rule definition, laws, mechanisms, processes, sanctions, and incentives.

Private regulation
Rules that are issued by business, business associations, or civil society actors to standardize and harmonize ethical business practices. Their force normally relies on market mechanisms.

which make governmental regulation strong and leads to its designation as **imperative regulation**. On the other hand, there is regulation issued by companies, industry associations or civil society groups—often referred to as **private regulation**. This results in rules that may also have a binding effect, even though the sanctioning mechanisms might be softer and more indirect—as we have seen in some of the previous chapters on consumers, suppliers, or civil society and their power to enforce business rules and behaviour.

This leads us to one final clarification about the relationship between business and government. When talking about government, the terms 'political' and 'politics' typically arise. Originally, these terms described the governance of the Greek people, the 'polis', and consequently included issuing laws, running the economy, international diplomacy, etc. Over the course of time, however, 'politics' has become a somewhat ambiguous concept, with all sorts of connotations, such as in 'office politics' or 'political correctness', etc. In this chapter, however, we will use the word 'politics' in its original sense. Therefore, when we discuss how companies are getting more involved in 'politics', we mean that they increasingly act in areas that have traditionally been the prerogative of governments, such as regulation.

Let us start by clarifying the nature of the relationship between business and government, and in particular the specific stake held by the government in corporations.

Basic roles of government as a stakeholder

When talking with managers about the government, or even simply skimming through the business press, it does not take long to realize that people in business tend to have a very ambiguous role towards the government. On the one hand, business likes to complain about an over-active government, perhaps because it demands 'excessive' taxes, imposes 'red tape', or because it restricts their activities, for example by blocking mergers or raising new standards for product safety. On the other hand, business also expects the government to be constantly active in protecting their interests, such as improving infrastructure or keeping foreign competitors out of the market.

If we look to this relationship from the government's perspective, the situation is by no means any more straightforward. While politicians like to surround themselves with powerful business leaders and are quite aware of the fact that a booming economy helps their chances at the ballot box, they also have to consider the interests of their electorate, who expect governments to 'police' business and to make sure that it acts for the benefit of society.

We could go on and list numerous examples of the rather complex, interwoven, and often quite contradictory ties between business and government. However, when discussing stakeholder theory in Chapter 2, we determined that a stakeholder of a corporation could be defined by the fact that it benefits or is harmed by the corporation, and/or that its rights were affected by the corporation. Applying this to government, we have to ask the question: how is government affected by business and how are certain governmental rights influenced by corporate action?

In order to sort out this slightly complicated relationship, we have to differentiate the two basic roles of government, which are shown in **Figure 11.1**. These are government as a representative of citizens' interests and government as an actor (or group of actors) with interests of its own.

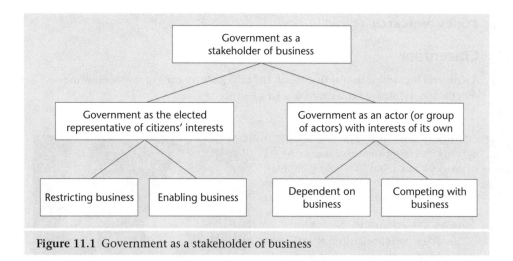

Figure 11.1 Government as a stakeholder of business

Government as a representative of citizens' interests

Unlike many other stakeholders, such as shareholders, employees, or suppliers, government in principle represents an *entire community*, since it is elected by the citizens of a certain town, region, country, or even continent (such as the European Parliament). In this respect, governments are similar to CSOs, which we discussed in Chapter 10, in that they represent the interests of a wider community. In this role as the *representative of citizens' interests*, governments mainly define the conditions for the licence to operate of business.

That said, we have to recognize that this aspect of the governmental role is of different strength in different political systems. In democratic systems, governments have a fairly strong incentive to act in their citizens' interests as they face elections on a regular basis. Of course, it is not always obvious what course of action actually is in the best interests of citizens. Consider the revelations about the US government's National Security Agency using information and communications technology (ICT) companies to spy on the public. While the government may have claimed that such actions were necessary for security reasons to protect the public interest, many took exception at the significant invasion of privacy it entailed. **Ethics on Screen 11** illustrates the major ethical quandaries this can raise on the part of companies by exploring the decision by Edward Snowden to blow the whistle on the government's activities.

In more authoritarian or dictatorial systems, governments might be less concerned about protecting citizens' interests—or at least having to justify their actions in such terms. However, even in such systems, governments cannot survive long term if they constantly violate the interests of their citizens, as the examples of the fall of communism in Eastern Europe in 1989, the end of apartheid in South Africa in the 1990s, or more recently the Arab Spring have shown.

In practice, this definition of the licence to operate normally becomes most visible in areas where governments—in their fulfilment of the electorate's mandate—try to *restrict business*. For example: they issue environmental regulation that forces companies to install filters or to recycle rather than dump waste; they impose taxes on corporate profits; and they investigate whether a merger bid is in the public interest. All of this is done

VISIT THE
ONLINE
RESOURCE
CENTRE
for links to
useful sources
of further
information

ETHICS ON SCREEN 11

Citizenfour

A tense and frightening thriller that blends the brisk globe-trotting of the 'Bourne' movies with the spooky, atmospheric effects of a Japanese horror film.

A.O. Scott, *New York Times*

Citizenfour is a fascinating documentary that not only deals with a range of issues covered in the book so far, but in focusing on internet privacy it does so in a context that has become one of the hottest areas of debate in contemporary business ethics (see also Case 11 for the wider context).

This 2014 documentary takes us to the tension-filled moments in early June 2013 when the former National Security Agency (NSA) employee Edward Snowden turns into a whistleblower (the NSA is the US agency set up after the September 11, 2001, terrorist attacks to gather more comprehensive information on potential terrorism threats). The core of the movie documents Snowden's first meeting with journalists in Hong Kong and sharing his 'intelligence' with them, while the outside world silently and slowly—but unstoppably—encroaches on the small group of twenty-first-century conspirators.

Citizenfour was directed, shot, and produced by Laura Poitras, who put this documentary together as the final piece in a trilogy on how the 9/11 events changed the US approach to human rights at home and further afield. The footage in the movie consists of real-time encounters between Snowden and Glenn Greenwald and Ewan MacAskill, two journalists from the *Guardian* who, together with the *Washington Post*, subsequently published a spate of articles on Snowden's revelations.

By the time of the meetings covered by the film, Snowden had worked for roughly a decade for the CIA and other US intelligence agencies as an IT specialist. In the movie he gives a powerful account of how being exposed to severe breaches of privacy and other constitutional rights of normal citizens caused him to expose the work of the agencies that employed him.

The movie is worth watching in the context of studying business ethics because it

Handout/Getty Images

provides a real-life showcase on how one might apply ethical reasoning in the context of business–government relations. Snowden is well aware that—in a Kantian sense—he breached some fundamental principles that should govern the work of intelligence analysts. But his urge to disclose is fuelled by a utilitarian insight that violating these principles—even putting his life and freedom on the line—is warranted because the revelations in his view would lead to the 'greatest good for the greatest number', i.e. would inform the American public and the global community of the violations of their rights being perpetrated by the US government.

Of course, there is also a business angle on the movie. After all, Snowden shares with the *Guardian* journalists how companies—from cellphone providers to Google, Apple, Yahoo, Facebook, and others—collaborated with the US government in getting access to people's phone records, email, and browsing data. It was revealed in a subsequent documentary on the Public Broadcasting Service (PBS) in the US how complicit Silicon Valley has been in facilitating the breaches in constitutional rights that brought Snowden to the point documented in *Citizenfour*.

The movie also achieves what no classroom discussion on the ethics of business–governmental relations can: how emotionally harrowing it can be to follow your conscience, and take the personal risk (as in Snowden's case) to be prosecuted as a traitor and sentenced to jail. The stakes in the context of government surveillance and antiterrorism are extremely high, and so ethical decision-making, as much as it is about applying thought and reflection, can also be at times such as this an emotional and very personal experience. *Citizenfour* shows us the reality of what it means to be an ordinary computer geek who has to wrestle with the simultaneously intellectual and emotional challenges of making an ethical choice in an intensely important situation.

Following its release, the movie won an Oscar, a BAFTA and a spate of international awards in 2015. This is because it not only deals with a crucial subject of public interest and delves into some quite dark areas of business–government relations, but it is also a gripping piece of cinema.

Sources

Packer, G. 2014. The Holder of Secrets. Laura Poitras's closeup view of Edward Snowden. *New Yorker*, 20 October 2014: http://www.newyorker.com/magazine/2014/10/20/holder-secrets.

PBS documentary *United States of Secrets—Part Two*: http://www.pbs.org/wgbh/pages/frontline/united-states-of-secrets/.

Scott, A.O. 2014. Intent on Defying an All-Seeing Eye. *New York Times*, 23 October 2014: http://www.nytimes.com/2014/10/24/movies/citizenfour-a-documentary-about-edward-j-snowden.html. https://citizenfourfilm.com.

because society wants business to operate in a way that, to stick with these examples: does not threaten the health of present or future generations; contributes to the maintenance of the infrastructure in a country; or maintains free and fair competition for the benefit of consumers.

Free and fair competition, however, is closely linked to the positive side of the government's role towards business (Carroll and Buchholtz 2015: 332–49). In forbidding a merger or regulating the behaviour of traders at the stock market, governments in fact take over a key role in *enabling business* activities in the first place. For instance, if the EU commissioner for competition forbids a merger and thus avoids the gradual emergence of monopolies, they make sure that there is still competition and—ultimately—still a free market as such. In fact, if we look to most of the regulatory functions of governments with regard to business, they have an enabling role more than anything else: markets can only function if basic rules are established and an appropriate regulatory framework exists.

However, the enabling role of the government is by no means confined to markets and other directly economic issues. It also pertains to a number of broader rules in society, such as a reliable and fair legal system, protection of private property, and efficient sanctioning mechanisms for illegal behaviour. Economic transactions rely heavily on safe expectations about the behaviour of the transaction partners. One of the problems of some less-developed countries is that a weak government does not tend to provide the stability that encourages foreign investors to enter these markets. An extreme case in the mid-2010s is Iraq, where next to a weak central government the emergence of an alternative quasi government in the form of ISIS has made it increasingly unattractive for companies to invest in, despite significant business opportunities in reconstruction and exploitation of its resources.

There is, of course, some debate about the degree of governmental responsibility necessary for a functioning economy (Carroll and Buchholtz 2015: 326–29). The options range from a passive, laissez-faire hands-off approach where government just sets the rules and controls the compliance of economic actors, to the other extreme where government assumes a forceful role in 'industrial policy' by actively interfering with the economy. The former approach was dominant in Anglo-American style economies for a considerable time, while many European governments have long operated a much more hands-on approach (Matten and Moon 2008). The financial crisis of the late 2000s, however, seems to have changed this: especially in the US and the UK, governments effectively took control of a number of banks and other companies. Whether this actually represents a general sea change in governmental approaches, though, remains to be seen. Looking beyond the Western context to regions such as South and East Asia, state influence, if not ownership, of business remains high—a phenomenon that we will return to later in this chapter.

Government as an actor (or group of actors) with interests of its own

The motivations for government to take an active role in the economy might be quite strong at times, but it is important to understand that this is not only because they are acting directly in the interests of their electorate. Government can also be seen as an actor (or group of actors), with interests of its own. One reason for this is that governments normally have a self-interest to be re-elected. One could also argue that, in most democracies, the control of the government by the electorate is somewhat indirect. This certainly applies to transnational governments such as the European Commission, but is increasingly an issue in many countries globally. As a result of this situation, we have to assume that government's stake in business is not only as an (indirect) representative of its electorate but also as a direct stakeholder with its own rights and interests.

As such, governments are first and foremost interested in a booming economy. Bill Clinton's by now proverbial US election slogan 'It's the economy, stupid!' (meaning that government success would mostly be judged in terms of competence in running the economy) could be said to be largely true now for many countries. This actually makes governments very *dependent on business*. On the one hand, their electoral success depends on maintaining high employment, increasing incomes, and expanding business activities. On the other hand, none of these things is *directly* influenced, let alone achieved, by government alone. This situation makes government a rather weak and dependent stakeholder, which many businesses are often only too aware of.

Government in this role, however, is not only *dependent* on business, but also *competes with business*. If we think about the privatization of telecommunications, the ownership of television companies, or the increasing usage of private companies in national health-care provision, we can see that business increasingly has also either taken over from, co-operated with, or competed with public organizations in certain industries. This has probably been displayed quite visibly in the recent wars in Iraq, Afghanistan, and several smaller conflicts around the world where we see a clear trend of outsourcing many traditional military tasks to private contractors, often putting army units under keen pressure to compete for their own jobs (Elms and Phillips 2009).

One could argue that in this context, governments are similar to those stakeholders described in Chapter 9, especially competitors. However, the delicate nature of the relations between business and governments when they compete in the same industry derives from their different and/or unequal positions of power. Government enjoys considerable authority and institutional power, since it can define industry rules and exercise legislative power. Corporations, on the other hand, might sometimes enjoy economic advantages, since they potentially have recourse to additional sources of finance for investment that government may be unable or unwilling to generate through taxation.

Having now set out in some detail the two main aspects of the stake held by government, we shall proceed to look at the ethical issues and problems that this complex relationship inevitably raises.

☑ **Skill check**

Distinguishing the dual stakes of governments. Government is an actor with competing interests and so it is important to distinguish between the two main types in evaluating its relationships with business.

■ Ethical issues in the relationship between business and government

From the discussion above, it should already be fairly obvious that the stake (or stakes) held by government puts it in an ambiguous position with business. However, most of the ethical issues that arise in this relationship pertain to the *closeness* of business–government relations. In particular, critics have questioned whether cosy relations between business and government can jeopardize the government's ability to fulfil its role of protecting the public's interest. **An Ethical Dilemma 11** gives you an opportunity to think about some of these problems in a specific example of 'close' business–government relations.

We will start with the basic issues here—essentially problems of legitimacy and accountability—and as we proceed through this section, we will examine the ethical case for different types and levels of business–government interaction. Towards the end of the section we will turn our attention to some further ethical issues that arise from government attempts at privatization and deregulation of industry.

Core problems: legitimacy, accountability, and modes of influence

Probably the main source of ethical problems in business–government relations is to be found in the fiduciary relationship that government has to society in general. What this means is that government is entrusted with the responsibility to act in society's best interests. As **Figure 11.2** shows, government here is in a somewhat ambiguous situation (Stigler 1971; Mitchell 1990). First, government is in a mutually dependent relationship with *society*: government receives consent from society and acts upon this to enact a regulatory environment that protects society's interests. But government also has a relationship with *business* where both partners are mutually dependent on each other for certain things: government is expected to provide a profitable and stable economic environment for business to act in; business is expected to provide taxes, jobs, and economic investment in return.

For government, the main ethical issue here lies in the necessity of carrying out the mandate that society has given it (in a democracy, this would be established through the

AN ETHICAL DILEMMA 11

Always good to have friends in politics

Business deals have always been fairly casual in the little Argentinian town of Bariloche, a popular mountain resort in the foothills of the Andes. Since Juan started his construction business 15 years ago he has won a lot of contracts from the municipal authority: redecoration of the town hall, a new kindergarten, even a nice chunk of the new circular road around town—all of which have kept his 20 employees busy and helped Juan and his family to enjoy a decent lifestyle. Sitting on the patio of his eighteenth-century farmhouse and watching the fumes of his Cohiba cigar slowly vanishing into the sunset, he feels quite at ease—if only there had not been this meeting with Santiago this afternoon.

Santiago is an old friend from Juan's childhood days. But when Juan started working at 15 years old, building houses with his father, Santiago had become a teacher. However, Santiago had soon got bored and before long he went into politics. For ten years now Santiago has been the mayor of Bariloche—but despite his lofty position, the two friends have continued to get on very well.

They normally meet once a month in the back room of a local café, share a glass of Malbec and exchange gossip. Of course, they also talk about business, and knowing what is coming up in the mayoral office has always helped Juan to tailor his bids to the municipal authority's priorities. Not that Santiago has directly pushed things for him—but among friends, they talked about projects and Juan was clever enough to integrate this information into his bids. Of course, he has known how to show his old friend some gratitude: whenever Santiago needed something fixed at his house it was never more than half an hour before one of Juan's employees turned up and sorted it out. And when Santiago gave a party for his fiftieth birthday last year, Juan took over the entire catering for 200 people, including drinks—but this was just a 'birthday present' for his friend.

However, today things seemed a little different. Santiago knew that Juan urgently needed new contracts to keep his company running, and so he mentioned the new municipal swimming pool that was about to be built. Santiago also mentioned that the project manager from another construction company, whom he had met last Sunday after church, had offered to build Santiago a swimming pool at his house if his company won the contract. Now Juan knows all too well that this has been Santiago's dream for years. Not that Santiago had asked for anything, but there was a funny tone to the conversation when he was telling Juan about his chat with the other contractor and about the pool.

Juan could easily fiddle the bills for labour and materials in such a way that a small swimming pool in a private house could be 'hidden' in the accounting of a project of the magnitude of the municipal pool project. But was that taking things a little bit too far? On the one hand, there were his employees and their families: without much other work in the pipeline, they needed Juan to find new work to keep them employed. Besides, doing a favour for an old friend here and there was hardly a crime, Juan reasoned. On the other hand, renewing Santiago's roof after last year's storms had already been a bit of a stretch for Juan. But building a swimming pool was clearly a bigger investment than any of the favours he had provided before. What would his employees say? And if they did not *say* anything, what would they *think*? And what about the rest of the people of Bariloche, what would they think?

The more he thought about it, the more angry Juan started to get—at his competitor for offering his friend the swimming pool; at Santiago for being so cheeky; and at himself for having been gradually dragged into this somewhat puzzling relationship. He decided to discuss the matter with his lovely wife Valentina when she returned from her shopping trip to Buenos Aires later that night. Maybe she would have some good ideas about how to sort out the dilemma.

Questions

1. What are the main ethical issues in this case?
2. What are the main ethical arguments for and against building the swimming pool for Santiago?
3. Would the situation be different if Santiago was a regular business customer rather than the mayor?
4. If you were Valentina, how would you advise Juan to proceed?
5. What should Juan do to deal with this situation in the long term?

electoral process) and to live up to what it has promised to its constituents. One aspect of this, of course, is its constraint and enabling of business. However, sometimes the relationship that government has with business can threaten its ability to live up to its duty to society. As Robert Reich (2007) argues, many of the decisions taken by the US government are not the reflection of citizen's voices but the result of special business interests who have lobbied government officials or paid for their campaigns. The activist and journalist Naomi Klein (2007), in her book *The Shock Doctrine*, shows how in many countries business has gained key influence over governments and provides many examples from developed, as well as developing, countries.

What it boils down to is that business obviously can have a significant influence on the implementation and direction of governmental policies. It is therefore no surprise that the issue of 'public sector ethics' has gained considerable momentum (Dobel 2007). The main ethical consideration arising from this situation is twofold: first, there is the problem of legitimacy of business influence; and second, there is the issue of accountability.

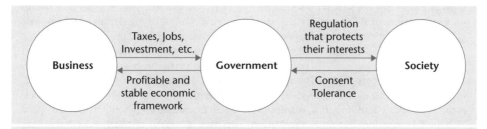

Figure 11.2 Government between business' and society's interests

The *legitimacy* of business influence on government has two sides. On one side, business is perfectly entitled to expect a stable legal and economic framework for its activities. On the other side, if these demands interfere with the mandate of government to act in the interests of its citizens, the line is clearly crossed. This then leads directly to the aspect of *accountability*: since the government acts as a representative of society's interests, the public has a right to be informed about governmental decisions with other constituencies (such as business), and to be able to determine whether it is acting in its interests or not.

Although not the same, accountability and legitimacy are fairly closely related to each other. Accountability will always be a problem when the influence of business on government is perceived as potentially illegitimate. We discussed the issue of accountability of corporations in Chapter 2, and to a certain degree this is an issue in all business relationships with stakeholders. However, the difference in accountability in business–government relationships is that the problem is not just business accountability to its stakeholders, but also the accountability of both parties to society about their relationship. As **Ethics Online 11** shows, the internet has become a crucial platform in providing more transparency and accountability around business–government relations.

VISIT THE ONLINE RESOURCE CENTRE
for links to useful sources of further information

▲   **ETHICS ONLINE** 11

Holding business and governments accountable

The internet has become a critical instrument in the struggle to hold business and government accountable for their dealings with each other and to tackle the complicity of business in human rights abuses by governments. There has been a veritable avalanche of sites emerging on the internet that monitor all sorts of business–government interactions globally.

The different actors in this virtual arena are quite a mixed bag. There are groups such as the London-based Business and Human Rights Resource Centre, which seeks to provide a neutral platform for information. It offers a balanced perspective by, for instance, inviting corporations to comment on allegations published on the site. With researchers on every continent it is certainly the most global source of information on business and human rights, and content is provided in various languages.

In a similar category there is Transparency International (TI), a global civil society organization dedicated to fighting corruption. TI is best known for its annual Corruption Perception Index (see Corruption of govern-

mental actors by business, pp. 507–509) and Bribe Payers Index (Chapter 9, Figure 9.4, p. 410), which are freely available to consult on its website and have become invaluable yardsticks for assessing corruption issues internationally. The organization also reports on stories of corruption around the world and offers resources for those seeking to address problems of corruption, including business–government bribery.

More recently, we have also seen a number of local initiatives emerging around the topic of corruption, such as Corruption Watch UK and Corruption Watch South Africa (the latter co-operates closely with TI). These include social media platforms, such as Corruption Watch Connected, where users can set up regional groups of experts and professionals interested in certain issues and industries.

Another site seeking to offer balanced evidence of business–government relations is the US-based Center for Public Integrity, whose mission is to 'produce original investigative journalism about significant public issues to make institutional power more transparent and accountable'. In the US the issue of business funding political campaigns is a huge issue, and websites such as the Center for Responsive Politics attempt to provide more transparency.

The Center for Responsive Politics also provides in-depth information about the lobbying activities of business in Washington. Interestingly, this topic is now also of wide public interest in the EU where we have seen the emergence of three web-based activist groups in recent years. Corporate Europe Observatory and LobbyFacts are two activist groups that offer in-depth information about corporate lobbying including searchable databases of statistics and other data. Similar work is done by the Alliance for Lobbying Transparency and Ethics Regulation that has roots in the European trade union movement.

Other players in the world of online watchdogs focus on specific issues, an example being Intellectual Property Rights Watch, which reports on a host of ethical issues relating to the involvement of business and other special interests in the design and implementation of intellectual property rights policy. Based in Switzerland and reporting mainly in English, the organization also provides reports in French, Spanish, Arabic, and Mandarin.

Organizations such as these have clearly started to play an important role in generating and disseminating news, data, and insights into specific elements of business–government relationships. In so doing, they help to facilitate, at least in some small way, accountability between governments, corporations, and citizens.

Sources
Alliance for Lobbying Transparency and Ethics Regulation (ALTER-EU): http://alter-eu.org.
Business and Human Rights Resource Centre: http://www.business-humanrights.org/Home.
Center for Responsive Politics: https://www.opensecrets.org.
Center for Public Integrity: http://www.publicintegrity.org.
Corporate Europe Observatory: http://corporateeurope.org.
Corruption Watch South Africa: http://www.corruptionwatch.org.za; social media platform: http://corruptionwatchconnected.org.
Corruption Watch UK: http://www.cw-uk.org.
Intellectual Property http://www.ip-watch.org/.
LobbyFacts: http://lobbyfacts.eu.
Transparency International: http://www.transparency.org/.

In the following, we will analyse some of the more common practices where these concerns of legitimacy and accountability arise from the relationship between business and government. Although both partners are able to influence the other, the main concerns for business ethics are where business has influence on government. This can happen in a variety of ways.

Modes of business influence on government

There are numerous ways that business can influence government. William Oberman (cited in Getz 1997: 59) distinguishes between different ways according to the following criteria:

- **Avenue of approach to decision-maker**. Business influence can range from very *direct* approaches to political decision-makers in person to more *indirect* forms of influence, such as advocacy advertising or media editorial that supports or challenges political decisions.

- **Breadth of transmission**. Influence can also be *public* (and therefore visible to all), or *private*, where politicians are approached behind closed doors.

- **Content of communication**. Finally, influence can either be *information-oriented*, i.e. focusing more on communication of information to persuade decision-makers, or *pressure-oriented*, which would involve more coercive types of approaches.

Ethical problems of accountability and legitimacy tend to arise in *direct* forms of *private* influence. Beginning with the weakest form of such influence—lobbying—we will explore progressively stronger influences that involve more pressure-oriented content, such as party donations, until we arrive at corruption, where government policy is virtually dictated (or 'captured') by business through illicit payments and other forms of bribery. Beyond corruption, we go on to discuss the problems of privatization and deregulation, which see business not so much merely *influencing* government as actually *replacing* it entirely. These different levels of influence that we will be examining are represented in **Figure 11.3**. As we shall see, they bring with them a range of ethical problems and issues.

Lobbying

Lobbying
Activities by business to directly influence governmental decision-making through private communication in the form of information provision and persuasion.

The weakest form of direct, private business influence on government is **lobbying** (McGrath 2005; Vining et al. 2005). For corporations, this area has become increasingly important, and today many major corporations employ professional lobbyists or have an internal manager or unit that is responsible for 'government relations' or 'public affairs' (van Schendelen 2002). Their role is to manage the corporation's attempts to communicate with and persuade government officials about issues relevant to the business. Other lobbying takes place through specialized lobbying firms (such as Burson-Marsteller), industry associations (such as the Confederation of Food and Drink Industries), or broader business associations (such as the Confederation of Indian Industry).

In whatever form it is carried out, lobbying has clearly become a prevalent form of corporate political action (Lord 2000). Lobbying is a rapidly growing industry: total spending on lobbying in the US was $3.3 billion in 2015, with some 12,000 lobbyists working

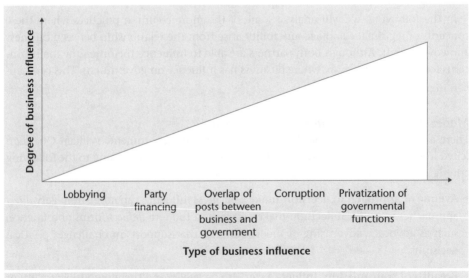

Figure 11.3 Business influence on government

in Washington (Collins 2015). Though the US is often said to lead this trend, recent trends in Europe seem to suggest that lobbying has even overtaken the US in some respects, with 30,000 lobbyists in Brussels allegedly shaping 75% of EU legislation in some form (Traynor 2015).

The key distinguishing feature of lobbying is that it is essentially an attempt by business to influence legislators through providing persuasive *information* rather than explicit *pressure* (Lord 2000). Such 'information' can be in the form of specific data, analyses, or opinions on business-related public policy issues. However, the persuasive nature of this provision of information often also introduces considerable pressure on government decision-makers. For this reason, although lobbying might be considered an important part of the policy-making process because it brings in greater plurality, it has often been regarded as a somewhat questionable activity (Anastasiadis 2014). However, the practice occurs in various guises, some more questionable than others, and includes a broad range of instruments and processes. To get a more concrete picture (and a more comprehensive idea of the ethical implications of lobbying), we might consider the different types of lobbying (see McGrath 2002).

- **Atmosphere setting**. This is essentially an awareness-raising process intended to enhance government appreciation of industry issues and products, and to create a climate or 'atmosphere' amenable to further influence. This may include events, dinners, or information rallies that create visibility for the interests of industry in the government sphere.

- **Monitoring**. An important part of lobbying consists of building up relations with government officials in order to receive reasonably detailed and up-to-date or 'advance' information about ongoing legislative trends and processes.

- **Provision of information to policymakers**. Government actors involved in policymaking cannot hope to know everything about the industries they are dealing with. As a result, they often seek out detailed, first-hand information from the very companies that are the subjects of proposed regulation. Strong relations between lobbyists and policymakers frequently mean that lobbyists are involved in the provision of this information.

- **Advocacy and influencing**. The ultimate goal of lobbying, of course, is not only to inform but ultimately to have an influence on decision-makers. Companies might attempt to do this by offering policy-oriented expertise and 'consultancy', often through industry associations, since they tend to have expert knowledge on certain issues.

- **Application of pressure**. Finally, business lobbying may use the opportunity to communicate with government actors to provide 'information' that is intended to put pressure on them to act in a certain way. This may include implicit or explicit 'warnings' about the potential consequences of particular policies, such as the likelihood of job losses or other politically sensitive outcomes.

In the case of these last three aspects of lobbying, it is not always entirely clear where relatively harmless information provision turns into advocacy or even more questionable forms of pressurization. In order to distinguish between info provision, advocacy, and pressurization, we have to examine specific examples in a particular context. Let us look at a couple of illustrations of successful lobbying in action.

- When President Obama started to draft the first plans to reform health care in the US, the industries related to this project sent 3,300 lobbyists to Washington to influence the reform package. This added no fewer than six lobbyists for each member of congress, and a total of $263 million in lobbying expenditure just in the first six months of 2009 (Salant and O'Leary 2009). It is no surprise then that while the 'Affordable Care Act' (otherwise known as 'Obamacare') led to some substantial gains in covering uninsured poorer Americans, for many critics the law does not go far enough—most notably due to the influence of the pharmaceutical and health-care lobbies in Washington (Brill 2015).

- In 2014 the member states of the European Union reached an agreement to reduce carbon emissions by 40% (from a 1990 base) by 2030. It only later transpired that this agreement was a watered-down version of what many member states and parts of the EU Commission initially had in mind—thanks to Brussels' sixth-biggest lobbyist: the Anglo-Dutch oil company Shell. Spending more than €4 million per year on lobbying in Brussels, Shell allegedly managed to avoid plans to make the 40% goal mandatory for all member states individually (Neslen 2015).

So how should we assess these forms of lobbying from an ethical perspective (see Ostas 2007)? It is obvious that weaker forms of lobbying, such as monitoring of legislative processes or communication with decision-makers in government, are fairly unproblematic. Indeed, they would be expected to potentially improve regulatory outcomes, and may indeed be desirable. However, there is a case to be made about the relative ease of the ability of business interest groups to gain access to political decision-makers, compared with other interest groups, such as civil society organizations, who may lack the resources or presumed *legitimacy* to exercise influence. The main ethical problem is that lobbying appears to enable powerful groups to have an unequal effect on the outcomes of public policy because of the huge investments they are able to make in putting their case and convincing others to pursue a course of action that defends their companies' private interests ahead of the public good. Lobbying therefore threatens the relations of *trust* between governments as supposed 'agents' and representatives of their electorate. The example of lobbyists shaping the health-care reforms in the US or Shell influencing EU regulations certainly raises the question of whether their 'private' interests are the same as those of the wider 'public' electorate.

However, there is still a further aspect. Many regulatory processes are fairly invisible to outsiders, and lobbying is often based on close personal ties between politicians and business. Corporations often use their 'recreational skills' (Dahan 2005) to gain access to politicians in a more relaxed, casual, and informal setting. Typical examples would be invitations to holiday resorts or big sporting events.

VISIT THE ONLINE RESOURCE CENTRE for a short response to this feature

? THINK THEORY

Which ethical theory would be best suited to judge whether the lobbying activity of a corporation or industry association is morally right or wrong? What would constitute 'responsible lobbying' according to this perspective?

Party and campaign financing

A similar situation occurs when industry makes donations to political parties or campaigns. Nowhere has the debate on these issues been more controversial than in the US where—after a number of previous reforms—the Supreme Court in 2010 opened up unprecedented opportunities for business to fund election campaigns. The so-called 'Citizens United' decision posits that corporations should enjoy the same right to free speech as individuals, and therefore should not face any limits on the amount with which they can support politicians running for election. While the effect of Citizens United is still debated (Hansen et al. 2015), the 2012 presidential elections saw a 600% increase in campaign spending, two-thirds of which went to conservative candidates.[2] For the 2016 presidential race, industrialists such as the Koch brothers, the principal owners of the oil conglomerate Koch Industries, have pledged to spend $1 billion on the Republican campaign.[3] Part of the Kochs' agenda is to avoid regulation on climate change, and there is evidence that their money supports candidates who share this view while their funding is used to campaign specifically against candidates that are supporting carbon-reducing regulation (Mayer 2010).

Practices such as these have led to widespread cynicism about business donations to politics. Again, the key issue is the legitimacy of these donations: even if parties are perfectly accountable for the donations—and in a number of countries, politicians are forced to disclose party donations—the temptation to link political decisions to financial support is substantial. Ultimately, some of these party 'donations' could easily be seen as a 'fee' to obtain a certain political decision or other personal favours—which of course raises the prospect of *preferential treatment*, and might even go so far as to threaten the very notion of a democratic process.

As we saw in Chapter 9, there are a number of ways we can look at such 'gifts' to try and determine whether they are acceptable, including the intention of the gift-giver, the impact on the receiver, and the perception of other parties. For business too, though, this situation is clearly a dilemma: while having good relations with political parties seems to be a necessity in many industries, the instrument of party financing can be a double-edged sword. It gains influence—but it could also severely harm the company's image and perhaps encourage questionable behaviour on the part of employees.

The ethical dilemma for corporations becomes even more complicated given that they are not the only ones who work hard at gaining influence with political parties: in an attempt to professionalize their strategies, CSOs have also increasingly sponsored political parties and events (Harris and Lock 2002). This partly brightens the moral terrain of party financing, since corporations then are more or less part of a general trend in society—although again the problem of the differential resources available to business actors compared with civil actors needs to be raised.

Of course, one possible way of dealing with these problems is for corporations to simply introduce rules that forbid political donations. For a while, this was supposedly the response of BP, one of the world's largest oil companies. In the early 2000s BP banned any funding of political parties, with its code of conduct stating that it would 'make no political contributions, whether in cash or in kind, anywhere in the world.' Although such a move was certainly commendable for making a stand on an issue of increasing contestability, there was more to BP's decision than initially met the eye. First, the firm continued to contribute millions of dollars to political groups and political action committees (PACs) that it regarded as outside the scope of its policy (Leonnig 2010). Second, with its tax contributions, spending power, and over 100,000 employees world-wide, BP is a typical representative of a group of multinationals that do not necessarily need to do extra party financing in order to be worthy of governmental attention. In addition, BP has been able to take advantage of close relations with the UK government through personnel shifts between the two organizations (Maguire and Wintour 2001), a widespread phenomenon often referred to as a 'revolving door' (Wilks 2015). This has created close informal ties between the company and the government, and of course, these ties conceivably allow the same kind of lobbying efforts that we mentioned earlier, without actually needing to specifically invest in formal 'lobbying'. But this, as we shall now see, raises a different kind of conflict of interest problem at the individual level.

Overlap of posts between business and government: individual conflicts of interest

'Revolving doors' between business and government are common in Europe or North America but have also been identified in other parts of the world. In Japan, for example, it is a common phenomenon for politicians to move into careers in the private sector and vice versa (Hayes 2009). However, if a company's managers go to work in govern-ment, we might reasonably ask whether they are acting for the government (as an agent of the general public) or for the company (as an agent for its shareholders). Clearly, this overlapping of posts raises quite substantial individual-level conflicts of interest when there is a clash between the two agency relations involved.

It is not only business people working for the government that is the problem though. The overlap works both ways. Many senior politicians have secured positions on the boards of large companies or in other senior advisory roles. In the UK, between 2000 and 2014, 600 former ministers and high-ranking civil servants were appointed to over 1,000 different business roles (Wilks 2015). In France, which still has a considerably high government ownership of corporations, the overlap of interests between business and government is so substantial that some elements of the media identify a 'crippling cronyism' in the French government.[4]

A particularly well-known case is that of former Italian Prime Minister, Silvio Berlusconi. During his times in power from 1994 to 1995, 2001 to 2006, and 2008 to 2011, Berlusconi, as the owner of Italy's three major television stations and largest publishing house, was able to virtually dominate the media and thereby marginalize criticism of his government.[5] Various contestable bills were debated in parliament without major media coverage inside the country. Moreover, revelations in 2009 about Berlusconi's alleged improprieties with prostitutes led to a swathe of writs from the prime minister in an ef-fort to block coverage in the non-Berlusconi owned newspaper *La Repubblica* as well as in several foreign magazines and newspapers. A controversial documentary, *Videocracy*, released in the same year and which was highly critical of Berlusconi's influence on de-mocracy and the media in Italy, was also refused airing by national TV networks RAI and Mediaset because it was 'offensive' to the reputation of their boss.[6]

The ethics of occupying a dual role in business and politics is therefore somewhat questionable. On the one hand, it could be argued that it has certain advantages if politi-cians have had experience of the business world and vice versa. It certainly makes politi-cians more aware of the economic realities underlying many of the issues about which they have to decide. It might be suggested even that industry experience can provide politicians with a more professional style of work and decision-making compared to what normally dominates the rather bureaucratic structures of the public domain. All of these factors could enable a more efficient approach to political work and therefore might be argued to be in the best interests of society. Close links between business and politics might also be an advantage in industries and projects whose success is strongly reliant on political factors. Examples could be entry into foreign markets, where the principle 'the flag goes and the trade follows' seems to have been a successful approach for some countries and industries. This more *utilitarian argument* would, in fact, see some benefit in a close overlap between business and politics.

On the other hand, there are also quite significant ethical problems linked to such a close amalgamation of business and politics. When the newly elected Obama administration appointed a former VP for public policy at Monsanto (a company manufacturing all sorts of controversial products such as genetically modified seeds or growth hormones for use in agriculture) to a senior position in the Food and Drug Administration (the top consumer safety agency in the US) this decision met with much controversy. Activists referred to this appointment as the 'fox watching the hen house' since one of the main responsibilities of his office included regulating his former employer (Flock 2012).

Whatever the rights and wrongs of appointments such as these, it makes obvious the problems that can arise when we have politicians who are entitled to set the rules of the economic game also acting as players in the game. If a company or an industry is able to influence and manipulate the rules towards its own interests, this potentially violates the principle of justice, most notably the notion of *procedural justice*. This particular notion of justice underlies the set-up of modern democracies since it focuses particularly on fairness and equality in the treatment of parties involved in the political process. Democratic institutions are tailored towards the representation and the pursuit of the interests of all members of society and not just towards those with the most economic power.

? THINK THEORY

Consider the principle of procedural justice in the context of the 'revolving door' between business and government. Are there ways to make these types of appointments fairer from a procedural justice point of view?

VISIT THE
ONLINE
RESOURCE
CENTRE
for a short
response to this
feature

Corruption of governmental actors by business

So far we have been discussing forms of business influence on government that, although they may be in the grey areas of business ethics, are legal in most countries. However, a more extreme form of business influence that occurs quite widely, but tends to be more often classified as illegal, is the direct payment of bribes to government officials by businesses. Where this is intended to 'buy' an influence on regulation, we refer to it as **corruption**.

Corruption can occur in many contexts and sectors, but when talking about government corruption in relation to business, we are mainly concerned with activities where private firms shape the formulation, implementation, or enforcement of public policies or rules by payments to public officials and politicians. In a certain sense, corruption is the most direct, private, and straightforward way of influencing governments. The

Corruption
Practices by
individuals or
organizations
that lead to
the abuse of
entrusted power
and authority for
private gain.

offer of bribes and other forms of corruption to gain influence over politicians is a major problem in many parts of the world. The international anti-corruption pressure group, Transparency International, produces an annual Corruption Perception Index (CPI), a listing of different states and the degree to which their public officials and politicians are perceived to be susceptible to corruption. Some highlights of the 2014 CPI are shown in **Figure 11.4**.

As the CPI shows, government officials in countries such as Denmark, New Zealand, Finland, and Sweden are among those perceived to be least susceptible to corruption, whilst countries with ongoing conflict, high levels of poverty, and failed institutions, such as Somalia, Iraq, Afghanistan, and Sudan, score very low. However, it is not just poverty (as some contend) that influences a country's place on the scale. Interestingly, countries such as Turkey and China—both emerging and relatively prosperous economies—have been downgraded on the 2014 index due to egregious incidents of government corruption. **Ethics in Action 11.1** features an example of corruption from Brazil—another emerging economy. But it also showcases potential avenues for companies to deal with this often-endemic phenomenon.

In light of the above, the ethics of corruption probably should be beyond much doubt. However, the dilemma for corporations in highly corrupt countries seems to be largely unavoidable. One might argue that when so many economic actors effectively 'buy' public officials, it becomes a necessity for all businesses to do so. This argument, however, leads us directly into the controversy about ethical absolutism and relativism that we introduced back in Chapter 3 and which has arisen a number of times throughout this book. Ultimately, from the perspective of Western democracies, this situation is beyond what we would regard as an ethically acceptable situation given the corrosive effects of corruption on societies. Moreover, if instead of the rule of law there is the rule of the most powerful corporations, then individual business is subject to governmental arbitrariness and despotism. When property rights are not granted, and contracts are not reliable, business ultimately becomes very difficult and uncertain (Hellman and Schankerman 2000). From an ethical theory perspective, this is a good example of Kant's theory, most notably the first part of the categorical imperative test: if state capture becomes a 'universal law', a normally functioning economy becomes nearly impossible.

VISIT THE ONLINE RESOURCE CENTRE for a short response to this feature

> **? THINK THEORY**
>
> Corruption has also been addressed from the perspective of consequentialist theories. How would these apply to state capture as discussed here?

Ethical issues in the context of privatization and deregulation

If corruption sometimes represents situations where business can dictate certain aspects of government policy, then privatization takes us into a situation where government effectively cedes responsibility for the provision of certain goods and services to business completely. Although we certainly would not want to suggest that privatization raises the same kind of fundamental ethical problems as corruption, there are a number of issues and dilemmas that we need to address.

Rank	Country	CPI score	Rank	Country	CPI score
1	Denmark	92	50	Malaysia	52
2	New Zealand	91	53	Czech Republic	51
3	Finland	89	54	Slovakia	50
4	Sweden	87	55	Bahrain	49
5	Norway	86	55	Saudi Arabia	49
5	Switzerland	86	61	Croatia	48
7	Singapore	84	61	Ghana	48
8	Netherlands	83	63	Cuba	46
9	Luxembourg	82	64	Turkey	45
10	Canada	81	67	Kuwait	44
11	Australia	80		South Africa	44
12	Germany	79	69	Brazil	43
12	Iceland	79		Bulgaria	43
14	United Kingdom	78		Greece	43
15	Belgium	76		Italy	43
	Japan	76		Romania	43
17	Barbados	74		Senegal	43
	Hong Kong	74	85	India	38
	Ireland	74		Thailand	38
	United States	74	100	China	36
21	Chile	73	103	Mexico	35
	Uruguay	73	107	Argentina	34
23	Austria	72		Indonesia	34
24	Bahamas	71	126	Azerbaijan	29
25	United Arab Emirates	70		Pakistan	29
26	Estonia	69	136	Iran	27
	France	69		Nigeria	27
	Qatar	69		Russia	27
31	Botswana	63	145	Bangladesh	25
	Cyprus	63		Kenya	25
	Portugal	63	161	Venezuela	19
	Puerto Rico	63	169	Turkmenistan	17
35	Poland	61	170	Iraq	16
	Taiwan	61	171	South Sudan	15
37	Israel	60	172	Afghanistan	12
	Spain	60	173	Sudan	11
39	Dominica	58	174	Korea (North)	8
	Lithuania	58		Somalia	8
	Slovenia	58			
42	Cape Verde	57			
43	Korea (South)	55			
	Latvia	55			
	Malta	55			
	Seychelles	55			

CPI Score relates to perceptions of the degree of corruption among government officials as seen by business people and risk analysts, and ranges between 100 (highly clean) and 0 (highly corrupt).

Figure 11.4 Corruption Perception Index (CPI) for selected countries

Source: Adapted from 2014 Corruption Perception Index. Copyright 2014 Transparency International: the global coalition against corruption. Used with permission.

VISIT THE ONLINE RESOURCE CENTRE for links to useful sources of further information

ETHICS IN ACTION 11.1   http://www.ethicalcorp.com

Corruption risk and opportunity
Andrea Bonime-Blanc, 17 February 2015

A widening corruption scandal is swirling around Brazil's state-run oil giant Petrobras amid allegations that former senior executives, construction companies, and politicians funnelled kickbacks from hefty oil contracts.

According to the police, federal prosecutors, and the testimony of former company executives involved in the scheme, Petrobras officials conspired with service companies to overcharge for goods and services. Some of the extra revenue from the inflated contracts was then kicked back to executives and politicians as bribes and campaign contributions. Brazilian authorities said on 29 January 2015 that the kickback scheme involved at least $800 million in bribes and other illegal funds, but the figure could change as the case develops. Several top executives from some of Brazil's biggest construction and engineering companies remain jailed as the investigation continues.

The scandal has dealt Petrobras a heavy financial blow. The company said it would cut its investments in 2015 because of its current financial situation and losses resulting from the corruption case. In an effort to repair its reputation, Petrobras has also hired a compliance officer to head the company's first compliance programme.

Yet, a smart, long-term strategic solution would require the CEO and the board to to proactively lead the anti-corruption effort in a broader, holistic manner, investing in creating a sustainable culture of integrity—with all the right policies, incentives, and performance metrics in place for the long term.

Turning the corruption challenge into a reputation opportunity

There are many and different opportunities for bribery and corruption in the oil and gas industry, each of them with related reputation consequences. Being prepared for corruption risks means protecting or even enhancing the company's reputation.

First, the central role of government agencies in overseeing virtually all aspects of the oil and gas sector presents multiple risks and opportunities for bribery and corruption. As governments at all levels grant or deny rights to oil and gas companies, businesses have an opportunity to improve their reputation by implementing an effective and predictable due diligence co-ordination and execution protocol that understands the role of the government. In practice, this means co-ordination of the legal, compliance, finance, project, and business development aspects of the business.

Second, the complex, extensive and diversified oil and gas supply chains mean that the sector is well exposed to third-party corruption. To mitigate these risks, companies should implement well-defined policies and effective platforms to proactively manage and oversee third parties in all aspects of the business.

Third, oil and gas companies are especially prone to suffering reputational losses from environmental, health and safety (EHS) corruption-related incidents. Again, there is an opportunity to enhance reputation by putting in place strong auditing and other EHS controls.

Finally, community relations at the local level can be fraught with human rights, labour rights, security, and corruption issues. To mitigate these risks, businesses should develop comprehensive community engagement strategies that work in parallel with their corporate anti-corruption policies.

The reputation risk from corruption goes along with other risks, especially ESG (environment, social, and governance) risks. Reputation damage typically arises when a company pretends to have proper anti-corruption measures in place but gets caught in a corruption scandal. As a result, the company incurs fines and suffers business losses, such as plummeting stock market prices. For example, last year the French industrial group Alstom agreed to pay a record $772.3 million fine for bribing officials to win power and transportation projects from state-owned entities around the world.

The corollary to such risks is the reputation opportunities associated with corruption—where a company has proper anti-corruption programmes and detectors in place that systematically investigate and report corruption incidents, when necessary, to the authorities. In this case, companies both meet their stakeholders' expectations and enhance their reputation and business value. In 2012 Morgan Stanley and in 2013 Ralph Lauren, for instance, investigated bribery incidents within their companies and voluntarily disclosed their findings to the government.

Sources

Ethical Corporation, Andrea Bonime-Blanc, 17 February 2015, http://www.ethicalcorp.com.
Reproduced with the kind permission of Ethical Corporation.

? THINK THEORY

Corruption is often criticized on the basis of non-consequentialist thinking. However, the Petrobras example can also be examined from the perspective of consequentialism. How would a utilitarian assess this situation and what does this tell you about the moral acceptability of corruption?

VISIT THE ONLINE RESOURCE CENTRE for a short response to this feature

---

Starting in the US and the UK during the 1980s, the world has experienced a strong move towards privatization of public industries such as public transport, postal services, telecommunications, and utility supply. This development coincided with, and was partly due to, quite substantial deregulation of certain industries and markets. This deregulation led to a situation where private businesses were allowed to enter industries that formerly were dominated, if not totally controlled, by public organizations. Similar developments took place later in the rest of Europe, Australasia, and Latin America and are still ongoing in many developing countries (Klein 2007). In a similar vein, the fall of the iron curtain propelled the major state-owned companies of Eastern Europe and the former Soviet Union into the privately owned capitalist system, entailing more or less similar consequences.

The common perception of state ownership is that large public service monopolies tend to be inflexible, bureaucratic, and typically deliver average quality at high costs (Wong 2009). So, for instance, the owner of Capita, one of the major private sector companies to have taken over provision of administrative services in the UK public sector service, boasted that it took his company seven hours to reach a decision that would have taken seven weeks in the civil service.[7] However, the results of the process of privatization have been mixed: while some of the newly privatized companies and industries, especially in the area of telecommunications and utilities, have been quite successful, other privatized corporations struggle and have not been able to provide reasonable quality and profitability. The picture is even more mixed from an ethical point of view (Jones 2001). Let us consider some of the common issues:

- **Privatization profits**. Considerable debate has taken place about the price at which formerly public companies should be 'sold' to private owners. If too high a price is charged, the new owners may feel exploited if their investment subsequently attracts a far lower valuation than their initial investment. For example, when Deutsche Telekom (owner of the T-Mobile brand) was privatized, the share price immediately sank dramatically below the price of the initial public offering (IPO), thereby infuriating shareholders. If too low a price is charged, a small group of investors taking over a former public utility might end up making huge profits on what were essentially public assets that ultimately belonged to the taxpayer. For instance, privatizations in Russia during transition resulted in super-rich oligarchs and an impoverished state and citizenry. Apart from the fact that stock-market prices ultimately are not predictable, a key ethical challenge in privatizing state-owned companies is to find a *fair price*.

- **Citizens turned consumers**. Postal services or public transport—to name just two examples—were originally under the care of governments because these services were considered a component of the social entitlements of citizens. One reason the state became involved in such services was to ensure that provision of basic services was supplied to all, regardless of where they lived or the cost of providing the service. However, a privatized postal service might argue that it cannot run a post office in rural Lapland or a Himalayan mountain village because there are only a few families in the village. It has to take these decisions on an economic rather than a political basis— which may mean that these families will no longer have a post office or bus service. In the absence of regulation, these issues typically cause controversy and confront corporations with difficult ethical dilemmas.

- **Natural monopolies**. Telecommunications, railways, and other utilities that deliver their services via networks—be they cables, rails, or tubes—cannot easily be privatized and opened up to competition because of the degree of integration that is necessary for them to function effectively. To give a simple example, it is technically and economically infeasible for a new rail company to build a new rail network next to a competitor's. For this reason, such industries are sometimes called *natural monopolies*. Generally, under the privatization of natural monopolies, access to and prices for using such networks are largely determined by governmental policy. However, experience shows that corporations may exploit this situation by either overcharging customers or delivering poor quality.

Next to full-on privatization, there has also been considerable debate about *public–private partnerships* (PPPs). The central idea of PPPs is that the government is still responsible for a considerable part of the project, while private companies bring in the investment. PPPs have been especially popular in the UK and Australia, while thousands of PPPs have also been documented in developing countries (Rufin and Rivera-Santos 2012). Well-known examples include the London Crossrail project, the Sydney Harbour tunnel, and India's Bangalore International Airport.

The performance of PPP projects, though, remains in question, with evidence suggesting mixed results so far on their effectiveness (Hodge and Greve 2007). In the UK, where PPPs have been extensively used for decades (most recently under the label of the Private Finance Initiative), a Treasury Committee report commissioned by the government found the initiative 'has the effect of increasing the cost of finance for public investments relative to what would be available to the government if it borrowed on its own account.' The general result seems to be that although PPPs can speed up infrastructure development and expand the range of finance possible, the profit-maximization rationale of the private sector can dominate PPPs at the expense of quality and value for money for the public. In addition, one of the key ethical challenges here is that PPPs often lack the kinds of reporting to the general public that would 'achieve accountability for public money that is increasingly spent in the private sector' (Shaoul et al. 2012).

Regardless of the possibility of raising ethical problems, it would appear that privatization, deregulation, and public–private partnerships are likely to continue to be a major feature of the economic landscape for firms, whether at home or further afield in developing countries. As this shows, governments are increasingly recognizing that new regulation is sometimes necessary to manage the involvement of private actors in providing public services. Moreover, as we shall now see, such developments are also part of a broader shift in relations between the state and business that has arisen from the process of globalization.

☑ **Skill check**

Analysing the ethical limits of modes of business–government influence. Understanding what constitutes appropriate and inappropriate influence on government by business is essential for determining the ethics of business–government relations.

■ Globalization and business–government relations

In Chapter 1 we defined globalization as 'the ongoing integration of political, social and economic interactions at the transnational level, regardless of physical proximity or distance'. Globalization thus has created a new space for the types of interactions between business and government that we have discussed so far in this chapter. To a large extent, these interactions can be conceptualized in terms of what is often referred to as global governance—namely the management of international affairs, whether

Global governance
The management of economic, social, ethical and environmental issues beyond national borders through rules, standards and norms. It involves governments, international organizations, civil society, and business.

social, economic, ethical, or environmental, by various actors including (not limited to) government.

The concept of **global governance** contrasts with how we might traditionally think about business–government relationships, where the governance of business was typically focused at the level of the nation state and was restricted primarily to governments setting and enforcing the rules for business. What we have seen throughout the book though is that the need to regulate and enforce ethical business behaviour clearly transcends national borders, as the examples of financial markets, the internet, or climate change illustrate quite vividly. Conspicuously then, it is often multinational corporations and CSOs rather than just national governments that get involved in governing business behaviour at the global level (Detomasi 2015). As we have seen in Chapters 9 and 10, these additional actors in the realm of global governance participate not just through conventional imperative regulation but also through forms of private regulation that involve various rules, standards, and norms.

One consequence of globalization is that it begins to change the roles of government and corporations. In the national context, governments are in the politically dominant position, since they hold the authority to govern business. In the global context, though, many argue that companies have gained significant political power (Fuchs 2005; Wilks 2013). The main reason for this is not so much that they find themselves in a position where they could wilfully violate national regulation. Rather, it is based on a phenomenon that Ulrich Beck (1998) has described as the 'corporate power of transnational withdrawal', namely that in a global economy, corporations can quite easily threaten governments that they will relocate to another country if certain 'undesirable' regulations—such as health and safety standards—are enforced. As national governments depend on corporations in terms of employment and tax payments, this situation puts companies in a position of relative power. Another source of political power of companies, however, is based on the fact that many multinationals have considerable economic power of their own. Corporations can have a substantial influence on global developments simply because of their size, scope, and resources.

The consequences of these changes is that business finds itself in a situation where it is still operating within the traditional national context, as well as being a key actor at the global level. This leads to four distinct constellations where business–government relations have been transformed through globalization, which we will discuss in the remainder of this section.

Business as an actor within the national context

Businesses are still located within nation states and they are therefore still subject to national imperative regulation. As we have already noted, globalization has weakened governments' ability to impose imperative regulation as companies have ample opportunity to escape national rules. A powerful example is the spate of tax scandals around US companies such as Amazon, Apple, eBay, Facebook, Google, and Starbucks who were found substantially reducing, if not eliminating, tax payments in some of their European subsidiaries. For instance in the UK, these six companies had revenues of an estimated $21 billion in 2014 on which they just paid a paltry 0.3% tax (Sommerlad 2015).

As with all general trends, there is of course considerable variation. In general, the ability of governments to use the more traditional imperative regulation remains powerful in areas where companies do not dispose of strong internationalization options (Rugman and Verbeke 2000). Furthermore, the increase in transnational regulation still results in a considerable increase in imperative regulation at the national level. Governments are responsible for the national implementation of, for instance, the Kyoto Protocol or certain EU directives. Since these treaties apply to many countries simultaneously, the power of transnational withdrawal for companies is certainly limited.

Business as an actor within the national context of authoritarian/ oppressive regimes

Considering business–government relations in the context of globalization, though, it is necessary to also highlight situations where business becomes an actor in authoritarian and oppressive regimes. Recent discussions of this issue have focused on countries such as Zimbabwe, Russia, China, Burma, and Sudan. The crucial ethical dilemma here is that multinationals that want to operate in these countries have to collaborate to a certain degree with the regime. This is shown quite visibly in the case of internet providers such as Yahoo or Google in China (see **Case 11**).

Next to collaborating, multinational presence in these countries also can be said to contribute to the economic stability and wealth of the existing regime. Therefore, even without directly collaborating with the regime, the presence of Western companies can be deemed to be contributing to their support. With the rise of multinationals from India, China, and Brazil, finding an ethical approach is by no means uncontroversial, as the case of Sudan and its government's alleged human rights abuses in the mid-2000s in Darfur has shown. While many Western pension funds started to divest in companies involved in Sudan and many companies pulled out of the country, the vacuum was filled by other players with less-favourable approaches to human rights, such as Chinese companies (Ethical Corporation 2006).

As Nien-hê Hsieh (2009) argues, multinationals in those contexts have a duty to contribute to the establishment of background institutions that normally protect human rights in democratic systems. He points to a number of areas where multinationals have a moral duty to become involved:

- Upholding human rights through normal business operations. This argument was used specifically in the case of multinationals in apartheid South Africa in the 1970s and 1980s, where in particular multinationals from the US refused to adopt the apartheid rules in their own operations.

- Contributing to economic development. As we have seen in the context of corruption, there is some form of link between poor governance and poverty. By operating in a developing country, a multinational can bring wealth and economic development to the country. This would also include multinationals becoming involved in providing education, infrastructure, or health care to the communities in which they operate.

- Direct involvement in creating background institutions for good governance. Companies such as Statoil in Venezuela or BP in Azerbaijan have run or sponsored programmes to train local judges or police officers in human rights and good governance. This might also include the encouragement of workers to join or found trade unions and other CSOs.

VISIT THE
ONLINE
RESOURCE
CENTRE
for a short
response to this
feature

> **? THINK THEORY**
>
> Reflect on the role of Western multinationals operating in oppressive regimes and countries with poor governance. What argument, based on one or more of the ethical theories in Chapter 3, can you make in favour of an obligation for multinationals to build fair background institutions in those countries?

Business as an actor in the global context

At a global level, we argued earlier that corporations assume a more dominant role, while governments—bound by their confinement to territorial boundaries—have only limited influence beyond national boundaries. The central ethical problem here is that business can find it easier in less-developed countries than in Western democracies to negotiate about tax levels, standards for environmental, health and safety protection, or human rights. As we saw in Chapter 1, the result of this process is the so-called 'race to the bottom' between developing countries, trying to attract foreign investment by offering ever lower standards of social and environmental protection (Scherer and Smid 2000).

Popular sentiment seems to be that this deterioration in standards is a real issue (e.g. Korten 1995; Hertz 2001b; Klein 2007), and some empirical evidence has supported the general hypothesis (e.g. Davies and Vadlamannati 2013). However, it is by no means uncontroversial (e.g. Rugman 2000). While some argue that there is an equally compelling case for a 'race to the top' in adopting standards (e.g. Saikawa 2013), others also point to the fact that multinationals in developing countries have a positive influence on standards. So, for instance, Christmann and Taylor (2001) argue that multinationals in China actually improve environmental performance since they introduce their environmental management systems (such as ISO 14000) in their Chinese subsidiaries.

This argument in itself is only partly convincing (environmental management systems tend to be process standards rather than a performance measures); it nevertheless leads us in an interesting direction. Although governments in developing countries may be unlikely to provide 'imperative' regulation that *forces* companies into more ethical behaviour—either because they do not dare or do not care—we increasingly witness that business *itself* assumes an active role in setting up certain types of regulation. We will have a closer look at these regulatory innovations in the next section as they are very closely linked to the corporate role as a citizen in civil society.

Business–government relations in international trade regimes

Despite the general point we made that governmental power at the transnational level is rather limited, there are however a number of transnational governmental institutions that have quite a significant influence on business. These can be regional bodies (such as the European Union (EU), the North American Free Trade Agreement (NAFTA), and the Association of South East Asian Nations (ASEAN) or global players (such as the World Trade Organization (WTO) and the World Bank). The general role of these bodies is to enable trade and exchange of goods and services. For business, this can be a double-edged sword. On the one hand, such bodies may enable firms to access cheap labour, reach larger markets, and other new opportunities. At the same time, these institutions increase competition and in some ways limit business, especially those outside the respective regional space. It is therefore no surprise that the regular meetings, for instance of the WTO, in which new regulation is discussed, are heavily lobbied by business, which often even has a direct mandate to take part in these negotiations (Woll and Artigas 2007).

One of the most influential regional bodies is the EU, as quite considerable legislative powers have been delegated from the member states to EU level. This not only concerns a lot of regulation on health, safety, and the environment, but the EU Commission is particularly active in making sure that fair competition is upheld in European markets for goods and services. This becomes particularly visible in the case of mergers and acquisitions, where the EU has a legacy of forbidding many planned mergers for fear of creating monopolies in certain markets.

■ Corporate citizenship and regulation: business as key player in the regulatory game

As we have seen in this chapter, the situation for companies is that imperative regulation at the national level remains important, but has decreased in intensity, whilst transnational regulation is still limited but has intensified. These transitions, coupled with concerns about 'over-regulation' stifling business innovation, have led to a fertile debate about how to improve the rule-making process governing social and environmental issues in business.

As a result, various innovations and new styles of regulation have emerged. These innovations pose a significant challenge to corporations in terms of how they might think about the notion of corporate citizenship. Specifically, new regulatory approaches usually include business (next to other actors) in the regulatory process itself, namely through private regulation (or 'self-regulation'). And because regulation is essentially about creating rules to benefit society, private regulation inevitably involves corporations more heavily in the governing of citizenship rights. In Chapter 2 we likened this to a political role for corporations in the era of globalization.

As we have explained, the central idea in private regulation is that private actors such as corporations and CSOs are involved in setting up rules and systems of monitoring and enforcement rather than these being solely in the hands of government. A typical example here is the regulation of financial markets in many countries, such as the UK, where this is handled by the Financial Conduct Authority—a self-regulating industry body rather than a government organization. Much of this regulation is *voluntary* in that business gets involved in these regulatory processes not because they are forced to do so by government, but because they see it as being in their own self-interest (Van Calster and Deketelaere 2001). Private regulation might therefore be regarded as 'softer' and more flexible since it can adjust reasonably easily to new circumstances, issues, and actors (Martínez Lucio and Weston 2000), and is frequently based on market mechanisms rather than hierarchical authority.

As Orts and Deketelaere (2001) point out, the greater involvement of companies in regulation is foremost a European approach, and one that has only fairly recently been adopted in other parts of the world and, most notably, on the global level. This collaborative approach has a long tradition in Europe and is often referred to by the term *corporatism* (Molina and Rhodes 2002). In particular, then, it has been countries such as France, Germany, and the Netherlands that have been among the early adopters of this approach since the 1970s.

There are a number of reasons why these forms of regulation have emerged. According to van Calster and Deketelaere (2001), the main goals for those trying to introduce new types of rule-making in this area are:

- **Encouragement of a proactive approach from industry**. Industry as an addressee of regulation (and hence the one that has to adapt to it) has typically been integrated rather late into the rule-making process—if at all. This means that governmental regulation has not always offered much encouragement for business and has not usually been very enthusiastically welcomed by companies. Self-regulation, therefore, has tried to encourage earlier and more proactive engagement from industry in the rule-making process, and has tried to make more use of the market to encourage ethical behaviour.

- **Cost-effectiveness**. Another goal of private regulation is to cut down on bureaucracy and costs on the part of government. To give an example: rather than telling companies which technology to use, or to measure the emissions at every single smoke stack, the introduction of a limited amount of tradable emission certificates for a certain industry has the same result without the costly administration and compliance control (Smalley Bowen 2003).

- **Faster achievement of objectives**. The average time for a proposal to be adopted by the EU is two years, followed by another two years for transposition by the member states. One of the motivations to change the regulatory process is to shorten this time lag. When engaging industry in regulation, the assumption is that the aims are attained faster since it offers a shortcut through the different institutions.

Figure 11.5 provides an overview of the changing field of regulation affecting business. It is based on Figure 10.1 in Chapter 10, which depicts the three main institutional sectors in society—government, business, and civil society. Figure 11.5 shows the relevant actors in each sector and gives some typical examples of the regulatory processes they are involved in. We have shaded the business sphere because this is the area that relates specifically to business involvement in private regulation.

☑ **Skill check**

Distinguishing forms of business regulation in a global context. Determining the different constellations of actors involved in specific forms of global governance enables you to identify and evaluate alternative modes of regulation.

Governments as regulators (segment 1)

First of all, we find governmental bodies as key actors in regulation. As we indicated earlier in this chapter, imperative regulation by government is still quite widely practised. This certainly applies to *national* governments, and while there is still some debate about the power and future of nation states it is certainly evident that the regulatory power of nation states, although diminished by globalization, will continue to be a significant influence on business (Taplin 2002). An example of a reinvigorated appetite of nation states to regulate business is the 2010 Dodd–Frank Act in the US that we discussed in Chapter 6

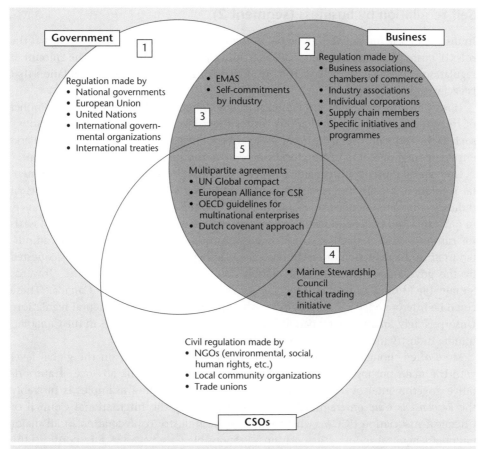

Figure 11.5 Players in the regulatory game and selected examples of private regulatory efforts

(Reforming corporate governance around the globe, pp. 255–259) as a reaction to the financial crisis of the late 2000s. But we see this appetite also in the area of law enforcement where, for instance, the EU Commission in recent years has significantly enhanced its scrutiny of antitrust behaviour in a number of industries, most notably pharmaceuticals (Esposito and Montanaro 2014). The ongoing EU antitrust investigations against Google and other technology companies are just another example of this trend (Arthur 2014).

What we see then is a growing importance for governmental bodies above the national level (sometimes called the 'supranational' level) such as the EU, treaty systems such as NAFTA, or supranational bodies such as the G20. However, if we analyse the role of governmental organizations with global scope, such as the UN or the OECD, we see that these organizations lack efficient mechanisms for sanctioning non-compliance with their regulation. An example are the ongoing efforts of the G20 to crack down on tax havens which have proven largely ineffective so far (Johannesen and Zucman 2014). Exceptions, however, are the World Bank and the IMF (International Monetary Fund), since they have the power to either grant or withdraw considerable amounts of money to/from developing nations (Woods 2001), and through this, also have considerable leverage on companies doing business in these countries.

Self-regulation by business (segment 2)

In discussing the roles of various actors in the field of regulation, it is apparent that the roles of business and government have increasingly become intertwined. The amount of regulation exclusively set by government is shrinking, as is the share of regulation that is exclusively set by business.

However, as we have seen throughout this book, there are still a considerable number of rules and norms that corporations set for themselves (and for other corporations), such as the codes of conduct introduced to govern business behaviour, or the social and environmental rules imposed on local subsidiaries and suppliers by large corporations.

One typical form of self-regulation which works as a direct counterpart to governmental regulation is collective agreements or commitments by industry—often sectors of industry—that are intended to avoid, forestall or soften potential laws: so, for instance, in order to avoid costly and restrictive regulation in the realization of the national goals for carbon dioxide reduction, the Confederation of German Industry (BDI) committed itself to the reduction of greenhouse gases far beyond the level originally requested by the government (Eberlein and Matten 2009). Another example is the 'Towards Sustainable Mining' principles developed by the Mining Association of Canada.[8] These could be interpreted as a straightforward attempt at avoiding governmental regulation. Unsurprisingly, an attempt by parliament to make responsible practices in the Canadian mining industry mandatory was voted down in 2010.

More often though we observe new business-driven regulation on the global level with the main purpose of addressing the vacuum created by the absence of authoritative governmental oversight. One of the most long-standing examples is probably the *Responsible Care* programme.[9] This was initiated by the International Council of Chemical Association (ICCA), which is the global industry confederation of all major national Chemical Industry Associations. Responsible Care began as a response to the devastating chemical-related disasters in Bhopal, Basle, and Seveso in the 1980s, and was adopted by the ICCA in 1991. The programme prescribes in quite some detail a large array of measures, practices, and policies intended to ensure responsible management in the industry. Member firms of the industry's national associations have to adopt these measures in order to be allowed to use the Responsible Care logo. As of 2015, the chemical industry associations of 60 countries worldwide had adopted the programme, thereby making its implementation for member firms mandatory.

An equally important standard that has been developed by industry is the *ISO 14000* standard series of the International Standard Organization in Switzerland.[10] These standards basically accredit environmental management systems for business as a way of setting rules for good practice in environmental management (Tarí et al. 2012). This is the most widely implemented environmental standard on a global level, mainly due to the fact that many corporations, especially multinationals, specify ISO 14000 certification for their suppliers (Corbett and Kirsch 2001; To and Lee 2014). The outcome of these standards, however, are by no means uncontested. Since many such standards, most notably ISO 14000, do not prescribe outcomes rather than management processes, recent research has cast doubt on their real effectiveness (Aravind and Christmann 2011; Delmas and Montes-Sancho 2011).

The ISO standards are a good example of how regulation and governance are changing. More recent standards, most notably ISO 26000 on social responsibility, show that business self-regulation gains legitimacy when it is drawn up in collaboration with governments and civil society groups—which we will discuss in the next section. In fact, where business engages in pure self-regulation, the literature remains somewhat ambivalent about the likely benefits (e.g. Tapper 1997; King and Lenox 2000). These approaches seem to have worked primarily in situations where corporate self-interest would suggest these measures anyway. So, for instance, the self-commitment of the German industry to reduce carbon dioxide emissions was easy to fulfil because large producers of these gases in East Germany were about to close down anyway in the early 1990s (Eberlein and Matten 2009).

Regulation involving business, governmental actors, and CSOs (segments 3, 4, and 5)

The design and implementation of regulation across sectors, whether at regional, national, or transnational levels, has become increasingly common. Although multi-sector co-operation is in itself not entirely new, it is the emergence of multi-sector initiatives to enact *global governance* that is most notable here. As David Detomasi (2007: 321) puts it, 'the strengths of state, market, and civil society actors combine to create an effective international governance system that overcomes the weaknesses afflicting each individually'. Typically, the main instrument used in such networks to regulate the social, ethical, and environmental impacts of business are codes of conduct and systems of monitoring and enforcement. We have already discussed these at some length in Chapter 5, including questions of effectiveness and the plausibility of developing worthwhile global codes of ethics. Nearly all large global governmental and multi-partite organizations, such as the UN, the OECD, the ILO (International Labour Organization), the FAO (Food and Agriculture Organization), and the WHO (World Health Organization), have issued codes intended to provide some degree of rule-setting for corporations in areas beyond the control of the nation state. There is such a rapidly expanding number of codes that it is hardly possible to provide a complete overview of this mushrooming field of regulation. In one study of codes relevant to multinationals, Fransen and Kolk (2007) identified almost 50 corporate responsibility standards issued over the previous decade, including six from intergovernmental organizations, seven from CSOs, 14 from business associations, and a further 22 multiple-stakeholder standards. This, of course, is in addition to the hundreds of individual company codes operated by companies across the globe.

Discussing these new forms of global business governance, two aspects seem worth highlighting. First, we see a growing number of regulatory frameworks where business is clearly stepping into policy fields that hitherto have been more the prerogative of governments. Examples are the Global Business Coalition for HIV/AIDS[11] or the Guiding Principles on Business and Human Rights[12]—both of which cover what are substantially public policy issues. This reflects what we discussed in Chapter 2 as the new role of business practising an extended view of corporate citizenship.

A second aspect is that a growing number of these global, private regulatory frameworks are no longer just trying to mimic traditional governmental regulation. Again, the ISO 26000 standard on 'social responsibility',[13] published in 2010, is a good example of a number of trends that have been emerging in this space of shared global governance between business, governments, and civil society more recently:

- **Deliberate rather than dictate**. While most standards were drawn up either unilaterally by business, or by business together with some NGOs and governmental agencies, a new generation of standards is characterized by increasing collaboration between all relevant stakeholders. In the case of ISO 26000 this resulted in a nine-year long process between a host of stakeholders from business, government and civil society representing not only all relevant constituencies but also representing all relevant regions of the globe (Balzarova and Castka 2012; Helms et al. 2012). The core goal of such a process is to enhance the legitimacy of the resulting standard.

- **Process rather than outcome orientation**. The core approach of many of these new standards is not so much to provide a tool that standardizes, monitors and benchmarks social or environmental performance. Rather the goal is to prescribe management processes which can be implemented in individual businesses and can guide management practices that then will be able to lead to the desired changes in performance (Hahn and Weidtmann 2012). This rather pragmatic approach is informed by the experience that widespread adoption of many standards has been hampered by firms' reluctance to accept binding forms of prescribed outcomes and measures.

- **Frameworks rather than specific norms**. In the process of global governance, multiple actors have to work together on a basis of mutual consent in the absence of the imperative authority that a single government would traditionally be able to exert. Therefore, such processes of deliberation, negotiation and experimentation cannot be prescribed by fixed rules and clear goals. Here this new generation of standards serves as a framework for guiding responsible business behaviour while leaving individual actors the space to adapt and implement these ideas on the ground. Globalization has created awareness for the global impacts of business from an ethical perspective; however, it appears that many of the solutions—as we have seen in many of the examples and cases in this book—are heavily dependent on local context. ISO 26000, for instance, has been used as a framework for local standards governing responsible business practices in countries as diverse as Australia, Brazil, Denmark, or Spain (Hahn 2013).

Ethics in Action 11.2 discusses the UN Global Compact as another of the more recent attempts to explore a different trajectory to fill the lack of regulatory bodies at the global level.

**VISIT THE
ONLINE
RESOURCE
CENTRE**
for links to
useful sources
of further
information

ETHICS IN ACTION 11.2

The UN Global Compact: talking about global regulation

In 2000 the UN launched the Global Compact in an attempt to address the ethical problems linked to corporate activities on a global scale. Rather than pursuing the top-down approach of earlier regulatory efforts, the UN Global Compact starts from the bottom up by working directly with corporations. As it states on the organization's webpage, the initiative is 'an initiative that provides collaborative solutions to the most fundamental challenges facing both business and society. The initiative seeks to combine the best properties of the UN, such as moral authority and convening power, with the private sector's solution-finding strengths, and the expertise and capacities of a range of key stakeholders'.

The UN Global Compact asks companies 'to embrace, support and enact, within their sphere of influence, a set of core values'. These are articulated in ten core principles in the areas of human rights, labour standards, the environment and anti-corruption.

Human rights:

- *Principle 1*: Businesses should support and respect the protection of internationally proclaimed human rights; and
- *Principle 2*: Businesses should make sure that they are not complicit in human rights abuses.

Labour:

- *Principle 3*: Businesses should uphold the freedom of association and the effective recognition of the right to collective bargaining;
- *Principle 4*: Businesses should uphold the elimination of all forms of forced and compulsory labour;
- *Principle 5*: Businesses should uphold the effective abolition of child labour; and
- *Principle 6*: Businesses should uphold the elimination of discrimination in respect of employment and occupation.

Environment:

- *Principle 7*: Businesses should support a precautionary approach to environmental challenges;
- *Principle 8*: Businesses should undertake initiatives to promote greater environmental responsibility; and
- *Principle 9*: Businesses should encourage the development and diffusion of environmentally friendly technologies.

Anti-corruption:

- *Principle 10*: Businesses should work against corruption in all its forms, including extortion and bribery.

Companies that want to join have to (a) provide a letter from their CEO indicating a commitment to these ten principles; and (b) annually report publicly on the firm's 'Communication on Progress' (COP) in implementing the principles. They are also asked to make an annual financial contribution to the Compact of several thousand dollars, depending on the size of the company. In return, companies can participate in Global Compact events and learning networks, use its various tools and resources, and signal to stakeholders that they are participants in the initiative with the 'We Support the Global Compact' logo.

The UN considers the Global Compact to be primarily a facilitator of dialogue and learning between business, government, and CSOs. It achieves this by establishing local networks within individual countries as well as working groups at a global, national, and local level to focus on specific challenges, for instance on the role of business in conflict zones or on business and child labour. Here, multi-partite participants work together to increase capacity to deal with the problem on a concrete business level, often resulting in new, specialized tools, principles, guidelines, or other resources.

As of 2015, the initiative had grown to more than 12,800 participants, including over 8,300 businesses in 145 countries around the world. Georg Kell, its executive director until 2015, argued that as a voluntary, facilitating initiative rather than a mandatory, imperative form of regulation, the compact has proven to be far more successful at gaining corporate 'buy-in' than any preceding initiative. The Compact, though, sees itself not as a substitute for regulation but as a network supplementing regulation at a global level.

This approach has not been without controversy. Critics have argued that signing up to the ten principles does not commit corporations to very much, since compliance is not monitored and defection is not substantially sanctioned. Ultimately, the critics see the Global Compact as a cheap 'bluewash' for corporations (meaning they cover up or 'wash' their problems with the blue of the UN flag), and a rather naïve approach to globalization that ignores the compelling economic rationalities of liberalized world markets.

Meanwhile, after becoming the largest such initiative in the world in terms of membership, the Global Compact has implemented a more formal structure of self-governance, including a board with representatives from business, civil society, labour, and the United Nations. The initiative also bolstered its integrity by firming up the rules of membership and has so far delisted nearly 5,200 companies for non-compliance with the rules or failure to provide a COP.

The relative success of the Global Compact in engaging with business has led to the emergence of more focused sector initiatives from the UN that apply a similar strategy. Realizing the importance of financial markets in pushing responsible corporate behaviour, the 'UN Principles for Responsible Investment' (PRI) were launched in April 2006 (see Chapter 6, Socially responsible investment, p. 266), while the 'UN Principles of Responsible Management Education' (PRME) were launched in 2007 to provide a set of principles for business schools to follow in their education of future business leaders. More than 500 business schools in more than 80 countries have since signed up to PRME, making it one of the most widely adopted initiatives in the sector.

Sources

Monbiot, G. 2000. Getting into bed with business: the UN is no longer just a joke. *Guardian*, 31 August: http://www.theguardian.com/Columnists/Column/0,5673,361716,00.html.
Rasche, A. and Kell, G. (eds.) 2010. *The United Nations Global Compact: achievements, trends and challenges*. Cambridge: Cambridge University Press.
Rasche, A., Waddock, S., and McIntosh, M. (eds.) 2013. The United Nations Global Compact Retrospect and Prospect. *Business & Society* 52 (1): 6–30.
http://www.unglobalcompact.org.
http://www.unprme.org.

VISIT THE ONLINE RESOURCE CENTRE for a short response to this feature

? THINK THEORY

Relate the UN global compact to the concepts of business–society relations, as outlined in Chapter 2. Where does the global compact fit into these concepts? Which areas does it not cover? By using these concepts, try to give a critical assessment of the potential and chances of the global compact.

In the final analysis, it would appear that the whole area of business involvement in self-regulation is multifaceted, multi-level, and highly dynamic. That business *is* involved in regulation is clear—thereby providing support for the argument that corporations have increasingly become involved in the protection (or otherwise) of citizens' rights and interests. What remains unclear, though, is whether voluntary initiatives by corporations can ever succeed in providing suitable and sufficient protection for citizens. While business conduct has clearly improved as a result of private regulation, particularly in respect of accepting responsibility for social and environmental conditions in the supply chain, its impact on the root problems it has been designed to address has been limited (Vogel 2010). Evidence suggests that the background presence of state regulatory capacity—or the 'gorilla in the closet'—is often a necessary precondition for effective enforcement (Verbruggen 2013). In the final section we shall address these questions in the specific context of sustainability.

■ Governments, business, and sustainability

In Chapter 1 we defined sustainability as 'the long-term maintenance of systems according to environmental, economic, and social considerations'. This definition certainly captures the broad understanding of the concept in business, politics, and wider parts of society. Reaching towards the end of the book, however, we should add that this definition by no means satisfies everybody, nor is it how it was originally thought of. Sustainability was certainly first considered a pre-eminently *ecological concept* prescribing rules and principles for the usage of natural resources in such a way that allows future generations to survive on this planet (see Pearce and Turner 1990).

A central idea of sustainability is to prescribe and implement changes to the usage of natural resources (Turner 1993). With regard to *renewable resources*, such as wood, agricultural products, water, or air, the key principle would be not to use those resources beyond their capacity of regeneration. With *non-renewable resources*, however, such as coal, oil, minerals, metals, and other key resources of modern industry, the original rules of 'strict' sustainability would suggest that none of these resources should be used if they would put future generations at a lower level of ability to meet their needs than the present generation. In the case of metals and other recyclables, this would result in fairly strict rules for circulating these resources in the economy; with regard to oil or coal, the consequences are more severe. Since resources such as these will ultimately be depleted, we have to be extremely cautious about their use, especially since they have major effects on the climate. Some have argued that sustainability does not allow their further usage at all. The Climate Tracker Initiative, for instance, promotes the concept of 'unburnable carbon' on the basis that burning today's known reserves of fossil fuels would lead to a greater than 2° Celsius increase in global warming—which is the level committed to by governments in 2010 in order to prevent the worst effects of global climate change from occurring.[14]

Without going into too much detail, sustainability in this sense is quite a tough and—from a business perspective—somewhat threatening concept. This applies particularly to industries that rely on non-renewable or carbon-intensive resources, such as the mining, oil and gas, or chemical industries. There has been some research that shows that the mutation of the sustainability concept from the original ecological view towards a 'softer' concept has been particularly driven by industry. For example, Mayhew (1997) showed how the World Business Council of Sustainable Development—a major international business association—introduced a systematically watered-down definition of sustainable development and by this gave a new, more industry-friendly meaning to the concept. By linking sustainability not only to ecological, but also to social and economic criteria, the strict rules for using resources are loosened and the concept becomes far more open to discretion.

Some authors, therefore, argue that the original agenda of sustainability has been 'hijacked' by industry and made less threatening and more ready to serve as a buzzword for corporate public relations (Welford 1997; Parr 2009). Unsurprisingly, many have argued that it is governments that should take the driving seat in achieving more sustainable business practices. Indeed, following the original Rio Summit in 1992, the industrialized world witnessed an avalanche of legislation in the 1990s aimed at tightening environmental standards for industry. However, in an assessment of the Rio + 20 summit in 2012, Peter Haas (2012) argued that by and large governmental bodies had failed to deliver on implementing sustainable development because in most countries they had not been able to stand up to entrenched economic interests. This pertains to both a failure in restricting business from engaging in unsustainable practices, and to promoting greener entrepreneurship and green business alternatives. The central ethical debate here focuses on the question of whether governments need to address sustainability primarily by imperative regulation or whether voluntary, market-based approaches provide more efficient and fair outcomes in pursuit of a more sustainable economy. We will illustrate these aspects by analysing the role of business and governments in the area of climate change and in the area of commodity management with regard to food security.

Global climate change legislation and business responses: support versus obstruction

One of the key political arenas of sustainability has been the debate on the regulation of global climate change (Begg, van der Woerd, and Levy 2005; Levy and Newell 2005; Klein 2014). As early as 1992, global warming and changes in the global climate were centre stage at the Rio Summit. Levy and Egan (2000) suggest that by this time, the World Business Council of Sustainable Development (a coalition of 200 international companies) had already subtly lobbied against any concrete measures to be implemented on a global level. However, as the political debate moved on, the Kyoto Protocol was ultimately signed in 1997 by nearly 200 countries. The protocol foresaw significant reductions by 2012 in the emission of greenhouse gases, most notably carbon dioxide. In 2009, the Kyoto process was followed up by the Copenhagen Climate Change Summit and a number of follow-up summits, which aimed to reach an agreement on policies for the period after 2012 (Schüssler et al. 2014).

Reductions in carbon dioxide, however, represent a severe threat for some industries. Kolk and Levy (2001) illustrate that among the fiercest opponents of imperative regulation with respect to climate action was the oil industry, which is fundamentally implicated in greenhouse gas emissions through the burning of fossil fuels. As a result, the industry founded the Global Climate Coalition (GCC) in 1989 in order to lobby against governmental regulation to cut back on greenhouse gas emissions. Depending on the home country context, however, companies have subsequently followed rather different trajectories (Kolk and Pinske 2007; Eberlein and Matten 2009).

Counted as among the main members of the GCC were the American companies ExxonMobil and Texaco, as well as the European companies BP and Shell, which left the GCC in 1996 and 1998, respectively. Despite their industry's profound scepticism towards regulating against greenhouse emissions, both European companies had to face the fact that their governments, and most notably the EU, were bound to implement Kyoto at some stage. In the US, and to a lesser degree also in Canada (see Case 3) and Australia, companies then saw considerable mileage in lobbying their governments to refrain from implementing climate protection legislation.

This strategy among North American oil companies met with considerable success: one of the first acts of the Bush administration in 2001 was to pull the US out of the Kyoto agreement, and the policies of the State Department on climate change in the early 2000s were directly based on the position of the GCC (Kolk and Pinkse 2007). ExxonMobil placed advocacy advertisements in the US press that questioned the 'uncertain' science of global warming, warned that regulation would 'restrict life itself', and argued that technological innovation and the market could meet any 'potential risks' of climate change (Livesey 2002). North American oil companies also sponsored their own scientific 'experts' (Rothenberg and Levy 2012) and engaged in media 'warfare' with NGOs such as Greenpeace (MacKay and Munro 2012). And while in Australia and Canada governments in the main turned out to side with industry on the denial of the need for major action on climate change throughout most of the last decade, the example of the US under Barack Obama shows how effective companies have been even in the face of governments more predisposed to act. As Andrew Hoffman (2015) argues, there is now an entire 'culture' of climate change denial in large parts of the American citizenry which appears to render serious governmental policies to restrict carbon emissions rather unlikely.

In Europe, conversely, the EU introduced the Greenhouse Gas Emission Trading Scheme (EU ETS) in 2005 in order to reach the goals of the Kyoto Treaty and European companies were heavily involved in lobbying efforts to shape the regulation. On the one hand the EU ETS represents one of the most comprehensive approaches to managing climate emissions globally. On the other hand it uses a market mechanism to reach these targets and leaves considerable freedom to business as to how exactly they want to address the issue. There is, then, considerable debate about the effectiveness of the EU ETS. Not only have key industries managed to avoid or delay inclusion (Buhr 2012) but there is also scepticism about whether the design of the market for carbon dioxide permits in fact incentivizes the desired reduction in emissions on the part of corporations (Veal and Mouzas 2012).

With the publication by the UK Treasury of the Stern Report (2006), which documented the severe economic impacts of climate change, a growing number of companies have begun to accept that measures to tackle climate change will be inevitable and that they might as well be part of the solution as opposed to resisting the inevitable (Pinkse and Kolk 2012). This is accompanied by the fact that implementation of climate change policies has given rise to new business opportunities, for example in solar and wind technologies, or alternative ways of powering cars, as the success of hybrid and electric vehicles has shown.

Achieving sustainability: securing the global supply of food and water

Another area of concern for governments in many countries, developed and developing nations alike, is the conservation of a sustainable livelihood for their citizens. Among the key challenges are the conservation of freshwater resources and the issue of food security. In both areas, business plays a key role, which has given rise to a number of ethical concerns.

An initial issue arising in the 1970s and 1980s in the industrialized world was the increasing water pollution caused by business, most notably the chemical industry. While these issues have been more or less successfully addressed through increased regulation and oversight, water pollution has become a major concern in rapidly industrialized countries such as China or India. In China, for example, the government has reported that 60% of its groundwater is polluted, giving rise to major public-health problems, including the existence of rural 'cancer villages', i.e. areas with high rates of cancer clustered around pollution hotspots (Chen 2015).

Another ethical debate has arisen around the privatization of water management and supply in many countries across the world (Rahaman et al. 2013). The most spectacular example of the ethical challenges of water privatization can be found in Bolivia (Spronk 2007). As many state-owned water suppliers in developing countries are challenged with corruption issues, efficiency problems, and poor-quality service, the World Bank has typically pushed countries towards privatization of the water supply. When Bolivian water was privatized in the early 2000s, American and French multinationals took over and began charging high fees or else refused to connect to the grid neighbourhoods that could not afford to pay. When, as part of their supply-chain management, the companies successfully lobbied the government to outlaw the use of rainwater, this led to violent protests and, ultimately, a change of government in the country. The problem by no means exists only in developing countries: Nestlé became a target of public outcry in the Spring of 2015 in California when it was found bottling and exporting water in the middle of a severe drought when water rationing was imposed by the state government (Walker 2015). Potential solutions to the problem seem to lie either in co-operatives (see Chapter 6; Douvitsa and Kassavetis 2014) or in novel, tripartite community enterprises, where Western multinationals bring capital and know-how and local governments and CSOs provide the infrastructure and human capital (Nwankwo et al. 2007).

In addition to water, with well over 7 billion people on the planet, the issue of food security is also becoming a growing sustainability concern for governments worldwide. Together with the depletion of key resources such as fish stocks, and the increasing proliferation of toxic chemicals such as DDT in the food chain, the issue is thought to be one of the major political challenges for the future. Again, the corporate sector plays a key role here, as private corporations control most elements of the global supply chains for food.

A major issue which has put substantial strain on poorer countries is the volatility of global food commodity markets (Clapp and Helleiner 2012). This has been exacerbated by another sustainability issue, namely the rise of biofuels to substitute for fossil fuels. As the consensus is growing that increased biofuel use will have a negative effect on food security (Nonhebel 2012), it is obvious that a good many of the decisions about these issues will have to be taken by private corporations, even if governments continue to play a role in setting the parameters and constraints on addressing these ethical issues.

■ Summary

In this chapter we have looked in some depth at the stake held by government in business, and set out how the role of government, and its central task of issuing regulation for business, affects this stakeholder relationship. We have seen that 'government' today is quite a complex set of actors and institutions that act on various levels, from local or regional level to a transnational or even global stage.

During the course of the chapter we have discussed the complex role of governments and the interdependencies and mutual interests that they have with business. As an actor that is primarily obliged to pursue the interest of the electorate, or society, the dominant ethical challenges in business–government relations are the issues of legitimacy and accountability. This particularly focuses on the question of how much influence business should have on governmental actors, and by what means this influence should be enacted. We discussed various forms of business intervention in governmental decision-making, from lobbying, to party financing, to far stronger forms of state capture and corruption.

We then took a closer look at the way globalization shifts the roles of business and government in regulating issues of relevance to business ethics. We discussed the notion of global governance, which assigns a new role to corporations as active players in the regulatory game, and discussed the various options and innovations in private regulation open to business and other players. We qualified this new role for business, though, when analysing the role of government in ensuring sustainable practices in business. While business is a key player in governments' attempts to implement sustainable development business, short-term interests may often hamper these initiatives, as we have seen particularly in the area of climate change regulation.

Study questions

1. What is regulation? What does it mean to say that actors other than government engage in regulation?

2. Explain the two basic roles of government that determine its stakeholder relationship with corporations.

3. What are the potential ethical problems associated with corporate lobbying of government?

4. 'Corporations should never do business with authoritarian or oppressive regimes. It is simply beyond the boundaries of ethical acceptability.' Critically examine this argument, outlining practical ways in which business can make decisions about which countries to do business in.

5. Why have corporations been increasingly involved in setting regulation for social and environmental issues and what are the main ethical challenges associated with their involvement?

6. Are strong governments necessary to achieve an effective response to climate change? Explain, using examples from contemporary business practice.

Research exercise

Conduct some research on the responsible care programme of the chemical industry (http://www.icca-chem.org/en/Home/Responsible-care/).

1. Explain the main details of the programme.

2. To what extent is the programme illustrative of private regulation?

3. What are the advantages and disadvantages of private regulation compared to imperative regulation for ensuring ethical conduct in the chemical industry?

4. Would you say the programme is likely to be sufficient to ensure ethical conduct in the chemical industry? If not, what else is necessary?

VISIT THE
ONLINE
RESOURCE
CENTRE
for links to
further key
readings

Key readings

1. Vogel, D. 2010. The Private Regulation of Global Corporate Conduct: Achievements and Limitations. *Business & Society*, 49 (1): 68–87.

This article from one of the leading academic voices in the business-government interface provides a concise overview and conceptualization of the private regulation of global business. It maps out why such forms of regulation have emerged, what benefits they bring, and what their limitations might be. It concludes quite critically, arguing that while private regulation has made some advances it should not be seen as a replacement for more effective state regulation.

2. Fransen, L.W. and Kolk, A. 2007. Global Rule-Setting for Business: A Critical Analysis of Multi-Stakeholder Standards. *Organization*, 14 (5): 667–84.

A useful companion piece to the first selection, this article sets out some of the different types of standards used in setting rules for global business and examines, in particular, the supposed benefits of multiple stakeholder initiatives in terms of membership, governance, and implementation. It offers a helpful and quite critical comparison of multiple stakeholder codes against other types of standards, using evidence from a comprehensive inventory of codes.

VISIT THE
ONLINE
RESOURCE
CENTRE
for links to
useful sources
of further
information on
this case

Case 11

Managing the ethics of censorship and surveillance: where next for the Global Network Initiative?

This case examines how information and communications technology (ICT) firms have gone about managing ethical challenges around internet censorship and surveillance by governments. In particular, it focuses on the Global Network Initiative, an industry-led programme aimed at building a framework for effective protection of human rights online. The case presents an opportunity to explore ways in which firms engage with governments around ethical issues, as well as attempts to build effective, multi-stakeholder initiatives to govern the behaviour of corporations with respect to global human rights problems.

In 2014, when it was revealed that millions of Yahoo users had images from their webcams intercepted by the UK surveillance agency GCHQ, it provoked a storm of controversy. It turned out that GCHQ, with the help of the US National Security Agency (NSA), had been collecting and analysing webcam images—including around 10% that involved what GCHQ referred to as 'undesirable nudity'—for several years without users knowing and regardless of whether they were actual intelligence targets suspected of any wrongdoing. Yahoo responded furiously stating, 'We were not aware of, nor would we condone, this reported activity. This report, if true, represents a whole new level of violation of our users' privacy that is completely unacceptable, and we strongly call on the world's governments to reform surveillance law consistent with [our] principles.'

This marked quite a change in circumstances for a company that only a few years before had received a major dressing-down from the US government over the firm's failure to protect the human rights of its users in China. 'Technically and financially, you are giants, but morally, you are pygmies' the US House Foreign Affairs Committee chair had scolded the firm's founder in 2007.

In the interim, Yahoo along with Google, Microsoft, and a host of academic institutions and human rights groups had formed the Global Network Initiative (GNI), a multi-stakeholder initiative aimed at 'protecting and advancing freedom of expression and privacy in information and communications technologies'. The US Government, meanwhile, had been the victim of a major whistleblowing incident that exposed the NSA's widespread, indiscriminate gathering of phone, email, chat, and social networking data through its PRISM surveillance system, which involved many large ICT firms. Protecting the human rights of technology users had clearly become much more complicated than simply obeying the law.

Governments, censorship, and surveillance

New information and communication technologies such as the internet and social media have been presented by many as a great force for connectivity, freedom of speech, and democracy. However, not all governments are quite as enamoured of the great freedoms that new technology brings. In authoritarian regimes, the internet and social media are often seen as a threat to the ruling authorities and therefore significant attempts are made to censor or monitor internet activity around politically sensitive subjects. Such restrictions can impede privacy and freedom of speech by internet users—and by extension, that of consumers of internet service providers, search engines, and other technology services. In a 2013 report, the press freedom organization Reporters Without Borders identified five countries as particular 'enemies of the internet' for their online surveillance activities—Bahrain, China, Iran, Syria, and Vietnam. In these countries, Reporters Without Borders claimed there were particularly high levels of 'active, intrusive surveillance of news providers, resulting in grave violations of freedom of information and human rights'.

Until the NSA revelations in 2013 catapulted the US into the surveillance headlines, much of the world's attention to internet surveillance and censorship had tended to focus on China. The country has the most internet users in the world—more than 600 million—yet internet use is highly restricted and the government regularly blocks websites and blogs that it views as a threat to state security. Reporters Without Borders has long marked out China as 'the world's biggest prison for netizens', with a total of 74 users and 30 journalists imprisoned for their internet activities according to its 2014 report. Many government departments are involved in mentoring and censoring the web, and the state reportedly employs thousands of workers to oversee online activity. The authorities main-tain strict enforcement of internet restrictions through sophisticated filtering technolo-gies (nicknamed the Great Firewall of China), rules requiring companies to prevent the circulation of banned material, and regular guidance to news media and websites. Black-outs are also used during particularly sensitive events. For example, on the annual anni-versary of the 1989 Tiananmen Square protests, hundreds of internet services are shut down to quell discussion of the pro-democracy movement, earning it the ironic epithet 'Internet maintenance day' in China.

Although China is a particularly serious case, it is not just authoritarian countries that engage in wide-scale surveillance of their citizens. The NSA revelations, precipitated by a massive leak of confidential files by the whistleblower Edward Snowden, made it clear that the US and the UK governments too were involved in mass surveillance previously unheard of in a democratic country. The leaked files revealed that the NSA and GCHQ were accessing information stored by major US phone and technology companies, and were engaged in mass intercepting of data from phone and internet networks. The NSA, for example, had direct access to the servers of Google, Apple, and Facebook without users' knowledge, and they legally required companies such as Yahoo and Verizon to hand over their users' data.

Complicity of ICT companies

Surveillance and censorship is a difficult area for ICT companies to navigate. Whilst coun-tries such as China offer huge potential for developing new markets, and the US is home to the world's largest ICT firms, dealing with host governments can raise a range of problems that firms are ill prepared to deal with. If they refuse to accept the demands of govern-ments they risk being fined or prevented from operating in the country. If they do accept them, they risk being complicit in human rights abuses.

Consider the experience of Yahoo. In the mid-2000s it had faced a major public relations problem after it was revealed that the company had complied with Chinese government requests to reveal personal details of journalists using its products who were considered crit-ical of the regime. One journalist was subsequently sentenced to ten years in a labour camp simply for emailing his newspaper's reporting restrictions to an overseas colleague. Yahoo, at the time, claimed it had no choice but to cede to the demands of the Chinese authori-ties, but following a stinging rebuke from Congress back home, the firm changed course. As part of its settlement of a lawsuit from the World Organization for Human Rights, Yahoo offered to pay legal bills for imprisoned customers, set up a fund to support human rights, and even lobbied the US government to press for the release of political dissidents detained by the Chinese authorities as a result of Yahoo's release of user information.

Google, which had faced similar criticisms to Yahoo in the 2000s, decided to partially pull out of China in 2010 due to concerns with censorship and privacy. It relocated its Chinese-language server outside the Chinese firewall in Hong Kong. However, its share of the crucial Chinese search market fell from 12% in 2010 to less than 2% by 2013. On the other hand, Microsoft, which competes with Google in the internet search market as well as many other areas of ICT, has resolutely remained in China and even criticized Google for pulling out of the country. The firm's CEO explicitly stated that Microsoft would comply with China's censorship requests in the same way that it follows the laws of every country where it operates.

A step forward for ICT companies and internet freedoms

The challenges of effectively managing censorship issues in a clear and consistent way have led to a range of responses from companies and their supporters and critics. A major breakthrough, however, came with the launch of the Global Network Initiative in 2008. Founded by Yahoo, Microsoft, and Google, three of the companies most in the firing line on such issues, the GNI is a partnership between tech companies, human rights groups, academic institutions, and other institutions involved in media and communications freedoms. The initiative was established following 18 months of development among the participants. It commits firms to a set of principles on freedom of expression and privacy that make clear the firms' commitments to protecting the human rights of their users. Some of the key principles are as follows:

- 'Participating companies will respect and protect the freedom of expression of their users by seeking to avoid or minimize the impact of government restrictions on freedom of expression, including restrictions on the information available to users and the opportunities for users to create and communicate ideas and information, regardless of frontiers or media of communication.'

- 'Participating companies will respect and protect the freedom of expression rights of their users when confronted with government demands, laws and regulations to suppress freedom of expression, remove content or otherwise limit access to information and ideas in a manner inconsistent with internationally recognized laws and standards.'

- 'Participating companies will respect and protect the privacy rights of users when confronted with government demands, laws or regulations that compromise privacy in a manner inconsistent with internationally recognized laws and standards.'

Beyond the principles themselves, the initiative also includes guidelines on implementation, including a commitment to human rights impact assessments. These are important in that such assessments provide companies with the knowledge necessary to identify when freedom of expression and privacy might be at risk, and to enable appropriate risk management strategies to be put in place.

Another critical element of the initiative is that since 2013 participating companies have also been subject to independent monitoring of their compliance with the commitments, and public reporting of the results. The first set of results was reported in 2014, concluding that each of the three founding companies was 'making a good faith effort to implement GNI's Principles on Freedom of Expression and Privacy, and to improve over time.' The GNI board chair, Jermyn Brooks, heralded the results, stating:

> these independent assessments—the first of their kind—present a major step forward on human rights accountability in the technology sector. They demonstrated in the many specific cases examined how companies, applying the GNI Principles, have in fact been able to limit the removal of content and the release of personal data as a result of government requests.

The GNI establishes for technology firms a much clearer framework for action than the piecemeal approach that was generally taken before—and one approved by a number of key stakeholders in the area of freedom of expression and privacy. Its embrace of independent assessment and reporting also means that it is the only initiative in the ICT industry that clearly demonstrates firms' accountability for human rights issues.

Despite these successes, the GNI still faces a number of challenges. One of the main problems encountered by the GNI has been its inability to bring in additional important stakeholders that would enhance its scope and legitimacy. For instance, although involved in some of the earlier discussions around the initiative, Amnesty International chose to drop out before the GNI was launched, citing what it saw as several weaknesses in the programme. Later, the Electronic Frontier Foundation (EFF), a non-profit organization that defends civil liberties in the digital world, withdrew from the GNI in 2013, citing 'a fundamental breakdown in confidence that the group's corporate members are able to speak freely about their own internal privacy and security systems in the wake of the National Security Agency (NSA) surveillance revelations'. Nevertheless, despite these high-profile critics, the GNI retains a substantial membership of NGO and academic members, including some from human rights hotspots such as Bolo Bhi (a Pakistan-based non-profit focused on internet access and digital security), Human Rights in China, and the Institute for Reporters' Freedom and Safety (an Azerbaijani civil society organization dedicated to protecting journalists' rights).

More critical has been the difficulty that the GNI has had in attracting corporate members beyond the three founding companies. By 2014 it had only expanded to six ICT companies, although this included two additional major players, Facebook and LinkedIn. Notably, however, as of 2014, not a single European or Asian ICT company had joined, stifling the GNI's ambition to become the global standard for the entire sector. In fact, many European telecommunications firms such as Vodafone, Orange, Telefonica, and Nokia had initiated their own programme, the Telecommunications Industry Dialogue on Freedom of Expression and Privacy, which launched in 2011 and published its guiding principles in 2013. This differs from the GNI in that it does not include non-business members such as civil society organizations (i.e. it is an industry body rather than a multi-stakeholder initiative) and has no commitment to independent assessment of members' performance against the guiding principles. These lower demands on companies have proven attractive to companies unwilling to sign up to the GNI. Despite their differences, however, the GNI and Telecommunications Industry Dialogue announced a two-year collaboration in 2013. This expanded the relationships of the GNI with other ICT companies without diluting the initiative's standards or giving the companies formal membership.

Another major problem facing the initiative is balancing the demands of the GNI principles with hard government regulations that may limit firms' ability to live up to their commitments. This was put into sharp relief by the NSA revelations that demonstrated that ICT companies were complicit in government snooping. Although the majority of technology companies initially denied that they knew anything about the practices, the senior lawyer for the NSA asserted that the agency had been operating with the 'full knowledge and assistance' of US technology companies such as Google and Yahoo. In fact, the companies had little option but to comply given that the US government not only amended a key law in 2007 that then enabled it to demand user information from online services, but even gave the companies millions of dollars to cover the costs of compliance with the law. Companies such as Yahoo that still tried to resist handing over users' data to the NSA did not have much success in legally contesting the changes and were even threatened by the US government with a fine of $250,000 a day for refusing to provide access to the data. If that was not enough, the fine was set to double each week that Yahoo refused to comply.

In the face of evidence that its members were complicit, willingly or otherwise, in government surveillance, the GNI made a number of official calls for the US and other governments to revise their surveillance practices and institute greater transparency. The initiative's corporate members also lobbied the US government for permission to disclose more information about the number and types of requests for data they received from national security programmes. With little indication of change from the US government, however, the companies went public with their frustration, setting up a website http://www.reformgovernmentsurveillance.com and sending an open letter to the US Senate, signed by the CEOs of Google, Facebook, Microsoft, Yahoo, and LinkedIn along with other major US tech companies, urging it to revise government rules on surveillance. As Mark Zuckerberg, the CEO of Facebook, declared: 'Reports about government surveillance have shown there is a real need for greater disclosure and new limits on how governments collect information. The US government should take this opportunity to lead this reform effort and make things right'. Yahoo even went so far as to publish the details of its court case with the NSA in a bid to 'demonstrate that it objected strenuously to the directives'.

Such moves could be seen as evidence that GNI members were taking seriously their commitments to actively lobby governments about privacy and surveillance issues. As the GNI principles state: 'Participants will also encourage government demands that are consistent with international laws and standards on freedom of expression. This includes engaging proactively with governments to reach a shared understanding of how government restrictions can be applied in a manner consistent with the Principles.' On the other hand, it had also become clear that the NSA revelations had seriously eroded trust in the security of user data held by US technology companies, causing a serious financial headache for the industry. With major clients shunning US providers due to concerns about government spying, lobbying among GNI members for reform of government surveillance procedures had become as much an economic imperative as it had an ethical one.

Questions

1. What are the main challenges for ICT firms in protecting human rights in the areas of freedom of expression and privacy?

2. Set out the main strengths and weaknesses of the GNI as a way of managing the human rights obligations of ICT firms.

3. How would you assess its level of success so far, and what would enhance its potential for achieving its aims?

4. Looking forward, what should the key performance indicators be for GNI companies, and how should these be measured?

5. Assess the appropriateness of GNI as a model for use in managing other ethical issues for ICT firms, or for other sectors entirely.

Sources

Ackerman, S. 2014. US tech giants knew of NSA data collection, agency's top lawyer insists. *Guardian*, 19 March 2014: http://www.theguardian.com/world/2014/mar/19/us-tech-giants-knew-nsa-data-collection-rajesh-de.

Custer, C. 2013. What to expect on June 4, China's unofficial and Orwellian 'internet maintenance day'. *Tech in Asia*, 3 June 2013: http://www.techinasia.com/june-4-china-unofficial-orwellian-internet-maintenance-day/.

Davis, P. 2008. Yahoo in China—censor turned freedom fighter. *Ethical Corporation*, 27 May: http://www.ethicalcorp.com.

Electronic Frontier Foundation 2013. EFF Resigns from Global Network Initiative. Electronic Frontier Foundation, 10 October 2013: https://www.eff.org/press/releases/eff-resigns-global-network-initiative.

GNI 2014. GNI report finds Google, Microsoft, and Yahoo compliant with free expression and privacy principles. *Global Network Initiative*. 8 January 2014. http://globalnetworkinitiative.org/news/gni-report-finds-google-microsoft-and-yahoo-compliant-free-expression-and-privacy-principles.

Helman, C. 2010. Microsoft's Ballmer calls out Google over China stance. *Forbes*, 22 January 2010: http://www.forbes.com/sites/energysource/2010/01/22/microsoft-ballmer-google-china-stance/.

Hille, K. 2009. Google has rude awakening in China. *Financial Times*, 19 June 2009: http://www.ft.com.

Johnson, B. 2008. Amnesty criticises Global Network Initiative for online freedom of speech. *Guardian*, 30 October 2008: http://www.guardian.co.uk.

Rhoads, C. and Chao, L. 2009. Iran's web spying aided by western technology. *Wall Street Journal*, 22 June: http://www.wsj.com.

Rushe, D. 2014. Yahoo $250,000 daily fine over NSA data refusal was set to double 'every week'. *Guardian*, 12 September 2014: http://www.theguardian.com/world/2014/sep/11/yahoo-nsa-lawsuit-documents-fine-user-data-refusal.

http://www.reformgovernmentsurveillance.com.

http://www.rsf.org.

Notes

1. Unless we explicitly state otherwise, it should be noted that we chiefly talk about democratic political systems with some form of parliamentary representation.
2. Cilizza, C. 2014. How Citizens United changed politics, in 7 charts. 22 January 2014, http://www.washingtonpost.com.
3. http://www.cbsnews.com/news/koch-brothers-network-will-spend-almost-1-billion-on-2016-election/.
4. Tieman, R. 2006. Crisis exposes crippling cronyism at heart of the French state. *Observer*, 25 June 2006: http://www.theguardian.com/business/2006/jun/25/france.
5. Jones, G. 2002. Conflicts continue: pressure mounts on prime minister to sell his TV stations. *Financial Times*, 22 July: 4.
6. See Hooper, J. 2009. Berlusconi declares war on European media over sex scandal reports. *Guardian*, 28 August: http://www.guardian.co.uk; Walters, B. 2009. TV network's attempt to stifle Silvio Berlusconi documentary backfires. *Guardian*, 3 September: http://www.guardian.co.uk.
7. Chrisafis, A. 2003. Fiascos that haunt 'can do' company. *Guardian*, 15 February: 13. http://www.theguardian.com/environment/2003/feb/15/londonpolitics.congestioncharging.
8. http://www.mining.ca/site/index.php/en/towards-sustainable-mining.html.
9. http://www.icca-chem.org/en/Home/Responsible-care/.
10. For details on the ISO norms discussed in this chapter visit the ISO website at http://www.iso.org/iso/home.html.
11. http://www.gbchealth.org.
12. http://www.ohchr.org/Documents/Publications/GuidingPrinciplesBusinessHR_EN.pdf.
13. http://www.iso.org/iso/home/standards/iso26000.htm.
14. http://www.carbontracker.org.

12

Conclusions and Future Perspectives

By the end of this chapter you should be able to

- Summarize the role, meaning, and importance of business ethics.
- Summarize the influence of globalization on business ethics.
- Summarize the value of the notion of sustainability.
- Summarize the role and significance of stakeholders as a whole for ethical management.
- Summarize the implications of corporate citizenship thinking for business ethics.
- Summarize the contribution of normative ethical theories to business ethics.
- Summarize the benefits of thinking about ethical decision-making.
- Summarize the role of specific tools for managing business ethics.

■ Introduction

We hope that by now you have a pretty good idea of what business ethics is all about, and what some of the main issues, controversies, concepts, and theories are that make business ethics such a fascinating subject to study. There is always a danger, though, that in reading a book such as this you are left at the end thinking something like: 'Fine, each individual chapter makes sense, but how does it all fit together?' In this last chapter, we will therefore attempt to remedy this by setting out a brief overview of the key topics of the book, and providing a round-up of our discussions during the preceding 11 chapters. We will in particular return to the subjects introduced in Part A of the book—such as globalization, sustainability, stakeholder theory, corporate citizenship, ethical theory, and management tools, etc.—and summarize how we have applied, developed, examined, and critiqued them in the context of individual stakeholders in Part B of the book. This final chapter should therefore help you to bring together what you have learnt so far and summarize the most important lessons about business ethics.

■ The nature and scope of business ethics

By now you should be quite aware that the simple question of 'what is business ethics?' does not exactly lend itself to a simple answer. In Chapter 1 we defined the subject of business ethics as 'the study of business situations, activities, and decisions where issues of right and wrong are addressed'. Clearly, the range of such situations, activities, and decisions is immense. We have certainly discussed most of the main ones, but existing problems sometimes go away or become more a matter of legislation, and new problems continue to arise, either because of new technologies, changes in business practices or markets, exposure to different cultures, changing expectations, or simply the arising of new opportunities for ethical abuse. Consequently, it is never possible to determine the exact extent of the business ethics subject—and nor indeed should it be.

The question of business ethics and the law that we first introduced in Chapter 1 has been substantially expanded upon throughout the book. In particular, we would like to reiterate the importance of seeing business ethics as largely, but by no means exclusively, starting where the law ends. We have shown this relationship to be an increasingly complex one, with corporations sometimes supplementing or replacing the law-making process with self-regulation, and sometimes challenging, resisting, and subverting legalistic approaches to enforcing ethical behaviour. Whichever way we look at it, the relationship between business ethics and the law would appear to be an area of continued change and evolution in the years to come. Moving forward, business ethics should be seen not so much as simply beginning where the law ends but as a practice that both influences and is influenced by the law.

■ Globalization as a context for business ethics

One of the main subjects covered in Chapter 1 was the context for business ethics provided by globalization. The subsequent chapters vividly illustrated that global economic, social, and political activities are constantly shaping and reshaping the role and context of business ethics. As we particularly emphasized in each of the stakeholder chapters in Part B, globalization results in a very specific demand for innovation in all firm–stakeholder relations.

The first aspect of globalization is that much corporate activity takes place in multiple national contexts. We have explained how shareholders, employees, consumers, suppliers, competitors, CSOs, and governments might all conceivably be located in other continents. As we said in Chapter 1, this typically exposes companies to different *cultural* and *legal* environments that leave considerable discretion to managers in determining and upholding ethical standards. While some studies point to multinationals taking advantage of this situation to essentially 'export' their irresponsible practices to their subsidiaries in the developing world (Surroca et al. 2013), others point to the key role played by local mid-level managers in these subsidiaries for driving social responsibility initiatives in host countries (Reimann et al. 2012). These questions of how Western companies engage with ethical issues in developing countries will clearly remain towards the top of the business ethics agenda for the foreseeable future.

A particular focus for us in discussing the consequences of globalization in this respect has been on emerging economies, such as the BRICS countries of Brazil, Russia, India, China, and South Africa. These have increasingly accounted for a significant proportion of global trade, and have become hugely important contexts for studying and practising business ethics. Some authors, for example, suggest that countries such as China (Ip 2009) and India (Berger and Herstein 2014) have unique cultures that require different understandings and models of business ethics.

Such attention to the ethics of BRICS companies is not just about Western companies doing business overseas or sourcing from emerging economies. The BRICS countries have also increasingly developed multinationals of their own that have a significant social, ethical and environmental impact on other countries. For example, when the Brazilian private equity firm 3G Capital took over the Canadian coffee chain, Tim Hortons, vigorous cost-cutting saw major job losses and cutbacks to the firm's lauded sustainability initiatives.[1] On the other hand, the Indian multinational Tata Sons, which is well known for its commitment to social responsibility at home, has also been active in Africa since the 1970s and asserts that it 'is involved in a range of community initiatives in Africa to stay true to its values and business ethos and contribute to the social and economic development of the continent.'[2] More broadly, Chinese multinationals in the resource sector have also made major inroads into Africa, raising important questions about their employment practices, community engagement, and impact on development (Jackson 2014). Clearly, Chinese companies operate differently to their Western counterparts in such contexts, but it is not clear yet whether this can necessarily be seen as more or less ethical (Pegg 2012). The question of how emerging economy multinationals address their social responsibilities overseas will be a growing part of the debate around business ethics in the years to come.

On a second level, we suggested at the outset that globalization creates a social space beyond the governing influence of single nation states. We particularly reiterated this in the context of global financial markets in Chapter 6 and the global regulation and civil regulation of corporations in Chapters 10 and 11. For many business ethics problems, no single nation state is able to regulate and control corporate actors, especially in contexts such as global financial markets. We have argued that a firmer governmental grip on such spaces is difficult to achieve. We also explored some of the mechanisms that have led to many other corporate activities escaping the direct control of nation states. This 'transnational space' creates an interesting arena where corporate actors appear to currently dominate the scene. This does not mean that ethical norms are not present here, but these spaces lack full governmental authority to effectively control corporate action. Especially in Chapters 10 and 11, we have discussed ways of filling this gap by self-regulation, or by selected initiatives of global CSOs, or even by initiatives driven by the UN. Attention is now shifting to examine how traditional state-based regulation might interact with business self-regulation to achieve positive outcomes in the transnational space rather than simply seeing them as discrete alternatives (Eberlein et al. 2014). Such considerations will no doubt be an area of increasing activity and interest in the future.

■ Sustainability as a goal for business ethics

The next major issue we raised in Chapter 1 was that of sustainability as a goal for business ethics. Throughout the chapters in the second half of the book, we discussed the nature of this goal and its challenges, and suggested some of the steps that corporations might take in order to enhance sustainability in the context of different stakeholder relations. We have found that in different contexts, contributions can be made in the different 'corners', as it were, of the sustainability triangle (see Figure 1.8, p. 33), as well as in providing a more even balancing of the triple bottom line of sustainability. Significant progress in sustainability reporting, sustainability share indices, industrial ecosystems, product recapture, and civil and intergovernmental regulation has been made and bodes reasonably well for the future.

However one looks at it, though, the challenge posed by sustainability for business ethics is a huge one. Appropriate balancing of the triple bottom line is extremely difficult to engineer, even if corporations have the will to attempt it. Some of our discussions around sustainability in the area of employees, consumers, suppliers, etc., have been quite speculative and potentially threatening to existing corporate ways of thinking, organizing, and behaving. Ultimately, sustainability implies goals that lie beyond the time horizons of business, and which might be thought to jeopardize traditional bottom-line goals. Progress towards sustainable solutions therefore appears to be possible, but slow, tentative, and at present often merely exploratory.

What remains to be said of the goal of sustainability? Our reflections in Chapter 11 have already been rather critical of the role of corporations in the sustainability area. This leaves us to reiterate two main conclusions. First, the triple bottom line definition of sustainability obfuscates the fact that corporations tend to focus primarily on *economic* aspects, and even the majority of companies pressing for greater sustainability tend to mainly emphasize *environmental* dimensions at the expense of *social* interests. There is often a trade-off between the different elements and, especially in the context of developing countries, many of those likely to be affected lack sufficient power and influence to have their interests effectively heard and represented.

Secondly, without strong governments issuing legislation and/or developing new institutional arrangements (such as carbon markets), business progress is unlikely to be sufficient to meet sustainability goals. As much as we have identified the eroding effects of globalization and increasing corporate power on governmental authority, sustainability is likely to demand that governmental actors—perhaps in concert with CSOs and corporations—retain a significant degree of influence over the globalizing economy. Calls by business leaders, including Richard Branson (the founder of Virgin) and Paul Polman (the CEO of Unilever), for governments to take more action on climate change suggest that we might see greater attention to finding ways for regulation to provide the kind of incentives to business that helps them positively align elements of the triple bottom line rather than having to make trade-offs.[3]

■ Corporate citizenship and business ethics

Back in Chapter 2 we also introduced the concept of corporate citizenship (CC) as the latest step in a number of developments in conceptual frameworks for ethical behaviour in business. Indeed, the subtitle of this book suggests that much of the content is about how to manage CC in an era of globalization. When first talking about the concept, two major points were evident. On the one side, CC in the 'extended' view identifies the corporate involvement in the governance of *citizenship rights*, most notably social, civil, and political rights. On the other hand, we have reiterated throughout the book that alongside this role, the question of accountability automatically surfaces. We have discussed these issues throughout the book, especially in Part B, raising a number of serious issues for consideration.

With regard to the first claim—that corporations take up the governing of citizenship—Chapters 6 to 11 have provided a convincing, though nonetheless varied, impression. When discussing the relationship to shareholders, we identified quite a substantial influence of corporations over civil rights, most notably the right to property of this constituency. We then made an extensive survey of the various rights that corporations have to govern for their employees, many of which touched on their social and civil rights.

In the arena of consumers and CSOs, corporations often provide a channel through which the public expresses its political choices rather than going to the ballot box. Corporate involvement in lobbying, as well as self-regulation and voluntary codes of conduct, further underlines their role in areas of politics traditionally occupied predominantly by governments.

In the context of competitors and suppliers, corporations might like to use practices that ultimately focus on infringing or circumventing the mechanisms of the market. In so doing, they can determine prices and the range of choices that we as citizens ultimately have. Corporations, in this area, assume some responsibility over the way markets operate and remain functioning. Large corporations, in particular, have significant influence over their suppliers, and through this they can dictate the way in which products are manufactured. If a large corporation requires certain ethical standards from its suppliers, such as environmental quality or human rights protections, they have considerable power to shape the manner in which the entitlements of third parties are actually enacted.

On the side of accountability, the picture developed over the previous 11 chapters of this book is not very bright. We have identified considerable power on the part of shareholders through their right to vote and initiate shareholder activism. In some forms of governance, such as is found in continental Europe or in worker co-operatives, employees too can exert a reasonable amount of influence on corporations. Such 'industrial democracy' (Engelen 2002), however, tends to remain limited to the rather narrow scope of societal interest that is closely linked to the interest of the corporation as a whole.

Consumers also have some, albeit quite limited, influence on corporations since their approval or disapproval of the company's stance on certain ethical issues can be expressed through the market. But certainly the most direct control of corporations in this respect requires the involvement of CSOs and formal campaigns of action. Indeed, it is exactly this sector that will probably play a central role in holding corporations accountable for the way in which they participate in society in the future. Nonetheless, the lack of accountability and legitimacy of CSOs themselves arguably remains one of the weaker foundations of CSOs' power to act as proxies for citizens.

Consequently, the relationship between companies and governments seems to be the most problematic one. It is apparent that under-resourced governments have ceded some influence and power to corporations—even in terms of their own party funding—but in the period following the financial crisis in the late 2000s there has been something of a revitalization of the governmental role. If anything, our discussions highlight the major gap between the influence of corporations on citizenship rights and the subsequent control and accountability issues involved for citizens. Throughout the book we clearly identify this institutional void; however, we also show some potential ways in which each stakeholder groups can use existing links in order to fill this gap.

■ The contribution of normative ethical theories to business ethics

In Chapter 3 we introduced normative ethical theories, suggesting that in a pluralistic perspective they can provide a number of important considerations for ethical decision-making in business. In so doing, we had already watered down the inherent claim of traditional ethical theories—that they provide codified rational solutions to every problem. Indeed, as you have progressed through the book it should have become extremely clear that these theories rarely provide us with a clearcut, unambiguous, and non-controversial solution. As such, this book could be argued to be closer to a postmodern perspective than anything else: ethical theories are at best tools to inform the 'moral sentiment' of the decision-maker and cannot predetermine solutions from an abstract, theoretical, or wholly 'objective' point of view. Ultimately, ethical decisions are taken by actors in everyday business situations. Ethical theories might help to structure and rationalize some of the key aspects of those decisions, but their status never can be one that allows a moral judgement or decision to be made without effectively immersing in the real situation. This is one of the key reasons that we introduced the Ethics on Screen and Ethics Online features into recent editions of the text since the medium of film and the interactive potential of the internet allow us to immerse ourselves into 'real-life' situations and, as it were, live the reality of ethical decision-making in business.

By positioning the role of ethical theory on this level, we by no means intend to play down the role of normative ethical theory (as a postmodernist would). These theories first of all help the individual actor to rationalize moral sentiments and to verbalize moral considerations in concrete business situations. Thus, we have emphasized the important role of ethical theory throughout the book, yet at the same time we have tried to encourage you to develop a critical perspective on theory. When discussing cases, ethics in action vignettes, and ethical dilemmas, our hope is that you will have discovered the value of ethical theories for communicating your views, and also for understanding the views and perspectives of others. Here, perhaps the main value of ethical theories lies in the fact that they help to rationalize and enable a discourse about ethical considerations in business decisions.

■ Influences on ethical decision-making

In Chapter 4 we examined descriptive ethical theories. This helped us to understand the way in which people in organizations actually make decisions about business ethics. In the subsequent chapters we have made evident the enormous range and complexity of ethical problems that continue to occur in business, suggesting that the factors influencing unethical decision-making continue to have a substantial role to play.

Given the increasing internationalization of business discussed throughout the book, we might first suggest that the national and cultural influences on decision-making, at both the individual and situational level, will progressively become more important, but less clearcut. Personal religious and cultural factors are increasingly challenged and reshaped by global business practices, and the influence of a specific, local, national context also shifts in the context of 'foreign' MNCs with global codes of practice.

Indeed, many of the more important influences identified in Chapter 4 were context based, and were often informal and cultural aspects, such as the moral framing of ethical issues in the workplace, organizational norms, and work roles. This suggests that more formal efforts to target improved ethical decision-making, such as codes of conduct and voluntary regulation, might ultimately have fairly limited impact unless they presage a more profound culture shift in business organizations. Some prospects for hope might be evident here when we consider that the mere fact of actively taking part in designing codes and rules could conceivably lead businesses to a deeper consideration of values in the longer term. Perhaps this is a little optimistic, but the opportunities for doing so would be enhanced if corporations continue to open themselves up to discourse with stakeholders—especially those that might challenge the dominant corporate mindset.

■ The role of management tools in business ethics

In Chapter 5, the last chapter in the first part of the book, we discussed the management of business ethics. Therefore, unlike, for instance, a book on finance or marketing, Crane and Matten has just one chapter dedicated to what we would traditionally call management instruments and tools. This might strike you as odd, especially if you are a business or management student, but it shows that business ethics is about more than just managing with tools and techniques. To our mind, it is much more about expanding horizons, deepening understandings, and developing critical thinking about business practices. The chapter on tools also suggests that business ethics is not really a separate branch of management at all. After all, it should be pretty clear by now that business ethics pertains to every traditional discipline of management, such as marketing, finance, strategy, etc., and more constitutes an additional set of criteria for typical decisions, and a different way of looking at 'normal' business situations.

This is not to say that the explicit management of business ethics is unimportant, and we have traced some of the potential for tools and techniques in the second part of the book. A crucial role, for example, is likely to be played by new forms of social auditing and reporting, particularly in helping customers, CSOs, and shareholders evaluate the corporation's performance against ethical criteria. This is closely linked to new forms of stakeholder dialogue that we discussed in Chapter 5. Employee participation, shareholder democracy, or business–CSO partnership, among other things that we discussed in Part B, clearly require active engagement by corporations with their stakeholders.

Another of the tools that we have made frequent reference to throughout Chapters 6 to 11 is codes of ethics. These are certainly one of the most commonly used tools of business ethics, and as we have discussed, the general lack of governmental regulation in a growing number of business areas means that codes are necessary to fill the rule-making gap. Certainly, in industry at the moment, codes and standards of various sorts have been the subject of enormous effort and interest. As we have discussed throughout the book, though, it remains to be seen where this development might lead and what real impact it might actually have in practice. Indeed, the multiplication and proliferation of more and more codes might actually be counterproductive to the original purpose of making decision-making more clear and companies more transparent and accountable. Moving forward it will be important to explore how the 'market' for such codes plays out, and whether competition among different standards for company's attention can actually be harnessed to improve corporate behaviour (Reinecke et al. 2012).

■ The role of different stakeholder constituencies in business ethics

In Chapter 2 we introduced a number of important concepts that help us to frame business ethics. Perhaps the most important of these was stakeholder theory, especially given that the major stakeholder constituencies of the corporation provided the structure for Part B of the book. Notwithstanding the fact that many managers will in practice probably deal with stakeholders on a much more instrumental basis, we have primarily developed a *normative* approach to stakeholder theory, namely the idea that certain groups have intrinsic rights and interests that need to be considered by managers. This has been an important element of the discussion in the second part of the book, not least because stakeholder rights often form the basis of many ethical issues and problems faced by business.

In Chapters 6 to 11 we discussed each individual stakeholder group separately, and it might appear as if they were all equally important to the corporation. Although in a certain sense they are, their significance certainly varies in different contexts, issues, and topics. *Shareholders* obviously remain a key stakeholder group for the corporation, especially at a time when globalized financial markets confront companies with the necessity to source their capital on a global level. With countries outside the US increasingly adopting a shareholder value ideology, the prospects of assigning a dominant role for shareholders appear to be advancing, notwithstanding a growing interest in alternative systems and corporate forms (such as social purpose companies). Another challenging area here is the topic of shareholder activism. Certainly, the field of SRI is an area of growing importance for corporations, and major institutional investors are increasingly responding to demands to add environmental, social and governance (ESG) criteria to their investment decisions.

Employees count among the most long-standing stakeholder groups of every business operation. In Europe and some other national contexts, there is still considerable ground for expecting employees to be a dominant stakeholder group, especially given the strong legal position this group generally has. However, new working practices, increased flexibilization, and challenges to legally codified protections all appear to have weakened the stake of employees somewhat in recent years. In the developing world, employee rights might be yet more open to contestation and abuse, requiring considerable attention to new practices and protections.

The role of *consumers* is particularly interesting, since although they have always been of utmost *instrumental* importance to business, their *normative* claims would seem to be somewhat weaker than those of certain other constituencies. While consumers might easily simply transfer their attention to another product or supplier, groups such as employees, suppliers, and local communities are more 'locked in' to the corporation and cannot so easily switch to an alternative. Nonetheless, it is easy to miss the fact that although the satisfaction of consumers appears to be in the self-interest of corporations, there is still much scope for exploitation and abuse of consumer rights. That said, the power of some consumers to exercise ethical purchasing is likely to sustain corporations' attention to consumers' ethical concerns.

The stake of *suppliers* appears to be one that although quite strong in certain contexts and industries, often has little legal protection, and will in practice often depend on the relative power balance with the corporation. *Competitors*, meanwhile, have one of the more contestable stakes in a firm, and although they have certain in-built rights that need to be considered, they will often be one of the lowest priorities for corporations. Interestingly, in environmentally exposed industries, competitors might be more strongly considered because of their role in setting up take-back and recycling schemes, just as suppliers might play a major role where integrated networks of recovery are intended. With an increasing trend towards just-in-time production and specialization, as well as strategic alliances and joint ventures, certain industries are more closely tied to their competitors and suppliers than others—a tendency that may also vary across different cultures and countries.

The stake of *CSOs* and *governments* is certainly the most complex and dynamic at the current time. CSOs, on the one hand, have heralded and pushed crucial ethical issues in the past, even initiating long-term processes of change on the part of corporations to respond, adopt, and incorporate the issues at stake. Over the course of time, CSOs have contributed to mainstreaming business ethics, but the legitimacy of their stake remains open to contestation in specific cases. The relationship of business with government meanwhile seems to be developing in an even more controversial direction. While governments may have lost some of their traditional power in issuing and enforcing regulation, they have by no means decreased in importance as a stakeholder. The crucial innovation, though, is that the relationship develops more into a partnership rather than the previously dependent role of business. This applies to the national level, but increasingly also to the global level, as the UN Global Compact as an 'institutionalized arena for addressing global governance gaps' illustrates quite well (Rasche et al. 2013).

■ Trade-offs and conflicts between different stakeholder groups

One final point that should be made clear at this stage is that one of the most challenging tasks for ethical management is to achieve an effective and appropriate balance between *competing* stakeholder expectations and claims. Different stakeholders are likely to diverge in the demands they place on corporations, making even a supposedly 'ethical' response a matter of some disagreement. Moreover, as we saw in Chapter 5, companies may well make their assessments based on largely instrumental grounds, meaning that those unable or unwilling to influence the corporation may be neglected, regardless of any intrinsic rights they might have.

On the surface, expectations of shareholders could be seen as clashing with all other stakeholders' interests nearly by default, as many of the latter are most likely to have a negative impact on profits, at least in the short term. Looking at the negative side, one could argue based on the numerous scandals we have discussed in this book (particularly in Chapter 6), that whenever shareholders are negatively affected we also see that other stakeholders, most notably employees and local communities, suffer as well from corruption and mismanagement. Looking at the ongoing popularity of ethical—or as we also termed it—socially responsible investment (SRI), we could argue that some of the most widely discussed and applied topics in business ethics in the business press are exactly those that attempt to reconcile shareholders' interests with those of other stakeholders. This 'business case' for business ethics is important, but it is critical that ethical issues are not always simply relegated to instrumental reasoning. Real rights and real responsibilities are at stake here.

More broadly, claims for more sustainability, accountability, and good citizenship from companies can be interpreted as demands for a better accommodation of competing and conflicting interests of their various stakeholders. In a sense, managing business ethics is almost always a matter of navigating a path through situations of multiple expectations and values that are in conflict. An essential starting point in this process is the acknowledgement and understanding of these divergent positions—and therefore finding a way of enabling stakeholders to give voice to their values. Here we can expect quite a bit of development over the coming years, in an arena sometimes couched in terms of 'stakeholder dialogue' or more optimistically 'stakeholder democracy' (Matten and Crane 2005). In the latter debate, the political metaphor of democracy is applied to the corporate engagement with stakeholders, suggesting that businesses are increasingly expected to allow all of their stakeholders opportunities to voice their interests and provide legitimate engagement in the governing of the corporation. In the context of our argument in this section, one of the key effects of these patterns of interaction would be to involve companies in a transparent process of simultaneous responses to divergent claims from various stakeholder constituencies.

■ Summary

In this chapter we have reviewed the main themes that were introduced in Part A of the book, and have synthesized and summarized the main contributions subsequently made to these themes in Part B. We have concluded that the nature and scope of business ethics is likely to remain complex and ever evolving, with the prospect that the subject will be increasingly important in the years to come. We explained how globalization has dramatically reshaped the role and context of business ethics, while sustainability has presented an important, yet extremely challenging, goal for business ethics to contend with. We then provided a summary of the different stakeholder contributions to our understanding of corporate citizenship thinking. In the remainder of the chapter we assessed the contribution of ethical theory, ethical decision-making, and business ethics management to our discussions in Part B. Here, we highlighted the need for a pragmatic, pluralistic approach that was both sensitive to the variety of contexts that corporations and managers are involved in, and that went beyond mere adherence to codified laws and procedures. Finally, we analysed the relative importance and relevance of each of the different stakeholder groups discussed in Part B, then went on to emphasize the profound problems of balancing competing stakeholder interests.

We hope that in reading this book, and thinking and talking about the issues and ideas that were raised, you will be better equipped to respond to the complex yet fascinating problems of business ethics. At the very least, we would like to think that we have opened your eyes to new problems and perspectives and hopefully excited you about the real-world challenges of business ethics. If the theories, concepts, and tools that you have learned along the way enable you to make better ethical decisions—by using empathy, imagination, and good judgement—then so much the better. The world of business ethics awaits you.

Study questions

1. What do you think will be the major new ethical issues and problems that businesses will have to face over the next decade?

2. Compare the challenges posed by globalization and sustainability to business ethics thinking and practice. Which do you think will prove to be the greatest challenge?

3. What are the particular ethical problems and issues that are likely to be faced by companies from emerging economies? What approaches to business ethics thinking and practice are likely to be appealing and suitable for such companies?

4. What are the major implications of corporate citizenship ideas for each major stakeholder group? How well placed is each group to influence the decisions and actions of corporations?

5. What are the benefits and drawbacks of adopting a pluralistic approach to normative ethical theory in business ethics?

6. Account for the prevalence of ethical codes in global business. To what extent do you consider such a development to be beneficial to the improvement of business ethics?

Research exercise

Select a controversial mining project currently under way in your country or involving a multinational company domiciled in your country and undertake research on the main stakeholders and ethical issues involved in the project. You might want to consult websites of major extraction companies, such as Anglo American, Barrick Gold, BHP Billiton, Freeport-McMoRan, Glencore, Rio Tinto, or Vale and/or review websites dedicated to identifying mining conflicts and empowering communities such as the following:

- Miningwatch Canada: http://www.miningwatch.ca.
- Latin American Mining Conflict Observatory: http://www.conflictosmineros.net.
- Mines and Communities: http://www.minesandcommunities.org.

1. Who are the main stakeholders involved in the project and what are their main concerns and interests?

2. Provide a ranking of these stakeholders according to either instrumental or normative principles, listing the criteria used in your ranking.

3. What methods has the company adopted so far in incorporating the interests of these stakeholders in its decision-making?

4. How would you recommend it proceed to enhance its stakeholder democracy?

VISIT THE ONLINE RESOURCE CENTRE for links to further key readings

Key readings

1. **Ip, P.K. 2009. The challenge of developing a business ethics in China.** *Journal of Business Ethics*, 88 (Supplement 1): 211–24.

   While the US has arguably had the biggest influence on twentieth-century business ethics, the future of the subject looks set to be bound up with developments in emerging economies, especially in China. This article discusses the challenge of developing business ethics in China by examining recent ethical scandals in the country and exploring some of their root causes. It concludes by offering some thoughts on what a uniquely Chinese version of business ethics might look like in the future.

2. **Reinecke, J., Manning, S., and Von Hagen, O. 2012. The emergence of a standards market: Multiplicity of sustainability standards in the global coffee industry.** *Organization Studies*, 33(5–6): 791–814.

   This article introduces the idea that different ethical codes or 'sustainability standards' compete against one another in a market. Using the multiplicity of codes in the coffee industry as an example, the article reports on interviews with industry participants to show how different standards seek to both differentiate from one another as well as build towards some form of convergence to enhance transnational business governance.

Notes

1. See http://craneandmatten.blogspot.ca/2015/04/has-tim-hortons-given-up-on.html.
2. See http://www.tataafrica.com/Our_commitment/community_initiatives.htm.
3. See http://ens-newswire.com/2015/02/10/business-leaders-urge-bold-climate-action-for-global-pact/.

REFERENCES

AccountAbility. 2005. *Towards responsible lobbying: leadership and public policy*. London: AccountAbility.

Ackers, P. and Payne, J. 1998. British trade unions and social partnership: rhetoric, reality and strategy. *International Journal of Human Resource Management*, 9 (3): 529–50.

Adams, J. 2008. Chinese union. *Newsweek*, 14 February 2008: http://www.newsweek.com.

Agle, B.R. and Caldwell, C.B. 1999. Understanding research on values in business. *Business and Society*, 38 (3): 326–89.

Aguilera, R.V. and Jackson, G. 2010. Comparative and international corporate governance. *The Academy of Management Annals*, 4 (1): 485–556.

Aguilera, R.V., Williams, C.A., Conley, J.M., and Rupp, D.E. 2006. Corporate governance and social responsibility: a comparative analysis of the UK and the US. *Corporate Governance*, 14 (3): 147–58.

Albert, M. 1991. *Capitalisme contre capitalisme*. Paris: Le Seuil.

Alexandridis, G., Petmezas, D., and Travlos, N.G. 2010. Gains from mergers and acquisitions around the world: New evidence. *Financial Management*, 39 (4): 1671–95.

Allenby, B.R. 1993. *Industrial ecology*. New York: Prentice Hall.

Altman, B.W. and Vidaver-Cohen, D. 2000. A framework for understanding corporate citizenship. Introduction to the special edition of Business and Society Review 'corporate citizenship and the new millennium'. *Business and Society Review*, 105 (1): 1–7.

Amaeshi, K.M., Osuji, O.K., and Nnodim, P. 2008. Corporate social responsibility in supply chains of global brands: a boundaryless responsibility? Clarifications, exceptions and implications. *Journal of Business Ethics*, 81 (1): 223–34.

Anand, V., Ashforth, B.E., and Joshi, M. 2004. Business as usual: the acceptance and perpetuation of corruption in organizations. *Academy of Management Executive*, 18 (2): 39–53.

Anastasiadis, S. 2014. Toward a View of Citizenship and Lobbying Corporate Engagement in the Political Process. *Business & Society*, 53 (2): 260–99.

Anderson, E. and Jap, S.D. 2005. The dark side of close relationships. *MIT Sloan Management Review*, 46 (3): 75.

Andreasson, S. 2011. Understanding Corporate Governance Reform in South Africa Anglo-American Divergence, the King Reports, and Hybridization. *Business & Society*, 50 (4): 647–73.

Aravind, D. and Christmann, P. 2011. Decoupling of standard implementation from certification. Does quality of ISO 14001 implementation affect facilities' environmental performance? *Business Ethics Quarterly*, 21 (1): 73–102.

Ariff, M. and Iqbal, M. 2011. *The Foundations of Islamic Banking: Theory, Practice and Education*. Cheltenham: Edward Elgar Publishing.

Arrow, K.J. and Hurwicz, L. 1977. *Studies in resource allocation processes*. Cambridge and New York: Cambridge University Press.

Arthur, C. 2014. European commission reopens Google antitrust investigation. *Guardian*, 8 September 2014. http://www.theguardian.com/technology/2014/sep/08/european-commission-reopens-google-antitrust-investigation-after-political-storm-over-proposed-settlement.

Arts, B. 2002. 'Green alliances' of business and NGOs: new styles of self-regulation or 'dead-end roads'? *Corporate Social Responsibility and Environmental Management*, 9: 26–36.

Artz, K.W. 1999. Buyer-supplier performance: the role of asset specificity, reciprocal investments and relational exchange. *British Journal of Management*, 10 (2): 113–26.

Ashman, D. 2001. Civil society collaboration with business: bringing empowerment back in. *World Development*, 29 (7): 1097–113.

Assael, H. 1995. *Consumer behaviour and marketing action* (5th edn.). Cincinnati: South-Western College.

Audi, R. 2012. Virtue ethics as a resource in business. *Business Ethics Quarterly*, 22 (2): 273–91.

Auger, P. and Devinney, T.M. 2007. Do what consumers say matter? The misalignment of preferences with unconstrained ethical intentions. *Journal of Business Ethics*, 76 (4): 361–83.

Auger, P., Devinney, T.M., and Louviere, J.J. 2006. Global segments of socially conscious consumers: do they exist? Paper presented at the Corporate Responsibility and Global Business: Implications for Corporate and Marketing Strategy, London Business School, 13–14 July.

Auletta, K. 2012. Paper Trail. *The New Yorker*, 25 June 2012.

Austin, J. 2000. *The* collaboration *challenge: how nonprofits and businesses succeed through strategic alliances*. San Francisco: Jossey-Bass.

Austin, J.E. and Seitanidi, M.M. 2012. Collaborative value creation: A review of partnering between nonprofits and businesses: Part I. Value creation spectrum and collaboration stages. *Nonprofit and Voluntary Sector Quarterly*, 41 (5): 726–58.

Babiak, K. and Thibault, L. 2009. Challenges in multiple cross-sector partnerships. *Nonprofit and Voluntary Sector Quarterly*, 38 (1): 117–43.

Badaracco, J.L., Jr., and Webb, A.P. 1995. Business ethics: a view from the trenches. *California Management Review*, 37 (2): 8–29.

Badenhorst, J.A. 1994. Unethical behaviour in procurement: a perspective on causes and solutions. *Journal of Business Ethics*, 13 (9): 739–45.

Bafilemba, F., Mueller, T., and Lezhnev, S. 2014. The Impact of Dodd-Frank and Conflict Minerals Reforms on Eastern Congo's Conflict. http://www.enough.org.

Bahena, A. 2009. *What role did credit rating agencies (CRAs) play in the financial crisis?* Des Moines, Ia.: University of Iowa Center for International Finance and Development.

Bailey, W. and Spicer, A. 2007. When does national identity matter? Convergence and divergence in international business ethics. *Academy of Management Journal*, 50 (6): 1462–80.

Bakan, J. 2004. *The corporation: the pathological pursuit of profit and power*. London: Constable and Robinson.

Balch, O. 2009. Access all areas. *Ethical Corporation*, April: http://www.ethicalcorp.com.

Ballwieser, W. and Clemm, H. 1999. 'Wirtschaftsprüfung'. In W. Korff (ed.), *Handbuch der Wirtschaftsethik*: 399–416. Gütersloh: Gütersloher Verlagshaus.

Balzarova, M.A. and Castka, P. 2012. Stakeholders' influence and contribution to social standards development: The case of multiple stakeholder approach to ISO 26000 development. *Journal of Business Ethics*, 111 (2): 265–79.

Banaji, M.R., Bazerman, M.H., and Chugh, D. 2003. How (un)ethical are you? *Harvard Business Review*, 81 (12): 56–65.

Banerjee, S.B. 2000. Whose land is it anyway? National interest, indigenous stakeholders, and colonial discourses. *Organization & Environment*, 13 (1): 3–38.

Banerjee, S.B. 2009. Necrocapitalism. *Organization Studies*, 29 (12): 1541–63.

Banerjee, S.B. 2011. Voices of the Governed: towards a theory of the translocal. *Organization*, 18 (3): 323–44.

Barak, M.E.M. 2013. *Managing diversity: Toward a globally inclusive workplace*. Thousand Oaks, CA: Sage.

Barkawi, A. 2002. Benchmarking sustainability investments am Beispiel der Dow Jones Sustainability Indexes. In R. von Rosen (ed.), *Ethisch orientierte Aktienanlage—Nische oder Wachstumsmarkt?*: 88–98. Frankfurt: Deutsches Aktieninstitut.

Barnett, M.L. and King, A.A. 2008. Good fences make good neighbors: a longitudinal analysis of industry self-regulation. *Academy of Management Journal*, 51 (6): 1150–70.

Barrett, E. 1999. Justice in the workplace? Normative ethics and the critique of human resource management. *Personnel Review*, 28 (4): 307–18.

Bart, C.K. 1997. Sex, lies and mission statements. *Business Horizons*, November–December, 40: 9–18.

Bartz, D. and Oreskovic, A. 2009. Facebook settles privacy case with FTC. *Reuters*, 29 November 2011: http://www.reuters.com/article/2011/11/30/us-facebook-privacy-idUSTRE7AS21J20111130.

Basil, D.Z., Runte, M.S., Easwaramoorthy, M. and Barr, C. 2009. Company support for employee volunteering: a national survey of companies in Canada. *Journal of Business Ethics*, 85: 387–98.

Baskerville-Morley, R.F. 2005. A research note: the unfinished business of culture. *Accounting, Organizations, and Society*, 30: 389–91.

Baudrillard, J. 1997. *The consumer society*. London: Sage.

Baughn, C.C. and Buchanan, M.A. 2001. Cultural protectionism. *Business Horizons*, 44 (6): 5–15.

Bauman, D.C. 2013. Leadership and the three faces of integrity. *The Leadership Quarterly*, 24 (3): 414–26.

Bauman, Z. 1989. *Modernity and the Holocaust*. Cambridge: Polity Press.

Bauman, Z. 1991. The social manipulation of morality. *Theory, Culture and Society*, 8 (1): 137–52.

Bauman, Z. 1993. *Postmodern ethics*. London: Blackwell.

Baumhart, R.C. 1961. How ethical are businesses? *Harvard Business Review*, 39 (July–August): 6.

Baur, D. and Palazzo, G. 2011. The moral legitimacy of NGOs as partners of corporations. *Business Ethics Quarterly*, 21 (4): 579–604.

Baur, D. and Schmitz, H.P. 2012. Corporations and NGOs: When accountability leads to co-optation. *Journal of Business Ethics*, 106 (1): 9–21.

BBC. 2012. Kent food workers held in 'slave-like' conditions. *BBC News*, 5 October 2012: http://www.bbc.com/news/uk-england-kent-19842821.

Beauchamp, T.L. 1997. Goals and quotas in hiring and promotion. In T.L. Beauchamp and N.E. Bowie (eds.), *Ethical theory and business* (5th edn.) 379–87. Upper Saddle River, NJ: Prentice Hall.

Beauchamp, T.L. and Bowie, N.E. 1997. *Ethical theory and business* (5th edn.). Upper Saddle River, NJ: Prentice Hall.

Becht, M. and Röell, A. 1999. Blockholdings in Europe: an international comparison. *European Economic Review*, 43: 1049–56.

Beck, U. (ed.). 1998. *Politik der globalisierung*. Frankfurt/Main: Suhrkamp.

Beck, U. 1992. *Risk Society: towards a new modernity*. London: Sage.

Becker, B. and Westbrook, D.A. 1998. Confronting asymmetry: global financial markets and national regulation. *International Finance*, 1 (2): 339–55.

Begg, K., van der Woerd, F., and Levy, D.L. (eds.). 2005. *The business of climate change: corporate responses to Kyoto*. Sheffield: Greenleaf.

Belal, A.R. 2002. Stakeholder accountability or stakeholder management: a review of UK firms' social and ethical accounting, auditing and reporting (SEAAR) practices. *Corporate Social Responsibility and Environmental Management*, 9: 8–25.

Bell, M.P., Özbilgin, M.F., Beauregard, T.A., and Sürgevil, O. 2011. Voice, silence, and diversity in 21st century organizations: Strategies for inclusion of gay, lesbian, bisexual, and transgender employees. *Human Resource Management*, 50 (1): 131–46.

Bendell, J. 2000. Civil regulation: a new form of democratic governance for the global economy? In J. Bendell (ed.), *Terms for endearment: business, NGOs and sustainable development*: 239–54. Sheffield: Greenleaf.

Bendell, J. and Murphy, D.F. 2000. Planting the seeds of change: business-NGO relations on tropical deforestation. In J. Bendell (ed.), *Terms for endearment: business, NGOs and sustainable development*. Sheffield: Greenleaf.

Berger, R. and Herstein, R. 2014. The evolution of business ethics in India. *International Journal of Social Economics*, 41 (11): 1073–86.

Berle, A.A. and Means, G.C. 1932. *The modern corporation and private property*. New York: Transaction.

Bernstein, S. and Cashore, B. 2007. Can non-state global governance be legitimate? An analytical framework. *Regulation & Governance*, 1 (4): 347–71.

Binford, L. 2009. From fields of power to fields of sweat: the dual process of constructing temporary migrant labour in Mexico and Canada. *Third World Quarterly*, 30 (3): 503–17.

Birchfield, V. and Freyberg-Inan, A. 2005. Organic intellectuals and counter-hegemonic politics in the age of globalisation: the case of ATTAC. In C. Eschle and B. Maiguashca (eds.), *Critical theories, international relations and 'the anti-globalization movement'*: 154–73. London: Routledge.

Bird, F.B. and Waters, J.A. 1989. The moral muteness of managers. *California Management Review*, Fall: 73–88.

Bloom, P.N. and Perry, V.G. 2001. Retailer power and supplier welfare: the case of Wal-Mart. *Journal of Retailing*, 77 (3): 379–97.

Blowfield, M. 1999. Ethical trade: a review of developments and issues. *Third World Quarterly*, 20 (4): 753–70.

Boatright, J.R. 2009. *Ethics and the conduct of business* (6th edn.). Upper Saddle River, NJ: Pearson Education.

Boatright, J.R. 2012. *Ethics and the conduct of business* (7th edn.). Upper Saddle River, NJ: Pearson Education.

Boele, R., Fabig, H., and Wheeler, D. 2000. The story of Shell, Nigeria and the Ogoni people—a study in unsustainable development. I—Economy, environment and social relationships. Paper presented at the Academy of Management Conference. Toronto.

Boli, J. and Lechner, F.J. (eds.). 2000. *The globalization reader*. Malden, MA, and Oxford: Blackwell.

Booth, P. and Whetstone, L. 2007. Half a cheer for Fair Trade. *Economic Affairs*, 27 (2): 29–36.

Borgerson, J.L. 2007. On the harmony of feminist ethics and business ethics. *Business and Society Review*, 112 (4): 477–509.

Borgmann, A. 2000. The moral complexion of consumption. *Journal of Consumer Research*, 26, March: 418–22.

Bowie, N.E. 1991. New directions in corporate social responsibility. *Business Horizons*, 34, July–August: 56–65.

Bowie, N.E. 2013. Business ethics in the 21st Century, *Issues in business ethics*. Dordrecht; New York: Springer.

Boyd, C. 1996. Ethics and corporate governance: the issues raised by the Cadbury Report in the United Kingdom. *Journal of Business Ethics*, 15: 167–82.

Brammer, S. and Pavelin, S. 2005. Corporate community contributions in the United Kingdom and the United States. *Journal of Business Ethics*, 56 (1): 15–26.

Brammer, S., Williams, G., and Zinkin, J. 2007. Religion and attitudes to corporate social responsibility in a large cross-country sample. *Journal of Business Ethics*, 71 (3): 229–43.

Braverman, H. 1974. *Labor and monopoly capital: the degradation of work in the twentieth century*. New York: Monthly Review Press.

Brenkert, G.G. 2010. The limits and prospects of business ethics. *Business Ethics Quarterly*, 20 (4): 703–709.

Bressers, H., De Bruijn, T., Lulofs, K., and O'Toole Jr., L.J. 2011. Negotiation-based policy instruments and performance: Dutch covenants and environmental policy outcomes. *Journal of Public Policy*, 31 (2): 187–208.

Brill, S. 2015. *America's bitter pill: money, politics, backroom deals, and the fight to fix our broken healthcare system* (1st edn.). New York: Random House.

Brodwin, E. 2013. Tobacco companies still target youth despite global treaty. *Scientific American*, 21 October 2013.

Brown, M.B. 1993. *Fair trade*. London: Zed Books.

Brown, M.E. and Mitchell, M.S. 2010. Ethical and unethical leadership. *Business Ethics Quarterly*, 20 (4): 583–616.

Brown, M.T. 2005. *Corporate integrity: rethinking organizational ethics and leadership*. Cambridge: Cambridge University Press.

Brugmann, J. and Prahalad, C.K. 2007. Cocreating business's new social compact. *Harvard Business Review*, 85 (2): 80–90.

Buchanan, D. and Huczynski, A. 1997. *Organizational behaviour* (3rd edn.). London: Prentice-Hall.

Buchholz, R.A. 1998. The ethics of consumption activities: a future paradigm? *Journal of Business Ethics*, 17 (8): 871–82.

Buhr, K. 2012. The Inclusion of Aviation in the EU Emissions Trading Scheme: Temporal Conditions for Institutional Entrepreneurship. *Organization Studies*, 33 (11): 1565–87.

Burke, L. and Logsdon, J.M. 1996. How corporate social responsibility pays off. *Long Range Planning*, 29 (4): 495–502.

Burke, R.J. and Black, S. 1997. Save the males: backlash in organizations. *Journal of Business Ethics*, 16: 933–42.

Burritt, R.L. and Schaltegger, S. 2010. Sustainability accounting and reporting: fad or trend? *Accounting, Auditing & Accountability Journal*, 23 (7): 829–46.

Butler, S. 2007. Levi's suspended by ethical group in living wage row. *The Times*: http://www.timesonline.co.uk.

Cannon, T. 1994. *Corporate responsibility*. London: Pearson.

Cao, M. and Zhang, Q. 2011. Supply chain collaboration: impact on collaborative advantage and firm performance. *Journal of Operations Management*, 29 (3): 163–80.

Cappelli, P. 2009. The future of the U.S. business model and the rise of competitors. *Academy of Management Perspectives*, 23 (2): 5–10.

Carney, M. 2008. The many futures of Asian business groups. *Asia Pacific Journal of Management*, 25 (4): 595–613.

Carr, A. 1968. Is business bluffing ethical? *Harvard Business Review*, 46 (January–February): 143–53.

Carroll, A.B. 1979. A three dimensional model of corporate social performance. *Academy of Management Review*, 4: 497–505.

Carroll, A.B. 1991. The pyramid of corporate social responsibility: toward the moral management of organizational stakeholders. *Business Horizons*, July–August, 34 (4): 39–48.

Carroll, A.B. 1998. The four faces of corporate citizenship. *Business and Society Review*, 100 (1): 1–7.

Carroll, A.B. 2008. A history of corporate social responsibility: concepts and practices. In A. Crane, A. McWilliams, D. Matten, J. Moon and D. Siegel (eds.), *The Oxford handbook of corporate social responsibility*: 19–46. Oxford: Oxford University Press.

Carroll, A.B. and Buchholtz, A.K. 2009. *Business and society: ethics and stakeholder management* (7th edn.). Cincinnati: South-Western.

Carroll, A.B. and Buchholtz, A.K. 2012. *Business and society: Ethics, sustainability and stakeholder management* (8th edn.). Mason, OH: South-Western Cengage Learning.

Carroll, A.B. and Buchholtz, A.K. 2015. *Business and society: Ethics, sustainability and stakeholder management* (9th edn.). Stamford, CT: Cengage Learning.

Cashore, B. 2002. Legitimacy and the privatization of environmental governance: how non-state market-driven (NSMD) governance systems gain rule-making authority. *Governance*, 15 (4): 503–29.

Cassell, C., Johnson, P., and Smith, K. 1997. Opening the black box: corporate codes of ethics in their organizational context. *Journal of Business Ethics*, 16: 1077–93.

CBCnews. 2014. GM recall linked to 57-cent ignition switch component: http://www.cbc.ca/news/business/gm-recall-linked-to-57-cent-ignition-switch-component-1.2593930.

Cederström, C. and Fleming, P. 2012. *Dead man working*. Alresford, Hants: Zero Books.

Cerin, P. and Dobers, P. 2001a. Who is rating the raters? *Corporate Environmental Strategy*, 8 (2): 1–3.

Cerin, P. and Dobers, P. 2001b. What does the performance of the Dow Jones Sustainability Group Index tell us? *Eco-Management and Auditing*, 8: 123–33.

Chen, A.Y.S., Sawyers, R.B., and Williams, P.F. 1997. Reinforcing ethical decision making through corporate culture. *Journal of Business Ethics*, 16: 855–65.

Chen, T.-P. 2015. China Cracks Down on Water-Polluting Industries. *Wall Street Journal*, 17 April 2015: http://www.wsj.com/articles/china-cracks-down-on-water-polluting-industries-1429267822.

Cheney, G. 1995. Democracy in the workplace: theory and practice from the perspective of communication. *Journal of Applied Communication*, 23: 167–200.

Chenting, S. 2003. Is Guanxi orientation bad, ethically speaking? A study of Chinese enterprises. *Journal of Business Ethics*, 44 (4): 303–15.

Chertow, M.R. 2007. 'Uncovering' Industrial Symbiosis. *Journal of Industrial Ecology*, 11 (1): 11–30.

Chhabara, R. 2008. Workplace equality—putting harassment on notice. *Ethical Corporation*, 22 October: http://www.ethicalcorp.com.

Chin, M.K., Hambrick, D.C., and Treviño, L.K. 2013. Political Ideologies of CEOs: The Influence of Executives' Values on Corporate Social Responsibility. *Administrative Science Quarterly*, 58 (2): 197–232.

Chiu, R.K. 2003. Ethical judgment and whistleblowing intention: Examining the moderating role of locus of control. *Journal of Business Ethics*, 43 (1–2): 65–74.

Christie, P.M.J., Kwon, I.-W.G., Stoeberl, P.A., and Baumhart, R. 2003. A cross-cultural comparison of ethical attitudes of business managers: India, Korea and the United States. *Journal of Business Ethics*, 46 (3): 263–87.

Christmann, P. and Taylor, G. 2001. Globalization and the environment: determinants of firm self-regulation in China. *Journal of International Business Studies*, 32 (3): 439–58.

Chryssides, G. and Kaler, J. 1996. *Essentials of business ethics*. London: McGraw-Hill.

Ciocchetti, C.A. 2011. The Eavesdropping Employer: A Twenty-First Century Framework for Employee Monitoring. *American Business Law Journal*, 48 (2): 285–369.

Ciulla, J.B. 2013. Leadership Ethics, *International Encyclopedia of Ethics*. London: Blackwell Publishing Ltd.

Claessens, S. and Fan, J.P.H. 2002. Corporate governance in Asia: a survey. *International Review of Finance*, 3 (2): 71–103.

Clancy, H. 2013. Dell Steps Up E-Waste Recycling With African Hub. *Forbes*, 12 May 2014: http://www.forbes.com/sites/heatherclancy/2013/2012/2005/dell-steps-up-e-waste-recycling-with-african-hub/.

Clapp, J. and Helleiner, E. 2012. Troubled futures? The global food crisis and the politics of agricultural derivatives regulation. *Review of International Political Economy*, 19 (2): 181–207.

Clarke, T. 2007. *International corporate governance: a comparative approach*. London and New York: Routledge.

Claydon, T. 2000. Employee participation and involvement. In D. Winstanley and J. Woodall (eds.), *Ethical issues in contemporary human resource management*: 208–23. Basingstoke: Macmillan.

Clegg, S., Kornberger, M., and Rhodes, C. 2007. Business Ethics as Practice, *British Journal of Management*, 18: 107–22.

Clifford, S. and Greenhouse, S. 2013. Fast and flawed inspections of factories abroad. *The New York Times*, 1 September 2013: http://www.nytimes.com/2013/09/02/business/global/superficial-visits-and-trickery-undermine-foreign-factory-nspections.html?pagewanted%20=%20all&_r%20=%20 2010.

Cludts, S. 1999. Organization theory and the ethics of participation. *Journal of Business Ethics*, 21: 157–71.

Colias, M. 2014. GM takes next step to strengthen relationship with suppliers. *Automotive News*, 26 February 2014: http://www.autonews.com/article/20140226/OEM10/140229907/gm-takes-next-step-to-strengthen-relationship-with-suppliers.

Collier, J. 1995. The virtuous organization. *Business Ethics: A European Review*, 4 (3): 143–9.

Collier, J. and Esteban, R. 1999. Governance in the participative organization: freedom, creativity and ethics. *Journal of Business Ethics*, 21: 173–88.

Collier, R. 2001. A hard time to be a father? Reassessing the relationship between law, policy, and family (practices). *Journal of Law and Society*, 28 (4): 520–45.

Collins, J.W. 1994. Is business ethics an oxymoron? *Business Horizons*, September–October, 37 (5): 1–8.

Collins, M. 2015. Buying Government With Lobbying Money. *Forbes*, 28 March 2015: http://www.forbes.com.

Connell, J., Gough, R., McDonnell, A., and Burgess, J. 2014. Technology, work organisation and job quality in the service sector: an introduction. *Labour & Industry: a journal of the social and economic relations of work*, 24 (1): 1–8.

Cooper, C. 1996. Hot under the collar. *Times Higher Education Supplement*, 21 June: 12–16.

Cooper, R.W., Frank, G.L., and Kemp, R.A. 2000. A multinational comparison of key ethical issues, helps and challenges in the purchasing and supply management profession: The key implications for business and the professions. *Journal of Business Ethics*, 23 (1/1): 83–100.

Copeland, L. 2014. Conceptualizing political consumerism: How citizenship norms differentiate boycotting from buycotting. *Political Studies*, 62 (S1): 172–86.

Corbett, C.J. and Kirsch, D.A. 2001. International diffusion of ISO 14000 certification. *Production and Operations Management*, 10 (3): 327–42.

Corbett, C.J. and Kirsch, D.A. 2001. International diffusion of ISO 14000 certification. *Production and Operations Management*, 10 (3): 327–42.

Cowton, C.J. 1999b. Playing by the rules: ethical criteria at an ethical investment fund. *Business Ethics: A European Review*, 8 (1): 60–9.

Cox, A., Sanderson, J., and Watson, G. 2000. *Power regimes: mapping the DNA of business and supply chain relationships*. Stratford-upon-Avon: Earlsgate Press.

Craft, J.L. 2013. A review of the empirical ethical decision-making literature: 2004–2011. *Journal of business ethics*, 117 (2): 221–59.

Crain, K.A. and Heischmidt, K.A. 1995. Implementing business ethics: sexual harassment. *Journal of Business Ethics*, 14: 299–308.

Crane, A. 1998. Culture clash and mediation: exploring the cultural dynamics of business-NGO collaboration. *Greener Management International* 24: 61–76.

Crane, A. 2000. *Marketing, morality and the natural environment*. London: Routledge.

Crane, A. 2013a. CSR and marketing to ethical consumers. In A. Crane, D. Matten, and L.J. Spence (eds.), *Corporate social responsibility: readings and cases in a global context* (2nd edn.). Abingdon: Routledge.

Crane, A. 2013b. Modern slavery as a management practice: Exploring the conditions and capabilities for human exploitation. *Academy of Management Review*, 38 (1): 49–69.

Crane, A. and Kazmi, B.A. 2010. Business and children: mapping impacts, managing responsibilities. *Journal of Business Ethics*, 91 (4): 567–86.

Crane, A. and Livesey, S. 2003. Are you talking to me? Stakeholder communication and the risks and rewards of dialogue. In B. Husted (ed.), *Unfolding stakeholder thinking*, Vol. II. Sheffield: Greenleaf.

Crane, A. and Seitanidi, M.M. 2014. Social partnerships and responsible business: what, why, and how? In M.M. Seitanidi, and A. Crane (eds.), *Social partnerships and responsible business: a research handbook*: 1–12. Abingdon: Routledge.

Crane, A. and Spence, L. 2008. *Competitive intelligence: ethical challenges and good practice*. London: Institute of Business Ethics.

Crane, A., Knights, D., and Starkey, K. 2008. The conditions of our freedom: Foucault, organization, and ethics. *Business Ethics Quarterly*, 18 (3): 299–320.

Crane, A., Matten, D., and Moon, J. 2008. *Corporations and Citizenship*. Cambridge: Cambridge University Press.

Cranford, M. 1998. Drug testing and the right to privacy: arguing the ethics of workplace drug testing. *Journal of Business Ethics*, 17: 1805–15.

Credit Suisse. 2013. *Global Wealth Report*. Zurich: Credit Suisse.

Crossland, C. and Chen, G. 2013. Executive accountability around the world: Sources of cross-national variation in firm performance-CEO dismissal sensitivity. *Strategic Organization*, 11 (1): 78–109.

Crotty, J. 2014. Corporate Social Responsibility in the Russian Federation A Contextualized Approach. *Business & Society*. doi: 10.1177/0007650314561965.

Culzac, N. 2014. Red Bull awards $13m to its customers for not giving them wings. *Independent*, 10 October 2014.

Cumming, D.J. and Johan, S.A. 2014. *Venture capital and private equity contracting: An international perspective* (2nd edn.). London: Elsevier.

Dahan, N. 2005. A contribution to the conceptualization of political resources utilized in corporate political action. *Journal of Public Affairs*, 5: 43–54.

Dahan, N., Doh, J.P., and Guay, T. 2006. The role of multinational corporations in transitional institutional building: a policy network perspective. *Human Relations*, 59: 1571–600.

Dahan, N.M., Hadani, M., and Schuler, D.A. 2013. The governance challenges of corporate political activity. *Business & Society*, 52 (3): 365–87.

Dahler-Larsen, P. 1994. Corporate culture and morality: Durkheim-inspired reflections on the limits of corporate culture. *Journal of Management Studies*, 31 (1): 1–18.

Daly, H.E. 1991. *Steady state economics* (2nd edn.). Washington: Island Press.

Daly, H.E. and Cobb, J.B.J. 1989. *For the common good: redirecting the economy towards community, the environment, and a sustainable future* (1st edn.). Boston: Beacon Press.

Dart, R. 2004. The legitimacy of social enterprise. *Nonprofit Management and Leadership*, 14 (4): 411–24.

Daugherty, P.J. 2011. Review of logistics and supply chain relationship literature and suggested research agenda. *International Journal of Physical Distribution & Logistics Management*, 41 (1): 16–31.

Dauvergne, P. and LeBaron, G. 2014. *Protest Inc.: The Corporatization of Activism*. Cambridge, UK: John Wiley & Sons.

Davies, I.A. and Crane, A. 2010. CSR in SMEs: investigating employee engagement in fair trade companies. *Business Ethics: A European Review*, forthcoming.

Davies, R.B. and Vadlamannati, K.C. 2013. A race to the bottom in labor standards? An empirical investigation. *Journal of Development Economics*, 103: 1–14.

Davis, K. 1973. The case for and against business assumption of social responsibilities. *Academy of Management Journal*, 16 (2): 312–22.

Davis, M., Kumiega, A., and Van Vliet, B. 2013. Ethics, Finance, and Automation: A Preliminary Survey of Problems in High Frequency Trading. *Science and engineering ethics*, 19 (3): 851–74.

Dawar, N. and Frost, T. 1999. Competing with giants. *Harvard Business Review*, 77 (March–April): 119–29.

Dawson, D. 2005. Applying stories of the environment to business: what business people can learn from the virtues in environmental narratives. *Journal of Business Ethics*, 58 (1/3): 37–49.

de Castella, T. 2014. Could work emails be banned after 6pm? *BBC News*, 10 April 2014.

De George, R.T. 1999. *Business ethics* (5th edn.). Upper Saddle River, NJ: Prentice Hall.

Dees, J.G. 1998. Enterprising nonprofits. *Harvard Business Review*, 76 (1): 54–67.

Defourny, J. and Nyssens, M. 2006. Defining social enterprise. In M. Nyssens (ed.), *Social enterprise: at the crossroads of market, public policies and civil society*. London and New York: Routledge.

Delmas, M.A. and Montes-Sancho, M.J. 2011. An institutional perspective on the diffusion of international management system standards. *Business Ethics Quarterly*, 21 (1): 103–32.

Delmas, M.A. and Montiel, I. 2009. Greening the supply chain: when is customer pressure effective? *Journal of Economics and Management Strategy*, 18 (1): 171–201.

Deloitte. 2013. *Turn on, Tune in, Turnover: Annual Review of Football Finance*. London: Deloitte LLP.

den Hond, F., de Bakker, F.G., and Doh, J. 2015. What prompts companies to collaboration with NGOs? Recent evidence from the Netherlands. *Business & Society*, 54 (2): 187–228.

Derry, R. 1987. Moral reasoning in work-related contexts. In W.C. Frederick (ed.), *Research in corporate social performance*. Greenwich, CT: JAI Press.

Des Jardins, J.R. and Duska, R. 1997. Drug testing in employment. In T.L. Beauchamp and N.E. Bowie (eds.), *Ethical theory and business* (5th edn.) 309–19. Upper Saddle River, NJ: Prentice-Hall.

Desmond, J. 1998. Marketing and moral indifference. In M. Parker (ed.), *Ethics and organizations*. London: Sage.

Desmond, J. and Crane, A. 2004. Morality and the consequences of marketing action. *Journal of Business Research*, 57: 1222–30.

Detomasi, D. 2007. The multinational corporation and global governance: modelling global public policy networks. *Journal of Business Ethics*, 71 (3): 321–34.

Detomasi, D. 2015. The Multinational Corporation as a Political Actor: 'Varieties of Capitalism' Revisited. *Journal of Business Ethics*, 128 (3): 685–700.

Devinney, T.M., Auger, P., and Eckhardt, G.M. 2010. *The Myth of the Ethical Consumer*. Cambridge: Cambridge University Press.

Dhir, A. 2015. *Challenging Boardroom Homogeneity: Corporate Law, Governance, and Diversity*. Cambridge: Cambridge University Press.

Diamond, J. 2008. What's Your Consumption Factor? *New York Times*, 2 January 2008: http://www.nytimes.com.

Dickinson, R.A. and Carsky, M.L. 2005. The consumer as economic voter. In R. Harrison, T. Newholm, and D. Shaw (eds.), *The ethical consumer*: 25–36. London: Sage.

Dijkhuizen, T. 2014. The EU's Regulatory Approach to Banks' Executive Pay: From 'Pay Governance' to Pay Design. *European Company Law*, 11 (1): 30–7.

Doane, D. 2013. What Goldman Sachs should admit: it drives up the cost of food. *Guardian*, 23 May 2013.

Dobel, J.P. 2007. Public management as ethics. In E. Ferlie, L.E. Lynn and C. Pollitt (eds.), *The Oxford handbook of public management*: 156–81. Oxford: Oxford University Press.

Dobson, A. 1996. Environmental sustainabilities: an analysis and typology. *Environmental Politics*, 5 (3): 401–28.

Doh, J.P. and Quigley, N.R. 2014. Responsible leadership and stakeholder management: Influence pathways and organizational outcomes. *The Academy of Management Perspectives*, 28 (3): 255–74.

Doh, J.P. and Teegen, H. (eds.). 2003. *Globalization and NGOs: transforming business, government, and society*. Westport, CT: Praeger Publishers.

Doh, J.P. and Teegen, H. 2002. Nongovernmental organizations as institutional actors in international business: theory and implications. *International Business Review*, 11: 665–84.

Doherty, B., Davies, I.A., and Tranchell, S. 2013. Where now for fair trade? *Business History*, 55 (2): 161–89.

Doherty, B., Haugh, H., and Lyon, F. 2014. Social enterprises as hybrid organizations: A review and research agenda. *International Journal of Management Reviews*, 16 (4): 417–36.

Dommeyer, C.J. and Gross, B.L. 2003. What consumers know and what they do: an investigation of consumer knowledge, awareness, and use of privacy protection strategies. *Journal of Interactive Marketing*, 17 (2): 34.

Donaldson, T. 1989. *The ethics of international business*. New York and Oxford: Oxford University Press.

Donaldson, T. 1996. Values in tension: ethics away from home. *Harvard Business Review*, 74 (September–October): 48–62.

Donaldson, T. 2008. Hedge fund ethics. *Business Ethics Quarterly*, 18 (3): 405–16.

Donaldson, T. and Preston, L.E. 1995. The stakeholder theory of the corporation: concepts, evidence, and implications. *Academy of Management Review*, 20 (1): 65–91.

Donleavy, G.D., Lam, K.C.J., and Ho, S.S.M. 2008. Does East meet West in business ethics: an introduction to the special issue. *Journal of Business Ethics*, 79 (1/2): 1–8.

Douvitsa, I. and Kassavetis, D. 2014. Cooperatives: an alternative to water privatization in Greece. *Social Enterprise Journal*, 10 (2): 135–54.

Drumwright, M. 1994. Socially responsible organizational buying. *Journal of Marketing*, 58, July: 1–19.

Dryzek, J.S. 2012. Global civil society: The progress of post-Westphalian politics. *Annual Review of Political Science*, 15: 101–19.

du Gay, P. 2000. *In praise of bureaucracy*. London: Sage.

Durkheim, E. 1993. *The division of labour in society*. Glencoe, Ill.: Free Press.

Duska, R. 2000. Business ethics: oxymoron or good business? *Business Ethics Quarterly*, 10 (1): 111–29.

Eaglesham, J. 2000. Staff privacy in the spotlight: workplace surveillance. *Financial Times*, 9 October: 22.

Easton, G. 1992. Industrial networks: a review. In G. Easton (ed.), *Industrial networks: a new view of reality*: 3–27. London: Routledge.

Eberlein, B. and Matten, D. 2009. Business responses to climate change regulation in Canada and Germany—lessons for MNCs from emerging economies. *Journal of Business Ethics*, 86 (2): 241–55.

Eberlein, B., Abbott, K.W., Black, J., Meidinger, E., and Wood, S. 2014. Transnational business governance interactions: Conceptualization and framework for analysis. *Regulation & Governance*, 8 (1): 1–21.

Edelman. 2014. *2014 Edelman Trust Barometer*. Retrieved 7 September 2013, from http://www.edelman.com/insights/intellectual-property/2014-edelman-trust-barometer/about-trust/global-results/.

Edwards, V. and Lawrence, P. 2000. *Management in Eastern Europe*. Basingstoke: Palgrave.

Egels-Zandén, N. 2007. Suppliers' compliance with MNCs' codes of conduct: Behind the scenes at Chinese toy suppliers. *Journal of Business Ethics*, 75 (1): 45–62.

Egels-Zandén, N. 2014. Revisiting supplier compliance with MNC codes of conduct: Recoupling policy and practice at Chinese toy suppliers. *Journal of Business Ethics*, 119 (1): 59–75.

Egels-Zandén, N. and Lindholm, H. 2015. Do codes of conduct improve worker rights in supply chains? A study of Fair Wear Foundation. *Journal of Cleaner Production*. doi:10.1016/j.jclepro.2014.08.096.

Eikenberry, A.M. and Kluver, J.D. 2004. The marketization of the nonprofit sector: civil society at risk? *Public Administration Review*, 64 (2): 132–40.

EIRIS. 2012. Evolving markets: what's driving ESG in emerging economies? *EIRIS Emerging Markets Report*, September 2012, London: EIRIS.

Elankumaran, S., Seal, R., and Hashmi, A. 2005. Transcending transformation: enlightening endeavours at Tata Steel. *Journal of Business Ethics*, 59 (1): 109–19.

El-Din, Y.G. 2014. Ethical banking to take over: Abu Dhabi Islamic Bank CEO. *CNBC*, 29 April 2104: http://www.cnbc.com/id/101624169.

Elkington, J. and Fennell, S. 2000. Partners for sustainability. In J. Bendell (ed.), *Terms for endearment: business, NGOs and sustainable development*: 150–62. Sheffield: Greenleaf.

Ellerman, D. 1999. The democratic firm: an argument based on ordinary jurisprudence. *Journal of Business Ethics*, 21: 111–24.

Elms, H. and Phillips, R.A. 2009. Private security companies and institutional legitimacy: corporate and stakeholder responsibility. *Business Ethics Quarterly*, 19 (3): 403–32.

Emmelhainz, M.A. and Adams, R.J. 1999. The apparel industry response to 'sweatshop' concerns: a review and analysis of codes of conduct. *Journal of Supply Chain Management*, Summer: 51–7.

Enderle, G. 1996. A comparison of business ethics in North America and continental Europe. *Business Ethics: A European Review*, 5 (1): 33–46.

Engelen, E. 2002. Corporate governance, property and democracy: a conceptual critique of shareholder ideology. *Economy and Society*, 31 (3): 391–413.

Entine, J. 2003. The myth of social investing: a critique of its practice and consequence for corporate social performance research. *Organization and Environment*, 16 (3): 352–68.

Entine, J. 2008. Crunch time for ethical investing. *Ethical Corporation*, November: 24–7.

Esposito, F. and Montanaro, F. 2014. A Fistful of Euros: EU Competition Policy and Reverse Payments in the Pharmaceutical Industry. *European Competition Journal*, 10 (3): 499–521.

Esty, D. and Winston, A. 2009. *Green to gold: How smart companies use environmental strategy to innovate, create value, and build competitive advantage*. Hoboken, NJ: John Wiley & Sons.

Ethical Corporation. 2006. Can investor activism have any effect on Sudan? *Ethical Corporation*, June: 6–7.

Ethics Resource Center. 2008. *National Business Ethics Survey 2007: An Inside View of Private Sector Ethics*. Arlington, VA: Ethics Resource Center.

Ethics Resource Center. 2014. *National business ethics survey of the US workforce 2013*. Arlington, VA: Ethics Resource Center.

Evan, W.M. and Freeman, R.E. 1993. A stakeholder theory of the modern corporation: Kantian capitalism. In W.M. Hoffman and R.E. Frederick (eds.), *Business ethics: readings and cases in corporate morality*: 145–54. New York: McGraw-Hill.

Evans, D. and Salas, C. 2009. Flawed credit ratings reap profits as regulators fail investors. *Bloomberg News*, 29 April 2009.

Farming Online. 2012. Arrests and suspension in Kent gangmaster abuse case. 2 November 2012: http://www.farming.co.uk/news/article/7461.

Farzad, R. 2013. Tesla is now worth 20 billion. *Bloomberg Businessweek*, 27 August 2013.

Faulks, K. 2000. *Citizenship*. London: Routledge.

Fearn, H. and Nesbitt, H. 2014. Lush to remove mica from all products over child labour fears. *Guardian*: http://www.theguardian.com/sustainable-business/lush-removes-mica-child-labour.

Featherstone, M. 1991. *Consumer culture and postmodernism*. London: Sage.

Ferner, A. and Hyman, R. 1998. *Changing industrial relations in Europe*. Oxford: Blackwell.

Ferrell, O.C., Fraedrich, J., and Ferrell, L. 2012. *Business ethics: ethical decision making and cases* (9th edn.). Mason, OH: Cengage Learning.

Ferrell, O.C., Fraedrich, J., and Ferrell, L. 2014. *Business ethics: ethical decision making and cases* (10th edn.). Mason, OH: Cengage Learning.

Ferrell, O.C., Gresham, L.G., and Fraedrich, J. 1989. A synthesis of ethical decision models for marketing. *Journal of Macromarketing*, 9 (2): 55–64.

Fineman, S. and Clarke, K. 1996. Green stakeholders: industry interpretations and response. *Journal of Management Studies*, 33 (6): 715–30.

Finnegan, W. 2014. Dignity—Fast-food workers and a new form of labor activism. *The New Yorker*, 15 September 2015.

Fisher, J. 2007. Business marketing and the ethics of gift giving. *Industrial Marketing Management*, 36 (1): 99–108.

Fiss, P.C. and Zajac, E.J. 2004. The diffusion of ideas over contested terrain: the (non)adoption of a shareholder value orientation among German firms. *Administrative Science Quarterly*, 49: 501–34.

Fitzgerald, R. 1999. Employment relations and industrial welfare in Britain: business ethics versus labour markets. *Business and Economic History*, 28 (2): 167–79.

Fleming, P. and Sturdy, A. 2011. 'Being yourself' in the electronic sweatshop: New forms of normative control. *Human Relations*, 64 (2): 177–200.

Flock, E. 2012. Monsanto petition tells Obama: 'Cease FDA ties to Monsanto'. *The Washington Post*, 30 January 2012.

Ford, R.C. and Richardson, W.D. 1994. Ethical decision making: a review of the empirical literature. *Journal of Business Ethics*, 13 (3): 205–21.

Forstater, M. 2006. Green jobs. *Challenge*, 49 (4): 58–72.

Foster, W. and Bradach, J. 2005. Should nonprofits seek profits? *Harvard Business Review*, 83 (2): 92–100.

Fraedrich, J., Thorne, D.M., and Ferrell, O.C. 1994. Assessing the application of cognitive moral development to business ethics. *Journal of Business Ethics*, 13 (10): 829–38.

Frank, R. and Efrati, A. 2009. 'Evil' Madoff Gets 150 Years in Epic Fraud. *Wall Street Journal*, 30 June 2009: http://online.wsj.com/news/articles/SB124604151653862301.

Frankental, P. 2002. The UN Universal Declaration of Human Rights as a corporate code of conduct. *Business Ethics: A European Review*, 11 (2): 129–33.

Frankental, P. 2006. Why socially responsible investment requires more risk for companies rather than more engagement. In R. Sullivan and C. Mackenzie (eds.), *Responsible investment*: 241–6. Sheffield: Greenleaf.

Fransen, L.W. and Kolk, A. 2007. Global rule-setting for business: a critical analysis of multi-stakeholder standards. *Organization*, 14 (5): 667–84.

Freeman, R. 2011. Speech at the OECD Policy Forum on Tackling Inequality, Paris. 2 May 2011.

Freeman, R.E. 1984. *Strategic management: a stakeholder approach*. Boston: Pitman.

French, P. 1979. The corporation as a moral person. *American Philosophical Quarterly*, 16: 207–15.

Frenkel, S.J. and Scott, D. 2002. Compliance, collaboration and codes of practice. *California Management Review*, 45 (1): 29–49.

Friedman, M. 1970. The social responsibility of business is to increase its profits. *New York Times Magazine*, 13 September 1970.

Friedman, M. 1999. *Consumer boycotts*. New York: Routledge.

Frizell, S. 2014. 7 Dead-Serious Uber Controversies That Somehow Didn't Sink the Company. *Time*, 18 November 2014: http://time.com/3592098/uber-controversy/.

Fuchs, D. 2005. Commanding heights? The strength and fragility of business power in global politics. *Millennium: Journal of International Studies*, 33 (3): 771–801.

Fuller, D.A. 1999. *Sustainable marketing: managerial-ecological issues*. Thousand Oaks, CA: Sage.

Galbraith, J.K. 1974. *The new industrial state* (2nd edn.). Harmondsworth: Penguin.

Geisel, J. 2012. Fewer Employers Offering Defined Benefit Pension Plans to New Salaried Employees. *Workforce*, 3 October 2012: http://www.workforce.com.

Getz, K.A. 1997. Research in corporate political action: integration and assessment. *Business & Society*, 36 (1): 32–72.

Ghoshal, S. 2005. Bad management theories are destroying good management practices. *Academy of Management Learning and Education*, 4 (1): 75–92.

Gichure, C.W. 2006. Teaching business ethics in Africa: what ethical orientation? The case of East and Central Africa. *Journal of Business Ethics*, 63 (1): 39–52.

Gilligan, C. 1982. *In a different voice*. Cambridge, MA: Harvard University Press.

Gini, A. 1997. Moral leadership: an overview. *Journal of Business Ethics*, 16 (3): 323–30.

Gioia, D.A. 1992. Pinto Fires and personal ethics: A script analysis of missed opportunities. *Journal of Business Ethics*, 11 (5/6): 379–89.

Gladwin, T.N., Kennelly, J.J., and Krause, T.S. 1995. Shifting paradigms for sustainable development: implications for management theory and research. *Academy of Management Review*, 20 (4): 874–907.

Glinska, G. 2014. Fighting Financial Exclusion: How To Serve 88 Million Americans Who Have No Bank. *Forbes*, 5 May 2014. http://www.forbes.com.

Gnuschke, J.E. 2008. Is the Green Revolution for real this time? Will green jobs be created in sufficient numbers to offset declines in other parts of the economy? Will green jobs replace real estate as the engine for the next round of economic expansion? *Business Perspectives*, 19 (3): 6–9.

Godwin, L.N. 2015. Examining the Impact of Moral Imagination on Organizational Decision Making. *Business & Society*, 54 (2): 254–78.

Goff, C. 2006. New standards in project finance. *Ethical Corporation*, May: 32–3.

Gond, J.P. and Crane, A. 2010. Corporate social performance disoriented: saving the lost paradigm? *Business & Society*, 49 (4): 677–703.

Goolsby, J.R. and Hunt, S.D. 1992. Cognitive moral development and marketing. *Journal of Marketing*, 56 (1): 55–68.

Gopal, P. 2009. Now hiring: green-collar workers. *BusinessWeek Online*: 23 July 2009: http://www.businessweek.com.

Goranova, M. and Ryan, L.V. 2014. Shareholder Activism A Multidisciplinary Review. *Journal of Management*, 40 (5): 1230–68.

Gordon, J.N. 2002. What Enron means for the management and control of the modern business corporation: some initial reflections. *University of Chicago Law Review*, 69: 1233–50.

Gordon, K. and Miyake, M. 2001. Business approaches to combating bribery: a study of codes of conduct. *Journal of Business Ethics*, 34: 161–73.

Gorz, A. 1975. *Ecologie et politique*. Paris: Editions Galilée.

Gould, S.J. 1995. The Buddhist perspective on business ethics: experiential exercises for exploration and practice. *Journal of Business Ethics*, 14 (1): 63–72.

Graham, G. 1990. *Living the good life: an introduction to moral philosophy*. New York: Paragon.

Grant, W. 2004. Pressure politics: The changing world of pressure groups. *Parliamentary Affairs*, 57 (2): 408–19.

Gray, R., Dey, C., Owen, D., Evans, R., and Zadek, S. 1997. Struggling with the praxis of social accounting: stakeholders, accountability, audits and procedures. *Accounting, Auditing and Accountability Journal*, 10 (3): 325–64.

Gray, R.H. 1992. Accounting and environmentalism: an exploration of the challenge of gently accounting for accountability, transparency and sustainability. *Accounting, Organizations and Society*, 17 (5): 399–426.

Gray, R.H., Bebbington, J., and Collinson, D. 2006. NGOs, civil society and accountability: making the people accountable to capital. *Accounting, Auditing and Accountability Journal*, 19 (3): 319–48.

Grayson, D. and Hodges, A. 2004. *Corporate social opportunity: seven steps to make corporate social responsibility work for your business*. Sheffield: Greenleaf.

Greening, D.W. and Turban, D.B. 2000. Corporate social performance as a competitive advantage in attracting a quality workforce. *Business & Society*, 39 (3): 254–80.

Greenwood, M.R. 2002. Ethics and HRM: a review and conceptual analysis. *Journal of Business Ethics*, 36: 261–78.

Greyser, S.A. 1972. Advertising: attacks and counters. *Harvard Business Review*, 50 (March–April): 22–36.

Gross-Schaefer, A., Trigilio, J., Negus, J., and Ro, C.-S. 2000. Ethics education in the workplace: an effective tool to combat employee theft. *Journal of Business Ethics*, 26: 89–100.

Guerrera, F. 2009. Welch denounces corporate obsessions. *Financial Times*, 13 March 2009.

Guide, V.D.R., Jr., and Wassenhove, L.N.V. 2006. Closed-loop supply chains: an introduction to the feature issue (part 1). *Production and Operations Management*, 15 (3): 345–50.

Gunter, B., Oates, C., and Blades, M. 2005. *Advertising to children on TV: content, impact, and regulation*. London: Routledge.

Gustafson, A. 2000. Making sense of postmodern business ethics. *Business Ethics Quarterly*, 10 (3): 645–58.

Haas, P.M. 2012. The political economy of ecology: Prospects for transforming the world economy at Rio plus 20. *Global Policy*, 3 (1): 94–101.

Habermas, J. 1983. Diskursethik—Notizen zu einem Begründungsprogramm. In J. Habermas, *Moralbewusstsein und kommunikatives Handeln*: 53–125. Frankfurt/Main: Suhrkamp.

Hahn, R. 2013. ISO 26000 and the standardization of strategic management processes for sustainability and corporate social responsibility. *Business Strategy and the Environment*, 22 (7): 442–55.

Hahn, R. and Weidtmann, C. 2012. Transnational governance, deliberative democracy, and the legitimacy of ISO 26000: Analyzing the case of a global multistakeholder process. *Business & Society*. doi: 10.1177/0007650312462666.

Håkansson, H. and Snehota, I. 2006. No business is an island: the network concept of business strategy. *Scandinavian Journal of Management*, 22 (3): 256–70.

Hall, M.H., Barr, C.W., Easwaramoorthy, M., Sokolowski, S.W., and Salamon, L.M. 2005. *The Canadian nonprofit and voluntary sector in comparative perspective*. Toronto: Imagine Canada.

Hallaq, J.H. and Steinhorst, K. 1994. Business intelligence methods—how ethical. *Journal of Business Ethics*, 13: 787–94.

Handfield, R.B. and Baumer, D.L. 2006. Managing conflict of interest issues in purchasing. *Journal of Supply Chain Management*, 42 (3): 41–50.

Hansen, W.L., Rocca, M.S., and Ortiz, B.L. 2015. The Effects of Citizens United on Corporate Spending in the 2012 Presidential Election. *The Journal of Politics*, 77 (2): 535–45.

Harris, P. and Lock, A. 2002. Sleaze or clear blue water? The evolution of corporate and pressure group representation at the major UK party conferences. *Journal of Public Affairs*, 2 (2): 136–51.

Hart, S.L. and Sharma, S. 2004. Engaging fringe stakeholders for competitive imagination. *Academy of Management Executive*, 18 (1): 7–18.

Hart, T.J. 1993. Human resource management—time to exorcise the militant tendency. *Employee Relations*, 15 (3): 29–36.

Hasan, M. and Dridi, J. 2010. The Effects of the Global Crisis on Islamic and Conventional Banks: A Comparative Study. *IMF Working paper* WP/10/201: http://www.imf.org/external/pubs/ft/wp/2010/wp10201.pdf.

Haslam, P.A. 2007. The corporate social responsibility system in Latin America and the Caribbean. In A. Crane and D. Matten (eds.), *Corporate Social Responsibility—A Three Volumes Edited Collection*, Vol. 3: 236–53. London: Sage.

Hauskrecht, A. 1999. Die asiatische Währungs- und Finanzkrise. In Landeszentrale für Politische Bildung (ed.), *Globalisierung als Chance*: 35–40. Stuttgart: Landeszentrale für Politische Bildung.

Hawkes, C. and Lobstein, T. 2011. Regulating the commercial promotion of food to children: a survey of actions worldwide. *International Journal of Pediatric Obesity*, 6 (2): 83–94.

Hayes, L.D. 2009. *Introduction to Japanese politics* (5th edn.). Armonk, NY: M.E. Sharpe.

Hayman, J.R. 2009. Flexible work arrangements: exploring the linkages between perceived usability of flexible work schedules and work/life balance. *Community, Work & Family*, 12 (3): 327–38.

Hediger, W. 1999. Reconciling 'weak' and 'strong' sustainability. *International Journal of Social Economics*, 26 (7/8/9): 1120–43.

Heilman, M.E. 1997. Sex discrimination and the affirmative action remedy: the role of sex stereotypes. *Journal of Business Ethics*, 16 (9): 877–89.

Heiskanen, E. and Pantzar, M. 1997. Toward sustainable consumption: two new perspectives. *Journal of Consumer Policy*, 20: 409–42.

Hellman, J.S. and Schankerman, M. 2000. Intervention, corruption and capture. *Economics of transition*, 8 (3): 545–76.

Helms, W., Oliver, C., and Webb, K. 2012. Antecedents of settlement on a new institutional practice: Negotiation of the ISO 26000 standard on social responsibility. *Academy of Management Journal*: 55 (5):1120–45.

Hemingway, C.A. 2013. *Corporate Social Entrepreneurship: Integrity Within*. Cambridge: Cambridge University Press.

Henderson, J.M. 2014. Why We Should Be Alarmed That Apple And Facebook Are Paying For Employee Egg Freezing. *Forbes*, 17 October 2014: http://www.forbes.com.

Herlin, H. 2013. Better safe than sorry: Nonprofit organizational legitimacy and cross-sector partnerships. *Business & Society*. doi: 10.1177/0007650312472609.

Hertz, N. 2001a Better to shop than to vote? *Business Ethics: A European Review*, 10 (3): 190–3.

Hertz, N. 2001b *The silent takeover*. London: Heinemann.

Higgs-Kleyn, N. and Kapelianis, D. 1999. The role of professional codes in regulating ethical conduct. *Journal of Business Ethics*, 19: 363–74.

Hilhorst, D. 2002. Being good at doing good? Quality and accountability of humanitarian NGOs. *Disasters*, 26 (3): 193–212.

Hilson, G. 2012. Corporate Social Responsibility in the extractive industries: Experiences from developing countries. *Resources Policy*, 37 (2): 131–7.

Hingley, M.K. 2005. Power to all our friends? Living with imbalance in supplier-retailer relationships. *Industrial Marketing Management*, 34 (8): 848–58.

Ho, C. and Redfern, K.A. 2010. Consideration of the role of guanxi in the ethical judgments of Chinese managers. *Journal of business ethics*, 96 (2): 207–21.

Hodge, G.A. and Greve, C. 2007. Public-private partnerships: an international performance review. *Public administration review*, 67 (3): 545–58.

Hoffman, A.J. 2015. *How culture shapes the climate change debate*. Stanford: Stanford University Press.

Hoffman, W.M., Driscoll, D.-M., and Painter-Morland, M. 2001. Integrating ethics. In C. Bonny (ed.), *Business ethics: facing up to the issues*: 38–54. London: The Economist Books.

Hofstede, G. 1980. *Culture's consequences: international differences in work related values*. Beverly Hills, CA: Sage.

Hofstede, G. 2001. *Culture's Consequences: Comparing Values, Behaviors, Institutions and Organizations Across Nations* (2nd edn.). Thousand Oaks, CA: Sage.

Hofstede, G., Hofstede, G.J., and Minkov, M. 2010. *Cultures and Organizations: Software of the Mind* (3rd edn.). New York: McGraw-Hill.

Holbrook, M.B. 1987. Mirror, mirror on the wall, what's unfair in the reflections on advertising? *Journal of Marketing*, 51, July: 95–103.

Hooper, S. 2013. UK aims to become centre for Islamic finance. *Aljazeera*, 1 November 2013: http://www.aljazeera.com/indepth/features/2013/10/uk-aims-become-centre-islamic-finance-201310319840639385.html.

Hopkins, W.E. and Hopkins, S.A. 1999. The ethics of downsizing: perceptions of rights and responsibilities. *Journal of Business Ethics*, 18: 145–56.

Hosmer, L.T. 1987. *The ethics of management*. Boston: Irwin Press.

Houlder, V. 1999. Wind power's zephyr builds to gale force. *Financial Times*, 25 June: 13.

Hsieh, N.-h. 2009. Does global business have a responsibility to promote just institutions? *Business Ethics Quarterly*, 19 (2): 251–73.

Hughes, A. 2001. Global commodity networks, ethical trade and governmentality: organizing business responsibility in the Kenyan cut flower industry. *Transactions of the Institute of British Geographers*, 26 (4): 390–406.

Hughes, A. 2005. Corporate strategy and the management of ethical trade: the case of the UK food and clothing retailers. *Environment and Planning A*, 37: 1145–63.

Hummels, H. 1998. Organizing ethics: a stakeholder debate. *Journal of Business Ethics*, 17: 1403–19.

Hunt, S.D. and Vitell, S.J. 1986. A general theory of marketing ethics. *Journal of Macromarketing*, 6, Spring: 5–16.

Hyatt, J.C. 2005. Birth of the ethics industry. *Business Ethics*, Summer: 20–6.

ILO. 2013. *World of Work Report—EU Snapshot*. International Labour Organization: http://www.ilo.org.

International Labour Organization. 1998. *World employment outlook*. Geneva: ILO.

Ip, P.K. 2009. Is Confucianism good for business ethics in China? *Journal of Business Ethics*, 88 (3): 463–76.

Ip, P.K. 2009. The challenge of developing a business ethics in China. *Journal of Business Ethics*, 88 (Supplement 1): 211–24.

Iwata, E. 2006. How Barbie is making business a little better. *USA Today*, 26 March 2006: http://www.usatoday.com.

Jackall, R. 1988. *Moral mazes*. Oxford: Oxford University Press.

Jackson, T. 2001. Cultural values and management ethics: a 10 nation study. *Human Relations*, 54 (10): 1267–302.

Jackson, T. 2014. Employment in Chinese MNEs: Appraising the Dragon's Gift to Sub-Saharan Africa. *Human Resource Management*, 53 (6): 897–919.

Jackson, T. 2014. Sustainable consumption. In G. Atkinson, S. Dietz, E. Neumayer, and M. Agarwala (eds.), *Handbook of sustainable development* (2nd edn.): 279–90. Cheltenham, UK: Edward Elgar.

Jacobs, A. and Gough, N. 2014. Alibaba, With Its I.P.O., Mints Millionaires and Risk-Takers. *New York Times*, 18 September 2014: http://dealbook.nytimes.com/2014/2009/2018/alibaba-with-its-i-p-o-mints-millionaires-and-risk-takers/.

Jensen, M. and Meckling, W. 1976. Theory of the firm: managerial behaviour, agency costs and ownership structure. *Journal of Financial Economics*, 3: 305–60.

Jeschke, M. 2007. Mining sector. In W. Visser, D. Matten, M. Pohl, and N. Tolhurst (eds.), *The A-Z of corporate social responsibility—the complete reference of concepts, codes and organisations*: 326–8. London: John Wiley.

Johannesen, N. and Zucman, G. 2014. The end of bank secrecy? An evaluation of the G20 tax haven crackdown. *American Economic Journal: Economic Policy*, 6 (1): 65–91.

Johansson-Stenman, O. 2012. Are most people consequentialists? *Economics Letters*, 115 (2): 225–8.

Johnson, G., Whittington, R., and Scholes, K. 2011. *Exploring corporate strategy* (9th edn.). Harlow: Pearson Education Ltd.

Johnson, P. and Smith, K. 1999. Contextualising business ethics: anomie and social life. *Human Relations*, 52 (11): 1351–75.

Jones, A. 2001. Social responsibility and the utilities. *Journal of Business Ethics*, 34: 219–29.

Jones, C., Parker, M., and ten Bos, R. 2005. *For business ethics*. Abingdon: Routledge.

Jones, G. and Hill, C. 2013. *Strategic management theory: an integrated approach* (11 edn.). Stamford, CT: Cengage Learning.

Jones, H.B. 1997. The Protestant Ethic: Weber's Model and the Empirical Literature. *Human Relations*, 50 (7): 757–78.

Jones, I.W. and Pollitt, M.G. 1998. Ethical and unethical competition: establishing the rules of engagement. *Long Range Planning*, 31 (5): 703–10.

Jones, T.M. 1991. Ethical decision making by individuals in organizations: an issue-contingent model. *Academy of Management Review*, 16: 366–95.

Joseph Rowntree Foundation. 2004. *Drug testing in the workplace: The Report of the Independent Inquiry into Drug Testing at Work*: http://www.jrf.org.uk/sites/files/jrf/185935212x.pdf.

Juggernath, S., Rampersad, R., and Reddy, K. 2013. Corporate responsibility for socio-economic transformation: A focus on broad-based black economic empowerment and its implementation in South Africa. *African Journal of Business Management*, 5 (20): 8224–34.

Jung, J.W. 2015. Shareholder Value and Workforce Downsizing, 1981–2006. *Social Forces*, 93 (4): 1335–68.

Kaler, J. 2000. Reasons to be ethical: self-interest and ethical business. *Journal of Business Ethics*, 27: 161–73.

Kalleberg, A.L. and Hewison, K. 2013. Precarious work and the challenge for Asia. *American Behavioral Scientist*, 57 (3): 271–88.

Kalliath, T. and Brough, P. 2008. Work-life balance: A review of the meaning of the balance construct. *Journal of Management and Organization*, 14 (3): 323–27.

Kaptein, M. and Schwartz, M.S. 2008. The effectiveness of business codes: a critical examination of existing studies and the development of an integrated research model. *Journal of Business Ethics*, 77 (2): 111–27.

Karnani, A. 2007. Doing well by doing good—Case study: 'Fair & Lovely' whitening cream. *Strategic Management Journal*, 28 (13): 1351–57.

Karnani, A. 2007. The mirage of marketing to the bottom of the pyramid: how the private sector can help alleviate poverty. *California Management Review*, 49 (4): 90–111.

Kempson, E. and Whyley, C. 1999. *Kept out or opted out? Understanding and combating financial exclusion*. Bristol: Policy Press.

Kerr, D. 2013. A U.S. judge gives the leader of the IMAGiNE file-sharing group a record prison term for camcording movies in the theater and distributing them on the Web. *CNET.com*, 3 January 2013.

Kershner, I. 2014. Scarlett Johansson and Oxfam, Torn Apart by Israeli Company Deal. *New York Times*, 30 January 2014: http://www.nytimes.com/2014/2001/2031/world/middleeast/scarlett-johansson-and-oxfam-torn-apart-by-israeli-company-deal.html?_r=2010.

Kieselbach, T. and Mader, S. 2002. Occupational transitions and corporate responsibility in layoffs: a European research project (SOCOSE). *Journal of Business Ethics*, 39: 13–20.

Kilbourne, W., McDonagh, P., and Prothero, A. 1997. Sustainable consumption and the quality of life: a macromarketing challenge to the dominant social paradigm. *Journal of Macromarketing*, 17 (1): 4–24.

Kim, S. and Rucker, D.D. 2012. Bracing for the psychological storm: Proactive versus reactive compensatory consumption. *Journal of Consumer Research*, 39 (4): 815–30.

Kimber, D. and Lipton, P. 2005. Corporate governance and business ethics in the Asia-Pacific region. *Business & Society*, 44 (2): 178–210.

King, A.A. and Lenox, M.J. 2000. Industry self-regulation without sanctions: the chemical industry's Responsible Care Program. *Academy of Management Journal*, 43 (4): 698–716.

King, A.A., Lenox, M.J., and Terlaak, A. 2005. The strategic use of decentralized institutions: exploring certification with the ISO 14001 management standard. *Academy of Management Journal*, 48 (6): 1091–106.

King, D.L., Case, C.J., and Premo, K.M. 2010. Current mission statement emphasis: be ethical and go global. *Academy of Strategic Management Journal*, 9 (2): 71–87.

Kirrane, D.E. 1990. Managing values: a systematic approach to business ethics. *Training and Development Journal*, November, 44 (11): 53–60.

Kirton, G. and Greene, A.-M. 2010. *The dynamics of managing* diversity. Abingdon: Routledge.

Kitts, D. 2013. In defence of bottled water, *The Inside Agenda Blog*: http://theagenda.tvo.org/blog/agenda-blogs/defence-bottled-water.

Klein, N. 2000. *No logo: taking aim at the brand bullies*. London: Flamingo.

Klein, N. 2007. *The shock doctrine: the rise of disaster capitalism*. Toronto: Alfred A. Knopf Canada.

Klein, N. 2014. *This changes everything: capitalism vs. the climate* (1st Simon & Schuster hardcover edn.). New York: Simon & Schuster.

Knibbs, K. 2014. Facebook loses privacy case in Germany, may help Europeans protect data, *Digital trends*, 18 February 2014: http://www.digitaltrends.com/social-media/facebook-must-comply-with-privacy-rules-in-germany-berlin-court-says/.

Knoepfel, I. 2001. Dow Jones Sustainability Group Index: a global benchmark for corporate sustainability. *Corporate Environmental Strategy*, 8 (1): 6–15.

Koch, E. 2000. *Globalisierung der wirtschaft*. Munich: Vahlen.

Koehn, D. 1999. What can Eastern philosophy teach us about business ethics? *Journal of Business Ethics*, 19: 71–9.

Kohlberg, L. 1969. Stage and sequence: the cognitive development approach to socialization. In D. Goslin (ed.), *Handbook of socialization theory and research*: 347–80. Chicago: Rand McNally.

Kolhatkar, S. 2014. A Lawsuit Peeks Inside the Goldman Sachs 'Boys' Club'. *Bloomberg Businessweek*, 2 July 2014.

Kolk, A. 2010. Trajectories of sustainability reporting by MNCs. *Journal of World Business*, 45 (4): 367–74.

Kolk, A. and Lenfant, F. 2012. Business-NGO collaboration in a conflict setting partnership activities in the Democratic Republic of Congo. *Business & Society*, 51 (3): 478–511.

Kolk, A. and Levy, D. 2001. Winds of change: corporate strategy, climate change and oil multinationals, *European Management Journal*, 19 (5): 501–9.

Kolk, A. and Pinske, J. 2007. Multinational's political activities on climate change. *Business & Society*, 46 (2): 201–28.

Kolk, A., Rivera-Santos, M., and Rufin, C.R. 2014. Reviewing a Decade of Research on the 'Base/Bottom of the Pyramid' (BOP) Concept. *Business & Society*, 53 (3): 338–77.

Korten, D.C. 1995. *When corporations rule the world*. London: Earthscan.

Koslowski, P. 2000. The limits of shareholder value. *Journal of Business Ethics*, 27: 137–48.

Kotler, P. and Lee, N. 2005. *Corporate social responsibility: doing the most good for your company and your cause*. Hoboken, NJ: Wiley.

Kotter, J.P. 1990. What leaders really do. *Harvard Business Review*, 68 (May–June): 103–11.

KPMG and RSM Erasmus University. 2008. *The business codes of the global 200: their prevalence, content and embedding*. KPMG Special Service BV: http://www.kpmg.com/CN/en/IssuesAndInsights/ArticlesPublications/Documents/business-codes-global-200-O-0804.pdf.

KPMG. 2013a. Integrity survey. KPMG Forensic: http://www.kpmg.com/CN/en/IssuesAndInsights/ArticlesPublications/Documents/Integrity-Survey-2013-O-201307.pdf.

KPMG. 2013b. International survey of corporate responsibility reporting. Amsterdam: KPMG.

Kurucz, E., Colbert, B., and Wheeler, D. 2008. The business case for corporate social responsibility. In A. Crane, A. McWilliams, D. Matten, J. Moon, and D. Siegel (eds.), *The Oxford handbook of corporate social responsibility*: 83–112. Oxford: Oxford University Press.

Laasonen, S., Fougère, M., and Kourula, A. 2012. Dominant Articulations in Academic Business and Society Discourse on NGO-Business Relations: A Critical Assessment. *Journal of Business Ethics*, 109 (4): 521–45.

Laczniak, G.R. and Murphy, P.E. 1993. *Ethical marketing decisions: the higher road*. Boston: Allyn and Bacon.

Lang, R. (ed.). 2001. *Wirtschaftsethik in Mittel- und Osteuropa*. Munich: Rainer Hampp.

Langevoort, D.C. 2010. Chasing the Greased Pig Down Wall Street: A Gatekeeper's Guide to the Psychology, Culture, and Ethics of Financial Risk Taking. *Cornell L. Rev.*, 96: 1209.

Langvardt, A.W. 2012. Ethical leadership and the dual roles of examples. *Business Horizons*, 55 (4): 373–84.

Lappin, J. 2014. Jury Finds Madoff Really Didn't Do It Alone, *Forbes Magazine*, 27 March 2014.

Larsson, L. 2007. Public trust in the PR industry and its actors. *Journal of Communication Management*, 11 (3): 222–34.

Lasprogata, G., King, N.J., and Pillay, S. 2004. Regulation of electronic employee monitoring: identifying fundamental principles of employee privacy through a comparative study of data privacy legislation in the European Union, United States and Canada. *Stanford Technology Law Review*, 4: https://journals.law.stanford.edu/stanford-technology-law-review/online/regulation-electronic-employee-monitoring-identifying-fundamental-principles-employee-privacy.

Lee, D.D., Humphrey, J.E., Benson, K.L., and Ahn, J.Y. 2010. Socially responsible investment fund performance: The impact of screening intensity. *Accounting & Finance*, 50 (2): 351–70.

Lee, M. and Koh, J. 2001. Is empowerment really a new concept? *International Journal of Human Resource Management*, 12 (4): 684–95.

Legge, K. 1998. Is HRM ethical? Can HRM be ethical? In M. Parker (ed.), *Ethics and organization*: 150–72. London: Sage.

Leonard, A. 2010. The Story of Bottled Water, *The Story of Stuff Project*: http://www.storyofstuff.org/movies-all/story-of-bottled-water/.

Leonard, D. 2014. Burger King Is Run by Children. *BloombergBusinessweek*, 24 July 2014: http://www.bloomberg.com/news/articles/2014-07-24/burger-king-is-run-by-children.

Leonnig, C.D. 2010. Despite BP corporate code, firm has made political contributions. *Washington Post*, 29 June 2010: http://www.washingtonpost.com/wp-dyn/content/article/2010/2006/2029/AR2010062903384.html.

Lertzman, D. and Vredenburg, H. 2005. Indigenous peoples, resource extraction and sustainable development: an ethical approach. *Journal of Business Ethics*, 56 (3): 239–54.

Levant, E. 2010. *Ethical Oil: The Case for Canada's Oil Sands*. Toronto: McClelland & Stewart.

Levitt, T. 1970. The morality (?) of advertising. *Harvard Business Review*, 48 (July–August): 84–92.

Levy, D. and Egan, D. 2000. Corporate politics and climate change. In R.A. Higgott, G.R.D. Underhill, and A. Bieler (eds.), *Non-state actors and authority in the global system*: 138–53. London: Routledge.

Levy, D.L. and Newell, P. 2005. *The business of global environmental governance*. Cambridge, MA: MIT Press.

Lewicka-Strzalecka, A. 2006. Opportunities and limitations of CSR in the postcommunist countries: Polish case. *Corporate Governance: The International Journal of Effective Board Performance*, 6 (4): 440–8.

Lewis, M. 2014. *Flash boys: a Wall Street revolt*. New York: WW Norton & Company.

Liket, K. and Maas, K. 2015. Strategic Philanthropy Corporate Measurement of Philanthropic Impacts as a Requirement for a 'Happy Marriage' of Business and Society. *Business & Society*. doi: 10.1177/0007650314565356.

Linthicum, K. 2014. No rest in the debate over Sabbath business hours in Jerusalem. *Los Angeles Times*, 14 April 2014: http://articles.latimes.com/2014/apr/14/world/la-fg-israel-sabbath-wars-20140414.

Livesey, S.M. 2002. Global warming wars: rhetorical and discourse analytic approaches to ExxonMobil's corporate public discourse. *Journal of Business Communication*, 39 (1): 118–49.

Locke, R. and Romis, M. 2007. Improving work conditions in a global supply chain. *MIT Sloan Management Review*, Winter: 54–62.

Locke, R. and Romis, M. 2007. Improving Work Conditions in a Global Supply Chain. *MIT Sloan Management Review*, Winter: 54–62.

Loe, T.W., Ferrell, L., and Mansfield, P. 2000. A review of empirical studies assessing ethical decision making in business. *Journal of Business Ethics*, 25 (3): 185–204.

Lokiec, P. 2008. Discrimination Law in France. In C. Barnard, H. Nakakubo, and T. Araki (eds.), *New developments in employment discrimination law*: 95–121. New York: Kluwer Law International.

Lord, M.D. 2000. Corporate political strategy and legislative decision-making. *Business & Society*, 39 (1): 76–93.

Louche, C. and Lydenberg, S. 2006. Socially responsible investment: differences between Europe and the United States. Vlerick Leuven Gent Working Paper Series 2006/22.

Lovins, A.B., Lovins, L.H., and Hawken, P. 1999. A road map for natural capitalism. *Harvard Business Review*, 77 (May–June): 145–58.

Lovins, H. 2015. The climate denier's guide to getting rich from fossil fuel divestment. *Guardian*, 14 April 2015: http://www.theguardian.com/environment/2015/apr/14/the-climate-deniers-guide-to-getting-rich-from-fossil-fuel-divestment.

Luce, E. and Merchant, K. 2003. India orders ban on advert saying fairer equals better for women. *Financial Times*, 20 March 2003: http://www.ft.com.

Lynas, M. 2008. Green v green. *Guardian*, 24 April: http://www.guardian.co.uk.

Lyotard, J.-F. 1984. *The postmodern condition: a report on knowledge*. Manchester: Manchester University Press.

MacDonald, C., McDonald, M., and Norman, W. 2002. Charitable conflicts of interest. *Journal of Business Ethics*, 39 (1–2): 67–74.

MacIntyre, A. 1984. *After virtue: a study in moral theory*. Notre Dame, Ill.: University of Notre Dame Press.

MacKay, B. and Munro, I. 2012. Information Warfare and New Organizational Landscapes: An Inquiry into the ExxonMobil-Greenpeace Dispute over Climate Change. *Organization Studies*, 33 (11): 1507–36.

Mackenzie, C. 1998. The choice of criteria in ethical investment. *Business Ethics: A European Review*, 7 (2): 81–6.

Maguire, K. and Wintour, P. 2001. The other woman in Blair's life walks out on him for job with BP. *Guardian*, 9 November 2001.

Maier, M. 1997. Gender equity, organizational transformation and challenger. *Journal of Business Ethics*, 16: 943–62.

Mainiero, L. and Jones, K. 2013. Sexual harassment versus workplace romance: Social media spillover and textual harassment in the workplace. *Academy of Management Perspectives*, 27 (3): 187–203.

Mäkinen, J. and Kourula, A. 2012. Pluralism in political corporate social responsibility. *Business Ethics Quarterly*, 22 (4): 649.

Manetti, G. 2011. The quality of stakeholder engagement in sustainability reporting: empirical evidence and critical points. *Corporate Social Responsibility and Environmental Management*, 18 (2): 110–22.

Marshall, T.H. 1965. *Class, citizenship and social development*. New York: Anchor Books.

Martínez Lucio, M. and Weston, S. 2000. European works councils and 'flexible regulation': the politics of intervention. *European Journal of Industrial Relations*, 6 (2): 203–16.

Mathiason, N. 2009. Private equity owned Boots ends ethical pledge. *Guardian*, 13 June 2009: http://www.guardian.co.uk.

Matten, D. and Crane, A. 2005. What is stakeholder democracy? Perspectives and issues. *Business Ethics: A European Review*, 14 (1): 6–13.

Matten, D. and Moon, J. 2008. 'Implicit' and 'explicit' CSR: a conceptual framework for a comparative understanding of corporate social responsibility. *Academy of Management Review*, 33 (2): 404–24.

Mayer, D.M., Nurmohamed, S., Treviño, L.K., Shapiro, D.L., and Schminke, M. 2013. Encouraging employees to report unethical conduct internally: It takes a village. *Organizational Behavior and Human Decision Processes*, 121 (1): 89–103.

Mayer, J. 2010. Covert Operations. *The New Yorker*, 30 August 2010.

Mayhew, N. 1997. Fading to grey: the use and abuse of corporate executives' 'representational power'. In R.J. Welford (ed.), *Hijacking environmentalism—corporate responses to sustainable development*: 63–95. London: Routledge.

McCabe, D.L. and Treviño, L.K. 1993. Academic dishonesty: honor codes and other situational influences. *Journal of Higher Education*, 64: 522–38.

McCabe, D.L., Dukerich, J.M., and Dutton, J.E. 1991. Context, values and moral dilemmas: comparing the choices of business and law school students. *Journal of Business Ethics*, 10 (2): 951–60.

McDonald, P. 2012. Workplace sexual harassment 30 years on: a review of the literature. *International Journal of Management Reviews*, 14 (1): 1–17.

McGrath, C. 2002. Comparative lobbying practices: Washington, London, Brussels. Paper presented at the Political Studies Association annual conference, University of Aberdeen.

McGrath, C. 2005. Towards a lobbying profession: developing the industry's reputation, education and representation. *Journal of Public Affairs*, 5: 124–35.

McGrew, A.G. 1997. Democracy beyond borders? Globalization and the reconstruction of democratic theory and practice. In A.G. McGrew (ed.), *The transformation of democracy? Globalization and territorial democracy*: 231–66. Cambridge: Polity Press.

McIntosh, M. and Thomas, R. 2002. *Corporate citizenship and the evolving relationship between non-governmental organisations and corporations*. London: British-North American Committee.

McIntosh, M. and Thomas, R. 2008. From risk to opportunity—how global executives view sociopolitical issues, *McKinsey Quarterly*, September: http://www.mckinseyquarterly.com.

McMurtry, J.J. 2009. Ethical value-added: fair trade and the case of Café Femenino. *Journal of Business Ethics*, 86: 27–49.

McNeely, J.A., Solh, M., Hiremath, R.B., Kumar, B., Suarez, P.A.Z., Uprety, K., Abdulrahim, M.A., Ruf, F., and Legoupil, J.-C. 2009. Viewpoints: 'Can the growing demand for biofuels be met without threatening food security?'. *Natural Resources Forum*, 33 (2): 171–3.

McPhail, K. 2001. The *other* objective of ethics education: re-humanising the accounting profession—a study of ethics education in law, engineering, medicine and accountancy. *Journal of Business Ethics*, 34: 279–98.

Meglino, B.M. and Ravlin, E.C. 1998. Individual values in organizations: concepts, controversies, and research. *Journal of Management*, 24 (3): 351–89.

Mellahi, K. and Wood, G. 2002. *The ethical business*. Basingstoke: Palgrave.

Michalos, A.C. 1988. Editorial. *Journal of Business Ethics*, 7: 1.

Millington, A., Eberhardt, M., and Wilkinson, B. 2005. Gift giving, Guanxi and illicit payments in buyer-supplier relations in China: analysing the experience of UK companies. *Journal of Business Ethics*, 57: 255–68.

Milne, G.R. and Culnan, M.J. 2004. Strategies for reducing online privacy risks: why consumers read (or don't read) online privacy notices. *Journal of Interactive Marketing*, 18 (3): 15–29.

Milne, M.J. and Gray, R. 2013. W(h)ither ecology? The triple bottom line, the global reporting initiative, and corporate sustainability reporting. *Journal of business ethics*, 118 (1): 13–29.

Milner, S. 2002. An ambiguous reform: the Jospin government and the 35-hour-week laws. *Modern and Contemporary France*, 10 (3): 339–51.

Mingers, J. and Walsham, G. 2010. Toward ethical information systems: the contribution of discourse ethics. *MIS Quarterly*, 34 (4): 833–54.

Mintzberg, H. 1983. The case for corporate social responsibility. *Journal of Business Strategy*, 4 (2): 3–15.

Mitchell, R.K., Agle, B.R., and Wood, D.J. 1997. Toward a theory of stakeholder identification and salience: defining the principle of who and what really counts. *Academy of Management Review*, 22 (4): 853–86.

Mitchell, W.C. 1990. Interest groups: economic perspectives and contribution. *Journal of Theoretical Politics*, 2: 85–108.

Moilanen, T. and Salminen, A. 2007. *Comparative study of the public-service ethics of the EU member states*. Helsinki: Finnish Ministry of Finance.

Molina, O. and Rhodes, M. 2002. Corporatism: the past, present and future of a concept. *Annual Review of Political Science*, 5: 305–31.

Monks, R.A.G. and Minow, N. 2011. *Corporate governance* (5th edn.). Hoboken, NJ: John Wiley & Sons.

Mont, O. 2004. *Product-service systems: panacea or myth?* Lund: International Institute for Industrial Environmental Economics.

Moody, M. 2008. 'Building a culture': the construction and evolution of venture philanthropy as a new organizational field. *Nonprofit and Voluntary Sector Quarterly* 37 (2): 324–52.

Moon, J. 1995. The firm as citizen: corporate responsibility in Australia. *Australian Journal of Political Science*, 30 (1): 1–17.

Moon, J. and Vogel, D. 2008. Corporate social responsibility, government, and civil society. In A. Crane, A. McWilliams, D. Matten, J. Moon, and D. Siegel (eds.), *The Oxford handbook of corporate social responsibility*: 303–23. Oxford: Oxford University Press.

Moore, E.S. 2004. Children and the changing world of advertising. *Journal of Business Ethics*, 52 (2): 161–7.

Moore, G. 1999. Corporate moral agency: review and implications. *Journal of Business Ethics*, 21: 329–43.

Moore, J. 1990. What is really unethical about insider trading? *Journal of Business Ethics*, 9: 171–82.

Morgan, G., Campbell, J., Crouch, C., Pedersen, O.K., and Whitley, R. 2010. *The Oxford handbook of comparative institutional analysis*. Oxford: Oxford University Press.

Morris, D. 2004. Defining a moral problem in business ethics. *Journal of Business Ethics*, 49: 347–57.

Mukherjee, R. 2014. From Jan 1, pharma cos can no longer gift freebies to doctors. *Times of India*, 23 December 2014: http://timesofindia.indiatimes.com/business/india-business/From-Jan-1-pharma-cos-can-no-longer-gift-freebies-to-doctors/articleshow/45610957.cms

Muller, A. and Whiteman, G. 2009. Exploring the geography of corporate philanthropic disaster response: a study of Fortune global 500 firms. *Journal of Business Ethics*, 84: 589–603.

Murphy, D. 2007. More Saudi women join the workforce, but limits remain strict. *Christian Science Monitor*, 24 April 2007: http://www.csmonitor.com.

Muskin, J.B. 2000. Interorganizational ethics: standards of behavior. *Journal of Business Ethics*, 24: 283–97.

Muthuri, J.N. 2008. Participation and accountability in corporate community involvement programmes: a research agenda. *Community Development Journal*, 43 (2): 177–93.

Muthuri, J.N., Matten, D., and Moon, J. 2009. Employee volunteering and social capital: contributions to corporate social responsibility. *British Journal of Management*, 20 (1): 75–89.

Nader, R. 1984. Reforming corporate governance. *California Management Review*, 26 (4): 126–32.

Nanto, D. 2008. *The U.S. financial crisis: the global dimension with implications for U.S. policy (November 10, 2008)*. Washington: Congressional Research Service.

NEF. 2010. *21 hours*. London: New Economic Foundation.

Néron, P.Y. 2010. Business and the Polis: What Does it Mean to See Corporations as Political Actors? *Journal of Business Ethics*, 94: 333–52.

Neslen, A. 2015. Shell lobbied to undermine EU renewables targets, documents reveal. *Guardian*, 27 April 2015.

New, S. 1998. The implications and reality of partnership. In B. Dale (ed.), *Working in partnership: best practice in customer-supplier relations*: 9–20. Aldershot: Gower Publishing.

Nicholls, A. 2006. Introduction. In A. Nicholls (ed.), *Social entrepreneurship: new models of sustainable social change*. Oxford: Oxford University Press.

Nicholls, A. and Opal, C. 2005. *Fair trade: market-driven ethical consumption*. London: Sage.

Nielsen, R.P. 2006. Introduction to the special issue. In search of organizational virtue: moral agency in organizations. *Organization Studies*, 27 (3): 317–21.

Nielsen, R.P. 2008. The private equity-leveraged buyout form of finance capitalism: ethical and social issues and potential reforms. *Business Ethics Quarterly*, 18 (3): 379–404.

Noland, J. and Phillips, R. 2010. Stakeholder engagement, discourse ethics and strategic management. *International Journal of Management Reviews*, 12 (1): 39–49.

Nomani, F. 2008. Islamic finance: law, economics. *International Journal of Middle East Studies*, 40 (2): 349–51.

Nonhebel, S. 2012. Global food supply and the impacts of increased use of biofuels. *Energy*, 37 (1): 115–21.

Nozick, R. 1974. *Anarchy, state, and utopia*. New York: Basic Books.

Nwankwo, E., Phillips, N., and Tracey, P. 2007. Social investment through community enterprise: the case of multinational corporations involvement in the development of Nigerian water resources. *Journal of Business Ethics*, 73 (1): 91–101.

O'Dwyer, B. and Owen, D.L. 2005. Assurance statement practice in environmental, social and sustainability reporting: a critical evaluation. *British Accounting Review*, 37 (2): 205–29.

O'Dwyer, B., Boomsma, R., and Parker, L. 2015. The co-construction of NGO accountability: Aligning imposed and felt accountability in NGO-funder accountability relationships. *Accounting, Auditing & Accountability Journal*, 28 (1): 36–68.

O'Dwyer, B., Owen, D., and Unerman, J. 2011. Seeking legitimacy for new assurance forms: The case of assurance on sustainability reporting. *Accounting, Organizations and Society*, 36 (1): 31–52.

O'Fallon, M.J. and Butterfield, K.D. 2005. A review of the empirical ethical decision-making literature: 1996–2003. *Journal of Business Ethics*, 59 (4): 375–413.

O'Neill, O. 2002. *A question of trust: the BBC Reith lectures 2002*. Cambridge: Cambridge University Press.

O'Rourke, A. 2003. A new politics of engagement: shareholder activism for corporate social responsibility. *Business Strategy and the Environment*, 12 (4): 227–39.

Oakley, J. and Bush, A.J. 2012. Customer Entertainment in Relationship Marketing: A Literature Review and Directions for Future Research. *Journal of Relationship Marketing*, 11 (1): 21–40.

OECD. 2001. Codes of corporate conduct—an expanded review of their contents. Paris: Organisation for Economic Co-operation and Development.

Ogbonna, E. and Wilkinson, B. 1996. Inter-organizational power relations in the UK grocery industry: contradictions and developments. *International Review of Retail, Distribution and Consumer Research*, 6 (4): 395–414.

Olney, W.W. 2013. A race to the bottom? Employment protection and foreign direct investment. *Journal of International Economics*, 91 (2): 191–203.

Olterman, P. and McClanahan, P. 2014. Tata Nano safety under scrutiny after dire crash test results. *Guardian*, 31 January 2014.

Orlitzky, M. 2008. Corporate social performance and financial performance: a research synthesis. In A. Crane, A. McWilliams, D. Matten, J. Moon, and D. Siegel (eds.), *The Oxford handbook of corporate social responsibility*: 113–36. Oxford: Oxford University Press.

Orlitzky, M., Schmidt, F.L., and Rynes, S.L. 2003. Corporate social and financial performance: a meta-analysis. *Organization Studies*, 24 (3): 403–11.

Orts, E.W. and Deketelaere, K. 2001. Environmental contracts and regulatory innovation. In E.W. Orts and K. Deketelaere (eds.), *Environmental Contracts*: 1–35. Dordrecht: Kluwer.

Ostas, D.T. 2007. The law and ethics of K street—lobbying, the first amendment, and the duty to create just laws. *Business Ethics Quarterly*, 17 (1): 33–63.

Ottensmeyer, E.J. and Heroux, M.A. 1991. Ethics, public policy, and managing advanced technologies: the case of electronic surveillance. *Journal of Business Ethics*, 10: 519–26.

Oulton, W. 2006. The role of activism in responsible investment—the FTSE4Good indices. In R. Sullivan and C. Mackenzie (eds.), *Responsible investment*: 196–205. Sheffield: Greenleaf.

Ovsey, D. 2014. Recourse for intellectual-property theft in China is improving, but new risks are emerging. *Financial Post*, 19 February 2014: http://business.financialpost.com/2014/2002/2019/recourse-for-intellectual-property-theft-in-china-is-improving-but-new-risks-are-emerging/.

Owen, D.L. 2005. Corporate social reporting and stakeholder accountability: the missing link. *ICCSR Research Paper Series* (32–2005).

Owen, D.L. and O'Dwyer, B. 2008. Corporate social responsibility: the reporting and assurance dimension. In A. Crane, D. Matten, A. McWilliams, J. Moon, and D. Siegel (eds.), *The Oxford handbook of corporate social responsibility*: 384–409. Oxford: Oxford University Press.

Oxfam. 2014. *Working for the few*. London: Oxfam International.

Packard, V. 1957. *The hidden persuaders*. New York: Pocket Books.

Pagell, M. and Wu, Z. 2009. Building a more complete theory of sustainable supply chain management using case studies of 10 exemplars. *Journal of Supply Chain Management*, 45 (2): 37–56.

Paine, L.S. 1994. Managing for organizational integrity. *Harvard Business Review*, 72 (March–April): 106–17.

Painter-Morland, M. 2010. Questioning corporate codes of ethics. *Business Ethics: A European Review*, 19 (3): 265–79.

Palazzo, B. 2002. US-American and German business ethics: an intercultural comparison. *Journal of Business Ethics*, 41: 195–216.

Parker, B. 1998a. *Globalization and business practice: managing across boundaries*. London: Sage.

Parker, M. 1998b. Business ethics and social theory: postmodernizing the ethical. *British Journal of Management*, 9 (special issue): S27–S36.

Parkin, F. 1982. *Max Weber*. London: Routledge.

Parkinson, J.E. 1993. *Corporate power and responsibility*. Oxford: Oxford University Press.

Parkinson, J.E. 2003. Models of the company and the employment relationship. *British Journal of Industrial Relations*, 41 (3): 481–509.

Parr, A. 2009. *Hijacking sustainability*. Cambridge, MA: MIT Press.

Pava, M.L. 1998. The substance of Jewish business ethics. *Journal of Business Ethics*, 17 (6): 603–17.

Peachey, P. 2014. Animal rights group ends 15-year campaign against experiments at Huntingdon. *Independent*, 24 August 2014: http://www.independent.co.uk/news/uk/crime/animal-rights-group-ends-15year-campaign-against-experiments-at-huntingdon-9687843.html.

Pearce, D. 1999. *Economics and environment: essays on ecological economics and sustainable development*. Cheltenham: Edward Elgar.

Pearce, D. and Turner, K. 1990. *Economics of natural resources and the environment*. New York: Harvester Wheatsheaf.

Pearce, J.A., II. 2009. The profit-making allure of product reconstruction. *MIT Sloan Management Review*, 50 (3): 59–65.

Peattie, K. and Crane, A. 2005. Green marketing: legend, myth, farce or prophesy? *Qualitative Market Research: An International Journal*, 8 (4): 357–70.

Pegg, S. 2012. Social responsibility and resource extraction: Are Chinese oil companies different? *Resources Policy*, 37 (2): 160–67.

Peloza, J. and Hassay, D.N. 2006. Intra-organizational volunteerism: good soldiers, good deeds and good politics. *Journal of Business Ethics*, 64 (4): 357–79.

Pfeffer, J. and Salancik, G.R. 1978. *The external control of organizations: a resource dependence perspective*. New York: Harper and Row.

Phillips, B.J. 1997. In defense of advertising: a social perspective. *Journal of Business Ethics*, 16: 109–18.

Phillips, R. 2011. *Stakeholder theory: impact and prospects*. Cheltenham, UK; Northampton, MA: Edward Elgar.

Pinkse, J. and Kolk, A. 2012. Addressing the Climate Change—Sustainable Development Nexus: The Role of Multistakeholder Partnerships. *Business & Society*, 51 (1): 176–210.

Pojman, L.P. 1997. The moral status of affirmative action. In T.L. Beauchamp and N.E. Bowie (eds.), *Ethical theory and business* (5th edn.) 374–79. Upper Saddle River, NJ: Prentice Hall.

Pollay, R.W. 1986. The distorted mirror: reflections on the unintended consequences of advertising. *Journal of Marketing*, 50, April: 18–36.

Poole, M. 2013. *Industrial relations: origins and patterns of national diversity*. Abingdon: Routledge.

Porter, M.E. 2008. The five competitive forces that shape strategy. *Harvard Business Review*, 86 (January): 79–93.

Porter, M.E. and Kramer, M.R. 2002. The competitve advantage of corporate philanthropy. *Harvard Business Review*, 80 (12): 56–69.

Porter, M.E. and Kramer, M.R. 2006. Strategy and society: the link between competitive advantage and corporate social responsibility. *Harvard Business Review*, 84 (December): 78–92.

Porter, M.E. and Kramer, M.R. 2011. Creating shared value. *Harvard Business Review*, 89 (2): 62–77.

Posner, B.Z. 2010. Another look at the impact of personal and organizational values congruency. *Journal of Business Ethics*, 97 (4): 535–41.

Prahalad, C.K. and Hammond, A. 2002. Serving the world's poor, profitably. *Harvard Business Review*, 80 (9): 48–57.

Premeaux, S.R. and Mondy, R.W. 1993. Linking management behavior to ethical philosophy. *Journal of Business Ethics*, 12: 349–57.

Preuss, L. 1999. Ethical theory in German business ethics research. *Journal of Business Ethics*, 18: 407–19.

Preuss, L. 2005. *The green multiplier: a study of environmental protection and the supply chain*. Basingstoke: Palgrave Macmillan.

Preuss, L., Gold, M., and Rees, C. 2014. *Corporate Social Responsibility and Trade Unions: Perspectives across Europe*. Abingdon: Routledge.

Prno, J. and Slocombe, D.S. 2012. Exploring the origins of 'social license to operate' in the mining sector: Perspectives from governance and sustainability theories. *Resources Policy*, 37 (3): 346–57.

Puppim de Oliveira, J.A. and Vargas, G. 2006. Corporate citizenship in Latin America: new challenges for business *Journal of Corporate Citizenship* (21). (special issue).

Rabelo, F.M. and Vasconcelos, F.C. 2002. Corporate governance in Brazil. *Journal of Business Ethics*, 37 (3): 321–35.

Rabouin, M. 1997. Lyin' T(*)gers, and 'Cares', oh my: the case of feminist integration of business ethics. *Journal of Business Ethics*, 16: 247–61.

Rahaman, A.S., Everett, J., and Neu, D. 2013. Trust, Morality, and the Privatization of Water Services in Developing Countries. *Business and Society Review*, 118 (4): 539–75.

Ram, M. 2000. Investors in people in small firms: case study evidence from the business services sector. *Personnel Review*, 29 (1): 69–91.

Rao, A. 2012. Managing diversity: Impact of religion in the Indian workplace. *Journal of World Business*, 47 (2): 232–39.

Rasche, A., Waddock, S., and McIntosh, M. 2013. The United Nations Global Compact Retrospect and Prospect. *Business & Society*, 52 (1): 6–30.

Rawls, J. 1971. *A theory of justice*. Cambridge, MA: Harvard University Press.

Reece, J.W. 2001. Business and the civil society: the missing dialectic. *Thunderbird International Business Review*, 43 (5): 651–67.

Reed, D. 2002. Corporate governance reforms in developing countries. *Journal of Business Ethics*, 37 (3): 223–47.

Reeves, R. 2005. Do the right thing. *Management Today*, 1 July 2005: http://www.clickmt.com.

Reich, R.B. 2007. *Supercapitalism: the transformation of business, democracy and everyday life*. New York: Alfred A. Knopf.

Reich, R.B. 2012. *Beyond Outrage*. New York: Random House.

Reich, R.B. 2015. Robert Reich: The sharing economy is hurtling us backwards. *Salon*, 4 February 2015: http://www.salon.com.

Reimann, F., Ehrgott, M., Kaufmann, L., and Carter, C.R. 2012. Local stakeholders and local legitimacy: MNEs' social strategies in emerging economies. *Journal of international management*, 18 (1): 1–17.

Reinecke, J., Manning, S., and Von Hagen, O. 2012. The emergence of a standards market: Multiplicity of sustainability standards in the global coffee industry. *Organization Studies*, 33 (5–6): 791–814.

Reitz, H.J., Wall, J.A., Jr., and Love, M.S. 1998. Ethics in negotiation: oil and water or good lubrication? *Business Horizons*, May–June, 41 (3): 5–14.

Renn, O., Webler, T., and Wiedemann, P.M. (eds.). 1995. *Fairness and competence in citizen participation*. Dordrecht: Kluwer.

Reuters. 2009. ECI Reveals Innovations in Training: Novartis Employees Play Video Games to Learn about Code of Ethics. Reuters, 12 March 2009: http://mobile.reuters.com/article/idUS195269+12-Mar-2009+BW20090312?irpc=932.

Rice, G. 1999. Islamic ethics and the implications for business. *Journal of Business Ethics*, 18 (4): 345–58.

Rifkin, J. 1995. *The end of work*. New York: Tarcher Putnam.

Roberts, M., Pettigrew, S., Chapman, K., Quester, P., and Miller, C. 2014. Children's exposure to food advertising: An analysis of the effectiveness of self-regulatory codes in Australia. *Nutrition & Dietetics*, 71 (1): 35–40.

Roberts, S. 2003. Supply chain specific? Understanding the patchy success of ethical sourcing initiatives. *Journal of Business Ethics*, 44 (2/3): 159–70.

Robins, N. and Humphrey, L. 2000. Sustaining the rag trade. London: International Institute for Environment and Development.

Robinson, S.R., Irmak, C., and Jayachandran, S. 2012. Choice of cause in cause-related marketing. *Journal of Marketing*, 76 (4): 126–39.

Robinson, W. 2005. Ethical considerations in flexible work arrangements. *Business and Society Review*, 110 (2): 213–24.

Rokeach, M. 1973. *The nature of human values*. New York: Free Press.

Romar, E.J. 2004. Globalization, ethics, and opportunism: a Confucian view of business relationships. *Business Ethics Quarterly*, 14 (4): 663–78.

Roodman, D. 2012. *Due diligence: An impertinent inquiry into microfinance*. Washington, DC: Center for Global Development.

Rorty, R. 2006. Is philosophy relevant to applied ethics? Invited address to the Society of Business Ethics annual meeting, August 2005. *Business Ethics Quarterly*, 16 (3): 369–80.

Rosenthal, S.B. and Buchholz, R.A. 2000. *Rethinking business ethics: a pragmatic approach*. New York: Oxford University Press.

Rossouw, G. 2005. Business ethics and corporate governance in Africa. *Business & Society*, 44 (1): 94–106.

Rothenberg, S. 2007. Sustainability through servicizing. *MIT Sloan Management Review*, 48 (2): 83–91.

Rothenberg, S. and Levy, D.L. 2012. Corporate Perceptions of Climate Science: The Role of Corporate Environmental Scientists. *Business & Society*, 51 (1): 31–61.

Rothschild, J. and Miethe, T.D. 1999. Whistle blower disclosures and management retaliation: the battle to control information about organization corruption. *Work and Occupations*, 26 (1): 107–28.

Rowan, J.R. 2000. The moral foundation of employee rights. *Journal of Business Ethics*, 24: 355–61.

Rowley, T.J. 1997. Moving beyond dyadic ties: a network theory of stakeholder influences. *Academy of Management Review*, 22 (4): 887–910.

Roy, R. and Whelan, R.C. 1992. Successful recycling through value-chain collaboration. *Long Range Planning*, 25 (4): 62–71.

Royle, T. 2005. Realism or idealism? Corporate social responsibility and the employee stakeholder in the global fast-food industry. *Business Ethics: A European Review*, 14 (1): 42–55.

Rudolph, B. 1999. Finanzmärkte. In W. Korff (ed.), *Handbuch der Wirtschaftsethik*: 274–92. Gütersloh: Gütersloher Verlagshaus.

Rudra, N. 2008. *Globalization and the race to the bottom in developing countries: who really gets hurt?* Cambridge, UK and New York: Cambridge University Press.

Rufin, C. and Rivera-Santos, M. 2012. Between Commonweal and Competition: Understanding the Governance of Public-Private Partnerships. *Journal of Management*, 38 (5): 1634–54.

Ruggie, J. 2008. Protect, respect and remedy: a framework for business and human rights. *Innovations*, Spring: 189–212.

Rugman, A.M. 2000. *The end of globalisation*. London: Random House.

Rugman, A.M. and Verbeke, A. 2000. Six cases of corporate strategic responses to environmental regulation. *European Management Journal*, 18 (4): 377–85.

Rushe, D. 2013. The 10 best-paid CEOs in America. *Guardian*, 22 October 2013.

Russell, J. 2006. A charter for success. *Ethical Corporation*, June: 11.

Saikawa, E. 2013. Policy diffusion of emission standards: is there a race to the top? *World Politics*, 65 (01): 1–33.

Salamon, L.M., Haddock, M.A., Sokolowski, S.W., and Tice, H.S. 2007. Measuring civil society and volunteering: initial findings from implementation of the UN handbook on nonprofit institutions, *Working Paper No. 23* Baltimore: Johns Hopkins Center for Civil Society Studies.

Salant, J.D. and O'Leary, L. 2009. Six lobbyists per lawmaker work on health overhaul. *Bloomberg News*, 14 August.

Sandberg, A. (ed.). 1995. *Enriching production: perspectives on Volvo's Uddevalla plant as an alternative to lean production*. Aldershot: Avebury.

Sarkar, J. and Sarkar, S. 2000. Large shareholder activism in corporate governance in developing countries: evidence from India. *International Review of Finance*, 1 (3): 161–94.

Sayer, A. 2009. Contributive justice and meaningful work. *Res Publica*, 15 (1): 1–16.

Scalet, S. and Kelly, T.F. 2012. The ethics of credit rating agencies: What happened and the way forward. *Journal of business ethics*, 111 (4): 477–90.

Schaefer, A. and Crane, A. 2005. Addressing sustainability and consumption. *Journal of Macromarketing*, 25: 76–92.

Scherer, A.G. and Palazzo, G. 2007. Toward a political conception of corporate responsibility—business and society seen from a Habermasian perspective. *Academy of Management Review*, 32 (4): 1096–120.

Scherer, A.G. and Palazzo, G. 2008a. Globalization and CSR. In A. Crane, A. McWilliams, D. Matten, J. Moon, and D. Siegel (eds.), *The Oxford handbook of corporate social responsibility*: 413–31. Oxford: Oxford University Press.

Scherer, A.G. and Palazzo, G. (eds.). 2008b. *Handbook of Research on Global Corporate Citizenship*. Cheltenham: Edward Elgar.

Scherer, A.G. and Palazzo, G. 2011. The New Political Role of Business in a Globalized World: A Review of a New Perspective on CSR and its Implications for the Firm, Governance, and Democracy. *Journal of Management Studies*, 48 (4): 899–931.

Scherer, A.G. and Smid, M. 2000. The downward spiral and the U.S. model business principles: why MNEs should take responsibility for improvement of worldwide social and environmental conditions. *Management International Review*, 40 (4): 351–71.

Schiesari, C. and Beat Grüninger. 2014. *Assessing the Benefits of Fairtrade Orange Juice for Brazilian Small Farmers*. http://www.fairtrade.net/fileadmin/user_upload/content/2009/resources/1404-Assessing_the_benefits_of_Fairtrade_Orange_Juice.pdf: BSD Consulting.

Schlosser, E. 2001. *Fast Food Nation*. Boston: Houghton Mifflin.

Schmidt, G. and Williams, K. 2002. German management facing globalization: the 'German model' on trial. In M. Geppert, D. Matten, and K. Williams (eds.), *Challenges for European management in a global context: experiences from Britain and Germany*: 281–93. Basingstoke: Palgrave.

Schnabel, C. 2013. Union membership and density: Some (not so) stylized facts and challenges. *European Journal of Industrial Relations*, 19: 255–72.

Schnackenberg, A.K. and Tomlinson, E.C. 2014. Organizational Transparency A New Perspective on Managing Trust in Organization-Stakeholder Relationships. *Journal of Management*. doi: 10.1177/0149206314525202.

Scholte, J.A. 2005. *Globalization: a critical introduction* (2nd edn.). Basingstoke: Palgrave.

Schrader, U. 1999. Consumer acceptance of eco-efficient services. *Greener Management International*, 25: 105–21.

Schumacher, E.F. 1974. *Small is beautiful: a study of economics as if people mattered*. London: Abacus.

Schüssler, E., Rüling, C., and Wittneben, B. 2014. On melting summits: The limitations of field-configuring events as catalysts of change in transnational climate policy. *Academy of Management Journal*, 57 (1): 140–71.

Schwartz, M. 2000. Why ethical codes constitute an unconscionable regression. *Journal of Business Ethics*, 23: 173–84.

Schwartz, M.S. 2004. Effective corporate codes of ethics: Perceptions of code users. *Journal of Business Ethics*, 55 (4): 321–41.

Schwartz, M.S. 2013. Developing and sustaining an ethical corporate culture: The core elements. *Business Horizons*: 56 (1): 39–50.

Scott, K., Park, J., and Cocklin, C. 2000. From 'sustainable rural communities' to 'social sustainability': giving voice to diversity in Mangakahia Valley, New Zealand. *Journal of Rural Studies*, 16: 443–6.

Seitanidi, M. M. and Ryan, A. 2007. A critical review of forms of corporate community involvement: from philanthropy to partnerships. *International Journal of Nonprofit and Voluntary Sector Marketing*, 12: 247–66.

Seitanidi, M.M. and Crane, A. (eds.). 2014. *Responsible business and social partnerships: a research handbook*. London: Routledge.

Selsky, J.W. and Parker, B. 2005. Cross-sector partnerships to address social issues: challenges to theory and practice. *Journal of Management*, 31 (6): 1–25.

Sen, S., Gurhan-Canli, Z., and Morwitz, V. 2001. Withholding consumption: a social dilemma perspective on consumer boycotts. *Journal of Consumer Research*, 28 (3): 399–417.

Sethi, S.P. 2002. Standards for corporate conduct in the international arena: challenges and opportunities for multinational corporations. *Business and Society Review*, 107 (1): 20–40.

Shankman, N.A. 1999. Reframing the debate between agency and stakeholder theories of the firm. *Journal of Business Ethics*, 19: 319–34.

Shaoul, J., Stafford, A., and Stapleton, P. 2012. Accountability and corporate governance of public private partnerships. *Critical Perspectives on Accounting*, 23 (3): 213–29.

Shaw, D. and Newholm, T. 2001. Voluntary simplicity and the ethics of consumption. *Psychology and marketing*, 19 (2): 167–85.

Shrivastava, P. 1995. Ecocentric management for a risk society. *Academy of Management Review*, 20 (1): 118–37.

Sillanpää, M. and Wheeler, D. 1997. Integrated ethical auditing: The Body Shop International. In S. Zadek, P. Pruzan, and R. Evans (eds.), *Building corporate accountability: emerging practices in social and ethical accounting, auditing and reporting*: 102–28. London: Earthscan.

Simms, M. 1994. Defining privacy in employee health screening cases: ethical ramifications concerning the employee/employer relationship. *Journal of Business Ethics*, 13: 315–25.

Simpson, R. 1998. Presenteeism, power and organizational change: long hours as a career barrier and the impact on the working lives of women managers. *British Journal of Management*, 9 (special issue): 37–50.

Simpson, R. 2000. Presenteeism and the impact of long hours on managers. In D. Winstanley and J. Woodall (eds.), *Ethical issues in contemporary human resource management*: 156–71. Basingstoke: Macmillan.

Sims, R.R. and Brinkmann, J. 2002. Leaders as moral role models: the case of John Gutfreund at Salomon Brothers. *Journal of Business Ethics*, 35 (4): 327–39.

Sims, R.R. and Brinkmann, J. 2003. Enron ethics (or: Culture matters more than codes). *Journal of Business Ethics*, 45 (3): 243–56.

Sinclair, A. 1993. Approaches to organizational culture and ethics. *Journal of Business Ethics*, 12: 63–73.

Singhapakdi, A. and Vitell, S.J. 1990. Marketing ethics: factors influencing perceptions of ethical problems and alternatives. *Journal of Macromarketing*, 10 (1): 4–18.

Sison, A.J.G. 2000. Integrated risk management and global business ethics. *Business Ethics: A European Review*, 9 (4): 288–95.

Sklair, L. 1991. *Sociology of the global system*. Baltimore: John Hopkins University Press.

Smalley Bowen, T. 2003. Reducing pollution—it's a bargain. *Financial Times*, 2 February: 16.

Smart, B. 2010. *Consumer Society: Critical Issues & Environmental Consequences*. Thousand Oaks, CA: Sage.

Smith, A. 1793. *An inquiry into the nature and causes of the wealth of nations*. London: A. Strahan and T. Cadell.

Smith, C. and Pun, N. 2006. The dormitory labour regime in China as a site for control and resistance. *International Journal of Human Resource Management*, 17 (8): 1456–70.

Smith, J. 2013. The World's Most Ethical Companies. *Forbes*, 6 March 2013: http://www.forbes.com/ sites/jacquelynsmith/2013/2003/2006/the-worlds-most-ethical-companies-in-2013/.

Smith, N.C. 1995. Marketing strategies for the ethics era. *Sloan Management Review*, 36 (4): 85–97.

Smith, N.C. 2003. Corporate social responsibility: whether or how? *California Management Review*, 45 (4): 52–76.

Smith, N.C. 2014. *Morality and the Market (Routledge Revivals): Consumer Pressure for Corporate Accountability*. London: Routledge.

Smith, N.C. 2015. *Morality and the market: consumer pressure for corporate accountability* (reprinted edn.). Abingdon: Routledge.

Smith, N.C. and Cooper-Martin, E. 1997. Ethics and target marketing: the role of product harm and consumer vulnerability. *Journal of Marketing*, 61, July: 1–20.

Smith, S. and Barrientos, S. 2005. Fair trade and ethical trade: are there moves towards convergence? *Sustainable Development*, 13: 190–8.

Smith, W.K., Gonin, M., and Besharov, M.L. 2013. Managing social-business tensions. *Business Ethics Quarterly*, 23 (3): 407–42.

Smithers, R. 2014. Global Fairtrade sales reach £4.4bn following 15% growth during 2013. *Guardian*, 3 September 2014: http://www.theguardian.com/global-development/2014/sep/03/global-fair-trade-sales-reach-4-billion-following-15-per-cent-growth-2013.

Solomon, A. and Lewis, L. 2002. Incentives and disincentives for corporate environmental disclosure. *Business Strategy and the Environment*, 11 (3): 154–69.

Solymossy, E. and Masters, J.K. 2002. Ethics through an entrepreneurial lens: theory and observation. *Journal of Business Ethics*, 38 (3): 227–41.

Somers, M.J. 2001. Ethical codes of conduct and organizational context: a study of the relationship between codes of conduct, employee behaviour and organizational values. *Journal of Business Ethics*, 30: 185–95.

Sommerlad, N. 2015. Six firms including Google and Facebook made £14BILLION last year but paid just 0.3% UK tax. *Daily Mirror*, 31 January 2015.

Sorge, A. 2005. *The global and the local: understanding the dialectics of business systems*. Oxford: Oxford University Press.

Sorrell, T. 1998. Beyond the fringe? The strange state of business ethics. In M. Parker (ed.), *Ethics and Organizations*: 15–29. London: Sage.

Spar, D. and Yoffie, D. 1999. Multinational enterprises and the prospects for justice. *Journal of International Affairs*, 52 (2): 557–81.

Sparkes, R. 2001. Ethical investment: whose ethics, which investment? *Business Ethics: A European Review*, 10 (3): 194–205.

Spence, L.J. 1999. Does size matter? The state of the art in small business ethics. *Business Ethics: A European Review*, 8 (3): 163–74.

Spence, L.J. 2002. Is Europe distinctive from America? An overview of business ethics in Europe. In H. von Weltzien Hoivik (ed.), *Moral leadership in action*: 9–25. Cheltenham: Edward Elgar.

Spence, L.J. and Lozano, J.F. 2000. Communicating about ethics with small firms: experiences from the U.K. and Spain. *Journal of Business Ethics*, 27 (1/2): 43–53.

Spence, L.J., Coles, A.-M., and Harris, L. 2001. The forgotten stakeholder? Ethics and social responsibility in relation to competitors. *Business and Society Review*, 106 (4): 331–52.

Spencer, J.W. 2008. The impact of multinational enterprise strategy on indigenous enterprises: horizontal spillovers and crowding out in developing countries. *Academy of Management Review*, 33 (2): 341–61.

Spicer, A., Dunfee, T.W., and Bailey, W.J. 2004. Does national context matter in ethical decision-making? An empirical test of integrative social contracts theory. *Academy of Management Journal*, 47 (4): 610–20.

Spronk, S. 2007. Roots of resistance to urban water privatization in Bolivia: the 'new working class,' the crisis of neoliberalism, and public services. *International Labor and Working-Class History*, 71: 8–28.

Stansbury, J. and Barry, B. 2007. Ethics programs and the paradox of control. *Business Ethics Quarterly*, 17 (2): 239–61.

Stanworth, C. 2000. Flexible working patterns. In D. Winstanley and J. Woodall (eds.), *Ethical issues in contemporary human resource management*: 137–55. Basingstoke: Macmillan.

Starik, M. and Rands, G.P. 1995. Weaving an integrated web: Multilevel and multisystem perspectives of ecologically sustainable organizations. *Academy of Management Review*, 20 (4): 908–35.

Stark, A. 1994. What's the matter with business ethics? *Harvard Business Review* 72 (May–June): 38–48.

Starkey, K. 1998. Durkheim and the limits of corporate culture: whose culture? Which Durkheim? *Journal of Management Studies*, 35 (2): 125–36.

Steger, M. 2013. *Globalisation. A very short introduction*. Oxford: Oxford University Press.

Steinmann, H. and Löhr, A. 1994. *Grundlagen der Unternehmensethik*. Stuttgart: Schäffer-Poeschel.

Stewart, J.B. 2014. Amazon's Shrinking Profit Sets Off a Seismic Shock to Its Shares. *New York Times*, 25 April 2014: http://www.nytimes.com/2014/04/26/business/amazons-shrinking-profit-sets-off-a-seismic-shock-to-its-shares.html.

Stigler, G.J. 1971. The theory of economic regulation. *Bell Journal of Economics and Management Science*, 2: 3–21.

Stonington, J. 2011. B-Schools' New Mantra: Ethics and Profits. 10 November 2011: http://www.businessweek.com/business-schools/bschools-new-mantra-ethics-and-profits-11102011.html.

Stout, L.A. 2012. *The shareholder value myth: how putting shareholders first harms investors, corporations, and the public* (1st edn.). San Francisco: Berrett-Koehler.

Strand, R. and Freeman, R.E. 2015. Scandinavian cooperative advantage: The theory and practice of stakeholder engagement in Scandinavia. *Journal of Business Ethics*, 127 (1): 65–85.

Su, B., Heshmati, A., Geng, Y., and Yu, X. 2013. A review of the circular economy in China: moving from rhetoric to implementation. *Journal of Cleaner Production*, 42: 215–27.

Sullivan, C. and Lewis, S. 2001. Home-based telework, gender, and the synchronization of work and family: perspectives of teleworkers and their co-residents. *Gender, Work and Organizations*, 8 (2): 123–45.

Sullivan, R. (ed.). 2003. *Business and human rights*. Sheffield: Greenleaf.

Surowiecki, J. 2008. All together now? *The New Yorker*, 9 June 2008.

Surowiecki, J. 2014. Le Divorce. *The New Yorker*, 3 November 2014.

Surroca, J., Tribó, J.A., and Zahra, S. A. 2013. Stakeholder Pressure on MNEs and the Transfer of Socially Irresponsible Practices to Subsidiaries. *Academy of Management Journal*, 56 (2): 549–72.

Tabuchi, H. 2011. Another scandal unsettles corporate Japan as paper maker accuses ex-chairman. *New York Times*, 28 October 2011: http://www.nytimes.com/2011/10/29/business/global/new-scandal-presses-corporate-japan.html?_r=10.

Taibbi, M. 2012. Greed and Debt: The True Story of Mitt Romney and Bain Capital. *Rolling Stone Magazine*, 29 August 2012: http://www.rollingstone.com/politics/news/greed-and-debt-the-true-story-of-mitt-romney-and-bain-capital-20120829.

Tamari, M. 1997. The challenge of wealth: Jewish business ethics. *Business Ethics Quarterly*, 7 (2): 45–56.

Taplin, I. 2002. The effects of globalization on the state-business relationships: a conceptual framework. In M. Geppert, D. Matten, and K. Williams (eds.), *Challenges for European management in a global context*: 239–59. Basingstoke: Palgrave.

Tapper, R. 1997. Voluntary agreements for environmental performance improvement: perspectives on the chemical industry's responsible care programme. *Business Strategy and the Environment*, 8: 287–92.

Tarí, J.J., Molina-Azorín, J.F., and Heras, I. 2012. Benefits of the ISO 9001 and ISO 14001 standards: A literature review. *Journal of Industrial Engineering and Management*, 5 (2): 297–322.

Taylor, R. 2000. How new is socially responsible investment? *Business Ethics: A European Review*, 9 (3): 174–9.

Taylor, R. 2001. Putting ethics into investment. *Business Ethics: A European Review*, 10 (1): 53–60.

ten Bos, R. 1997. Business ethics and Bauman ethics. *Organization Studies*, 18 (6): 997–1014.

ten Bos, R. and Willmott, H. 2001. Towards a post-dualistic business ethics: interweaving reason and emotion in working life. *Journal of Management Studies*, 38 (6): 769–93.

Tepper, R. 2013. Dannon Under Fire For Use Of Carmine, Insect-Based Color Additive. *Huffington Post*, 24 July 2013: http://www.huffingtonpost.com/2013/2007/2024/dannon-carmine_n_3645757.html.

Terrachoice. 2009. *The seven sins of greenwashing: environmental claims in consumer markets*. Toronto: Terrachoice Group Inc.

The Economist. 2005. The ethics of business. *The Economist,* 20 January 2005: http://www.economist.com/node/3555286.

The Economist. 2012. Firms with benefits. *The Economist*, 7 January 2014: http://www.economist.com/node/21542432.

The Economist. 2013. Free speech or knowing misrepresentation? *The Economist*, 5 February 2013: http://www.economist.com/blogs/schumpeter/2013/2002/rating-agencies.

The Economist. 2014a. Big interest, no interest. *The Economist*, 13 September 2014: http://www.economist.com/news/finance-and-economics/21617014-market-islamic-financial-products-growing-fast-big-interest-no-interest.

The Economist. 2014b. Corporate upgraders. *The Economist*, 15 February 2014.

The Economist. 2014c. Enter the Chinese NGO. *The Economist*, 12 April 2014: http://www.economist.com/news/leaders/21600683-communist-party-giving-more-freedom-revolutionary-idea-enter-chinese-ngo.

Thomas, A. 2004. The rise of social cooperatives in Italy. *Voluntas: International Journal of Voluntary and Nonprofit Organizations*, 15 (3): 243–63.

Thompson, P. and McHugh, D. 2002. *Work organizations* (3rd edn.). Basingstoke: Palgrave.

Thorne LeClair, D. and Ferrell, L. 2000. Innovation in experiential business ethics training. *Journal of Business Ethics*, 23 (3/1): 313–22.

To, W. and Lee, P. 2014. Diffusion of ISO 14001 environmental management system: global, regional and country-level analyses. *Journal of Cleaner Production*, 66: 489–98.

Topham, G. 2014. Richard Branson's domestic airline dream dies, but BA rivalry lives on. *Guardian*, 12 October 2014: http://www.theguardian.com/business/2014/oct/12/richard-branson-rivalry-british-airways-virgin-atlantic.

Topping, A. 2009. Disabled worker wins case for wrongful dismissal against Abercrombie & Fitch. *Guardian*, 13 August 2009.

Torrington, D. 1993. How dangerous is human resource management? A reply to Tim Hart. *Employee Relations*, 15 (5): 40–53.

Traynor, I. 2015. 30,000 lobbyists and counting: is Brussels under corporate sway? *Guardian*, 8 May 2014.

Treviño, L.K. and Brown, M.E. 2004. Managing to be ethical: debunking five business ethics myths. *Academy of Management Executive*, 18 (2): 69–81.

Treviño, L.K. and Nelson, K.A. 2014. *Managing business ethics: straight talk about how to do it right* (6th edn.). Hoboken, NJ: John Wiley.

Treviño, L.K. and Youngblood, S.A. 1990. Bad apples in bad barrels: a causal analysis of ethical decision making behavior. *Journal of Applied Psychology*, 75 (4): 378–85.

Treviño, L.K., Brown, M.E., and Nelson, K.A. 2007. *Managing business ethics: straight talk about how to do it right* (4th edn.). Hoboken, NJ: Wiley.

Treviño, L.K., Weaver, G.R., and Reynolds, S.J. 2006. Behavioral ethics in organizations: A review. *Journal of Management*, 32 (6): 951–90.

Treviño, L.K., Weaver, G.R., Gibson, D.G., and Toffler, B.L. 1999. Managing ethics and legal compliance: what works and what hurts. *California Management Review*, 41 (2): 131–51.

Tsalikis, J. and Fritzsche, D.J. 1989. Business ethics: a literature review with a focus on marketing ethics. *Journal of Business Ethics*, 8: 695–743.

Tucker, E. 2014. Justice Department announces charges against Chinese cyberspies. *PBS Newshour*, 19 May 2014: http://www.pbs.org/newshour/rundown/justice-department-announce-charges-chinese-cyberspies/.

Turner, E.A.L. 2010. Why Has the Number of International Non-Governmental Organizations Exploded since 1960? *Cliodynamics*, 1 (1): 81–91.

Turner, K. (ed.). 1993. *Sustainable environmental economics and management: principles and practice*. London: Belhaven Press.

Ufford, S. 2015. The Future Of The Sharing Economy Depends On Trust. *Forbes*, 10 February 2015. http://www.forbes.com.

UN. 2005. *2005 Report on the world situation*. New York: United Nations Publications.

UN. 2008. *Embedding Human Rights in Business Practice II*. New York: UN Global Compact.

UNEP. 2011. *Decoupling natural resource use and environmental impacts from economic growth*. Nairobi: UNEP.

United Nations. 2005. *The inequality predicament*. New York: United Nations Publications.

Uppal, J.Y. and Mangla, I.U. 2014. Islamic Banking and Finance Revisited after Forty Years: Some Global Challenges. *Journal of Finance Issues*: 13 (1): 16–27.

Vaara, V. 2014. Did Apple Fix E-Book Prices for the Greater Good? *The New Yorker*, 16 December 2014.

Valente, M. and Crane, A. 2010. Private enterprise and public responsibility in developing countries. *California Management Review*, 52 (3): 52–78.

Van Calster, G. and Deketelaere, K. 2001. The use of voluntary agreements in the European Community's environmental policy. In E.W. Orts and K. Deketelaere (eds.), *Environmental contracts*: 199–246. Dordrecht: Kluwer.

van Gerwen, J. 1994. Employers' and employees' rights and duties. In B. Harvey (ed.), *Business ethics: a European approach*: 56–87. London: Prentice Hall.

van Luijk, H.J.L. 1990. Recent developments in European business ethics. *Journal of Business Ethics*, 9: 537–44.

van Luijk, H.J.L. 2001. Business ethics in Europe: a tale of two efforts. In R. Lang (ed.), *Wirtschaftsethik in Mittel- und Osteuropa*: 9–18. Munich: Rainer Hampp.

van Schendelen, R. 2002. The ideal profile of the PA expert at the EU level. *Journal of Public Affairs*, 2 (2): 85–9.

van Tulder, R., Seitanidi, M.M., Crane, A., and Brammer, S. 2015. Enhancing the impact of cross-sector partnerships: four impact loops for channelling partnership studies *Journal of Business Ethics*, forthcoming.

Vanhamme, J., Lindgreen, A., Reast, J., and van Popering, N. 2012. To do well by doing good: Improving corporate image through cause-related marketing. *Journal of business ethics*, 109 (3): 259–74.

Vaughan, A. 2014. Lego ends Shell partnership following Greenpeace campaign. *Guardian*, 9 October 2014: http://www.theguardian.com/environment/2014/oct/09/lego-ends-shell-partnership-following-greenpeace-campaign.

Veal, G. and Mouzas, S. 2012. Market-Based Responses to Climate Change: CO2 Market Design versus Operation. *Organization Studies*, 33 (11): 1589–616.

Verbruggen, P. 2013. Gorillas in the closet? Public and private actors in the enforcement of transnational private regulation. *Regulation & Governance*, 7 (4): 512–32.

Verstegen Ryan, L. 2005. Corporate governance and business ethics in North America: the state of the art. *Business & Society*, 44 (1): 40–73.

Vidal, J. 2013. Toxic 'e-waste' dumped in poor nations, says United Nations. *Observer*, 14 December 2013: http://www.theguardian.com/global-development/2013/dec/14/toxic-ewaste-illegal-dumping-developing-countries.

Vining, A.R., Shapiro, D.M., and Borges, B. 2005. Building the firm's political (lobbying) strategy. *Journal of Public Affairs*, 5: 150–75.

Visser, W. 2008. CSR in developing countries. In A. Crane, A. McWilliams, D. Matten, J. Moon, and D. Siegel (eds.), *The Oxford handbook of corporate social responsibility*: 473–99. Oxford: Oxford University Press.

Visser, W. 2010. The Age of Responsibility: CSR 2.0 and the New DNA of Business. *Journal of Business Systems, Governance and Ethics*, 5 (3): 7–22.

Visser, W., McIntosh, M., and Middleton, C. (eds.). 2006. *Corporate citizenship in Africa—lessons from the past; paths into the future*. Sheffield: Greenleaf.

Vives, A. 2007. Social and environmental responsibility in small and medium enterprises in Latin America. In A. Crane and D. Matten (eds.), *Corporate social responsibility—a three volumes edited collection*, Vol. 3: 245–66. London: Sage.

Vogel, D. 1992. The globalization of business ethics: why America remains different. *California Management Review*, 35 (1): 30–49.

Vogel, D. 1998. Is US business obsessed with ethics? *Across the board*, November–December, 30: 31–3.

Vogel, D. 2005. *The market for virtue: the potential and limits of corporate social responsibility*. Washington: Brookings Institution Press.

Vogel, D. 2008. Private global business regulation. *Annual Review of Political Science*, 11 (1): 261–82.

Vogel, D. 2010. The private regulation of global corporate conduct: achievements and limitations. *Business & Society*, 49 (1): 68–87.

Wagemans, F.A., Koppen, C. van, and Mol, A.P. 2013. The effectiveness of socially responsible investment: a review. *Journal of Integrative Environmental Sciences*, 10 (3–4): 235–52.

Walker, T. 2015. California drought: Nestle accused of bottling and selling water from national forest spring using permit that expired over 25 years ago. *Independent*, 15 April 2015.

Wallace, M. 1989. Brave new workplace: technology and work in the new economy. *Work and Occupations*, 16 (4): 363–92.

Walsh, J.P. 2008. CEO compensation and the responsibilities of the business scholar to society. *Academy of Management Perspectives*, 22 (2): 26–33.

Wang, H., Appelbaum, R. P., Degiuli, F., and Lichtenstein, N. 2009. China's New Labour Contract Law: is China moving towards increased power for workers? *Third World Quarterly*, 30 (3): 485–501.

Wansink, B. and Chandon, P. 2006. Can 'Low-Fat' Nutrition Labels Lead to Obesity? *Journal of Marketing Research*, 43 (4): 605–17.

Watson, T.J. 1994. *In search of management: culture, chaos and control in managerial work*. London: Routledge.

Watson, T.J. 1998. Ethical codes and moral communities: the gunlaw temptation, the Simon solution and the David dilemma. In M. Parker (ed.), *Ethics and Organizations*: 253–68. London: Sage.

Watson, T.J. 2003. Ethical choice in managerial work: the scope for moral choices in an ethically irrational world. *Human Relations*, 56 (2): 167–85.

Watts, J. 2009. China plastic bag ban 'has saved 1.6m tonnes of oil'. *Guardian*, 22 May 2009: http://www.guardian.co.uk.

Weaver, G., Treviño, L.K., and Cochran, P.L. 1999. Corporate ethics programs as control systems: influences of executive commitment and environmental factors. *Academy of Management Journal*, 42 (1): 41–57.

Webb, T. 2006. Is Asian corporate governance improving? *Ethical Corporation*, May: 25–6.

Weber, J. 1990. Managers' moral reasoning: assessing their responses to three moral dilemmas. *Human Relations*, 43 (7): 687–702.

Weber, M. 1905. *Die protestantische Ethik und der 'Geist' des Kapitalismus*, Vols. 21 and 22. Tübingen: Archiv für Sozialwissenschaft und Sozialpolitik.

Weber, M. 1947. *The theory of social and economic organization* (T. Parsons, trans.). Oxford: Oxford University Press.

Webley, S. (ed.). 2008. *Use of codes of ethics in business: 2007 survey and analysis of trends*. London: Institute of Business Ethics.

Webley, S. and Le Jeune, M. 2005. *Corporate use of codes of ethics: 2004 survey*. London: Institute of Business Ethics.

Weiskopf, R. and Willmott, H. 2013. Ethics as Critical Practice: The 'Pentagon Papers', Deciding Responsibly, Truth-telling, and the Unsettling of Organizational Morality. *Organization Studies*, 34 (4): 469–93.

Welford, R.J. 1997. *Hijacking environmentalism: corporate responses to sustainable development*. London: Routledge.

Werhane, P.H. 1998. Moral imagination and the search for ethical decision-making in management. *Business Ethics Quarterly*, Ruffin Series: 75–98.

Werhane, P.H. 1999. The Role of Self-Interest in Adam Smith's Wealth of Nations. *Journal of Philosophy*, 86 (11): 669–80.

West, J.P. and Bowman, J.S. 2015. Electronic Surveillance at Work: An Ethical Analysis. *Administration & Society*, forthcoming.

Whawell, P. 1998. The ethics of pressure groups. *Business Ethics: A European Review*, 7 (3): 178–81.

Wheeler, D., Fabig, H., and Boele, R. 2002. Paradoxes and dilemmas for stakeholder responsive firms in the extractive sector: lessons from the case of Shell and the Ogoni. *Journal of Business Ethics*, 39: 297–318.

Whitley, R. 1999. *Divergent capitalisms: the social structuring and change of business systems*. Oxford: Oxford University Press.

Whitley, R. 2009. U.S. capitalism: a tarnished model? *Academy of Management Perspectives*, 23 (2): 11–22.

Wickramasekara, P. 2008. Globalisation, international labour migration and the rights of migrant workers. *Third World Quarterly*, 29 (7): 1247–64.

Wieland, J. 2014. *Governance Ethics: Global value creation, economic organization and normativity*: 161–78. Cham, Switzerland: Springer.

Wienen, I. 1999. *Impact of religion on business ethics in Europe and the Muslim world: Islamic versus Christian tradition*. Oxford: Peter Lang.

Wilks, S. 2013. *The Political Power of the Business Corporation*. Cheltenham: Edward Elgar.

Wilks, S. 2015. *The revolving door: how big business has colonised UK politics*. High Pay Centre: http://highpaycentre.org/blog/the-revolving-door-how-business-has-colonised-uk-politics.

Williams, S., Heery, E., and Abbott, B. 2011. The emerging regime of civil regulation in work and employment relations. *Human Relations*, 64 (7): 951–70.

Willke, H. and Willke, G. 2008. Corporate moral legitimacy and the legitimacy of morals: A critique of Palazzo/Scherer's communicative framework. *Journal of Business Ethics*, 81: 27–38.

Winstanley, D., Clark, J., and Leeson, H. 2002. Approaches to child labour in the supply chain. *Business Ethics: A European Review*, 11 (3): 210–23.

Witkowski, T.H. 2005. Antiglobal challenges to marketing in developing countries: exploring the ideological divide. *Journal of Public Policy and Marketing*, 24 (1): 7–23.

Wolff, R. 2012. Yes, there is an alternative to capitalism: Mondragon shows the way. *Guardian*, 24 June 2012: http://www.theguardian.com/commentisfree/2012/jun/24/alternative-capitalism-mondragon.

Woll, C. and Artigas, A. 2007. When trade liberalization turns into regulatory reform: the impact on business-government relations in international trade politics. *Regulation & Governance*, 1: 121–38.

Wong, S.C.Y. 2004. Improving corporate governance at SOEs: an integrated approach. *Corporate Governance International*, 7 (2): 6.

Wong, S.C.Y. 2009. Government ownership: why this time it should work. *McKinsey Quarterly* (June): http://www.mckinsey.com.

Wood, D.J. 1991. Corporate social performance revisited. *Academy of Management Review*, 16: 691–718.

Wood, D.J. 2010. Measuring Corporate Social Performance: A Review. *International Journal of Management Reviews*, 12 (1): 50–84.

Woodruffe, H. 1997. Compensatory consumption: why women go shopping when they're fed up and other stories. *Marketing Intelligence and Planning*, 15 (7): 325–34.

Woods, N. 2001. Making the IMF and the World Bank more accountable. *International Affairs*, 77 (1): 83–100.

Woods, P.R. and Lamond, D.A. 2011. What would Confucius do?—Confucian ethics and self-regulation in management. *Journal of Business Ethics*, 102 (4): 669–83.

World Commission on Environment and Development 1987. *Our common future*. Oxford: Oxford University Press.

Woywode, M 2002. Global management concepts and local adaptations: working groups in the French and German car manufacturing industry. *Organization Studies*, 23 (4): 497–524.

Wray-Bliss, E. and Parker, M 1998. Marxism, capitalism and ethics. In M. Parker (ed.), *Ethics and organizations*. London: Sage: 30–52.

Wylie, I. and Ball, C. 2006. Out with the old? *Guardian*, 25 February: 3.

Yardley, J. 2013. Report on Deadly Factory Collapse in Bangladesh Finds Widespread Blame. *New York Times*, 22 May 2013: http://www.nytimes.com/2013/2005/2023/world/asia/report-on-bangladesh-building-collapse-finds-widespread-blame.html?_r=2010.

Yaziji, M. and Doh, J. 2009. *NGOs and corporations: conflict and collaboration*. Cambridge: Cambridge University Press.

Yip, G. 1995. *Total global strategies*. London: Prentice Hall.

Yoshikawa, T. and Rasheed, A.A. 2009. Convergence of corporate governance: critical review and future directions. *Corporate Governance: An International Review*, 17 (3): 388–404.

Zadek, S. 1998. Balancing performance, ethics and accountability. *Journal of Business Ethics*, 17: 1421–41.

Zadek, S. 2001. *The civil corporation: the new economy of corporate citizenship*. London: Earthscan.

Zadek, S. Pruzan, P., and Evans, R. (eds.) 1997. *Building corporate accountability: emerging practices in social and ethical accounting, auditing and reporting*. London: Earthscan.

Zhao, X. and Belk, R.W. 2008. Politicizing consumer culture: advertising's appropriation of political ideology in China's social transition. *Journal of Consumer Research*, 35 (2): 231–44.

Zhexembayeva, N., Fedoseeva, O., and Martyschenko, S. 2007. Towards a revolution in cross-boundary partnership: complex socio-economic development in the Regions of SUAL Group Presence. *Centre for Business as an Agent of World Benefit Newsletter*, 3 (2).

SUBJECT INDEX

NAME INDEX

COUNTRIES AND REGIONS INDEX

COMPANIES, ORGANIZATIONS AND BRANDS INDEX